A Global History of Modern Historiography

The first book on historiography to adopt a global and comparative perspective on the topic, *A Global History of Modern Historiography* looks not just at developments in the West but also at the other great historiographical traditions in Asia, the Middle East, and elsewhere around the world over the course of the past two and a half centuries.

This second edition contains fully updated sections on Latin American and African historiography, discussion of the development of global history, environmental history, and feminist and gender history in recent years, along with new coverage of Russian historical practices. Beginning in the mid-eighteenth century, the authors analyze historical currents in a changing political, social, and cultural context, examining both the adaptation and modification of the Western influence on historiography and how societies outside Europe and America found their own ways in the face of modernization and globalization.

Supported by online resources including a selection of excerpts from key historiographical texts, this book offers an up-to-date account of the status of historical writing in the global era and is essential reading for all students of modern historiography.

Georg G. Iggers is Distinguished Professor Emeritus at the State University of New York (SUNY), Buffalo. His publications include *Marxist Historiographies: A Global Perspective* (2015, co-edited with Q. Edward Wang), *Historiography in the Twentieth Century* (1997), and *The German Conception of History* (1968).

Q. Edward Wang is Professor of History at Rowan University in Glassboro, New Jersey, and Changjiang Professor of History at Peking University in China. Among his publications are *Chopsticks: A Cultural and Culinary History* (2015), *Mirroring the Past: the Writing and Use of History in Imperial China* (2005, co-authored with On-Cho Ng), and *Inventing China through History: The May Fourth Approach to Historiography* (2001).

Supriya Mukherjee teaches at the University of Manitoba in Winnipeg. Her research interests include German history and the history of historical writing in India.

A Global History of Modern Historiography

Second edition

Georg G. Iggers, Q. Edward Wang, and Supriya Mukherjee

Routledge
Taylor & Francis Group

LONDON AND NEW YORK

This edition published 2017
by Routledge
2 Park Square, Milton Park, Abingdon, Oxon OX14 4RN

and by Routledge
711 Third Avenue, New York, NY 10017

Routledge is an imprint of the Taylor & Francis Group, an informa business

© 2008, 2016 Georg G. Iggers, Q. Edward Wang and Supriya
Mukherjee

First published 2008 by Pearson Education Limited

British Library Cataloguing in Publication Data
A catalogue record for this book is available from the British Library

Library of Congress Cataloging-in-Publication Data
Names: Iggers, Georg G., author. | Wang, Q. Edward, 1958– author. |
   Mukherjee, Supriya, author.
Title: A global history of modern historiography / Georg G. Iggers,
   Q. Edward Wang and Supriya Mukherjee.
Description: Seond edition. | New York, NY : Routledge, [2016] | Includes
   bibliographical references and index.
Identifiers: LCCN 2016004725 | ISBN 9781138942271 (hardback : alk.
   paper) | ISBN 9781138942264 (pbk. : alk. paper) | ISBN 9781315543499
   (ebook)
Subjects: LCSH: Historiography—History.
Classification: LCC D13 .I34 2016 | DDC 907.2—dc23
LC record available at http://lccn.loc.gov/2016004725

ISBN: 978-1-138-94227-1 (hbk)
ISBN: 978-1-138-94226-4 (pbk)
ISBN: 978-1-315-54349-9 (ebk)

Typeset in Sabon
by Apex CoVantage, LLC

Contents

5   The appeal of nationalist history around the world:
Historical studies in the Middle East and Asia in the
twentieth century   158

Preface and Acknowledgments to the Second Edition

Some years ago, Longman Publishers asked Georg Iggers to write a history of modern historiography. Both agreed on a concept that would have dealt primarily with Western historiography since the Enlightenment. As Iggers proceeded with the manuscript, he became increasingly uncertain about the project. Several histories of historiography had appeared in English and other Western languages in recent years, including Michael Bentley's *Modern Historiography* (1999) and Georg Iggers' own book, *Historiography in the Twentieth Century* (1997). However, none took into consideration the interaction between historical studies in the West and the rest of the world in the last two and a half centuries. As he proceeded with the manuscript, Iggers began to see the need for writing a history of modern historiography differently, namely from a global perspective, with greater attention paid to the political, social, and intellectual context of historical studies. He then asked Q(ingjia) Edward Wang, educated at East China Normal University in Shanghai with a PhD in East Asian and European intellectual history and historiography from Syracuse University, to cooperate with him. Wang and he had already exchanged manuscripts since Wang attended Iggers' lectures in Beijing in 1984. Iggers had read Wang's dissertation on the modernization of Chinese historical thought and writing in the twentieth century, which examines the interaction of Western and traditional Chinese historiographical practices. The dissertation was followed by Wang's book, *Inventing China through History: The May Fourth Approach to Historiography* (2001), one of his many publications in English and Chinese in which he has developed these ideas further. In 1999 the two organized an international conference at the State University of New York at Buffalo with contributions on changing historical thought in various Western and Asian societies and in Sub-Saharan Africa. The papers of the conference were published as *Turning Points in Historiography: A Cross-Cultural Perspective* (2002), which served to prepare their joint project. In early 2006, they asked Supriya Mukherjee to assist them with the Indian part of the book. She had studied in New Delhi with Sumit Sarkar, a leading historian of modern India and Indian historiography, before she came to Buffalo to study with Georg Iggers and obtained a PhD in modern European intellectual history and historiography. Since then she has not only written the sections of the book dealing with modern Indian historical and social thought but also contributed a great deal with critical suggestions on all parts of the manuscript. Without her help, it would have been very difficult to complete the project.

The three contributors are very grateful for the support and advice that they received in the course of their work. In December 2002, when Iggers and Wang were at the early stage of their work, Jürgen Kocka invited them to Berlin to an international conference, which included historians and social scientists from East Asia, to discuss the project. Subsequently, they were invited by universities in Germany, Austria, Italy, Hungary, Spain, Great Britain, the United States, Mexico, China, Japan, and South Korea to present the project. In addition, Georg Iggers is particularly thankful to the Max Planck Institute for History in Göttingen, which with its extensive historiographical library provided him with an excellent setting for this work and the opportunity to discuss it with the researchers attached to the Institute and its many foreign visitors. It is a great loss to the international community that the Institute, which over the years has provided a unique forum for scholars from all over the world, was closed. We would like to thank the many persons whom we were able to consult, including Guido Abbatista, Shigeru Akita, Julia Arnautova, Doris Bachmann-Medick, Arndt Bauerkämper, Stefan Berger, Werner Berthold, Corinne Blake, Gerhard Botz, Ernst Breisach, Qineng Chen, Youssef M. Choueiri, Gustavo Corni, Albert Cremer, Natalie Z. Davis, Andreas Daum, Roger Des Forges, Gerald Diesener, Prasenjit Duara, Vera Dubina, Benjamin A. Elman, Axel Fair-Schulz, Franz L. Fillafer, Eckhardt Fuchs, Effi Gazi, Frank Hadler, Chun-chieh Huang, Peng Jiang, Vandana Joshi, Stefan Jordan, Donald Kelley, Jürgen Kocka, Kazuhiko Kondo, Peter Kriedte, Wei-ying Ku, Wolfgang Küttler, Hal Langfur, Antonis Liakos, Jiehyun Lim, Chris Lorenz, Renato Mazzolini, Hans Medick, Alan Megill, Matthias Middell, Achim Mittag, Masake Miyake, On-cho Ng, Michihiro Okamoto, Jan Piskorski, Attila Pók, Ilaria Porciani, Jörn Rüsen, Dominic Sachsenmeier, Masayuki Sato, Edith Saurer, Hans Schleier, Jürgen Schlumbohm, Ernst Schulin, Shen Han, Gabrielle Spiegel, Bo Stråth, Jeremy Telman, Edoardo Tortarolo, Johan van der Zande, Rudolf Vierhaus, Adelheid von Saldern, Rudolf von Thadden, Peter Th. Walther, Gregory Witkowski, Daniel Woolf, Yashushi Yamanouchi, Jason Young, and Zhilian Zhang, and to Carl Sieverling at the Max Planck Institute for History for his help with Georg Iggers' many computer problems. More recently we were able to consult several persons who offered their advice on the revision of our book for the new edition. Michael Antolovic, Jürgen Kocka, Sasha Pack, and Daniel Woolf carefully read Chapter 8; Istvan Jaksic, Juan Maiguashca, Jurandir Malerba, Ignacio Chuecas Saldias, and Felipe Soza made useful suggestions on the Latin American section of Chapter 6; and Toyin Falola, Martin Klein, Ndubueze Mbah, Chris Saunders, Wessel Visser, Claude Welsh and Jason Young helped with the Sub-Saharan section of Chapter 6. Also, the making of the index for the new edition was assisted by Lin Man and Zhang Yibo, two graduate students at Peking University.

Finally, Georg Iggers would like to express warm thanks to his wife, Wilma, who not only encouraged him in the project but spent many hours reading and discussing the manuscript. Edward Wang is grateful to his wife Ni for her understanding and support that enabled him to spend months during his sabbatical year in Asia, where he focused on writing certain parts of the book. Supriya Mukherjee would like to thank her husband Pinaki, who carefully read her part of the work and then asked the right questions.

Georg G. Iggers, Q. Edward Wang, and Supriya Mukherjee

December 2015

Preface and Acknowledgments to the First Edition

In the meantime in 2012, the three of us revised the English text and brought it up-to-date for a forthcoming German edition of the book, which was published by the renowned Vandenhoeck & Ruprecht publishing house. We thank the Fritz Thyssen Foundation for providing a grant that made the translation possible. We also thank Jürgen Kocka, who steadily followed our work, not only for having mediated the grant from the Fritz Thyssen Foundation but also for valuable suggestions. The German text differs from the book as it was published in English in 2008. The literature that has appeared since we submitted the manuscript to the publisher in 2007 and the discussions that have ensued from this literature have been taken into account. Whole sections of the English text have been rewritten, including those on feminist and gender historiography, on history and memory, on global history, among other topics. The final chapter dealing with current trends since 1990 was thoroughly rewritten, and we are thankful to Peter Burke, Richard Evans, Natalie Davis, and once more Jürgen Kocka for their advice. Georg wants to thank his wife Wilma who read large parts of the text. And finally he wants to thank Daniel Plassche, a graduate student, who not only solved the many computer problems that came up but assisted him in the bibliographical research.

Georg Iggers, Q. Edward Wang, and Supriya Mukherjee
December 2012

Introduction

We are living today in an age of rapid globalization.[1] Its pace has accelerated in the past several decades, particularly since the end of the Cold War. The main thrust for globalization came from the West, but in most recent times important impulses also came from elsewhere, particularly East Asia and India. But while globalization involved a high degree of Westernization, it by no means resulted in homogenization but everywhere produced diverse responses to the West rooted in indigenous cultures. In fact, we have witnessed homogeneity resulting from processes of globalization and at the same time increasing heterogeneity. Globalization thus is extremely complex and variegated, on the one hand indeed leading to high degrees of homogeneity in economic organization, technological and scientific developments, and even lifestyles following Western patterns, on the other hand to marked divergences from Western outlooks and practices and even to pronounced resistance to Western influences.

Yet despite this trend to globalization, historical studies have lagged behind. In this volume we intend to examine the transformation of historical thinking and writing within this larger global context. In the past two centuries and particularly in the twentieth, a number of histories of historiography have been written. Yet the focus has been Western or national, and where it has been Western, it has generally not been comparative but subdivided into national traditions. As far as historical studies in general have been concerned, writings, particularly in the past two and a half decades after the momentous developments since 1989–1991, have increasingly turned to the non-Western worlds and to a much greater extent than earlier have included aspects of culture and society. But this has not been the case with histories of historiography, including those published as recently as the turn from the twentieth to the twenty-first centuries.[2] A fair number of studies, increasingly anthologies, have treated historical cultures in various non-Western societies. And the larger histories of historiography continued to be Western oriented and generally have continued to be restricted to the English, French, German, and occasionally Italian literature. Only in the last few years in Markus Völkel's *Geschichtsschreibung: Eine Einführung in globaler Perspektive* (2006), Daniel Woolf's *A Global History of History*

(2011), and the five-volume *Oxford History of Historical Writing* (2010–2012) have there been comprehensive histories from a global perspective.[3]

Our book is different, much smaller than *The Oxford History* and more modest in scope than either it or the books by Völkel and Woolf, which deal with the history of historical writings since the very beginnings of historical time, and as a result can devote only limited space to the period with which we are dealing. Only Woolf is truly comparative; Völkel deals with separate historiographical cultures in isolation. We are dealing with a time when increasing interactions made comparisons possible. We are restricting ourselves to the period from the late eighteenth century until the present. Our interest lies in the interaction of the Western and non-Western historiographical traditions in a global context. Although on the economic level there was considerable interaction earlier, there were as yet only isolated contacts between historians in different cultures. In East Asia and in the Muslim world from the Maghreb to Southeast Asia, well established traditions of historical scholarship existed; in Hindu India there were ancient literary traditions and in Sub-Saharan Africa oral traditions of history, but there was as yet little transcultural exchange. However, the early impact of the Arabs in India and in parts of Sub-Saharan Africa should not be overlooked.[4] This isolation changed in India as early as the last third of the eighteenth century with the establishment of British colonial rule and somewhat later in the nineteenth century in the Muslim countries and in East Asia.

But the interaction was largely one way, from the West to the non-Western world. What we are portraying are processes of Westernization – processes again in the plural – that underwent modifications everywhere in the face of resistance from traditional outlooks and institutions. We do not see Western patterns of thought inherently as positive or normative but view them within a certain historical and cultural setting. In dealing with Western influences, we are very much aware that the West is not an organic unit but that it is highly heterogeneous, marked by political and intellectual divisions, so that we can talk of Western influences but not of a Western influence. One task of the study will be to explore aspects that are common to the West. Similarly, the cultures that interact with the West are highly complex, and therefore the reception of Western influences is highly variegated as well. Thus Max Weber's famous attempts to characterize the West by contrasting it with other civilizations such as China and India must be taken with a great deal of caution, even if Weber considered these characterizations not as actual descriptions but as ideal types, heuristic devices for better understanding them. We are aware of the problems when we make the interaction of Western and non-Western historical cultures in all their complexity the core of our study. As we have already indicated, we begin in the late eighteenth century because at that point the various traditions of historical thinking that until then had existed relatively, although not totally, apart from each other began to interact.

Before we proceed, the question regarding the proper subject of historiography needs to be addressed. Since the institutionalization of historical studies in the nineteenth century, works on historiography have focused heavily on professional historians. A relatively sharp dividing line has been drawn between history and literature. We shall conceive of historiography not only as representation of the past as it was, but also as it was remembered. But memory is often deceiving. The great interest in history and in the study of history in the modern period is closely associated with the emergence of powerful nationalisms, not only in Western societies but also, in the twentieth century, in the countries once under Western colonial domination, like India, or threatened by domination like China, by Japan. Nations that never existed as nations, such as India, invented themselves through the use of history, often using imaginary, legendary pictures of their past to justify their present.[5] Historical scholarship plays an important role in this construction of national memories. In theory, there is a clear dividing line between scholarship and legend; in practice, they are closely related in the historical imagination not only of Western but also of non-Western countries.

A key weakness of the existing histories of historiography is that they take historical scholarship too seriously, more or less at face value, not fully recognizing the extent to which scholarship in the West and in the non-Western societies was very much a part of a broader historical culture. Thus on the one hand, historical scholarship as it emerged as a professional discipline, first in nineteenth-century Germany but soon generally in the West and simultaneously in Meiji Japan (1868–1912), sees itself as committed to scientific objectivity but in practice uses its research techniques to support national myths. The German historical school did this under the guise of scientific objectivity to legitimize German unification under the Prussian Hohenzollerns in the nineteenth century;[6] Jules Michelet (1798–1874) immersed himself in the archives in defense of French democratic nationalism, and Japanese historians employed Rankean methods of critical scholarship to criticize Confucian historiography and then turned around to extend support to Japanese imperial traditions in advancing Japanese nationalism. This does not mean that historians should not aim to be truthful, but they should be aware of their own biases. A prime task of the historian must be to criticize distortions of the past.

This leads us to a dilemma. On the one hand we see the limits not only of historical scholarship but more generally of historical writing as the basis of a comparative, intercultural history of historical thought. On the other hand, we too shall rely primarily on historical texts. There is a practical reason for this. Historical consciousness expresses itself in many forms, not only in scholarship but also in imaginative literature, in the plastic arts, in monuments and architecture, in festivals, in song, in various intangible and unarticulated expressions of collective memory. To include all of these manifestations in our account would be an undertaking beyond our ability, requiring a "thick description" in the mode of Geertzian cultural anthropology to reconstruct the web of meanings that constitute the historical outlook of a culture. And even then we may fall victim to the illusion that cultures are integrated systems while in fact they may contain many contradictory aspects that resist being subsumed in a system. We shall deal with texts and with the historians who produced them but at the same time be aware that these historical writings reflect climates of opinion in the cultures in which they originated. Thus while focusing on historiography we shall view the writings we examine in their broader institutional, political, and intellectual framework. It will be important to examine the organization of historical studies and instruction in the modern period from a comparative, intercultural perspective, for example the formation of university-centered disciplines of professional historians, the governmental support that these innovations received, the place historical studies occupied in the political setting of middle-class opinion, and the effect of notions of popular science such as those of social Darwinism in the late nineteenth and early twentieth centuries on historical writing.

The theme of our book is by no means a history of culture or society on a large scale but rather involves the recognition of the interrelatedness of historical writing with other aspects of the society. One important question will also be the audience at which historical works are directed. This audience underwent changes during the period with which we are dealing. On the one hand the institutionalization and professionalization of historical studies led to progressive specialization so that history was increasingly written by specialists for specialists who are part of the profession but often are isolated from the broader public. Yet much history writing, also on the part of professional historians such as Leopold von Ranke (1795–1886) and Jules Michelet, was read as literature by audiences that often coincided with the readers of the great historical novels. And finally the role of school textbooks in the Western as well as in the non-Western countries must be considered – the extent to which they rely on scholarly findings but even more the function they serve in conveying the images of the national past that the governments want to implant in the minds of the younger generation. Moreover, both in the West and in the non-West, the media used for the dissemination of historical materials and with them their audiences underwent changes, from heavy reliance on the printed word in the nineteenth century, not only of scholarly but also of popular publications, including newspapers, illustrated journals, and historical fiction, to the twentieth century when they were supplemented first by film, than by radio, television, videos, and most recently by the Internet.

In dealing with the history of historical thought and writing in the period since the beginning of interaction among the historical cultures, we employ two concepts to give structure to our account. The first, which we have already discussed, is globalization; the second is modernization. Globalization and modernization are not identical but are interwoven. Globalization, of course, precedes the recent period. Already very early in the history of civilizations there were exchanges, not only military and commercial but also cultural. The spread of the Phoenician alphabet, derived from Egyptian hieroglyphics, became the basis of the Hebrew, Greek, and Roman alphabets. The Hellenization of the Roman world is another example, as is the spread of the major world religions, Buddhism, Christianity, and later Islam. Yet with the age of discoveries in the fifteenth and sixteenth centuries, a particular form of Western-dominated globalization began.

We would like to distinguish among three distinct phases in this process. The first involved the emergence of a capitalist world market together with an early phase of colonization by the West. The prime targets at that point were less the countries in East Asia and in parts of the Muslim world, Persia, and the Ottoman Empire, with well established political structures, ancient civilizations, and functioning economies, than regions of the world that were less able to defend themselves such as the Americas, Sub-Saharan Africa, Southeast Asia, Oceania, and to an extent the Indian Peninsula. Immanuel Wallerstein has distinguished between the European "core states," in which expansive capitalist economies were firmly established, and the colonial "peripheries," which became the subjects of Western penetration and exploitation.[7] Not that these areas were totally passive. The slave trade was possible only with the cooperation of African chieftains and merchants, and, in turn, the slave-based economies in the Caribbean, the North American English colonies, and Brazil were integrated with the European economies. In Europe this was the age of the consolidation of centralized states, with standing armies and bureaucratic structures, some of which (Spain, Portugal, England, France, the Dutch Netherlands, Sweden, and Denmark) already constituted incipient nation-states, Yet in this period, the European states were not yet able to penetrate into the well established states in East and West Asia. This changed with industrialization in Europe, in the United States, and by the late nineteenth century also in Japan and with the superior military strength that accompanied it. The refusal of the British envoy in 1793 to kowtow in front of the Chinese emperor is symptomatic of this changed situation. This is the age of imperial expansion, of the colonization of the African continent, North and South, and the consolidation of colonial control in South and Southeast Asia. The defeat of China by Great Britain in the Opium Wars in 1839–1842 ushered in a period in which China was no longer able successfully to resist Western and ultimately also Japanese penetration.

But not only the political, military, and economic but also the civilizational balance had shifted in a second phase. While prior to the eighteenth century, Europeans had admired Chinese and to an extent Persian and Arab civilizations, they now considered them inferior. As Jürgen Osterhammel, a leading historian of the European-Asian encounter, noted: "In the eighteenth century Europe compared itself with Asia, in the nineteenth century it no longer accepted such comparison."[8] Certain elements of Asian culture received attention in the West, such as Japanese and to an extent

Chinese art and architecture and even acupuncture medicine. A Bengali poet, Rabindranath Tagore (1861–1941), was awarded the Nobel Prize for literature in 1913. Western Oriental studies dealt with classical Indian, Chinese, Persian, and Arab literature. But the main sources of science, technology, philosophy, literature, art, music, and of course economic penetration went from the West eastward. The non-Western world in the course of the nineteenth and the first half of the twentieth centuries increasingly adopted Western ideas as well as technology and weaponry to protect its autonomy and culture, but generally, as in the case of Japan, it was less a direct adoption than an adaptation of Western ideas and institutions to the indigenous cultures. It is striking how many Western books in all fields from the late nineteenth century on and even before were translated into Chinese, Japanese, Korean, and to a lesser extent also into Farsi, Arabic, and Turkish, and how few were translated into Western languages. This holds true to this day.[9]

The period after the end of the Second World War marked a new third phase. At least on the surface the political balance changed with the independence of almost all the former colonies and with the reemergence of China as an important power. Yet the older formal imperialism was replaced by a new informal imperialism, by the economic penetration and domination of the former colonies in the so-called Third World by the economically highly developed countries. The main impact of globalization has been economic, the emergence of a financial capitalism that knows few national borders. Capitalism now is to a much greater extent international and global than it was earlier, as shown in the dramatic increase of MNCs (multinational corporations) and INGOs (international nongovernment organizations) in today's world. With the end of the Cold War, the state capitalism of the Soviet bloc gave way to finance capitalism, and the same was true of states such as the nominally communist People's Republic of China and somewhat later the Democratic Republic of Vietnam. New information techniques not only transformed society and economy but also tied the world more closely together. But culture and lifestyles too were globalized. Examples of the latter are the McDonaldization of food consumption, Hollywood films, jeans, and popular music. To be sure, older patterns of consumption have not disappeared but have kept their specific cultural character. At the same time new uncertainties arose, a discomfort with many aspects of modern – that is, Western – civilization, resulting in reactions and even revolts against Western modernity, not only outside but also within the West. The late 1960s – for which 1968 has become a symbol – marked a sharper break with older patterns of thought than did 1945. Independently but concurrently with this, fundamental scientific-technological changes took place, the so-called information revolution, which transformed the material conditions of life. Thus while broad segments of opinion rebelled against the growing impact of science and technology, the changes that took place in the economy and in all aspects of society seem irreversible.[10]

How has all of this affected historical thinking and historical inquiry? Again we would like to tie the history of historical writing and consciousness to the phases of globalization that we have outlined, aware that this classification is tentative and oversimplifies a complex development. Interestingly the first phase of globalization, prior to the breakthrough of industry and imperial power in the nineteenth century – in other words following the early overseas discoveries – witnessed more examples of a global outlook in historical writing than did the second phase. A prime example of such an approach to history is the many-volume *A Universal History: From the Earliest Account of Time to the Present*,[11] launched by a group of English primarily amateur historians in 1736, which was truly universal, with volumes dedicated not only to Western but also to non-Western countries and regions, not only in Asia but also in Sub-Saharan Africa and the Americas. This history was made possible by the immense increase in geographic knowledge in the course of overseas explorations. In this history, Europe, while occupying many volumes, was seen as but one among many civilizations.

A second stage, the age of imperial expansion after 1800, in fact witnessed a serious contraction in historical scope. The center of historical attention was now Europe, and the non-Western world was approached from the viewpoint of European domination. Specialized studies of so-called Oriental cultures, with a focus on their early beginnings, persisted but were generally not integrated into a broader view of world history. The view of Europe – and that meant Western and Central Europe and later also North America – as the apex of civilization, largely precluded taking the rest of the world seriously. But even a European perspective was largely lacking as historical studies concentrated on the nation-state. This focus on the nation-state reflected not only the new nationalism but also the heavy reliance on archival sources that made it difficult to go beyond national borders and even more beyond the confines of Europe and the Americas. Moreover, this reliance on state documents contained in the archives led to the neglect of broader social and cultural factors although the archives, as we shall see later, could very well serve as a basis of social and economic history.

At last in the third phase, in the second half of the twentieth century, greater attention was paid to the non-Western world and also to cultural and social dimensions. Paradoxically, the idea of the supremacy of Western culture was abandoned and the equal dignity of other cultures was recognized, but the economic stranglehold of Western and increasingly also East Asian capitalist economies over the former colonies was strengthened.

Like Woolf, we maintain that historical consciousness was not a privilege of the West but existed in all cultures. The idea that only the West has a sense of history, as put forward in the late eighteenth century among others by David Hume (1711–1776) and Edward Gibbon (1737–1794) and reiterated in the nineteenth century by thinkers as diverse as James Mill (1773–1836), Georg Friedrich Wilhelm Hegel (1770–1831), Leopold von

Ranke, and Karl Marx (1818–1883), a conception that dominated much Western thought until well past the middle of the twentieth century, cannot stand in the face of the rich historiographical traditions of other cultures throughout the ages. Yet the idea is still not entirely dead but now is used not to claim the superiority of Western culture with its Enlightenment heritage and yet to hold this heritage responsible for the ills of the modern world. Thus Hayden White from a postmodern perspective too has held that "historical consciousness" is "specifically Western" but now sees it negatively as "a prejudice by which the presumed superiority of modern industrial society can be retroactively substantiated."[12] And Ashis Nandy, from a postcolonial perspective, has linked the Western intellectual heritage since the Enlightenment with its "secular world view," its "scientific rationality," and its "theories of progress . . . and development" to the "world wars, gulags, and genocides of the twentieth century" which replaced the supposedly healthier cultures that depended on "myths, legends, and epics to define themselves."[13]

We begin our history with an examination of historical thought and writing immediately prior to the impact of Western influences, that is, toward the end of the eighteenth century. Different historical cultures can be identified, each reflecting different outlooks and values and different institutional and political settings. Specifically we shall look at the West, as well as Latin America, the Islamic countries, East Asia, India, and, in the twentieth century, Sub-Saharan Africa. We are aware that there are national and regional diversities in each of these units, determined in the West in part by national and linguistic separations, as in France, Scotland, Italy, Russia, Germany, and also in Latin America. Moreover, within each of these national entities, as well as in Latin America which is not such an entity, differences exist in religious and political orientation; in East Asia there are Korean and Japanese traditions with a common source in classical Chinese civilization transformed, however, in different national settings; in China itself, Confucian, Buddhist, Daoist, and Neo-Confucian currents interact in various historical periods; in the Islamic world, ethnic and linguistic divisions exist among Arabs, Turks, Persians, and Southeast Asians and again between the Sunnis and Shiites. Nevertheless, we wish to define certain common characteristics that mark each of these cultures, in addition to elements that transcend the divisions of the cultures with which we are dealing.

Our second concept is that of modernization.[14] Some types of modernization occurred in specific societies, for example in early nineteenth-century Europe, but did not immediately have a worldwide impact. In Japan, until 1854 when Admiral Perry put an end to its self-imposed isolation, important transformations had already taken place earlier in the economic and administrative spheres, which were neither as yet directly influenced by Western culture nor had yet any impact outside of Japan. As a matter of fact, many economic and social developments associated with modernization took place progressively since the beginnings of the

Tokugawa shogunate in the seventeenth century, and despite the country's hermetic isolation, European studies were conducted based on translations from the Dutch, who alone among Westerners were permitted to have a small island enclave.

A good deal of Western social theory since the late eighteenth century, long before the term was coined in the mid-twentieth century, assumed that all of modern history was subject to a process of modernization. Modernization suggested a break with traditional patterns of thought and institutions, in religion, economics, and politics, marked by the threefold "revolutions": the emergence of modern science and of a scientific outlook; the political revolutions of the eighteenth century, the American but even more the French Revolution with its impact on Europe and its focus on national sovereignty based at least in theory on the consent of the governed; and the process of industrialization under capitalist conditions. From Adam Smith (1723–1790) and Adam Ferguson (1723–1816) in Scotland and the Marquis de Condorcet in France (1743–1794) in the late eighteenth century to much of social science theory in the second half of the twentieth century, modernization envisaged a uniform process pointing to the advances of science, the establishment of a capitalist world market, followed by the consolidation of civil societies and the establishment of liberal democracies in progressive stages throughout the world. In the meantime, the idea of modernization has been widely discredited. One reason for the critique is the assumption of classical modernization theories that Western societies, such as the United States, can serve as models for the world, while in the eyes of the critics it actually serves to legitimize the capitalist control over the economically less developed parts of the world. Another reason is that transformations of the world under modern conditions have obviously not led to uniformity. Thus a distinguished Indian historian, Dipesh Chakrabarty, in a recent series of essays, *Provincializing Europe*, sought to demonstrate the parochialism of a Western view of historical development that recognized only one form of modernity and argued that present-day Indian culture, including its indigenous religious roots, just as much represents forms of modernity.[15]

Nevertheless, the realization that there are marked breaks with traditional ways of thinking and of political, economic, and social organization and that there have been radical movements away from traditional thought patterns and institutions remains useful for an examination of the history of historical writing in the Western and non-Western worlds. This process was most advanced in the West but by no means restricted to it. One of these changes was the attempt to transform history from a literary to a scientific enterprise. Scientific in this context meant the insistence that history be written on the basis of the critical examination of evidence by professional scholars. We are aware that this increased emphasis on source criticism was not restricted to the West but occurred at the same time, hardly influenced by the West, in China and Japan and to an extent also in the Islamic countries and India. In both China and the West, there occurred what Benjamin

Elman, in a famous study of Chinese scholarship,[16] called the transformation from philosophy to philology, in Europe perhaps better described as the shift from theology and religion to philology, but in both cultures involving a more secular outlook, so that in China the classical Confucian writings and in the West Homer and the Bible were no longer seen as canonical texts but increasingly as historical documents. This new conception of historical inquiry as a rigorous science was accompanied in both cultures by the professionalization of historical studies. Although history in China had for many centuries been written for the most part for the ruling dynasty by bureaucrats who were professionals of a sort, the seventeenth and eighteenth centuries saw the establishment of academies more free from such direct control and in Europe the emergence of research-oriented academies. The similarities must not be overstressed. The political, social, and cultural contexts were very different in East Asia and Europe, but the changes in historical thought and inquiry reflect a move, partial to be sure, to new attitudes and practices.[17] To an extent these reorientations were integrated in other aspects of modernization operating not only in East Asian countries but also in India and the Muslim world such as the extension of a market economy that, as André Gunder Frank (1929–2005) and others argue, provided a stimulus for the growth of capitalism in the Western world.[18]

There was, however, a complex of ideas that were specifically Western and transmitted to the non-Western world while the latter sought to protect itself against Western domination. One idea, closely linked to the notion of modernity, was the view that history was a coherent process involving scientific, technological, and social advancement in the direction of modern conditions of life. History was transformed from a chronicle of events to coherent narratives. There emerged now the conception of a world history leading from early beginnings to its high point in the West in modern times. This development was defined differently in historical works reflecting different ideological positions. What they had in common was the conviction that everything human was subject to change, not arbitrary but purposeful change. Man, as José Ortega y Gasset (1883–1955) argued, has no nature but only a history.[19] Linked to this idea was the firm belief that not philosophy but history offered the best key to the understanding of things human, so that philosophy too, such as that of Hegel, must be historical. Almost all Western historians – and not only they but the broad educated public – accepted this idea of the primacy of history. They also accepted a second idea, namely that history was a science, although there were fundamental differences in views about what sort of a science. While French and British positivists, Social Darwinists, and Marxists searched for laws of history, other historians, such as Leopold von Ranke, denied that there were such laws and stressed that the task of the historian was not to explain but to understand human actions in their historical context. But even advocates of this view, who like Ranke rejected the idea of progress, still firmly believed in historical development and the superiority of Western civilization.[20]

Increasingly in the course of the nineteenth century, historians as well as many intellectuals in East Asia, India, and the Muslim countries, accepted the Western idea of historical development and believed that they must take over Western standards to protect their culture against the military and economic might of the West. The Western idea of the primacy of the nation-state replaced the focus on dynasties in East Asian and Muslim historical writings as the institution that gave structure to their historical narratives. Thus historiography outside the West was increasingly Westernized and modernized without losing contact with older indigenous traditions. Yet at no point was there a consensus among historians in the West and elsewhere on the nature of history and the way in which it should be written. And at all times there were countermovements to the dominant historical approaches.

The last few decades – the period that we have termed the third phase of globalization – witnessed fundamental reorientations both in historical thought and in the broader context in which history is written. There was an expansion of historical studies with a greater interest in transnational and intercultural themes and a turn away from a focus on elites to a "history from below," which included not only the ordinary lives of broad masses of the population, who had largely been excluded from histories and were now given special attention, but also the role and status of women in history. At the same time there was a growing uneasiness about the conditions that modernization had brought about, as well as a critique of the faith in science and in the beneficial character of modern civilization, assumptions on which much Western historiography and social science theory and research rested. A good deal of this critique had already originated in the eighteenth century, although for a long time it represented a minority position. Similar critical attitudes existed elsewhere, foremost in India. Thus there were elements of consensus between the radical critique of scientific rationality and of progressive history that we have associated with postmodernism in the West and with postcolonial thought in India and Latin America.

In the chapters that follow, we shall pursue these developments in historical thought and writings in their broader intellectual, social, and economic context from the eighteenth century to the beginning of the twenty-first century, focusing on the interaction between Western and non-Western historical cultures, yet keeping in mind the complexities that preclude the writing of any simple narrative. In Chapter 1, we begin our narrative by offering a general survey of various historiographical traditions around the world, centering on the West, the Middle East, the East and Southeast Asia as well as India, and focusing on their important developments in the eighteenth century. Then we proceed to Chapter 2, discussing changes in historical practices in the modern age, centering on the advance of nationalism in the wake of the French Revolution from the West to the rest of the world and its impact on historical writing. This modern transformation of historical writing was characterized by the rise of academic history and, along with it and because of it, the emergence of the historical profession, which are discussed in some detail in Chapter 3, focusing on the paradigmatic influence of Rankean historiography in the West as well as in East Asia, particularly Japan. Notwithstanding its significance in shaping the modern historical profession, Rankean historiography and German historicism faced a serious crisis in the beginning of the twentieth century, especially in the years between the two World Wars. As a result, as we demonstrate in Chapter 4, a new orientation of historical thought occurred in the West whose influence was also to be well appreciated in the historical practices during the post–World War II period. In the worlds outside the West, as shown in Chapter 5, the attraction of nationalist history persisted throughout the twentieth century, which played an instrumental role in shaping the historical practices in the world in uniformity. But it is also important to note that voices critical of nationalist historiography and the nationalist constellation of the modern world have arisen in historical communities in such countries as India and also, to a lesser extent, Japan in postwar periods. These criticisms joined forces with postmodern challenges to modern historiography in the West after World War II, discussed in Chapter 6, where we also saw the effort, initiated by the French *Annales School* but expanded by the social and social science historians in Anglo-America and Germany, to broaden the scope of historical study and transcend the nation-state paradigm. Another important challenge to modern nationalist historiography came from postcolonial critiques associated with the publications of the *Subaltern Studies* by a group of Indian scholars and Edward Said's *Orientalism* in the 1970s and 1980s. Both publications were significant in changing the historical thought and writing not only in the West, Latin America, and Africa (Chapter 6) but also in the Middle East and Asia (Chapter 7). In addition to the influence of postcolonialism, other forces (ideological as well as religious) that affected the historical writings in the Middle East and Asia during the late twentieth century were the rise of Islamism and the decline of Marxism; both phenomena have contributed to the questioning of the nation-state emphasis in historiography in the historical community, as detailed in Chapter 7. In Chapter 8, we offer a general discussion of the recent changes in historical practices around the world in light of the impact of globalization. We consider the following five trends important in mapping the historical practices around today's world and perhaps also in its foreseeable future: (1) the continuing cultural and linguistic turn that gave rise to the so-called new cultural history; (2) the ever greater expansion of feminist and gender history; (3) the new alliance between historical studies and social sciences in light of the postmodern critique; (4) the challenges to national historiography associated with (though not exclusively) the study of postcolonialism; (5) the rise of world history and global history and, distinct from them, the history of globalization. At the same time, we are fully aware that these are tentative characterizations, open for further discussions with our readers.

Finally, two concerns run through the book and give it a degree of unity; the first is our rejection of Eurocentric approaches to history, the second our defense of rational inquiry. Few would disagree with us today on the first that all peoples have had an historical consciousness that they expressed in written or other forms. Our book seeks to dismantle the preconception of the superiority of Western historical thought by showing that there were in fact long-standing traditions of historical thought and writing in all the cultures with which we deal.

Our second concern is directed against that part of the postmodern critique of the intellectual heritage of the West that holds that an objective study of history is not possible because the past has no basis in objective reality but is a construct of the mind or of a nonreferential language and that therefore all historical writing constitutes a form of imaginative literature and lacks clear criteria for establishing the truth or falsehood of historical accounts. We are fully aware of the limits of rational inquiry, of the impossibility of arriving at definitive answers in which many of the professionally trained historians in the nineteenth century still believed. We recognize the extent to which historical accounts reflect different, often conflicting perspectives that defy convincing proof. It is hardly possible to reconstruct the past with clear certainty, but it is often possible to demonstrate the falsity of historical statements, the distortions that feed into political ideologies. One of our concerns is to show in what ways history in all of the cultural communities with which we deal is abused in the pursuit of political, particularly nationalist, agendas. Because this is the case, we have in all the chapters, in Western and non-Western settings, examined the political, social, and to an extent religious context in which history has been written. This could lead to the disturbing conclusion that all history is an expression of ideology and thus result in an extreme epistemological relativism. But if there is a real core to history, if human beings actually inhabited the past, as we believe, then there are ways of approaching this reality, imperfect and colored as the perception of it may be. It is an important task of the historian, to which we set ourselves in this book, to dismantle distortions and myths. Because this is only very partially possible, the history of historiography is a continuous dialogue that does not tell a single story but that offers varying, often conflicting interpretations. These enrich our picture of the past but nevertheless remain subject to critical examination following standards of inquiry shared by the scholarly community as to their factual basis and their logical consistency. Every historian is entitled to ethical and political commitments that color his or her perception of history, but these do not free historians to fabricate a past for which there is no evidential basis. Here we sharply disagree with a great deal of postmodern literary theory. Historical writing has many of the characteristics of literature but at the same time differs from imaginative literature, even though the two overlap. Historical writing involves imagination, and serious literature always has a reference to reality. But the latter is not bound by the same standards of inquiry that govern the community of scholars. Without this distinction, history would be indistinguishable from propaganda. There is a dangerous conflict between the efforts by postmodern theorists to reject the Enlightenment heritage of rational inquiry at the very time when the precarious condition of today's conflict-laden world requires such inquiry.

Notes

1 Jürgen Osterhammel and Niels P. Peterson, *Globalization: A Short History* (Princeton, 2005); Bruce Mazlish and Akira Iriye, eds., *The Global History Reader* (London, 2004); Bruce Mazlish, *The New Global History* (New York, 2006); Sebastian Conrad, Andreas Eckert, Ulrike Freitag, Thomas Bertram, Gerhard Hauck, and Reinhart Kößler, eds., *Globalgeschichte: Theorien, Ansätze, Themen* (Frankfurt, 2007); *The Oxford Handbook of World History* (Oxford, 2011); Jürgen Osterhammel, *The Transformation of the World: A Global History of the Nineteenth Century* (Princeton, 2014); Lynn Hunt, *Writing History in the Global Era* (New York, 2014), and Crossley Pemela Kyle, *Thinking History Globally* (New York, 2015).

2 Mirjana Gross, *Von der Antike zur Postmoderne. Die zeitgenössische Geschichtsschreibung und ihre Wurzeln* (Vienna, 1998); Michael Bentley, *Modern Historiography* (London, 1999); Anna Green and Kathleen Troup, eds., *The Houses of History: A Critical Reader in Twentieth-Century History and Theory* (New York, 1999); Ralf Torstendahl, ed., *An Assessment of Twentieth Century Historiography* (Stockholm, 2000) (does include chapters on China, Japan, and Africa); Hans-Ulrich Wehler, *Historisches Denken am Ende des 20. Jahrhunderts* (München, 2001); Lloyd Kramer and Sarah Maza, eds., *A Companion to Western Historical Thought* (Malden, 2002); Joachim Eibach and Günther Lottes, eds., *Kompass der Geschichtswissenschaft* (Göttingen, 2002); Donald Kelley, *Fortunes of History: Historical Inquiry from Herder to Huizinga* (New Haven, 2003) and *Frontiers of History: Historical Inquiry in the Twentieth Century* (New Haven, 2006); Georg G. Iggers, *Historiography in the Twentieth Century: From Scientific Objectivity to the Postmodern Challenge* (Hanover, 2005, re. ed.). Lutz Raphael, *Geschichtswissenschaft im Zeitalter der Extreme: Theorien, Methoden, Tendenzen von 1900 bis zur Gegenwart* (München, 2003) does deal briefly with historical studies outside the West in the twentieth century.

3 D. R. Woolf, ed., *A Global Encyclopedia of Historical Writing* (New York, 1998), in two volumes, should also be mentioned here.

4 There were indeed traditions of historiography in Sub-Saharan Africa, going back to the Moslems, and in the case of Black African, even if not Sub-Saharan Africa, to classical Greek sources. See the UNESCO *General History of Africa*, 8 vols. (London, 1981–1993).

5 E.g., Q. Edward Wang, *Inventing China through History: The May Fourth Approach to Historiography* (Albany, 2001).

6 Georg G. Iggers, *Deutsche Geschichtswissenschaft: Eine Kritik der traditionellen Geschichtssuaffassung*, 4th ed. (Wien, 1997).

7 Immanuel Wallerstein, *The Modern World System*, 3 vols. (Minneapolis, 1974–1987).

8 Jürgen Osterhammel, *Geschichtswissenschaft jenseits des Nationalstaats: Studien zu Beziehungsgeschichte und Zivilisationsvergleich* (Göttingen, 2001), 84.

9 Dominic Sachsenmaier, *Global Perspectives on Global History: Theories and Approaches in a Connected World* (Cambridge, 2011).

10 Cf. Mazlish and Iriye, *Global History Reader.*

11 23 vols. (London, 1736–1765), initiated by Georg Sale (1697?–1736), an orientalist who had translated the *Qur'ān* into English.

12 Hayden White, *Metahistory: The Historical Imagination in Nineteenth-Century Europe* (Baltimore, 1973), 2.

13 Ashis Nandy, "History's Forgotten Doubles," *History and Theory*, theme issue, 34 (1995), 44.

14 See P. Nolte, "Modernization and Modernity in History," *International Encyclopedia of the Social and Behavioral Sciences* (Amsterdam, 2001), vol. 15, 9954–9962. See also Stephen R. Graubard, ed., "Multiple Modernities" *Daedalus*, special issue, 129:2 (Winter 2000); and Dominic Sachsenmaier, Jens Riedel, and Shmuel N. Eisenstadt, eds., *Reflections on Multiple Modernities: European, Chinese and Other Interpretations* (Leiden, 2002), 120.

15 Dipesh Chakrabarty, *Provincializing Europe: Postcolonial Thought and Historical Difference* (Princeton, 2000).

16 Benjamin A. Elman, *From Philosophy to Philology: Intellectual and Social Aspects of Change in Late Imperial China* (Cambridge, MA, 1984).

17 On-Cho Ng stresses the East–West differences in his "The Epochal Concept of 'Early Modernity' and the Intellectual History of Late Imperial China," *Journal of World History*, 14 (2003), 37–61.

18 Andre Gunder Frank, *ReOrient: Global Economy in the Asian Age* (Berkeley, 1998); also Kenneth Pomeranz, *The Great Divergence: China, Europe and the Making of the Modern World Economy* (Princeton, 2000).

19 José Ortega y Gasset, *History as a System and Other Essays toward a Philosophy of History* (New York, 1961). See also Frederick C. Beiser, *The German Historicist Tradition* (Oxford, 2011); Frank Ankersmit, *Meaning, Truth, and Reference in Historical Representation* (Ithaca, 2012), ch. 1 "Historicism," 1–28.

20 Leopold von Ranke, "On Progress in History" in Georg G. Iggers, ed., *The Theory and Practice of History* (London, 2011), 20–23.

1 Historiographical traditions in the world

A view of the eighteenth century

Where do we begin?

Transcultural comparisons

We are beginning our discussion of the history of modern historiography on a comparative global scale in the eighteenth century for two main reasons: First, as we already mentioned in the Introduction, this was the eve of the period when Western historiography exerted an important influence on the historical cultures of the rest of the world. Second, the eighteenth century was marked by fundamental changes in historical perspective, primarily but not exclusively in the West. It is then that a modern outlook, as we have described it in the Introduction, emerged that dominated the ways of thinking about history throughout the nineteenth and well into the second half of the twentieth centuries.

The question immediately arises how historiographical traditions can be compared. In the Introduction we have identified several traditions of historical thought and writing; at the same time we are aware that the cultures within which these traditions originated include very different subcultures; thus in the time period we are covering national lines are important. But these traditions of historical thought cannot be defined in exclusively national terms; many important trends are transnational. Notable examples are the broad influence of the Enlightenment in Europe and elsewhere and the spread of "evidential learning" in East Asia. We must be aware that none of these cultures are stagnant, as was often maintained by Eurocentric thinkers from the eighteenth to the mid-twentieth centuries but that all have undergone changes in time. Yet for purposes of comparison, we can work with certain characteristics that they share or do not share.

Characteristics of historiographical thought in different cultures

We shall outline three such characteristics.

1. All have a tradition, which, notwithstanding the changes in outlook that these historiographies undergo, give them a degree of continuity.

All go back to classical models in distant antiquities, which determined the way history was conceived and written. In the West, the great Greek historians, particularly Herodotus (ca. 484–420 BCE) and Thucydides (ca. 460–400 BCE), provide two very different models that shaped historiography until the modern period.[1] The Islamic world has also been very much aware of the philosophers and the historians of the ancient Hellenic and Hellenistic world. In East Asia, the influence of Confucius, who built and expanded on an earlier tradition of recording and writing history by the *shi* (scribe/historian) on various levels of government, was felt not only in China but also in Japan, Korea, and Vietnam. In India, the origins of a historiographical tradition go back to the Sanskrit Vedas and the Indic traditions of Itihasa and Purana, a body of ancient Indian lore about past times and events.

2. Intertwined with the classical origins of each tradition is a religious component. In the West, it is Christianity with its sources not only in the New Testament but also in the Hebrew Bible. These are also crucial to Islam in addition to the *Qur'ān*. Both share a conception of historical time as directional with its origin in Genesis, its central event (for Christianity, the crucifixion of Jesus and for Islam, Muhammad's flight to Medina), and for both, the fulfillment of time with the final judgment. In East Asia, the creation of the *shi*, an official position, which was hereditary up to about the first century CE, stemmed from the practice of shamanism in ancient China. Though teleological notions are generally absent in East Asian historical thought, they do occasionally occur.[2] The role of Confucius as a very worldly figure is, of course, very different from Jesus as the son of God or of Muhammad as God's prophet. Nevertheless, the notion of a heavenly order, *tian*, which was referred to frequently by Confucius himself and his followers, guides the writings of Chinese historians as they judge the actions of the preceding dynasty. Various forms of Buddhism affect East Asian thought generally with cyclical ideas of history also shared by Hinduism. But cyclical ideas are by no means absent in classical Western thought.

3. Third, the institutional framework in which historical writing takes place differs in each of the cultures we have identified, and in each it reflects changing political and social conditions. Perhaps the greatest divergence in this regard is between East Asian and Western historiography. A determining factor for the former, at least in China but to a lesser extent also in Japan and Korea, is the existence from very early times on, albeit with some interruptions, of an empire or, in Korea, a kingdom, in the service of which historians write history. From very early on, historians in China are integrated in the government bureaucracy; from the seventh century on, there exists a History Bureau, whose task it is to write an evaluative history of the previous dynasty. History is thus written by bureaucrats for bureaucrats.[3] On the regional and local level, history is written by collectives similarly organized. Nevertheless, these historical writings do not always serve the interest of the ruler;

inspired by their duty to the *tian*, historians often censure his behavior in their works. Nor are historians always anonymous; we have information about the biographies of many historians. And there are histories written by private individuals. In the West, the situation is almost the reverse. In Classical Antiquity and again in the period since the Renaissance, history is mostly written by individuals not in the service of the state. Particularly in the Middle Ages, it is written within monastic orders, in some cases by historians attached to a court. In the Islamic world, especially in Persia but also in the Greek Orthodox Byzantine Empire, religious orders and court historians play an important role, and again we also have considerable information about individual historians. History was written for a different audience in the West than in China. In Classical Antiquity, historians like Thucydides read their work to an assembled public, and in the period after the Renaissance, printing and a book market made historical writings available to a broad readership. Thus history was written for a broad public more than was the case in China. Book markets were, however, not restricted to the West and were well established in China and Japan.

The West

Characteristics of Western historiography

At this point we shall address the elusive question about the character of the West. This was attempted at a recent international conference in Germany, which included participants from various non-Western countries.[4] In his opening paper, Cambridge historian Peter Burke, one of the most knowledgeable writers on modern Western historiography, posed ten theses on what specifically constitutes Western historical thought. For him "[t]he most important, or at least the most obvious characteristic of Western historical thought," which distinguishes it from other cultures, "is its stress on development or progress, in other words its 'linear' view of the past." This is linked to a "historical perspective," which avoids "anachronisms" and recognizes the individuality of the past. It is further distinctive in its preoccupation with epistemology, that is, with the problem of historical knowledge, its search for causal explanations, and its commitment to objectivity. Moreover "the quantitative approach to history is distinctively Western."[5] The problem with this definition is that the characteristics that Burke describes are not Western but modern.[6] They describe aspects of modern thought that today are shared by many non-Western historians but do not to the same extent apply to historical thought in the West in the medieval or even the Classical period. The linear approach and the idea of progress, the occupation with the problem of historical knowledge – the latter shared by East Asian and Moslem thinkers – and the search for causal explanations emerge in the discussions in the West in the eighteenth century, while the quantitative approach to history belongs to the late twentieth century and is by no means generally accepted.

The emergence of an Enlightenment worldview

What is new in the eighteenth century is a view of the world, which is held by many historians, reflecting the impact of the scientific revolution, a loosening of the earlier reliance on Biblical chronology, and a turn to the critical analysis of sources, which to an extent also took place in East Asia[7] and which in the West goes back to the Renaissance[8] and the Reformation.

There occurs in the West in the eighteenth century a gradual and uneven decline in once firmly held religious convictions. This age is often identified as the Enlightenment,[9] although we have to be aware that the Enlightenment includes very different, often conflicting outlooks, in different national and religious settings, and that the eighteenth century is marked not only by a widely shared belief in science but also by religious revivals, such as Pietism, Methodism, Hasidism, Quietism, and Jansenism, and by the early stirrings of Romanticism. Nevertheless, there is a reorientation in outlook among segments of the upper and the educated middle classes that may be associated with the Enlightenment, which ushers in a modern view of the world.[10]

As we just noted, this change in the West was deeply influenced by what has been called the "scientific revolution," which, as in the case of Isaac Newton (1643–1727), did not question established Christian beliefs but rejected supernatural intervention in the sphere of nature and explained nature in terms of laws that could be validated empirically. While Bishop Bossuet (1627–1704), in his *Discourse on Universal History* (1681), once more defended a traditional Christian theology, Pierre Bayle (1647–1706), in his *Historical and Critical Dictionary* (1695), demanded that all philosophical notions must be subjected to the scrutiny of critical reason. In Great Britain this turn to empiricism was reflected in the philosophy of John Locke (1632–1704), which in turn asserted an important influence on the French *philosophes*, including Voltaire (1694–1778),[11] Denis Diderot (1713–1784), and Jean-le-Rond d'Alembert (1717–1783), who in the mid-century launched the multivolume *Encyclopédie*.[12] For historical writing, this meant an enhanced commitment to cleansing the narration of the past from legend and a commitment to truth. The great historical narratives of the eighteenth century in Great Britain by David Hume (1711–1776), Catherine Macaulay (1731–1791),[13] William Robertson (1721–1793),[14] and Edmund Gibbon (1737–1794)[15] undertook such a task, with Hume seeking to dismantle Whig and Tory constructions of the evolution of British political institutions and Robertson and Gibbon directly confronting Christian traditions. In France, the most notable histories by Charles-Louis de Secondat, Baron de Montesquieu (1689–1755),[16] Voltaire, and the Abbé Guillaume Raynal (1716–1796)[17] took on a more analytical character, seeking causal explanations of historical change. Moreover, Robertson, Gibbon, and Voltaire, although still focusing on high politics, took into consideration social and cultural aspects, with Voltaire in his *History of Manners* (1753) dealing with scientific and technical advancement and with such elements of material life as the invention of eyeglasses and the innovation of street lighting. The Göttingen historian August Ludwig Schlözer (1735–1809) wrote in 1772 that the historian was "no longer to follow the military road where conquerors and armies marched to the beat of the drum. Instead he should travel the unnoticed route followed by traders, apostles, and travelers. . . . The invention of fire, bread, brandy etc. are just as worthy facts as the battles of Arbela, Zama, and Magdeburg."[18]

The past few years have seen the attempt to see the Enlightenment not in primarily Western terms but from a global perspective. But there are fundamental differences in the ways in which the globalization of the Enlightenment is interpreted. Although there is general agreement that the ideas of the Enlightenment, involving a secular, rational worldview and a firm belief in universal human rights, became part of movements toward modernity throughout the world, Sebastian Conrad, in an important essay in 2012, "Enlightenment in Global History: A Historiographical Critique,"[19] emphatically rejects the notion of the essentially European origin of the Enlightenment and argues that parallel ideas existed independently of Western influence in non-Western societies. We have already pointed at the emergence of evidential scholarship in seventeenth- and eighteenth-century China, independently but in some ways similar to what was occurring in Europe, in its move away from theological to secular, historical interpretations. Jürgen Osterhammel, a pioneer in global history, who in his early work more than any other historian dealt with the interrelation of Europe and Asia in the eighteenth century,[20] nevertheless concludes that "[t]he Enlightenment was a European phenomenon that had multifaceted effects around the world but originated in Europe."[21] Conrad, while denying this, concedes that the Enlightenment and the legacy of the French Revolution served as models for movements of modernization and democratization in much of the non-Western world in the nineteenth century and since. Dipesh Chakrabarty, in *Provincialyzing Europe*,[22] has pointed at the different forms of modernization that, despite their diversity, nevertheless shared in European traditions of the Enlightenment, although giving them different forms reflecting their historical and cultural diversity.

Erudition and critical historical scholarship

Yet there was another orientation, which derived from different historiographical origins, with a much more rigorous emphasis on methods of establishing the truth of historical assertions, that of erudition.[23] It wanted to transform history into a scientific enterprise but was less concerned with creating historical accounts than with rigorously examining the veracity of the sources on which such accounts rested. From the perspective of critical scholarship, the authors of the great narrative histories to which we just referred had not been sufficiently careful in their use of sources. To be sure, Gibbon had the best erudite sources available as a basis of his grand history; however, they were not primary sources but accounts by others that needed to be tested.

While the British and French historians we mentioned had all distanced themselves from religious orthodoxy, many of the erudite scholars continued to consider themselves to be good Christians, whether Catholic or Protestant, as they applied critical methods of text analysis not only to secular but also to religious history. Major contributions to the development of such methods were already made in the seventeenth century by scholars from two Catholic religious orders, the Jesuit Bollandists situated in Antwerp and the Benedictine Maurists in Paris, who sought to free the hagiographic stories of the lives of the saints from their legendary segments.[24]

In the course of the eighteenth century, erudition, which narrowly dealt with texts, turned into philology, which placed the text into a broader historical and cultural context. With a focus on the critical examination of texts, the Académie des Inscriptions et des Belles Lettres was established in Paris in 1701. Patterned on it, academies were created in the course of the century, and similar institutions arose in Germany, Italy, Spain, and elsewhere on the continent and in Latin America.[25] Ludovico Muratori (1672–1750) already undertook a critical edition of medieval Italian sources in the first part of the eighteenth century.[26] New methods of textual criticism played a central role in the evolution of Protestant church history in Germany at the new universities at Halle and Göttingen[27] and at the venerable University of Leipzig founded in 1409. Now first steps were taken in the criticism of the Bible. This did not mean that religious belief was abandoned but that the Bible had to be seen in its historical context. Similarly, the Homeric texts were subjected to historical analysis. Friedrich August Wolf (1759–1824) in *Prolegomena to Homer* (1795)[28] sought to demonstrate through an examination of language and style that these poems were not one integral body but were produced by separate poets at different times. Hermeneutics became an important part of philology in search of the historical understanding of the sources. Hermeneutics was not satisfied with establishing the meaning of texts through the analysis of the language as it was used at the time these texts were produced but with understanding the intentions of its authors. This in turn involved seeing these authors within their cultural setting. The basis was laid for a historiography that was more critical than the great narrative histories of the British historians and yet saw history not in terms of fragmented texts but as a coherent story.

Enlightenment historiography

This leads us once more to the question of what constitutes Enlightenment in historiography. The philosophical orientation was much more

dominant in Great Britain and France than in Germany where a herme-
neutical philology was highly developed. Yet both orientations coexisted.
Giambattista Vico (1668–1744) in his *Szienza Nuova* (*New Science*) of
1725[29] had made a classical distinction between nature and history. While
nature was not human-made and thus was incapable of being understood,
history was made by humans and thus, in contrast to nature, could be
understood. Vico was little known outside of Italy until the first part of
the nineteenth century, but this separation between nature and history was
later basic to much historiographical thought, particularly in Germany but
not only there. By the end of the eighteenth century, German historians in
the hermeneutic tradition were just as committed to a scientific approach
as the philosophically oriented British or French historians. However, they
understood science differently, not in terms of the uniformity of human
nature that Hume and Gibbon assumed but rather in terms of the multiplicity of human cultures requiring a methodology that could deal with
this diversity.

Germany in the eighteenth century was obviously different from Great
Britain or France not only because of the absence of a national state, which
was also absent in Italy, but also because the political and social conditions
corresponded much less to the model of modernity we had drawn in the
Introduction. Great Britain and France, of course, were also very different from each other, with capitalism and a civil society most developed in
Great Britain, or at least England, and less developed but not absent in
Germany. Side by side with strong absolutist states, foremost Prussia, there
still existed in Germany local corporate (*ständisch*) institutions that had
virtually disappeared in England and had become considerably weakened in
France. The conditions under which historical writing took place differed
from those in England and to a lesser extent from those in France. While
in England history was most frequently written by men of leisure and in a
few cases, such as Catherine Macaulay, also by women,[30] who wrote for a
market, in Germany many historians and fewer in France were attached to
universities; in Germany, history had been taught at the universities since
they had been reorganized by Melanchton during the Protestant Reformation. As yet, however, historical instruction took the form of lectures in
courses that profited little from original research; this changed in the new
university of Göttingen.[31] Historians, using the newly developed critical
methods, were now most frequently professionals attached to the universities or academies, whereas in England they tended to be men or, in the case
of Catherine Macaulay, women of leisure. There were chairs of history at
Oxford and Cambridge dedicated not to professional training but to the liberal education of aspiring Christian gentlemen, as were also the colleges and
universities established in the American colonies. In Scotland the situation
resembled in some ways more closely that in Protestant Germany, with serious philosophers and historians attached to the universities at Edinburgh,
Glasgow, and Aberdeen.[32]

German forms of Enlightenment

The German intellectual and academic scene in Germany was similarly fashioned by notions of Enlightenment, but *Aufklärung*, the German term for "Enlightenment," took different forms from those in Great Britain and France.[33] In the *Aufklärung*, religion continued to play a much more important role. The historians and philosophers, whether Lutherans or Pietists, were believing Christians who held that their conceptions of an enlightened social order were compatible with their Christian faith. They did not want to free the world in which they lived from religion, as Voltaire did, but like Gotthold Ephraim Lessing (1729–1781) saw the history of the world in terms of the education of humankind. The greatest goal, compatible with Lutheran doctrine, was the achievement of spiritual freedom. The German Enlightenment thinkers, like their French counterparts, wanted to reform what remained of the medieval order and to end the restrictions on free thought and inquiry but did not challenge the established political system. They rather trusted the enlightened monarchs, foremost Frederick the Great (1712–1786), to carry through these reforms. In contrast to the French *philosophes* of the *Encyclopédie*, for whom reason was identical with logical thought or empirical inquiry, German thinkers tended to view reason and understanding, as Vico already had done, as involving the total personality, including its volitional and emotional aspects. They thus viewed the Middle Ages more charitably than Voltaire or Robertson, Thus Justus Möser (1720–1794)[34] in his *Osnabrückische Geschichte* (1768) saw the evolution of his hometown Osnabrück positively since early days as an expression of what he called *Lokalvernunft*, a *Vernunft* (reason) that manifested itself not in abstract terms of human rights but in concrete local institutions that had grown historically. In a somewhat similar way, Edmund Burke (1729–1797) in *Reflections on the Revolution in France* (1790) had defended the British constitution, which he considered an outgrowth of history, against the determination of the French revolutionaries to reshape the political and social order in France along radical lines of abstract human rights.

Yet there are elements of Enlightenment thought that fit well into our definition of modernity as we have delineated it in the Introduction as a heuristic device to compare Western and non-Western historiographies.[35] There came into existence a republic of letters. Similarly as in the natural sciences, the findings and interpretations of historians were submitted to review by a community of scholars. Scholarship acquired a cosmopolitan character with the rapid translation of important works into various European languages. There were scholarly journals in all European countries, and beyond the relatively restricted circle of academic historians and philosophers there was a host of journals such as the *Edinburgh Review* in Scotland read by a broad educated public. The fact that such a public existed, also in Germany, reflected the presence of a civil society. And there was a flourishing book market in addition to lending libraries. Hume, Gibbon, and Robertson received major advances for their works, which became best sellers. Yet the most striking characteristic, which marks the historical outlook of the Enlightenment as modern, was the conception of time in linear directional terms.

From universal history to Eurocentric ideas of progress

The shift to a modern conception of time is best illustrated by the transformations that the writing of universal history underwent in the course of the eighteenth century. There had been a long history of universal histories since early Christian times, the first important representative of which was St. Augustine (354–430). We already mentioned the English *Universal History* in the first half of the eighteenth century. Yet despite its commercial success, the *Universal History* soon came under criticism from Enlightenment perspectives.[36] One of the most outspoken critics was Schlözer, who not only criticized its insufficient adherence to scholarly standards but even more its lack of an overall conception of historical development. For him it constituted a mere compilation of information without a systematic idea. He himself in the 31st volume of the German edition of the *Universal History*, his famous *Nordic History* (1771), went in a very different direction, seeking to reconstruct the culture of Slavic and Central Asian peoples and using anthropological and archeological evidence and an analysis of the languages of these various peoples to gain an understanding of their cultures.

The interest in the broad universal approach of the *Universal History* markedly declined in the second half of the eighteenth century. Voltaire still dealt with China, India, and Persia in his *Essay on Manners and the Spirit of Nations* (1756), but the center of civilization for him was Europe, as it also was in his *Age of Louis XIV* (1751). As the title suggested, Voltaire in this work focused not on the person of Louis XIV but on the age, which he considered the most enlightened in world history. While the German philosopher Gottfried Wilhelm Leibniz (1646–1716) at the turn to the eighteenth century still spoke of two great civilizations on the Eurasian continent, China and Europe, China was now seen as having reached its high point in distant antiquity but as then having become immobile and stagnant.

By the second half of the eighteenth century, several theories of progress were formulated, most notably those by A.R. Jacques Turgot (1727–1781) and the Abbé Etienne Condillac (1714–1780) in France and Isaac Iselin (1728–1782) in Switzerland, who saw the development of mankind from primitive, superstitious beginnings to modern enlightenment, as did the Marquis de Condorcet (1743–1794) in his *Sketch of a Historical Picture of the Progress of the Human Mind* (1794).[37] In a similar vein, Immanuel Kant (1724–1804), in his essays "Eternal Peace" and "The Idea of a Universal History from a Cosmopolitan Point of View," foresaw the Enlightenment as leading to a worldwide society of confederated republics in which wars would be abolished. The driving force would be in Europe. A conception in many ways parallel was put forward by the Scottish moralists in the late eighteenth century, by Adam Ferguson (1723–1816),[38] Adam Smith (1723–1790), and John Millar (1735–1801), for whom the most important factor was the advancement of trade in four stages from nomadism to the urban, commercial societies of their day, again a development centered in a Europe that would bring civilization and culture to the rest of the world. Christian Meiners (1747–1810) in Göttingen wrote broad cultural studies that included aspects of everyday life such as culinary preferences, dress, and housing. And he was one of the first historians to turn to a history of women.[39] Yet he was outspokenly racist in his interpretation of history. Influenced by the discussions taking place in Göttingen among anthropologists who wanted to put the study of man on a scientific basis through the measurements of skulls, he argued that there was a hierarchy of races that could be empirically validated. Meiners asserted that the yellow peoples were inferior to the whites in intelligence and physical beauty and that the blacks were barely different from the apes, thus justifying imperial expansion and slavery. Meiner's racism was by no means unique; it was shared by many distinguished Enlightenment thinkers, including Voltaire, Kant, and Benjamin Franklin.[40]

Meiners was an extreme case, but the belief in white European superiority was held widely and linked to the idea of progress. There were nevertheless dissident voices. The best known of these was Johann Gottfried Herder (1744–1803),[41] who accepted the basic premises of the Enlightenment that related to the equal dignity of all human beings, their *Humanität*. He disputed the idea that mankind was moving to a unified enlightened civilization, possessing a European imprint, and argued instead that there were multiple cultures, European and others, each with its own character and an equal right to exist. Humankind consisted of a multiplicity of ethnic units that he called a *Volk* – a concept difficult to translate into English as "people" or "nation." But while the terms "people" (French *peuple*) and "nation" acquired a very different connotation with the French Revolution – the nation consisting of its citizens – Herder saw the *Volk* as an organic unit, a super individual, passing like individual persons through stages of growth from birth to death. Critical of the Enlightenment notion of abstract reason, he emphasized the role of the nonrational and emotional aspects in the process of knowing.[42] The poetry of a people was a prime indication of its character, and the earlier and more original the poetry was, the less contaminated by civilization and therefore the more valuable it was. Herder was later interpreted by German and Slavic nationalists to justify their rejection of the democratic values of the Western Enlightenment. But Herder greeted the French Revolution in its early, nonterrorist phases. And he was critical of how the expansion of European power had destroyed the cultures of indigenous peoples, such as that of the American Indians.

The Middle East

From the West, we now turn to the Middle East, not only because the region is adjacent to Europe but also because the path of its historical culture crossed and intersected with that of the Western tradition. As early as the eighth and ninth centuries, evidence "for an exchange of historiographic ideas amongst Muslims, Christians and Jews" was already discernible.[43] More specifically, a certain biblical influence was detected in the early historical practices among the Muslims in the Middle East.[44] But the exchange was hardly unilateral. Centuries later when Jean Bodin (1529/30–1596), one of the earliest historiographers in Europe, penned his *Method for the Easy Understanding of History*, he reminded his readers that the Muslims had developed a rich tradition in historical writing.[45]

The rise of Islam and the origin of Muslim historiography

Muslims perceived and fashioned the human relation with God in a similar way as Europeans. The Islamic religious tradition shaped Muslims' worldview and outlook on history. Indeed, the rise of Islam in the early seventh century constituted a major turning point in world history in general and in the history of the Middle East in particular. It resulted in a cultural transformation in the region where the early seeds of human civilization had been sown. In 610 CE when Muhammad ibn Abdallah began receiving revelations, what he, the Prophet for the Muslims, brought to the Arabs was not only a divine plan but also the *Qur'ān*, or "a new literary form and a masterpiece of Arab prose and poetry."[46] Verse thus became the earliest and most respected style in historical writing among the Muslims. It was used to write battle day epics and genealogies. As prototypes of Islamic historiography, epics and genealogies had existed in their crude form in pre-Islamic times. But it was after the rise of Islam that they became important genres in Islamic historiography.[47]

Following Muhammad's *hijrah* from Mecca to Medina in 622, the successful expansion of Islam in the Middle East marked the beginning of the Islamic calendar, or the anchoring point for writing history among the Muslims. Muhammad himself also became a definitive stimulus to Islamic historical writing, not only in that he cast religious importance to past actions and events but also in that, to early Muslim historians, Muhammad's appearance was a "dividing line in the whole course of history."[48] Drawing on the tradition of epics and genealogies, there emerged two kinds of historical literature among the early Muslims. One was *hadīth*, which focused on recording the Prophet's deeds and words. The other was *khabar*, which described the Prophet's and his associates' epic accomplishment. The development of *khabar* and *hadīth* learning also enabled the Muslims to gain the sense of change in time: the stories entered in the *khabar* and *hadīth* were usually preceded by the *isnād* (chain of transmitters/authorities), which provided information that distinguished the stories' original compilers (who were not necessarily their authors) from their transmitters of later generations. The compilation of the *isnād* thus also showed that *hadīth* and *khabar* scholars were concerned with the authenticity of historical records.[49]

For the Muslims, if the *Qur'ān* was a legal and moral compass, the *hadīth* literature, which illustrated the social and legal aspects of the early Muslim community (*ummah*), preserved useful historic precedents.[50] Traditionalism thus was the raison d'être for early Islamic historiography. After the death of Muhammad in 632, it was further fueled by the desire to recount the Prophet's feats, or his campaigns (*maghāzī*) against the Meccans. As a result of the Muslims' military success in conquering present-day Iraq, Syria, Iran, and Egypt, paper, especially Egyptian papyrus, was made available to them. During the eighth and ninth centuries, *hadīth* and *khabar* learning exploded; Islamic historiography also entered its classical period, which witnessed a tremendous growth of Prophetic biography, or the *maghāzī* and *sīra*.[51]

From 610, when Muhammad received his first revelation, to the crisis during the reign of the Caliph Uthman (644–656), these four decades were a "crucial moment" in Islamic history. On the one hand, *Dar al-Islam* (land under Muslim rule) expanded swiftly from the corner of Western Arabia and founded a multiethnic and multilingual empire, spanning from North Africa, through Asia Minor, to Central Asia. On the other hand, the Muslim community experienced severe internal crisis and civil war after the death of Muhammad in 632. This tumultuous period was a Golden Age for the Muslims because it offered "the standard of belief and conduct against which all later ages must measure themselves."[52] To fully comprehend and appreciate the meaning of this Golden Age, Muslim historians searched for more tools to make sense of history, which resulted in the creation of new forms in historiography.

Main styles in Muslim historiography

Toward the end of the tenth century, three genres had emerged as distinct forms of historical learning. In addition to the *sīra*, or biography, there were *tabaqāt* and *ta'rīkh*. The former stood for prosopography and the latter chronography, or chronicle/history, exemplified by Abū Ja'far al-Tabarī's (838?–923) voluminous *Ta'rīkh al-rasul wa al-muluk* (*History of the Prophets and Kings*). The emergence of these three genres suggested that by that time, historical writing had more or less departed from the *Qur'ānic* and *hadīth* tradition and assumed a position of its own. This was evidenced by a much more broadened and diversified interest by historians in recording the past. Ibn Sa'd (784–845), for example, wrote an eight-volume *tabaqāt*, the oldest extant today, which offered biographic sketches of 4,250 people, including 600 women.[53] Al-Tabarī's masterpiece, as mentioned, excelled in the massive amount of sources he culled and cited, as well as in his all-encompassing framework. His *Ta'rīkh* began with creation and ended in

915, only several years before his death. It applauded the rise and triumph of Islam. But despite its ethnocentrism, Al-Tabarī's *Ta'rīkh* was well qualified to be a universal history, whose breadth of coverage was unrivaled by any work of his European contemporaries. As an inspiring model of chronography, it had a paradigmatic influence on Islamic historical writing.[54]

Also around the tenth century, Muslim historians began to experiment with a continuous narrative in historical writing. Ahmad ibn Abī Ya'qūb al-Ya'qūbī (?-ca. 897), whose broad worldview might have been an inspiration for al-Tabarī, was a noted example. To al-Ya'qūbī and like-minded historians, to write history in a continuous narrative might already be a matter of course, for their works were intended to extend coverage well beyond the Arabic world. Al-Ya'qūbī also managed to uphold a high standard with respect to ensuring the accuracy of his sources. His success helped turn the continuous narrative style into a predominant form of historical writing in the Muslim world during the eleventh and thirteenth centuries.[55]

Al-Ya'qūbī and al-Tabarī's catholic worldview and their attempt at universal history mirrored the early success of the Muslim expansion, which was exemplified by the establishment of the Umayyad/Abbasid dynasties. The Umayyad/Abbasid dynastic transition during 747–750 also heightened political awareness among Muslim historians. In view of this transition of power, historians tackled the issue of political legitimacy – namely, whether the Abbasid indeed represented, as they proclaimed, a new phase in Islamic history and whether their reign restored the Muslim community's covenant with God and enabled the Muslims to embark on the course of redemption. A religious paradigm – Covenant-Betrayal-Redemption – was thus used to address a political interest in historiography. To a great extent, this theoretical paradigm also served as a grand narrative underpinning the future development of Islamic historiography among the Persians and Ottomans, for such questions as political legitimacy and right government remained a major concern for Muslim historians.[56]

The bureaucratization and secularization of historiography

In many ways, the development of Persian historiography from the eleventh century highlighted the characteristics of medieval Islamic historiography. First, efforts were made to continue and expand on the writing of universal/ world history. During the Mongol period, Rashīd al-Dīn (1247–1318), a Jewish convert to Islam and the vizier of the Mongol khanate, assembled a group of scholars (including two Chinese) and produced a multivolume universal history, covering a variety of regions stretching from Ireland to China.[57] Second, together with the interest in universal history, new attempts were made to write local and regional history – to some extent, the rise of Persian historiography itself had attested to this interest – that bore on the future development of Islamic historiography. Third, historical study received court patronage and institutional support. Motivated by a pragmatic interest in searching in history for useful political lessons and inspiring moral exemplars, not only court historians but also retired ministers and generals turned to the writing of history. The proliferation of *Fürstenspiegel* (mirror for princes) literature was a telling example, albeit not exclusively historical.[58] Ibn Khaldūn (1332–1406), though a Tunisian, pursued a similar interest in his acclaimed *Muqaddimah* in the fourteenth century, which, in a crystallized form, offered useful political insights for the Muslims of his time. It also became an exemplar of historiography that exerted far-reaching influence in the modern Western world.[59] Fourth, though the Golden Age of the past remained significant, more and more historians turned to the writing of contemporary history, giving rise to dynastic history as well as to autobiography.

The bureaucratization, or secularization, of Islamic historiography would continue more forcefully in the Ottoman centuries. Beginning in the fifteenth century, the Ottomans commissioned historians to compile official chronicles for the empire, though at the peak of Ottoman power, the best history was produced by Mustafa Âli (1541–1600), a retired bureaucrat. Âli's *Künhü'l-ahbar* (*Essence of Histories*) carried on the tradition of universal history in Muslim historiography, as much as Ibn Khaldūn had done a century earlier. But it was also a work of historiography that offered candid and thoughtful discussions on the Islamic and Ottoman tradition of historical writing.[60] By the late seventeenth century, the Imperial Historiographer (*vak'anüvis*) was established by the Ottomans. Mustafa Naima (1665–1716) was the first to assume the position. His political utilitarianism and moral didacticism, his insistence on source verification, his use of unembellished style, and his neutral stance helped set his work apart from that of his contemporaries;[61] to please their court patrons and impress their learned peers, the latter had often employed ornate prose and grandiloquent verse in their historical writings at the expense of accuracy.[62]

In his life, Naima also began to witness a seismic change in the Ottomans' relation with Europe. Over the centuries, Muslims had held contempt for their neighbors in Europe, including the Byzantines, chiefly because "Christian Europe had little or nothing to offer" and "was visibly and palpably inferior."[63] Beginning in the seventeenth century, however, sporadic efforts were made by Muslim/Ottoman historians to acquaint themselves with European history and to use European historical sources to enrich their accounts. A new universal history, compiled by Münedjdjim Bashi (1631–1702), was a prime example. Modeling on the work of Rashīd al-Dīn, Münedjdjim Bashi's history included descriptive and up-to-date coverage of such contemporary events as the English Revolution, based primarily on translated European sources.[64]

The decline of the Muslim world and Muslim historiography?

Münedjdjim Bashi's attempt to expand the tradition of universal history writing harbingered the coming of a new era in the history of the Muslim world;

beginning in the eighteenth century, the Ottomans were no longer able to maintain their military superiority over that of European powers. Modern historians have identified the peace treaty signed between the Ottomans and the Austrians in Karlowitz in 1699 a turning point in the history of Muslim–European relations. The Ottomans began to take an interest in the military technology of the Europeans. But this interest soon spilled over to other areas. Since diplomacy became a viable option for the Ottomans in their dealings with the Europeans, some of their bureaucrats began to learn about the European diplomatic system.[65] The importation of printing technology was another example. Ottoman historians, including the Imperial Historiographers, began to study European languages and write more about European history. Some even came to the realization that their Empire's future lot might depend on "an accurate understanding of European developments."[66] The initiatives for integrating Europe into Muslim historiography were also observable on the local, community level, in the writings of local/regional history and even autobiographies.[67] All this contributed to a marked change in Muslim historical practice and historical thinking. Against the backdrop of the rise of Europe, Ottoman history in the eighteenth century, as well as the history of the Muslim world in general, seemed to have entered a period of stagnation, even decline. In contemporaneous historical discourses, there were also many discussions on the "imperial crisis," which seemed to have corroborated the observation. However, recent scholarship has found that this "decline" thesis needs substantial qualification because the Ottoman Empire remained quite able to regularize its government and maintain a stable hierarchy throughout the eighteenth century.[68] With respect to historical writing, it was also generally agreed that after Mustafa Naima, the Ottoman Empire failed to produce another giant in the century. But in Egypt there was Abd al-Rahmān al-Jabartī (1753–1825), a first-rank historian not only in Egypt but also in the entire Muslim world. In his works, al-Jabartī recorded and reflected on the impact of Napoleon's invasion in his country, to which we shall turn in the next chapter.

India

Western views on Indian historical consciousness

A major problem with including Indian historiography in this chapter on the eighteenth century is that not only Western historians but also, until recently, Indian historians have maintained that India possessed no history until the British colonizers introduced it in the nineteenth century.[69] At that time, Western observers in particular regarded "no history" to imply two things. On the one hand, it referred to the supposed unchanging character of Indian civilization. South Asian society before the advent of the Europeans was not only an Oriental Despotism but also a static society that did not undergo any historical change. From Hegel and Ranke to Marx, the notion prevailed that Indian society was stagnant and immobile. Karl Marx assigned to the two large civilizations of India and China an Asiatic mode of production that did not participate in the progressive course of Western history, whereas for Ranke, India possessed only a "natural history."[70] From this basic premise of an unchanging society, it followed that the Indians had no conception of historical thinking, although for Hegel, who inverted the problematic, it was the lack of historical consciousness that was responsible for India's remaining outside the world historical dynamic.[71] In general it was maintained that history was a British import, that no Indian historian had written history, and that James Mill's (1773–1836) *History of British India* in 1817 constituted the first history of India. This assumed that the Western conception of writing history with its roots in Classical Antiquity, Renaissance Humanism, and the Enlightenment represented the standard by which historical studies were to be measured. Moreover, although many Indian historians in the late nineteenth and early twentieth centuries challenged the theory of Oriental Despotism, they too, like most Western writers of the same period, argued that history was fundamentally different from poetic imagination and that this distinction was absent in India. Recent postmodernist Indian scholarship also held the view that precolonial India lacked proper historical consciousness. India recaptured its past, if at all, through myths and legends.[72]

One may, of course, question whether such a clear distinction existed in the medieval Christian West or whether in an unqualified form it is still accepted by many historical thinkers today who have come to question the possibility of objective history and, like Hayden White, argue that every historical narration is at its core a work of poetic imagination. But we must also appreciate the role of dehistoricization for the imperial project. During the seventeenth and especially the eighteenth centuries, there had been a great admiration for Indian culture, as there had been for China. Indology developed as a discipline at the Académie des Inscriptions et des Belles Lettres in Paris after 1700 and in Germany as well. As we saw earlier, in Great Britain, there were positive portrayals of foreign cultures such as in Sales' *Universal History*, and this was followed by accounts of Indologists such as Sir William Jones (1746–1794), who regarded the civilizational accomplishments of ancient India equal to those of ancient Greece and indeed, saw in them common cultural roots. Although Jones was an official of the colonial government in Bengal, he did not accept the classical Enlightenment model of progress, which placed India at a primitive stage of development in comparison to Europe. Indian civilization possessed its own unique value, even though her ancient glory had suffered a decline ever since and needed the "protection and welfare" of the British.

However, Jones's views were not shared by other, later commentators, many of whom were in the employ of the East India Company, such as the Utilitarian James Mill. Mill accused Orientalists like Jones of performing a disservice by presenting a glorified version of the Indian past, when in fact, both the past and present of India had little to recommend it. The Indians were indeed at a low stage of evolution. "By conversing with the Hindus of the present day, we, in some measure, converse with the Chaldeans and Babylonians."[73] It remained to the British to free the Indians from their primitive culture and bring them into the stream of history.

By the nineteenth century, therefore, the mosaic perspective of culture as seen in writers like Jones and, of course, Herder, whom we mentioned earlier, had given way to a much more critical assessment which also became complicit in the project of colonization. James Mill and Thomas Babington Macaulay (1800–1859) denied that the Indians possessed any civilization in any meaningful sense, and this was said to be evident in their marked lack of historical consciousness. To cite Macaulay, "All the historical information which has been collected from all the books written in the Sanskrit language is less valuable than what may be found in the most paltry abridgements used in preparatory schools in England."[74] Yet even Jones maintained that the Indians lacked a historical sensibility; unlike the Greeks, they had buried their past in a "cloud of fables." Nor were the British the only Europeans to lay bare such inadequacies. Even al-Biruni, the tenth-century Persian historian and Indologist remarked that Indians paid little attention to "the historical order of things."[75]

Indian forms of historical writing

It is true, of course, that ancient India did not have a tradition of history writing in its modern form as a rational, objective, and specialized academic discipline. Yet while ancient (and largely Hindu)[76] India lacked the more familiar forms of history writing, there existed numerous texts of historical intent and memory. "Even Hindu kingdoms had elaborate records, genealogies, and annals which could be as precise as those found in other early modern societies."[77] The literary concept of *itihasa* (translated as "thus it was") and the *Purana* writings, comprising stories from ancient times about the past and written in a variety of genres and forms, played a powerful role in the social culture of ancient India and included, in its corpus, biographies, genealogies, and annalistic accounts of various sorts, "embedded," to use Romila Thapar's term, in nonhistorical narratives.[78] Gabrielle Spiegel has noted the function of annals and genealogies, in the premodern context, in establishing a sense of continuity, linear progression, and social identity.[79] Romila Thapar has also shown that the genres of biography and genealogy in particular became more frequent with the strengthening of the monarchical state, as a means to establish the political authority of the ruler. Additionally, there appears to be a link between the quantum of such texts and the levels of organized bureaucratic power. Thus royal biographies start appearing more frequently after the seventh century, although it was not until the Islamic kingdoms of the Delhi Sultanate and the Mughal Empire in particular that historical accounts of various kinds become much more numerous.

During this period, Persian became the dominant language of administration and much historical writing. The latter were characterized by an impressive attention to individual military and administrative events and their causes couched in nonreligious terms. The contrast they present with the earlier Sanskrit texts is unmistakable. In the latter, the religious and mythological content was primary and the historical content secondary. The Islamic texts were primarily historical but were nonetheless informed by a religious and moral outlook. In this they were not too different from the theodicy of medieval Christian historians, along with a unidirectional sense of time, and while this contrasted quite strongly with the *yuga* (age) concept of cyclical time to be found in the Sanskrit texts, it is important to recognize the commonality of a religious basis.[80] Also, as it has been pointed out, the linear/cyclical binary is not absolute, since within each of the Hindu ages of time there is room for linearity and process, although the sequence of the ages was irreversible.[81]

Indo-Islamic history writing was characterized by narrative histories and commentaries on political issues, and many of these were written by government officials. Their texture was instructional and panegyric, exalting and warning rulers and their courts. At the same time, history remained a narrowly conceived discourse about political power and government rather than a wider social process. It took as its model Persian traditions of historical writing, leading to a distinctive Indo-Persian historiographic tradition comprising chronographic-form political narratives, regnal accounts (*ta'rikh*), and biographies (*tazrika*) of rulers, poets, *ulema*, and saints, as well as memoirs.[82] And remarkably, it was during the reign of the Mughal emperor Akbar (1542–1605) that a rationalist and secular "official history," using archival material and based on a critical examination of sources, was developed to buttress the emperor's imperial ambitions and weaken the influence of the religious elements in government.[83] Mill's was not the first general history of the subcontinent. It was during Akbar's reign that first and second general histories of India were written.[84] It is also important to recall that India during its so-called Islamic phase witnessed a blending of Hindu and Muslim literary traditions, expressed in genre and authorship. Thus, the Indo-Persian *ta'rikh* tradition made an imprint on Sanskrit and vernacular narratives, albeit in selective and creative ways. Numerous Persian histories of dynasties, biographies, and local histories of clans, castes, and towns were written by Hindus of the scribal classes who were employed in the Mughal bureaucracy. But older traditions of writing did not die out. Multiple cultures of writing history coexisted in the early modern period and even well into the twentieth century.[85]

Social and intellectual transformations during the early modern period

In the period between 1500 and 1800, which began with the establishment of the Mughal Empire and ended with the British presence, fundamental transformations took place in the subcontinent that intensified in the seventeenth and eighteenth centuries. These transformations, which have parallels elsewhere in the Muslim as well as in the European worlds and in East Asia too, permit one to speak of an incipient process of modernization as we defined the concept earlier.[86] And these changes are not limited to Muslim India. Two things have to be kept in mind. There is not yet a hard line of separation between Muslims and Hindus, as well as other religious groups. Despite Muslim governmental dominance in much of India, Hindu beliefs and customs permeated Muslim ones and vice versa. "Syncretic" religious practices were prevalent in many parts of the country, such as Bengal and Kashmir. Also, Muslim governments were marked by a high degree of tolerance for the Hindus, many of whom entered high positions in the administration. Second, India was not sealed off hermetically from the surrounding world. From the Aryan conquests ca. 1500 BCE until the European incursions beginning in the fifteenth century CE, India was repeatedly invaded, and the invaders – whether Hellenistic Greeks, Arabs, Persians, Afghans, Mongols, and finally Europeans – left their cultural impact. Nor was invasion the only conduit of culture. From the early first millennium, there began an extensive trade circuit encompassing the Indian Ocean area, and this circuit extended from the Maghreb in the West to South China in the East. The Arab traders joined this circuit in the eighth century, and unlike their predecessors, many of them made their homes in South Asia while continuing to be a part of the Muslim world. On the level not only of trade but also of ideas and scholarship, Indians were in touch with the intellectual centers in Cairo, Istanbul, Baghdad, Damascus, and Teheran, which in turn maintained contact with Europe. Also, an important consequence of trade was bilingualism and even multilingualism. This suggests that, beyond trade, forms of knowledge were also transmitted along trade routes.

Some scholars have argued that the eighteenth and to an extent the seventeenth centuries were marked by intellectual transformations that differed from country to country and within each country, including India, but had certain common traits.[87] This change began already before the impact of colonialism. It was connected with the emergence of a world market that brought India into closer contact with Europe. This development took place largely in the major urban centers such as Delhi and Lucknow, but with the decline and dissolution of the Mughal empire, the residential cities in the new smaller territorial principalities also became centers of intellectual and literary life. All this contributed to a new civil society that sprang up in the urban centers side by side with more traditional modes of thinking. Similarities are pointed out with eighteenth-century Europe. The monopoly of the scholars and theologians was broken as reading circles sprang up in the towns. Salons came into existence, in some ways similar to those in Paris and Berlin, in India frequently headed by a courtesan. In addition to the salons attended by well-to-do traders and nobles, there were study circles attended by members of lower social classes, soldiers, artisans, and small traders and businessmen. Coffee houses and bath houses became places for the exchange of ideas. The colloquial language, foremost Urdu, replaced Persian as the language of communication in these circles. It involved a turn away from religious orthodoxy but not necessarily from religion. Reminiscent of Western currents in the eighteenth century, stress was placed on the development of the individual personality. As A. Ali writes in *The Golden Tradition* (1973) of India:

> By the middle of the eighteenth century, doubts begin to assault the mind, the spirit of inquiry awakens, curiosity raises its head, questionings are heard like the rumblings of thunder, the critical spirit, the spirit that refuses to take things on mere authority, is born as the modern age has already begun. . . . It is now that the spirit of freedom awakens, surprisingly coincidentally with a similar movement in Europe where the floodgates of Revolt and Romanticism were opened.[88]

But we must be careful. Political, economic, and social conditions were still very different in Europe and India. The caste system was still in place. The transformations that made possible the French Revolution in France or pressures for reform elsewhere in Europe were absent in India. India was a society in transition but still largely traditional in its social structure and intellectual outlook. But was historical writing in India then a "derivative discourse," a Western import brought by the British?

Recent research suggests otherwise. The changes of the early modern period had varied effects. The emergence of new principalities in the seventeenth and eighteenth centuries brought with it a new class of civil servants and legal scholars. Bureaucratization led to the establishment of archives and the employment of historians attached to the courts with the task of researching legal rights. An emerging middle class resorted to archival records to secure its property claims in the courts. In East India, an already existent Persianized historiography was, by the late eighteenth century, being written in service of the first colonial authorities desirous of acquiring knowledge about the regions they were conquering. As such, they became "acts of self-representation" in the transition from precolonial to colonial rule, as they attempted to transmit indigenous notions of good government to the new rulers. But structurally they remained in the Indo-Islamic tradition, writing narrative discourses about political power as articulated through the institutions of government.[89]

In South India, however, among a growing class of "service gentry" that included scribes, court functionaries, and village officials, we see the emergence, frequently in the regional vernacular, of a "new and specific historical awareness."[90] Its members came from a tradition of graphic rather than oral literacy, privileged prose over poetry, and were multilingual. Their works do not have royal or other patrons, nor are they dedicated to the gods, although the moral framework that underlies them suggests a politically prescriptive significance. They wrote in Telegu, Tamil, Marathi, Sanskrit, and Persian, and it is in Telegu that the word for history, *caritramu*, emerges in the sense of *histoire* and *storia*. Not least, their writings appear to conform to modern criteria of historical writing.[91]

The primary reason why these texts have been overlooked is ascribable to their genre. Written either as courtly poetry, folk epics, or diplomatic reports, their historical content is "hidden" to us but understood by their contemporaries by their "texture," the subgeneric markers, shifters, and the like within texts that informed their audience of their historical intent. As yet, history *sui generis* did not exist as an independent discipline, or *shastra*, to use the Sanskrit equivalent for the term. But historical consciousness did and was written in literary modes prevalent in the culture.

Of course, these were still regional histories. But taken together with a flourishing Indo-Persian tradition, which had also influenced extant genres and styles contributing to a diverse array of historical cultures, one can argue that although premodern Indian historiography did not correspond to the modern definition of the subject as a secularized, scientific, and factual professional discipline, it was not by any means lacking in historical consciousness. Nor did it lack elements of rationality and factuality, even in the "embedded" histories of ancient India, when these were seen as required forms of remembrance. Further, early modern historical styles, such as the Indo-Persian *ta'rikh* tradition, had rigorous rules of authority and method. If historical writing is seen as a reflection of the social, political, and cultural imperatives of its time, then premodern Indian historical writing was sensitive to the exigencies of its evolving culture.

East and Southeast Asia

Shamanism and history: The origin of the shi

Finally we turn to East and Southeast Asia, where we see a long tradition of historical writing established first in China. In its formative years, shamanism played an important role in the gestation of both the written language and the historical culture in ancient China. The earliest records of history were found in oracle inscriptions on animal bones and tortoise shells during the Shang period (ca. 1600–1066 BCE). These records were mostly entered by a shaman-cum-king for the purpose of divination and incantation. In a later time, a position called *shi* was created, and during the long course of the Zhou dynasty (1046–256 BCE), the *shi* multiplied and became ubiquitous at the Zhou court. The modern Chinese now tend to translate *shi* as "historian." But in Zhou times, the *shi*'s responsibility was not exclusively historical – it was also a scribe and an astrologer.[92]

That historical writing originated from shamanic activities, and that the *shi* was initially a government position left an enduring imprint in Chinese historical thinking. Writing history in China was often an official undertaking, though prior to the seventh century, many historical works were not written per government orders, and after the seventh century, there was still a vigorous practice in private history writing. In ancient texts, such as the Six Classics, which Confucius (ca. 551–479 BCE) might have helped edit and preserve, there was already reference to history as a mirror, reflecting the past rights and wrongs that were deemed beneficial for the present. History thus was regarded as a repository of political wisdom, which became a lasting belief broadly held in China's imperial period, if not also today. It prompted new dynastic rulers to order the compilation of the history of the preceding dynasty. From the seventh century, this became a standard practice of historical writing in China, which, in no time, also exerted a notable influence in Korea, Vietnam, and Japan.

The formation of Confucian historiography

The nature of dynastic history writing was written "by the bureaucrats for the bureaucrats," as well as for the rulers. However, private interest in historical writing was both persistent and lively throughout China's imperial era. Sima Qian (145–87 BCE), arguably the greatest historian in imperial China, for example, pursued by and large the same interest as did Herodotus when he set out to compile the *Records of the Historian* (*Shiji*), which was to satisfy his curiosity for extraordinary occurrences and preserve historical memory. Though he was born into a hereditary *shi* family, Sima wrote his magnum opus on his own without the emperor's patronage. And his goal was "to explore the boundary between the realm of Heaven and the realm of humanity, to comprehend the process of changes in times past and present, and to establish the tradition of one family."[93] Sima did not intend it simply as a service to the emperor.

At the time when Sima Qian began his writing, narrative history had already taken root in China, to which Sima was indebted in developing his own style – "to establish the tradition of one family."[94] Yet in his effort to "comprehend the changes in times past and present" or to seek out the governing law in history, Sima was inspired more by Confucius, who had established that history writing ought to help establish a normative sociopolitical order. By revising the existent *Spring and Autumn Annals* (*Chunqiu*), compiled by the *shi* of his home state Lu, Confucius altered slightly the records in the *Annals* by replacing certain words (e.g., from "killed" to "murdered") in them in order to achieve a stronger moral condemnation on the illicit behavior seen rampantly at his time. By exercising the so-called "pen-law of the *Spring and Autumn*" (*Chunqiu bifa*), Confucius demonstrated that the historian's pen was used not only to record the past but also to pass moral and political judgment.

In the works of Confucius and Sima Qian, there were frequent references to the *tian* (Heaven), or the Chinese notion of God. This showed that during their times, the shamanic belief in the Heaven–humanity correlation remained influential. However, by moralizing the writing of history, Confucius injected a worldly turn to the historiographical tradition and enhanced the agency of historical writing: He hoped to restore what he considered a Heavenly order by the historian's pen, whereby the good and evil were made known to the public. To Confucius and his followers, the historian's straightforwardness was not devoid of a moral standard; it rather meant that the historian should set his record "straight" to uphold the moral standard, not "bend" to political pressure or coercion.[95]

Given the influence of Confucianism, which became a state ideology in the Han dynasty (206 BCE–220 CE), historiographical compilation thus pursued a dual goal. It was both historical and normative, motivated as much by the desire to build a repository of historical knowledge as by the pursuit of an ideal sociopolitical order. Thus Sima Qian's *Records* follows a hierarchical structure, a microcosm of his own ideal world perhaps, to house his vividly and colorfully styled biographies.[96] By ranking and grouping historical figures this way, Sima demonstrated what the ideal sociopolitical order was supposed to be. The annals-biography style Sima invented was later adopted, after some modification, as the standard form for dynastic history writing in imperial China and elsewhere in the Sinitic world.

The History Bureau and dynastic history

Beginning in the Tang dynasty (618–907), history writing was turned into an official undertaking by the establishment of the History Bureau. The Tang rulers showed a great interest in making history a resourceful mirror from which useful political lessons could be learned to improve their rule and prolong the dynasty. The Bureau's task, or the task of its historians, was, on the one hand, to compile histories of previous dynasties and collect and preserve documents and sources for the current regime on the other. These sources were vetted and organized under such categories as "court diaries," "daily calendar," and "veritable records," on whose bases a contemporary history, called "national history" (*guoshi*), would be compiled.[97]

The Tang system of official historical writing exerted a paradigmatic influence in Korea, Vietnam, and, in a later time, also in Japan, so much so that dynastic histories in these places were written in Chinese as late as the end of the nineteenth century. Conversely, valuable records of early histories of Japan, Korea, and Vietnam were found in Chinese historical works. In Japan, the *Six National Histories* (*Rikkokushi*), written originally in Chinese, were patterned on the Tang model of official history writing.[98] The notion that history was a mirror for the present, as propagated by Tang rulers and historians, also resonated well in Japan. During the eighth and twelfth centuries, there appeared a group of historical texts, *Ōkagami*, *Imakagami*, *Mizukagami*, and, more famously, *Azumakagami*, all bearing the word "mirror" (*kagami*) in their titles. But their content and style were becoming increasingly more Japanese than Chinese, indicating that the Chinese influence had gradually waned. Indeed, unlike in Korea and Vietnam, the Chinese tradition of dynastic history was never solidified in feudal Japan, partially because prior to the seventeenth century, Japan had not established a unified dynastic power. But despite the frequent warfare, efforts were continually made by Japanese historians to record history and examine the causes of the rise and fall of powers. The proliferation of the "battle-day literature" (*Gunki monogatari*) was a case in point.[99]

The Tang practice of historical writing and its idea of history as a mirror were not particularly moralistic, if judged by the Confucian standard. After the fall of Han in the third century, Buddhism had entered China proper and Tang culture was characteristically Buddhist, especially with respect to its influence in Japan and Korea. Buddhist hagiographic writing, as well as its exhortative intent, succeeded in merging with the existing tradition of biographic writing in Tang historiography. But Confucianism revived during the Song dynasty (960–1279), which, sometimes known as Neo-Confucianism in Western scholarship, reasserted the moralist position in historical writing. This assertion, however, was not immune to Buddhist influence. In the Song discourse of history, historians deployed such metaphysical concepts as the "principle" (*li*) or "Heavenly principle" (*tianli*) to moralize historical writing, which was unseen before in classical Confucianism.[100]

The spread and influence of dynastic historiography

The Song practice of history thus differed from that of the Tang, and the Neo-Confucian practice differed from that of the early Confucians. Empowered by their knowledge of the cosmological order, members of the literati class turned to history to remonstrate with their emperor against any deviating behavior from the Heavenly principle. Sima Guang's (1019–1086) undertaking of *The Comprehensive Mirror for Aid in Government* (*Zizhi tongjian*) was a famous example. On first look, this general history, covering over 1,300 years, exercised the time-honored idea in making history a political mirror for government. But Sima Guang perhaps sought to go beyond that; his masterpiece could be viewed as offering a master narrative that generalized the rise and fall of dynasties in the past. It distilled valuable political wisdom for the ideals of proper rulership.[101]

In other words, from the Song period onward, dynastic historiography became increasingly monarch centered. It had departed from the model established by Sima Qian in the Han period, which now looked almost panoramic in its coverage. While dynastic historians narrowed the scope of their work, they increased tremendously its size. Many dynastic histories comprised of a great number of volumes. Because of its stupendous size, once completed, one dynastic history was printed in only several copies. They were usually kept in the royal palace and imperial library, inaccessible to the general public. And this was not just a Chinese phenomenon. As China's closest neighbors, Korea and Vietnam both established the system of official history writing under the Chinese influence from the twelfth century on, if not earlier.[102] In 1145, Kim Pu-sik (1075–1151) compiled the *Historical Records of the Three Kingdoms (Samguk sagi)*, which is the earliest surviving history in Korea.[103] During the Chosŏn dynasty (1392–1910), which saw more Chinese influence in the form of Neo-Confucian learning, more efforts were made to promote history writing.[104] The *History of Korea (Koryŏsa)*, compiled in 1451, was Korea's first complete dynastic history. *The Comprehensive Mirror in the Eastern Kingdom [Korea] (Tongguk t'onggam)*, on the other side, was an emulation of Sima Guang. In their effort to uphold the Confucian world order, Korean historians followed the principle of flunkeyism (*sadae*) and affirmed Chosŏn Korea's tributary bondage to China.[105] However, this might be an isolated case because dynastic histories in Vietnam of the same period were intended to glorify the feats of *Dai Viet* ("Great Viet"), as in *An Outline History of Great Viet (Dai Viet su luoc)* and *Historical Records of Great Viet (Dai Viet su ky)*. The *Complete Version of the Historical Records of Great Viet (Dai Viet su ky toan thu)*, compiled by a court historian Ngo Si lien in 1479, was another example, even though all these historical texts invariably also registered the influence of Confucian moral values.[106] Meanwhile, the Buddhist, or South Asian, influence in Vietnamese historiography was not to be ignored. The *Compilation of the Departed Spirits in the Realm of Viet (Viet dien u linh tap)* from the thirteenth century was written by a custodian of a Buddhist library.[107] Finally, in Japan, dynastic history writing entered a period of revival from the seventeenth century, which saw the compilations of the *Comprehensive Mirror for Our Dynasty (Honchō tsugan)* and *History of Great Japan (Dai Nihonshi)*; the latter was launched by a member of the Tokugawa family, the *shogun* (general) who ruled a unified Japan in the emperor's name.

As dynastic historiography established itself as the norm of historical writing in the Sinitic world, back in China where it originated, its quality deteriorated. During the Ming dynasty (1368–1644), the augmentation of imperial power meant that it became more and more difficult for the historians of the History Bureau to record faithfully the events happening around the court, let alone those from elsewhere. Private history writing flourished in the Ming period, in part because historians worked in private, inspired continually by the Neo-Confucian political ideals and intent on exposing concealments in official historiography.[108] The proliferation of private history writing in the Ming period also benefited from the growth of a commercial culture and a book market beginning in the sixteenth century. Thanks to the development of trade and commerce, an urban society emerged in southeast China, which created a new readership among the urban dwellers who turned to history mainly for entertainment. Tailored to such an interest, new genres appeared in Ming private historiography in which the line between history and fiction became increasingly porous.[109]

"To seek the truth from facts": The rise of evidential learning

After the Mings' fall in the seventeenth century, the Manchus established the Qing dynasty (1644–1911) in China. To Confucian scholars, including those in Korea and Japan, the collapse of the Ming dynasty marked the end of a historical era. Korean Confucians attempted to turn Korea into Sojunghwa (Little China), or a new center of Chinese culture.[110] Japan under Tokugawa's reign (1603–1868) saw a notable development of commercial culture, parallel to that of Ming and Qing China. In response to the need and interest of the growing number of townspeople, Japanese scholars employed different hermeneutic strategies in interpreting the Confucian classics, which came to unravel and fragment the Neo-Confucian orthodoxy endorsed by the shogunate. Of the many schools emerging at the time, the National Learning School, led by Motoori Norinaga (1730–1801), was particularly significant; buoyed by a protonationalist sentiment, it doubted the universal value of Confucian teaching and questioned its cultural relevancy to Japan.

In China, a similarly critical attitude toward Neo-Confucianism was manifest in the school of evidential learning (*kaozhengxue*), which arose in the wake of the Ming-Qing dynastic transition from the mid-seventeenth century. Intent on promoting practical learning and statecraft knowledge, Qing scholars became displeased and disillusioned with the Neo-Confucian interpretation of Confucian teaching. They distanced themselves from the Ming Neo-Confucian metaphysics and endeavored to restore the classical Confucianism of the Han period and earlier. To this end, which was analogous to the Renaissance humanists' efforts to restore Greco-Roman classical culture, Qing scholars turned to the methods of philology, phraseology, phonology, etymology, and epigraphy, hoping to fathom and wrest the original (hence true) meaning of the Confucian classics.

This reorientation of intellectual culture, characterized by Benjamin Elman as a process "from philosophy to philology," exerted a significant impact on the study of history.[111] It pointed to a marked change in historical thinking in that the evidential scholars' rejection of Neo-Confucianism was predicated on the notion that since the Neo-Confucians lived over a thousand years after Confucius, there was no reason to worship their works as orthodox and authoritative interpretations of Confucian teaching. This idea of anachronism had appeared before, such as in the Song period.[112] But never before had it become so widespread and influential as in the eighteenth century.

For evidential scholars, *Shishi qiushi* (to seek truth in actual facts) was a motto. This was embodied most typically in Dai Zhen's (1724–1777) scholarship, a luminary in the Qing scholarly constellation. Dai's scholarship was encyclopedic, ranging from phonology, etymology, and phraseology to geography, astronomy, and mathematics. Though he was not primarily a historian, he studied ancient institutions and regulations. His main goal in

pursuing such a broad array of knowledge was to achieve a better understanding of Confucian teaching. Different from the Neo-Confucians, especially those of the Ming who had prized intuition and epiphany, Dai focused
on restoring the apposite historical context in order to apprehend the meaning of the Confucian classics on their own terms. He maintained that if one
hoped to understand the meaning of the text, one had first to understand
the meaning of the words.[113] Similar to the humanists and antiquarians in
Europe of the same period, Dai and his followers believed that philology
was the queen in classical learning. In particular, they emphasized the study
of ancient phonology because pronunciations changed over time, and, in
ancient times, many characters had been interchangeable due to their then
similar pronunciations.[114] The Qing scholars' interest in ancient history was
not unprecedented. Given the long tradition of historical writing in China,
the Chinese had possessed a good knowledge about their past, perhaps
better than any other in the world of the same period. They acquired this
knowledge by studying and mastering the masterpieces bequeathed to them
from the past. The towering status of Sima Qian, for example, spawned
many imitations across the Sinitic world. However, at times efforts were
also made to evaluate the master's work critically, checking the validity and
reliability of its content. Liu Zhiji (661–721), a Tang historian, was a good
example. In his *Comprehensive Perspectives on Historiography (Shitong)*,
arguably the first historiographical study ever produced in the Sinitic world,
Liu offered a critical, sometimes scathing, evaluation of previous histories
and classics.[115] Indeed, historiographical study was a respected scholarly
tradition in imperial China; scholars had made tremendous effort to gloss,
examine, and annotate previous historical works.

The Qing evidential project built and expanded on this tradition. Wang
Mingsheng's (1722–1797) *Critical Studies of the Seventeen Histories (Shi-
qishi shangque)*, Qian Daxin's (1728–1804) *Critical Notes on the Twenty-
two Histories (Ershi'ershi kaoyi)*, and Zhao Yi's (1727–1814) *Notes on the
Twenty-two Histories (Nian'ershi zhaji)* were the best examples of Qing
evidential scholarship, showcasing its critical spirit and sophisticated methods. As shown in their titles, the subject of their critical study was revered
dynastic histories that had been previously regarded as "standard histories"
(*zhengshi*). Yet Wang, Qian, and Zhao subjected them to critical scrutiny,
comparing their records with myriad other sources, including inscriptions on
bronze and stones. Armed with their erudition, they also provided detailed
and usually correct explanations for the people, events, official titles, places,
and institutions mentioned in them. In addition, they, especially Zhao Yi,
discussed general patterns and trends of social, cultural, and institutional
developments.[116]

To conduct the studies as such, these historians were motivated by the
traditional desire to establish history as a mirror. Yet meanwhile they argued
that history played an equally important role as the study of the Confucian classics, a bold argument unseen before. To these evidence-oriented

historians, historical study had a value equal to that of classical study. This trend of historicism in Qing intellectual culture led to a "historicization" of classical learning.[117] This process was best summarized in the statement that "all Six Classics were histories," entered emphatically by Zhang Xuecheng (1738–1801) in his *General Principles of Literature and History (Wenshi tongyi)*, even though Zhang's own scholarly interest extended beyond evidential study. By emphasizing and restoring the historicity of the classics, Qing evidential scholars succeeded in unraveling the Neo-Confucian hermeneutic edifice, which had considered the classics as sacred and immutable, and raised the agency of history by emancipating it from its traditional auxiliary status to classical study. They pursued and maintained the belief that the right and wrong or the greatness of the classics would reveal themselves once the historical truth was established. This belief was not dissimilar to Leopold von Ranke's in his well-known maxim, *"wie es eigentlich gewesen."* Zhao Yi, for example, criticized the Neo-Confucian project on historiography, for it rewrote some previous historical works not for correcting their mistakes but for better espousing Confucian ideals.[118]

All these scholars – Wang Mingsheng, Qian Daxin, Zhao Yi, and, to a lesser extent, Zhang Xuecheng – were contemporaries of Dai Zhen. In fact, they befriended one another; Qian, for example, was a friend of Dai's and related to Wang by marriage. Together with many others, they formed a scholarly community, a Republic of Letters, which consisted of several schools emerging from where these savants worked as school teachers and independent scholars. The emergence of this Republic of Letters benefited from the boom of a book culture in the Ming and Qing period. According to one estimate, by 1750, this book culture had printed more books in China than the sum of all books printed in the rest of the world.[119] Qing scholars often published their works in a number of volumes, even though some of them, such as Zhang Xuecheng, lived in poverty.

This explosive growth of the book culture in Qing China extended the vigorous development of commercial culture, associated with impressive economic development and consistent population growth. As mentioned earlier, an urban society in southeast China had already emerged in the Ming period. By the eighteenth century, a national market had formed, characterized by its long-distance trade both at home and abroad. As merchants gained more social respect, they interacted and associated, through marriage, with the literati class. To some extent, the augmented interest in practical learning and evidential study in the Qing suited the need of merchants in an increasingly urban and commercialized cultural setting.

Associated with this social change, the Republic of Letters also grew; many scholars who had succeeded in the civil examinations retired early from government in order to devote themselves to teaching and scholarship. Qian Daxin and Wang Mingsheng were well-known examples. Their decision was facilitated by the availability of teaching positions in many academies. During Ming and Qing China, the number of academies reached

an unprecedented high level. Many scholars thus were able to support themselves and, more importantly, exchange their ideas with one another by
teaching in an academy. The development of the commercial culture already
mentioned also provided financial support to some members of the literati
class for their interest in scholarly pursuit. Wealthy merchants, for example,
usually offered a handsome amount of royalty and commission to a noted
scholar or a poet for writing a eulogy or a poem for a deceased family member or an ancestor. During the eighteenth century, though the odds of passing the highest level of the civil examination appeared to have worsened, the
number of candidates succeeding at the lower levels increased, suggesting
the rise of literacy – estimated between 20 and 30 percent among the male
population – and an expanded readership for books in history and other
genres.[120] If a "reading public" indeed was emerging in Ming-Qing China,
it was also benefited from the increase of literacy rate among women, as
revealed by recent studies of Chinese women's history.[121]

The interest in evidential learning, too, spilled over to the Qing court.
Emperor Qianlong (r. 1735–1795), who was well-known for his grandiose
ambitions and extravagant projects, commissioned the compilation of the
Complete Works of the Four Treasuries (*Siku quanshu*). It was a stately
attempt to screen, abstract, and catalog all worthy books published in the
past and organize them under the four categories of classics, history, philosophy, and belles lettres, a traditional bibliographical system first used during
the pre-Tang period. The completion of the *Four Treasuries* project reaped
the fruits of evidential study; the latter's ideas and techniques in textual and
historical criticism were applied to examine and ascertain the authenticity
of the books and to investigate and ensure the integrity and veracity of their
contents. In fact, Dai Zhen, the doyen of evidential learning, was made an
editor for the project.[122]

In other aspects, the emperor's interest in and patronage of the *Four
Treasuries* project could be an insidious scheme, aiming at thought control
of the literati class. It might be intended to channel the intellectual energy
to something meticulous and time-consuming in order to thwart preemp-
tively subversive acts. During the Qing period, there indeed occurred several
bloody and notorious cases of "literary crimes" (*wenziyi*), in which a writer,
historian, or a poet was executed by the emperor, along with his family, rela-
tives, and even disciples, for alleged treasonous ideas found in his writings.
Emperor Qianlong might come across as a dilettante in literati culture. Yet
insofar as his political consideration was concerned, he was certainly more
dependent on Neo-Confucian learning for its emphasis on moral cultivation
and sociopolitical order. Thus viewed, evidential learning was tinged with a
dissident overtone. At least, it showed an unwillingness among some members of the literati class to lend overt support to Manchu rule.

The Tokugawa shogun in Japan also detected the potentially subversive
power in evidential study, though as an intellectual movement it did not
reach Japan until the end of the eighteenth century. The Kansei Prohibition

(1790) was an example.[123] It was shogunate's attempt to shore up the Neo-Confucian orthodoxy and fend off its critics and challenges from various schools, including the emergent evidential learning advocated by Inōe Kinga (1732–1784) and Yoshida Kōtan (1745–1798) in Japan.[124] Despite the prohibition, evidential learning continued to attract a following and reached maturation during the nineteenth century, whereas it declined apparently in Qing China.

In Chosŏn Korea, critics of Neo-Confucian learning, including those with a bent for evidential learning, were gathered together in the School of Practical Learning whose rise mirrored the Ming-Qing intellectual change in China.[125] An Chŏng-bok (1712–1791), an acclaimed evidential historian, demonstrated his excellent skills in source criticism and enviable erudition in both Korea and Chinese histories in his *An Outline History of Eastern [Korean] History* (*Tongsa kangmuk*), a chronicle bearing a deceiving Neo-Confucianist title. Noticeably, spurred on perhaps by an embryonic nationalist sentiment in light of Ming's fall, he and especially his followers began to shed doubt on the Sinocentric world order that had traditionally undergirded Chosŏn Korea's tributary relation with China.[126] In the work of Le Quy Don (ca. 1726–1784), a well respected Vietnamese historian, similar efforts were made to broaden the use of sources, thanks to the influence of evidential learning. Le's multivolume *Complete History of the Le Dynasty* (*Le Trieu Thong Su*) departed from official Vietnamese historiography. Enriched by vivid biographic accounts, it was more a prosopography than a chronicle, reminding one of Sima Qian's *Records*.[127] In sum, prior to the intrusion of Western powers, the intellectual life of the Sinitic world exhibited a great deal of vitality and dynamism, highlighted by the ebb and flow of evidential learning. In the following centuries, the interest and focus nurtured by evidential learning were to condition and characterize the efforts by the historians in the region to accommodate and appropriate the Western influences, to which we will turn in the next chapter.

Notes

1 See Ernst Breisach, *Historiography: Ancient. Medieval, & Modern* (Chicago, 1983); Arnaldo Momigliano, *The Classical Foundations of Modern Historiography* (Berkeley, 1990).
2 Masaki Miyake, "Millennial Movements and Eschatologies in Europe and Asia: A Comparative Approach" in Marlene Soulsby, ed., *Time: Perspectives of the Millennium* (Westport, 2001), 213–227; for Europe: Karl Löwith, *Meaning in History: The Theological Implications of the Philosophy of History* (Chicago, 1949).
3 See W. G. Beasley and E. G. Pulleyblank, eds., *Historians of China and Japan* (Oxford, 1961), 5; also E. Balacz, "L'histoire comme guide de la pratique bureaucratique," ibid., 78–94.
4 Jörn Rüsen, ed., *Western Historical Thinking: An Intercultural Debate* (New York, 2002).
5 Peter Burke, "Western Historical Thinking in a Global Perspective," ibid., 15–30.

6 Georg G. Iggers, "What Is Uniquely Western about the Historiography of the West in Contrast to That of China?" ibid., 101–110.

7 On China, see Benjamin Elman, *From Philosophy to Philology: Intellectual and Social Aspects of Change in Late Imperial China* (Cambridge, MA, 1984).

8 See Donald R. Kelley, *Foundation of Modern Historical Scholarship: Language, Law, and History in the French Renaissance* (New York, 1970).

9 There is a tremendous literature on the Enlightenment. The following is a selective list of mostly recent literature: For a very comprehensive trans-European discussion of the Enlightenment, see the Wikipedia article "Age of Enlightenment," updated on August 13, 2015. Some titles: Dorinda Outram, *The Enlightenment* (Cambridge, 2005); Martin Fitzpatrick, Peter Jones, Christa Knellswolf, and Iain McCalman, *The Enlightenment World* (New York, 2004); Ellen Judy Wilson and Peter Hanns Reill, *Encyclopedia of the Enlightenment* (New York, 1996); James Schmidt, ed., *What Is Enlightenment? Eighteenth-century Answers and Twentieth-century Questions* (Berkeley, 1996); Peter Gay, *The Enlightenment: An Interpretation*, 2 vols. (New York, 1966–1969); Carl Becker, *The Heavenly City of the Eighteenth-century French Philosophers* (Ithaca, 1931); Isaiah Berlin, *Three Critics of the Enlightenment: Vico, Hamann, Herder* (Princeton, 2000); Peter Hanns Reill, *Vitalizing Nature in the Enlightenment* (Berkeley, 2005); Jonathan Israel, *A Revolution of the Mind: Radical Democracy and the Intellectual Origins of Democracy* (Princeton, 2010); Harvey Chisick, *Historical Dictionary of the Enlightenment* (Lanham, MD, 2005); Daniel Brewer, ed., *Cambridge Companion to the Enlightenment* (Cambridge, 2014). Most recently, Sebastian Conrad's attempt to place the Enlightenment in a global context, "Enlightenment in Global History: A Historiographical Critique," *American Historical Review*, 117 (2012), 999–1027.

10 Paul Hazard, *La Crise de la conscience européenne 1680–1715* (Paris, 1935); English: *The European Mind* (Cleveland, 1963); also Paul Hazard, *European Thought in the 18th Century: From Montesquieu to Lessing* (New Haven, 1964).

11 J. H. Brumfitt, *Voltaire, Historian* (Oxford, 1958).

12 *Encyclopédie, ou dictionnaire raisonné des sciences, des arts, et des métiers*, published between 1751 and 1776 with later supplements. Diderot was chief editor; contributors included d'Alembert, Condillac, Baron d'Holbach, Montesquieu, Rousseau, Turgot, and Voltaire, among many others. See Robert Darnton, *The Business of the Enlightenment: A Publishing History of the Encyclopédie, 1775–1800* (Cambridge, MA, 1979); Philipp Blom, *Enlightening the World: Encylopédie, The Books That Changed the Course of History* (New York, 2005).

13 Catherine Macaulay, *History of England from the Accession of James I to That of the Brunswick Line*, 8 vols. (London, 1763–1783).

14 A useful selected edition of Robertson's works is Felix Gilbert, ed., *The Progress of Society in Europe* (Chicago, 1972).

15 John Pocock, *Barbarism and Religion*, vol. 1, *The Enlightenment of Edmund Gibbon, 1737–1764* (Cambridge, 1999); Arnaldo Momigliano, "Gibbon's Contributions to Historical Method" in Arnaldo Momigliano, ed., *Studies in Historiography* (New York, 1966), 40–55.

16 Baron de Montesquieu, *Considerations of the Causes of the Greatness of the Romans and Their Decline* (New York, 1965).

17 *Histoire philosophique et politique des établissements et du commerce des Européens dans les deux Indes*, originally published in Amsterdam in 1770.

18 Cited in English in Georg G. Iggers, "The European Context of German Enlightenment Historiography" in Hans-Erich Bödeker, Georg G. Iggers, Jonathan Knudsen, and Peter Hans Reill, eds., *Aufklärung und Geschichte* (Göttingen, 1986), 240.

19 *American Historical Review*, 117 (2012), 999–1027.

20 Jürgen Osterhammel, *Die Entzauberung Asiens Europa und die asiatschen Reiche im 18. Jahrhundert* (München, 1998).

21 Cited in Conrad, "Enlightenment in Global History: A Historiographical Critique," 1005.

22 Dipesh Chakrabarty, *Provincializing Europe* (Princeton, 2000).

23 Anthony Grafton, *Defenders of the Past: The Traditions of Scholarship in an Age of Science, 1450–1800* (Cambridge, MA, 1981).

24 David Knowles, *Great Historical Enterprises: Problems in Monastic History* (London, 1963).

25 Daniel Roche, *Le Siècle de Lumières en Province: Académies et academicians provincials*, 2 vols. (Paris, 1975); Outram, *The Enlightenment*, with bibliography on academies in the French, British, and Spanish worlds; Notker Hammerstein, "The Enlightenment" in Lawrence Stone, ed., *The University in Society* (Princeton, 1974), vol. 2, 625.

26 Lodovico A. Muratori, ed., *Rerum italicarum scriptores* (Milan, 1723–1751).

27 Peter Reill, *The German Enlightenment and the Rise of Historicism* (Berkeley, 1975); Herbert Butterfield, *Man on His Past: The Study of the History of Historical Scholarship* (Cambridge, 1955).

28 English: (Princeton, 1985).

29 *The New Science*, translation of the 1744 edition by Thomas G. Bergin and Max Fisch (Ithaca, 1984); Isaiah Berlin, *Vico and Herder: Two Studies in the History of Ideas* (London, 1976).

30 On women historians, see Natalie Z. Davis, "History's Two Bodies," *American Historical Review*, 93:1 (February 1988), 1–30; also Davis, "Gender and Genre: Women as Historical Writers, 1400–1820" in Patricia Labalme, ed., *Beyond their Sex: Learned Women of the European Past* (New York, 1980), 153–182.

31 Charles McClelland, *State, Society and University in Germany, 1700–1914* (Cambridge, 1980); R. S. Turner, "University Reformers and Professorial Scholarship in Germany 1760–1860" in Stone, *The University in Society*, vol. 2, 495–531.

32 Nicholas Phillipson, "Culture and Society in the 18th Century Province: The Case of Edinburgh and the Scottish Enlightenment" in Stone, *The University in Society*, vol. 2, 449–494.

33 Hans-Erich Bödeker et al., eds. *Aufklärung und Geschichte: Studien zur deutschen Geschichte im 18. Jahrhundert* (Göttingen, 1986); Reill, *The German Enlightenment and the Rise of Historicism*.

34 See Jonathan B. Knudsen, *Justus Möser and the German Enlightenment* (Cambridge, 1986).

35 Ibid., 14–19; Schlözer contrasts a world history that is an "aggregate" of all special histories – implicitly a critique of the English *Universal History* – and one that seeks to construct a "system in which the world and mankind are a unity," 14.

36 See Eduard Fueter, *Geschichte der neueren Historiographie* (München, 1936), 322, who argues that the *Universalgeschichte* does not belong in the Enlightenment. For an excellent discussion of the critical reception of the *Universal History*, see Johan van der Zande, "August Ludwig Schlözer and the English *Universal History*" in Stefan Berger, Peter Lambert, and Peter Schumann, eds., *Historikerdialoge: Geschichte, Mythen und Gedächtnis im deutsch-britischen kulturellen Austausch 1750–2000* (Göttingen, 2003), 135–156.

37 English: (Westport, 1979); Keith Michael Baker, *Condorcet: From Natural Philosophy to Social Mathematics* (Chicago, 1975).

38 *An Essay on the History of Civil Society* (1763).

39 *Geschichte des weiblichen Geschlechts*, 4 vols. (Hannover, 1788–1800).

40 See the *Wikipedia* article on Voltaire; Google "18th-Century Racism."

41 See E. M. Bernard, *Herder on Social and Political Culture* (Cambridge, 1969).

42 *Ideas on the Philosophy of the History of Humanity* (1784–1791); *Letters for the Advancement of Humanity* (1793–1797).

43 Chase Robinson, *Islamic Historiography* (Cambridge, 2003), 48. Robinson cites the example that Orosius's *Historiae adversus paganos* was translated into Arabic in Spain in the tenth century. But Franz Rosenthal does not think that this particular translation had "any sort of influence on Muslim historiography." *A History of Muslim Historiography* (Leiden, 1968), 80–81.

44 Franz Rosenthal, "The Influence of the Biblical Tradition on Muslim Historiography" in Bernard Lewis and P. M. Holt, eds., *Historians of the Middle East* (London, 1962), 35–45.

45 See Rosenthal, *Muslim Historiography*, 50–51. It has been noted that Jean Bodin's *Method* is comparable to Ibn Khaldūn's (1332–1406) *Muqaddimah*, for the latter also deals with, among other things, historical methodology.

46 Karen Armstrong, *Islam: A Short History* (New York, 2000), 5. Also, A. A. Duri, *The Rise of Historical Writing among the Arabs*, ed. & tr. Lawrence I. Conrad (Princeton, 1983), 137–138.

47 Tarif Khalidi, *Arabic Historical Thought in the Classical Period* (Cambridge, 1994), 4–5. Duri, *Rise of Historical Writing among the Arabs*, 12–20. Also, Rosenthal, *Muslim Historiography*, 18–24, though Rosenthal disputes the historical nature of the battle day literature because it usually was not presented "under the aspect of historical cause and effect."

48 Rosenthal, *Muslim Historiography*, 26.

49 Duri, *Rise of Historical Writing among the Arabs*, 23.

50 For a brief discussion of the importance of *Qur'ān* and *hadīth* in guiding the Muslims, see R. Stephen Humphreys, *Islamic History: A Framework for Inquiry* (Princeton, 1991), 21–23.

51 Khalidi, *Arabic Historical Thought*, 30–34; Robinson, *Islamic Historiography*, 20–30.

52 R. Stephen Humphreys, "Turning Points in Islamic Historical Practice" in Q. Edward Wang and Georg G. Iggers, eds., *Turning Points in Historiography: A Cross-Cultural Perspective* (Rochester, 2002), 92–93 and his "Modern Arab Historians and the Challenge of the Islamic Past," *Middle Eastern Lectures*, 1 (1995), 121–122.

53 Robinson, *Islamic Historiography*, 28–30.

54 Al-Tabarī's work has been translated by various translators into English under the title *The History of Al-Tabarī* (Albany, 1985).

55 Robinson, *Islamic Historiography*, 35–36, 97–100; Khalidi, *Arabic Historical Thought*, 81–82; also, Tarif Khalidi, "Ahmad ibn Abī Ya'qūb al-Ya'qūbī" in *Global Encyclopedia of Historical Writing*, ed. Daniel Woolf (New York, 1998), vol. 2, 981.

56 Humphreys, "Turning Points in Islamic Historical Practice," 90–94 and his *Islamic History*, 72, 91. Also, Julie Scott Meisami, *Persian Historiography to the End of the Twelfth Century* (Edinburgh, 1999), especially 281–283; and Bernard Lewis, *From Babel to Dragomans: Interpreting the Middle East* (Oxford, 2004), 411–412.

57 Bernard Lewis, *The Muslim Discovery of Europe* (New York, 1982), 150–157.

58 Rosenthal, *Muslim Historiography*, 113–118.

59 Warren E. Gates' article, "The Spread of Ibn Khaldūn's Ideas on Climate and Culture," offers evidence for Ibn Khaldūn's influence on European thinking in the seventeenth century, *Journal of the History of Ideas*, 28:3 (July–September 1967), 415–422.

60 Cf. Cornell Fleischer, *Bureaucrat and Intellectual in the Ottoman Empire: The Historian Mustafa Âli (1541–1600)* (Princeton, 1986).

61 Lewis V. Thomas, *A Study of Naima*, ed. Norman Itzkowitz (New York, 1972), 110–119.

62 Bernard Lewis describes certain works of Ottoman historians as "mere verbiage and bombast." See his *From Babel to Dragomans*, 422. But entertainment had always been a major reason for Muslims to turn to history, for which a work's orality and aurality were usually prized. See Robinson, *Islamic Historiography*, 171–177.

63 Bernard Lewis, *Islam in History* (Peru, IL, 1993), 100.

64 Ibid., 109–110.

65 Virginia H. Aksan, *An Ottoman Statesman in War and Peace: Ahmed Resmi Efendi, 1700–1783* (Leiden, 1995), xv–xvi, 18–23, and her *Ottomans and Europeans: Contacts and Conflicts* (Istanbul, 2004), 32.

66 Lewis, *Islam in History*, 111.

67 See Thomas Philipp, "Class, Community, and Arab Historiography in the Early Nineteenth Century: The Dawn of a New Era," *International Journal of Middle East Studies*, 16:2 (May 1984), 161–175; Steve Tamari, "Biography, Autobiography, and Identity in Early Modern Damascus" in Mary Ann Fay, ed., *Auto/Biography and the Construction of Identity and Community in the Middle East* (New York, 2001), 37–50.

68 Whether the Ottomans represented a declining age for the Muslims has been questioned by Rifa'at 'Ali Abou-El-Haj's *Formation of the Modern State: The Ottoman Empire, Sixteenth to Eighteenth Centuries* (Albany, 1991) and analyzed in Gabriel Piterberg's *Ottoman Tragedy: History and Historiography at Play* (Berkeley, 2003). For a historiographical review, see Jane Hathaway, "Rewriting Eighteenth-Century Ottoman History," *Mediterranean Historical Review*, 19:1 (June 2004), 29–53.

69 It has been pointed out that such views were often noticeable among the local intelligentsia of many ex-colonies during the nineteenth and twentieth centuries. See Kumkum Chatterjee, *The Cultures of History in Early Modern India* (New Delhi, 2009), 5.

70 Leopold von Ranke, "On the Character of Historical Science (A Manuscript of the 1830s)" in Georg G. Iggers, ed., *Leopold von Ranke: The Theory and Practice of History* (London, 2011), 16. The passage reads: "Finally we can devote but scant attention to those peoples who remain today in a kind of state of nature and who lead us to assume that they have been in this state from the beginning – that the prehistoric condition has been preserved in them. India and China claim an old age and have a lengthy chronology. But even the cleverest chronologist cannot understand it. Their antiquity is legendary, but their condition is rather a matter of natural history."

71 "As Indians do not have any history in the sense of historiography, they do not have history as actions (*res gestae*), i.e., no development towards a truly political status." Cited in Michael Gottlob, ed., *Historical Thinking in South Asia: A Handbook of Sources from Colonial Times to the Present* (New Delhi, 2003), 8.

72 Thus the Indian historian R. G. Bhandarkar (1837–1925) stated: "The historical curiosity of the Indian people was satisfied by legends." Cited in Gottlob, *Historical Thinking in South Asia*, 2. Also Romila Thapar, "Indian Historiography – Ancient" in Woolf, *Global Encyclopedia of Historical Writing*, 455–458.

73 Cited in Gottlob, *Historical Thinking in South Asia*, 7.

74 Cited in ibid., 9.

75 Cited in Asim Roy, "Indo-Persian Historical Thoughts and Writings: India, 1350–1750" in José Rabasa, Masayuki Sato, Edoardo Tortarolo, and Daniel Woolf, eds., *The Oxford History of Historical Writing: 1400–1800* (New York, 2012), vol. 3, 150.

76 It should be kept in mind that in ancient India there were also Buddhist and Jaina writings that, reflecting the particular worldviews of those sects and their social backgrounds, expressed a different type of historical consciousness and form.

The monastery chronicles of both these religions are rich in secular information and have a temporal eschatology based on the historicity of their founding fathers.

77 C. A. Bayly, "Modern Indian Historiography" in Michael Bentley, ed., *Companion to Historiography* (London, 1997), 678.
78 Romila Thaper, "Society and Historical Consciousness: The Itihasa-Purana Tradition" in Romila Thapar and Sabyasachi Bhattacharya, eds., *Situating History: Essays in Honour of Sarvapalli Gopal* (New Delhi, 1986), 353–386.
79 Gabrielle Spiegel, "Genealogy, Form and Function in Medieval Historiography" in Gabrielle Spiegel, ed., *The Past as Text* (Baltimore, 1997).
80 In the high-Hindu conception of time, there were four *yugas* in endless recurrence: from the *yugas* of *Satya*, to *Treta*, *Dwapar*, and finally *Kali*, there is a progressive degeneration from a "golden age" (*Satya-yuga*) to social chaos (*Kali-yuga*), until the cycle is repeated again.
81 Sumit Sarkar, *Writing Social History* (New Delhi, 1998), 8.
82 Roy, "Indo-Persian Historical Thoughts," 153–157.
83 Ibid., 159–161.
84 Ibid., 161.
85 Chatterjee, *The Cultures of History*, 253–255.
86 Thus also John F. Richards used his own set of criteria and refers to this period as "early modern" instead of Mughal India or late medieval India or late pre-colonial India. See "Early Modern India and World History," *Journal of World History*, 8 (1997), 197–209.
87 On intellectual transformation in India in the eighteenth century, see Jamal Malik, "Mystik: 18. Jahrhundert" in Stephan Conermann, ed., *Die muslimische Sicht (13. bis 18. Jahrhundert)* (Frankfurt a/M, 2002), 293–350.
88 Cited in ibid., 305.
89 Kumkum Chatterjee, "History as Self-Representation: The Recasting of a Political Tradition in Late Eighteenth Century Eastern India," *Modern Asian Studies*, 32 (1998), 913–948.
90 V. N. Rao, David Shulman, and Sanjay Subrahmanyam, *Textures of Time: Writing History in South India, 1600–1800* (New York, 2003), 136.
91 Ibid., 136.
92 A number of modern Chinese scholars have offered their explanations for the origin and function of the *shi* in ancient China, and their works are collected in Du Weiyun and Huang Jinxing, eds., *Zhongguo shixueshi lunwen xuanji (Selected Essays in the History of Chinese Historiography)* (Taipei, 1976), vol. 1, 1–109. For an updated English summary, see On-cho Ng and Q. Edward Wang, *Mirroring the Past: The Writing and Use of History in Imperial China* (Honolulu, 2005), 1–7.
93 Ng and Wang, *Mirroring the Past*, 62.
94 Ronald Egan, "Narratives in *Tso Chuan*," *Harvard Journal of Asiatic Studies*, 37 (1977), 323–352, and *The Tso Chuan: Selections from China's Oldest Narrative History*, tr. Burton Watson (New York, 1989) and Watson's introduction.
95 Cf. Q. Edward Wang, "Objectivity, Truth, and Hermeneutics: Re-reading the *Chunqiu*" in Ching-i Tu, ed., *Classics and Interpretations: The Hermeneutic Tradition in Chinese Culture* (New Brunswick, 2000), 155–172.
96 Wai-yee Li, "The Idea of Authority in the *Shih chi* (Records of the Historian)," *Harvard Journal of Asiatic Studies*, 54:2 (December 1994), 345–405; Ng and Wang, *Mirroring the Past*, 53–67. For monographic studies of Sima Qian's historiography in English, see Burton Watson, *Ssu-ma Ch'ien: Grand Historian of China* (New York, 1958); Stephen W. Durrant, *The Cloudy Mirror: Tension and Conflict in the Writings of Sima Qian* (Albany, 1995); and Grant Hardy, *Worlds of Bronze and Bamboo: Sima Qian's Conquest of History* (New York, 1999).

97 Denis Twitchett, *The Writing of Official History under the T'ang* (Cambridge, 1993).

98 Sakamoto Tarō, *Rikkokushi (Six National Histories)* (Tokyo, 1972).

99 Sakamoto Tarō, *Nihon no shūshi to shigaku (Historical Compilation and Study in Japan)* (Tokyo, 1991), 67–86, 132–137. Cf. Hugh Burton, "A Survey of Japanese Historiography," *American Historical Review*, 43:3 (April 1938), 489–499, especially 490–492.

100 Peter Bol, *"This Culture of Ours:" Intellectual Transitions in T'ang and Sung China* (Stanford, 1992); Yu Yingshi, *Zhu Xi de lishi shijie (The Historical World of Zhu Xi)* (Taipei, 2003); and Wm. Theodore de Bary, "Some Common Tendencies in Neo-Confucianism" in David Nivison and Arthur Wright, eds., *Confucianism in Action* (Stanford, 1959) and Wm. Theodore de Bary, ed., *The Unfolding of Neo-Confucianism* (New York, 1975).

101 E. G. Pulleyblank, "Chinese Historical Criticism: Liu Chih-chi and Ssu-ma Kuang" in W. G. Beasley and E. G. Pulleyblank, eds., *Historians of China and Japan* (Oxford, 1961), 135–166; Xiao-bin Ji, "Mirror for Government: Ssu-ma Kuang's Thought on Politics and Government in *Tzu-chih t'ung-chien*" in Thomas H. C. Lee, ed., *The New and the Multiple: Sung Senses of the Past* (Hong Kong, 2004); and Xiao-bin Ji, *Politics and Conservatism in Northern Song China: The Career and Thought of Sima Guang (1009–1086)* (Hong Kong, 2005).

102 Zhu Yunying, "Zhongguo shixue duiyu Ri, Han, Yue de yingxiang (The Influence of Chinese Historiography in Japan, Korea and Vietnam)" in Du and Huang, *Zhongguo shixueshi lunwen xuanji*, vol. 2, 1056–1057. It was also said that during the twelfth century, a civil service examination system and a national university modeled on the Tang were instituted in Vietnam. See K. W. Taylor, "Vietnamese Confucian Narrative" in Benjamin A. Elman, John B. Duncan, and Herman Ooms, eds., *Rethinking Confucianism: Past and Present in China, Japan, Korea, and Vietnam* (Los Angeles, 2002), 343–344 and K. W. Taylor, *The Birth of Vietnam* (Berkeley, 1983), 250–251.

103 Li Runhe (Lee Yun-hwa), *Zhonghan jindai shixue bijiao yanjiu (A Comparative Study of Modern Chinese and Korean Historiography)* (Beijing, 1994), 17.

104 Cf. Wm. Theodore de Bary and JaHyun Kim Haboush, eds., *The Rise of Neo-Confucianism in Korea* (New York, 1985), and Martina Deuchler, *The Confucian Transformation of Korea: A Study of Society and Ideology* (Cambridge, MA, 1992).

105 Zhu, "Zhongguo shixue duiyu Ri, Han, Yue de yingxiang," 1060; Li, *Zhonghan jindai shixue*, 13–20.

106 See Alexander Woodside, *Vietnam and the Chinese Model: A Comparative Study of Nguyen and Ch'ing Civil Government in the First Half of the Nineteenth Century* (Cambridge, MA, 1971), 18–22.

107 Taylor, *Birth of Vietnam*, Appendix O, 349–359, and John K. Whitmore, "*Chung-hsing* and *Cheng-t'ung* in Texts of and on Sixteenth-century Vietnam" in K. W. Taylor and John Whitmore, eds., *Essays into Vietnamese Pasts* (Ithaca, 1995), 116–136.

108 Ng and Wang, *Mirroring the Past*, 193–222.

109 Also Kai-wing Chow, *Publishing, Culture, and Power in Early Modern China* (Stanford, 2004), and Cynthia Brokaw and Kai-wing Chow, eds., *Printing and Book Culture in Late Imperial China* (Berkeley, 2005).

110 JaHyun Kim Haboush, "Contesting Chinese Time, Nationalizing Temporal Space: Temporal Inscription in Late Chosŏn Korea" in Lynn Struve, ed., *Time, Temporality and Imperial Transition: East Asia from Ming to Qing* (Honolulu, 2005), 115–141.

111 Benjamin A. Elman, *From Philosophy to Philology: Intellectual and Social Aspects of Change in Late Imperial China* (Los Angeles, 2000, rev. ed.);

also Luo Bingliang, *18 shiji Zhongguo shixue de lilun chengjiu* (*Theoretical Advancement in Chinese Historiography of the Eighteenth Century*) (Beijing, 2000), and Q. Edward Wang, "The Rise of Modern Historical Consciousness: A Cross-Cultural Comparison of Eighteenth-Century East Asia and Europe," *Journal of Ecumenical Studies*, XL:1–2 (Winter–Spring 2003), 74–95.

112 Cf. Lee, *The New and the Multiple*, particularly Lee's introduction.

113 Dai Zhen's major work, *Mengzi ziyi shuzheng*, has been rendered into English, entitled *Tai Chen on Mencius: Explorations in Words and Meaning*, tr. & intro. Ann-ping Chin & Mansfield Freeman (New Haven, 1990).

114 Cf. Hamaguchi Fujiō, *Shindai kōkyogaku no shisōshi teki kenkyū* (*A Study of Intellectual History on Qing Dynasty's Evidential Learning*) (Tokyo, 1994).

115 E. G. Pulleyblank, "Chinese Historical Criticism: Liu Chih-chi and Ssu-ma Kuang," 135–166; Ng and Wang, *Mirroring the Past*, 121–128.

116 Du Weiyun, *Qingdai shixue yu shijia* (*Historiography and Historians in the Qing Period*) (Beijing, 1988), and idem, *Zhao Yi zhuan* (*Biography of Zhao Yi*) (Taipei, 1983).

117 On-cho Ng, "A Tension in Ch'ing Thought: 'Historicism' in Seventeenth- and Eighteenth-century Chinese Thought," *Journal of the History of Ideas*, 54:4 (1993), 561–583, and Benjamin Elman, "The Historicization of Classical Learning in Ming-Ch'ing China" in Wang and Iggers, *Turning Points in Historiography*, 101–146.

118 Ng and Wang, *Mirroring the Past*, 245.

119 The estimate is in Ping-ti Ho, *The Ladder of Success in Imperial China: Aspects of Social Mobility, 1368–1911* (New York, 1962), 214.

120 Cf. Yu Yingshi, *Rujia lunli yu shangren jingshen* (Nanning, 2004); Elman, *From Philosophy to Philology*; and Du, *Qingdai shixue yu shijia*. For the information on the literacy rate, see Brokaw and Chow, *Printing and Book Culture*, 30–31.

121 See Dorothy Ko, *Teachers of Inner Chambers: Women and Culture in Seventeenth-century China* (Stanford, 1994), and Susan Mann, *The Precious Records: Women in China's Long Eighteenth Century* (Stanford, 1997).

122 Cf. R. Kent Guy, *The Emperor's Four Treasuries: Scholars and the State in the Late Ch'ien-lung Era* (Cambridge, MA, 1987).

123 Robert Backus, "The Kansei Prohibition of Heterodoxy and Its Effects on Education," *Harvard Journal of Asiatic Studies*, 39:1 (1979): 55–106.

124 Zhu, "Zhongguo shixue duiyu Ri, Han, Yue de yingxiang," 1053–1054; Benjamin Elman, "The Search for Evidence from China: Qing Learning and Kōshōgaku in Tokugawa Japan" in Joshua A. Fogel, ed., *Sagacious Monks and Bloodthirsty Warriors: Chinese Views of Japan in the Ming-Qing Period* (Norwalk, 2002), 158–184; and Nakayama Kyūshirō, "Kōshōgaku gaisetsu (General Discussion of Evidential Learning)" in Fukushima Kashizō et al., eds., *Kinsei Nihon no jugaku* (*Confucianism in Early Modern Japan*) (Tokyo, 1939), 710–729.

125 Cf. Mark Setton, *Chŏng Yagyong: Korea's Challenge to Orthodox Neo-Confucianism* (Albany, 1997).

126 Shin Yong-ha, *Modern Korean History and Nationalism*, tr. N. M. Pankaj (Seoul, 2000), 5–14.

127 Cf. Li Tana, "Le Quy Don" in Kelly Boyd, ed., *Encyclopedia of Historians and Historical Writing* (London, 1999), vol. 1, 210.

2   The advance of nationalism and nationalist history

The West, the Middle East, and India in the nineteenth century

Historiography in a revolutionary age between 1789 and 1848

The political context

There is no question that the French Revolution and the Napoleonic regime which followed it fundamentally changed the conditions under which history was studied, written, and read in the West. The Revolution reflected both the extent to which a process of modernization, as we described it in the Introduction, took place and the limits of this process. By 1815, the Revolution had been effectively defeated, and the attempt was made to restore many aspects of the old order. Yet in fact, although monarchical governments were reinstituted, the basic social and to an extent even political reforms of the Revolutionary period remained intact. Except to an extent in Eastern Europe, society on the Continent had been transformed profoundly. Already in its early stages, the Revolution had abolished the remnants of the feudal order in France, established equality under the law, and loosened the fetters that had stifled a free market economy. The result of the Napoleonic conquests was that these basic reforms were carried to large areas of Continental Europe – to Germany, the Low Countries, Switzerland, and important parts of Italy. In Great Britain many of these institutions were already well established before. In Prussia in the aftermath of defeat by the Napoleonic forces, reforms pointing in these directions were initiated from above. The result was the strengthening of the middle class – the *bourgeoisie* in France, the *Bürgertum* in Germany – and the growth of civil society. The period after 1815 did not undo this development but rather gave it a new impetus. Even in the political sphere the old order was not restored. Louis XVIII (1755–1824), upon his return from exile, issued a charter that transformed France into a constitutional monarchy. And although Austria, Prussia, and some of the smaller German and Italian states refused to make concessions, the movements for constitutionalism gained strength. By 1830 various German states had constitutions. In England, the Reform Act of 1832 strengthened the representation of the middle classes, but apart from England and Belgium the Industrial Revolution had not yet begun in earnest and left little impact on historical thought.

All this affected the way in which history was written. Although the developments we have just mentioned pointed to a modern outlook, the immediate reaction among historians during and immediately after the revolutionary events was to turn against the Enlightenment ideals that had inspired the Revolution. The Revolution was seen as a repudiation of history, the unfortunate objection to building society on new rational lines. The introduction of the metric system symbolizes this state of mind, the replacement of older, involved patterns of measurement by new clear-cut ones. A first important response to the French Revolution, well before the Revolution entered its terroristic phase, was Edmund Burke's already mentioned *Reflections on the French Revolution*, written in 1790. Burke did not argue against change and reforms – he had been a supporter of the American Revolution – but he believed that reforms that represented a marked break with existing institutions would lead to turmoil and violence. Burke thus offered a theoretical basis for conservative programs in the first half of the nineteenth century, yet a good deal of historical thought went beyond Burke to outright reaction.

Romanticism and historiography

Enlightenment was replaced by Romanticism[1] as the dominant outlook in the first half of the nineteenth century. But as we saw in the previous chapter, Enlightenment perspectives in the eighteenth century were multifaceted and by no means neglected history; in fact, history occupied a very central role in the thinking of Montesquieu, Voltaire, Hume, and Gibbon – and in a different way in that of Herder. And Romanticism also was multifaceted, on the one hand glorifying the past, on the other hand championing very diverse political ideals for the transformation of modern society, ranging over the whole spectrum of political opinions.

The reaction against the ideals of the French Revolution took the form of the idealization of the Middle Ages, but the Middle Ages could be seen in very different ways. They could be viewed nostalgically as a harmonious society held together by the hierarchical order of feudalism and the religious faith of Roman Catholicism, as Vicomte René de Chateaubriand (1771–1835) did in his widely read *Génie du Christianisme* (1802),[2] or they could be seen as sources of modern liberty and even democracy, as they were by Augustin Thierry (1795–1856) and Jules Michelet (1798–1874). Joseph de Maistre (1753–1821) placed the origins of what he considered to be the crisis of modern society in the Protestant Reformation, which by introducing the principle of an individual conscience destroyed the harmony of the medieval Christian world. Yet the great Romantic poets of the early nineteenth century, Percy Bysshe Shelley (1792–1822) and Lord Byron (1788–1824) in England, championed democratic reforms, and Lord Byron sacrificed his life in the struggle for Greek liberty.

The impact of emergent nationalism on historiography

Out of the reaction against the French Revolution and the Enlightenment came the discovery of the nation as the key force in modern history. In Germany, the cult of the nation was part of the struggle against French domination after the defeat of Prussia by Napoleon in 1806 and the so-called Wars of Liberation against him in the years 1813 and 1814. In the place of the equality of men as a universal principle valid at all times, as it had been proclaimed in the American Declaration of Independence (1776) and the French Declaration of the Rights of Man and of the Citizen (1789), the nation as an inclusive community rooted in the past was now perceived as central to the course of history.[3] But the very idea of the nation as a community involved an almost democratic idea, namely that all the members of the nation were not merely subjects of princely authorities but equal partners and that these authorities were not divinely ordained but represented the nation. While Berlin was under French occupation in 1807, Johann G. Fichte (1762–1814) delivered his *Addresses to the German Nation*,[4] in which he saw the German nation not as part of mankind as a whole but as a unique body distinct from all other nations. While the French Revolution had defined France as the fatherland of all liberty-loving humans worldwide, so that one could obtain French citizenship by adhering to the ideals for which the French republic stood, Fichte now defined German nationality in racial terms. In other words, one could not be a Jew or a Pole and at the same time a German. While not using biological terms of race, Fichte saw the Germans as an exclusive linguistic community into which one had to be born. For him, language was not merely a value-free medium for the representation of objective reality but rather shaped the way in which humans understood the world in which they lived. Language was conditioned by culture and embodied culture. For him, there was nothing universal about language. Languages embodied the spirit of the nations by which they were spoken. But there were two classes of languages, those that had originated at the very beginning of a national community and continued to the present and those that had been imposed from the outside. German, for Fichte, belonged to the first class, French to the second. The Germans, he argued, spoke a tongue that had continued to live since the origins of the Germanic peoples in primeval times and embodied the depth of an unbroken national spirit; the continuity of French culture had been broken by Roman domination and was thus artificial and rationalistic. It was up to the Germans now to create a nation-state to give political expression to their nationhood.

Although allegiance to the Christian religion, whether Protestant or Catholic, was not repudiated, the nation now emerged as the primary point of reference, more powerful than the established religions. In the course of the first half of the nineteenth century, a similar exclusionary notion of the nation was shared throughout Europe, most powerfully in Germany and in the countries to the East from Bohemia to Greece that were struggling to establish their national identity and independence. In these countries, historiography followed more closely the German rather than the French example.[5] This nationalism had a considerable impact on historical scholarship. The cosmopolitan perspective of the eighteenth century was now replaced by a focus on the nation not only in Germany but in Europe generally. At the same time, the attempt was made to give historical studies a more rigorous character. There was a close relationship between the development of professional scholarship and the new nationalism.[6]

The relationship between professional scholarship and nationalism

Attention was now given to the collection and edition of medieval sources that would provide a basis for writing national histories. As already mentioned, the first great effort in this direction had already been made in Italy by Ludovico Muratori's edition of medieval Italian documents in the early eighteenth century. German scholars played a leading role in the first half of the nineteenth century in the development of historical studies from a national perspective. As we saw, philological methods had been well developed in the seventeenth century by the Maurists and Bollandists in Paris and Belgium and further refined in the studies of church history and the Greco-Roman classics at the eighteenth-century German universities. But none were as yet intended to serve national interests. This changed with the launching of large projects, such as the *Monumenta Germaniae Historica*, established in 1819 with an explicit national orientation, to help create a national identity through the critical edition of medieval sources. The Middle Ages were now seen as a high point of German history in which the preeminent role of the Holy Roman Empire in Europe preceded the fragmentation of Germany.

By the mid-nineteenth century, similar projects had been launched elsewhere. In France a special Ecole des Chartes was established in 1821 for the critical study of medieval sources, followed in 1836 by a systematic collection and edition of medieval documents initiated by François Guizot (1787–1874),[7] then premier. By 1844 when the Rolls Series was initiated in Great Britain, several European countries from Spain to Scandinavia had already followed suit.

This occupation with the edition of medieval sources of national history was accompanied, particularly in Prussia, by a concerted effort by the government to transform history into a rigorous academic discipline that would serve the national cause. In 1810, as part of the reforms that had been carried out by the Prussian state in the aftermath of the defeat of 1806, the University of Berlin was established as an institution in which teaching would be combined with research.[8] History was to be raised to the level of a rigorous academic discipline committed to reconstructing the past free of fictional elements. Two historians of antiquity should be mentioned here, Barthold Georg Niebuhr (1776–1831), the historian of Rome, and August Böckh (1785–1867), the historian of Greece, both of whom were appointed to the university in Berlin when it opened. Niebuhr and Leopold von Ranke,[9] who came to the university in 1825 and applied Niebuhr's methods to modern European history, were soon regarded as the fathers of historical science. This reputation stemmed from their insistence that all historical writing must rest on the critical examination of primary sources. For Niebuhr no existing accounts of Roman history and for Ranke none of early modern history were sufficiently acceptable because they were based partly on secondary sources. Niebuhr saw it as his task to demonstrate the unreliability of the Roman historian Livy (59/64 BCE–17 CE), and Ranke that of the Florentine historian Francesco Guicciardini (1483–1540). We shall deal with Ranke, who only became influential in the middle and the second half of the nineteenth centuries, later when we examine the professionalization of historical studies. In the lectures he delivered in Berlin beginning in 1810 and in his *History of Rome* (1811–1812),[10] Niebuhr set out to rewrite Roman history. Methodologically, he was influenced by eighteenth-century German philologists, foremost Friedrich August Wolf. With the analysis of Roman law and the reliance on inscriptions, he began to reconstruct the Roman state as he believed it had functioned. His approach fitted into the spirit of the time, for example, his idealization of a Roman society of free peasants that according to him preceded the Roman Republic for which he had no evidence but that corresponded to his Romantic inclinations. Perhaps more innovative than the work of Niebuhr was that of his colleague August Böckh, who using material sources, inscriptions, coins, and whatever information he could find on prices, wages, and property values, reconstructed the political economy of Athens.[11]

By this time, historical studies in Germany were largely centered at the universities as they already had been to an extent in the eighteenth century. And the universities expected that these studies would be conducted according to the methods of source criticism considered as the methodological norm, which posited that there was a sharp distinction between professional scholarship and the imaginative literature written by amateurs. But, in fact, there was no such clear distinction. The great majority of historians continued to be amateurs, at least outside of Germany.[12] And in an age marked by a profound interest in history, scholarly works were also seen as literature. Much of history throughout Europe was still read in the form of novel or drama. For instance Walter Scott's (1771–1832) novels had an immense influence on the writing of history. He made the Middle Ages come alive, placing his heroes in concrete historical settings. Turning to the modern period, Honoré de Balzac (1799–1850), in his multivolume *Human Comedy*, attempted to do the same for the various sides of French society in his day. Even at the German universities, history was not yet written solely for a scholarly community but also with a broader public in mind. And this public, already immense before the French Revolution in France, Great

Britain, and the Netherlands, when works by Hume, Gibbon, and Catherine Macaulay were best sellers, became even larger with the expansion of a civil society in Central Europe and Italy in the first half of the nineteenth century.

The liberal reinterpretation of the Middle Ages

After about 1830, the fascination with the Middle Ages wore off, and historians dealt more with the historical roots of the society in which they lived. Already before 1830 A. H. L. Heeren (1760–1842), trained by Christoph Friedrich Schlosser (1776–1861) at the University of Göttingen in the 1780s, had dealt with the history of trade worldwide in the framework of the evolving modern state system. He and particularly Schlosser, the author of a world history and a history of the eighteenth century, who were little concerned with archival research and the careful analysis of sources, were probably the most widely read German historians in the first half of the nineteenth century. In France beginning in the 1820s, a number of historians, foremost the already mentioned Augustin Thierry[13] and François Guizot,[14] wrote histories of the emergence of the Third Estate since the Middle Ages, while Jules Michelet saw, from an outspokenly democratic perspective, the French people as the moving force of French history since early times.[15] The Middle Ages were seen differently now, not nostalgically as a source of order and hierarchy but as a stage in the development of a modern civil society. Michelet was without doubt the most widely read French historian, generally revered by broad segments of the French population as the greatest French historian, an academician and professor for some years at the prestigious Collège de France and head of the national archives but nevertheless seen more as a poet than as a critical historian. His histories of France and of the French Revolution are essentially an epic of the French nation. He went into the archives not to let the documents determine his writing but to seek inspiration for his narratives. He was inspired by the revolutionary ideals of the Enlightenment and yet was deeply influenced by Vico, whom he translated, and by Herder. Romanticism and Enlightenment thus merged. Michelet was an embattled democrat who repeatedly experienced persecution by the authorities, under the Bourbon monarchy, under Guizot in the July monarchy, who at first supported him, and under Napoleon III (1808–1873). While German scholarship focused on the state and identified the nation with the state, the French historians we have mentioned gave much greater attention to the social and cultural aspects. The attention they gave to class as a factor in political conflict and social change led Karl Marx (1818–1883) to remark that they foreshadowed his own conception of history.[16]

In Great Britain and Italy, academic history played an even less important role. None of the important British historians were academics. The two who stand out in this time period are Thomas Babington Macaulay (1800–1859)[17] and Thomas Carlyle (1795–1881),[18] both immensely popular and little concerned with rigorous scholarship. Carlyle poked fun at a fictional Professor Dryasdust who represented the scholarly tradition. Macaulay, an active politician and for many years a member of Parliament, in his *History of England from the Accession of James II* (1849–1861), became the prime advocate of the "Whig Interpretation of History" relating the success story of the development of liberal institutions in England.[19] From 1834 to 1838, he lived in India where he served on the Supreme Court of India and concluded that the Indians had to be freed from their primitive culture by the English. While Macaulay sang a peon about human progress best manifested in the ascent of English liberty, Carlyle looked with disdain at the modern world, saw the French Revolution as a catastrophe, admired the great authoritarian heroes in history, but also, as a critic of industrial society, he expressed his concern for the impoverished masses and his scorn for the ruling classes. In contrast to the optimistic complacency of Macaulay, he emerged as a conservative critic of the culture and the society of his time.

The colonial perspective and historiography

There are thus considerable varieties of historical thought during the period from the aftermath of the French Revolution to the Revolutions of 1848 at the midpoint of the nineteenth century. Nevertheless, there existed a broad consensus in the West on what the relation between the European and the non-European worlds should be. Western powers now dominated the non-Western world even more than they had in the eighteenth century. India was firmly in the hands of the British, East India of the Dutch. The year 1840 marked the humiliation of the once proud Chinese empire. Western military power was unchallenged. The gulf in prosperity between West and East, North and South had widened dramatically with industrialization,[20] as did the flow of raw materials from the non-Western world to the West, which sent its products to the former and through various devices prevented it from developing its own industries. The role that slavery in the Caribbean and the Americas played in the development of capitalist industry and trade must not be overlooked.[21]

The world market was now firmly established, but the scope of historical writing had narrowed. While the eighteenth century still produced the English *Universal History*, historians now focused exclusively on the West and more specifically on Europe or dealt with the non-West from the perspective of Western colonial control. This development already began in the eighteenth century. Enlightenment thinkers assumed the superiority of Western culture and found the non-Western world uninteresting, although William Robertson (1721–1793) wrote a history of the Americas[22] and the Abbé Raynal (1713–1796) wrote a scathing indictment of the European exploitation of the indigenous populations in the colonial world.[23]

Historians in the first part of the nineteenth century, with few exceptions, no longer wrote histories of Europe but focused increasingly on the historians' national affiliations. One notable exception was Leopold Ranke who considered the nations as the basic units in postrevolutionary Europe but saw Europe still as a whole held together by the balance of the European powers. His first book, *Histories of the Latin and Germanic Nations, 1494–1514* (1824),[24] examined the origins of the modern European state system and was followed by books on the Roman papacy, on Germany in the age of the Reformation, and on Serbia, France, and England in the modern period, viewed in terms of the interaction of the European powers. But Ranke was an exception; his students were more narrowly nation oriented. Not historians but philologists continued to be interested in Indian and to a lesser extent Chinese studies. But they were interested in ancient India and China from a romantic perspective, particularly in Indian mysticism. National history, moreover, particularly but not only in Germany, tended to focus on the state and the elites, largely ignoring society and the broad masses of the population. As we saw, this was less true in the writings of Guizot and Michelet in France and of Macaulay in England, who reflected a more liberal political tradition.

The decline of liberalism in historiography

Perhaps we can say that at least in the period before 1848, nationalism was closely intertwined with liberalism. This was also true of the so-called Prussian historians until the failure of their political programs in the 1848 Revolutions.[25] Not all historians were liberals, although almost all were nationalists. Particularly in the early years during and after the French Revolution, there were so-called counterrevolutionary thinkers in France and Germany – and the Slavophiles in Russia[26] – who fought constitutionalism and sought a return to regimes in which an absolute monarchy would be closely allied with an authoritarian and fundamentalist Church.[27] It is striking that a number of the leading German Romantics converted to Catholicism. In France throughout the nineteenth and well into the twentieth centuries until the Vichy regime under the Nazis, there was an important royalist historiographical tradition outside the universities that fought the heritage of revolutionary and republican France.[28]

   After 1830, there emerged a democratic and, under the impact of incipient industrialization, even a socialist historiography. Karl Marx and Friedrich Engels (1820–1895), who on the eve of the 1848 Revolution in *The Communist Manifesto* outlined a course of history leading to a communist society, wrote two important historical sketches analyzing the German and French historical settings to explain the defeat of the revolutions.[29] From a somewhat different and more moderate socialist position, Louis Blanc (1811–1882)[30] employed economic class as an explanatory category for the history of the French Revolution and of the July Monarchy, as did Lorenz von Stein (1815–1890)[31] from a conservative perspective in his analysis of class conflicts in the1830s and 1840s. Yet the bulk of the liberals reflected their own social origin. And liberalism meant to them the rejection not only of absolutism but also of democracy. Guizot, not only a leading historian but a political figure who dominated the July Monarchy from its beginnings in 1830 until its overthrow in 1848, is an example of this. Democracy for the liberal historians meant the rule of the masses, and the masses represented the mob as they did in the Reign of Terror in the French Revolution. And the rule of the masses, they warned, meant the destruction of European civilization as it had been known. Although liberalism stood for the free exchange of ideas and the rule of law, it also justified police methods that curbed the subversive movements and ideas that threatened the liberal status quo. The vote was to be restricted to the propertied and cultured classes, as it also was in England by the Reform Act of 1832. The leading German historians of the 1830s and 1840s – Friedrich Christoph Dahlmann (1785–1860), Heinrich von Sybel (1817–1895), and Johann Gustav Droysen (1808–1884)[32] – shared these ideas with their West European colleagues. Dahlmann wrote histories of the French and the English revolutions, identifying with the moderate English as against the radical French tradition. Nationalism and liberalism for them were inseparable. Both would merge in the future German nation-state. But German nationalism, as it was born out of the struggle against Napoleon, and culminated in the War of Liberation, contained a strongly xenophobic and aggressive note.[33]

For the most part, liberals, democrats, and socialists alike were optimistic. They believed that history would lead to a stage at which high levels of education would be reached, civil society would be strengthened, and immense progress would be made in the conditions of human life. Europe was the undisputed leader in this process and would spread its civilization to the less fortunate and more benighted corners of the world.

Ideas of progress and of crisis

But there were also the dissident voices of those who were not convinced that history was moving in the direction of a liberal society or that such a society was desirable. Instead, like the Saint-Simonians[34] and the young Auguste Comte (1798–1857),[35] they held that the modern world was in a deep crisis, marked by individualism and lacking a unifying belief. Taking over parts of the Catholic counterrevolutionary critique of modernity, they yearned for a new order that would combine the unity of medieval society and its faith with greater social justice made possible by an authoritarian regime, guided not by religious doctrine but by scientific experts. From a very different perspective, Alexis de Tocqueville (1805–1859), a statesman and historian, pointed at the dangers in modern political development. Basically committed to liberal values, he nevertheless saw them threatened by the emergence of a modern mass society. In his *Democracy in America* (1833), he foresaw the inevitable development of democracy in the modern Western world, with America revealing the picture of this world as it would be.

Tocqueville did not oppose democracy but feared that it would impose a new despotism of the masses, destroying the variety and individualism of traditional European society. Yet he believed that America also showed how democracy could be combined with the protection of individual liberties and the role played by voluntary associations that counteracted the centralism of the modern state. In a subsequent work, *The Ancient Regime and the Revolution* (1856), Tocqueville presented a view of the French Revolution that revised the counterrevolutionary and the liberal interpretations of the Revolution. To him the basic issue in the Revolution was neither liberty nor equality. Rather it was part of a process, begun in the French monarchy in the seventeenth and eighteenth centuries, by which the monarchy dismantled older liberties and centralized the power of the state. By proclaiming the sovereignty of the nation, the Revolution did not revise this trend but consolidated and extended it.

In many ways the liberal ideologies of the first half of the nineteenth century built on ideas of the Enlightenment, but there were fundamental differences. Both Condorcet and Kant in the late eighteenth century had foreseen a development that would lead to perpetual peace and a world confederation of republican governments. As we saw, their cosmopolitanism gave way to nationalism. But the future was no longer envisaged in terms of the peaceful coexistence of nations, as Herder had believed, but was marked by conflict in the form of war. Neither the idea of a peaceful confederation of European states nor that of a world without war any longer played a role in the historical literature. War between nations was now considered natural and inevitable, as it had been in Europe since the emergence of the modern state system in the sixteenth century. As Carl von Clausewitz (1780–1831)[36] formulated it in *On the Philosophy of War* (1832), war was an extension of policies pursued in peace by other means. Hence the great role that diplomatic and military history played in European historiography, particularly but not exclusively in Prussia. Yet few historians still thought of ideological wars as they had been propagated in the militant phases of the French Revolution. Also still absent was the idea of wars of annihilation. Wars might lead to the expansion of frontiers or to shifts in the balance of power, but they are aimed ultimately at a restoration of peace. In fact the period from the Congress of Vienna in 1814 and 1815, which established a system of collective security among the major powers that soon fell apart, saw no major international conflicts until the Crimean War of the 1850s.

Hegel's philosophy of history

Georg Wilhelm Friedrich Hegel's (1770–1831) philosophy of history[37] is not unrepresentative of historical thought in this period, even if it reflects the peculiarities of early nineteenth-century Germany. His speculative notions rooted in German Idealism were not shared by less metaphysically oriented thinkers in Western Europe or Italy and reflect the specifically bureaucratic character of the Prussian state. Prussia had had no revolution but, as we noted, had had reforms imposed from above that created the basis for a civil society but left in place the autocratic powers of the monarchy and the central role of the bureaucracy. These were the differences between Germany and Western Europe. But certain ideas were shared, even if Hegel gave them a more dogmatic and linguistically involuted, if not obscure, formulation. The first central idea was that all reality was historical. History thus replaced abstract philosophy. There were no abstract truths; all truths had to be understood in concrete historical settings. The world was constantly evolving, following a definite pattern. Hegel now saw this development as a process in which reason, which at the beginning of time had a purely abstract character, took on a concrete form in the course of history. During this process, liberty was embodied progressively in social and political institutions. For Hegel, freedom in the abstract as a universal principle, as Enlightenment thinkers and the authors of the French Declaration of the Rights of Man had envisioned it, did not exist; it emerged in the course of history that began with Oriental Despotism in East Asia, in empires in which no one was free except the despot, and then through various stages led to the world of postrevolutionary Europe where reason and freedom achieved their full development. But change for Hegel was not brought about by the direct actions of men, although great men such as Alexander the Great (356 BCE–323 BCE) or Napoleon (1769–1821) seized the right historical moment and thus became unwitting instruments of history. Rather, change was affected by the impersonal agency of what Hegel defined as a dialectical process, in which every stage of history and its institutional manifestations, because they embodied reason and freedom only imperfectly, were replaced by a higher stage that represented the next level of progress and that, again because of its imperfections, was followed by a still higher stage, until a world embodying reason and guaranteed freedom was finally achieved in postrevolutionary Europe. For him, the French Revolution paved the way for this state but because of its universalism remained imperfect. It knew freedom only in the abstract, in terms of universal human rights. In his own time, he believed, freedom was firmly anchored in the existing postrevolutionary states, foremost in Restoration Prussia, which recognized the place of civil society (*bürgerliche Gesellschaft*) embedded in a powerful monarchy, in which an enlightened bureaucracy represented the welfare of the whole of society, not that of special interests as in constitutional or parliamentary regimes. History had thus come to an end.

Hegel was as yet read relatively little outside of Germany. Yet stripped of its peculiar metaphysics, several of his key ideas were shared by his contemporaries throughout the Western world. One was that there was only one history, world history, which found its culmination in modern Europe. Europe alone, because it represented the high point of progress, had both the right and the obligation to carry its civilization to the rest of the world.

Ranke criticized the schematism of Hegel's philosophy, which forced history into a straightjacket that permitted little room for diversity or human freedom.[38] But on two points, Ranke held views very similar to those of Hegel. He saw the states as manifestations of historical reason, in his words "thoughts of God,"[39] and like Hegel he viewed wars as main agents of change. For Hegel, the victor represented the higher stage of reason and hence of morality. Similarly, Ranke commented: "You will be able to name few significant wars for which it could not be proved that genuine moral energy achieved the final victory."[40]

Nationalism and the transformation of historiography in the Middle East

The Muslim "discovery" of Europe

Beginning in the 1790s, a series of reforms was introduced by Selīm III (r. 1789–1807), the new Sultan of the Ottoman Empire, marking the prelude to the modernization that the Muslim world was to experience in the nineteenth century. Despite external challenges of European powers and internal upheavals that the Ottoman Empire had faced through most of the eighteenth century, the imperium weathered the crisis of territorial losses and fragmentation. Toward the end of the eighteenth century, the movement for provincial independence and autonomy slowed down. And in a new war between the Empire and Russia and Austria, its archenemies, in 1791–1792, the Ottomans were able to conclude it on relatively lenient terms. All this paved the way for Selīm III to rise to power and to introduce the reform. Selīm, however, well understood that despite the war's outcome, the Ottoman army paled in comparison with its European counterparts in weaponry and training. Thus in 1793 he set up new military and naval schools and staffed them with French instructors.

Its military focus notwithstanding, the reform had broad implications. It was regarded as the New Order (*Nizam-i Cedid*), or a new phase in Ottoman history. It instituted channels for Western ideas to flow to the Middle East, one of which was through Ottoman diplomats now stationed permanently in London, Paris, Berlin, and Vienna, a practice established by Selīm III to reciprocate the gestures of his European neighbors. These diplomats, following the example of Ahmed Resmi Efendi (1700–1783), a special envoy to Europe of the previous century, brought back firsthand knowledge about the West, helping generate interest in European culture and history in general and in the ideas and ideals of the French Revolution in particular. While the influence of the Revolution was by no means comprehensive, its ideas of liberty, equality, and nationality – though not fraternity – had a far-reaching effect on changing the identity and loyalty among the subjects of the Ottoman Empire.[41] This change would also exert its influence in reorienting the way history was written among Muslim Turks and beyond.

Yet in Egypt, the French Revolution had an immediate and direct impact. In the wake of Napoleon Bonaparte's invasion of Egypt in 1798, his solo flight back to France in 1799, and the Anglo-French rivalry, an Ottoman military officer from Albania, Muhammad 'Alī (1769–1869), seized power and made himself the new master of Egypt. In his reign between 1805 and 1848, 'Alī spearheaded the modernization in Egypt, setting it apart from other parts in the Middle East. By contrast, after Selīm III's deposition in 1807, the pace of modernization in the Ottoman government came to a temporary halt. But in Egypt and Syria, occupied by Egypt from the 1830s, it was expedited at full speed. Under 'Alī, the Egyptian government hired French advisors, established translation schools, and sent students to France and other European countries to learn about military technology, international law, and public administration. Muhammad 'Alī also showed some interest in history, insofar as he could compare himself with Alexander the Great.[42]

Indeed, though the French occupation of Egypt was short-lived, it had an enduring impact. Napoleon's expedition into Egypt was both military and scientific; he brought 170 Orientalists (European intellectuals interested and specialized in studies of non-Western cultures), archaeologists, scientists, and engineers (many of them belonged to the Institut d'Égypte) along with his foot soldiers and cannons. Moreover, they stumbled on the Rosetta Stone, which piqued tremendous interest among Europeans in mysterious ancient Egypt. The later decipherment of the hieroglyphic inscriptions on the Stone also contributed to the birth of modern Egyptology. As the French took stock of Egyptian culture and history, shown in their compilation of the *Description de l'Égypte*, the Muslims too entered their presence in historical records; most of the entries were, however, not flattering. In the chronicle of the years 1791–1808, for example, the Ottoman Imperial Historiographer Ahmed Asım Efendi (?–1819) likened the French political system to "the rumblings and crepitations of a queasy stomach." He also warned his fellow Muslims to watch out for the licentious behavior and dangerous ideas of the French, lest they undermine "the principles of the Holy Law."[43]

There were less hostile and dismissive descriptions of the French by Muslim historians, one of which was by Abd al-Rahmān al-Jabartī (1753–1825), whom we mentioned in the previous chapter. As an observant historian with an inquisitive mind, al-Jabartī also saw something most of his cohorts had failed to notice at the time. He noticed the French scholarly exploration of his homeland. In his magnum opus, *Wondrous Vestiges in Biographies and Reports* ('*Ajā'ib al-Āthār fī'l-Tarājim wa'l-Akhbār*), he described vividly the scientific activities of the French scientists and scholars, to which he was apparently intrigued. He also recorded his own interactions with the French. Yet in general, al-Jabartī pursued quite a different interest in history than did his French counterparts. He was, for instance, unfazed by the growing interest of the French and other Europeans in ancient Egypt. His *Wondrous Vestiges* consisted of four volumes, covering the period between

1688 and 1821. It was a contemporary and local history (insofar as it deals mostly with Egypt) written in the traditional chronographic style.

As a "giant" in Islamic historiography, al-Jabartī was credited with his careful investigation of his material, his rich and detailed presentation, his detached stance and unabashed candor, all of them were characteristics of a first-rate historian. While writing under 'Alī's reign, al-Jabartī offered a critical account of this modern-day Alexander the Great, in contrast to a good number of panegyrical works (some of them written by Western scholars and travelers) heaped on the monarch at the time.[44] Al-Jabartī's contemporaneous records of French rule and his interpretative approach to the change of his time also helped his work to be praised enthusiastically by modern Western historians.[45] It perhaps helped open the latter's eyes to the rich tradition of historical writing in the Islamic world. Thus, if Selīm III stood midway between old and new in Ottoman history,[46] al-Jabartī occupied the same position in the development of Ottoman historiography. His work connected tradition and modernity, the latter of which was already emerging on the horizons.

But tradition and modernity did not form a dichotomy in the transformation of Islamic historiography. The Islamic tradition of historical writing remained quite alive at the threshold of its modern transformation. Al-Jabartī's excellence, as some have argued, suggests that the tradition had actually entered a period of "spontaneous revival" at the beginning of the nineteenth century. However, the argument goes, this revival was "interrupted by the advent of the French expedition," in that the French occupation injected a new turn by which Muslim historians became more engaged in translation than in composition.[47] Moreover, there was no absolute line of demarcation between traditional and modern historiography.

Thanks to the position of Imperial Historiographer and the preservation of government archives during the Ottoman period, nineteenth-century Islamic historians were endowed with abundant historical records. In order to sort through these records and put them into use, they developed certain expertise in textual criticism, characterized by the deftness in tackling the seemingly infinite wealth of archival materials located in either Istanbul or other provincial capitals. Moreover, this deftness, or the fetish of it, exemplified by the works of bureaucratic historians as specimens of the growth of Ottoman and Egyptian historiography in the nineteenth century, has still commanded the attention and interest of the students of Ottoman history to this day. It provides to some extent a "documentary framework" that at once conditions and constrains the expansion of historical scholarship.[48]

Whose pharaohs? (Re)writing the history of Egypt

Prior to the eighteenth century, Muslim historians were known for their indifference to the history and culture of Europe, which was due as much to their religious bias and cultural arrogance as to the backwardness of Europe. Yet they held a different attitude toward pharaonic Egypt; not only were they intrigued by the formidable size of the pyramids and the sphinx, but some of them also attempted to reckon the pagan history of ancient Egypt with the rise of Christianity and, more splendidly and significantly, the rise of Islam.[49] To be sure, the number of works on ancient Egyptian culture and history written by Muslim authors during the medieval period remains fairly small, especially in comparison with the impressive body of literature in other areas. What they have written is also mostly inaccurate, unsystematic, and even fanciful. The great Ja'far Muḥammad ibn Jarīr al-Ṭabarī (839–923) of the tenth century, for example, offered not much more information on ancient Egypt than did the Old Testament. It accorded little attention to Egypt's Greco-Roman millennium in his otherwise panoramic coverage of the Islamic rule of the Mediterranean.[50] All the same, medieval Muslims were not uninterested in pharaonic Egypt, nor were they indifferent to its cultural accomplishment.

As Muslims expanded their worldview from the late eighteenth century, they also developed increasingly more interest in their "own" pasts, namely the pre-Islamic history of the Mediterranean world. During the nineteenth century, ancient Egypt drew more and more attention from Muslim scholars, and the study of Egyptian history marked the most notable achievement by Egyptian historians of the age. This achievement constituted an example of the modernization of Islamic historiography, for the endeavor to make anew of past traditions was part and parcel of the nationalist state-building project pursued by the Muslims in the face of a growing Western influence in the Middle East. The nationalist impulse compelled scholars and historians first to imagine a community of inhabitants in a given land and then to search its past for useful and inspiring elements to justify its formation, legitimize its existence, and promote and strengthen the cohesiveness and affinity among its inhabitants.[51] Thus the imagination of the community is at times arbitrary, reflecting a historical temporality and, in many non-Western regions, a form of resistance to Western colonialism. The historiography produced by and for the national imaginary is invariably teleological, in which the historians trace and document the origin and development of their nation in a remote past in order to transform the extant cultural tradition and reconfigure the historical memory.

The work of Rifā'ah al-Tahtāwi (1801–1873), an outstanding intellectual figure in modern Egypt, represented this surge of interest in ancient Egypt in the nineteenth-century Middle East. An educator, journalist, translator, and littérateur, al-Tahtāwi played a multifaceted role in the transformation of modern Islamic culture. Yet his main scholarly achievement lay in his effort to introduce seminal changes to the study of history and engender interest in ancient Egypt within the Muslim scholarly community. Having traveled widely and witnessed the increasing influence of European culture, al-Tahtawi came to realize the need for the Muslims to engage in cultural reform.

While in Europe, al-Tahtāwi acquainted himself with some of the leading French Orientalists – Silvestre de Sacy (1755–1838), Caussin de Perceval, Armand-Pierre (1795–1871), Joseph Reinaud (1795–1867), and Edmond-François Jomard (1777–1862) – Jomard was credited with the publication of the *Description de l'Égypte*. From these scholars, al-Tahtāwi learned new ways in studying history, which he later applied in his own writings. He also developed an interest in ancient Egypt. Different from the European Orientalists, however, al-Tahtāwi was attracted to ancient Egypt because it was a useful subject for advancing Egyptian nationalism.

The growing influence of nationalism in the Middle East was also shown in the attempt by nineteenth-century Muslim historians to search for and identify with a cultural and historical legacy (usually in pre-Islamic times) characteristic of their imaginary of a national past. Al-Tahtāwi's pioneering work in Egyptian history, *The Radiance of the Sublime Tawfīq in the Story of Egypt and Ishmael's Descendants* (*Anwār Tawfīq al-Jalīl fī Akhbār Misr wa-Tawthīq Banī Ismā'īl*), is a telling example. Different from the earlier works on Egyptian history by al-Jabartī and others, al-Tahtāwi's survey of the Egyptian past centers on its pre-Islamic period, which comprised the pharaonic eras, Alexander and the Ptolemies, the Romans, and the Byzantines up to the Islamic conquest. This represents a significant and seminal move by an Islamic historian. As mentioned earlier, al-Tabarī, arguably the greatest historian from the traditional Muslim world, had been quite oblivious of the entire millennium of Greco-Roman Egypt. By contrast, al-Tahtāwi gives it a detailed description and, from an Islamic perspective, assigns it with historical significance. Moreover, in his writings of pharaonic Egypt, al-Tahtāwi had incorporated recent archaeological findings by European scholars, suggesting his familiarity with Orientalist scholarship. While pursuing the translation project, al-Tahtāwi and his disciples had rendered into Arabic some important contemporary European works on ancient Egypt, including that of Auguste Mariette (1821–1881), a renowned Egyptologist.

While al-Tahtāwi's study of pre-Islamic Egypt was indebted to Egyptology in Europe, he wrote his *Story of Egypt* clearly for Egypt with an unmistakable nationalist overtone. His work proclaims that unlike other cultures, Egyptian culture had shone through the centuries. In its beginning, or "at the time of the pharaohs it [Egypt] was the mother of all the nations of the world." During the subsequent Greco-Roman periods, it maintained its robust cultural development and became a center of learning for the ancient world. After the rise of Islam, it became a pole of Islamic culture and helped spread civilization to Europe. Even in his own time, al-Tahtāwi opines, Egypt retained its strength and glory, evidenced by its victory over the French in the early 1800s and by the vigorous forward movement led by Muhammad 'Alī.[52]

Aside from its nationalist interest, al-Tahtāwi's *Story of Egypt* departed from traditional Islamic historiography in both method and style. Al-Tahtāwi used both Arabic and non-Arabic sources, as well as archaeological and geographical explorations, in constructing his account, which was inspiring to Muslim historians of later generations. He also treated historical movement both chronologically and topically. Indeed, if the "demise of the chronicle" indicated the transformation of Muslim historiography in the modern period, this process found its best illustration in al-Tahtāwi's *Story of Egypt*. In contrast to earlier historical works, al-Tahtāwi experimented with the use of narrative in recording and interpreting history.[53] In spite of all this novelty, al-Tahtāwi was quite content with being a reformist in politics and historiography and reluctant to introduce more radical changes. As a former student at *al-Azhar*, he maintained his loyalty to the Islamic cultural tradition, which was shown both in his interpretation of history and in his devotion to the Prophet Muhammad, to whom he dedicated a new biography completed in his twilight years.

National identity and historical writing

While the Egyptians were busy searching for a cultural legacy distinct to their land and culture, the Ottomans (or the Turks), the Syrians, the Tunisians, and the Persians too embarked on a similar cause in their efforts at nation-building. To construct the historical narrative of modern Persia/Iran, for example, the Persians harked back to the great and glorious Persian civilization in ancient, pre-Islamic times. On the one hand, having revived such mythical epics as the *Dasatiri* and *Shahnamah*, they attempted to dissociate Iran from Islam and extolled Persia as a polyglot and multiethnic empire of the ancient world. Their effort involved revoking and reviving pre-Islamic myths, symbols, and heroes for help in creating a new Iranian national identity. On the other hand, having synchronized and/or substituted the eras of Adam, Noah, Moses, and Jesus with those of Kayumars, Hushang, Tahmuris, and Jamshid – all reputed figures of history symbolizing ancient Persia – they created a grand narrative of history, in which a new, national-oriented genre of historiography was to be grounded. Drawing on epical sources and the works of European Orientalists, the nationalist historical narrative often begins with Kayumars, the putative primogenitor of humankind in Persian legends, and proceeds through contemporary Iran. Having cast the Muslim period as one of "alien" rule and the cause of Iran's weakness, it rejects the previous consideration of the rise of Mohammad as beginning a new civilization and restores Zoroastrian mythologies as quintessentially Iranian, representing the national "spirit and character" of modern Iran. Moreover, this anti-Muslim and Arabophobic approach to reinventing Iran's past also involved the project to purify and simplify the Persian language by cleansing the Arabic influence; such influence, again, was blamed for contributing to the unscientific elements in Farsi.[54]

Compared with the Egyptians and the Iranians, the Ottomans faced a greater challenge in constructing the nationalist historical narrative, for their knowledge of early Turkish history was fragmentary, to say the least.

Traditionally, the Ottomans had entertained two kinds of loyalty, the religious loyalty to Islam and political loyalty to the Ottoman state. Since the Ottomans regarded themselves as the legitimate Muslim rulers of a Muslim Empire and the heirs to the great rulers of the Muslim past, their historians accorded little attention to the pre-Islamic history of the Turks and of Turkey. During the nineteenth century, as Turkish nationalism, or so-called Turkism, began to emerge, some efforts were made by such journalists and historians as 'Alī Su'āvī (1839–1878) and Süleymān Pasha (?–1892) to trace the origin of pre-Islamic Turkish history and the early Turks' military prowess. And for the most part, their writings relied on Western sources. Other nationalist histories appearing at the time, such as those by Namık Kemāl (1840–1888), an important intellectual leader of his time for his advocacy of freedom and liberty espoused by the French Revolution and his devotion to the defense of traditional Islamic values, remained committed to extolling the grandeur of the Muslim past. Kemāl showed no intention of distinguishing between what was Islamic and what was Ottoman. In his writings, he reminded his readers that their fatherland had produced such "national" heroes as Saladin, Sultan Mehemmed II, Sultan Selīm I, and Emīr Nevrūz. In other words, "he saw nothing incongruous in including medieval Arab and Persian Muslims, and an ancient Arabian Caliph, in his appeal to 'Ottoman' pride." And Kemāl's view of history was "in line with the feeling of his times."[55]

The ideas of liberty and nationalism appealed to the Ottomans because, as we saw in Egypt, the Ottoman Empire also embarked on a series of reforms throughout most of the century. The deposition of Selīm III in 1807 was a setback to the reformist movement. But it did not stall its momentum completely. In the face of increasing Western influence and the menacing threat from the modernizing Egypt under Muhammad 'Alī, the Ottoman Sultans Mahmud II and his son Abdülmecid decided to continue Selīm III's pioneering work. To compete with Muhammad 'Alī, Mahmud made the revolutionary move to send students to study in Europe. Not only did he revive the military and naval schools established by Selīm III, he also founded new ones. While retaining Selīm's military focus on training army and naval officers, Mahmud took on new initiatives to modernize traditional schooling by establishing grammar and translation schools, in hopes of educating civil officials. Assisted by Şanizade (aka Ataullah Mehmed, 1769–1826), the Imperial Historiographer, modern science and technology found their way from Europe into the Empire and also into the classrooms of Ottoman schools. For his instrumental role in modernizing/Westernizing the Ottoman Empire, Mahmud II was compared to Peter the Great in Russia. In actuality, he moved more closely in the footsteps of his cousin, Selīm III, as later did his son Abdülmecid. Under Abdülmecid, the Empire entered a new course of development, the *Tanzimat*, or Reorganization. This *Tanzimat* period of 1839–1876 marked the heyday of Westernization in the Ottoman Empire.

As the Ottoman Empire's military, financial, legal, administrative, and educational systems underwent a comprehensive transformation, so did the practice of history writing. This was shown first and foremost in the works of the Imperial Historiographers. Despite his conservatism and contempt for European civilization, as we saw earlier, Ahmed Asım Efendi painted a positive image of Peter the Great and praised the Tsar's effort in strengthening Russia, which had left an indelible impression on Mahmud II. Ahmed Cevdet Pasha (1822–1895), another Imperial Historiographer and later the Minister of Education, used translated European sources found in Egypt and elsewhere to compile his voluminous imperial chronicle, turning it into the most important historical work in the *Tanzimat* period. Though Cevdet Pasha did not abandon the traditional use of the chronicle, like al-Jabartī, he offered colorful descriptions and cogent analyses of events and personages as occasion permitted and on scrutinized sources.[56]

A more visible change was shown in the broadening of the scope of historical writing. During the *Tanzimat* period, the Ottoman Empire faced a swelling threat posed not only by the Russians and the Austrians but also by the rebellious Greeks and rival Egyptians. The urgency for reviving the Empire and shoring up its borders prompted Ottoman historians to expand their study, shifting the attention from recording contemporary events – which had preoccupied the work of the Imperial Historiographer – to early Ottoman history, in hopes of constructing a continuous historical narrative and bolstering national self-esteem. Hayrullah Efendi (1834–1898), for example, set out to write about every sultan in the past. Having gotten as far as the seventeenth century, his *History of the Imperial Ottoman State* (*Tārīkh-i devlet-i 'aliyye-i 'osmāniyye*), though incomplete, bespoke the rising influence of Ottomanism, one of the major intellectual trends in nineteenth-century Ottoman history. This Ottomanism also found a strong and eloquent voice in the works of Namık Kemāl, a powerful intellectual figure we have encountered earlier.

A major driving force for introducing changes in Islamic historiography came from the incentives for educational reform in the period. Since the beginning of the nineteenth century, as more and more Muslims became interested in learning about Western culture, new-type schools had mushroomed across the Middle East. Egyptians and Syrians took the lead, but the Ottomans were not far behind. During the *Tanzimat* period, for example, debates were raging in the Ottoman Empire over establishing a national university and a system of primary and secondary schools, not only in Istanbul but also in the provinces.[57] The creation of new-type schools transformed the content of schooling by expanding its subjects. For example, historical study, which had been regarded as secondary, if not downright unimportant, slowly found its way into the school curriculum at the time. To meet the need of students interested in studying history, new-style textbooks on Western models were compiled, which were usually written as narrative and arranged by chapters and sections, rather than following the traditional chronicle style. Ahmed Vefīq Pasha's (1823–1891) *An Outline of Ottoman History* (*Fezleke-i tārīkh-i 'osmānī*) constituted a good experiment, which was written during his diplomatic sojourn in France. Decades later, this new style was also adopted by such Imperial Historiographers as 'Abdurrahmān Sheref (1833–1925), who compiled a vastly popular school history text-book of Ottoman history.[58]

As Minister of Education of the Ottoman Empire, Ahmed Cevdet Pasha not only attempted innovations in his own historical writing, but he also assisted others to attempt the same, such as Ilyās Matar (1857–1910), the author of the first history of Syria. Matar's history glorified Syria's past as the cradle of the civilized world, where many inventions and virtuous people had appeared. Though Matar did not present Syria essentially as "a politi-cal national entity," his nationalist overtone was unequivocal. His endeavor reflected the growing Syrian nationalist consciousness, which was encour-aged by the Ottoman government at the time as the latter was then promot-ing more autonomous cultural development within the Empire. Moreover, Matar had had some noted predecessors, and his writing had benefited from the educational reform in Syria. Though initiated by the Egyptians, the edu-cational reform in Syria gained more momentum as the region opened more to Western influences, after the Egyptians' withdrawal. Matar was educated, for example, at the Syrian Protestant College, founded by American mis-sionaries in 1866. Aside from his friendship with Cevdet, he was quite close to Butrus al-Bustāni (1819–1883) and his son Salīm Bustāni (1848–1884), two liberal-minded educators and journalists. Though they were not pri-marily historians, the Bustānis influenced Matar by their secularized under-standing of Islamic history, which encompassed pre-Islamic Arabia and a new historical outlook characterized by their love for Syria. The Bustānis promoted and propagated these new ideas of history in a new-type school they founded in Beirut and in their essays serialized in the *al-Jinān*, one of the first modern Arabic journals they edited and published.[59]

The Minister of Education in Egypt under Khedive Ismā'īl (r. 1863–1879) was 'Alī Mubārak (1823–1893), an able administrator and versatile scholar with training in engineering. Mubārak pushed for more history teaching in secondary schools and, after founding the Teachers' College (*Dār al-'Ulūm*) in 1871, also in higher education. Indeed, though Mubārak was not formally trained as a historian, he played an instrumental role in promoting histori-cal education and preserving historical knowledge in nineteenth-century Egypt. During his tenure as the Minister of Education in the 1870s, his-tory was taught every year in the four-year secondary schools. Al-Tahtāwi's groundbreaking book on Egyptian history was adopted as the basic text. It was also much to Mubārak's credit that a National Library (*Dar al-Kutub*) was established in Egypt.[60]

Bridging the old and the new: The encyclopedists and the neochroniclers

During Mubārak's time, a new generation of historians with interesting characteristics emerged in Egypt. Like Mubārak, they received scientific training in the West and, after their return, held important administrative positions in education and public works. Amīn Sāmī, for example, served at one time as director of the Teachers' College, although he was better known for his long directorship at a peerage school reputed for academic excellence. Educated in both Western scientific culture and classical Islamic learning, Amīn Sāmī and like minds were equally conversant in both, for which they were reputed as the "encyclopedists."[61] In their writings, "they referred to al-Tabarī, Ibn 'Abd al-Hakam, al-Mas'ūdī, Ibn Khaldūn, al-Maqrīzī, al-Suyūtī, as well as to Voltaire, Rousseau, Montesquieu and the orientalist Quatremère."[62] And this was not confined to only Egypt. During the same period, encyclopedists emerged in other regions, such as in the equally Westernized Syria. Salīm Shihādah (1848–1907) and Salīm al-Khūrī (1834–1875), two Beirutis, published their encyclopedias, as did Butrus Bustānī (1819–1883)[63] Perhaps the most notable commonality in them was their interest in writing history. Mahmūd al-Falakī (1815–1885), an astronomer and engineer, later developed a distinguished career in pre-Islamic history by publishing not only in Egypt but also in Europe. 'Alī Mubārak, despite his various administrative duties, was a prolific writer, best known for compiling the encyclopedic *al-Khitat al-Tawfīqiyyah al-Jadīdah* in 20 volumes. His scientific interest, which led him to study the measurement system of the pyramid builders, and his rich and thorough description of the changes in both the nature and civilization of ancient Egypt rendered him a noted Muslim Egyptologist of his time.[64]

While distinctly "modern" with regard to their scientific training and knowledge, these historians retained notable elements found in traditional Islamic historiography. Mubārak's *al-Khitat al-Tawfīqiyyah*, as its title indicates, adopted the *Khitat* form, which might be translated as "descriptions." Amīn Sāmī, Mubārak's protégé, compiled *The Nile Almanac* (*Taqwīm al-Nīl*) in many volumes, tracing the evolution of Egyptian civilization through the previous ages to his own. This trend for reviving the traditional forms of historical writing continued well into the late years of the century, in the works of Mīkhā'īl Shārūbīm (1861–1920) and Ismā'īl Sarhank Pasha (1854? –1924). Throughout the nineteenth century, traditional and modern historiography indeed developed in parallel in Egypt and elsewhere in the Middle East. On the one hand, Muslim historians began taking interest in pre-Islamic times, especially in Egypt. From the mid-nineteenth century, not only had 'Alī Mubārak's work caught attention among Western Egyptologists, but there also appeared a bevy of Muslim Egyptologists, such as Mahmūd al-Falakī, 'Alī Bahjat (1859–?), and Ahmad Kamāl (1860–?), who frequently published essays in European scholarly journals. Kamāl also won the honor as the first modern Egyptian to have mastered hieroglyphics, whereas Nejib Asım (1861–1935) became the first Turcologist in the Ottoman Empire, conversant with the emerging Turcological study in Europe.

On the other hand, however, Islamic tradition remained quite attractive to many Muslim historians, and for good reasons.[65] Under Ahmad Bey

(1837–1855), Muhammad 'Alī's counterpart in Tunisia, reforms toward Westernization were launched in full speed, Tunisian historians, however, harked back intensively to Ibn Khaldūn, their putative predecessor, and used Khaldūn's ideas to accommodate the ideas of Locke, Voltaire, and Montesquieu, adumbrate the ebb and flow of the Muslims in the past, and assist the formation of Muslim nations in their own times. Through the efforts of these historians, Khaldūn thus became "a dominant intellectual figure throughout the second half of the nineteenth century," whose works generated interest not only in Tunisia but also in Egypt and elsewhere. Indeed, Khaldūn's influence was appreciated in the Muslim world well into the twentieth century.[66]

In their historical writings, many first-rank historians of the century, such as Sāmī, Shārūbīm, and Sarhank in Egypt and Ahmed Cevdet Pasha in the Ottoman Empire, adopted creatively and innovatively traditional styles. That is, as so-called neochroniclers, they have attempted a marriage between chronography and analytical, critical history. Though written in chronicle and gazetteer style, their works are not devoid of the critical spirit and analytical flavor commonly associated with modern historiography, nor are they inadequate in depicting a monographic study. Sarhank's *A Precise History of the Maritime States* (*Haqā'iq al-Akhbār 'an Duwal al-Bihār*) is a good example. In this topical history, Sarhank appears quite at ease in using Arabic and European historical sources and sharing his historical insights on the complex rise and fall of maritime nations. In fact, the chronicle style seems to have enabled these historians to maintain a detached position. Shārūbīm's *A Definitive History of Ancient and Modern Egypt* (*Al-Kāfī fī Ta'rīkh Misr al-Qadīm wa'l-Hadīth*) is a case in point. Though it often treated controversial periods of history, such as the reign of Muhammad 'Alī, the book was praised for its fairness in judgment and perceptiveness in analysis. While guarding the tradition, Shārūbīm also judiciously avoided its defects – his *History of Ancient and Modern Egypt* clearly was not a mélange of historical sources as one often found in earlier scholarship but rather a reliable and coherent account of history.[67]

Combining traditional and modern historiography, these historical works were products of their times, or the reform era. The Muslims launched these reforms to respond to the challenge of the West. But the reforms were also aimed to renew and revive the Islamic tradition. Toward the last two decades of the century, this reform movement experienced a notable change. The outcome of the Franco-Prussian War caused the decline of French influence in the region, which affected negatively the reformers' cause in the Ottoman Empire. Having expanded its military force for several decades, Egypt encountered a severe financial crisis, which resulted in the 'Urābī Revolution (1881–1882), arguably the first nationalist movement in the Middle East. It also led to the British Occupation of Egypt (1882–1922/1952), which further weakened and fragmented the Muslim world. In order to fend off Western imperialism and colonialism, more and more Muslims turned to the ideology of nationalism and embarked on the cause of nation-building.

Nationalist historiography thus was to be developed in full swing and became the dominant trend in twentieth-century Muslim historiography.

Nationalism and the transformation of Indian historiography

Historiography during early colonialism

In discussing Indian historical literature during the transition from the preco-lonial to the colonial period, from the eighteenth to the nineteenth centuries, we are confronted with the problem of trying to assess the relative impact of European modes of historical thinking on a society that was already under-going a process of modernization to varying degrees. As noted previously, in South India, in the eighteenth century and even earlier, there was a tradition of historical writing that in significant ways conformed to modern criteria for the discipline, although this was embedded in older literary genres and textual traditions. In Bengal, there was a Persianized historiography written in prose and with a narrow political focus but a historiography nonetheless, which aimed to come to grips first with the decline of Mughal power and later with the new political presence of the East India Company (EIC). This Persian historiography was fundamentally moral in its outlook, although it acknowledged secular notions of causality. It chronicled the corruption and decline in virtue among the Mughals; likewise, it also pointed to the moral failings of the English. But Persianized historians such as Ghulam Husain Tabatabai (1727/28–?), author of the eighteenth-century magnum opus *Seir Mutaqherin* (1781), were also aware of the differences in the politi-cal culture of the EIC, and this engendered a new political and historical consciousness. The Company had achieved its victory at Plassey in 1757 using underhanded means against the local potentate Siraj-ud-daula. This event was followed by a period of violence, rapacity, and plunder until, threatened by the instability it had caused, the Company underwent self-regulation and reform, bringing a peace and stability to the region that had been lacking on account of an existing fractious local political situation to which the Company also contributed. Such complexities found comment in the writings of indigenous historians such as the aforementioned Tabatabai. Tabatabai chronicled the strategies of cunning and deviousness employed by the Company in its bid for power, the "drunken and licentious" character of the English, and the failure of the new rulers to live up to standards of good government according to the moral canons of classical Mughal politi-cal philosophy. Yet he also inserted a note of practicality in acknowledging the stability brought about by the British presence. More significantly, he showed an understanding of the essential character of modern imperialism, namely, economic exploitation coupled with a sense of cultural superiority. Thus, "Ghulam Hussain may have been the first to characterize the nature of the East India Company's early government of Eastern India as a system of colonial rule."[68] Interestingly, Tabatabai's critical account was translated into English in 1789.

Writers such as Tabatabai represented a genre of writing that character-ized the old educated bureaucratic literati that, although critical of Com-pany rule, still aspired to find employment with the new administration. They hoped, through their writings, to highlight the role of an informed and experienced bureaucracy in ensuring good government. But the British remained wary of them. That these works had little influence on the emerg-ing colonialist historiography is seen in the fact that virtually all colonialist historians portray the pre-British Muslim governments as despotic, violent, and exploitative. As noted in the previous chapter, this was the theme of Oriental Despotism, the foil against which Company rule was justified. As we shall see, this particular characterization of the Mughal/Muslim king-doms also became a critical element in the nationalist historiography of the late nineteenth century.

At the beginning of the nineteenth century, we see two types of histori-cal writing, both owing their articulation to the EIC's presence. The first of these were the histories written by British servants of the Company who found time outside their administrative duties to pen historical narratives. These were the so-called administrative historians and some, such as James Mill, the Chief Examiner of Correspondence in London, had never even been to India. The second genre was represented mainly by Bengali Hindu literati (*pandits*, or scholars) commissioned by the Company College at Fort William, Calcutta, to write history texts as language primers. Further, continuing a trend already begun in the eighteenth century with the politi-cal ascendancy of the EIC, the period witnessed the development of new patronage networks and institutional sites for purposes of cultural and his-torical preservation, such as the Asiatic Society of Bengal, founded by the aforementioned Sir William Jones in 1784.

A primary motivation for the administrator historian was to garner infor-mation that would rationalize and facilitate Company rule. Knowledge of local customs, usages, and the like was needed to govern and to collect revenue. The result was a type of administrative history that was later the standard fare of the *District Gazetteers, Reports on Revenue Settlements*, etc. But because local information was not always forthcoming or manage-able in terms of volume, it problematized the question of colonial histori-cal knowledge. According to Ranajit Guha, the need to end dependence on local sources of information, which was often regarded as suspect and even deliberately misleading, gave rise to a historiography that was wholly instru-mental in its scope, that is to say, a colonialist historiography.[69] Bernard Cohn has shown that the early period of colonial governance relied heav-ily on an understanding of India's past.[70] Thus the Company's scholar offi-cials proceeded to build textual and artifactual collections, namely archives, while Orientalists studied languages as source material for historical infor-mation. This preservationist impulse, intended to promote and legitimize colonial rule, had important consequences. On the one hand, it led to "the production of an archive of (and for) rule."[71] Colonialist narratives relying on native material constructed histories that weaved in the triumph of the British. On the other hand, the engagement with native texts and artifacts, coupled with the need for accurate administrative data, led to a sharpening of a sense of methodology and a disciplining of historical practice, of which an important element was the turn to a more rigorous empiricism with an emphasis on "facts." Thus "ideas of historical truth were conditioned by the classificatory practices of the early colonial state."[72] This had important repercussions on precolonial narrative traditions as well, which were differently structured for their historical content and which were now divested of their legitimacy other than as raw material and "sources" from which "facts" could be gleaned. The task of appraisal and establishing authenticity was often the work of the colonial antiquarian, who advanced the new historical method.[73] It is also important to note that, despite instrumentalist motivations, the universalist impulse of the Enlightenment continued to be an important factor. Studying the history of India would shed light on the history of mankind.[74] At the same time, the enterprise of collecting, with the help of native assistants, often scholars in their own right, had important repercussions. It delegitimized Indian practices of history, making way for the ascendance of a positivist history in India, but it also put its stamp on colonialist historiography. Within the institutional space of centers of Orientalist learning, Britons and Indians came together to thrash out the significance of the diverse textual traditions they encountered. Rama Sundari Mantena writes in his excellent book on historiography in South India, "[N]ative Indian assistants did not simply imbibe new practices of history but also shaped them while immersed in daily collection, collation, assessment and translation activities."[75] In time, they began their own historical researches as well as promoting Indian societies of learning, which functioned as institutional sites for the production of historical knowledge, although, in the first half of the nineteenth century, the latter were few and far between.

In contrast, the historical works of the Indian literati writing for Fort William College were written at the behest of the Company, which required books that would serve as language primers (in Bengali and not Persian) for a growing English bureaucracy. Three of the works that come to our attention are Ramram Basu's *Raja Pratapaditya Charita* (*The Story of King Pratapaditya*, 1801), Rajiblochan Mukhopadhyay's *Maharaj Krishnachandra Rayasya Charitram* (*The Life of King Krishnachandra*, 1805), and Mritunjoy Bidyalankar's *Rajabali* (*Chronicle of Kings*, 1808). According to Ranajit Guha, "All three works were textual sites of a conflict between archaism and modernism at both the literary and historiographical levels."[76] Additionally, these works reveal both Sanskrit/Puranic and Indo-Persian *ta'rikh* influences, the latter in terms of incisive narratives of political ambition and power that, despite admittedly numerous references to providence and divine intervention, were purely temporal in their analysis. A noteworthy element of these texts was their authors' awareness of divergent accounts of the same incident, the emphasis on credibility in choice of account, the search for accuracy in reporting facts, and, lastly, a sense of narrative continuity and completeness. Whether these elements mirrored the Western model of historiography, as Ranajit Guha states, or provides yet another example of the influence of Persian and other types of indigenous traditions is not clear. Kumkum Chatterjee argues that there appears to be little evidence of a Western influence in these compositions.[77] However, this does not contradict our earlier comment on the hybrid nature of the Indian historiographical culture of the late eighteenth century, which was reflected in the accounts of the Bengali pandits. By this time the Asiatic Society of Bengal, under the leadership of Sir William Jones, had begun its pathbreaking work on the Indo-European languages concept. Philology played a key role in colonialist historiography, in part because native accounts were deemed poorly developed and untrustworthy. Besides the Asiatic Society, the College of Fort St. George in Madras, another center for Orientalist scholarship, also carried out philological research, particularly in the vernaculars. Here the discovery of what Thomas Trautmann calls the Dravidian Proof was made, namely, that the languages of South India were not derivative of Sanskrit but formed a separate category altogether. Trautmann has argued that research into the Dravidian Proof was conducted with the help of Indian traditions of language analysis,[78] and Rama Sundari Mantena writes that "historical philology would not have emerged had it not been for the British Orientalists' reliance on Indians and Indian forms of knowledge"[79] and that further, through a historical and organicist understanding of the Indian languages, Orientalist philology contributed to a linear and progressive conception of historical development, insofar as language in its temporality was assumed to be a sign of a society's cultural development.[80] These conclusions suggest that a "domination" model of Indian historiography, regarding Indians as passive recipients of colonialist knowledge forms, needs to be modified, at least for the early colonial period.

The new pedagogy and the emergence of a modern historical consciousness

As we noted, during the earlier decades of the nineteenth century, Indian assistants with scholarly ambitions had also begun original work of their own. Often they were able to present their conclusions in colonial literary societies, suggesting that there was a colonial "public sphere" in which natives and Britons could engage in common intellectual pursuits. But we must be careful not to overvalue the social implications of this inclusion. Indian intellectuals were allowed involvement only at the behest of individual patrons, and further they were never regarded as having fully made the transition from native *pandit* to modern scholar.[81] It was not until the latter half of the nineteenth century that this situation changed, and Indians were seen as capable of a rationalistic and empirical historiography.

Indeed, as the century progressed, a positivist historiographical model became increasingly prevalent among Indian scholars, as older paradigms were displaced (but not eliminated) and new methods and views were developed including an increasingly historicist outlook. The partisan nature of much colonial historiography also played a role in this development. Colonialist arguments about good governance and civilizational progress under the British portrayed the precolonial past in a deplorable way. This provoked, among Indian historians, a defense response that had to be framed in the same rationalist paradigm.

Additionally, we have to take into account the role played by history in formal education in the emergence of a modernized historical consciousness. History was taught not only in the missionary schools and colleges but also in the newer vernacular schools that were created to train the clerks and servants of the Empire. These modern schools, which gradually displaced the traditional *tols*, *pathshalas*, and *madrasas*, emphasized a curriculum aligned with colonial educational values. The traditional *pathshalas* (elementary schools) had imparted the basic skills necessary for everyday life; their focus was on language, arithmetic, and accountancy, not on history. But during the second decade of the nineteenth century, many of these were provided with, free of charge, printed material in keeping with a liberal (and not just secular) educational philosophy. History was one of the most important subjects of the new pedagogy, and in 1844 Governor-General Hardinge gave the orders for the establishment of some hundred odd vernacular village schools that reflected this new curricular emphasis.[82] The new pedagogical and intellectual importance of history led to a growing interest in the subject. The Utilitarian emphasis, particularly in the mission schools, on the exemplar achievements of European antiquity and, equally, the less than exemplar achievements and record keeping skills of the Indian ancients, evoked curiosity regarding the "facts" and "accomplishments" of the Indian past, about which an earlier generation of liberal Orientalists such as William Jones had written with some favor and sympathy.

Religious revivalism and the search for a glorious past

Further, since the colonialist narratives ascribed the British presence in India to the reason of history itself, it became necessary to produce a counter-mythology to invalidate this assertion. One important metanarrative to emerge contrasted a materialistic West with a spiritual East; although the West would have its moment, history would end with the triumph of the Indian spirit. Such assertions were made by the prominent social and religious reformers of the time. Reformers such as Rammohun Roy (1772–1833), Dayanand Saraswati (1824–1883), and Vivekananda (1863–1902) were not, of course, historians. They wished to resuscitate an older, more pristine Hinduism, one uncorrupted by time and priestly venality, through reform movements that some scholars have described as a "Protestanization of Hinduism." But they strove to discover the civilizational foundations of India's renewal and destiny in the traditions of the ancient past where already, they asserted, mankind's creativity had reached its spiritual and intellectual perfection. Reform therefore was linked to a revival of a past that also implied a break with the recent dismal and corrupted past but not with the specificity of India. This did not, however, imply a rejection of modernity. Indeed, the reformers saw their agenda as being compatible with modernity since, they asserted, ancient Indian civilization had already anticipated the achievements of rational-technological modernity. This was one way of reconciling tradition with the challenges of modernity. Roy even provided evidence to counter the supposed ahistoricity of India, and Dayanand, the religious reformer and founder of the Arya Samaj sect of Hinduism, argued that the Vedas contained all of modern science. Of course, this last statement betrayed a very simplistic understanding of Vedic culture or its scientific potential. Further, by equating India's ancient past with a Hindu past, it framed the argument for an exclusivist and homogeneous definition of ancient Indian society, presuming as well the existence of a well-defined religion called "Hinduism" for the ancient period, when this was not the case. More significantly, the ideas of the Hindu revivalist/reform movements could be and were utilized by a strand of nationalist historiography that formed the ideological basis of the political Hinduism movements of the twentieth century. A singularized version of Hinduism, one that glossed over its social and philosophical heterogeneity, came to be regarded as a necessary precondition for both social reform and political mobilization. And it provided a definition of Indian-ness that could be harnessed by some of the radical nationalist historiographies of the independence movement.

Social reform efforts along religious lines also developed among the Indian Muslim intelligentsia, such as the educationist Sayyid Ahmad Khan (1817–1898), who endeavored to reconcile Western education and science with the injunctions of the Koran. But the Islamic tradition posed greater difficulties partly because its tenets were more structured and defined, as compared to Hinduism, which could be interpreted more flexibly. Further, because the Golden Age of Islam was located outside India, it problematized the issue of Islam as an indigenous element in Indian culture. Ultimately, however, the recourse to religion among both communities "hardened the lines of demarcation"[83] and diminished the syncretist trends of earlier times. This was to have an impact on later nationalist writing and, in particular, on the development of the two-nation theory that would underline the Partition of India in 1947.

Of course, these social reformers were not professional historians and made scant reference to actual historical data. But their views, which stood in stark contrast to the colonial ones taught in the colonial schools, led to a growing "hunger for history" among the Indian intelligentsia so that history became a way of recovering one's dignity as well as "a way of talking about the collective self, and bringing it into existence."[84] In 1838, the Society for the Acquisition of General Knowledge was formed in Calcutta; its purpose was to hold lectures on aspects of European learning. The very first of these, given by Rev. Krishna Mohun Bannerjee, "On the Nature and Importance of Historical Studies," made the point that the success of the West was due to its historical self-understanding, its appreciation of its own past.[85] This was soon followed by the appearance of numerous regional and national histories, mostly in Bengali. Thus, for example, we have the educationist Ishwar Chandra Bidyasagar's *History of Bengal* (*Bangalar Itihas*, 1848) and Kedar Nath Datta's *History of India* (*Bharatbarsher Itihas*, 1859), among others. This new history took many of its cues from colonialist historiography, but also questioned many of its presumptions. Thus, for example, Mill's tripartite periodization schema of Hindu-Muslim-British rule was adopted, but his negative depiction of Indian society as an area of civilizational darkness was rejected. Indian historians looked more toward liberal Orientalists such as William Jones and Mountstuart Elphinstone (1779–1859), who compared ancient India to the civilizations of Greece and Rome and celebrated its achievements in philosophy, astronomy, mathematics, and other sciences. Many of them also, in depicting the ancient period as a golden age, concluded that the subsequent era of 'Muslim rule' was one of loss and decline. This too was partially the result of Mill's periodization, which in turn drew on the European periodization of ancient/medieval/modern, with the middle period being characteristically, the Dark Ages. Nineteenth-century European historiography's prejudice toward Islam, which was very much prevalent in its books on Indian history, also had its influence in the formation of a Hindu Indian identity as a historical subject, serving in the process, to "communalize" Indian history, although anti-Muslim prejudices were by no means absent in indigenous writings prior to Mill's, such as the Fort William College *pandit* Rajiblochan's account of the conspiracy against Siraj-ud-daula.[86] Sumit Sarkar has argued that the middle-class (*bhadralok*) strata of Hindu society, even though in a position of colonial dependency, nonetheless experienced a relative improvement in its status with the advent of British rule. The critical attitude toward the Islamic past was therefore the displaced status anxiety of a social group unable to freely criticize the source of its economic well-being.[87]

The rationalist paradigm

Indigenous historians also began to accept the Western notion that there was no tradition of historical writing in India prior to the British. Thus the historian Rajendralal Mitra (1822–1891), the first Indian president of the Asiatic society, stated, "Indian literature is almost void of all authentic historical accounts."[88] As Partha Chatterjee points out, this notion was "a singular discovery of European Indology";[89] it would not have occurred to the Fort William College historians. At the core of this conception was a greater consciousness of method and rules of evidence and authenticity, and the acceptance of the rationalist-positivist model of history. We must also keep in mind that over the course of the nineteenth century the discipline of history was disaggregated into the separate disciplines of archaeology, history, and art history in the various professional organizations such as the Asiatic Society, as well as in colleges and universities, in which Indian historians, such as the aforementioned Rajendralal Mitra, as also the well-known Sanskrit scholar and historian of ancient India R. G. Bhandarkar (1837–1925), made their mark as well. Bhandarkar was a fervent advocate of rationalist-positivist history. Echoing Ranke, as he interpreted him, he insisted that the facts must speak for themselves. "One must in the first place be impartial, with no particular disposition to find in the materials before him something that will tend to the glory of his race and country, nor should he have an opposite prejudice against the country or its people. Nothing but dry truth should be his object."[90] Bhandarkar was in favor of social reform and in his numerous public lectures brought to light the discrepancies between the Hindu practices of his day and those of ancient times. But he also insisted that only correct methodology could assure the correct direction of reform. "By a clear perception of our great national defects we prepare the ground for healthy progress in the future."

In many ways, Indian historical writing of the second half of the nineteenth century replicated the subjects and themes of colonial writing. Social history was equated with "folklore," economic history dealt with land grants and productivity data, issues that had administrative significance. Political history was the history of kings and then of governor-generals. But this historicization of Indian thinking did not automatically mean "colonialism by consent."[91] The colonial concept of historical change did not allow Indians any role in the historical dynamic. This view was no longer accepted. And since it was difficult to openly criticize colonialism, indigenous historical writing provided the means for recovering agency, even though instances of such agency were to be located in the remote past.

The birth of the nationalist paradigm

Increasingly, history was used to contest many of the disparaging assumptions of the Orientalists. Thus, according to Partha Chatterjee, by 1870, the principal elements of a nationalist historiography were already in place.[92] We must keep in mind, however, that a nationalist historiography can be nationalist in several ways. First and foremost, it must presume a consciousness of the nation as a discrete formation coextensive with a geographical and civilizational coherence. Second, it possesses an intimate sense of its past and often of its ancient past as the foundational source of identity and historical destiny. This also becomes the rationale for agency and subjectivity, which is also an aspect of nationalist historical writing. Finally, a nationalist historiography is premised on an awareness of the Other. This consciousness, however, may or may not lead to a critique of the Other. Thus, it may lead to a critique of colonialism. It may also prompt an exclusivist definition of the Self that seeks to excise elements that are inimical to the aforementioned first two definitions of a nationalist historiography.

It was not until the first decade of the twentieth century, with the rise of the *Swadeshi* (self-sufficiency) movement and revolutionary terrorist movements, that a nationalist historiography of India characterized by an emphatic and vehement critique of colonial rule came into its own, although aspects of colonialism had been brought under critical scrutiny earlier, even as far back as the late eighteenth century, as Kumkum Chatterjee has shown. However, the first indigenous writings about an Indian, and not just a regional past began to appear in the 1850s. Two of the most important of these were Nilmani Basak's and Tarinicharan Chattopadhyay's *History of India (Bharatbarsher Itihas)*, two separate books with the same title authored by Bengali historians.[93] Basak's *History*, in three volumes and published over two years, expressed in its preface the wish to disabuse the reader of the Anglophone notion that "the ancient Hindus were a very stupid lot." It also asserted that the representation of the past could be done more authentically and attractively in Bengali rather than in English. Language was now beginning to be recognized as an index of identity, which fed into the emerging national consciousness. It is important to keep in mind that the Indian nationalist thinking created many types of discourses regarding identity. In India, the sense of region and the sense of nation emerged together. To say that there was a rising arc of nationalist consciousness that eventually subsumed the regionalisms does not bear up to the facts.[94] In that sense, there was no contradiction between a linguistic pride in the *matribhasha* (mother tongue) and nationalist consciousness, and, as Guha points out, throughout the 1850s, "national language" was used interchangeably with *matribhasha*, suggesting language as the ideological marker of ethnicity and political agency.[95]

Thus it was the bonding of colonial education with the vernacular that led to the new historiography. As Anglophone histories came to be translated for use in schools and universities, their inadequacies and fallacies were remarked on. In the second half of the nineteenth century, a number of "textbook historians" (generally college professors) began to write histories of India for the Bengali schools. These texts sought to revive pride in the native heritage by disputing the disparagements of the colonial narratives. Thus Kshirodchandra Raychaudhuri in 1876 stated in the preface of his book, "I have written this book for those who have been misled by translations of histories written in English."[96] One claim that was rejected was that British rule had the inevitability of historical necessity. Indian historians, now schooled in European history, statecraft, and political philosophy, argued instead that colonial victory was the result of Machiavellian machinations. The British won the Battle of Plassey because of Clive's intrigues and Mir Jafar's treachery. Nawab Siraj-ud-daulah lacked virtue and was a tyrant. But his defeat was the outcome of power politics, not personal failings or divine retribution.

Much more influential than Basak's multivolume *History* was Tarinich-aran Chattopadhyay's *History of India*. Already in its 18th edition by 1878, it was the most popular history textbook in Bengali schools in the latter part of the nineteenth century. As with Basak, "India" is now a discrete entity, a country (*desh*), and *desh* is now the framework for the narrative, not king lists. Much like the other textbook authors of his generation, Tarinicharan's formulation relied on Anglophone frameworks such as the Hindu-Muslim-British schema, in which the notion of India as a coherent geographical unit was also implicit. Tarinicharan also relied on the Indological accounts of ancient India, although, of course, this was a very selective reliance. Mill's utterly damning account of the Indian past was rejected; much more to his liking was Mountstuart Elphinstone's *History of India* (1841), by no means the "hegemonic textbook"[97] of Mill's that had to be wrestled with at every turn but that took a much more favorable view of the achievements of the ancient Indians in, as described in Elphinstone's chapter titles, "Philosophy," "Astronomy and Mathematical Science," "Medicine," and so on. However, to fully recover Indian agency, it was necessary to address two areas of concern. First, one had to explain why this glorious civilization underwent a decline. Second, one had to show what was required for the Indians them-selves to carry out what the British had already begun, that is to say, India's modernization. Both issues could be easily addressed by a reformulation of the British tripartite division of Indian history. Thus, "ancient India had to become the classical source of Indian modernity, while the 'Muslim period' would become the night of medieval darkness."[98] For Tarinicharan, all of the negative depictions in the colonial narratives of the Muslim period and the Muslim kings, "slunk in sloth and debauchery, and emulating the vices of a Caligula or Commodus," as Sir Henry Elliot put it, make perfect sense. The cruel, dissolute, but also religiously fanatical conquerors (no longer Turko-Afghans or Mughals, but Muslims), who are not the original inhabit-ants of India like the Hindus, but come from outside as does their religion (from Arabia), manage to defeat the Hindus not because of divine interven-tion but because of bad luck and unforeseeable circumstances. The nation-alist historiography of the late nineteenth century, therefore, was directed against both the British as well as the Muslims.

Nationalism, communalism, and historical writing

Taricharan and Basak adumbrated a recurring theme, namely, the civiliza-tion greatness of the ancient Indian past and its subsequent decline under Muslim rule. But this representation also raised the problematic question of the role of the British, who had freed the Hindus from the tyranny of Muslim misrule. However, if Indian-ness was defined in terms of geographi-cal and religious identity, then the Christian English were outsiders too. Nor were their (admittedly beneficial) modernizing efforts alien to the ancient Hindu culture, as the social and religious reformers had argued.

Late nineteenth-century Indian nationalist historiography therefore created the discourse of the ethnical singularity of India, which was magnanimous enough to give outsiders a place. It was by no means the only one and, as Partha Chatterjee has argued, there were also faint rumblings of an alternative, "de-centered" historiography.[99] Additionally, we see in Basak the hints of an interesting historiographical shift that in the beginning of the next century would become more evident, namely, a move away from state-centered political history to "a fairly remarkable and precocious interest in social and cultural history," which came into its own precisely at a time when the Rankean model was establishing its hegemony in Europe.[100] This valorization of culture over kings and wars was partly in response to the paucity of chronologically firm data on the Hindu period, which by this time was an important methodological consideration. It also represented a politics of identity that gave a cultural rather than a political priority to the Indian past, within the broader political agenda of establishing historical agency. The culture of this historiography, however, was mainly that of the religious or caste-based community.

The Muslim ripostes to the various sectarian versions of the Indian past were equally defensive; these, too, had to struggle with the colonialist narratives (and their Hindu versions). One response was to explain some of the negative aspects of Muslim rule in terms of the exigencies of political responsibility and, by implication, as acts that were contrary to the tenets of Islam (as maintained by the Bengali writer Sayyid Abdul Rahim). The other was to emphasize the civilizational greatness of Islam, which had its own classical age and contributory role in the culture of mankind. The English and Hindu portrayal of Muslims as warlike, fanatical, and oppressive was slanderous. A true account of the Muslim past could be portrayed only by Muslims, and writers such as Abdul Karim (1863–1943) set out to do so.

Secular narratives and the emergence of economic nationalism

Historical writing in the vernacular developed in other parts of India as well. In 1864 Shiva Prasad (1823–1890) wrote the first history of India in Hindi; the title of his book, *Itihasa Timirnasak* (literally, *History as the Destroyer of Darkness*) indicated the practical rationale of the book – history as a guide to positive change. Thus, history was not just the foundation for collective self-understanding; it was also the way to progress. And progress derived from a sense of history implied agency. Self-understanding led to self-development, and self-development was an autonomous act. Thus by the 1870s there appeared a new strand in indigenous historical thinking, one that increasingly questioned the possibility of progress under British rule. Harishchandra of Benaras (1850–1885), a student of Shiva Prasad, was an early critic of colonial rule. This development also coincided with a secularization of the cause of reform. Among a new generation of socially active reformers such as Dadabhai Naoroji (1825–1917) and

Mahadev Govind Ranade (1842–1901), social change came to be separated from religious concepts, which in turn suggested a concept of progress that was more fully modern. And although Naoroji and Ranade remained politically loyal to British rule, they did not hesitate to criticize it on the basis of its own claims. For Naoroji, "The present system of government is destructive and despotic to the Indians and un-British and suicidal to Britain."[101] Of special relevance to the reformers was the economic consequences of British rule, the "drain of wealth" caused by heavy taxes, and the repatriation of income in the form of Home Charges. These assertions were strongly informed by Marxist frameworks of analysis, in particular those regarding the international division of labor and the imperialism of free trade. Their "economic nationalist" perspective also signaled a turning away from religious politics and issues pertaining to ancient Indian culture; increasingly, the Mughals as well as other regional dynasties were portrayed as being humane and benevolent. Ranade was very critical of revivalist historiography of the religious kind and asked the revivalists which origin they wanted to go back to, since there were many and since all origins are conditioned by history.[102] In turn, the economic nationalists encouraged a scrutiny of the political context of British economic policy, which became the focus of the debates of the Indian National Congress founded in 1885.

The conclusions of Naoroji and Ranade influenced the writings of the well-known historian and politician Romesh Chunder Dutt (1845–1909). Dutt was also a historical novelist, and the historical novel was also a form of political action in India, one that often openly confessed its instrumental agenda, as we will see later. In 1897, he published his *England and India: A Record of Progress during One Hundred Years*, which in addition to the drain of wealth also pointed to the deindustrialization of India brought about by mass-produced British goods. Dutt relied on the Government of India's "blue books" for his source material, thus challenging the orthodoxy of the benefits of British rule on the basis of colonial records. He did not deny some of the blessings of colonial rule, in particular the value of Western education. But like Naoroji, he challenged its claim as an agent of progress and used the concept of progress itself to deny that claim.

The conclusions of the economic nationalists, particularly the theme of the "drain of wealth," became a very important component of political action in the early twentieth century. The *Swadeshi* movement of 1905 was very much based on its arguments, although it has also been argued that the nationalist movement was much more radical than the historiography of the economic nationalists, which in many ways remained loyalist. However, by invoking the economic explanation, they exhibited an openness to global processes that was far more forward-looking than the arguments of the revivalists with their consolidation of agency along communitarian lines.

The colonial histories of India had contributed to the emergence of a modernized historical consciousness during the nineteenth century. Indigenous historians came to accept modern, rationalistic criteria of historical representation. The discipline of history itself became an acknowledged and important area of knowledge. Historical writing also became an important tool in the fashioning of an emergent national consciousness. This national-ist historical consciousness tended to be reactive and imitative, insofar as much of it aimed at invalidating the belittling colonial accounts of Indian culture but on the basis of colonial principles of determination. Thus Indian history, too, was divided into three historical ages, and the first, ancient age was deemed in no way inferior to the classical glory of Greece and Rome. But the existence of a glorious past was not enough to explain the present state of colonial domination and indignity. One strand among the national-ist historians attributed India's weakness and decline to its period of Muslim rule, and in this they echoed the Anglophone historians. The nationalist his-torians were, of course, members of an urban elite that was itself the prod-uct of colonial rule. Their hostility toward India's Islamic heritage therefore contradicted the syncretic traditions that had flourished, particularly in the rural areas of Bengal.

Notes

1 See a very comprehensive, "Romanticism," comparing tthe romantic move-ment in various European countries and North and South America, *Wikipedia*, updated August 18, 2015. Stephen Bann, *Romanticism and the Rise of His-tory* (New York, 1995); also his *The Clothing of Clio: A Study of the Rep-resentation of History in Nineteenth Century Britain and France* (Cambridge, 1984); Hugh Trevor-Roper, *The Romantic Movement and the Study of History* (London, 1969); Isaiah Berlin, *The Roots of Romanticism* (Princeton, 1999); still valuable are two older works, George P. Gooch, *History and Historians in the Nineteenth Century* (London, 1913) and Georg Brandes, *Main Currents in Nineteenth-Century Literature* 6 vols. (New York, 1901), vol. 2, *The Romantic School in Germany*, vol. 4, *The Romantic School in France*, and also relevant, vol. 1, *Emigrant Literature* on the French émigrés. Stefan Berger, "The Invention of European National Traditions in European Romanticism" in Stuart Macin-tyre, Juan Maiguashca, and Attila Pok, eds., *The Oxford History of Historical Writing*, vol. 4: 1800–1945 (Oxford, 2011), 19–40.
2 François-René Chateaubriand, *The Genius of Christianity* (New York, 1975).
3 See Georg G. Iggers, *The German Conception of History: The National Tradi-tion of Historical Thought from Herder to the Present* (Middletown, 1983); also Ernst Breisach, *Historiography: Ancient, Medieval, & Modern* (Chicago, 1983), 228–267; Ernest Gellner, *Nations and Nationalism* (Oxford, 1983); Hans Kohn, *The Idea of Nationalism: A Study in the Origin and Background* (New York, 1944); Eric J. Hobsbawm, *Nations and Nationalism since 1780: Programme, Myth, Reality* (Cambridge, 1990); Stefan Berger, *The Search of Normality: National Identity and Historical Consciousness in Germany Since 1800* (Provi-dence, 1997); Stefan Berger, Mark Donovan, and Kevin Passmore, eds., *Writing National Histories: Western Europe Since 1800* (London, 1999). See the 9-vol. series, Stefan Berger, Christoph Conrad, and Guy Marchal, eds., *Writing the Nation* (New York, 2011–2015).
4 English: *Addresses to the German Nation* (Westport, 1979).
5 Effi Gazi, *Scientific National History: The Greek Case in Comparative Perspec-tive (1850–1920)* (New York, 2000); see Monika Badr, "East-central European

Historical Writing" in *The Oxford History of Historical Writing*, vol. 4, 326–348; Marius Turda, "Historical Writing in the Balkans," ibid., 349–368.

6 Erik Lönnroth, Karl Molin, and Ragmar Björk, eds., *Conceptions of National History: Proceedings of Nobel Symposium 78* (Berlin, 1994), which also includes chapters on India, China, Japan, and postcolonial Africa; Berger, Conrad, and Marchal, eds., *Writing the Nation*.

7 *Collection de documents inédits sur l'histoire de France.*

8 William Clark, *Academic Charisma and the Origins of the Research Universities* (Chicago, 2006); Charles E. McClelland, *State, Society, and Universities* (Cambridge, 1980).

9 Theodor H. Von Laue, *Leopold von Ranke: The Formative Years* (Princeton, 1950); Leonard Krieger, *Ranke: The Meaning of History* (Chicago, 1977); Santi Di Bella, *Leopold von Ranke: Gli anni della formazione* (Soveria Mamell, 2005); Andreas D. Boldt, *The Life and Work of the German Historian Leopold von Ranke (1795–1886)* (Lewiston, NY, 2014); Georg G. Iggers, ed., *Leopold von Ranke, The Theory and Practice of History* (London, 2011), see the Introduction, xi–xlv. The von in front of Ranke's name is actually not applicable at this point; he was ennobled only late in life.

10 English: *The History of Rome* (London, 1851).

11 August Böckh, *Der Staatshaushalt der Athener* (Berlin, 1817).

12 On nonacademic historians, see Martin Nissen, *Populäre Geschichtsschreib ung¨Historiker, Verleger und die deutsche Öffentlichkeit 1848–1900* (Köln, 2009).

13 Augustin Thierry, *The Formation and Progress of the Third Estate*, 2 vols. (London, 1859). On Thierry: Friedrich Engel-Janosi, *Four Studies in French Romantic Historical Writing* (Baltimore, 1955); Stanley Mellon, *The Political Uses of History* (Stanford, 1958); and Lionel Gossman, *Augustin Thierry and Liberal Historiography* (Middletown, 1976).

14 François Guizot, *History of France from the Earliest Times to the Year Eighteen Forty-Eight*, 8 vols. (Chicago, 1869–1898); idem, *History of Europe from the Fall of the Roman Empire to the French Revolution* (London, 1854); idem, *History of Civilization in Europe* (New York, 1899). On Guizot: Mellon, *The Political Uses of History*; also Gooch, *History and Historians in the Nineteenth Century*.

15 Jules Michelet, *History of France* (1855); *History of the French Revolution* (1847), and *The People*; on Michelet: Roland Barthes, *Michelet* (Oxford, 1987); Linda Orr, *Jules Michelet: Nature, History, and Language* (Ithaca, 1976); Arthur Mitzman, *Michelet, Historian: Rebirth and Romanticism in Nineteenth-century France* (New Haven, 1990).

16 Karl Marx to Joseph Wedemeyer, March 5, 1852 in *Marx-Engels Werke*, vol. 28 (East Berlin, 1963), 507–508.

17 Thomas Macaulay, *History of England from the Accession of James II* (New York, 1968); John Clive, *Macaulay: The Shaping of the Historian* (New York, 1974).

18 Thomas Carlyle, *The French Revolution: A History* (Oxford, 1989); *History of Frederick the Great*, ed. and abridged John Clive (Chicago, 1969); *Heroes and Hero-worship and the Heroic in History* (London, 1888). On Carlyle: John D. Rosenberg, *Carlyle and the Burden of History* (Oxford, 1985).

19 See Herbert Butterfield, *The Whig Interpretation of History* (London, 1931).

20 Kenneth Pomeranz, *The Great Divergence: China, Europe, and the Making of the Modern World Economy* (Princeton, 2000).

21 Edward E. Baptist, *The Half Has Never Been Told: Slavery and the Making of American Capitalism* (New York, 2014); Michael Zeuske, *Handbuch Geschichte der Sklaverei. Eine Globalgeschchte von den Anfängen bius zur Gegenwart* (Berlin, 2013).

22 William Robertson, *The History of America*, 2 vols. (New York, 1798).

23 See ch. 1, Abbot Guillaume-Thomas Raynal, *Histoire philosophique et politique des établissemens et du commerce des Européens dans les deux Indes* (Amsterdam, 1770).

24 English selections in Georg G. Iggers, ed., *Leopold von Ranke: Theory and Practice of History*, which contains a section of the *History of the Popes*, and Roger Wines, ed., *The Secret of World History* (New York, 1981).

25 See Iggers, *German Conception of History*.

26 On the Russian Slavophiles, see *The Oxford History of Historical Writing*, vol. 4, 307–309.

27 On the émigrés from France during the French Revolution and Romanticism in Germany and France, see an old but still useful book, Brandes, *Main Currents in Nineteenth-Century Literature*, 6 vols, vols. 1, 2, and 4.

28 William Keylor, *Jacques Bainville and the Renaissance of Royalist History in the Twentieth Century* (Baton Rouge, 1979).

29 Friedrich Engels and Karl Marx, *Revolution and Counterrevolution or Germany in 1948*; Karl Marx, *The Eighteenth Brumaire of Louis Bonaparte* (New York, 1852).

30 Louis Blanc, *The History of Ten Years, 1830–1840* (London, 1844).

31 Lorenz von Stein, *Socialism and Communism in Contemporary France* (Leipzig, 1842); *The History of the Social Movement in France, 1789–1850*, tr. Kaethe Mengelberg (Totowa, 1965).

32 On Dahlmann, von Sybel, and Droysen, see Iggers, *German Conception of History*, passim.

33 See Iggers, *German Conception of History* and Robert Southard, *Droysen and the Prussian School* (Lexington, 1995).

34 Georg G. Iggers, *The Cult of Authority: The Political Philosophy of the Saint-Simonians* (Amsterdam, 1970, 2nd ed.); also Georg Iggers, ed. and tr., *The Doctrine of Saint-Simon: An Exposition: First Year, 1828–1829* (Boston, 1958); *Actualité du saint-simonisme* (Paris, 2004).

35 Henri Gouhier, *La jeunesse d'Auguste Comte et la formation du positivisme*, 3 vols, (Paris, 1933–1941); Mary Pickering, *Auguste Comte: An Intellectual Biography* (Cambridge, 1994); Mike Gane, *Auguste Comte* (London, 2006); F. A. Hayek, *Counter Revolution of Science* (Glencoe, 1952).

36 See Peter Paret, *Clausewitz and the State* (Oxford, 1976).

37 See *Lectures on the Philosophy of World History: Introduction. Reason in History*, ed. Johannes Hoffmeister (Magnolia, 1970); Herbert Marcuse, *Hegel and the Rise of Social Theory* (Boston, 1960); Shlomo Avineri, *Hegel's Theory of the Modern State* (Cambridge, 1972); Joachim Ritter, *Hegel and the French Revolution* (Cambridge, MA, 1984); Frederick Beiser, ed., *Cambridge Companion to Hegel* (Cambridge, 1993); Jerry F. Pinkard, *Hegel: A Biography* (Cambridge, 2000); Frederick Beiser, *Hegel: A Biography* (Cambridge, 2005).

38 See Leopold von Ranke, "On the Relations of History and Philosophy" ms. of the 1830s, in Iggers, ed., *Leopold von Ranke*, 5–7, "On the Character of Historical Science" ms. of the 1830s, ibid., 8–16.

39 Leopold von Ranke, "A Dialogue on Politics" (1836), ibid., 119.

40 Ibid., 117.

41 Bernard Lewis, *The Emergence of Modern Turkey* (London, 1968), 53–54; Erik J. Zürcher, *Turkey: A Modern History* (London, 1993), 27–29.

42 Jack A. Crabbs, Jr., *The Writing of History in Nineteenth-century Egypt: A Study in National Transformation* (Cairo, 1984), 67–68.

43 Lewis, *Emergence of Modern Turkey*, 71–72. For a critical review of the French influence in modernizing the Middle East, see Dror Ze'evi, "Back to Napoleon? Thoughts on the Beginning of the Modern Era in the Middle East," *Mediterranean Historical Review*, 19:1 (June 2004), 73–94.

44 Ibid., 398–399.
45 Crabbs, *Writing of History in Nineteenth-century Egypt*, 43–66.
46 Norman Itzkowitz, *Ottoman Empire and Islamic Tradition* (New York, 1972), 109.
47 Gamal el-Din el-Shayyal, "Historiography in Egypt in the Nineteenth Century" in Bernard Lewis and P. M. Holt, eds., *Historians of the Middle East* (Oxford, 1962), 403.
48 Cf. Gabriel Piterberg, *An Ottoman Tragedy: History and Historiography at Play* (Berkeley, 2003), 185–186; Anthony Gorman, *Historians, State and Politics in Twentieth-century Egypt: Contesting the Nation* (London, 2003), 12–15.
49 Ulrich Haarmann, "Medieval Muslim Perceptions of Pharaonic Egypt" in Antonio Loprieno, ed., *Ancient Egyptian Literature: History and Forms* (Leiden, 1996), 605–627.
50 See Donald M. Reid, *Whose Pharaohs? Archaeology, Museums, and Egyptian National Identity from Napoleon to World War I* (Berkeley, 2002), 30.
51 Cf. Bernard Lewis, *History: Remembered, Recovered, Invented* (New York, 1975). Also Benedict Anderson, *Imagined Communities: Reflections on the Origin and Spread of Nationalism* (New York, 1991).
52 Cf. Reid, *Whose Pharaohs?* 108–110.
53 Crabbs, *Writing of History in Nineteenth-century Egypt*, 14, 74–82; El-Shayyal, "Historiography in Egypt in the Nineteenth Century," 417–418.
54 Mohamad Tavakoli-Targhi, *Refashioning Iran: Orientalism, Occidentalism and Historiography* (Houndmills, 2001), 96–104, and idem, "Historiography and Crafting Iranian National Identity" in Touraj Atabaki, ed., *Iran in the 20th Century: Historiography and Political Culture* (London, 2009), 5–22. "Iran" as the name for the country was adopted officially as late as 1935, though it had been used by the people before in referring to their land.
55 Lewis, *Emergence of Modern Turkey*, 336; Ercüment Kuran, "Ottoman Historiography of the Tanzimat Period" in Lewis and Holt, *Historians of the Middle East*, 426–427; Zürcher, *Turkey*, 71–72.
56 Kuran, "Ottoman Historiography of the Tanzimat Period," 422. Also Supraiya Faroqhi, *Approaching Ottoman History: An Introduction to the Sources* (Cambridge, 1999), 156–157.
57 Cf. Selçuk Akşin Somel, *The Modernization of Public Education in the Ottoman Empire, 1839–1908: Islamization, Autocracy and Discipline* (Leiden, 2001).
58 Kuran, "Ottoman Historiography of the Tanzimat Period," 424–425.
59 Cf. Youssef M. Choueiri, *Modern Arab Historiography: Historical Discourse and the Nation-State* (London, 2003), 39–53.
60 Crabbs, *Writing of History in Nineteenth-century Egypt*, 94.
61 Ibid., 109–129.
62 El-Shayyal, "Historiography in Egypt in the Nineteenth Century," 405.
63 Choueiri, *Modern Arab Historiography*, 3–4.
64 Reid, *Whose Pharaohs?* 179–181.
65 Cf. Faroqhi, *Approaching Ottoman History*, 157–158.
66 Choueiri, *Modern Arab Historiography*, 4, 22, 191–192.
67 Cf. Crabbs, *Writing of History in Nineteenth-century Egypt*, 130–145.
68 Kumkum Chatterjee, "History as Self-Representation: The Recasting of a Political Tradition in Later Eighteenth Century India," *Modern Asian Studies*, 32 (1998), 942. Chatterjee also suggests that the "strategies of self-representation" employed by Tabatabai and others imply an incipient 'nationalist' historiography, one that reflected the transition from precolonial to colonial rule.
69 Ranajit Guha, *An Indian Historiography of India: A Nineteenth Century Agenda and Its Implications* (Calcutta, 1988), 14.

70 Bernard Cohn, *Colonialism and Its Forms of Knowledge: The British in India* (New Jersey, 1988).

71 Nicholas Dirks, *Castes of Mind: Colonialism and the Making of Modern India* (New Jersey, 2001), 144.

72 Rama Sundari Mantena, *The Origins of Modern Indian Historiography in India. Antiquarianism and Philology, 1780–1880* (New York, 2012).

73 Ibid., 51.

74 Ibid., 39.

75 Ibid., 181.

76 Guha, *An Indian Historiography*, 28.

77 Chatterjee, *The Cultures of History*, 143.

78 Thomas R. Trautmann, *Languages and Nations: The Dravidian Proof in Colonial Madras* (Berkeley, 2006).

79 Mantena, *The Origins of Modern Indian Historiography*, 18.

80 Ibid., 156.

81 Ibid., 121.

82 Sumit Sarkar, *Writing Social History* (Delhi, 1997), 14.

83 Michael Gottlob, ed., *Historical Thinking in South Asia: A Handbook of Sources from Colonial Times to the Present* (New Delhi, 2003), 21.

84 Quotation by Sudipta Kaviraj in Sarkar, *Writing Social History*, 13.

85 Vinay Lal, *The History of History: Politics and Scholarship in Modern India* (New Delhi, 2003), 27–28.

86 Sarkar, *Writing Social History*, 18.

87 Ibid., 19.

88 Cited in Gottlob, *Historical Thinking in South Asia*, 2.

89 Partha Chatterjee, *The Nation and Its Fragments: Colonial and Postcolonial Histories* (Princeton, 1993), 95.

90 Cited in C. H. Phillips, ed., *Historians of India, Pakistan and Ceylon* (London, 1961), 281.

91 Gottlob, *Historical Thinking in South Asia*, 12.

92 Chatterjee, *The Nation and Its Fragments*, 88.

93 Basak's book, in three volumes, appeared in 1857–1858, and Chattopadhyay's in 1878.

94 Sunil Khilnani, *The Idea of India* (New Delhi, 1997), 153.

95 Guha, *An Indian Historiography of India*, 42.

96 Chatterjee, *The Nation and Its Fragments*, 91.

97 Ronald Inden, *Imagining India* (Oxford, 1990), 45.

98 Chatterjee, *The Nation and Its Fragments*, 102.

99 This tended to be a Bengal-centered historiography that acknowledged that Pathan rule (unlike Mughal rule) was actually good for Bengal, that unlike other areas of India, Islam did not spread in Bengal by force, and that the Bengali Muslims were, in fact, a particular type of Bengali. See Chatterjee, *The Nation and Its Fragments*, 113–114.

100 Sarkar, *Writing Social History*, 24.

101 Gottlob, *Historical Thinking in South Asia*, 48.

102 Ibid., 49.

3 Academic history and the shaping of the historical profession

Transforming historical study in the nineteenth-century West and East Asia[1]

The cult of science and the nation-state paradigm (1848–1890)

The political context of historiography

The Revolutions of 1848 and 1849 did not have the impact on society and historiography that the French Revolution and the Napoleonic era had. Nevertheless, they were part of fundamental changes in the political, social, and intellectual climate in the Western world. Like the French Revolution, the revolutions of 1848 did not achieve what its participants intended; in many ways, they were dismal failures. They contributed to the survival of the old structures but also gave way to important reforms. The revolutions in the German and Italian states and in parts of the Habsburg Empire had a democratic undercurrent that was linked to national aspirations, in Germany and Italy for national unification and in Hungary for independence, while in France, where nationalism was not a pressing issue, socialist stirrings mingled with democratic ones. And they failed everywhere. By 1849, the dreams of the German and Italian revolutionaries of achieving unification by democratic means were shattered; in Hungary, the Russian army called in by the Habsburg government put a bloody end to Hungarian autonomy; in France, the workers' uprising of June 1848 was crushed by the National Guard, and class conflicts led to the plebiscitarian dictatorship of Napoleon III. Events were less spectacular in Great Britain where attempts by the Chartists to obtain the vote for the working classes were rebuffed.

Nevertheless, ultimately the aims of the revolutionaries were attained almost everywhere, although only partially. Universal male suffrage was established in France in 1848, in Great Britain in two stages but only in part by the Reform Acts of 1867 and 1884. In Italy, Austria, and Scandinavia, the vote was restricted; in Prussia and in some of the German states, there was a weighted system of votes by class; in the German Empire in 1871, universal male suffrage was introduced in the Reichstag, the powers of which, however, were limited. Nowhere in Europe were women as yet given the vote, although movements for women's suffrage emerged in Great Britain,

Germany, and Scandinavia at the end of the century and somewhat earlier in the United States where some of the Western states enfranchised women. Nevertheless, there emerged a mass electorate everywhere and with it mass parties and a mass political press.

The movements for national unification succeeded in Italy and Germany respectively in 1870 and 1871, and Hungary received its autonomy within the Habsburg Empire in 1867. But Italian and German unification were accomplished not by parliamentary decisions but, as the Prussian chancellor Prince Otto von Bismarck (1815–1898) proclaimed, "by blood and iron" in a series of wars. The historians played an important role in Germany and Italy in mobilizing the public for the national cause. Many of the German historians, who in 1848 as members of the Frankfurt Parliament had espoused liberal causes, after the failure of the revolutionary movement swung to the support of the Prussian Hohenzollern monarchy. They surrendered their liberal principles to an autocratic regime that nevertheless satisfied their pursuit of a political order, achieved national unification, and implemented the economic and social reforms wanted by the middle classes and protected them against the revolutionary threat from below.[2] The French Revolution and more recently the Paris Commune of 1871 inspired this fear. The peculiar balance in a rump Germany, excluding Austria but including Polish, Danish, and French minorities, that combined autocracy with limited parliamentarism was to have an effect on the direction in which historical studies went in Germany with a strong focus on the state in contrast to more liberal Western nations.

The social context of historiography

But these political developments have to be seen in the framework of the fundamental changes in Western societies, including the United States, and as yet to a lesser extent Eastern Europe. They were brought about by the rapid pace of industrialization after 1850, which in turn affected historical thought. A predominantly rural society gave way to an urban one, and an industrial working class emerged. Yet while this process was rapid, it must be stressed that much of the traditional order remained. Politically this meant that the new mass electorate decreased the power of the middle-class liberal parties and gave strength not only to the socialists but also to agrarian and artisan interest groups and to the small shopkeepers who felt threatened by economic modernization. One by-product of this was that, while Jews were finally emancipated at least in Central and Western Europe, a new political anti-Semitism arose in Germany, Austria, and France, as Jews were identified with the new society.[3]

The full impact of the technological revolution made itself felt. Karl Marx and Friedrich Engels wrote in *The Communist Manifesto* in early 1848: "The bourgeoisie, during its rule of scarce one hundred years, has created more massive and more colossal productive forces than have all preceding generations together, subjection of Nature's forces to man, machinery, application of chemistry to industry and agriculture, steam navigation, railways, electric telegraphs, clearing of whole continents for cultivation, canalization of rivers, whole populations conjured out of the ground – what earlier century had even a presentiment that such productive forces slumbered in the lap of social labor?"[4] This was only the beginning of a process that accelerated in the course of the second half of the nineteenth century. And technological advance was inseparable from the progress of scientific discovery. Romanticism in literature and art partly gave way to a new realism, which in turn, with the emergence of an industrial society with its conflicts and deprivations, turned into a harsh naturalism focused on the social dislocations of modern society.

The turn to "scientific" history

In the study and writing of history, these transformations resulted in a cult of science that assumed different forms but, as we shall see, generally assumed the progressive character of history and the superiority of Western civilization over the rest of the world. Historiography was to become "scientific," but there were three dominant conceptions of scientific history, distinguished according to their methodological approaches. All claimed that they had freed themselves from the philosophic and metaphysical assumptions of earlier historiography and that they were strictly scientific, and yet, as we shall see, they all were rooted in philosophical presuppositions without empirical validation.

The positivist paradigm

The term "positivism" is generally associated with the work of Auguste Comte (1798–1857),[5] who built on a tradition that went back to the French Enlightenment and to an extent even to Francis Bacon (1561–1626): the notion that the history of mankind reflected a progressive path from superstition in its various religious expressions through a metaphysical phase to modern "positive" science, freed of the blind spots of religion and metaphysics. Yet Comte's positivism, widely hailed as the high point of intellectual progress, contained serious contradictions. Although he argued that positive science rested on empirical validation, he offered no validation for his system. In fact, he was deeply committed to the early nineteenth-century Catholic thinkers, who bitterly opposed the French Revolution and the Enlightenment and who wanted to restore what they considered an organic society, a modern version of the Middle Ages.[6] Comte argued that modern man lacked a common doctrine; he saw freedom of thought and inquiry as a disease of the modern world. Science, rather than religion, was to provide this doctrine. In his later years, he proclaimed positivism as a "religion of humanity" and the scientists as its priests. Comte's positivism had clearly conservative implications that appealed to those who wanted to be scientific in outlook, yet rejected a liberal and even more a democratic society.

Comte wrote no history, and no history was written in his vein. The historian who was generally credited as a positivist was Henry Thomas Buckle (1821–1862),[7] who in his *History of Civilization in England* (1857, 1861) applied what he considered a scientific method to the writing of history. For Buckle there is only one science, namely natural science. For him, "there can be no history without the natural sciences."[8] History must use the same methods as the natural sciences, beginning with empirical evidence and proceeding through analysis of this evidence to the formulation of general laws. Buckle is convinced "that the marked tendency of advancing civilization is to strengthen our belief in the universality of order, of method, and of law."[9] In contrast to Comte, Buckle sees the high point of history in the liberal institutions of modern England. But in the final analysis, all human behavior, including such personal acts as marriage, has to be understood in statistical terms as part of collective phenomena. He himself was a self-educated, widely read amateur with no university training. His contribution lay in including aspects of civilization, science, but also literature and art in his narrative. In his history Buckle's focus was not Western or world history but national history. He wanted, after his English history, to write similar national histories of France, Spain, and Scotland but died before he could do so. In Europe his influence was limited because he made no concrete contributions to historical method. But in Japan, Buckle's emphasis on "collective phenomena" was inspirational to a generation of historians interested in writing the history of "civilization," or "civilizational history" (*bunmei-shi*), by which the Japanese hoped to help revamp their historiographical tradition.[10]

A similar positivist attempt was made by the French historian Hyppolite Taine (1828–1893), a professor of history, in his *History of English Literature* (1863), in which he applied the concepts *"race, milieu et moment,"* roughly translated as "race, setting, and time," which were too vague to be useful analytical tools. This and his histories of France, with their very critical approach to the French Revolution and its heritage, won him election in 1878 to the French Academy. Ultimately this analytical approach was taken more seriously later in the century by the emerging discipline of sociology than by historians.

The paradigm of the German historical school

A very different approach to historical science emerged in Germany. In contrast to France, the historians were exclusively trained professionally and held academic positions. They insisted as much as their French colleagues or Buckle that their approach to history was scientific and called their discipline *Geschichtswissenschaft* ("historical science"). The term *Wissenschaft* ("science"), however, in German has a different meaning than the term "science" has in English and in French. Its model of scientific inquiry and explanation differs from that of the natural sciences. Any field of study, including the humanities and history, can be scientific if it follows a systematic procedure of inquiry. Thus the humanities and therefore also history can be scientific if they proceed on the basis of a well-defined methodology. In a review essay in 1861 in the *Historische Zeitschrift*, the newly founded central journal of the German historical profession, Johann Gustav Droysen (1808–1884), professor of history in Berlin, directly challenged Buckle's conception of historical science.[11] He argued that while the natural sciences assume total determinism, history deals with those aspects of life that are not fully predetermined, the sphere of human freedom. And they require special methods that take into consideration the meaning of actions that cannot be reduced to general laws but require the understanding of intentions as they manifest themselves in particular events, personalities, and institutions. This line of argument goes back to Leopold von Ranke. The core of this science rests in the rigorous examination of primary sources but does not stop there.

Ranke, as we saw, became identified with the dictum that it is not the task of the historian to judge the past but "merely to show what essentially happened" (*wie es eigentlich gewesen*).[12] *Eigentlich* in English can, however, have the meaning of "actually" or "essentially." Outside of Germany, particularly in America and France, Ranke was often understood as wanting to show what "actually" happened, in other words not to go beyond the facts,[13] and thus was seen as a positivist, not in the sense of Comte and Buckle, seeking generalizations, but by restricting his inquiry to the objective reconstruction of events. In Germany he was generally understood as seeking to comprehend what "essentially" happened. The starting point of historical studies must in fact be the rigorous examination of original sources. But Ranke was fully aware that history does not stop with facts but that it must present a story. Thus, he wrote: "History is a science in collecting, finding, penetrating; it is an art because it recreates and portrays what it has found and recognized. Other sciences are satisfied simply with recording what has been found; history requires the ability to recreate." And while history "has to rely on reality . . . as an art it is related to poetry."[14]

But Ranke was still convinced that the element of artistic imagination that enters into serious historical study does not prevent careful source criticism from yielding the data with which narratives that correspond to reality can be recreated. He solved this problem by having recourse to an idealistic philosophical, we might even say religious assumption that he does not acknowledge as contrary to his scientific outlook. Yet there is a problem in the transition from the facts established through the criticism of sources to the historical narrative that involves artistic creativity. Ranke sought to solve this problem in a way similar to that which had already been well formulated by Wilhelm von Humboldt in his famous essay, "On the Historian's Task" (1821). "The historian's task," Humboldt wrote, "is to present what actually happened." "An event, however," he continued, "is only partially visible in the world of the senses; the rest has to be added by intuition, inference, and guesswork."[15] For Humboldt, the human world consisted of individualities, and these include individual persons as well as the great social institutions. Each individuality manifests a unique idea, rooted in the actual world but yet eternal. The ideas are thus highly individual and cannot be reduced to sheer abstractions. Ranke was convinced that "world history does not present a chaotic tumult" but that "there are forces, and indeed life-giving, creative forces, moral energies" that reveal themselves to us once we immerse ourselves in the sources. "They cannot be defined or put in abstract terms, but one can behold them and observe them."[16] As noted in the previous chapter, the state for Ranke is a prime moral force, in his words a "thought of God," which holds society together. There are no states in the abstract. "There is an element which makes a state not a subdivision of general categories, but a living thing, an individual, a unique self."[17] It has a need to expand, to maintain itself in the struggle for power. Yet in that struggle and in war, as we cited, mere force does not triumph but rather "genuine moral energy." From this follows the conclusion that the liberal conception of civil society that recognizes the needs and pursuits of individuals, while it has its place, must be subordinated to the authority of the state. Welfare is not the primary aim of the state.

Ranke's conception of historical science occupies a central role in the so-called Prussian School, which dominated German historical studies in the second half of the nineteenth century.[18] The School consisted partly of students of Ranke, such as Heinrich von Sybel (1817–1895) and others like Droysen, who nevertheless in their commitment to the German unification under Prussia, distance themselves from Ranke's avowed value of neutrality. Droysen, more than any other nineteenth-century German historian, proceeds to formulate a systematic theory of history and of historical method in his *Grundriss der Historik* (first 1858) (*Outline of the Principles of History*), which continues to be taken seriously by German historians today.[19] Droysen, going beyond Ranke, stresses that we never perceive the data contained in the sources directly but that they require the active role of the historian who must reconstruct them. For Droysen, historical knowledge requires what he calls "interpretation."[20] Yet like Ranke, he is satisfied that immersion into the sources results in truthful knowledge of the past. But neither he nor Ranke has a clear method for attaining this knowledge. Both ultimately depend on intuition, which for them reveals the past as it really is, notwithstanding the subjectivity of the historian. And at this point they return to metaphysical assumptions that they refuse to recognize as such. Droysen is as convinced as Ranke that moral forces are at work in history and that states are moral forces (*sittliche Mächte*).[21] Grasping this order does not involve the analysis of the data acquired from the criticism of sources, but involves a process of *Verstehen* ("understanding"). Understanding is not attained through an act of thinking in terms of abstract logic; it involves, to cite Droysen, "the whole spiritual-physical nature" of the inquirer. It is "like an act of creation, like a spark of light between two electrophoric bodies, like the act of conception."[22] Thus the historian grasps the forces that constitute the moral order of the universe and of society spontaneously. Although both Ranke and Droysen reject Hegel's philosophy of history as too dogmatic and inflexible, they agree that the basic institutions of society, the family, civil society, religion, and the state constitute this order in an ascending scale.

But is this a methodology? The result is that while Ranke as well as the Prussian School after him assert that their way of proceeding from the critique of sources is scientific, their reliance on intuition opens them to ideological distortions and introduces a political bias. In essential ways, the political philosophy of the Prussian School proceeding from Rankean principles justifies Germany's expansionism in Europe as well as its attempts to establish itself as a world power imposing its imperialist control over colonial peoples. Assuming the moral character of the state, Droysen argues that power (*Macht*) in contrast to force (*Gewalt*) is always ethical. Thus, if the soldier "wounds and kills, desolates and burns because he has been ordered to do so, he acts not as an individual and in accordance with his individual opinions. . . . He acts so to speak from a higher Ego . . . The individual may often find this difficult. . . . But he can feel secure in his conscience when he complies with this higher duty."[23] Here Nazi morality is foreshadowed.

Heinrich von Treitschke (1834–1896),[24] who filled Ranke's chair in 1873 at the University of Berlin after the latter's retirement and Droysen's colleague there, argued similarly, even with less recourse to Idealistic language, when he wrote that "only in war does a nation become a nation. . . . Without war there would be no State at all."

No civilization is possible without masses that serve elites and make possible that the latter possess the leisure to be creative. In war, he counsels, the life and property of civilians should be respected if it does not interfere with military operations, but this applies to "civilized," that is, Western people; the laws of war do not protect "barbarians," primarily blacks.[25]

A next generation of German historians, including Max Lenz (1850–1932) and Erich Marcks (1861–1939), called for a return to Ranke's supposed objectivity and value neutrality, but in fact were uncompromisingly partisan from a conservative point of view, calling in their apotheosis of Bismarck for authoritarian leaders and applying Ranke's conception of the great European powers to the world scene to legitimate German imperialism.[26]

Nevertheless we must separate the peculiar notion of the state of the Prussian historians from the conception of historical science in which it is embedded. The latter understands itself as an alternative to what we have described as positivistic approaches stressing generalization, susceptible in many cases to quantitative, statistical methods. Instead, it proposes an approach centering on diversity and meaning that requires the consideration of qualitative factors. We have not assigned a term to the latter orientation, which has often been labeled as "historism" or "historicism," a term that we have wanted to avoid in a nineteenth century context because it has had divergent meanings and, although occasionally used earlier, came into use in this sense only at the turn to the twentieth century.[27]

The German tradition just discussed, with its emphasis on the state, focused heavily on military and diplomatic history as made by leading political leaders, mostly excluding social, economic, and cultural factors. There were, however, exceptions. The impact of industrialization and the emergence of a radical working class movement led in Germany to the so-called Historical School of National Economics most prominently represented by Gustav von Schmoller (1838–1917).[28] The two contrasting views of the study of social phenomena in the positivistic and historical orientation were formulated clearly in the so-called controversy between Schmoller and the Austrian economist Carl Menger (1840–1921) sparked by Menger's attack on the German historical school of economics in his *The Errors of Historicism in German National Economics* (1884). For Menger, economics as a science in the tradition of Adam Smith and David Ricardo had to work with abstract models that possessed a degree of universal validity across historical and national lines. Schmoller argued that this was not the case, that the economy functioned differently in different national settings and in different historical times, apportioning an important role to political factors and to the centrality of the state.

The Marxist paradigm

Marxism provided a third conception of historical science. Although we often think of Marxism as a well-formulated, systematic doctrine, in fact the writings of Karl Marx and Friedrich Engels (1820–1895) were more doctrinaire than systematic and contained many contradictions.[29] Marxist doctrine in the twentieth century then took on very different, often opposing forms. We would like to point at two different aspects of Marx's thought that are difficult to reconcile; the first was his and Friedrich Engels' materialistic conception of history, which shared many assumptions with the positivist tradition we have discussed, and the second involved a critique of positivism that shared certain assumptions with the historical school. A concise definition of the first is contained in the preface to Marx's *Contribution to the Critique of Political Economy* (1859), in which he expresses views he held throughout his life, from the *German Ideology* in 1845 until his death in 1883. Thus he writes:

> In the social productions of their life, men enter into definite relations that are indispensable and independent of their will, relations of production which correspond to a definite stage of development of their productive forces. The sum total of these relations of production constitutes the economic structure of society, the real foundation, on which

rises a legal and political superstructure and to which correspond definite forms of social consciousness. The mode of production of material
life conditions the social, political, and intellectual life process in general. It is not the consciousness of men that determines their being, but,
on the contrary, their social being that determines their consciousness.[30]

This posits a strict determinism; men are governed by irresistible laws of
development. Like Buckle and the positivists, Marx conceives laws of historical development that govern mankind. And like the positivists he sees
the progressive replacement of religion and metaphysics by positive science.
But unlike positivism, the driving force of history is economic, not intellectual, and takes the form of class conflict. In every period of history, there
are oppressors and oppressed; the state is the instrument by which the former keep the latter in check and exploit them. History is seen as a dynamic
process driven by the evolving modes of production and the social conflicts
resulting from them. Marx and Engels differentiate between utopian and scientific socialism, the latter brought about not by the pious intention of well-
meaning individuals but by the inevitable force of economic development.

Yet there is another side to Marx's scientism that, in a sense, contradicts
his harsh economic determinism. Very early, already in the "Theses on Feuerbach" (1845), he sees the chief defect of the materialist doctrines of that
time in their seeing "the thing, reality, sensuousness only in the form of the
object, but not as human sensuous activity."[31] And knowledge is always a
social act, which takes place in a concrete social setting and which influences
the course of development. Therefore the achievement of communism is not
purely the result of impersonal forces but includes the agency of a revolutionary class. And the vision of an ongoing history toward a sane society
involves a fundamental critique of positivistic science and economics. Thus
in *Capital*, he criticizes classical economics on two grounds. Capitalism has
to fail because of its inherent contradictions, but also because it places economic values over human values.[32]

Common aspects of the three paradigms

Yet despite the fundamental differences between the conceptions of what
constitutes historical science, the positivism, the historical school, and the
Marxism we have described share certain common beliefs that cannot be
justified scientifically. All believe in progress, although the historical school
avoids the term and even in the case of Ranke argues against it. Droysen for-
mulates it in a way that all three orientations share, that history is a unified
process finding its fulfillment in the modern West. Droysen distinguished
between transactions (*Geschäfte*), which relate to the private sphere, and
History (*Geschichte*), which in English would have to be written with a capital "H," which relates to the political sphere. There are historical peoples
and nations and those that are not historical and therefore do not matter.

Even Ranke who in another famous dictum argues against a formal idea of progress by proclaiming that "every epoch is immediate to God,"[33] in fact holds that China and India indeed have an "antiquity that is legendary" but no history.[34] For Buckle, Droysen, and Marx, history, seen as world history, is limited to the West. For Droysen and Treitschke, there are also persons who count for world history and the masses who do not; for Marx, it is classes, in the modern age the bourgeoisie and the proletariat, which occupy an active historical role, while he compares the French peasantry to a "sackful of potatoes,"[35] playing no role in the course of modern history. And all three justify the expansion of Western power over the non-Western world and its exploitation. As for Asia, Marx speaks of an "Asian mode of production," distinct from the West, that remained static and thus played no role in the historical development of the last three millennia. Marx, in a series of articles on the occasion of the Sepoy Rebellion in India (1857), pointed at the exploitative character of British rule but also saw it as a necessary stage if India was to be brought into the modern world in which it would develop along the lines of the modern bourgeois world, which on a global scale would ultimately usher in a communist, postcapitalist society.[36] They also share with the German school the belief in the civilizing mission of Germany over the peoples of Eastern Europe.

The professionalization of historical studies

But there is also a basic flaw in the claim of all three orientations to have "raised history to the level of a science," as Droysen formulated it.[37] All three insist that they have liberated history from metaphysics, but all operate with metaphysical assumptions. In the case of the German historical school, which is openly theistic, this is obvious. But also Marx, despite his avowed atheism, is deeply entrenched in Judeo-Christian teleology, something that he denies. Nevertheless, he is committed to a highly teleological vision of a moral order, which is admittedly still in the process of becoming but beckons around the corner. Social conflict will come to an end in "an association in which the free development of each is the condition for the free development of all."[38]

All three of these paradigms claimed to be scientific, and none of them in fact was. All proceeded on the basis of metaphysical assumptions, which they did not recognize as such but which defied empirical validation. Increasingly in this period, historical studies were professionalized and situated at universities or at research institutes. Up to the nineteenth century, history was written by men, and to a lesser extent women, of letters, often with experience in public life, rarely associated with universities outside of Germany and Scotland. As already mentioned, this changed with the founding of the University of Berlin in 1810, which combined teaching with research. To a lesser extent, this had already been practiced at the University of Göttingen since it was founded in 1737, but the way history was researched and written at the University of Berlin soon became a model for universities throughout Germany and ultimately worldwide. It was the second paradigm, that of the German historical school, that dominated professional historiography, although in each country outside Germany it underwent changes, reflecting different national traditions and conditions. History now for the first time became an academic discipline. Although historians distinguished their conception of science from that of other sciences, particularly the natural sciences, they adopted the institutional framework in which the latter were practiced. To be a historian involved a comprehensive way of life. Historians went through extensive training, had to pass examinations, and received degrees much like scientists and scholars in other disciplines. Professional associations of historians and professional publications came into being, making possible a community of scholars. A sharp distinction arose between the professional and the amateur historian. Only the former would be considered scientific in any serious sense.[39] Historical research was increasingly centered at the universities.

Yet from the beginning there was a sharp contradiction between the scientific ethos of the historian and his political commitment. I am intentionally saying "his" because women were effectively excluded from the profession. This had not been the case to the same extent before. Women historians had been rare but existed.[40] We have already mentioned Catherine Macaulay, the eighteenth-century liberal critic of David Hume's history of England enjoyed a broad readership. And nationalistic history was not restricted to Germany. We have already pointed at the close connection between nationalism and the major scholarly projects for the collection and edition of medieval sources, such as the *Monumenta Germaniae Historica* in Germany, established in 1819, soon to be followed by similar projects in other countries. This project, centered in Munich, was not linked directly to a university but nevertheless involved professional historians. The recruitment of scholars at the universities involved a selection that influenced the political orientation of the historians,[41] even where they were able to write and study relatively independently of direct state interference. Certain groups of persons were automatically barred from university appointment. We have already mentioned women. Jews also were for a long time excluded unless they converted, although later in the century as religious anti-Judaism turned into racial anti-Semitism, conversion no longer sufficed.[42] There was generally no place for Catholics at the predominantly Protestant universities in Germany. The process of recruitment also provided that there was a high degree of political conformity,[43] although prior to 1848 a fair number of historians urged liberal reforms. Yet they played an important role in propagating the idea of national unity, anachronistically seeking its origins in the medieval or early modern past, as Droysen and Sybel did, and thus inventing a national history.

It is interesting that the system of the modern university along the pattern of the University of Berlin first took shape in Germany rather than in countries like England and the United States, which were farther ahead on the road to political and economic modernization and where the modern research-oriented university on the German pattern was introduced relatively late and only in part. The purpose of the reformed German university was not to convey a liberal education – that was the task of the academic secondary schools, in the first place the humanistic *Gymnasium* – but rather to train students to pursue research. The lecture that was so important at the German universities prior to the nineteenth century was supplemented by the research seminar. Soon after the mid-nineteenth century, the Berlin model was widely accepted at German-speaking universities and soon afterward outside Germany as well. Historical journals, which laid claim to being professional, were founded in many European countries, the United States, and Japan, modeling themselves on the *Historical Magazine* (*Historische Zeitschrift*), founded in Germany in 1859 under the editorship of Heinrich von Sybel. The *History Journal* (*Revue Historique*) was founded in 1876 in France, the *Italian Historical Magazine* (*Rivista Storica Italiana*) in 1884, the *English Historical Review* in 1886, the *Historical Journal* (*Shigaku zasshi*) in Japan in 1889, and the *American Historical Review* in 1895. The Danish *Historical Journal* (*Historisk Tijdsskrift*) had appeared already in 1840. In the last three decades of the nineteenth century, a host of historical journals appeared in all Southeastern European countries, as well as in Hungary, Poland, and Russia. At the same time instruction in history was transformed in all Western countries, including Latin America, and in Japan where a young German, Ludwig Riess (1861–1928), who had been trained in the Rankean manner, was invited in the 1880s to establish the Department of History at the University of Tokyo.[44] In 1868, the Ecole Pratique des Hautes Etudes was founded in Paris and introduced the seminar method into historical instruction. After France's defeat in the Franco-Prussian War in 1870–1871, the French university system was thoroughly revamped with a strong research orientation.[45] Something similar occurred in the United States, although to a lesser extent.[46] The function of the American colleges similar to that of the English and Scottish universities had been to convey a liberal education. In 1876, the first graduate program in the field of history leading to a PhD after the German model was instituted at the newly founded research-oriented Johns Hopkins University in Baltimore, soon followed by major American private and Midwestern state universities. Throughout Southeastern Europe, beginning in Greece, a similar transformation of higher education with the express purpose of furthering the national cause, took place.[47] By the 1880s, professional associations of historians had been formed in almost all Western countries, including Russia and Southeastern Europe, and in Japan.

The new historical professions for the most part shared two characteristics: (1) They were intensely nationalistic, and (2) they tended to concentrate on politics on the state level and on diplomacy and the military to the exclusion of social and cultural history. Ranke had seen the nation correctly as the major unit of the Europe of his time, but he had still written histories of non-German states such as France and Great Britain. In his attitude he remained in fact a European. But Prussian historians who came after him, including such of his students as Heinrich von Sybel, criticized him for not taking a strong stand on national unity and particularly for his insistence that the historian must be impartial. Actually the "impartiality" Ranke had in mind was not neutral at all. He was committed to the idea that the historian who regarded the course of history impartially would reject both the reactionary forces that wanted a return to the ancient regime and the radicals who wanted liberal and democratic reforms[48] and who, as Edmund Burke had done earlier, would very much recognize the conservative status quo as the outgrowth of historical forces. Sybel, while committed to the critical study of sources, nevertheless maintained that "every historian who has had any significance in our literature has had his colors. There have been believers and atheists, Protestants and Catholics, liberals and conservatives, historians of all parties, but no longer any objective, impartial historians devoid of blood and nerves."[49]

There were few comprehensive European histories and no world histories. Even in Latin America there were no comprehensive histories of Latin America but almost only national histories. Ranke in his last years as an octogenarian finally began to write the world history that he had always wanted to write, but it was strictly a history of the European world with its ancient Mediterranean origins.

Ranke was often misunderstood outside of Germany where his dictum *"wie es eigentlich gewesen"* was separated from its theoretical basis. In 1885, a year before his death, the American Historical Association elected him as its first honorary member whom they considered the "father of historical science." Ranke was now turned into a positivist, who, however, had little in common with the positivism of Comte or Buckle. Thus Herbert Baxter Adams (1850–1901) at Johns Hopkins University wrote: "Ranke determined to hold strictly to the facts of history, to preach no sermon, to point no moral, to adorn no tale, but to tell the simple historical truth." Ephraim Emerton (1851–1935) at Harvard University saw in Ranke the founder of "the doctrine of true historical method" and commented: "If one must choose between a school of history whose main characteristic is the spirit and one which rests upon the greatest attainable number of recorded facts, we cannot long hesitate . . . Training has taken the place of brilliancy and the whole world is today reaping its benefit."[50] Ranke was thus made into a narrow specialist, although he disclaimed writing for specialists and wished to address a broad public on the great forces operating in history.

But not all historical writing fitted into these three paradigms. In *A Short History of the English* People (1874), John Richard Green (1837–1883) asserted that the history of England must take into consideration the anonymous masses that had been neglected in all previous national histories. There were important works of cultural history that turned away from the dominant concentration on politics. Two important works should be mentioned: One is *La Cité antique* (The Ancient City) (1864) by Numa Denis Fustel de Coulanges (1830–1889), which deals broadly with the culture of the ancient Greek cities, culture in the sense of patterns of life and beliefs in which religion occupies a determining role. Perhaps even more important was Jacob Burckhardt's (1818–1897)[51] *Civilization of the Renaissance in Italy* (1860). The book was conceived not as narrow scholarship but as an artistic work that recreated the outlook of an age with art and literature as sources. Its main thesis was that the culture of the Middle Ages, in which the individual was always part of a corporate group, was replaced by a new outlook in which individuals could express and fulfill their individuality. In a sense this was an attempt to construct a comprehensive history of an age in which many aspects of life were considered, including the state, which, however, was presented not in the form of a narrative account of political events but "as a work of art" in which a new modern outlook came to fruition. In this as in his other works, Burckhardt consciously broke with the theoretical and methodological assumptions of the German Historical School. A Swiss, he received part of his training at the University of Berlin, where he was a student of Ranke, before he returned to his native Basel. It is striking that despite the new directions in which he went, he was invited to fill Ranke's chair of history in Berlin upon Ranke's retirement, before it was offered to Treitschke. His decision to decline the chair in Berlin appears to have had to do a good deal with the way in which he saw the developments in Germany in the wake of the creation of the German Empire in 1871 under Bismarck. He criticized the new German state not from a democratic but from a conservative position because he feared the forces of a mass society behind German unification. This led him to question the basic philosophic presupposition of much of the historiography of the time. He emphatically rejected the idea of progress and the idea that there was a unitary history. Thus he rejected the very concept of a philosophy of history. His colleague in Basel, Friedrich Nietzsche (1844–1900) at this time wrote his polemical essay against the historians, "Vom Nutzen und Nachteil der Historie für das Leben" ("Of the Benefits and Disadvantages of Historical Writing for Life," 1874), in which he totally misunderstood what the professional historians were doing, accusing them of retiring into ivory towers, not realizing the extent to which, notwithstanding their claims of objectivity, they wrote history with a political purpose, distorting the past in the service of ideology.

But much history continued to be written and to be read outside of academe. Two German writers combined historical study with imaginative literature to create an idealized image of a German nation going back to Germanic origins. Both as historians and as novelists, they were able to attract an immense German readership and feed into an extreme nationalism. Gustav Freytag (1816–1895) in *Bilder aus der deutschen Vergangenheit* (1859–1867), translated as *Pictures of German Life*,[52] gave a popular account of German history since Teutonic times with the aim of portraying a German folk character through the ages. Freytag felt indebted to the English historical novelists, particularly to Walter Scott and Charles Dickens. In a later work, *Die Ahnen* (*The Ancestors*) (1873–1881), Freytag drew an imaginative story of one family from the fourth century to his own time. Perhaps his best known and most translated work was his novel *Soll und Haben* (*Debit and Credit*) (1855), which celebrated the solid qualities of the German merchants and contrasted them negatively with those of a Jewish merchant. Felix Dahn (1834–1912), in a similar nationalistic vein, reached an immense public in his partly historical but largely imaginative novel, *Ein Kampf um Rom* (*A Struggle for Rome*) (1876–1878) from the time of the great migrations.

Russia and Southeastern Europe

Generally, Russia and East Central Europe have been omitted from histories of Western historiographies until very recently. Interestingly, one exception is a history of historiography, published very early in the twentieth century, in 1913, George P. Gooch, *History and Historians in the Nineteenth Century*. In a chapter entitled "Minor Countries,"[53] Gooch deals briefly with the countries he had left out, Italy, Spain, Portugal, Switzerland, Scandinavia, the Low Countries, but also Bohemia and Hungary. It is striking that he considers all of these countries, including Italy, Spain, and Russia, minor for purposes of historiography and devotes a minimum of space to them. In many ways, the development of historiography in those countries in the nineteenth century was parallel to that of the countries with which we have dealt, the growing reliance on critical documentary methods and the professionalization of historical studies in conjunction with history serving the national state. Yet among them there were also differences, shaped in part by differing ideological orientations within different political contexts. Effi Gazi has traced the emergence of a historical profession committed to critical methods of dealing with the sources as part of the strengthening of the national state in Greece and compared it with developments in various Southeast European countries that went in similar directions.[54] In Serbia, Ilarion Ruvarac (1832–1905) undertook the task to free Serbian history, which rested largely on national myths, from these myths and placed it on a factual basis.[55] Much of his work as a monk, however, took place outside an institutional academic setting. This setting was well established before the end of the nineteenth century in Greece, Romania, and Russia. In Romania, Alexandru Dimitrie Xenopol (1847–1920)[56] participated in the international discussions in Henri Berr's *Revue de synthèse historique*, which sought to go beyond the Rankean state-oriented paradigm to a history seeking an interdisciplinary approach linking historical studies to the new disciplines of sociology and economics.

The institutionalization of historical studies was well established in Russia by the second half of the nineteenth century. Already very much earlier, the German historian August Ludwig Schlözer (1735–1809, mentioned in Chapter 1), often considered the father of modern Russian historical writing, from 1761 to 1769, spent a considerable amount of time in St. Petersburg and placed ancient Russian history on a solid documentary basis. He was the first to undertake the textual and linguistic analysis necessary to produce a definitive rendition of the ancient Russian past.[57] Going beyond Russian history in his *Nordic History*,[58] he undertook reconstructing the history of a multitude of ethnic groups in the Russian East and beyond, using methods of linguistic, anthropological, and statistical analysis, not undertaken again on this scale until the twentieth century.

By the mid-nineteenth century, historical studies in Russia were split between a state-oriented historiography that concentrated on the monarchy and the Church and one that placed greater emphasis on the regions and on the broader population. A sharp division existed between Slavophiles, who ardently rejected the modern civilization of the West, and the Westernizers, who affirmed Western modernity. Universities were already well established when the reforms of 1863 granted them greater autonomy. By the 1870s two important centers of historical studies, the St. Petersburg School and the Moscow School, stood out. Historical studies now were professionalized according to the international pattern. The historical generation of the 1870s widely embraced the scientific ethos of international scholarship and achieved the independence of history from literature and philosophy. The outstanding historian of the Moscow School was Vasily Osipovich Kliochenskii (1841–1911), followed by his pupil Pavel Nikolaevich Miliukov (1859–1943).[59] What marked their work was their movement away from the political focus of the State School that preceded them and a greater consideration of social and particularly economic factors. In this way they prepared the way for the increased trend from 1890 onward toward Marxist economic materialism.

The crisis of Confucian historiography and the creation of the modern historical profession in East Asia

A dramatic increase of contacts between Asia and the West characterized the history and historiography in nineteenth-century Asia. But this was not the first time that the Europeans made their appearance in the region they called "the Far East." During the sixteenth and seventeenth centuries, the Jesuits had extended their missionary work to Asia. Having lived and worked in East Asia for about a century, the Jesuits brought back to Europe firsthand knowledge about the mysterious powers in the Orient, leaving strong impressions on and even arousing admiration in such intellectual figures as Voltaire and Leibniz. While in Asia, they also introduced to the Asians the European accomplishments in mathematics and astronomy. Thus, some have speculated that the scientific knowledge brought by the Jesuit missionaries might have prodded the Chinese to pursue exacting scholarship as exemplified by "evidential learning."[60] Whatever the influence of the Jesuits' work, however, by the early eighteenth century, just as the Muslims began to "discover" Europe and the Indians saw their land being colonized by the Europeans, China and Japan reclosed their doors to the outside world (in Vietnam, the ban of Christianity had already taken place several decades earlier). And they did it more resolutely than before; the Japanese aptly described the policy as *sakoku*, or "locking up the country."

Accommodating the Western influence

But the lockup was not airtight. Japan's Tokugawa shogunate, for instance, granted Chinese and Dutch merchants with limited trading rights; through the latter, European learning, under the rubric of *Rangaku* (Dutch learning), continued to filter into the country. The *Rangaku* nurtured interest in European language and culture among Japanese students, from whom emerged the first generations of "Western experts" in Japan, such as Mitsukuri Genbo (1799–1863) and Nishimura Shigeki (1828–1902), who either translated or wrote about Western histories during the later years of the Tokugawa era.[61] In China, from the seventeenth century, Portuguese colonists managed to retain Macau, a small fishing town, though its role in facilitating cultural exchange appeared relatively insignificant. Nonetheless, from the early nineteenth century, Western missionaries reemerged in China. Having learned Chinese, some, such as Karl F. A. Gützlaff (1803–1851) and Elijah C. Bridgman (1801–1861), made efforts to teach the Chinese about the changes in the world outside China, hence broadening the worldview among some of the Chinese.

Parallel to the missionary work was European economic expansion. Around the same time when the Jesuits traveled to Asia, the Dutch and Portuguese, who had mastered Euro-Asian long-distance trade, also reached Asia and established entrepots. The English followed suit, and throughout the eighteenth century, the English government had appealed repeatedly to the Qianlong Emperor of China's Qing dynasty for establishing a trade relation, only to no avail. Though the Chinese emperor appeared unmoved by the English requests, his subjects had become more and more addicted to opium smoking, which was fetched from India, England's newly acquired colony, where it was grown in large quantity. This began to tip the trade balance in favor of the English beginning in the nineteenth century, in that their merchants not only made up their trade deficit with China but also forced the Chinese, for the first time, to pay silver for their goods, namely opium. The world was indeed changing. And the change did not go entirely unnoticed in China. Gong Zizhen (1792–1841) and Wei Yuan (1794–1857), two leading literati of their age, registered in their writings concerns over the Western incursion and pondered solutions to mitigate its detrimental impact. They reiterated the need of promoting statecraft knowledge, an idea that had been prevalent in the early Qing, and revisited the interest in ancient history forged by the evidential school, hoping to shore up defense. However, their ideas of and approaches to history also differed markedly from that of the evidential scholars. Compared with the evidential scholars' restorationist interest, for example, Gong and Wei were more contemplative and theoretical in their attitude toward the function of historical study. Their primary goal was not to reconstruct the past, as their predecessors had attempted, but to distill a general law from the study of ancient history, or the age of Confucius in pre-Han China, in hopes of guiding and ordering the present world. As intellectual leaders of their time, Gong's and Wei's departure from the historicist interest of evidential learning was an indication that evidential learning as an intellectual movement had declined in nineteenth-century China. The cultural climate was indeed changed, for when he was young, Gong had been schooled in evidential study by his grandfather, Duan Yucai (1735–1815), then a renowned evidential scholar.

The decline of evidential scholarship put an end to the project launched by some of the evidential savants on historicizing classical learning. But the interest in history persisted. In two aspects, Gong's and Wei's work bore on the change of Chinese historical thinking and writing through the remainder of the nineteenth and the early twentieth centuries. One was their firm belief in the relevance of Confucian teaching, which was translated into a relentless effort to search in the Confucian tradition for useful elements in order to better understand and cope with new changes. The other was the enduring interest in historical study, which not only reflected the residual influence of evidential learning but also extended the traditional idea of seeing history as a mirror, or a repository, of wisdom for solving problems of the present. Though appearing to have followed a traditional line of thinking, Gong's and Wei's ideas of history revealed a nuanced and perceptible change. Drawing on the New Text interpretation of the Confucian classics, they called great attention to Confucius's ingenuous interpretation of ancient culture, particularly his revision of the *Spring and Autumn Annals*, in which, as Wei and Gong both believed, were embedded the Confucian theory of historical change. This theory, abbreviated simply as the Three-Age Doctrine (*sanshi shuo*), appeared to be a cyclical understanding of historical movement. However, since the doctrine expounded the notion that history at times experiences epochal changes, Gong and Wei maintained that it was useful and germane for their time because China was encountering such a moment.[62] Thus the Chinese were not oblivious and indifferent to the expansion of Western powers. During most of the nineteenth century, many historical works were written prima facie according to convention. But a discernible change in both style and scope was also unmistakable. The proliferation of the study of historical geography and frontier studies, for example, furthered the evidential interest in empirical knowledge. But its boom at the time also reflected a growing concern with foreign encroachment of China's borders by Russia in the north and by England and France in the south.[63]

Though Gong Zizhen and Wei Yuan, as well as the exponents of frontier studies, foresaw the need for the Chinese to brace for the changing trend of history, they might not have expected how soon it did come. Gong died during the Opium Wars (1838–1842), and Wei actually participated in the war and therefore witnessed China's defeat firsthand. The defeat irreversibly opened China's door to the West. Having seen the Western military superiority, Wei enjoined the Chinese to learn from the West, that is, in his words, "to learn about the barbarians' knack in order to rein them in" (*shiyi zhiyi*). And he put it into practice by offering a historical account of the Opium Wars and, in another work, by invoking the memory of the early Qing's success in pacifying China's coastline by annexing such islands as Taiwan. A more influential work attributed to Wei Yuan was *An Illustrated Treatise on the Sea Kingdoms* (*Haiguo tuzhi*), which was the first yet not the only attempt by a Chinese historian to write a world history during the period.[64] That the *Sea Kingdoms* was written in a composite of treatises also merits attention. It suggested that, aside from official historiography, private historical works were increasingly written in styles other than the prescribed annals-biography, of which the "treatise/monograph" (*zhi*) and the "narrative from beginning to end" (*jishi benmo*), invented by Yuan Shu (1131–1205), were the clear favorites. This shift indicated a slow yet significant change in the Chinese ideas of history and their worldview: The disfavoring of the annals-biography was coupled with the decline and demise of the traditional agenda for depicting political hierarchy and legitimacy in historical writing. The appearance of Western works translated by missionaries at the time also helped spark the growing interest in narrative history, for most Western histories were written in a continuous narrative. Despite its notably enlarged worldview, the *Sea Kingdoms*, as well as others of its kind, was not meant to challenge Sinocentrism in the Chinese worldview. Its survey of world history, for example, does not include China, suggesting that the Chinese had not yet considered their country on a par with other nations in the world. In sum, though Wei Yuan advocated and used Confucian theory to expound the need of knowing the outside world, he and his cohorts continued to see the world beyond China as the "outside."

Civilization and history: A new worldview

Wei Yuan's *Sea Kingdoms* struck a quite different reading in Japan. Having watched closely China's defeat in the Opium Wars, the Japanese were wary about their relation with China vis-à-vis the expanded world and appeared more eager to seek an adaptation. While Chinese books like the *Sea Kingdoms* offered much needed information for the Japanese about the (Western) world, with the benefit of *Rangaku* learning, the Japanese also readily detected its residual Sinocentrism and factual mistakes.[65] Their own renderings of world history, such as Okamoto Kansuke's (1839–1904) *Records of World History* (*Bankoku shiki*), included that of Japan, indicating an interest in placing their country in the emerging community of nations in the new world.

Indeed, after the fall of the Tukugawa shogunate, a new worldview emerged in Meiji Japan (1868–1912). The moves by the new Meiji government were particularly indicative in this regard. Shortly after its establishment, the new government sent an official delegation to tour the West, hoping to acquire firsthand knowledge about Western culture, politics, and society, as well as the conditions on which it could modify the unequal treaties signed by the Tokugawa shogunate with Western powers during the previous decades. This two-year-long trip, cut short by a policy dispute at home, led many Japanese to conclude that in order to join the world now led by the West, they had to sever their cultural ties with China and Asia in general and promote "civilization" and "Enlightenment" pursuant to the Western model.

This Westernization movement occasioned a notable change in historical thinking, which was best shown in Fukuzawa Yukichi's (1835–1901) *Outline of A Theory of Civilization (Bunmeiron no gairyaku)* of 1875. Inspired by Henry Buckle's *History of Civilization in England* and François Guizot's *Histoire de la Civilisation en Europe*, Fukuzawa, whose early training had straddled both *Rangaku* and Confucian learning, argues that Confucianist historiography had become outdated and should be replaced by civilizational history (*bunmeishi*), a neologism he coined in describing Buckle's and Guizot's approach to national history. For history, Fukuzawa proclaims, should now be written for a different purpose. It is not for espousing a normative moral and political order but for narrating the progress of civilization in a nation. By standard of civilization, he acknowledges, Japan and China are only "semi-civilized," falling behind Europe. Fukuzawa thus has not only adopted the unilinear historical outlook propagated by modern Western historians, but he also used it to make the case for Japan's departure from the Sinitic world and joining the Western world. A decade later, he put his thoughts into the famous "Datsu-A ron" ("Thesis on Leaving Asia"), arguing more forcefully and explicitly for such need.

Taguchi Ukichi (1855–1905), a young journalist and an enthusiastic convert to civilizational history, extended Fukuzawa's unilinear understanding of world history into the writing of Japanese history. Beginning in 1877, Taguchi published his seminal book, *A Short History of Japanese Civilization (Nihon kaika shōshi)*, in which he delineated Japan's cultural development from its beginning to the present in a composite narrative. Taguchi intended to present and analyze the zeitgeist and its vicissitudes throughout Japanese history, emulating what Buckle and Guizot had done with European history. Both Buckle's and Guizot's works, incidentally, by the time had appeared in several translations in Japan.[66] The influence of their work enabled Taguchi and his followers to sidestep the traditional focus on regal succession in Japanese historical writing and draw attention instead to the cultural development shown in religion, literature, philosophy, and social customs. As a new genre, this civilizational history introduced a sea change to both the idea and style of historical writing. Having shifted the historian's attention from monarchy to civilization, which in turn obliterated the need of moral didacticism, it freed Japanese historians to adopt the narrative style prevalent in Western historical writing. However, as Taguchi Ukichi reminds us, this adoption is at once an innovation and a renovation, for in the long tradition of Chinese historical writing, there had emerged three styles in historiography. In addition to the annals-biography and chronicle, there was a third one that Taguchi called "historical discussion style" (J. *shirontai*; C. *shilunti*), which too had been used by historians long before.[67] By writing the *Short History of Japanese Civilization*, Taguchi hoped to revive that style, even though his organization of the book in chapters and sections clearly reflected Western influence. While the "historical discussion style," as well as the treatise format used by Wei Yuan in his *Sea Kingdoms*, employs a narrative structure, it does not usually follow a continuous narrative, divided only by chapters and sections. However, Taguchi's self-professed revivalism merits our attention. As an overt advocate of Western learning, he had no apparent reason to conceal his direct borrowing from the West in experimenting with civilizational history. His revivalist claim, perhaps, was a genuine effort to locate indigenous elements in the past in order to better accommodate the Western influence. And Taguchi was by no means alone in making such a syncretic effort. Syncretism, or the dialogues between the traditional and modern, native and foreign, rather constituted a recurrent leitmotif in the processes of modern transformation of historical writing across non-Western regions.

The interplay of the old and the new

Indeed, during Meiji Japan, though the interest in Western culture and institutions appeared robust, the revivalist desire was also apparent. After all, Japan's "modern" era was ushered in by the restoration of imperial power in Emperor Meiji in 1868. A year later, the Meiji government established a History Bureau and ordered it, in the name of the new emperor, to compile a "national history," which was however *not* an example of Western influence but rather extended the tradition of dynastic historiography. The establishment of the History Bureau by the government was purported to resume the practice of official historical writing imported from Tang China in the seventh century. More specifically, as the Imperial Rescript stated, this new national history was meant to be a sequel to the "Six National Histories" (*Rikkokushi*) from the seventh and tenth centuries, with the purpose to "affirm the prince-minister hierarchy, distinguish the foreign and the native and promote the cardinal [moral] principle in the country." These reasons, as well as their wordings, were reminiscent of many previous projects on dynastic historical writings in the Sinitic tradition.[68]

Thus, despite the new ideas from the West, the tradition of dynastic history writing remained vivacious in most parts of Asia throughout the nineteenth century. The Western incursion had actually prompted many dynastic rulers to seek useful historical lessons in the past in order to deal with the challenge. The History Bureau in both Qing China, Chosŏn Korea, and Vietnam, for example, remained operative in collecting sources and compiling "veritable records." The *Ming History* (*Mingshi*), completed by Qing official historians, received a better mark than its predecessor did in the Ming. The "veritable records" in Chosŏn Korea, which amounted to a great number of volumes, displayed its court historians' painstaking effort to preserve historical sources faithfully and fastidiously. The effort made by Vietnamese court historians was equally impressive, if not more so.[69] In 1855, three years after the French began their full-scale encroachment in Southeast Asia, King Tu-doc (r. 1847–1883) of the Nguyen dynasty (1802–1887) ordered the compilation of the *Outline and Details of the Comprehensive Mirror of Vietnamese History, with Imperial Annotation* (*Kham dinh Viet su thong giam cuong muc*). This massive work, written in Chinese, took almost 30 years to complete. It represented an earnest attempt to seek a historical solution to the growing menace to the Vietnamese dynasty. But it was focused, as indicated by its title, on espousing the need of legitimate regal succession in history from the Neo-Confucian perspective. Despite its value as a general history of Vietnam, this stupendous work thus was an anachronistic undertaking, rendering little help in saving the dynasty. One year after its completion, Vietnam was divided into three and became a protectorate of the French.[70]

If the tradition of dynastic historiography began to lose its appeal, it only happened slowly and gradually. The compilation of an official history for Japan, by imperial fiat, went through a meandering course, reflected in the name change of the History Bureau and its frequent staff turnover during the 1870s and 1880s.[71] Since *A Chronological History of Great Japan* (*Dai Nihon hennenshi*), the project's title decided eventually by the Bureau, was to be written in Chinese, the Bureau was staffed mostly by China scholars (*Kangaku sha*). However, these scholars were divided by two main schools, if not more, due to their scholarly interest and pedigree. One adhered to the Neo-Confucian advocacy of moralistic didacticism in historiography, whereas the other pursued an evidential interest in source criticism, suggesting the ascending influence of evidential learning in Japan at the time. Beginning in 1882, the Bureau fell into the hands of Shigeno Yasutsugu (1827–1910), an evidential scholar, who was assisted by Kume Kunitake (1839–1931) and Hoshino Hisashi (1839–1917) with similar scholarly interest and training. Under Shigeno's leadership, the Bureau focused on culling and criticizing historical sources in preparation for compiling a comprehensive account of "national history."[72]

The *Chronological History of Great Japan* was so named because the project was now aimed to continue and complete the *History of Great Japan* that had begun during the Tokugawa period. But it also distinguished from the latter in that, as a chronological history or a contemporary draft of historical sources, it constituted only the first stage in dynastic historical compilation; convention had required that a formal compilation of dynastic history occur after the end of a reign. Executing the project as such made perfect sense to Shigeno Yasutsugu and his colleagues, for it allowed them to demonstrate and apply their skills of evidential research in scrutinizing historical sources.

By placing source criticism at the center of the historian's work, this empiricist interest also helped bridge evidential learning and modern Western historiography and transform the Japanese tradition of [official] historical writing. To pursue his evidential interest in source verification, for example, Shigeno Yasutsugu found that many factual mistakes, including those in the *History of Great Japan*, had occurred because traditional historians were overly concerned with moral exhortation and political legitimacy. Kojima Takanori, for instance, was a mysterious hero from the fourteenth century who, over the centuries, had received plenty of praises and admiration from pre-nineteenth-century historians because he supposedly lent important support and encouragement to Emperor Go Daigo (r. 1318–1339) in the latter's restoration endeavor. But Shigeno's scrutiny of the sources led him to disbelieve Kojima Takanori's existence as a historical figure. Along with his colleague Kume Kunitake, he came to challenge the veracity of the story, an oft cited perfect case by Confucian scholars of the past in espousing the Confucian ideal of political loyalty, orthodoxy, and order.[73] By disclosing the fabrication of Kojima Takanori, Shigeno also exposed the flaws of Confucian historiography. Like his contemporaneous "civilizational historians," he now considered it outdated and inconsequential to his work.

Moreover, Shigeno Yasutsugu discovered that Western historiography could aid his relentless evidential overhaul of the existing body of historical literature. Compared with Fukuzawa Yukichi and Taguchi Ukichi, the members of the History Bureau were not Western oriented, nor was there much official contact between the "civilizational historians" and those in the Bureau. However, Shigeno and his Bureau members were not immune from Western influences. Kume Kunitake, for example, had been a junior staff member of the Meiji government's official entourage to the West. Shigeno also noted the works of Western historians, especially those on Japanese history. He was impressed by the latter's richness in narrating historical details and inquisitive interest in historical causality; he deemed both as valuable and helpful in improving the work of the Japanese historian.[74] Yet his interest in Western historiography remained noticeably different from Fukuzawa Yukichi's; as an official historian, for example, Shigeno was not as concerned as Fukuzawa was with the expansion of historical writing into covering sociocultural areas.

George Zerffi, Ludwig Riess, and the Rankean influence in Japan

In order to learn more about the Western tradition of historical writing, the History Bureau, through the help of a Japanese diplomat in London,

commissioned George G. Zerffi (1820–1892), an exiled Hungarian diplomat and a self-made historian teaching at the University of London, to write
a history of Western historiography in 1879. Zerffi completed the assign-
ment in several months, and the end result was *The Science of History*, one
of the earliest attempts at the history of history by a European historian.
Though now little known among Western and Japanese historians, the latter were ironically its targeted audience; Zerffi's study of historiography
suggested that cross-cultural contact not only extended Western influence
to non-Western regions but also prompted Westerners to engage in self-
examination of their own culture from a comparative perspective. That
Zerffi, in his writing, made a foray into drawing comparisons between
Western and Asian cultures and histories was illuminating.[75]

Indeed, as indicated by his book's title, Zerffi intended to emphasize the
scientific nature of historical practice in the West, perhaps as a contrast
to the Confucian historiographical tradition with which he dabbled while
preparing his writing. Ironically, during much of the nineteenth century,
scientific, or critical, historiography in the Rankean fashion had not yet
become a dominant historiographical trend in England where he resided.
Many English historians, such as Thomas Macaulay, appeared much more
at home in the liberal tradition of historical writing. Nonetheless, Zerffi
not only considered scientific historiography a major characteristic of the
historical practice in the modern West, in this 773-page-long book, he also
offered a general survey of the origin and development of scientific history
from the classical Greek and Roman times to its culmination in German/
Rankean historiography of his time. He obviously believed that modern
scientific historiography was characteristic of the Western cultural tradition.

Zerffi perhaps was a bit carried away by his teleologism. Intent on tracing
the scientific history from the ages of the Greeks and Romans to that of his
own, he seemed to have run out of space to leave enough pages in his *The
Science of History* to cover the ascendance of Rankean historiography, the
exemplar of scientific history in his reckoning. But his message did manage
to get across to the Japanese historians in the History Bureau. Even though
Zerffi's book was not translated into Japanese in a timely manner, that Ludwig Riess (1861–1928), a distant disciple of Ranke's, was invited to teach in
Japan in 1887 spoke to the book's effect on its intended audience. Being a
Jew, Riess had failed to land a full-time job in Germany; when the invitation
from Japan arrived, he was doing research in England. But in Japan, Riess
was appointed the first history professor at the newly founded Tokyo University; the university administration was convinced that a Westerner was
needed to carry out the task of introducing modern historical education to
the country. This was, however, eventually changed after the Meiji government moved the History Bureau to the university in 1888. Consequently,
Shigeno Yasutsugu, Kume Kunitake, and Hoshino Hisashi were made history professors and Riess's colleagues at the university. In 1889, they and
Riess worked together to found the Japanese Historical Association and

published the *Shigaku zasshi* (*Journal of History*), a professional journal of historical study. Thanks to Riess and his introduction of the German model of modern historiography, Japanese historians established a historical profession in tandem with their counterparts in Germany, France, England, and the United States.[76]

The emergence of the historical profession in Japan coincided with and benefited from the modernization of Japanese education. Compared with its Asian neighbors such as China, Japan realized more quickly the need of establishing a modern-type institution of higher education and of promoting and propagating scientific education in the country. Modern education in Japan, however, was not a sheer outgrowth of foreign influence but was instead grafted onto the existing tradition of schooling. The prototype of Tokyo University, for example, was the *Shōhei kō*, a famous Confucian school in Edo where Shigenot Yasutsugu and others had received their education. Having merged with other schools, it was reorganized into Tokyo University in 1877 and became Japan's first modern institution of higher learning at the national level. Before 1886, when the university changed its name to Tokyo Imperial University, it was not yet a comprehensive school; the design of its curriculum was Western oriented with a clear bias for science education. Its history curriculum, for example, concentrated on teaching the history of the West and, having failed to recruit adequate teachers, was discontinued in two years. It was not until Ludwig Riess was hired in 1887 (one year after the school became the Imperial University) that history teaching was revived at Tokyo University. After Shigeno and his colleagues at the History Bureau joined its faculty, the curriculum of history was expanded to include the teaching of Japanese history. In historical study and education, therefore, professionalization and nationalization complemented one another, which was another recurrent phenomenon in the development of modern historiography across the world.

That Japan went ahead of its Asian neighbors in professionalizing historical writing bespoke the fast pace of Westernization in the country. Yet insofar as the change of historical study was concerned, Riess's presentation of Rankean historiography, which was characterized by a strong advocacy of Ranke's critical and objective approach to historiography, was not particularly foreign to Shigeno and his colleagues trained in the evidential school. That is, perhaps due to his own Jewish background or his consideration of the difficulty for the Japanese to fully understand the German idealism and Lutheran pantheism underpinning Ranke's historical practice, Riess chose to focus his presentation of his mentor's work on the methodological level. His most remembered course at Tokyo University was Historical Methodology, in which he used Ernst Bernheim's *Lehrbuch der historischen Method und der Geschichtsphilosophie*, leaving out the book's discussion on the philosophy of history.[77] It appears clear that Riess, in his introduction of German historiography, wanted to tailor it to the empirical interest inherent in the Japanese tradition of evidential learning whereby he could turn Rankean historiography into a universal model of historical study. In his research, Riess also tried to demonstrate that the Rankean method was applicable to the study of Japanese history, or to the execution of the nation-building or even empire-building project. It was worth mentioning that during his stint in Japan, Riess wrote a short history of Taiwan, an island coveted by the Japanese government at the time. Judging from the publications of his Japanese colleagues of the period, it seemed that Riess's strategy worked out well. Shigeno Yasutsugu, for example, enjoined that "historians must learn to be neutral and fair-minded" and Hoshino Hisashi advocated that "historical study and writing must base on carefully selected sources." Kume Kunitake, their more radical colleague, declared that "one must eschew the habit of commending the good and condemning the bad in order to see history [per se]." These statements clearly extended the agenda of Rankean historiography. Meanwhile, they also expanded on the interest of evidential learning.[78]

The Japanese tradition of historical study thus was reformed and transformed via a cross-cultural exchange, in which evidential learning not only paved the way for the Japanese to accommodate the Rankean model of Western historiography but also experienced a reincarnation in itself: Evidential scholars now became professional historians working in academic settings. And the change was hardly unilateral; as Rankean historiography extended its influence to Asia and elsewhere, it also acquired a different image than it had had in Germany.[79] In Riess's presentation of and his Japanese audience's perception of Ranke, this German master's image experienced a metamorphosis in that his political conservatism and religious belief were relegated to an insignificant level, in much the same way as, in its gestation, evidential learning had originally risen as an alternative to the metaphysical understanding of Confucian moral and political philosophy. Both Rankean historiography and evidential learning were now perceived as consequential only in advancing historical methodology, whereas their religious and ideological underpinnings were overlooked.

But methodology is hardly neutral. Ranke's emphasis on archive-based research, as discussed earlier, foregrounded the rise of nation-states, for the archives were usually established by the government and were also about the government. Shigeno's and Kume's critical examination of traditional sources for their project also had political implications, though at the time, it seemed at odds with the Japanese government's project on nation-building. Both of them, as well as Hoshino, interrogated the validity of many reputed sources and revealed their fallacy and falsity. Drawing on scrupulous source criticism, Kume Kunitake went so far as to demythologize the hallowed Shinto tradition in ancient Japan and declare that it was nothing but a custom of Heaven worship. Preoccupied with his interest in straightening out the facts, Kume challenged, perhaps inadvertently, the sanctity of Shintoism deemed fundamental by the government in its espousal of the purity of Japan's imperial house, a key component in its nation-/empire-building endeavor. In 1892, succumbing to mounting public pressure wielded by the Shintoists, Tokyo University fired Kume. Shigeno Yasutsugu, in a few years, was also forced into retirement. A setback for academic research and freedom in Japan's higher education, their dismissals from Tokyo University illustrated modern historiography's invariable entanglement in national politics.[80]

Japan's "Orient" and the changing of the Sinitic world

From the 1890s, as Japan expedited its pace in nation and empire building, it not only imposed more government restriction on academic research but also opened up a new era with respect to Japan's relation with the West. In contrast to the overt enthusiasm for Westernization in the early Meiji era, the new generation of intellectuals developed a more prudent attitude toward the Western influence and a more inward interest in discovering the value of Japan's past tradition and that of East Asian tradition in general.[81] Emperor Meiji's Imperial Rescript of Education, issued in 1890, symbolized this cultural turn, for the Rescript restated the need for imparting such Confucian moral values as loyalty, obedience, filiality, and harmony in Japanese schools. But this restatement hardly signaled that Japan was to cultivate friendship with China at the time. Quite the contrary, Japan's goal was to turn itself into the leader of Asia, replacing and even subduing China whereby it could make itself an equal to the West. That is, in order to become the "West," Japan had to find its "Orient."[82] The burgeoning study of Chinese and Asian history, under the rubric of *Tōyōshi* (history of the East), a neologism coined at the time in Japan's historical circle and school curriculum from the 1890s on, prefigured the trend. In retrospect, this changing climate of Japan's political culture was partially to blame for the dismissals of Kume Kunitake and Shigeno Yasutsugu from Tokyo University, for it gave rise to the revival of cultural nativism and political conservatism. Shigeno's and Kume's attacks on Japanese legends, their empiricist bend for historical factuality rather than didacticism, and their insistence on compiling the *Chronological History of Great Japan* in Chinese had made them the prime targets. Their departure marked the end of official history writing in modern Japan. But government sponsorship of and interference in history writing continued, as shown in the area of textbook compilation where government supervision and intervention were to become the norm that has lasted more or less to this day.[83]

Meanwhile, the study of civilizational history advanced. From the 1880s, Taguchi Ukichi and other advocates of civilizational history and its variant, "people's history" (*minkan shigaku*), began working out a closer relationship with their academic counterparts. In the *Shikai* (*Sea of history*), a journal edited by Taguchi aimed to promote popular and people's history, many academic historians became its frequent contributors. During the 1890s, the exponents of people's history organized the Society for the Friends of the People (*Minyūsha*), led by Tokutomi Sohō (1863–1957), Takekoshi Yosaburō (1865–1950), and Yamaji Aisan (1864–1917), whose writings represented prominent voices in charting Japan's cultural reorientation. Insofar as their historical studies were concerned, these intellectuals expanded Taguchi's interest in searching for a law-like generalization to adumbrate the progress of Japanese civilization. They also improved his approach by examining such important historical events as the Meiji Restoration from the people's perspective. In their reckoning, the Meiji Restoration became a social revolution, engendered by the awakening of the national consciousness among the Japanese people, who rose to fight the unjust authority.[84]

On two grounds, these historians' interest converged with that of their academic counterparts. First, like the academic historians who were now mostly Western-educated, these "people's historians" strove to establish a parity between Japanese history and European history and advocated that the two adopt a similar approach to interpreting their movements. More bravely than the seemingly bloodless academicians, they thus refuted the exaltation of Japan's unique cultural and religious traits, promoted by the Shintoists and the political oligarchy. Second, as ideologues of liberalism and populism, they were equally excited by Japan's victory in overseas expansion and eager to deliver their service. Tokutomi, for example, was well noted for his zealous support of the government in the Sino-Japanese War and Russo-Japanese War. During the early twentieth century, having changed notably his political stance and his public image, he by and large jettisoned his liberal image and became a chief spokesperson for Japan's imperialist foreign policy.

Japan's rise and China's decline changed the landscape of the Sinitic world and exerted a direct impact on Korea. In the late nineteenth century, Korean historians began seeking a way to emerge from the shadow of China and establish Korea's cultural independence by rewriting its history. This trend, which coincided with the rise of *Tōyōshi* in Japan, represented an embryonic form of modern Korean nationalism. Its origin, however, could be traced back in the Koreans' reaction to the Ming-Qing transition in seventeenth-century China and the subsequent rise of Practical Learning, the Korean extension of evidential learning during the eighteenth and early nineteenth centuries.[85] Owing to the influence of nationalism, many Korean historians grumbled that the Koreans in the past had made an earnest effort to know about what happened in Chinese history but that, in the meantime, they unfortunately had ignored and neglected their own history. In actuality, the Koreans should be proud of their country's history because, among others, its length is comparable to China's. As early as 2333 BCE, the legend goes, Tan'gun, the ancient king born of a divine being and a female bear, had founded the Korean kingdom. Thus, toward the turn of the nineteenth and twentieth centuries, the Koreans started shaking off their country's long bondage with China, or flunkeyism (*sadae*), a derogatory characterization of Korean culture and history during most of the Chosŏn dynasty

(1392–1910).[86] From that time to this day, nationalism has underscored the major course of development in modern Korean historiography, in part because Korea lost its independence to Japan at the turn of the twentieth century and in part because after gaining independence after World War II, the peninsula has remained divided.

When Japan eyed China as its "Orient," China, however, appeared unalarmed. Beginning in the 1860s, the reigning Qing dynasty had embarked on a course of Westernization, though on a much smaller scale than that of Japan. Its halfhearted approach reflected the Chinese reluctance to forsake their entrenched worldview that their land was the so-called Middle Kingdom under Heaven and to acknowledge the rise of the West. But it also had something to do with the outbreak of the Taiping Rebellion (1850–1864), which was sparked by a self-claimed Christian movement. Though the Western powers, out of their economic interest, sided with the dynasty, the Chinese literati were alarmed by the danger of Western religious and cultural influence in eroding traditional beliefs in Confucianism. When the Qing army appeared incapable of dealing with the Taiping rebels, the literati organized militia forces to lend their support to the dynasty; together, they succeeded in putting down the rebellion. This victory paved the way for the Qing dynasty's restoration (1862–1874), in which more attempts were made to harmonize China's relation with Western powers and Japan. At the same time, the regime renewed its effort to reinforce the Confucian tradition. Zhang Zhidong (1837–1909), a ranking Qing official, propounded a theoretical formula in which Chinese learning was exalted as the "substance" (*ti*), whereas Western learning was deemed as the "functional" (*yong*). This *ti-yong* formula became the guiding principle for the restoration, in that while many new offices were established in the government – the General Office for Managing Foreign Affairs (*Zongli yamen*) being the most notable and most important – aiming to acquaint the Chinese with new knowledge of international affairs, no serious attempt was made to reform and modernize the Chinese educational system. To be sure, there were also new schools being established to teach foreign languages and scientific knowledge, funded either by provincial governments or by Western missionaries. But these schools generally lacked appeal to the Chinese youth because they failed to prepare the students for the civil service examination, which before 1905 remained an important aim for schooling Chinese students and the usual channel for them to enter officialdom.

Thus, though the Qing restoration paralleled the early Meiji period, unlike Japan, China had not felt the need for establishing a modern institution through which Chinese students could acquire a systematic knowledge of the West and the world. There were, of course, exceptions, of which Wang Tao (1828–1897) was a noted example. Born into a literati family in Southeast China, Wang had a solid training in Confucian learning and later got a chance to work in Hong Kong for several years, where he assisted James Legge (1815–1897), a Scottish missionary, to translate Confucian classics into English. Invited by Legge, Wang also spent three years in England. Compared with his predecessors of the previous generation – e.g., Wei Yuan – Wang thus acquired firsthand knowledge of the West and gained a much better understanding of the changing tide of world history. If to Wei Yuan, the Westerners' "knack" was military technology, Wang Tao extended it into institutions and culture, which he felt necessary to introduce to his compatriots. Influenced by Western journalism, his writings attended to contemporary events, such as the Franco-Prussia War, and offered descriptions and analyses in a narrative structure, an attempt comparable to Taguchi Ukichi's in Japan. But Wang was also very much a person of his time. Arguably the most cosmopolitan person in late nineteenth-century China, he maintained that Confucian moral values were universal and pertinent for analyzing the trend of world history.[87]

Wang Tao could be regarded as China's "civilizational historian," whose historiographical innovations had inspired his Japanese counterparts. In Wang's visit to Japan in the 1870s, he had been warmly welcomed by Shigeno Yasutsugu and his colleagues at the History Bureau.[88] But back home, Wang's work was received less enthusiastically; throughout his life, Wang remained somewhat a maverick with respect to both his lifestyle and literary accomplishment. Qing official historians or Shigeno Yasutsugu's counterparts in China showed little interest in Wang's Western-influenced approach to historiography. They were instead more concerned with the quality of such "standard histories" as the *Ming History* and *Yuan History* (*Yuanshi*) compiled by their predecessors in the previous dynasties. And their criticism of these two histories was usually directed at these histories' supposed lapses in expounding the Confucian moral and political agenda. Yet a closer look at the historians' preoccupation with dynastic historiography at the time revealed that they did not hole up completely in the old tradition. At least in their study of Yuan history, their work seemed to have benefited from the Western sources regarding the Mongol conquest of Euro-Asia that had been recently made available. More specifically, these Western sources enabled such historians as Hong Jun (1839–1893), Ke Shaomin (1850–1933), and Tu Ji (1856–1921) to take advantage and examine the accuracy of the *Yuan History* through cross-reference. These new specimens of Yuan historical study also received attention in Japan, where Mongol history was considered an integrated part of the *Tōyōshi*. All this suggested that by the end of the nineteenth century, the Chinese had also gradually expanded their worldview, which resulted in some discernible changes in historical writing. Not only had more Western historical works been translated into Chinese by such missionaries as Young J. Allen (1836–1907) and Timothy Richard (1845–1919), whose activities had received much more tolerance – even patronage – from the Qing court, but Xue Fucheng (1838–1894), Xu Jianyin (1845–1901), and other Chinese diplomats who had traveled overseas also offered historical accounts and travelogues about the West, as well as Japan. Huang Zunxian's (1848–1905) *Japan: A National History (Riben guozhi*) was considered the best in the category. That Huang decided to write a general history about Japan was a significant move in itself, for previously Japanese history was either overlooked or inaccurately portrayed by Chinese historians, even by Wei Yuan in his *Sea Kingdoms*. By comparison, Huang not only provided a comprehensive and detailed account of Japanese history, but he also praised Japan's recent success in modernization.

But few Chinese, including perhaps such "Japan hands" as Huang Zunxian, had foreseen the direct and dire impact Japan's modernization would exert on China and the Sinitic world order as a whole. Having watched the impressive "progress" of Japanese civilization with an envious eye, they enjoined their compatriots to quickly follow suit, less China fall behind. During the 1890s, the ideas of evolution and social Darwinism thus were gaining currency in China. Robert Mackenzie's *The Nineteenth Century*, an otherwise banal survey of modern European history, was rendered by Timothy Richard into Chinese and became an instant best seller because of its zealous espousal of the ideal of progressive history. But by and large, prior to 1895 when the Qing was shatteringly defeated by Japan in the Sino-Japanese War, even the most open-minded Chinese appeared not just impressed but alarmed by Japan's quick pace in modernization. The war's outcome, however, came to shock them. Having put an end to the restoration era of the Qing, it also ushered in a new era of change for Chinese historical thinking. Japan's blatant challenge to China proved convincingly to the Chinese that the world had now followed a different historical trend, best encapsulated in the Darwinian principle of survival of the fittest. The Chinese then painfully realized that if their country failed to catch up the trend, it would then lose not only the vaunted Middle Kingdom status but also its national independence. Paradoxically, therefore, Japan's quick ascendance also proved inspirational to the Chinese: it goaded them to take more action and launch similar political and social reforms whereby they hoped to reclaim their past glory. By 1898, both the court and the literati seem to have agreed on the need of a more thorough reform. However, after the emperor decreed the 1898 Reform, the more powerful Empress Dowager smothered it after a mere hundred days – she was afraid of losing her power.

Thus, in contrast to the transformation of Japanese historical writing, where evidential empiricism meshed successfully with Rankean critical historiography, the Chinese interaction with the Western historiographical influence was shown in their acceptance of evolutionism, or social Darwinism, a more urgent agenda in their continued struggle for national survival and regeneration. Aside from Robert Mackenzie's *Nineteenth Century*, Thomas Huxley's *Ethics and Evolution*, translated by Yan Fu (1853–1921), a student returned from England, also became a best seller in fin de siècle China. In the meantime, the Darwinian emphasis on change and evolution prompted Chinese scholars to delve again in their own tradition for compatible elements. In this light, Gong Zizhen and Wei Yuan's reinterpretation of Confucianism as harboring the idea of change in history continued to attract attention. Drawing on the Three-Age Doctrine advanced by Gong and Wei, Kang Youwei (1858–1927), the protagonist of the 1898 Reform, went as far as to recast the image of Confucius as a social reformer from the perspective of Darwinian evolutionism in a series of controversial works.[89] Kang's reincarnation of Confucius was not accepted by many, but his attempt at merging New Text Confucianism with evolutionism, or social Darwinism, inspired historians and scholars of the future generation to accommodate foreign ideas and introduce more changes into modern Chinese historiography during the next century.

Notes

1 On a comparative view of the process of professionalization, see Gabriele Lingelbach, *Klio macht/Karriere: Die Instituionalisierung der Geschichtswissenschaft in Frankreich und den USA in der 2. Hälfte des neunzehnten Jahrhunderts* (Göttingen, 2003).

2 Georg G. Iggers, *The German Conception of History: The National Tradition of Historical Thought from Herder to the Present* (Middletown, 1983).

3 Peter Pulzer, *The Rise of Political Anti-Semitism in Germany and Austria* (Cambridge, 1960); Sulamit Volkov, *The Rise of Popular Antimodernism* (Princeton, 1978); Georg G. Iggers, "Academic Anti-Semitism in Germany 1870–1933: A Comparative Perspective," *Tel Aviver Jahrbuch für Deutsche Geschichte*, 27 (1998), 473–490.

4 Karl Marx and Friedrich Engels, "Manifesto of the Communist Party" in Robert C. Tucker, ed., *The Marx-Engels Reader* (New York, 1978, 2nd ed.), 477.

5 Mary Pickering, *Auguste Comte. An Intellectual Biography*, vol. 1 (Cambridge, 1993); Mike Gane, *Auguste Comte* (London, 2006); Henri G. Gouhier, *La Jeunesse d'Auguste Comte et la formation du positivisme*, 3 vols. (Paris, 1933–1941).

6 See Georg G. Iggers, *The Cult of Authority, The Political Philosophy of the Saint-Simonians* (The Hague, 1958); Robert Carlisle, *Saint-Simonianism and the Doctrine of Hope* (Baltimore, 1987); *Actualités du Saint-Simonisme* (Paris, 2004).

7 Eckhardt Fuchs, *Henry Thomas Buckle: Geschichtsschreibung und Positivismus in England und Deutschland* (Leipzig, 1994).

8 See Buckle, excerpts from the *History of Civilization in England* in Fritz Stern, *The Varieties of History: From Voltaire to the Present* (Cleveland, 1956), 121.

9 Ibid., 125.

10 Henry Buckle's work, along with François Guizot's, was translated into Japanese in the 1880s. It also had a Chinese translation shortly afterward. Ōkubo Toshiaki, *Nihon kindai shigaku no seiritsu (The Establishment of Modern Japanese Historiography)* (Tokyo, 1988), 94–95; Ozawa Eiichi, *Kindai Nihon shigaushi no kenkyū: Meiji hen (Study of the History of Modern Japanese Historiography: Meiji Period)* (Tokyo, 1968), 169–176; Hu Fengxiang and Zhang Wenjian, *Zhongguo jindai shixue sichao yu liupai (Ideas and Schools in Modern Chinese Historiography)* (Shanghai, 1991), 201–205.

11 Droysen, "Art and Method" in Stern, *Varieties of History*, 137–144.

12 Leopold von Ranke, Introduction to *Histories of Latin and Germanic Nations* (1824) in Georg Iggers, ed., *Leopold von Ranke: The Theory and Practice of History*, 86.

13 See Georg G. Iggers, "The Image of Ranke in German and American Historical Thought," *History and Theory*, 2 (1962), 17–40.

14 Leopold von Ranke, "On the Character of Historical Science" in Iggers, *Leopold von Ranke: The Theory and Practice of History*, 8.

15 Von Humboldt, "On the Historian's Task" in Georg G. Iggers and Konrad Von Moltke, eds., *Leopold von Ranke: The Theory and Practice of History* (Indianapolis, 1973), 5.

16 Leopold von Ranke, "The Great Powers" in Iggers, *Leopold von Ranke, The Theory and Practice of History*, 52.

17 Leopold von Ranke, "A Dialogue on Politics," ibid., 112.

18 See Iggers, *German Conception of History*, ch. 5, "The High Point of Historical Optimism: The 'Prussian School'," 90–123; Robert Southard, *Droysen and the Prussian School of History* (Lexington, 1995).

19 Jörn Rüsen, *Begriffene Geschichte: Genesis und Begründung der Geschichtstheorie Johann Gustav Droysens* (Paderborn, 1969).

20 Johann G. Droysen, "Interpretation" in *Historik: historisch-kritische Ausgabe*, by Peter Leyh (Stuttgart, 1977), 22, 169–216.

21 See Iggers, *German Conception of History*, 112–114; Günter Birtsch, *Nation als sittliche Idee: der nationale Staatsbegriff in Geschichtsschreibung und Gedankenwelt* (Göttingen, 1964).

22 Iggers, *German Conception of History*, 111.

23 Ibid., 115.

24 Andreas Dorpalen, *Heinrich von Treitschke* (New Haven, 1957).

25 Georg G. Iggers, "Heinrich von Treitschke" in Hans-Ulrich Wehler, ed., *Deutsche Historiker*, vol. 2 (Göttingen, 1972), 66–80.

26 See Wolfgang J. Mommsen, "Ranke and the Neo-Rankean School in Imperial Germany: State-oriented Historiography as a Stabilizing Force" in Georg G. Iggers and James M. Powell, eds., *Leopold von Ranke and the Shaping of the Historical Discipline* (Syracuse, 1990); Hans-Heinz Krill, *Die Ranke-Renaissance: Max Lenz und Erich Marcks: ein Beitrag zum historisch-politischen Denken in Deutschland 1880–1935* (Berlin, 1962).

27 Georg G. Iggers, "Historicism: The History and Meaning of the Term," *Journal of the History of Ideas*, 56 (1995), 129–152; Frederick C. Beiser, *The German Historicist Tradition* (Oxford, 2011); Jörn Rüsen and Friedrich Jaeger, *Geschichte des Historismus* (München, 1992); Charles Bambach, *Heidegger, Dilthey, and the Crisis of Historicism* (Ithaca, 1995).

28 Gustav Schmoller, *The Economics of Gustav Schmoller*, tr. W. Abraham and H. Weingast (New York, 1942).

29 On recent discussions of Marx and Marxism, see Paul Blackledge, *Reflections on the Marxist Theory of History* (Manchester, 2006); Kevin B. Anderson, *Marx at the Margins: On Nationalism, Ethnicity, and Non-Western Societies* (Chicago, 2010); Eric Hobsbawm, *How to Change the World: Reflections on Marx and Marxism* (New Haven, 2011); also Q. Edward Wang and Georg Iggers, eds., *Marxist Historiographies: A Global Perspective* (London, 2015).

30 Karl Marx, "Marx on the History of His Opinions" in Tucker, *Marx-Engels Reader*, 4.

31 Karl Marx, "Theses on Feuerbach," ibid., 143–144.

32 Karl Marx, "The Fetishism of Commodities and the Secret thereof" from *Capital* vol. 1, ibid., 319–329.

33 Leopold von Ranke, "On Progress in History" (1854) in Iggers, *Leopold von Ranke: The Theory and Practice of History*, 21.

34 Leopold von Ranke, "On the Character of Historical Science," ibid., 46.

35 Karl Marx, "The Eighteenth Brumaire of Louis Bonaparte" in Tucker, *Marx-Engels Reader*, 608.

36 Karl Marx, "The British Rule in India," ibid., 653–664.

37 Johann Droysen, "Erhebung der Geschichte zum Rang einer Wissenschaft" in *Historik*, 451–469; this is Droysen's review of T. H. Buckle, *Civilization in England*, vol. 1.

38 Karl Marx and Friedrich Engels, "Manifesto of the Communist Party" in Tucker, *Marx-Engels Reader*, 491.

39 On the role of "amateur" historians and the lack of any clear distinction between amateur and professional historiography, see Martin Nissen, *Populäre Geschichtsschreibung Historiker, Verleger und die deutsche Öffentlichkeit (1848–1900)* (Köln, 2009). See also Peter Burke, "Lay History: Official and Unofficial Representations: 1800–1914" in Stuart Macintyre, Juan Maiguashca, and Attila Pok, eds., *Oxford History of Historical Writing*, vol. 4 (Oxford, 2011), 115–132.

40 On women historians, see Natalie Z. Davis, "History's Two Bodies," *American Historical Review*, 93:1 (February 1988), 1–30; and "Gender and Genre: Women as Historical Writers, 1400–1820" in Patricia Labalme, ed., *Beyond Their Sex: Learned Women of the European Past* (New York, 1980); Joan W. Scott, "American Women Historians, 1884–1984" in her *Gender and the Politics of History* (New York, 1988), 178–198.

41 On the recruitment of the German historical profession, see Wolfgang Weber, *Priester der Klio: Historisch-sozialwissenschaftliche Studien zu Herkunft und Karriere deutscher Historiker und zur Geschichte der Geschichtswissenschaft 1800–1970* (Frankfurt a/M, 1984).

42 Iggers, "Academic Anti-Semitism in Germany 1870–1933."

43 Weber, *Priester der Klio* and *Geschichte der Europäischen Universität* (Stuttgart, 2002); Fritz Ringer, *The Decline of the German Mandarins: The German Academic Community, 1890–1933* (Middletown, 1990).

44 Margaret Mehl, *History and the State in Nineteenth-Century Japan* (New York, 1998), 95–107.

45 William R. Keylor, *Academe and Community: The Foundation of the French Historical Profession* (Cambridge, MA, 1975).

46 Peter Novick, *That Noble Dream: The "Objectivity Question" and the American Historical Profession* (Cambridge, MA, 1988).

47 Effi Gazi, *Scientific National History: The Greek Case in Comparative Perspective* (New York, 2000).

48 "Über die Verwandtschaft und den Unterschied der Historie und der Politik," Ranke's inaugural lecture as a full professor (*Ordinarius*) at the University of Berlin in 1836, translated from Latin in Ranke's *Sämmtliche Werke*, 24, 280–293.

49 Cited in Iggers, *German Conception of History*, 117.

50 Cited in Iggers, "The Image of Ranke in German and American Historical Thought," 21–22.

51 See Felix Gilbert, *History: Politics and Culture. Reflections on Ranke and Burckhardt* (Princeton, 1990); John R. Hinde, *Jacob Burckhardt: The Crisis of Modernity* (Montreal, 2000); and Lionel Gossman, *Basel in the Age of Burckhardt* (Chicago, 2000).

52 *Pictures of German Life in the XVth, XVIth, and XVIIth Centuries*, tr. Malcolm (London, 1862).

53 George P. Gooch, *History and Historians in the Nineteenth Century* (London, 1955, rev. ed.), 397–416.

54 *Scientific National History: The Greek Case in Comparative Perspective, 1850–1920.*

55 See Božidar Pejović, ed., *Stojan Novaković i filološka kritika: izabrani kritic?ki radovi Stojana Novakovića i filososk kritika: Izabrani kritiški radovi Stojana Novakovića, Ilariona Ruvarca, Jovana živanovića* (Belgrade, 1975).

56 A. D. Xenopol, *Histoire des Romains de la Dacie trajane, depuis les origines jusqu'à l'union des principautés en 1859* (Paris, 1896).
57 See, for example, Schlözer's *Russische Annalen in ihrer Slavonischen Grundsprache* (V Sanktpeterburgie, 1809–1819) and *Münz-, Geld- und Bergwerks-Geschichte des Russischen Kaiserthums* (Göttingen, 1791).
58 See *Allgemeine nordische Geschichte. Aus den neuesten und besten nordischen Schriftstellern und nach eigenen Untersuchungen beschrieben, und als eine geographische und historische Einleitung zur richtigern Kenntniss aller skandinavischen, finnischen, slavischen, lettischen und sibirischen Völker, besonders in alten und mittleren Zeiten* (Halle, 1771).
59 *Gosudarstvennoe khoziʾaʾistvo Rossiĭ v pervoĭ chetverti XVIII stoliʾeʾtiʾaʾi reforma Petra Velikago* (St. Petersburg, 1905) and *Ocherki po istorīi russkoĭ kul'tury*, which was translated into English as *Outlines of Russian Culture* by Valentine Ughet and Eleanor Davis (South Brunswick, 1960).
60 Benjamin Elman, *From Philosophy to Philology: Intellectual and Social Aspects of Change in Late Imperial China* (Cambridge, MA, 1984), 116–122; Joanna Waley-Cohen, "China and Western Technology in the Late Eighteenth Century," *American Historical Review*, 98:5 (1993), 1525–1544, especially 1534.
61 Ōkubo Toshiaki, *Nihon kindai shigakushi (A History of Modern Japanese Historiography)* (Tokyo, 1940), 161–222; Sakai Saburō, *Nihon seiyō shigaku hattsushi (History of the Development of Western Historiography in Japan)* (Tokyo, 1969), 44–47.
62 On-cho Ng and Q. Edward Wang, *Mirroring the Past: The Writing and Use of History in Imperial China* (Honolulu, 2005), 250–258.
63 Hu Fengxiang and Zhang Wenjian, *Zhongguo jindai shixue sichao yu liupai (Trends and Schools in Modern Chinese Historiography)* (Shanghai, 1991), 34–90.
64 Jane Kate Leonard, *Wei Yuan and China's Rediscovery of the Maritime World* (Cambridge, MA, 1984), and Q. Edward Wang, "World History in Traditional China," *Storia della Storiografia*, 35 (1999), 83–96.
65 Yoda Yoshiie, *Nitchū ryōkoku kindaika no hikaku kenkyū josetsu (An Introduction to the Comparative Study of Japanese and Chinese Modernization)* (Tokyo, 1986), 44, 66–67.
66 Ozawa Eiichi, *Kindai Nihon shigakushi no kenkyū. Meiji hen (Study of Modern Japanese Historiography: Meiji Period)* (Tokyo, 1968), 105–106.
67 Taguchi Ukichi made this statement in another similarly structured book, *Shina kaika shōshi (A Short History of Chinese Civilization)* (Tokyo, 1887), preface.
68 Sakamoto Tarō, *Nihon no shūshi to shigaku (Historical Compilation and Study in Japan)* (Tokyo, 1991), 234; Mehl, *History and the State in Nineteenth-century Japan*, 16–17.
69 Li Tana, "Vietnamese Chronicles" in Kelly Boyd, ed., *Encyclopedia of Historians and Historical Writing* (London, 1999), vol. 2, 1265–1266.
70 Jin Xudong, "*Qinding Yueshi tongjian gangmu* jianlun (A Brief Discussion of the Outline and Details of the Comprehensive Mirror of Vietnamese History, with Imperial Annotation)," in Wang Qingjia and Chen Jian, eds., *Zhongxi lishi lunbianji: liumei lishi xuezhe xueshu wenhui (History and Its Scholarly Approach: Essays by Chinese Historians in the U.S.)* (Shanghai, 1992), 255–267.
71 Mehl, *History and the State in Nineteenth-century Japan*, passim.
72 Jiro Numata, "Shigeno Yasutsugu and the Modern Tokyo Tradition of Historical Writing" in W. G. Beasley and E. G. Pulleyblank, eds., *Historians of China and Japan* (Oxford, 1961), 264–287; Nagahara Keiji, *20 seiki Nihon no rekishigaku (20th Century Japanese Historiography)* (Tokyo, 2005), 13–16.
73 John Brownlee, *Japanese Historians and the National Myths, 1600–1945* (Vancouver, 1997), 86–89.

74 Ibid., 82.
75 See Numata Jirō, "Meiji shoki ni okeru seiyō shigaku no yunyū ni tsui te: Shigeno Yasutsugu to G. G. Zerffi, *The Science of History*" "The Importation of Western Historiography in the Early Meiji Period: Shigeno Yasutsugu and G. G. Zerffi's *The Science of History*" in Itō Tasaburō, ed., *Kokumin seikatsushi kenkyū* (*Studies of the History of National Life*) (Tokyo, 1963), vol. 3, 400–429; Mehl, *History and the State in Nineteenth-century Japan*, 74–80. For George G. Zerffi's life and career, see Tibor Frank, *From Habsburg Agent to Victorian Scholar: G. G. Zerffi, 1820–92*, tr. Christopher Sullivan and Tibor Frank (Boulder, 2000).
76 Mehl, *History and the State in Nineteenth-century Japan*, 87–112.
77 Brownlee, *Japanese Historians and the National Myths*, 73–80; also Leonard Blussé, "Japanese Historiography and European Sources" in P. C. Emmer and H. L. Wesseling, eds., *Reappraisals in Overseas History* (Leiden, 1979), 193–222.
78 These were all article titles in the *Shigaku zasshi* (*Journal of History*) during 1889 and 1890. That the establishment of academic history converged and cemented evidential learning and Rankean historiography has been maintained by most Japanese scholars of historiography. See Jiro Numata, "Shigeno Yasutsugu and the Modern Tokyo Tradition of Historical Writing" in Beasley and Pulleyblank, *Historians of China and Japan*, 273–287; Ōkubo, *Nihon kindai shigakushi*, 74–81; Sakamoto, *Nihon no shūshi to shigaku*, 247–248; and Nagahara, *20 seiki Nihon no rekishigaku*, 15.
79 Iggers, "The Image of Ranke in German and American Historical Thought."
80 Brownlee, *Japanese Historians and the National Myths*, 92–106. Also, Byron K. Marshall, *Academic Freedom and the Japanese Imperial University, 1868–1939* (Berkeley, 1992).
81 Kenneth Pyle, *The New Generation in Meiji Japan: Problems of Cultural Identity, 1885–1895* (Stanford, 1969); Carol Gluck, *Japan's Modern Myth: Ideology in the Late Meiji Period* (Princeton, 1985).
82 Stefan Tanaka, *Japan's Orient: Rendering Past into History* (Berkeley, 1993); Nagahara, *20 seiki Nihon no rekishigaku*, 43–45.
83 Mehl, *History and the State in Nineteenth-century Japan*, 113–147.
84 See Peter Duus, "Whig History, Japanese Style: The Min'yusha Historians and the Meiji Restoration," *Journal of Asian Studies*, 33:3 (May 1974), 415–436.
85 Cf. Remco E. Breuker, "Contested Objectives: Ikeuchi Hiroshi, Kim Sanggi and the Tradition of Oriental History (*Tōyō shigaku*) in Japan and Korea," *East Asian History*, 29 (June 2005), 69–106.
86 Li Runhe (Lee Yun-hwa), *Zhonghan jindai shixue bijiao yanjiu* (*A Comparative Study of Modern Chinese and Korean Historiography*) (Beijing, 1994), 87–90.
87 See Paul A. Cohen, *Between Tradition and Modernity: Wang T'ao and Reform in late Ch'ing China* (Cambridge, MA, 1974), 91–96, 110–139; Q. Edward Wang, *Inventing China through History: The May Fourth Approach to Historiography* (Albany, 2001), 36–42.
88 Shiteng Huixiu (Sanetō Keishū), *Mingzhi shidai Zhongri wenhua de lianxi* (*Cultural Exchanges between Meiji Japan and Qing China*), tr. Chen Guting (Taipei, 1971).
89 See Hsiao Kung-ch'uan, *A Modern China and a New World: K'ang Yu-wei, Reformer and Utopian, 1858–1927* (Seattle, 1975).

4 Historical writings in the shadow of two world wars

The crisis of historicism and modern historiography

The reorientation of historical studies and historical thought (1890–1914)

The changing political and cultural climate

The year 1890 is not a climactic date, like 1789, 1848, or 1871, although it marked the dismissal of Otto von Bismarck as Chancellor of Germany. But generally in Western and Northern Europe, including Germany, Austria-Hungary, Italy, as well as the United States, the political systems that had been in place in 1871 remained intact. The situation was more volatile in the Balkans and in Russia. The social changes that we had observed after the mid-nineteenth century, industrialization and urbanization and on the political level the emergence of a mass electorate, mass parties, and a mass press, accelerated and created a setting that, as we shall see, directly affected the ways in which history was written. By 1890 strong socialist movements, often shaped by Marxist ideas, had become vocal in all continental European countries, foremost in Germany, and by 1900 a non-Marxist Labour Party had come into existence in Great Britain. Everywhere universal male suffrage had been introduced, belatedly in Austria in 1907 and in Italy in 1912, and while women generally did not yet have the vote, there were vocal movements for their suffrage in Great Britain, the United States, Germany, and Scandinavia, which set the stage for granting women the vote in all of these countries very shortly after the end of World War I. Moreover, middle-class democratic parties gained in strength, even in Germany where the power of parliament was seriously curbed, In France, Great Britain, and Scandinavia, close cooperation between these parties and labor came about, as exemplified by the entry of the socialists into the government in France in 1900 and in Great Britain by the coalition of the Liberal and Labour parties in 1906. Labor parties begin to play an important role in Australia and New Zealand, as did Social Democrats in Scandinavia. In the United States, the Progressive party emerged as an advocate of social and democratic reform, but it avoided taking a stand on the discrimination of blacks. There were also anti-Semitic and chauvinistic movements in Germany, Austria, and

France representing agrarian interests, traditional craftsmen, and shopkeepers threatened by the emergence of large corporate businesses.

The period between 1890 and 1914 was also marked by major changes in the intellectual and cultural spheres. In physics, theories of relativity and indeterminacy moved away from older mechanistic notions. Sigmund Freud's (1856–1939) psychoanalysis explored the role of the subconscious. The new art in France and Germany moved away from older forms of realism, as did the novelists James Joyce (1882–1941) and Marcel Proust (1871–1922). In music, harmony began to give way to atonality.

The challenge to traditional historiography

The critique of the Rankean model

Although the patterns of professional scholarship established by the Rankean School continued to dominate historical studies at the universities, voices of dissent challenged the stress on political, diplomatic, and military history and the narrow concentration on written official documents. It is striking that just as the professionalization of historical studies loosely following the Rankean model was adopted internationally in the 1870s and 1880s,[1] the model was criticized throughout Western countries, including Latin America, and with only a short delay in Japan. As we shall see, the Japanese critique of Rankean historiography was inspired by Karl Lamprecht, whose works were translated into Japanese in the early twentieth century.[2] The critique centered on two important points: One was that the Rankean model of historiography reflected a society prior to extensive industrialization and ignored the political and social consequences of the emergence of a mass public. The second critique, connected with the first, was that it operated with a much too narrow concept of historical science that neglected the social context of historical development. In the United States and in France, the model of scholarship that professional historical studies followed in the universities was to be criticized not because it was too scientific, as Friedrich Nietzsche had claimed, but because it was not sufficiently scientific. Science involves causal explanation. An increasing number of historians throughout the West and Japan began to move to social, economic, and cultural history and in some cases attempted to formulate theories of historical development on the basis of their empirical observations.

Karl Lamprecht and the Methodenstreit in Germany

In Germany, the controversy about the proper methods of historical studies, the so-called *Methodenstreit*, initiated a bitter debate between the established profession and Karl Lamprecht (1856–1915),[3] professor of history at the University of Leipzig, who in 1891 had published the first volume of his ultimately 12-volume *Deutsche Geschichte* (*German History*).[4] Unlike the

mainstream German histories that traced the course of political developments that ultimately led to the unification of Germany under Bismarck and
focused on the great personalities who guided this development, Lamprecht wrote a history in which society and culture, not great men, provided
the context in which political history had to be understood. Lamprecht's
Deutsche Geschichte was attacked because it called into question the idealistic presuppositions of the national tradition of German historiography
and because it took economic factors into consideration, and it was accused
of being Marxist, which it was not. Lamprecht's history was considered to
be subversive, calling into question the legitimacy of the Prussian-German
state, which it also did not. His own politics tended in the direction of
moderate democratic reforms. The *Deutsche Geschichte* was held to be
positivistic in the sense of Comte and Buckle. It set out to formulate laws
of historical development by which German history went through regular
upward cycles, each lasting about five hundred years. His history continued
to be thoroughly nation oriented, only that the center of the nation was not
to be found in its political organization but in its culture, in what Lamprecht, in terms derived from German Romanticism, termed the *Volksgeist*.
The book was rightly criticized by the German historical establishment for
its superficial scholarship and its unproved speculations. Max Weber, the
sociologist, who was very critical of the scholarship represented by the German academics and who wanted to give the studies of history and society a
more rigorous character, strongly attacked Lamprecht who, in claiming to
elevate history to the level of a science, actually with his loose speculation
and Romantic notions did a serious disservice to the efforts to achieve this.[5]

Lamprecht's *Deutsche Geschichte* was preceded by his doctoral dissertation of 1884, *An Economic History of the Moselle Region in the Middle
Ages*,[6] which has generally been respected as a serious, innovative work. In
it Lamprecht undertook to write a comprehensive economic and social history of a specific region, placing it in a concrete geographic setting, based on
the careful examination of the archives. At about the same time, the French
historian Charles Seignobos (1854–1942) wrote a very similar dissertation
on Burgundy[7] in approximately the same period. Both set examples for
later intensive regional histories in a concrete time frame, but Seignobos
afterwards reverted to more traditional historiography. Despite the hostile
reception of Lamprecht's *Deutsche Geschichte* by his colleagues, it was very
popular among nonacademic readers, unlike his book on the economic
history of the Moselle region. Nevertheless, the latter paved the way for
Lamprecht's pioneering work in *Landesgeschichte* (regional history), which
became an important field in German scholarship.

The reorientation of historical studies in France

A parallel but in many ways different reaction against the political and diplomatic history along the German pattern as represented by Gabriel Monod

(1844–1912), the founder of the *Revue Historique*, took place in France. The intellectual traditions were different. The idealistic tradition that played such an important role in Ranke's conception of history was absent. The single most influential historian in nineteenth-century France was Jules Michelet (1798–1874), who had written a vivid history covering broad segments of everyday life, not only centering on select charismatic personalities but also including common men and women. The most important exponent of a modern comprehensive history was Henri Berr (1863–1954), a philosopher by training, who in 1900 founded the *Revue de synthèse historique*, to which he invited Lamprecht to contribute, although there is little indication of direct influence. As the title of the review suggested, Berr wanted a history that would integrate all aspects of the society and culture of a time. Berr was profoundly influenced by the sociologist Emile Durkheim (1858–1917),[8] the French geographer Paul Vidal de la Blache (1843–1918), and the German geographer Friedrich Ratzel (1844–1904). Vidal de la Blache and Ratzel saw geography primarily not as a natural but as a human science and maintained that history cannot be separated from geography.[9] Durkheim held that history, as traditionally pursued, could not be a science because it has no system, but it could serve sociology in dealing with societies in a historical perspective. Unlike the German tradition, which insisted that history is a science that deals with individuals, whether persons or societies, and seeks to understand their unique qualities, Durkheim insisted that sociology, which subsumes history, deals with the "collective conscience" of social groups. Turning in his book, *Suicide* (1897), to the modern, industrial world of his day, he undertook to analyze suicide in terms of what he defined as *anomie*, the isolation of individuals in the anonymous mass society that has replaced the sense of belonging in older traditional societies. Berr was convinced that history could and should place collective phenomena, as outlined by Durkheim, into a historical framework. His review later became an important forum for international discussions of historical theory and method that in turn influenced the new social history in France.

While serious Marxist scholarship was still lacking and no important Marxist historians held an academic post anywhere, an avowedly Marxist history appeared in France at the turn of the century, *The Socialist History of the French Revolution* by Jean Jaurès (1859–1914), a leading politician in the French Socialist party. Jaurès employed Marxist concepts of class conflict to focus on the role that peasants and workers, until then largely neglected, played in the course of events. Jaurès wrote a scholarly history that used archival sources. Accompanied by extensive illustrations, it was written in such a manner that it could also be read by peasants and workers. He stressed the role of economic factors without being an economic determinist, indebted, as he said, not only to Marx's analysis but also to Michelet's "mysticism" in which charismatic individuals, including common men and women, played an important role. It is striking that the French academic response to Jaurès was very different from that of the

German academic community to Lamprecht. Jaurès was taken seriously as a scholar. In 1903, he asked the French government to appoint a commission to collect and publish the scattered sources for the economic and social history of the French Revolution, a request that was granted. Jaurès became chair of the commission that included the leading French historians of the Revolution. In Germany, the universities were dominated by scholars committed to the Prussian monarchy, and advocates of democratic reform were largely excluded;[10] in France, the majority of scholars in the universities, as they were reformed in the Third Republic, espoused republican ideals.[11] There was a royalist historiography, opposed to the Republic and critical of the French Revolution, but its members, with the notable exception of the already mentioned Hyppolite Taine, were largely outside the academy, some of them politically active in the ultranationalist, anti-Semitic *Action Française*.[12]

The "New History" in the United States

In the United States a similar turn to social history took place with the "New History," which settled accounts with the self-styled "scientific history" of the generation of professional historians preceding it. An important impetus came from Frederick Jackson Turner (1861–1932),[13] professor at the University of Wisconsin, who in an essay on the "Frontier in American History" (1893) challenged the notion of the origins of English and American free institutions in ancient Germanic tribal society, widely held by the earlier professional generation, and argued that American freedom was unique, originating in the struggle for the frontier. The true America was not that of the Eastern elite establishment but that of the common people in the heartland and the Western regions of America. The historians must take into account the geographic setting of American society, the crucial role of the Western frontier, and the social and cultural context of America's political history.

Turner's history coincided with the rise of the Progressive Movement in American politics, which strove for democratic reforms. It was preceded by the Populism of the 1870s and 1880s, which was primarily an agrarian movement challenging the power of the banks and railroads. The Progressive Movement took into consideration the condition not only of farmers but also of workers in an industrial society. James Harvey Robinson (1863–1936), professor at Columbia University since 1893, in a series of articles in the 1900s and in his "New History" (1912) outlined a program for such a history, which for him would center on culture and society. Culture in turn for him meant intellectual history, which he viewed as not restricted to great thinkers but seeking to understand the mental outlook of a time. Unlike Turner, this history did not restrict itself to America but saw America as part of a Western civilization in which Europe played a decisive role. In 1919 the first undergraduate course in Western Civilization was introduced at Columbia University. Also at Columbia University, a circle of similarly oriented historians and social scientists gathered, including the philosopher John Dewey (1859–1952). Carl Lotus Becker (1873–1945) devoted a number of studies to major currents in European intellectual history and the European influence on American notions of democracy.[14]

It is striking that the "New History," which was committed to democracy, still almost totally neglected the fate of the African American population in America. The president whom many of them supported, Woodrow Wilson (1856–1924), elected in 1912, opposed any reforms of the system of racial segregation. In general, the advocates of a "New History" sought a close cooperation between history and the incipient social sciences. Yet unlike Lamprecht and Berr, they did not believe that this "New History" could formulate laws of the historical development of social processes, although they were optimistic about the general development of the modern world toward greater democracy and social equality.

Yet unlike Turner, who promoted an American exceptionalism, some of the "progressive" historians were very aware of the imperfections of American democracy. In 1913, Charles Beard (1874–1948)[15] published *The Economic Interpretation of the American Constitution*. Although he did not consider himself to be a Marxist, he adopted two concepts that were close to the Marxian interpretation of history and society. One, as the title of the book suggests, was the centrality of economic forces; the second was the extent to which political power rested on economic power and was applied to preserve social and economic inequalities. Beard undertook to shatter the American myth that the fathers of the American constitution were motivated primarily by ideals of freedom and to show instead that private economic interests guided their decisions. Unlike Lamprecht and Berr, who were convinced that scientific objectivity was possible in the study of history and of society, Carl Becker and Charles Beard were much more guarded and stressed the role of subjective factors.

Economic and social history in Great Britain

In Great Britain the move from traditional erudition to an interdisciplinary social history was slower. Many historians continued to write along the lines of the Whig Interpretation of History[16] with a focus on parliamentary and legal developments. Nevertheless, outside academe there were important works dealing with labor history, focused on the life of the poor. Arnold J. Toynbee (1851–1883), not to be confused with his famous nephew by the same name, in *Lectures on the Industrial Revolution in England*, published posthumously in 1884, focused attention on the social consequences of industrialization on the towns and on the enclosures in the countryside. There were two husband-and-wife teams, John Lawrence Hammond (1872–1949) and Barbara Hammond (1873–1961), who in 1911 published *The Village Labourer*, and Beatrice Webb (1858–1943) and Sydney Webb

(1859–1947), who published *History of Trade Unionism* (1894) and *Industrial Democracy* (1897). In France, two important works on the conditions of labor appeared by Emile Levasseur (1828–1911) and Henri Hauser (1866–1946).

Economic history, as a discipline apart from economics but also from history, began to occupy an important role in the 1920s but had its origins already in the 1890s when the British economist W. J. Ashley (1860–1927) was appointed to the world's first chair in economic history at Harvard University. Soon chairs of economic history were established on both sides of the ocean.

The new social history elsewhere

The turn away from the state-oriented paradigm to an interdisciplinary social and cultural history proved to be an international development occurring throughout the West, including Latin America, and soon also in East Asia. In Poland, at the relatively autonomous universities of Krakow and Lwów under Austria but also at the University of Warsaw in the Russian-dominated part of Poland, this reaction was closely tied in with the commitment to endow a national culture with a historical foundation in order to pave the way to the restoration of national independence and to counter the attempts at Russification and Germanization by the occupying powers. In Russia, where the concentration on the empire as a political and religious entity had been extraordinarily strong, the Moscow School of Vasily Osiovich Kluchevskii (1841–1911) and his student Pavel Nikolaevich Miliukov (1859–1943) pursued an interdisciplinary approach in which political structures and processes were placed in a broader economic and social context to account for Russia's alienation from the West.[17] Beginning in the early twentieth century, Lamprecht's works were rendered into Japanese, sparking the interest in sociocultural history as exemplified by the work of Tsuda Sōkichi, which set out to examine the collective mind of the Japanese people.[18] In China, a similar move toward broadening the field of history was inspired by James H. Robinson's *The New History*, which appeared in Chinese in the early 1920s. It aided the historians there in their critical reflection on the imperial tradition of monarch-centered historiography while experimenting with the writing of national history.[19]

The move to a new paradigm of social and cultural history thus took place on an international scale. Of course, the older patterns of doing history continued in most places. Many historians in all the countries we have mentioned still worked in the traditional mode, seeking to avoid theoretical questions although almost never free from political biases. Important impulses came from Germany with Karl Lamprecht's initiative in his *German History*, but Germany was the one country in which this "New History" was vociferously ostracized. Lamprecht was neither a radical democratic reformer nor a Marxist, but he was made to appear as such. This undoubtedly had a good deal to do with the semiautocratic government of Germany and the fear by broad segments of the middle classes that democratization and political reforms in this direction would strengthen the power of the Social Democratic working classes. Moreover, German historians, as we saw in the previous chapter, had played a very important role in mobilizing public opinion in support of the semiautocratic solution of 1871, which fulfilled middle-class demands for a constitution that satisfied many of their political and social demands and at the same time bolstered the status quo. Lamprecht's challenge to the traditional historiography with its idealistic assumptions was thus seen as subverting the established political and social order.

International exchanges

For the first time since the eighteenth-century Enlightenment, close scholarly exchanges took place across national lines. Many American, French, and Eastern European historians had come to study in Germany in the course of the second half of the nineteenth century, soon joined by students from Japan and the Middle East. This continued into the early twentieth century. Robinson, the central figure of the American "New History," had studied with Lamprecht in Leipzig, which had become a center where a small group of like-minded scholars in the social sciences met regularly, including the economist Karl Bücher (1847–1930), the psychologist and philosopher Wilhelm Wundt (1832–1920), and the geographer Friedrich Ratzel. They formed a circle of scholars interested in interdisciplinary studies that met regularly and of which Lamprecht was an active member. Durkheim had also studied in Leipzig, as had the leading Romanian historian, Nicolae Iorga (1871–1940), who completed his doctorate in Leipzig in 1893 under the supervision of Lamprecht. Others studied in Berlin, including Robinson and the African American sociologist and historian W.E.B. Du Bois (1868–1963), who attended the lectures of the economic historian Gustav von Schmoller and corresponded with Max Weber.

One example of the new international cooperation in historical studies was the founding in 1893 by the Austrian Social Democratic historian Lujo Moritz Hartmann (1865–1924) and the conservative German historian Georg von Below (1858–1927) of a quarterly review for economic and social history, *Vierteljahrschrift für Sozial- und Wirtschaftsgeschichte*, with articles in German, French, English, and Italian, as well as contributors from all over Europe and North America. In 1904 at the Congress of Arts and Sciences at the Universal Exposition in St. Louis, the main exponents of a "New History" – Karl Lamprecht, Frederick Jackson Turner, James Harvey Robinson, and J.B. Bury from England (1861–1927) – in a session moderated by Woodrow Wilson – discussed new directions in historical and social studies. Also present at the Congress were the sociologist Max Weber, the sociologist of religion Ernst Troeltsch (1865–1923), and the church

historian Adolf von Harnack (1851–1930) from Germany.[20] Lamprecht
then gave a series of lectures at Columbia University in 1904, which were
published in English the following year under the title *What Is History? Five
Lectures in the Modern Science of History.*[21] He received a fair amount of
attention in the United States; in 1906, he was elected an honorary member
of the American Historical Association, as Ranke had been a generation earlier, but it is questionable whether, with his speculative conceptions of laws
of history, he exerted any direct influence on the American scene.

Discussions of historical theory

The 1890s and early 1900s also witnessed lively discussions on the nature
of historical knowledge. Two important guidebooks to historical method
appeared at this time. Ernst Bernheim (1850–1942), *Lehrbuch der historischen Methode* (*Textbook of Historical Method*, 1889) and Charles-
Victor Langlois (1863–1929) and Charles Seignobos, *Introduction aux
études historiques* (*Introduction to the Study of History*, 1898) set forth
standards for scholarly research. They were translated into various languages, parts of Bernheim's book very quickly into Japanese. We already
mentioned Henri Berr's *Revue de synthèse historique* as an international
forum for exchanges on new approaches to historical studies. The most
intensive theoretical treatments of history as a field of inquiry, however, took
place in Germany. In a sense, this was a renewed discussion that went back
to Droysen's *Grundriss der Historik*, and his critique of Buckle, which we
dealt with previously. This debate was revived in 1883 in Wilhelm Dilthey's
(1833–1911) *Einleitung in die Geisteswissenschaften* (*Introduction to the
Humanities*),[22] an attempt to formulate a "critique of historical reason,"
parallel to Kant's *Critique of Pure Reason*. He took up an assumption that
played a key role in the historiographical tradition going back to Ranke and
Droysen, namely that history was a science but a humanistic science that differed from the natural sciences in not seeking abstract causal explanations
but rather was committed to "understanding" (*Verstehen*) human motivations that defied such explanation. Dilthey agreed with Kant that the nature
of the human mind prescribed a strict logic of inquiry. He was convinced
that real knowledge was possible in the *Geisteswissenschaften* (cultural sciences). Its truth did not exist in its correspondence to an outside reality; it
rather involved the active construction or reconstruction of the past by the
mind. As he commented, "[W]hat I experience within me is there for me as
a fact of consciousness because I become aware of it. . . . All experience has
its original connectedness in the condition of our consciousness in which it
appears, in the totality of our nature."[23] He stressed that all knowledge is
subjective, yet at the same time was convinced that the process of subjective
cognition nevertheless led to knowledge. Here he did not really go beyond
the role that Ranke and Droysen assigned to the function of understanding
(*Verstehen*), which made up the subject matter of history. *Verstehen* was

ultimately an act of intuition. But he was no more able to develop a methodology that could test the validity of intuitions. He emphatically wanted to free history from metaphysics but in fact fell back to the same metaphysical assumption as Ranke and Droysen in assuming that *Verstehen*, although an essentially subjective act, was rooted in an underlying reality.

Wilhelm Windelband (1848–1915) and Heinrich Rickert (1863–1936),[24] agreed with Droysen and Dilthey that intuitive understanding (*Verstehen*) provided a bridge between intuition and objective reality, yet they too were unable to develop a methodology by which intuitive knowledge could be tested against objective reality. Windelband was known for the strict division he made between the "nomothetic" methods of the natural sciences seeking generalizations and laws, and the "idiographic" method of history, aiming to grasp the individual character of historical phenomena, a distinction that fitted in well with the German historians' critique of Lamprecht, a critique that, as we saw, carried with it political implications. Rickert continued in this direction of thought, but he introduced two important ideas into the discussion that he shared with Max Weber, namely that the human sciences cannot dispense with concepts and that the defining aspects of a culture are the values they embody.

Yet the most important attack on the lack of clear method of the Historical School and at the same time on the positivistic approach of Lamprecht came from Max Weber. Like his Heidelberg colleague Rickert, Weber stressed that cultures must be studied in terms of the central values they embody but insisted, as Rickert did, that this study must not insert the values of the observer. Weber now speaks of social rather than of cultural sciences (*Geisteswissenschaften*) and is committed to formulating a methodology that will elevate the study of society to the rigor of other sciences.[25] Much more emphatically than Rickert or the Neo-Kantians in general, he denied that there are any values that possess validity beyond their respective cultures. The world of men is marked by conflicting values, none of which have a basis in science or reason. The thin link between ethics and reason, on which Windelband and Rickert still insisted, is cut.[26] But despite his extensive reading of Dilthey and Sigmund Freud – and of Friedrich Nietzsche – Weber maintained his firm belief in the possibility of rational thought unaffected by emotions or by the Freudian subconscious. None of the values of the cultures studied have any objective validity. But, he writes: "[I]t is and will remain true that methodologically correct proof in the social sciences, if it is to achieve its purpose, must be acknowledged as correct, even by a Chinese, who on the other hand may be deaf to our conception of the categorical imperative."[27] Weber recognizes that the cultural and social sciences deal with unique and qualitative events that require methods different from the natural sciences; nevertheless, all sciences, including the cultural and social sciences, require clear concepts, theories, and generalizations. But insofar as cultures are webs of meaning, they require concepts that seek to understand these meanings in their concrete setting. Thus he calls for what he terms a *verstehende Soziologie*, which unlike the German Historical School sees *Verstehen* not as an intuitive act but as one involving rational concepts. He therefore sides with the Viennese economist Carl Menger (1840–1921) in his critique of the one-sided historical approach of Gustav von Schmoller and of the German Historical School of National Economics,[28] which ignored regularities in economic behavior, but he also criticized Menger and classical political economy for reducing economics to ahistorical laws.[29] Social science was possible because, within cultures and societies, individuals behave according to certain accepted standards. Weber rejects the idea of the Historical School that the behavior of individuals and social groups is incommensurable. According to Weber, to assume that "freedom of will is identical with irrationality of action is a mistake. . . . Unpredictable behavior (*Unberechenbarkeit*) is the privilege of the insane."[30] Thus there are patterns inherent in every society, and the task of the social scientist is to reduce them to concepts. Although Weber believed in the possibility of rational thought, he stressed that the character of a society and culture does not reveal itself directly to the observer but reflects the questions that the latter poses. Like Durkheim, Weber believed that a science of societies must operate with typologies but that they do not fully correspond to reality. They are attempts to grasp reality. Weber calls them "ideal types," which must be tested empirically and conceptually against social reality.

Yet there was a contradiction between Weber's radical ethical relativism and his insistence on the meaninglessness of the world on the one hand and his actual philosophy of history on the other. Although he would not acknowledge it, he held positions that came close to social Darwinism. Weber was an ardent German nationalist who saw history as a struggle for national survival. The world was marked by a perpetual struggle of *Weltanschauungen* (world outlooks). The task of politics was not to decide on the validity of these outlooks but, with a sense for reality, to decide how this outlook can be implemented. An ethics like that of the Sermon on the Mount overlooked these realities and was thus irresponsible.[31] In one of his early writings arguing against the influx of Polish agricultural workers into Germany, he adopted an outspokenly racist position. Thus the Germans who had competed with the Poles in an age-old struggle in which they had proved their cultural superiority were being threatened with displacement by an "inferior race" (*tieferstehende Rasse*).[32] He did not repeat this later, when he praised W. E. B. Du Bois as an outstanding intellectual and published him in the *Archiv für Sozialwissenschaft*. He continued to stress that Germany in the international struggle for survival must move in the direction of a parliamentary democracy, not because he championed democracy but because he believed that the only way to survive in the international power struggle was to overcome the alienation of the working classes and to curb the outdated power of the aristocracy and the bureaucracy. In the early stages of World War I, he championed extensive annexations, but his sense of reality led him by 1917 to call for a negotiated peace without annexations and for political reforms and, in November 1918, to support the German republic.[33]

Throughout his scholarly career, Weber undertook a comparison of Western civilization with those of the non-West. This assumed that each of these civilizations, past and present, possessed a set of values that determined its character. Yet despite his value relativism, this comparison led him to the assumption that the West represented a superior culture. He saw the West as possessing a particular form of rationalism. Science, in the form of abstract logical or empirical thinking, existed only in the West. Other cultures had forms of science too but never in this abstract form. The history of the West was marked by a process of intellectualization in which old religious and metaphysical illusions were abandoned in favor of scientific ones. On the one hand, the West represented one culture among others; on the other hand, its conception of reason and science corresponded to universally valid criteria of logical thought.[34] In the final analysis this process of intellectualization meant not only intellectual progress but also the destruction of cherished values and the confrontation of modern man with the meaninglessness of existence.

The existential crisis of modern civilization

These conceptions of progress in Western history, leading on the one hand to a better world and on the other hand to conditions created by this very progress in which old beliefs and values would be destroyed and humanity plunged into an existential crisis, existed side by side in the same thinkers: Durkheim, Freud, and Weber are among the more striking examples. We have been dealing with historians and philosophers most of whom occupied moderate positions. But a broad segment of public opinion went much further in the direction of notions of Western supremacy and outright racism. The 1890s and early 1900s saw anti-Jewish pogroms in the Russian Empire and Romania, as well as the Dreyfus Affair in France, although in the last instance Dreyfus and the Third Republic were vindicated. The decision of the United States Supreme Court in 1896 in *Plessy vs. Ferguson* that racial segregation, as it was practiced in the South, did not violate the U.S. Constitution reflected the climate of opinion at the time, just as the Court's decision in *Brown vs. Board of Education* in 1954, declaring racial segregation in the schools unconstitutional, reflected a changed climate. Indicative of the climate at the turn of the century was that the world looked on when the Germans exterminated a large part of the native population in the so-called Herero War (1904–1908) in German Southwest Africa (now Namibia). In an effort to create a positive historical image of these actions, monuments were built in Germany to commemorate the German soldiers who died in the war. Already earlier, millions of Africans had been murdered in what became the Belgian Congo. These incipient genocides were legitimated by historical conceptions of the racial and cultural superiority of the West.

Historiography between two world wars (1914–1945)

The historians during World War I[35]

On July 31, 1914, on the immediate eve of the outbreak of hostilities, a French fanatic nationalist assassinated Jean Jaurès, the socialist political leader and historian who had issued a last appeal for France to stay out of the war. The assassination reflected the strength of nationalistic sentiment that resulted in a change in the political climate.

The period between 1890 and 1914 had been marked, at least in the West but to an extent also elsewhere, by a broadening of the historical perspective away from a narrow focus on state-oriented history with a concentration on diplomatic and military history relatively isolated from interdisciplinary approaches to social, economic, and cultural history. Moreover, despite persistent nationalist sentiments, the period also saw increasing international communication. The latter trend was interrupted and in some cases even reversed with the outbreak of the war in 1914.

It is frightening to see how broad the consensus was in all belligerent countries in support of the war. There were jubilant mass demonstrations in Berlin, Paris, Vienna, St. Petersburg, and London. Everywhere the churches – Lutheran, Roman Catholic, Russian Orthodox in England, not only the Anglicans but with the exception of the Quakers also the Dissenting churches – invoked God's blessings on their respective armies. And the intellectuals and writers solidly supported the war, at least in its early stages as a war of defense of their culture, among them such thinkers as Sigmund Freud, Emile Durkheim, Max Weber, and Thomas Mann (1875–1955). There were few dissident voices, foremost in Germany Albert Einstein (1879–1955) and in France the novelist Romain Rolland (1866–1944). Open critics of the war, such as the philosopher Bertrand Russell (1872–1970) in England and Rosa Luxemburg (1871–1919) in Germany and, in 1917 after America's entry into the war, the socialist leader Eugene Debs (1855–1926) were incarcerated.

It is a shame how intellectuals and historians in particular subordinated their scholarship to what they considered their patriotic duty of serving the war effort. Given the growing influence of nationalism, this was by no means a solely Western phenomenon. In France, Ernest Lavisse (1842–1922) and Emile Durkheim, who had both studied in Germany and had held a high regard for German intellectual traditions, now invented a line from Luther to the Hohenzollern monarchy, Bismarck, and Treitschke's glorification of ruthless *Macht* (power). Members of the faculty of modern history at Oxford University followed a similar line of argument in a series *Why We Are at War: Great Britain's Case*.[36] The war was seen as the confrontation of two cultures, the one of the Western Allies based on the "state of law," the other represented by Prussia on Machiavellian raison d'état, the pursuit of political power, if necessary by war. The authors recognized two Germanies, the militaristic Germany of Potsdam and that of German culture of Weimar, which was subordinated to the former. The official counterpropaganda of the Germans, which had broad support from the historians and intellectuals generally, was that this was a clash of two cultures, the "Ideas of 1914," embodied in the political status quo in Germany with its alleged sense for social justice and its roots in a rich cultural tradition, in contrast to the "Ideas of 1789" of democratic France and England lacking this sense of responsibility. The writer Thomas Mann argued that Germany embodied *Kultur* (culture) with its philosophic idealism and depth and sense of community, whereas the Western Allies represented *Zivilisation* with its rationalistic mind set and its crude materialism.[37] The international cooperation among historians in the prewar period broke down, not to be revived soon after the war. The *Vierteljahrschrift für Sozial- und Wirtschaftsgeschichte*, which had been published in four languages pointing in the new directions of social history, now became a strictly German journal that specialized more narrowly on institutional and administrative history. The breakdown in crossnational communication was reflected in the rupture between Karl Lamprecht and Henri Pirenne (1862–1935), a Belgian, who had been a mediator between German and French social historians. When Karl Lamprecht, who had been a good friend of Pirenne but was an ardent supporter of the German cause including the invasion of Belgium, sought to visit Pirenne, Pirenne slammed the door in front of him.[38] Pirenne also well into the 1920s opposed inviting German historians to international conferences.

Never before had governments enlisted historians as effectively in the propaganda efforts as during World War I and were able to find support among the historians. This was true in all belligerent countries, interestingly most so in the United States where the mass circulation of modern media was most developed. Almost immediately after the U.S. entry into the war in 1917, President Woodrow Wilson created the Committee of Public Information, which with the full cooperation of the American Historical Association distributed propaganda pamphlets to tens of thousands potential readers. The American Historical Association, moreover, founded a history teacher's magazine instructing high school teachers how to teach the historical background of the war. Proportionately more teachers were dismissed from American universities and colleges than in any other country involved in the war. The way historians were recruited in the various European countries made for greater social and political homogeneity than in the academic profession in the United States. Although many intellectuals saw a threat to Western democracy if Germany were victorious, there were also pacifists. A fair number of historians and others were dismissed from both state and private institutions of higher learning. Charles Beard, who thought it was necessary for the United States to enter the war against Germany, resigned his position at Columbia University in 1917 to protest the violation of academic freedom after a number of his colleagues opposing the war were dismissed. Also at Columbia University, James Harvey Robinson was pressured to revise his widely circulated textbook, *Medieval and Modern Times*, to introduce a more anti-German note, and he complied.[39]

In Germany, this pressure to comply was not necessary because of the solid consensus among the historians. One exception occurred when Veit Valentin lost his *venia legendi* in 1917 (his permission to teach at the university level) because of his supposed lack of patriotism.[40] His *venia legendi* was not restored after the war. German historians massively supported the calls for public support of German war policy. The most famous and ultimately infamous of these declarations was the *Aufruf an die Kulturwelt* (Proclamation to the World of Culture),[41] signed by 93 of the most distinguished German intellectuals, scientists, artists, and writers, who defended the invasion of Belgium and who saw no conflict between the German military tradition and German culture. A similar declaration was signed by 4,000 teachers at institutions of higher learning. The Proclamation of the 93 contained an ominous racist note when it accused the Allies of "inciting shamefully Mongols and Negroes against the white race" and "thus hav(ing) no right to call themselves defenders of civilization." A dissenting proclamation, supported by Albert Einstein, was signed by eight persons.[42]

Nevertheless, the consensus among German historians and intellectuals generally broke down in the course of the war. In 1917, the Reichstag adopted a Peace Resolution, which had no parallel in other belligerent countries, and called on the German government to negotiate a peace of understanding with no territorial annexations. The Resolution was ignored by the government, now dominated by the military under Generals Paul von Hindenburg (1847–1934) and Erich Ludendorff (1865–1937). At this point a number of important intellectuals, including the historian Friedrich Meinecke, the historically oriented social scientists Max Weber, Alfred Weber (1868–1958), and Ernst Troeltsch formed a loose political group that called for moderation in the pursuit of the war and political reforms in the direction of parliamentary democracy. This division – between historians who held fast to the established political order and the established ways of doing history and a minority of historians and social scientists who were moderate in the aims but nevertheless saw the need of reforms both in politics and in scholarship – would significantly shape the intellectual and scholarly climate in post–World War I Germany.[43]

The critique of rationality and modernity and the defenders of the Enlightenment

Woodrow Wilson had proclaimed that the war was being fought "to make the world safe for democracy" and had, in his Fourteen Points, called for the self-determination of nations. Instead, the period between the two wars was marked by political instability in all but the old established democracies in Western and Northern Europe and in the United States. Democratic governments were established in the new national states that emerged with the dismemberment of the prewar empires – Germany, Austria-Hungary, Ottoman Turkey, and Russia – but all of these new democracies with the exception of Czechoslovakia gave way to authoritarian regimes, as did Italy, Portugal, Germany, and ultimately Spain. Territories were so distributed by the victorious Allies that the defeated states had to yield land to the new states so that large restive minorities found themselves in these states. The October Revolution in what became the Soviet Union created an authoritarian state, committed to state socialism, that perceived itself as a challenge to the established social order of the capitalist world and was seen as such by the latter. The Nazis in Germany saw themselves as a bulwark against Bolshevism and at the same time wished to even scores with the Western democracies who had humiliated and punished Germany in the peace treaties of 1919.

This instability was reflected in a growing disenchantment with democracy and with modern civilization. This negative attitude was already voiced in the late nineteenth century by various historians and social thinkers coming from different political directions, such as Friedrich Nietzsche, Vilfredo Pareto (1848–1923), Georges Sorel (1847–1922), and in the interwar period by Johan Huizinga (1872–1945), the philosopher Martin Heidegger (1889–1976), the poets T. S. Eliot (1888–1965) and Ezra Pound (1885–1972), and many others. Their basic assessment of the world was that all sense of community had been lost in modern society and that democracy had led to the rise of the masses who destroyed all cultural values. Generally, as already in Nietzsche's writings in the 1870s and 1880s and still half a century later in José Ortega y Gassett's (1883–1955) *Revolt of the Masses*,[44] this critique emphatically rejected the idea of progress that had pointed to an enlightened, democratic modern world and that, as in the case of Italian Futurismo and Fascism and in a sense also in the Nazi movement, despite the latter's idealization of the medieval rural world, wanted to create a new social and political order led by a charismatic leader and inspired by an ultranationalistic myth.[45] This revolutionary idea of the myth also permeated the thought of Georges Sorel, a syndico-anarchist who rejected both the Marxist confidence in progress and scientific socialism, as well as the democratic socialist endorsement of reform, and urged revolutionary violence to sway the masses into concerted action. It is not surprising that Sorel was invoked by both Lenin and Mussolini.[46]

One of the key elements of this critique of modernity was the attack on rational thinking. Again, ideas propagated already before 1914, including Dilthey's stress on subjectivity, became important in philosophical discourse, at least on the Continent. An example for this antirationalism is the vitalistic philosophy of Henri Bergson (1859–1941), for whom the basic reality was life. For him, intelligence could deal only with the mechanical world of dead nature, but life could be understood only immediately, not rationally or empirically, but through intuition. The conception of what constitutes reality is thus totally transformed and a special role assigned to myth. This rejection of reality is carried even further by Martin Heidegger who sought an escape from scientific thinking in poetry and abandoned the Enlightenment heritage of reason and human rights. In Germany, this outlook was embraced particularly by the political right, to which Heidegger, who in 1933 as Rector of the University of Freiburg endorsed the Nazi program, belonged. A highly pessimistic note was struck in Oswald Spengler's (1880–1936) *Der Untergang des Abendlandes* (*Decline of the West*),[47] written during the war and published between 1918 and 1922 and widely read also outside of Germany; Spengler's conception of history is guided by an extreme fatalism. He presents a number of supposedly high cultures, one of which is the West, with each going through predetermined cycles. Each has its own character that determines its ways of reasoning. Thus there is no universal science or even mathematics; each culture has its own science and mathematics, and no communication is possible between these cultures. All begin in a heroic age of war and religious faith and lose their essential quality with urbanization and a turn from myth to science and technology. In the West, the age of classical culture was followed by that of civilization, which possesses the very characteristics of a society in which the masses dominate and culture is destroyed by commercialization. No creative thought is possible, as the Western world dissolves into an inchoate barbarism, to be replaced by a new civilization that begins from the heroic, mystic stage that marked the early West. The modern world stands at the edge of the abyss.

But the heritage of the Enlightenment was by no means dead, although it was very much embattled on the continent. Particularly in the Anglo-Saxon world but also in the Vienna Circle in the 1920s and 1930s, a version of logical positivism reaffirmed their confidence in a scientific approach. And the thinkers of this orientation, philosophers like Alfred Whitehead (1861–1947) and Bertrand Russell (1872–1970) in Great Britain and Karl Popper (1902–1994) and Rudolf Carnap (1891–1970), who were forced to emigrate from Vienna, remained firmly committed to democratic values.

The United States

How do these intellectual currents affect historical studies and historical writing? If we deal with the historical profession in the democratic countries in the West, relatively little. These historians remain sheltered in the institutional setting in which they worked, although we saw during World War I that their work was not immune to pressures for conformity from the outside. In the United States, the persecution of dissidents during the war continued during the Red Scares in the immediate postwar years. The professionalization of historical studies had everywhere increased specialization with the result that the historians within the universities were much more isolated from the general public than they had been in the nineteenth century. There were relatively few historians now who like Charles Beard were public intellectuals. The main trend toward a broad social and cultural history, begun at the turn of the century, continued in the interwar period. In the United States, the Progressive historians, whom have we already mentioned, continued to play an important role in their quest for a democratic history. Charles Beard coauthored the popular *The Rise of American Civilization* (1926) with his wife Mary (1876–1958). But despite their aim to be inclusive of the whole population, the Progressive historians still largely ignored women[48] and evaded the question of the subordination of blacks in American society.

There was also a current that went in a very different direction from the Progressive Movement, namely the outspokenly racist Dunning School,[49] which in its meticulous search of archives considered itself to be Rankean and objective. In this vein James G. Randall (1881–1953), in *Civil War and Reconstruction* (1937), sought to prove the innate inferiority of blacks as demonstrated by their allegedly total irresponsibility when they briefly were represented in the legislatures during the Southern Reconstruction immediately after the American Civil War. W. E. B. Du Bois, in *Black Reconstruction*[50] (1935), showed a very different picture in pointing at the positive achievements of black legislators in introducing much needed social reforms, reforms that survived the Reconstruction period. In a masterful final chapter, "The Propaganda of History,"[51] he argued how historical scholarship, in the guise of Rankean scrutiny of archival sources, could be used to sustain ideological, in this case racist, assumptions. Combining a Marxist analysis of class conflict with that of racial conflict, he set out to write a history in which the black lower classes were not silent passive subjects devoid of political ideas but active participants in the political process of the Reconstruction with an understanding of what they wanted. Nevertheless, it is striking that in 1935 he still almost totally ignored the place of women in the struggle for equality. At this point, there were no blacks and almost no women on the faculties of prestigious or even less prestigious universities and colleges in the United States or for that matter in Canada, and very few Jews.

An offspring of the "New History" in the United States was the history of ideas or intellectual history. Intellectual history represented a conscious attempt to go beyond the conventional political history and beyond the social history of the Progressive historians in order to reconstruct the mental outlooks underlying such histories. In the works of James H. Robinson, already discussed, and Carl Becker (1873–1945), for example in his *The Heavenly City of the Eighteenth-century Philosophers* (1932), there were attempts to understand broader social and political movements through the ideas that motivated them. Arthur Lovejoy (1873–1962), in *The Great Chain of Being*,[52] gave a further impulse to the history of ideas and in 1940 founded the *Journal of the History of Ideas*. The interest in a history of ideas was not new. Already in 1918 a series, *Studies in the History of Ideas*, was launched by the philosophy department at Columbia University.

Great Britain

As in the United States, World War I did not represent a marked break in British historiography from that of the prewar period. Much more so than in the United States, social history was closely related to economic history. As a matter of fact, a clear academic division existed between economic history and history as such. The latter continued largely along lines of traditional scholarship; the former opened up areas of social history. Two major topics occupied historians primarily in this period, what came to be called the crisis of the gentry in the transition from the sixteenth to the seventeenth centuries and the condition of the working class in the Industrial Revolution. Marxist theories did not yet occupy the role in these discussions that they played in Great Britain after World War II. None of the important historians, including Thomas Ashley (1860–1927), R.H. Tawney (1880–1962), M.M. Postan (1899–1981), and Eileen Power (1889–1940), were Marxists. Tawney, who was a founding editor in 1927 of the *Economic History Review*, in his *Religion and the Rise of Capitalism*, built on Max Weber rather than on Marx. All at one time were associated with the London School of Economics. Power had the distinction not only of being the first woman full professor at the London School of Economics but in her work, of which *Medieval People* (1923) became best known, of having shown that archival sources could be used to reconstruct the lives of ordinary people, including women. The occupation with intellectual and cultural history as later represented in the work of Isaiah Berlin (1909–1997) and Quentin Skinner still occupied a much more marginal role than in the United States.

Germany in the interwar period

The situation in Germany in the interwar period was different. It is striking how little the experience of the war affected the attitudes of the majority of the German academic historians. The historians, as were the intellectuals generally, were divided along the lines that, as we have already indicated, occurred during the war, between ultranationalists, for whom Bismarck's solution of the German question in 1871 constituted the high point of history, and moderate nationalists, who also were monarchists at heart but wanted to face the realities of defeat, recognize the Weimar Republic, and worked for a reconciliation with the former enemies in the West. They were much less willing to recognize the new borders in the East. The first group was ardently opposed to the Weimar Republic and wanted a return to authoritarian government. As historians, they maintained the prewar nation-oriented political history opposed to the social or cultural history initiative. There were few committed democrats, at least not in the older generation. Meinecke was the foremost of the moderate historians. They were joined by the historically oriented social thinkers, Max Weber and Ernst Troeltsch, who, however, both died in the very early years of the Weimar

Republic. The *Ideengeschichte* (history of ideas) that Meinecke pursued rested on German philosophic and historiographic traditions very different from Weber's sociological approach. His focus was on individual great personalities who through their ideas shaped political developments. Nevertheless this represented an opening away from the narrow power political orientation of the German historical establishment. Meinecke went through a transformation of his political outlook. In his first important book from this perspective, *Weltbürgertum und Nationalstaat* (*Cosmopolitanism and the National State*) (1907), he still maintained that the German cultural tradition and the power politics that led to the unification of Germany under Bismarck were in harmony and belonged together, a theme repeated by the signatories of the 93 intellectuals in 1914, which Meinecke incidentally did not sign.[53] In his more pessimistic book, *Die Idee der Staatsräson* (*Machiavellism*) (1924), he conceded that the experience of World War I had led him to give up his earlier belief in the ethical nature of power as pursued by Germany. In his *Entstehung des Historismus* (*Historism: The Rise of a New Historical Outlook*) (1936), in the face of Nazism, he completely isolated historical ideas from politics yet argued that the German tradition of historical thought constituted the highest point in the development of philosophy and, together with Luther, represented the two gifts that Germany had given mankind.

Nevertheless, it is to Meinecke's credit that despite his relatively conservative political and historiographical outlook and the fact that he was not entirely free of anti-Semitic prejudices, he was willing to work with younger historians, almost all of whom were committed democrats and many of Jewish ancestry, who came to Meinecke because they respected him but also because there was hardly anyone among the conservative historians with whom they could study.[54] They believed that historical studies must go in a new direction, toward a political history closely linked to other disciplines, foremost to sociology, particularly that of Max Weber, but also to psychology and economics. They were not satisfied with a history of events but wanted to analyze the political and social structures in which these events took place. And from a democratic perspective they wanted to examine critically the antidemocratic heritage of Bismarckian and post-Bismarckian Germany. Had they been permitted to remain in a democratic Germany, they might have contributed to the revitalization of the German historical profession. But all of them were forced to emigrate when the Nazis came to power in 1933 because of their Jewish ancestry, their liberal opinions, or in most cases both.[55] A historian from an older generation must be mentioned here, Otto Hintze (1861–1940), who had studied with Droysen and Schmoller and had devoted himself before 1918 to a study of Prussian administrative and economic institutions but who in the Weimar Republic underwent a change both in his political attitudes and in his methodological orientation. He now saw the state no longer as sacrosanct, as much of the Prussian School had done, but as an institution among others. His procedure in the great essays he wrote in the 1920s on feudalism and modern capitalism was no longer narrative but analytical in the manner of Max Weber. Hedwig Hintze (1884–1942),[56] his wife, should also be mentioned here, the first woman historian to receive the *venia legendi* at the University of Berlin, permitting her to teach there. She concentrated on a topic not popular in Germany at the time, namely the French Revolution. She was viewed critically because of her sympathy for the democratic aspects of the Revolution. Her work has been recognized only in recent years and is now considered innovative and significant. Because of her Jewish ancestry, she was forced to emigrate to the Netherlands, where she died just as she was scheduled to be deported to Auschwitz, apparently a suicide. She had been appointed to a professorship at the New School for Social Research in New York City but was denied a U.S. visa.

There was another, very different reaction in interwar Germany against the historical establishment, this time from young historians of the ultra-nationalistic right.[57] They regarded the state orientation of their elders as antiquated and elitist. They wanted a history that encompassed the population generally, focusing on the German *Volk*, defined as a racial community, bonded by blood and language, and excluding Jews and ethnic minorities. They rejected the borders of Germany imposed by the Allies at Versailles but also the pre-1918 borders and wanted Germany to expand to include all areas in which ethnic Germans lived, primarily in the East but also in the West, and they were prepared to expel non-Germans from these lands. In Social Darwinian terms, they saw history as the struggle of the races for survival. They looked forward to a war that would establish German supremacy in Europe at the cost of peoples whom they considered inferior. They thus foreshadowed the program of the Nazis in their opposition to the parliamentary democracy of the Weimar Republic, their call for legislation excluding Jews from public life, and their readiness to reshape the ethnic map of Europe, if necessary, by war. On the one hand they rejected the urban and cosmopolitan modernity of their time and dreamed of a return to a world of agrarian communities as it existed in premodern times. On the other hand they applied highly modern methods in their historical studies, as Werner Conze (1910–1986) did in his dissertation of 1934 on the small isolated German-speaking community of Hirschenhof[58] in Livonia. Conze, who combined historical, sociological, ethnographic, demographic, and statistical methods, except for his political assumptions was not very different from historians around the *Annales* journal in France. After 1945, Conze, who had cast off his racist doctrines and his Romantic agrarianism, played a key role in the West German profession in laying the foundations of a social history of modern industrial society.

It is striking how the German historical profession, which before 1914 had bitterly opposed Karl Lamprecht's turn to a cultural history and rejected the social history of Friedrich Meinecke's students in the 1920s, accepted the young advocates of a *Volk*-oriented history. This had a good deal to do with the antagonism against the parliamentary democracy of the Weimar Republic and their determination to revise the limitations that the Versailles Treaty had placed on Germany. Although few historians joined the Nazi Party, they agreed with much of its program, with the result that the Nazis made little effort to coordinate the work of the historians. Those historians who dissented or were of Jewish origin or both were forced to emigrate. In the course of the war, a large number of historians contributed to the studies necessary for the removal of non-German ethnic populations.[59] It is shameful that in 1933, when it would not yet have endangered their lives, no historian of note had the courage or conviction to protest the dismissal of their colleagues, and few showed any eagerness to welcome them back after 1945. Repression in Fascist Italy resulted in two of the leading historians, Gaetano Salvemini (1873–1957) and Arnaldo Momigliano (1908–1987) being forced into exile.[60] In Romania, Nicolae Iorga (1871–1940) was murdered by the political police.[61]

Marxist forms of historiography

Another form of authoritarian rule was practiced in the Soviet Union beginning shortly after the Bolshevik seizure of power. Its control was even more total than in the Fascist states and in Nazi Germany. We must be careful, however, with the use of the term "totalitarianism" because in both Fascist states and in Nazi Germany, state and party aimed for total control, but there were always niches in which historians could work independently. But nowhere were historians in the interwar period in Europe threatened as directly and physically as with the purges, which included deportation and actual execution, as under Stalin (1880–1953) after 1929. Historical studies were guided by a doctrine that called itself Marxist-Leninist. Although it proceeded from a materialistic conception of history holding that the clash of economic forces determined history, Vladimir Ilich Lenin (1870–1924) had introduced a voluntarist element into Marxism, which assigned a central role to the party to intervene and to guide the historical process. While Marx and Engels had still believed that there is an objective past that makes possible the scientific study of history, Marxism, as reinterpreted by Lenin, held that there was no such thing as science for science's sake, that all cognition reflected ideological positions, and that historical study, instead of reconstructing the past as it actually occurred, served the political needs of party and state. Nevertheless institutes of higher learning, foremost the central Institute of History at the Academy of Sciences of the USSR as well as the universities, trained historians in classical methods of source criticism. The further the topic was removed from issues of current politics, the greater was the degree of autonomy, provided Marxist language was preserved. Thus Soviet historians made important contributions to areas less directly subjected to party dogma such as medieval and ancient history and archaeology, and the edition and publication of sources. A good deal of Soviet historiography in the interwar and post–World War II period tended to be positivistic in the sense that historians avoided interpretation and let the facts speak for themselves, protecting themselves (and there was an increasing number of women historians) with copious references to the works of Marx, Lenin, and Stalin. And Soviet historians made important contributions to areas that had been insufficiently explored, not only the history of the working class but also of that of the lower classes generally, and turned to what came to be known as material culture, which touched on aspects of everyday life.[62]

But Marxism began to play an important but different role in historical thought in continental Europe outside the Soviet Union, which has led to the coinage of the term "Western Marxism." Two interpreters of Marxist theory, Georg Lukács (1885–1971) and Antonio Gramsci (1891–1937), wrote their key works in the interwar period but had their main influence only in the 1960s. Lukács, originally from Budapest, who had played an important role in the Communist revolution in Hungary in 1919, belonged to the intellectual circle around Max Weber in Germany and was very much aware of the discussions of the time. A committed Marxist and Communist, who viewed history as a dialectical process driven by class conflict, he nevertheless believed that the materialist interpretation of Marx was out of tune with the intellectual climate of twentieth-century Europe. In *History and Class Consciousness* (1923), he argued that Marx had been misunderstood by vulgar Marxists as a materialist and a determinist. A careful reading of *Das Kapital* would show that Marx's key concern was the critical examination of what Marx had called the "fetishism of commodities," which places the accumulation of capital and profit ahead of human needs. Lukács placed Marx in a philosophic tradition that went back to Hegel. Marx now emerged as a critic of a civilization who wished to reduce all knowledge to abstract, dehumanized, rather than dialectical reason. Modern science, Lukács argued, reflected this insistence to reduce the qualitative aspects of life to quantities and needed to be replaced by a new Marxist science that put human values and needs in the foreground. *History and Class Consciousness* was immediately condemned by the Communist International, and Lukács bowed to the dictate of Moscow and withdrew the book, which was only republished in 1967 in a changed political and intellectual climate but was nevertheless widely circulated in pirated editions. Antonio Gramsci, who headed the Italian Communist party in the immediate post-World War I period, was incarcerated by Mussolini in 1926. After 11 years in prison, he was released because of his poor health and died very shortly afterward. In prison he confronted the question why a proletarian revolution did not occur in Italy and why instead Fascism seized power and consolidated the capitalist order. On scraps of paper, published as *Prison Notebooks*[63] after the demise of Fascism, Gramsci held that the victory of Fascism could obviously not be explained in classical Marxist terms of economic determinism. It had to take into account the "hegemony" (Gramsci's term) that the governing classes exerted over the minds of the working classes. A successful proletarian revolution required the creation of a proletarian consciousness and an alternative revolutionary culture.

These two works, which had an immense impact on Marxist thought only in the 1960s, did not yet replace classical notions of class in historical writing. The most important center of Marxist historiography in the interwar period outside the Soviet Union was France. The major topic to which Marxist historians turned was the French Revolution. Now, for the first time, Marxist-oriented historians were represented at the French universities. Briefly, they tried to interpret the French Revolution in classical Marxist terms as a bourgeois revolution that put an end to the remnants of the feudal order. The most innovative of these historians was doubtless Georges Lefebvre (1874–1959). Lefebvre began his publishing career in 1924 with an in-depth study based on careful analysis of archival sources in a specific locality, the Département du Nord, still maintaining the thesis of the bourgeois revolution but showing significant differences within social groups and in *The Coming of the French Revolution* (1939) showed the extent to which various classes beside the bourgeoisie – the lower middle classes, the peasantry, and the nobility – each played a role in the upheaval of 1789. His most important contribution, however, was his *The Great Fear of 1789: Rural Panic in Revolutionary France* (1932), in which he modified a purely economic interpretation of the peasant uprisings in the summer of 1789 by introducing psychological analyses of mass behavior. In an essay that followed on the collective mentalities of the revolutionary crowds, Lefebvre disputed the claim by the conservative psychologist Gustave Le Bon (1841–1931) that the crowds in their fury had no clear ideas of what they wanted by arguing that in fact the archival sources showed that they were more than an impassioned mob but had a conception of a moral order that motivated them, thus endowing them with a human face.

The early Annales *School*

The most innovative initiative in social history in the interwar period came from two French historians, Lucien Febvre (1878–1956) and Marc Bloch (1886–1944), the founders in 1929 of the journal *Annales d'histoire économique et sociale*. Febvre and Bloch very much expanded and modified what had been understood as social and economic history since the turn of the century in North America, Great Britain, Belgium, and Scandinavia, and by Schmoller and Weber in Germany. Two early works exemplify what Febvre and Bloch had in mind: Febvre's dissertation of 1911, *Philippe II et la Franche Comté*[64] and Marc Bloch's *Les rois thaumaturges* (*The Royal Touch*)[65] of 1924. Febvre took Henri Berr's call for a historical synthesis seriously when he wrote the history of a region, the Franche Comté at the time of the Protestant Reformation. He aspired to create an integrated history that portrayed the interplay of geographic, economic, social, religious, and political factors and at the same time sought to recapture everyday culture. Febvre built on French historiographic rather than on German scholarly traditions, which had influenced French professional studies in the last third of the nineteenth century, on Jules Michelet's combination of social, cultural, and political history, and on Vidal de la Blache's human geography, which stressed the physical framework in which all history takes place but which, in contrast to the environmental German determinist Friedrich Ratzel, whom we have already mentioned, stressed the role that humans play in the shaping of their environment. Like Jean Jaurès, whom he admired, he portrayed the conflict between nobility and bourgeoisie in the emergence of a modern world but even more than Jaurès tried to show that this conflict could not be understood primarily in economic terms but involved outlooks and cultural patterns. Bloch's *Royal Touch* dealt with the belief in late medieval and early modern France and England that the king could cure scurvy by touching the afflicted person, a belief that this was part of the sacred character of kingship that persisted even among those who were not healed. Bloch here touched on the question of collective mentality. He was aware of what anthropologists like James Fraser (1854–1941) in *The Golden Bough* (1890) and Lucien Lévi-Bruhl (1857–1939) had to say about sacred kingship and primitive mentality.

Unlike Bloch, Febvre showed a great interest in the history of religion, particularly at the time of the Reformation, with a focus on collective attitudes. Thus in his *Martin Luther* (1928),[66] he did not deal primarily with the man but with a theme similar to that of his dissertation on the *Franche Comté*, a new religious outlook that reflected the bourgeoisie's desire for greater rationality and clarity than Catholicism offered. He attempted to relate religious to social history and yet avoid a reduction of the former to the latter. Febvre's most important work was most certainly his book on the religion of Rabelais, *The Problem of Unbelief in the Sixteenth Century: The Religion of Rabelais* (1942),[67] in which he raised the question whether Rabelais was an atheist as has often been maintained and concluded that he could not have been one because the *"outillage mental"* (mental tool, Febvre had language in mind) for being an atheist was lacking. Foreshadowing the later linguistic turn, he examined the language of the sixteenth century, which did not provide the concepts needed for unbelief. To declare Rabelais an atheist was therefore anachronistic.

This structuralist note was even more pronounced in Bloch's work. In 1931, he published his *French Rural History*, an attempt to write a comparative history of agriculture in France and England but particularly between the North and the South of France. His approach in this work was of pronouncedly material orientation. He wanted to establish what tools were used in the various regions and at various times and compare the management of fields. He decided to proceed from the present, about which we know the most, to the past and through aerial photography to discover how fields were organized through time. Bloch was aware, however, that cultural factors influenced the use of tools and field patterns. Yet his most important work was doubtless his *Feudal Society* (1939–1940), an examination of four hundred years of European history from the ninth to the fourteenth centuries. Several things are striking. This was not a history along national but along European lines. It did not concentrate on the political structure of feudalism but on the interrelation of the various aspects of the culture. It paid attention to how medieval people viewed the world around them – their perceptions of life, death, nature, time, and space – but also emphasized the role of money in the transformation of medieval society in the rise of towns and commerce. This historical sociology is more indebted to Durkheim's conception of collective representation than to Weber's more institutional approach. Like Weber, Bloch wanted to create an ideal type of a society that can then be compared with other societies. In his final chapter, he suggests that forms of feudalism may have existed in other cultures; he mentions Japan as a possible subject of comparative studies. Incidentally, Durkheim's sociological approach also influenced the work of modern Turkish historians.[68] What is striking in Durkheim's sociology and in Bloch's history is the neglect of individuals. *Feudal Society* is a history in which mankind is seen in collective terms, but we do not meet real people.

From 1920 to 1933, Febvre and Bloch were colleagues in Strasbourg, which only very recently had been returned to France. With offices next to each other, they steadily exchanged views. Together with Henri Pirenne in Belgium, they planned the creation of a journal that, although only in French, would serve the purposes that the *Vierteljahrschrift für Sozial- und Wirtschaftsgeschichte* had served for international communication and would have an even broader conception of what constituted economic and social history. In 1933 Febvre went to the prestigious Collège de France in Paris, while Bloch in 1936 was appointed to the professorship of economic history at the Sorbonne in Paris, succeeding the already mentioned author of French labor history, Henri Hauser (1866–1946). It is noteworthy that Bloch's conception of economic history was sufficiently recognized in France for him to be offered this chair. The *Annales d'histoire économique et sociale*, now located in Paris, received acceptance not only among many French historians, although by no means a majority, but also historians in Scandinavia, Great Britain, Brazil, and elsewhere. In Poland a journal with the almost identical Polish title, *Annals of Social and Economic History*, was founded in 1931 by Franciszek Bujak (1875–1953) and Jan Rutkowski (1886–1949) who were in close contact with the French *Annales*.

A final remark: Although Febvre and Bloch were French patriots – Bloch volunteered for the French army at an advanced age, fought in the *Résistance*, and was executed by the Germans – neither wrote nation-oriented history. Their histories either centered on a region or more often were transnational and comparative. Moreover, it is important to note that in contrast not only to traditional historical narratives but also to most sociological approaches at the time, Febvre and Bloch in their work abandoned the linear chronology pointing to the progress of the Western world that had been widely accepted by historians in Europe and North America since the professionalization of historical studies in the nineteenth century.

Notes

1 On a comparison of professionalization in France and the United States with that of Germany, see Gabriele Lingelbach, *Klio macht Karriere. Die Institutionalisierung der Geschichtswissenschaft in Frankreich und den USA in der zweiten Hälfte des 19. Jahrhunderts* (Göttingen, 2003).

2 Karl Lamprecht's influence in Japan was mainly seen in the so-called "Cultural History School," which arose in the 1920s and was represented by the work of Tsuda Sōkichi and Nishida Naojirō. See chapter 5 for more details and Naramoto Tatsuya, "Bunka shigaku (Cultural History)" in Association of Historical Research and Association of the Study of Japanese History, ed., *Nihon rekishi Kōza* (*Lectures on Japanese History*), vol. 8 (Tokyo, 1968), 221–245; Nagahara Keiji, *20 seiki Nihon no rekishigaku* (*20th Century Japanese Historiography*) (Tokyo, 2005), 81–87.

3 Roger Chickering, *Karl Lamprecht: A German Academic Life (1856–1915)* (Atlantic Highlands, 1993); Luise Schorn-Schütte, *Karl Lamprecht: Kulturgeschichtsschreibung zwischen Wissenschaft und Politik* (Göttingen, 1984); Matthias Middell, *Weltgeschichtsschreibung im Zeitalter der Verfachlichung und Professionalisierung: Das Leipziger Institut für Kultur- und Universalgeschichte*, 3 vols. Vol. 1, *Das Institut unter der Leitung Karl Lamprechts* (Leipzig, 2005).

4 (Leipzig, 1891–1911).

5 Chickering, *Karl Lamprecht*, 268–269.

6 Karl Lamprecht, *Deutsches Wirtschaftsleben im Mittelalter: Untersuchung über die Entwicklung der materiellen Kultur des platen Landes auf Grund der Quellen* (Leipzig, 1885–1886).

7 Charles Seignobos, *Regime féodale en Bourgogne jusqu'en 1360: étude sur la société et les institution d'une province au Moyen-Âge* (Paris, 1882).

8 Steven Lukes, *Emile Durkheim: His Life and Work: A Historical and Critical Study* (Stanford, 1985).

9 Paul Vidal de la Blache, *Géographie universelle* (Paris, 1927–1948) and *Principles of Human Geography* (New York, 1926).

10 On the political and intellectual atmosphere at the German universities and its divisions, see Fritz Ringer, *The Decline of the German Mandarins: The German Academic Community, 1890–1933* (Middletown, 1990).

11 William Keylor, *Academy and Community: The Foundation of the French Historical Profession* (Cambridge, MA, 1975).

12 William Keylor, *Jacques Bainville and the Renaissance of Royalist History in the Twentieth Century* (Baton Rouge, 1979).

13 Richard Hofstadter, *The Progressive Historians: Turner, Beard, Parrington* (New York, 1968); Ernst Breisach, *American Progressive History: An Experiment in Modernization* (Chicago, 1993).

14 Carl Lotus Becker, *The Declaration of Independence: A Study in the History of Political Ideas* (New York, 1922) and *The Heavenly City of the Eighteenth-century Philosophers* (New Haven, 1932).

15 On Beard, see Hoftstadter, *The Progressive Historians*; Peter Novick, *That Noble Dream: The "Objectivity Question" and the American Historical Profession* (Cambridge, 1988); Breisach, *American Progressive History*; and Ellen Nore, *Charles A. Beard: An Intellectual Biography* (Carbondale, 1983).

16 See Herbert Butterfield, *The Whig Interpretation of History* (London, 1931).

17 Anatole G. Mazour, *Modern Russian Historiography* (Westport, 1975); Thomas M. Bohn, *Russische Geschichtswissenschaft von 1880 bis 1905: Pavel N. Miljukov und die Moskauer Schule* (Köln, 1998).

18 For a comprehensive study of Tsuda Sōkichi's ideas of history and historiography, see Ueda Masaki, ed., *Tsuda Sōkichi* (Tokyo, 1974).

19 Q. Edward Wang, *Inventing China through History: The May Fourth Approach to Historiography* (Albany, 2001), 67–72.

20 *Congress of Arts and Sciences: Universal Exposition, St. Louis 1904*, vol. 2 (Boston, 1906).

21 (New York, 1905).

22 English: *Introduction to the Human Sciences: An Attempt to Lay a Foundation for the Study of Society and History* (Detroit, 1988). On Dilthey, see Jacob Owensby, *Dilthey and the Narrative of History* (Ithaca, 1994); Charles Bambach, *Heidegger, Dilthey, and the Crisis of Historicism* (Ithaca, 1995); Frederick C. Beiser, *The German Historicist Tradition* (Oxford, 2011).

23 Cited in Georg G. Iggers, *The German Conception of History: The National Tradition of Historical Thought from Herder to the Present* (Middletown, 1983), 135.

24 On Windelband and Rickert and Neo-Kantianism, see Thomas Willey, *Back to Kant* (Detroit, 1979); Klaus Köhnke, *Entstehung und Aufstieg des Neokantianismus* (Frankfurt, 1986); Erich Kreiter, *Philosophy as Weltanschauung ib Trendelenburg, Dilthey und Windelband* (Amsterdam, 2007); Sebastian Luft and Rudolf Makreel, eds., *Neo-Kantianism in Contemporary Philosophy* (Amsterdam, 2010).

25 Max Weber, " 'Objectivity' in Social Science and Social Policy" in H. H. Gerth and C. Wright Mills, eds., *Max Weber on the Methodology of the Social Sciences* (Glencoe, 1949).

26 Max Weber, "Politics as a Vocation" in H. H. Gerth and C. Wright Mills, eds., *From Max Weber: Essays in Sociology* (New York, 1946), 76–128.

27 Weber, " 'Objectivity' in Social Science," 58.

28 Carl Menger, *Die Irrtümer des Historismus in der deutschen Nationalökonomie* (Vienna, 1884).

29 Max Weber, "Roscher und Knies und die logischen Probleme der historischen Nationalökonomie" in J. C. B. Mohr and Paul Siebeck, eds.,*Gesammelte Aufsätze zur Wissenschaftslehre* (Tübingen, 1968), 1–145.

30 Cited in Iggers, *German Conception of History*, 163.

31 Weber, "Politics as a Vocation," 119.

32 Cited in Iggers, *German Conception of History*, 169. See also Wolfgang J. Mommsen, *Max Weber and German Politics 1890–1920* (Chicago, 1984).

33 Mommsen, *Max Weber and German Politics 1890–1920*.

34 Max Weber, *The Protestant Ethic and the Spirit of Capitalism* (New York, 1958), "Introduction," 13–31.

35 On the universities in Germany, Russia, France, and Great Britain in World War I, see Trude Maurer, ed., *Kollegen-Kommilitonen-Kämpfer: Europäische Universitäten im Ersten Weltkrieg* (Stuttgart, 2006); also Notker Hammerstein, "The First World War and Its Consequences" in Walter Rüegg, ed., *A History of the Universities in Europe*, vol. 3 (Cambridge, 2004), 641–645.

36 Stuart Wallace, *War and the Image of Germany: British Academics 1914–1918* (Edinburgh, 1988).

37 See Thomas Mann, *Betrachtungen eines Unpolitischen* (1918); English: *Reflections of an Unpolitical Man* (New York, 1983).

38 Chickering, *Karl Lamprecht*, 439.

39 Novick, *That Noble Dream*, ch. 5, "Historians on the Home Front," 11–132.

40 Hans Schleier, "Veit Valentin" in his *Die bürgerliche Geschichtsschreibung der Weimarer Republik* (e. Berlin, 1975), 346–398; Elisabeth Fehrenbach, "Veit Valentin" in Wehler, *Deutsche Historiker*, vol. 1, 69–85.

41 The complete text of *Aufruf an die Kulturwelt* with the 93 signatories can be found in Google (see also http://planck.bbaw.de/onlinetexte/Aufruf_An_die_Kulturwelt.pdf).

42 Albert Einstein, "Manifesto to the Europeans" (with G. F. Nicolai and F. W. Förster), mid-October 1914, in *The Collected Papers of Albert Einstein*, 8 vols. (Princeton, 1987–2002), vol. 6, 28–29.

43 Ringer, *Decline of the German Mandarins*.

44 José Ortega y Gasset, *The Revolt of the Masses* (London, 1932).

45 Jeffrey Herf, *Reactionary Modernism: Technology, Culture and Politics in Weimar Germany and the Third Reich* (Cambridge, 1986).

46 Jack Roth, *The Cult of Violence: Sorel and the Sorelians* (Berkeley, 1980).

47 English: (New York, 1926).

48 But see Mary Beard, ed., *America through Women's Eyes* (New York, 1933).

49 See William A. Dunning, *Reconstruction, Political and Economic* (New York, 1907).

50 W. E. B. Du Bois, *Black Reconstruction in America: An Essay on the Role Which Black Folks Played in the Attempt to Reconstruct Democracy in America 1860–1920* (New York, 1935).

51 W. E. B. Du Bois, "The Propaganda of History" in his *Black Reconstruction: An Essay toward a History of the Part Which Black Folk Played in the Attempt to Reconstruct Democracy in America, 1860–1880* (New York, 1956), 711–729.

52 Arthur Lovejoy, *The Great Chain of Being: A Study of the History of an Idea* (Cambridge, MA, 1936).

53 See note 41; also the article "The Manifesto of the Ninety-Three" in Wikipedia, which lists all 93 signatories, Meinecke is not among them.

54 Gerhard A. Ritter, ed., *Friedrich Meinecke – Akademischer Lehrer und emigrierte Schüler. Brief und Aufzeichnungen 1910–1977* (München, 2006).

55 Mario Keßler, *Deutsche Historiker im Exil (1933–1945)* (Berlin, 2005); Gabriele Eakin-Thimme, *Geschichte im Exil: Deutschsprachige Historiker nach 1933* (München, 2005); Peter T. Walther, "Von Meinecke zu Beard? Die nach 1933 in die USA emigrierten Neuhistoriker," Ph. D. Dissertation, State University of New York at Buffalo, 1989. See also Axel Fair-Schulz and Mario Kessler, eds., *German Scholars in Exile* (Lanham, 2011).

56 Schleier, "Hedwig Hintze" in his *Bürgerliche Geschichtsschreibung*, 272–303; Steffen Kaudelka, *Rezeption im Zeitalter der Konfrontation: Französische Geschichtswissenschaft und Geschichte in Deutschland 1920–1940* (Göttingen, 2003), 241–408; Peter Th. Walther, "Die Zerstörung eines Projekts. Hedwig Hintze, Otto Hintze und Friedrich Meinecke" in Gisela Bock and Daniel Schönplug, eds., *Friedrich Meinecke in seiner Zeit* (Stuttgart, 2006), 211–226; Peter Th. Walther, "Hedwig Hintze in den Niederlanden 1939–1942" in Keßler, *Deutsche Historiker im Exil*, 197–222; also Otto und Hedwig Hintze, *"Vergangenheit und laß nicht auf zu kämpfen": die Korrespondenz 1929–1940* (Essen, 2004). Walther's "Hedwig Hintze in den Niederlanden 1939–1942" says it is not certain that it was a suicide.

57 Willi Oberkrome, *Volksgeschichte: Methodische Innovation und völkische Ideologisierung in der deutschen Geschichtswissenschaft* (Göttingen, 1993); Winfried Schulze, *Deutsche Geschichtswissenschaft nach 1945* (München, 1989), ch. 17.

58 *Hirschenhof: die Geschichte einer deutschen Sprachinsel in Livonien* (*Hirschenhof: The History of a German-Speaking Community in Livonia*) (Berlin, 1934).

59 Ingo Haar and Michael Fahlbusch, *German Scholars and Ethnic Cleansing 1920–1945* (New York, 1945).

60 Edoardo Tortarolo, "Objectivity and Opposition: Some Emigré Historians in the 1930s and Early 1940s" in Q. Edward Wang and Franz Fillafer, eds., *The Many Faces of Clio: Cross-cultural Approaches to Historiography* (New York, 2007), 59–70.

61 William O. Oldsen, *The Historical and Nationalistic Thought of Nicolae Iorga* (Boulder, 1973). Iorga received his doctorate in 1893 from Karl Lamprecht. He was not a democrat and in fact was active in an anti-Semitic, xenophobic party. Apparently as a result of his conflicts with the Fascist Iron Guard and his opposition to the domination of Romania by Germany, he was murdered in November 1940.

62 T. Sanders, "Soviet Historiography" in Daniel Woolf, ed., *A Global Encyclopedia of Historical Writing* (New York, 1998), 854–856; Yuri L. Bessmertny, "August 1991 as Seen by a Soviet Historian, or the Fate of Medieval Studies in the Soviet Era," *American Historical Review*, 97:2 (June 1992), 803–816.

63 See Antonio Gramsci, *Selections from the Prison Notebooks of Antonio Gramsci* (London, 1971); David Forgacs, ed., *Antonio Gramsci: Selected Writings 1916–1935* (New York, 1988).

64 Lucien Febvre, *Philippe II et la Franche-Comté, etude d'histoire politique, religieuse et morale* (Paris, 1911); preceded by *La Franche-Comté* (Paris, 1905).

65 English: *Royal Touch: Sacred Monarch and Scrofula* (London, 1973).

66 English: *Martin Luther: A Destiny* (New York, 1929).

67 English: (Cambridge, MA, 1982).

68 Bernard Lewis, "History Writing and National Revival in Turkey" in *From Babel to Dragomans: Interpreting the Middle East* (London, 2004), 425–426.

5   The appeal of nationalist history around the world

Historical studies in the Middle East and Asia in the twentieth century

Ottomanism, Turkism, and Egyptianization: Nationalist history in the Middle East

The rise of modern education

Entering the twentieth century, two lines of development in historical practices occurred in the Middle East: the growth of national history and the professionalization of historical research and teaching. Both phenomena had a good deal to do with the Muslims' increasing contacts and interaction with the West. When Western powers intensified their pace for colonizing the world, heralding the age of new imperialism, they also exported nationalism to non-Western regions. In the 'Urābī Revolution in Egypt, nationalism had already become an effective weapon for the Muslims – and peoples of non-Western regions in general – to fight off the brunt of colonialism and imperialism. For nation-building, nationalizing the production of cultural and historical discourses was crucial, which led to educational reforms. As early as 1845, the Ottomans had already contemplated establishing a national university, though it (the University of Istanbul) was not founded until 1900. From the mid-nineteenth century on, a number of modern-type schools at secondary levels emerged in various parts of the Ottoman Empire (some were older ones after some refurbishment), and from their graduates, there emerged many political and intellectual leaders. The *Mülkiye* school, for example, produced, among others, Murad Bey (?–1912), a future leader of the Young Turks Movement, and 'Abdurrahmān Sheref, the last Imperial Historiographer and a transitional figure in the emergence of modern Ottoman/Turkish historiography.[1]

Syria and Egypt made similar attempts at "national schools," either privately such as through the work of Western missionaries or officially by khedivial fiat. In 1908, Prince Ahmad Fu'ad founded the Egyptian University (Cairo University after 1952), which became a state institution after the prince became King Fu'ad in 1925. In these modern schools, history teaching constituted a part of its core curriculum, marking a stark contrast to its neglectful status in such traditional institutions as the *Madrasah* and *al-Azhar*. This change paved the way for the professionalization of historical study; more and more histories were written by history professors working in these schools. By the 1920s, the first generation of professional historians appeared in the Middle East.

To the Ottomans, the rise of nationalism meant further fragmentation of their empire and weakening of the imperial power. Throughout the nineteenth century, as more and more regional powers sought independence and autonomy, such as in the Balkans and other European territories where the imperial strength had traditionally lain, the empire saw itself increasingly become the "sick man of Europe." Yet the Ottomans were not ready to concede to their fate. The last two decades of the nineteenth century saw the Young Ottomans rise to power, which ushered in a constitutional era in Ottoman history. By making attempts at establishing representative government, the empire seemed to have regained its strength by appealing to Ottomanism and pan-Islamism.

Ottomanism had its spokespersons in historiography, such as Ahmed Midhat (1844–1912), a versatile littérateur and prolific writer. Drawing on Western material, Midhat authored a universal history and a number of national histories of Europe, though his style was more journalistic than historical, which perhaps helped to render him one of the most widely read authors of his time. Midhat's broad influence reflected the zeitgeist of the constitutional era, characterized by an unprecedented interest in Western culture and history, including, needless to say, the idea of nationalism.[2] To a great extent, the nationalist influence was borne out in the Young Ottomans Movement, in that the movement prompted patriotism, or the love for *vatan* (fatherland), even though its main agenda was to restore the Ottoman *millet* (nation) as the owner and master of all Muslims. These ideas found their expressions in the writings of Ebüzziya Tevfik (1849–1913), the historian of the Young Ottomans, who was also influenced by Namık Kemāl's ideas of pan-Islamism. Different from Ahmad Midhat in interest and style, Ebüzziya was another noted figure in disseminating Western ideas and culture of the era.[3]

Thus, at the turn of the twentieth century, Ottomanism represented a prevalent form of nationalism in the Middle East. It not only held sway in Istanbul and its immediate surrounding areas in Anatolia but also precipitated positive and sympathetic responses in such faraway places as in Egypt, a chief challenger to the Ottoman imperium through much of the nineteenth century. Yet then after the 'Urābī Revolution of 1881–1882, Egypt had become quite different than before. The various reforms initiated by Muhammad 'Alī and continued by most of his followers had drained its revenue and, worse still, following the Revolution, it entered the period of British Occupation. In their resistance to foreign rule, Egyptians contemplated many options, including forming an alliance with the Ottoman Empire. Mustafa Kāmil (1874–1908) and Muhammad Farīd (1868–1919), two important nationalist historians of the time, were chief advocates of the Egyptian-Turkish cooperation against European powers. Kāmil was a protégé of 'Abdullāh al-Nadīm (1845–1896), a spokesman of the 'Urābī Revolution; together they founded the Nationalist Party, the first political party in Egypt. Farīd, who had a Turkish ancestor, also worked closely with the Nationalist Party and authored two histories, one on Egypt under Muhammad 'Alī and the other on the Ottoman Empire. Obviously, his decision to write these two books had a good deal to do with his political interest and perhaps even his Turkish ethnicity. Like the Young Ottomans, Kāmil and Farīd were ardent believers in pan-Islamism; on its tenets they developed a culturalist approach to describing and examining the conflict between the West and the Middle East. In his magnum opus, *The Eastern Question (Mas'alah al-Sharqiyyah)*, Kāmil analyzed, in both historical and religious terms, the modern woes that haunted the Ottoman Empire and its provinces. A major source of the problem, he opined, lay in the enmity between the Muslims and Christians, which could be traced back to the time of the Crusades. The Ottomans' expansion in Europe exacerbated the problem because ever since the end of the eighteenth century as the Europeans gained strength, they had been on a campaign to challenge the Ottoman Empire and nibble away at its territories. The British Occupation of Egypt was but one example. Unfortunately, it took a long time for the Ottomans to realize the Europeans' true intention. Kāmil lamented the internecine fights among the Muslims and campaigned for pan-Islamism. He went so far as to inveigh against the 'Urābī Revolution because, in his opinion, it caused the British invasion and that the British were the villain of all Muslims. In order to shore up the Muslim world against the European intrusion, all Muslims needed to work together. To this end, Kāmil advocated Egyptian-Turkish unity as well as the renunciation of Egyptian national territory.[4]

Kāmil and Farīd are modern historians of Egypt, not only because of their nationalist ideas but also because of their decidedly "modern" interest; their writings are both centered on Muslims' relations with the Europeans in modern times. To conduct this sort of bilateral research, they benefited from frequent trips to Europe and the availability of European source material in governmental archives and official documents. Yet despite their shared conviction in nationalism, Kāmil and Farīd employed different styles in writing their works. Kāmil's work is well noted for its analytical depth, whereas Farīd is more a stylist in a traditional sense, shown in his mastery of the *'saj* in constructing historical narrative. Farīd's success in blending the traditional and modern attests to the vitality of the Islamic tradition in historiography, for what he achieved is by no means an isolated case. The influence of the chronicle, a staple form in traditional Islamic historiography, for example, remains discernible in the writings of Turkish historians on Ottoman history to more or less this day.[5]

Writing Turkish history in/for modern Turkey

Kāmil and Farīd advocated Egyptian-Ottoman unity, or all-Arabic solidarity, at the beginning of the twentieth century because they had high hopes for the Young Ottomans in their endeavor to introduce the constitutional era and revive the Empire. However, the era was short-lived and was quickly replaced by the despotism of Sultan Abdülhamid II (r. 1876–1908). But the trend of nationalism did not recede but saw a new high tide in Turkism. As we discussed in Chapter 2, the ideas of Turkism had already emerged in the works of 'Alī Su'āvī and Süleymān Pasha in the mid-nineteenth century. During the Hamidian reign (the reign of Abdülhamid II), Turkism gained a tremendous momentum. Though pan-Islamism never died completely (it later assumed a secular form in the revival of pan-Arabism during the 1950s and 1960s) and the word "Ottoman" persisted in its usage, during the last years of the nineteenth century, the Turks had undoubtedly developed interest in searching for two new notions – the notion of Turkey and the notion of Turks – in history. If in the late nineteenth century, the term "Turk" rarely appeared in daily usage, the Greco-Turkish war (1897) prompted Mehmed Emin, a young poet, to proudly pronounce himself a Turk: "[W]e are Turks, with this blood and with this name we live."[6]

This pronouncement was significant in that, though the term "Turks" had appeared long before, it mainly referred, somewhat derogatorily, to the Turkish-speaking villagers in Anatolia. But in declaring his identity, Mehmed Emin used the name "Turk" with both pride and passion. This declaration mirrored the experience of identity change among Muslim Turks in the Ottoman Empire, promoted by the Young Turks Movement at the time. Like the Young Ottoman Movement, the Young Turks Movement was nationalistic, but it was also distinctly more secular, more Westernized (with respect to both its intellectual origin and its political interest in representative government, including republicanism), and Turkish oriented. Indeed, the growth of Turkism bore clear imprints of Western Turcology; the latter found its way into the Ottoman Empire through Russia and the Balkans or the Empire's more Westernized neighbors and regions. Shemseddin Sami Frasheri (1850–1904), an Albanian, for example, conducted philological studies of pre-Ottoman history and culture, inspiring the self-awareness among the Turks. Ziya Gökalp (1876–1924), who had a Kurdish origin and an inclination for pan-Turkism, or Turanism, produced a series of important historical works expounding the need for renewing Islam for modern life and providing the intellectual foundation for the Turkist movement.[7]

After the Young Turks seized power in 1908, especially after Mustafa Kemal (Kemal Atatürk, 1881–1938) founded the Republic of Turkey in 1923, the study of Turkish history entered a period of rapid growth. This growth benefited from the attempts at professionalizing historical study, such as the establishment of the Ottoman Historical Society in 1910. In 1923, after the founding of the Republic, the society changed its name to Turkish Historical Society, a move that underscored its new role in promoting Turkish national history. But even in the pre-Republic period, the society had already played its part in facilitating the transition from traditional to nationalist historiography. 'Abdurrahmān Sheref (1833–1925), the last Imperial Historiographer, served its first president who, as we already mentioned in Chapter 2, authored a popular textbook of Ottoman history in a narrative style. Having collaborated with Mehmed Arif (1873–1919), Nejib Asım (1861–1935), another prominent member, compiled a history of the pre-Ottoman period based on his knowledge of Western Turcological studies. The society also promoted a high scholarly standard in its journal, exemplified by Ahmed Refik's (1881–1937) many important contributions that examined and analyzed valuable sources for the study of Turkish history. Meanwhile, Ziya Gökalp and his followers published essays in scholarly journals, pronouncing and espousing Turkism in historiography. A student of Emile Durkheim (1858–1917), Ziya Gökalp, along with his comrades, extended the study of Turkish history geographically to such regions as Central and South Asia where the Turks had once resided. They also expanded it historiographically by drawing attention to the development in law, institutions, folklore, and culture, in addition to the more traditional focus on political changes.[8]

Yet Kemal Atatürk, the country's founder, was perhaps a more important driving force behind the progress of nationalist historiography in Turkey. A true patriot, Kemal's interest in history was not narcissistic, such as comparing himself to certain past heroes, but nationalistic with an intent on promoting a distinct Turkish national identity through history writing. This interest seemed to have resonated well in the country's fledgling community of academic historians; in the same year as Kemal Atatürk founded the Republic, he was conferred the title of honorary professor of history at the University of Istanbul. In contrast to some of his contemporaries' expectations, Kemal was a true convert to the ideas of the Young Turks Movement. He envisioned a different future for the new country by focusing his effort on creating a new country, centered in Anatolia, and on promoting secularism by severing its ties with Islam. To this end, a "New History," one that foregrounds the non-Islamic dimension of the Turkish people and glorifies the feats of Turkish civilization, was in order. Kemal was irked by the notion prevalent among European historians that the Turks were part of the "Orient." He was determined to develop a new historical interpretation of the country's past on which the modern Turkey's future was to be based.[9]

In the first Turkish Historical Congress held in 1932, Kemal saw his interest in assuming a distinct Turkish historical identity come into fruition. To dissociate Turkey from both Islam and the Ottomans in its past, Turkish historians, many working at the Faculty of Geography, History and Language newly founded by Kemal in Ankara,[10] the country's new capital, came up with a theory known as the Turkish Historical Thesis (*Türk Tarih Tezi*), which consists of three parts. First, Turkish history is not only different from but also older than the history of the Ottomans. Second, the Turkish race is brachycephalic, hence white, instead of yellow. Third, as offspring of Central Asiatics, Turks brought civilizations to Anatolia, Iraq, Egypt, and the Aegean. This thesis, which has its origin in Orientalist scholarship,[11] is based on two assumptions that were later worked out in detail by Turkish historians of the era. One is that Turks were and are brachycephals of the

Alpine kind, whose ancestors included the Hittites; the Turkish ancestors were related more to the Europeans than to the Asians. The other is that Anatolia in Central Asia was the geographic center of ancient civilizations from which other civilizations derived, including Egyptian, Mesopotamian, Chinese, Greek, and Indian. In other words, of all these ancient civilizations, only Turkish was the original, whereas the rest were but its derivatives.[12]

Grotesque and chauvinistic as it may appear, the radicalness of this assertion about Turkish history and civilization matched up to the extent of other reform measures Kemal initiated for the new country. Determined to make Turkey a modern European country, he wanted to break off its ties with the Islamic and Ottoman past and make anew its cultural tradition. To secularize Turkey, he launched attacks on the religious establishment as well as on such customs as the fez and veil, though only with limited success. Had he lived longer, one could reasonably surmise that Turkey's Westernization and secularization would have made more strides. All the same, Kemal's iconoclasm has become a lasting legacy in modern Turkey. Insofar as the Turkish Historical Thesis is concerned, professional historians might have had some reservations. But they, such as Mehmet Fuat Köprülü (1890–1966), a contemporary of Kemal's as well as a leading historian of twentieth-century Turkey, apparently shared Kemal's nationalist sentiment. In his presentation of early Turkish history, Köprülü, under the influence of Durkheimian sociology (which had already been perceptible in Ziya Gökalp's works of an earlier time), accorded attention to a variety of socioeconomic factors in order to avoid one-sided interpretation. Yet he remained quite convinced that Turkdom, rather than any foreign factors, played an essential role in the evolution of early Turkish history.[13]

Needless to say, Kemal Atatürk's design for modern Turkey was Western oriented. And Westernization was becoming a dominant trend in the Middle East and, as we shall see later, also in East Asia and elsewhere, from the turn of the twentieth century to about the 1950s.[14] Despite the catastrophe of World War I, Western powers sped up their imperialist and colonial expansion into more non-Western regions. In 1911, for example, Italy took over Libya and, in the aftermath of the collapse of the Ottoman and Austrian-Hungarian Empires, Britain and France carved out modern–day Syria, Lebanon, Jordan, and Palestine and extended their influence in Iraq and, less successfully, also Iran. To fend off Western imperialism, nationalism became a powerful weapon. This was particularly apparent in the case of Egypt, where the British had established a colonial rule since 1882. But in the face of the growing Egyptian nationalism, Britain had to acknowledge Egypt's independence in 1922, though its influence remained afterwards.

The Egyptianization of historical writing

As we saw in Turkey, national independence did not mean a return to the past. Rather, it generated more incentives for the people to borrow from the

West in carrying out the nation-building project. In the process, those who had earlier exposure to Western learning played a more notable and useful role. A case in point was the activities of Syrian intellectuals in modern Egypt. Thanks to the region's geographical proximity to Western Europe, many Syrians and Lebanese, who were often Christians, boasted language proficiency in both Arabic and European languages. During the British occupation of Egypt, they immigrated to Egypt and quickly assumed an instrumental role in promoting modern journalism and education. Some of them, such as Jirjis Hunayyin (1854–1924) and Ya'qub Artīn (1842–1919), though an Armenian, also held important government positions in Egypt. Hunayyin in 1904 published *Land and Taxation in Egypt* (Al-Atyān wa'l-Darā'b fi'l-Qutr al-Misrī), which contained rich information in economic history. Artīn authored two books in Egyptian history and published a number of articles in the *Bulletin de l'Institut Egyptien*, a scholarly journal devoted to Egyptian studies in France. Carefully documented, these writings drew on governmental archives, to which their authors had easy access, thanks to their distinguished social stature. Artīn also published mostly in French, suggesting the extent of his Western education.[15]

Though they were immigrants, these Syrians were by no means less enthusiastic than the Egyptians for advancing the cause of Egyptian nationalism. In their newspapers and magazines, Ya'qūb Sarrūf (1852–1927) introduced nationalism and Darwinism to Egypt, as did Farah Antūn (1861–1922) of the works of Jean-Jacques Rousseau and Ernest Rénan. In his *Egypt for Egyptians* (Misr li'l-Misriyyīn), Salīm al-Naqqāsh (?–1884) provided a detailed analysis of the 'Urābi Revolution, which he witnessed firsthand, though his overall position was not as prorevolutionary and nationalistic as the title of his book might suggest. In both scholarly production and intellectual influence, Jurjī Zaydān (1861–1914), a Beiruti, seemed to have eclipsed all his peers. During his youth, Zaydān learned German, French, and English, as well as Syriac, Latin, and Hebrew, in addition to Arabic, his mother tongue. He received part of his education, in medicine, at Syrian Protestant College, an American university, but later realized that his real passion lay in literature, history, and journalism. After coming to Egypt, he first launched a successful career in journalism. His editorship of the popular magazine *al-Hilāl* earned him a distinct voice at the national level, which was, however, both good and bad. Along with Mustafa Kāmil, the nationalist historian, and Ya'qūb Sarrūf, his fellow Syrian, he advocated the creation of a national university in Egypt, which was to be the Egyptian University established in 1908, as we previously mentioned. But his Syrian/Lebanese background and Western training also brought suspicion and enmity to the Egyptians. Zaydān was, for instance, rarely acknowledged for his role in founding the Egyptian University.[16] Though agreeing with him on the need for creating a national university, Mustafa Kāmil was known for his unfriendliness toward Syrian émigré intellectuals, whom he often derided as the "intruders."[17]

Indeed, though Zaydān won such accolades as "the dean of the Syrian Egyptian historians" and, on another occasion, even "the dean of Arab historians of his day," he was disallowed to teach Islamic history at the Egyptian University that he had helped establish. His contribution to modern Egyptian historiography, therefore, lay mainly in his prolific publications in Islamic history and literature, including the much acclaimed, five-volume *History of Islamic Civilization* (Ta'rīkh al-Tamaddun al-Islāmīn), published in 1902–1906. As a Westernized scholar steeped thoroughly in Orientalist scholarship, Zaydān was known for his secular approach and his disdain for traditional Islamic historiography. In the *History of Islamic Civilization*, he duly acknowledged the importance of the Prophet Muhammad and the significance of Islamic civilization, considering the Arab the jewel of civilizations in the Fertile Crescent. However, Zaydān refused to describe the rise of Islam as a triumph of God's will over its heathen enemies from the orthodox Muslim perspective.[18]

It was not surprising for the Egyptian nationalists to distrust the Syrian émigré scholars, for nationalism at times bred xenophobic sentiments. The founding and development of the Egyptian University are illustrative in this regard. As one of the earliest modern institutions of higher education in the Middle East, it was created for nationalizing and professionalizing scholarly activities in and for Egypt. To the extent that it was a modern university, it rivaled, and at times also antagonized, such old institutions as the *al-Azhar* and even the more recently founded *Dār al-'Ulūm*, in its mission to bring modern academic culture to the country. The university employed Western scholars and scientists in its formative years. But over the course of its development, it also made great efforts to Egyptianize its faculty by hiring native scholars with European qualifications.

The Egyptianization of the faculty at the Egyptian University first took place in the Faculty of Arts. In 1919, the university welcomed Tāhā Husayn (1889–1973), its former student and a recent doctorate from France, to teach such courses as History of the Ancient East and Philosophy of History. Tāhā Husayn's contract stipulated he was not to undertake any work outside the university with permission.[19] Thus, historical study in the Middle East was ushered into the period of professionalization. Though blind, Tāhā Husayn excelled in his academic works while at the university and proceeded to study at Sorbonne with a scholarship, where he worked with Emile Durkheim and Paul Casanova (1861–1926), an Orientalist scholar. As one of the first Egyptian students receiving a Western doctorate, Tāhā Husayn later developed a sterling career in university administration, serving at one time as Minister of Education and became a leading voice for modern education in Egypt.

The same fortune also fell upon Muhammad Rif'at Bey (1857–1949), one of the founding fathers of Egypt's historical profession. A contemporary of Tāhā Husayn, Muhammad Rif'at went to Europe during the early twentieth century. Having received a master's degree from the University of Liverpool, he became a professor of history at the Higher Teachers' College after his return. Almost at the same time, he launched a career in educational leadership and eventually became Minister of Education in the 1950s. In spite of his administrative duties, Muhammad Rif'at managed to continue publishing in history. In 1947, he published an important book in English, *The Awakening of Modern Egypt*, though his earlier books were mostly written in Arabic. An avowed nationalist, Muhammad Rif'at not only participated in and later promoted the Egyptianization of university faculty in Egypt, but he also truly believed and advocated its necessity. "It is the nationals of a country," he declared, "who are best fitted to express the true feelings and reactions of their fellow-countrymen to the ideas and the events that confront them."[20]

Muhammad Rif'at's nationalism found its echoes in the writings of Muhammad Shafiq Ghurbāl (1894–1961), the doyen of Egyptian historical study of the early twentieth century. A former colleague of Muhammad Rif'at's after his return from England at the Higher Teachers' College, Shafiq Ghurbāl joined the faculty at the Egyptian University in 1929, where Tāhā Husayn was the dean of the Faculty of Arts. Like Muhammad Rif'at, Ghurbāl received his master's degree in history at the University of Liverpool, though he continued his study by earning a PhD from the University of London, under the supervision of the then budding historian, Arnold Toynbee (1889–1975). As a typical example of the first generation of academic historians in Egypt, Ghurbāl published his works mostly in English. His first book, *The Beginnings of the Egyptian Question and the Rise of Mehemet Ali*, based on his doctoral thesis and published in 1928, was regarded as "a landmark" in modern Egyptian historiography by marking "a new stage of its development."[21] In his foreword to the book, Arnold Toynbee unabatedly praised his student's work: "[Ghurbāl] is so thoroughly detached from the passions and prejudices that enter into his field of study that . . . it would be difficult to guess from internal evidence whether the author was an Englishman, a Frenchman, or an Egyptian, or none of these."[22]

Ghurbāl might appear more detached in his writings than, perhaps, Muhammad Ibrahim Sabrī (1894–1978), a fellow academic historian, and 'Abd al-Rahmān al-Rāfi'i (1889–1966), a political activist-cum-historian and protégé of Mustafa Kāmil. But he was no less nationalistic or short of political predilection. To Ghurbāl, historical study served a mission, which was to advance national interest. In fact, his appointment at the Egyptian University represented an important pawn in the university's Egyptianization scheme. In 1935, Ghurbāl succeeded Arthur J. Grant (1862–1948), a reputed English historian of modern European history, as the first Egyptian professor of modern history at the university. This change of the guard represented a symbolic and significant step in advancing national education in Egypt: Not only was Ghurbāl an Egyptian, but he also specialized in Egyptian history instead of European history. In his position, which he held subsequently for over 20 years, Ghurbāl trained and nurtured scores of young historians who came to dominate the field of historical study in today's Egypt. And these historians all have worked on Egyptian history, studying myriad topics ranging from political and institutional changes to social and economic development.

If Ghurbāl's influence was comprehensive and far-reaching, it was also because, like Tāhā Husayn and Muhammad Rif'at, he held several important government positions throughout his career, helping direct the country's education. Though he never became Minister of Education, he served many terms as the undersecretary of the Ministry under several regimes. His political position was known to be a bit conservative, since he seemed close to the royal house. Yet this might result from his nationalist inclination, for the opposition force to the king was led by the Wafd, a nationalist party responsible for obtaining Egypt's independence from the British in 1922, though afterward, the party often received support from the British in its attempt to uphold power. At the same time, the British also were interested in maintaining their influence in Egypt.

In many aspects, Muhammad Ibrahim Sabrī (1894–1978), another leading figure in Egypt's academic historical circle, was a foil to Ghurbāl, his erstwhile colleague at the Egyptian University. A student who returned from France instead of Britain, Sabrī received his doctorate at Sorbonne under the supervision of Alphonse Aulard (1849–1928), an expert on the French Revolution. Compared with Ghurbāl's steadily upward path to the Parthenon, Sabrī encountered a few turns in launching his career. In addition to college teaching, which he did first at the Higher Teachers' College, then at the Egyptian University and *Dār al-'Ulūm* and in 1950, returned to the Egyptian University, he served once as the deputy director of the National Library (*Dar al-Kutub*). But in contrast to Ghurbāl's relatively thin record in publication, Sabrī was prolific, though most of his writings were in French, hence circumscribing his intellectual influence in his own country. But his *La Révolution égyptienne* (1919–1921), which described the events of 1919 and clearly bore his mentor's influence, rivaled Ghurbāl's *The Beginnings of the Egyptian Question and the Rise of Mehemet Ali* in shaping the direction of academic historical study in Egypt. Published about a decade earlier, it had been regarded as marking "the advent of professional Egyptian historiography."[23]

As representative figures of the first generation of academic historians in modern Egypt, the careers of Muhammad Rif'at, Shafiq Ghurbāl, and Ibrahim Sabrī, while different to some extent, revealed that since the 1920s, historical study in Egypt had entered a new phase: It had become an academic discipline researched and taught by professional historians. Like their Western counterparts, these historians all based their writings on carefully scrutinized sources, mostly comprised of government archives. Yet they also expanded on the Muslim tradition in that, during the Ottoman period, historians in the Middle East had developed sophisticated techniques in employing archival material in recording and writing history. These modern

Egyptian historians distinguished themselves from their predecessors more in style than in method; they strove to deliver their research findings in direct, if also detached, Arabic prose, without the versification in 'saj. In addition, they played a leadership role in establishing professional societies in Egypt. Learned societies had existed in Egypt before, founded mostly by the Westerners. The *Institut de'Egypte*, for example, was established in 1859, which was a reincarnation of Napoleon's *Institut Égyptien* of 1798. Though it was dominated by European Orientalists, there were also prominent non-European members, such as Rifā'ah al-Tahtāwi and Ya'qub Artīn. During the first half of the twentieth century, the *Institut de'Egypte* also participated in the process of Egyptianization; Tāhā Husayn, for example, was elected a member in 1924, as was Ghurbāl in 1947, though by then, in 1945, Ghurbāl had already founded the Royal Association for Historical Studies (later Egyptian Association for Historical Studies), a more important, less elitist, organization for the historical community in Egypt. In 1949, the association published the *Royal Egyptian Historical Review* in both Arabic and English, and after 1952, the journal was renamed *Egyptian Historical Review*. In 1951, the association had a list of 350 members and, since then, it has grown to a membership of over 3,000 at present.

Academic history and national politics

Having acquired all the trappings of academic historiography, the emergence of the historical profession in Egypt was closely linked to and intimately reflected changes in the political arena. Indeed, as we have already seen in the case of Europe, while the establishment of historical study as an academic discipline improved the autonomy of the historian and the quality of his (her?) work, it has by no means immunized the writing and study of history from outside influences, for academic historiography was often (but not in every case!) established by state patronages and government sponsorships. In the Middle East, save for a few missionary schools, academic institutions of a modern sort were founded by the state as part and parcel of its nation-building project. The history professors at the University of Istanbul, as we have mentioned, endorsed enthusiastically and expanded diligently on Kemal Atatürk's proposition on early Turkish history, hoping to bolster national self-esteem. Since then, the study of Turkish history had dominated the field of history, though the Ottoman period remained unpopular because it represented a bygone era with antinationalist ideologies.[24]

As the Turkish historians turned their backs on the Ottoman imperium, their counterparts in other parts of the region also assailed Ottoman rule as imperialist and oppressive. In order to forge their own distinct national identity, they strove to trace their countries' origins in a more remote past. Iraqi historians, for example, discovered a past in the Assyrians, whereas the Tunisians staked out a claim on their past glory in the Carthaginians, and the Lebanese evoked the accomplishment of the Phoenicians.[25] In Iran, amid many sensible efforts at modernization associated with the dynastic change in 1925, following the Constitutional Revolution, academic history made considerable strides and was highly nationalistic. Continuing their predecessors' cause in shaping up the Iranian national identity through dearabicization, intellectuals in the post-Constitutional period aspired to search for ways to conceive and construct a distinct Persia/Iran, emphasizing its ethnic and linguistic homogeneity as well as its historical and cultural continuity. Impressed by the development of such ancillary disciplines as archaeology, epigraphy, and numismatics to historical study in modern Europe, Hassan Pīrnīyā (1874–1935), who wrote on ancient Iranian history, felt that these methods could be readily applied to explaining the grandeur of Persian civilization (e.g., Sassanid dynasty) and its superior characteristics to that of Indian civilization. Mahmud Mahmud (1881–1965), another politician-cum-historian, turned to Iran's more recent past. He reckoned that, despite foreign invasion, Iran proved itself to be a unique nation, thanks to God's blessing and the glorious deeds performed by the Iranian elites. Ahmad Kasravī (1890–1946), their contemporary, actually paid the price of his life for condemning the Islamic "pollution" of Persian culture and language. He argued strongly that despite the invasion of the Muslims resulting in the Islamic "pollution" of Persian culture, Persians had maintained their racial and ethnic "purity" over the subsequent centuries. His radical stance caused his assassination by an extreme Islamicist at a court trial on March 11, 1946. All these examples helped illustrate the entangled development between historiography and politics in modern Iran, as the country strove to organize itself as a nation-state under Reza Shah (1878–1944) and his successors in the Pahlavi era.[26]

Back to Egypt again. The major concern for twentieth-century Egyptian historians was not whether their culture had had a long history – it seemed that their nineteenth-century predecessors like Rifā'ah al-Tahtāwi and 'Alī Mubārak had succeeded in grounding it in the rich cultural heritages of ancient Egypt[27] – but how to assess and analyze the rise of modern Egypt in the reigns of such famous reformers as Muhammad 'Alī and Ismā'īl, as well as the ebb and flow of Egyptian nationalism toward the end of the nineteenth century. Muhammad Rif'at and Shafiq Ghurbāl, provided their royal connection, endorsed reform-minded khedives while not taking a blind bit of notice to their autocratic policy. Muhammad Rif'at had written a popular textbook of modern Egyptian history, in which he contrasted the success of these khedives to the failure of the 'Urābī Revolution because the former strengthened Egypt whereas the latter caused the British invasion. The more liberal Ibrahim Sabrī also portrayed the 'Urābī Revolution in an unfavorable tone because, given his close tie with the Wafd, he intended to accord more credit to Sa'd Zaghlul and his party for achieving Egypt's independence. Interestingly, 'Abd al-Rahmān al-Rāfi'i, the widely read amateur historian, seemed to be the only exception. In his writings, al-Rāfi'i took a more neutral approach in assessing both the khedives and the 'Urābīsts, even though his mentor Mustafa Kāmil had held a negative opinion of the latter.[28] These different interpretations of modern Egyptian history suggest, once again, that academic historians were not immune to political influences. Beginning in the 1950s, it seemed that the changing politics, shaped by the onset of the Cold War and, more recently, by the far-reaching impact of globalization, have come to exercise a more direct influence in prefiguring the direction and development of historical study in Egypt and elsewhere in the Middle East.

Nationalism, scientism, and Marxism: Modern historiography in East and Southeast Asia

As a turning point in modern East Asian history, the Sino-Japanese War of 1895 exerted a tremendous impact on transforming the traditional order of the Sinic world. Thanks to the budding news media introduced by the Western missionaries and established by Western-influenced Chinese journalists, China's defeat in the war was made known to its people much more quickly and effectively than in the previous times.[29] It awakened the Chinese once and for all. In the ensuing 1898 Reform, though the reform-minded Emperor and his confidants, Kang Youwei (1858–1927) and Liang Qichao (1873–1929), lost their bid for power to the Empress Dowager and her associates, the latter also believed that certain change was necessary. The Empress Dowager, for instance, kept the national institution founded by the reformers in 1898, which was to become Peking (Beijing) University, China's first modern university. Advised and administered by Zhang Zhidong (1837–1909), who now earned Empress Dowager's trust for engineering China's cultural borrowing from the West, the Qing reform was ushered in a new course characterized by its attempt to follow Japan's model. In its formative years, Peking University not only employed Japanese or Japan-educated Chinese instructors, it also set up its departments and curricula according to the Japanese model. To Zhang and like-minded officials, Japan was attractive also because beginning in the 1890s, the wholesale Westernization policy of the early Meiji period had given way to the new interest in "returning" to Japan's Asian and native roots.[30]

"New historiography" in China

At the turn of the twentieth century, a great number of Chinese students flocked into Japanese schools; from these students emerged a generation of future political and intellectual leaders, of whom Liang Qichao was the most notable. Though not officially a student (Liang in fact went to Japan in exile because of his leadership role in the 1898 Reform), Liang's political stature enabled him to befriend prominent Japanese intellectuals and political leaders. Inspired by the endeavor of Fukuzawa Yukichi and Taguchi Ukichi, Liang launched a journalist career in Japan, aiming to promote the need for more political reform back in China. In his advocacy of constitutionalism, he introduced, via Japanese translations of which he managed to have acquired a reading knowledge, the works of many liberal thinkers from the West.[31] He also realized that paving the way for establishing constitutional monarchy and representative government in China entailed the alteration of the Chinese way of thinking and cultural tradition, including reforming the practice of historical writing. Thus, in 1902, in his *New Citizen's Journal*, Liang serialized a seminal work, *New Historiography* (*Xin shixue*), in which he disparaged the Chinese tradition of dynastic historiography, in much the same way as did Fukuzawa, and declared the need for a "Historiographical Revolution" (*shijie geming*). At the outset of the *New Historiography*, Liang states that though historical writing has had a long tradition in China, it has become fusty and inadequate because, in contrast to modern Western historiography, where historical writing had engendered nationalism, the Chinese tradition had focused instead on the monarch or the rise and fall of dynasties. Moreover, engrossed with moral didacticism, Chinese historians lacked incentive to discover and explain historical causality, resulting in the want of novelty and creativity in their works. In fact, Liang avers, over the past two millennia, the compilation of the 24 dynastic histories from the Han dynasty to the Qing amounted to only a mere act of repetition, for all of them served just one purpose – helping the reigning monarch to prolong his rule.[32]

As the first salvo fired at the Chinese tradition of historical writing, Liang's *New Historiography* also outlines ideas of New Historiography. First, Liang writes, it should become an integral part of the nation-building endeavor, a compelling task for the Chinese in the wake of their country's repeated defeats by foreign powers. Second, pursuant to the example of Japanese civilizational history, it should describe and analyze the progress, or evolution, of the nation as a whole, rather than focus on the successes and failures of monarchical power.[33]

Though sketchy, these two areas represented the foci of the so-called Historiographical Revolution at the time, pursued by Liang's many cohorts sojourning and studying in Japan, of whom Zhang Taiyan (1868–1936), Huang Jie (1873–1935), and Deng Shi (1877–1951) were most visible. In 1905, Zhang, Huang, Deng, and other Japan-educated Chinese students published the *National Essence Journal* (*Guocui xuebao*), in which Liang Qichao's formulations of national and "civilizational" history reverberated in their writings and considerations of the historiographical problem facing China. Like Liang, they maintained that the Historiographical Revolution was then in a dire need because people's history (*minshi*) should supersede the "monarchical history" (*junshi*) in order to make history writing useful for the nationalist cause. By espousing such needs, they called for the revival of the National Essence – a neologism appearing amid Japan's search for its Eastern roots during the 1890s – though they used it not to reclaim the relevance of the Confucian legacy but to seek a *pre*-Confucian past in a more remote past, much as the Renaissance humanists did in recovering Greek and Roman culture, in hopes of finding compatible elements to accommodate the modern ones from the West.

In his delineation of the evolution of the so-called *Yellow History* (*Huangshi*) in China proper, Huang Jie called special attention to the Yellow Emperor, the putative progenitor of the Chinese people, in China's high antiquity. Huang's work, though incomplete, was an early attempt at national history in China, which centered on the evolution of the yellow race. But to Huang, Zhang Taiyan, Liu Shipei (1884–1919), and other journal contributors, the Chinese race was not indigenous but rather emigrated from Central Asia, or Chaldea, some five millennia previously, as propounded by Terrien de Lacouperie (1844–1894), a French sinologist. By accepting Lacouperie's theory, these intellectuals hoped to link the origin of Chinese civilization historically and ethnically to Central Asia, the accepted cradle of human civilizations whence Greek civilization, the fountainhead of Western civilization, also originated.[34] Their move was similar to the one made by Turkish historians in the 1920s to claim Central Asia as the origin of ancient Turkish culture and people; both projects were motivated by the desire to bolster national self-esteem and prestige for their people, an essential feature of nationalist historiography.

At the time when these new, nationalist ideas of history were propounded and propagated, education in China was also entering a period of reform. In addition to Peking University, the Qing dynasty permitted the establishment of more universities as well as primary and secondary schools of the modern sort, in which such new subjects as mathematics, physics, chemistry, and foreign languages were taught. History, along with other "old" subjects, also stood at the core of the curriculum, though taught increasingly in a new way, reflecting the impact of the Historiographical Revolution. After 1905, when the dynasty abolished the time-honored civil service examination system, Chinese students became now more enthused to embrace the new knowledge system, to which the shortcut was via Japanese texts. To satisfy the swelling need for new schoolbooks, Japan-educated students supplied translations of Japanese textbooks. In the area of history, thanks to the thriving *Tōyōshi* study, Japanese historians had already written a number of texts on Chinese history, some of which were simply written in Chinese, such as Naka Michiyo's (1851–1908) *A General History of China* (*Shina tsūshi*).

In the early twentieth century, Naka's book, along with Kuwabara Jitsuzō's (1870–1931) *A Brief History of the East* (*Tōyō shiyō*), quickly became popular history textbooks in Chinese schools. These texts distinguished themselves in three areas: (1) Unlike the traditional annals-biographic dynastic histories, they followed a narrative structure with a clear periodization, which usually adopted the tripartite division (ancient, medieval, and modern) from Western historiography; (2) while political change remained the center of the narrative, influenced by civilizational history or people's history, the authors noted changes in such other areas as religious activities, cultural customs and literary accomplishments in a more comprehensive, yet succinct manner; and (3) though moral education remained heeded in their selection of events and personages for narration, the authors' main interest was to depict the continuous development of national history from the ancient to the contemporary age and, occasionally, also offer a causal explanation for the flow of historical events. In short, brevity (covering the entire span of Chinese history in one or two volumes), periodization, and narrativity were the main attractions of these Japanese texts. And these characteristics were deemed well suited for teaching Chinese history from a new, nationalist perspective.

To profit from the lucrative textbook market, Chinese publishers also quickly caught up. In 1905, the Commercial Press, for example, issued *The Newest Middle School Textbook of Chinese History* (*Zuixin zhongxue Zhongguo lishi jiaokeshu*), authored by Xia Zengyou (1863–1924), a friend of Liang Qichao's who shared Liang's belief in progressive history. Xia's book might be the first Chinese attempt to write a history of the country's past in the new narrative style. But almost at the same time, similar attempts were made by others, including Liu Shipei, a member of the National Essence group and China's first convert to anarchism. As the Chinese were reading, studying, and writing their country's past from myriad new perspectives (social Darwinism or evolutionism, nationalism, anarchism, and even racism), these theories too helped point to the possible directions in which their country's history could move at the time when the fall of the Qing dynasty was imminent. Indeed, despite its last-ditch effort at introducing modern reform, the dynasty was unable to save its fate: In 1911, it was overthrown by Sun Yat-sen's (1866–1925) nationalist party. In waging the revolution, the party's spokesperson Zhang Taiyan, another member of the National Essence group, had explained to his compatriots that, founded by the Manchus, the Qing dynasty had been an alien and illegitimate regime because China should belong to the Han Chinese.[35]

The tension between national history and scientific history

The proclamation of the Republic of China in 1912, the first republic in Asia, ushered the country into a new era with great optimism and expectation. However, they were quickly supplanted by pessimism and despair, for in competing for the first presidency, Yuan Shikai outmaneuvered Sun Yat-sen and reaped the fruit of the revolution. As Sun Yat-sen was now preparing for the so-called Second Revolution in Southern China, Chinese intellectuals at Peking University continued their search for a cultural reform, or revolution, in order to help the country to cope with its modern woes. Drawing on Liang Qichao's iconoclasm of the past decade, this new generation of Chinese intellectuals advocated the needs for introducing "Mr. Democracy" and "Mr. Science" to China and for a critical overhaul of the Chinese cultural tradition. Thanks to the influence of the Historiographical Revolution and the teaching of newly styled history textbooks, evolutionism had been readily accepted by the May Fourth generation to interpret the progress and movement of history. Moreover, it also became a means for them to create a New Culture. Hu Shi (1891–1962), a Peking University professor with a doctoral degree from the United States and the leader of this New Culture Movement, proclaimed that the idea of evolutionism was not foreign to the Chinese. Yet in contrast to Kang Youwei who had made the same observation at the end of the previous century, Hu examined evolutionism on the methodological level and established it as both a scientific method and a historical theory. In common parlance, Hu called evolutionism a "genetic method" or the "method of grandparents and grandchildren." Writing his dissertation at Columbia University where he worked with John Dewey (1859–1952), a prominent American philosopher of pragmatism, Hu had traced the development of this method in ancient Chinese thought. After his return to teach at Peking University in 1917, Hu shifted his attention to the evidential learning of the Qing period, in which he found what he believed was the most matured application of evolutionism as a scientific method in the Chinese intellectual tradition. For Qing evidential scholars in their study, he posited, examined the "evolution" of one text through the ages and compared its various versions in order to track and identify the embedded interpolations, modifications, and distortions. And in so doing, the scholars followed a scientific procedure, marked by questioning, hypothesis, experiment, and verification. This procedure was identical with the application of modern scientific method, summarized in his mentor Dewey's book *How We Think* (1909). By adopting the Qing method, or textual and historical criticism, Hu ascertained and authenticated the true authorship of several famous novels popular both in the Qing and his own time. He also scrutinized the validity of many texts in areas of philosophy and history. Thus, by characterizing evidential learning as scientific and comparing it with modern Western scientific scholarship, Hu Shi rediscovered and revived that Qing scholarly tradition.[36] What he achieved also was to orient the changes in modern Chinese historiography similarly to what Shigeno Yasutsugu had done in meshing evidential learning with Rankean historiography in Japan several decades previously.

The changes Hu Shi introduced to the study of Chinese history began modestly with a research project named "National Studies" that he introduced at Peking University. Gu Jiegang (1893–1980), Hu's student and protégé, was hired as his assistant. Galvanized by the May Fourth iconoclastic spirit, Hu and Gu held a critical and skeptical attitude toward China's extant literary and historical corpus, intent to subject it to a critical overhaul. Upon Hu's request, Gu began the project by following the example of Qing scholars to sift the extant body of literature by winnowing authentic texts from forged and falsified ones. Their effort and interest were akin to that of the National Essence group in that, inspired by the attempt of

Renaissance humanists at reviving Greek and Roman classical culture, Hu and Gu were hoping to effect a "Chinese renaissance" by recovering an authentic and trustworthy literary tradition. When Hu was asked to recall the significance of the National Studies project in the 1940s, he indeed compared it with the Renaissance.[37]

The analogy, however, has its shortcomings, for the tradition they wanted to recover was not buried, so to speak, in the dust of history but had been extolled, worshiped, and cherished by generations of Chinese scholars. The real issue, however, is, to the May Fourth scholars baptized by the scientific culture, this enormous corpus has been riddled by fraudulence and falsity; it is not authentic and reliable by the scientific standard. In his critical examination of the historical texts regarding China's high antiquity, for example, Gu Jiegang developed strong suspicion about their validity and authenticity. Influenced by May Fourth iconoclasm, he ventured a bold hypothesis that the ideal reigns of the "Three Dynasties" of ancient China, romanticized and idolized by past historians and literati, were not a real but a trumped-up story. Instead, Gu surmised, Yu, one of the sage-kings of the time, might just be a totemic symbol, not a real historical figure. Gu's suspicion received support from Hu Shi, his mentor, because Hu believed that a bold hypothesis is the first step to launch scientific research and investigation. Encouraged, Gu continued his endeavor to expose the unreliability of traditional historical sources. Characterizing his activity as an act of "doubting antiquity" (*yigu*), Gu instigated the "Discussion of Ancient History," debating the historicity of China's high antiquity. This was akin to what his Japanese counterparts had done with regard to the age of gods in prehistoric Japan. In the discussion, Gu also aired doubts on the historicity of the Yellow Emperor, the widely accepted ancestral figure for the Chinese people.[38]

Like Shigeno's and Kume's revelation of the deficiency and unreliability of historical records and writings in premodern Japan, Gu Jiegang's "doubting antiquity" activity stirred up a public debate in China, for if his presupposition were accepted, then the course of Chinese history would be shortened from 5,000 years to about 3,000 years, a radical move that surely would have caused strong protest from such historians as the National Essence group. Though the idea came from Gu, its radicalness, however, was already anticipated in Hu Shi's course on Chinese intellectual history at Peking University, which Gu had taken as a student.[39] Different from Japan where the discussion of the unreliability of historical sources had faced pressure from politicians and the religious establishment, the Discussion of Ancient History remained by and large an academic discussion in China. In fact, the discussion helped the advance of academic historiography in China. In order to challenge Gu, who incidentally came to become a shining star in the fledgling academic community, wooed by many universities, his critics also had to go to the sources and examine them in much the same way as Gu did in developing his thesis. Through their leadership role of the National Studies project, Hu Shi and Gu Jiegang became leading figures of the so-called

Historical Source School, so named for its emphasis on source evaluation and verification. During the late 1920s and 1930s, the school dominated the world of Chinese historians, now comprised mostly of history professors working in an academic setting. These historians also organized historical associations and published historical journals, most of which, however, had rather short lives.

In promoting scientific history, the Historical Source School questioned the longevity of Chinese history, which might hurt the pride of the people. But this scientization of historical study was unmistakably for the nationalist purpose. Cognizant of the development of sinological study in both the West and Japan, Hu Shi and Gu Jiegang were concerned with its "backward" status in China. That is, if Chinese scholars remained insensitive to the question of source criticism and verification, their work was not going to command respect from their foreign counterparts. A decade earlier, Shiratori Kurakichi (1865–1942), a Japanese sinologist trained in the Rankean method, had challenged the reliability of the ancient historical texts pertaining to China's high antiquity, though his argument was rebutted by Hayashi Taisuke (1854–1922), a fellow sinologist.[40]

In the heat of the Discussion of Ancient History in 1926, Fu Sinian (1896–1950), Hu Shi's other student and protégé at Peking University, returned from Europe where he had studied for seven years. Having dabbled in a wide array of subjects in Europe, Fu, while at Berlin University, eventually found his real interest in philology, philosophy, and history. Upon his return, he established the Institute of History and Philology, China's first research institution in historical study. Championing the idea that philological study ensures the reliability of historical sources, the institute's name reflected the German/Rankean influence. Yet the history-philology combination also extended the tradition of evidential learning, to which Fu had had an early exposure. But Fu Sinian sought more. Under his leadership, the Institute conducted archaeological digs in Anyang, the putative capital of the Shang dynasty (ca. 1600–1066 BCE). Beginning in the early twentieth century, a number of inscribed oracle bones had surfaced in Anyang, from which such scholars as Wang Guowei (1877–1927), Hayashi Taisuke, and Paul Pelliot (1878–1945), the French sinologist, obtained valuable information on the dynasty's history and ancient China in general. Fu's excavation did not yield more oracle bones as he had hoped. But using the archaeological method, he and his colleagues were able to prove that the Shang dynasty had not only been a real historical entity but also a thriving and sophisticated civilization. Thus, on hard scientific evidence, Fu rebutted his former classmate Gu Jiegang's thesis on the unhistoricity of Chinese antiquity. His success, too, was a boon to the Historical Source School to which he belonged because Fu proved that examining old sources *and* finding new ones advance modern scientific history. Propitiously, his finding also restored the validity of ancient Chinese history, lending support to the people's pride in their country.[41]

Modifying the Rankean model: National history in Japan

By defeating China in 1895 and subsequently also Russia in 1905, Japan was on its path to becoming a world power. But historical scholarship faced a new challenge. To rally people behind the war machine, Japanese government exercised thought control. When Kōtoku Shūsui (1871–1911), a socialist thinker, spoke out against the war, he was thrown into jail and eventually put to death for treason in 1911. The government also attributed Japan's overseas victories partially to the "omnipotence" of Japan's imperial house, which, as more and more people were now led to believe, boasted an unbroken line of succession from the age of gods to the present day – or *Bansei ikkei* – a "unique" phenomenon unseen elsewhere except in Japan. In 1911, when the government received complaints that its history textbook stated that during the fourteenth century, two imperial courts had existed simultaneously, vying for legitimacy, it decided to intervene and ruled eventually in favor of the southern court in order to uphold the *Bansei ikkei* claim. In this battle, former leaders of the historical community Shigeno Yasutsugu, Kume Kunitake, and their successors Mikami Sanji (1865–1939) and Kita Sadakichi (1871–1939) lost ground – they failed to persuade the public that the two courts' coexistence was a historical fact and that it was meaningless to debate whether one was more legitimate than the other. In a self-serving way, they had to take comfort by drawing the difference between historical research and historical education; as "applied history," they consented, it was nothing wrong for the latter to serve directly the need of the nation-state.[42]

During the early twentieth century, Japanese academic historians made notable efforts to advance Japanese nationalism and later imperialism in historical research. In addition to Mikami and Kita, the constellation of Japanese academic historians then included Tsuboi Kumezō (1858–1936), who had been Riess's junior colleague after earning his doctorate in Germany, Fukuda Tokuzō (1874–1930), who also had a German doctorate, and Shiratori Kurakichi, a student of Riess's; all of them were known for their effort to extend Western historical scholarship in many areas of historical study in Japan. After Riess returned to Germany, for example, Tsuboi continued teaching the Historical Methodology course and preaching the tenets of Rankean historiography. Fukuda, along with Hara Katsurō (1871–1924), Uchida Ginzō (1872–1919), and Nakata Kaoru (1877–1967), all received their advanced education in Europe, adopted a comparative approach to analyzing the characteristic and aspects of Japanese history, aiming to draw an analogy to those of European nations. Shiratori, along with Naka Michiyo (1851–1908) and Naitō Konan (1866–1934), both respected China scholars, were pioneering scholars in *Tōyōshi* study in whose scholarship one unmistakably found Japan's territorial interest in the region. Shiratori Kurakichi, for instance, proposed a hypothesis on the shared racial origin of Japanese and Korean people – *Nissen dōsoron* – for justifying Japan's annexation of Korea in the wake of these two wars.[43] In no time, Shiratori would also extend the hypothesis to include the Manchus, presaging his country's interest in Manchuria.

By the end of World War I, the landscape of modern Japanese historiography had thus notably changed. The dominance of academic historiography, marked by its transformation of evidential scholarship in emphasizing source criticism and its focus on political history, had given way to several new schools, some of which were based in such newly founded universities as the Kyoto University, which rose in no time to become an archrival of Tokyo University. The rise of socioeconomic history, represented by the works of Fukuda Tokuzō, Uchida Ginzō, and others, was a good example.[44] The work of Yanagita Kunio (1875–1962), which pioneered folklore study, was another. Yet perhaps a more interesting example was the school of "cultural history" (*bunka shigaku*), or "*Geistesgeschichte*" (*seishin shigaku*), pioneered by Tsuda Sōkichi (1873–1961) and Nishida Naojirō (1886–1964) and expanded by Muraoka Tsunetsugu (1884–1946) and Watsuji Tetsurō (1889–1960), for it explored the cultural and psychological side of history. From this perspective, the school developed a novel and comprehensive interpretation of Japan's historical development, in much the same way as did Karl Lamprecht with German history in the early twentieth century. Its "rebellion" against the empiricist historiography of the previous period also had the same effect as did Lamprecht's battle against Rankean historiography. Auspiciously in 1919, Lamprecht's *Moderne Geschichtswissenschaft* (1909) appeared in Japanese. Nishida, while studying in Europe in the 1920s, had taken an interest in the works of Condorcet, Hegel, and Lamprecht. Indebted to Lamprecht, Nishida came to realize the limits of critical historiography for its preoccupation with source criticism and its inadequacy in advancing theories in historical explanation and periodization, in contrast to the focus of Condorcet and Hegel. Inspired by Heinrich Rickert and Wilhelm Dilthey, Nishida also pondered over the relationship between individuality and universality in historical study. He concluded that while it is imperative for historians to straighten out historical facts, it is more important for them to wrest and identify the true spirit that moves behind the surface of historical events and offer plausible interpretations of historical movement.[45]

Though a student of Shiratori Kurakichi, the new leader of critical and empirical historiography, Tsuda Sōkichi, drew the same conclusion as did Nishida: He too believed that the historian's work was not confined to source criticism. Instead, he argued, a more compelling task was to discover and reveal the "national mind/psyche" (*kokumin shisō*) and its characteristics of different time periods. From this nationalist perspective, Tsuda set out to reveal and amplify Japan's unique cultural traits in both the premodern and modern periods. Despite the Chinese influence in the premodern period, he contended, the Japanese had developed its own cultural tradition, which was fundamentally different from the Chinese one. The same could also be said about Japan's cultural development in the modern period, despite the Western cultural influence. Though he had not studied abroad as did Nishida, perhaps by working with Shiratori who had been Riess's disciple, Tsuda absorbed elements of Rankean historicism and maintained that a general coherence was embedded in the fabric of Japanese history. However, as mentioned previously, Riess's version of Rankean historiography had been lopsided in that it emphasized only *Quellenkritik* in Rankean historiography. Tsuda's interest in the fluidity and vitality of historical movement might suggest that he perhaps was more influenced by such neohistoricists as Wilhelm Dilthey and Friedrich Meinecke.[46]

In many ways, Tsuda Sōkichi's cultural history epitomized the advancement of Japanese historiography in the post-Meiji, or the Taishō, period (1912–1926). Joining the effort by other contemporary schools, such as the socioeconomic school and the folklore study, it explored new areas in historical study, overcoming the narrow focus on political history characterizing the work of the first generation of academic historians. More specifically, drawing on the legacy of civilizational history and "people's history," Tsuda and like-minded contemporaries strove to shift the interest of the historian from political elites to the ordinary masses and take a holistic approach to historical interpretation. All this was consistent with the zeitgeist of the Taishō era. Though at times turbulent and unstable, the Taishō period witnessed a remarkable progress in advancing democratic, representative government. This progress undermined and eventually overthrew the dominance of the oligarchy in the Meiji government, and in its place a two-party system was established. Thanks to Japan's economic boom in World War I, the numbers of the middle class were on the rise, and so was the working class. Interest in universal male suffrage, workers' rights, civil rights, social welfare, feminism, unionism, socialism, and communism were also growing tremendously. All this had aided and, to a great extent, also pushed for more democratic changes at the government level. By asserting and amplifying Japan's independent and coherent cultural development in its past, Tsuda's and others' work reflected this growing public confidence in and high expectation for Japan's ascending stature as a modernizing country in pursuit of an equal standing with Western powers.

Perhaps more so than the others, Tsuda Sōkichi's historiography was representative of the historiographical changes of the time because it ingeniously expanded on the extant projects introduced by his predecessors. For instance, armed with the critical method, his teacher Shiratori Kurakichi had examined critically the historical literature of China's antiquity and shed doubts on its validity. Following Shiratori's interest, as well as that of Shiratori's teachers (e.g., Shigeno, Kume, and Hoshino), in ancient history, or the age of gods, Tsuda examined the reliability of the *Kojiki* (Records of Ancient Matters) and *Nihon shoki* (Chronicles of Japan), two of the earliest history texts in the Six National Histories, for understanding prehistoric Japan. Like his predecessors, he questioned their validity as historical sources, yet in the meantime, he acknowledged their value for offering clues to understanding the psyche and mind-set of the ancient people, a focus of his historiography. By refuting the historicity of these texts, which had been deemed fundamental by Shitonists and politicians to the sacredness of the imperial house, Tsuda, like his predecessors, later had to pay a hefty price. In the late 1930s, he was incarcerated briefly, and his works were prohibited from circulation.

Though the Taishō era marked a progressive turn in Japan's domestic politics, insofar as the country's foreign policy was concerned, it moved in the same direction dictated by the Meiji oligarchy. During the Meiji-Taishō transition in 1910, Japan formally annexed Korea, ending the 500-year rule of the Chosŏn dynasty. Following Taiwan, Korea now became Japan's other colony. It also expanded its interest in China by presenting the "twenty-one points plan" to the Chinese government, at the time presided over by Yuan Shikai (1859–1916), a former Qing official and the father of Chinese warlordism. Japan's ascendance in stature in world politics thus was achieved at the expenses of China and Korea. In the wake of World War I, Japan became the prime target in a new wave of the nationalist movement taking place in both countries. Hoping to regain the independent status for their country at the Versailles Conference, Koreans mounted the March First Movement of 1919, in which 2 million people participated, equaling about 10 percent of the country's population. Two months later, indignant at the agreement reached at the Versailles Conference according to which Japan was to expropriate Germany's sphere of influence in China, Chinese college students took to the Beijing streets and launched the May Fourth Movement. As landmarks for the growing nationalist movements, both events were significant in charting the cultural development in Korea and China.[47]

Myth and history: In search of the origin of the Korean nation

During the 1920s and the 1930s, nationalism was on the rise in both China and Korea. After the failure of the March First Movement of 1919, the Koreans had to cope with more brutal oppression under Japanese colonial rule. This rule had a scholarly dimension in that in support of their government's colonial policy, Japanese Korea scholars not only presumed the "backwardness/stagnation" of Korean civilization but also articulated reasons as to why it was so. In the main, their theory goes as follows. First, over its history, Koreans had never gained an independent status. Squeezed and bullied by powerful neighboring empires, they had been accustomed to depending on others (e.g., China), which explained the prevalence of flunkeyism (J. *jidai shugi*; K. *sadae juŭi*) in Korean history, particularly during the Chosŏn period. Second, via studies of archaeology, ethnography, philology, and history, Japanese Korea scholars, such as Shiratori Kurakichi, postulated that the Koreans and Japanese belonged to the same racial lineage (*Nissen dōsoron*), whose ancestors lived in many regions across Northeast

Asia in prehistoric time, and that during the fourth and seventh centuries, Korea had been ruled by the Japanese. In other words, Japan's rule of Korea liberated the Koreans from their historical subordination to China, and, now more civilized and more advanced, the Japanese were justified to "improve" the welfare of the racially related Korean brothers and sisters by ruling their country.[48]

In addition to developing the *Nissen dōsoron* theory, Shiratori took stock of Tan'gun, the mythic founder of ancient Korea, and took apart this creation myth cherished by the Korean people. By comparing the *Memorabilia of the Three Kingdoms* (*Samguk yusa*), a thirteenth-century text in which the Tan'gun story first appeared, with some earlier and contemporary historical texts found in both Korea and China, he concluded that the Tan'gun legend could not be created earlier than the fourth century CE because the *Memorabilia of the Three Kingdoms* bore Buddhist influence and Buddhism was not introduced into Korea until the fourth century and after.[49] A meticulous textual study, Shiratori's conclusion, however, was unacceptable by Koreans because it cut short their history, hurting their national pride in the most unpropitious time when it was much needed to withstand Japan's colonial rule.

Thus in the 1920s, Sin Ch'ae-ho (1880–1936), later hailed "the father of modern Korean historiography," published a series of works, debating and repudiating Shiratori and other Japanese *Tōyō* scholars of their interpretations of Korean history, surrounding the Tan'gun legend. Contrary to Shiratori, Sin Ch'ae-ho considered ancient Korean history, or the period of Three Chosŏn stretching from the prehistoric past to the first century BCE that began with Tan'gun, the most valuable because of its remarkable independent spirit and splendid cultural development. Of the Three Chosŏn, again, the Tan'gun period was the most significant because it quintessentially displayed *the* Korean cultural characteristics. In the same vein, Sin dismissed the importance of the second Chosŏn, or Kija Chosŏn, because Kija, a successor to Tan'gun, was a Chinese prince related to the Shang royal family and exiled to Korea after the dynasty's fall and because, during the Kija Chosŏn, there was tremendous Chinese cultural influence in Korea.[50] To some extent, Sin's work was comparable to that of the Chinese National Essence group; it amounted to a valiant effort to rediscover the "National Essence" in ancient Korea, for Kija had long been regarded as the founder of the Korean state during the 500-year rule of the fallen Chosŏn dynasty as an effort to strengthen Korea's tie with China.[51]

An original thinker, Sin Ch'ae-ho trekked a rather difficult path. On the one hand, in order to seek new ways in which Koreans could rebuild their country, he holds a negative, though sympathetic, stance toward the Chosŏn dynasty because it had cultivated a close relation with China for many centuries. In so doing, he seems to have acquiesced to the Japanese claim that his people had been heavily influenced by foreign, especially Chinese culture and that the Chosŏn period had been passive and inconsequential. On the other hand, by rediscovering and restoring Tan'gun, a legendary figure of divine descent supposedly born in 2333 BCE, as the first Korean king, he rejects the Japanese claim that Korea had always been dependent on the others. In fact, by establishing Tan'gun as the founder of Korea in such a remote past, he extends considerably the length of his country's history, making it comparable to if not longer than its neighbors'.

Sin Ch'ae-ho's delicate and daring endeavor proved inspirational to fellow Korean historians, even to this day.[52] In the writings of Ch'oe Nam-son (1890–1957), a wunderkind well-known for his literary and intellectual talent and his draft of the Korean Declaration of Independence in the March First Movement, we found a continual effort to emphasize the longevity of Korean history around Tan'gun. Influenced by modern historical scholarship, exemplified in the Japanese *Tōyō* study, Ch'oe combed through a number of historical sources and conducted folkloric and linguistic analysis of the Tan'gun legend. His conclusion was that the Tan'gun story offered clues to a particular practice of shamanism not only in ancient Korea but also in a broad region across Euro-Asia. This shamanistic practice, characterized by its worship of heaven, the human, and the underworld, had originated in Korea and spread to its neighbors in a later time. To make such a claim, Ch'oe first asserted that the T'aebaek Mountains, stretching from North Korea to Manchuria, where Tan'gun was born, were the birthplace of the shamanistic practice. He then took pains to argue, using fastidious and arbitrary linguistic evidence, that there had existed a northeast Asian cultural sphere, centering in ancient Korea. Thus, Korea was not only an independent entity but also a leader of the cultural development in Northeast Asia.[53]

During and despite Japan's rule, historical writing in Korea hence experienced a sea change. Sin Ch'ae-ho's and Ch'oe Nam-son's interest in the Tan'gun myth and even their theories about it, for example, had a good deal to do with the development of popular religion in modern Korea. In the religion of Tan'gun (*Tan'gun-gyo*), founded in 1905, Tan'gun was not only regarded as the founder of Korea but also worshiped as a savior of the Korean people from their plight. Other sects of popular religion also played an indispensable role in the course of Korean history. The uprising of the Tonghak religion in 1895, for example, triggered the Sino-Japanese War. The mobilization of the March First Movement also benefited from the participation of various religious sects. In modern times, the extent to which religious beliefs exerted their impact on the writing of history was greater in Korea than in Japan and China.[54]

The changes of Korean historiography also bore influences of nationalism, racialism, and social Darwinism, which came to Korea via not only Japan but also of China. In the early twentieth century, Liang Qichao's many writings and his call for the Historiographical Revolution had exerted great influence among Korean scholars. Sin Ch'ae-ho had translated some of Liang's essays into Korean. Like Liang, Sin, in his *New Reading of History (Toksa sillon)* (1908), vilified Confucian moralist historiography and advocated the need for historical writing to serve the cause of national salvation. Drawing on social Darwinism, he maintained that history is a struggle and that the struggle is between the "self" and the "other," a thesis that clearly reflects the grim reality of Korea's fight against Japanese colonialism.[55] Lastly, on a methodological level, Japanese *Tōyō* study apparently left its marks on the development of modern Korean historical scholarship, as shown in the founding of the Chindan Academic Association (*Chindan hakhoe*) in 1934. Dovetailing the empirical interest of *Tōyō* scholarship with the preexisting tradition of evidential learning in Korea, the CAA remains an influential academic society to this day, suggesting the persistent attraction of textual-critical study among modern Korean scholars.[56] Another example was found in Ch'oe Nam-son's proposition on the ancient Northeast Asian cultural sphere, which expanded on the *Nissen dōsoron* theory advanced by Shiratori and others. During the 1930s, Japanese politicians and scholars were working on establishing the so-called Greater East Asian Co-prosperity Sphere to justify their country's invasion of Manchuria and future territorial ambitions. Incidentally, Ch'oe had a thriving career under Japanese rule; unlike Sin Ch'ae-ho, who died tragically as an exiled revolutionary in 1936, Ch'oe, three years later in 1939, became a professor at Kenkoku University in Manchukuo, the Japanese puppet state, marking a stark contrast to his earlier image as an author and signer of the Korean Declaration of Independence.[57]

War and revolution: The appeal of Marxist historiography

Beginning in its occupation of Manchuria in 1931 and its large-scale invasion of China in 1937, Japan's military aggression turned the 1930s into a trying period for all Asian historians. Under the war threat, the Historical Source School in China, for example, gradually lost its dominant position and its appeal to the younger generation of students and scholars; its emphasis on careful source analysis and its preference for monographic study appeared distant to the harsh social reality. Instead, Marxist influence, shown in the writings of Li Dazhao (1888–1927) and Chen Duxiu (1879–1942), leaders of the May Fourth Movement and founders of the Chinese Communist Party, was growing markedly. Its influence in historical study precipitated the so-called Social History Controversy of 1931–1933, in which participants debated the nature of Chinese society in order to seek a tangible solution to the national crisis facing the people. These Marxist-oriented historians were contemplating the options of socialist and communist revolution and weighing and vacillating among the doctrines of Leninism, Trotskyism, and Stalinism.[58]

After Japan occupied many cities in China's coast regions in 1937–1938, Chinese universities retreated to inland areas, which made it impossible for historians to conduct monographic studies using original sources. Leaders of the Historical Source School also adapted their ideas of and approach to

history to the new environment. Fu Sinian, for example, tried to use historical evidence to condemn Japan's occupation of Manchuria. In contrast to
his earlier emphasis on monographic study, he now considered teaching the
general history of China, one that emphasized its longevity and vitality for
boosting the people's morale, a necessary component in college education.
A number of such general Chinese history textbooks thus were published, of
which Qian Mu's (1895–1990) *The Outlines of National History* (*Guoshi
dagang*) (1940) and Liu Yizheng's (1880–1956) *The Essentials of National
History* (*Guoshi yaoyi*) (1948) were most popular.

Beginning in the 1930s, historical writings in Vietnam, to which we have
so far paid little attention, also embarked on a new, modern course, characterized by its reception of a wide array of ideological influences from
abroad via the writings of Vietnamese scholars educated overseas, mostly
in France. Before that period, however, Vietnamese historical writing had
followed two parallel yet seemingly independent tracks of development.
On the one hand, French Orientalist scholars, particularly those working
at École Française d'Extrême Orient produced historical studies of Vietnam
in a modern fashion and disseminated such knowledge through their missionary schools to the Vietnamese. On the other hand, historical works by
native Vietnamese historians more or less adhered to the style and format
established by Confucian historians of the past. Tran Trong Kim (1883–
1953), a respected scholar and a nationalist, for example, published the
Brief History of Vietnam (*Viet-nam Su-luoc*) in 1928, which was written in
a modified traditional style. The book subsequently went through several
editions well into the 1960s, a testimony to its popularity and the tenacity of
tradition. But meanwhile it was evident that such new ideologies as Marxism, socialism, Trotskyism, and anarchism were increasingly filtering into
the Vietnamese ideas and writings of history. Dao Duy Anh's (1904–1988)
Short History of Vietnamese Culture (*Viet Nam van hoa su cuong*) (1938),
for example, marked the attempt to adopt the Marxist interpretive framework. Vietnamese scholars proficient in French also began publishing historical works about their country and its relations with France and Europe
in French scholarly journals. All this forecasted and, to some extent, also
fostered a more sweeping change in Vietnamese historiography after the end
of World War II.[59]

The rise of Marxist influence in the 1930s had in part to do with the
worldwide economic crisis triggered by the U.S. stock market crash in 1929,
which also hit Japan. But since the beginning of the twentieth century, Marxist, socialist, and communist ideas had already been present in Asia. *The
Communist Manifesto*, for example, was rendered into Japanese by such
scholars as Kōtoku Shūsui and Kawakami Hajime (1879–1946), the famous
Marxist teaching at Kyoto University, one of the centers of socioeconomic
history. During the Taishō period, many of Marx's works including *Capital*
also appeared in Japanese, inspiring, for example, Noro Eitarō (1900–1934),
a precocious Marxist historian, to analyze the historical development of

Japanese capitalism from a comparative perspective. Unfortunately, Noro was arrested by the government for his involvement in the labor movement in 1933 and died in police custody the following year. Noro's fellow comrades, including Hani Gorō (1901–1983), who had earned his history education at Tokyo University and Heidelberg University respectively, continued the project Noro had started on publishing a series of important books on Japanese capitalism. Hani's volume on the Meiji period, for example, was particularly well received, as was Hattori Shisō's (1901–1956) theoretical analysis of the nature of the Meiji Restoration. Rather than simply label it a bourgeois revolution, Hattori noticed the difference of the Meiji Restoration and other bourgeois revolutions in history and conducted an in-depth investigation in the formation of the bourgeois/landlord class in Japan.[60]

More importantly, joining other schools in expanding the field of history, Japanese Marxist historians were the first to promote the study of family and women's history. Takamure Itsue (1894–1964), a devoted feminist and a former anarchist, was an interesting example. Out of her feminist concern for female power and women's status, Takamure launched her study on the matriarchy system in ancient Japan. In her opinion, while women were given rights to own and inherit property during the Meiji period, they were still far from liberated, due mostly to the influence of the patriarchal tradition, which she identified as China's Confucian culture. In conducting her study, Takamure consulted Friedrich Engels' *Origins of the Family, Private Property and the State*, Lewis H. Morgan's *Ancient Society*, and Johann J. Bachofen's *Das Mutterrecht*, though oddly, her contact with other Japanese Marxists seemed infrequent. After World War II broke out, she became an ardent supporter of the government and assumed a leadership role in pro-war women organizations. She believed that the war against China extended her feminist cause because she blamed Chinese Confucian culture for undermining the matriarchal system indigenous to ancient Japan.[61]

In conclusion, the outbreak of World War II constituted yet another turn in the development of modern Asian historiography. In Japan, while the growth of Marxist historiography was suppressed, the so-called imperial historical school, led by Hiraizumi Kiyoshi (1895–1984), held sway. It offered staunch support to the militarist government, extolling Japan's sacred imperial rule as the basis for its unique "national body" (*kokutai*), in hopes of proving the invincibility of Japanese army. The theoretical contemplation on the national body was found in the works of Nishida Kitarō (1870–1945), "the father of modern Japanese philosophy" and the founder of the influential Kyoto School in modern Japan. In the 1930s, Nishida and his disciples philosophized Japan's rise as a new world power and its impact on the course of world history, lending justifications for their country's military aggression.[62] Indeed, during wartime, few could uphold dissenting views as the government had stepped up its persecution of dissidents. Tsuda Sōkichi's incarceration is worth mentioning again because it was by no means an isolated case at the time. In wartime China, there were also efforts to shore up the nationalist government for fighting the Japanese invasion. The decline of the Historical Source School was conducive to developing new schools, of which Marxist historiography was most notable. In Yan'an, the communist base, a new generation of Marxist historians competed and challenged the stature and influence of Hu Shi, Gu Jiegang, and Fu Sinian. They were to become new leaders of the Chinese historical circle after the communists took over power in 1949. In postwar Japan, Vietnam, and Korea, as we shall see in the next chapter, Marxist historiography too constituted a major trend in historiography, though the extent of its influence varied from one to the other and over time.

Nationalist historiography in modern India

Late nineteenth-century antecedents: Romantic nationalism

In 1924, Mohandas Karamchand Gandhi, by then the undisputed leader of the Indian nationalist movement, made the following remarkable observation:

> I have no desire to engage the reader's attention upon my speculations on the value of history considered as an aid to the evolution of our race. I believe in the saying that a nation is happy that has no history. It is my pet theory that our Hindu ancestors solved the question for us by ignoring history as it is understood today and by building on slight events their philosophical structure. Such is the *Mahabharata*. And I look upon Gibbon and Motley as inferior editions of the *Mahabharata*.[63]

Gandhi's distrust of history was not shared by his fellow nationalist travelers. In 1899, the Indian poet Rabindranath Tagore remarked on the noticeable "enthusiasm for history" among the Indian public. Here the question arises as to when a nationalist historiography that embraced the idea of an independent Indian nation came into being. We have seen that colonialist historiography had provoked a response as early as the 1850s, a response that critiqued the Orientalist presumptions about the Indian past. Another strand of writing, as represented by the economic nationalists such as Naoroji, Ranade, and Dutt, emphasized the negative economic impact of British rule but remained in the main politically loyalist. An openly anti-colonialist historiography rose to the fore only with the radicalization of the Indian politics in the early twentieth century. But this is not to say that groundwork had not already been prepared decades earlier. The pivotal role of history and historical consciousness in the articulation of nationhood was clearly understood among the Indian literati. R. C. Dutt had claimed, "No study has so potent an influence in forming a nation's mind and a nation's character as a critical and careful study of its past history."[64] Dutt, of course, was known for his economic analysis of British rule, but he was also the author of a three-volume work on the history of ancient India and a historical novelist who made conscious use of the genre, as did Sir Walter Scott, whose fictional works he admired, to generate a sense of patriotic valor and interest in the past.

As in Europe, the historical novel played a critical role in the rise of nationalist consciousness, and Dutt's writings in the genre owed much to the encouragement of another Bengali, the well-known writer Bankimchandra Chatterjee (1838–1894), whose own historical novels were avidly consumed by the Bengali reading public. Bankim, who has been credited with "dreaming up the icon of the nation" with his various agenda-setting essays and historical novels, was a powerful stimulus for historical reflection among the Bengali intelligentsia in particular. If Gandhi rejected history and the pull of the past, Bankim conceived history as the only possible cure for India's political weakness. His fierce outcry "We have no history! We must have a history!" was in effect a struggle for power and a call to action since, as we have already seen, when this statement was made in 1880, there was already a considerable body of indigenous historical writing. But for Bankim, these writings did not represent a real history since they did not recount the heroic and glorious deeds of Indians past. That such a recounting was necessary showed his cognizance of the political value of history. Who will write such a history, he asked? "You will write it, I will write it, everyone will write this history." The writing of history would be a collective act, an act of praxis that would give rise to a national collective pregnant with possibilities. Bankim's agenda therefore went much further than that of an earlier generation of historians like Basak whose primary aim was to counter the colonial stereotypes. And it showed a canny awareness of the myth-making potential of the historical novel, a form in which he excelled. As in Europe and elsewhere during the second half of the nineteenth century, there was in India a conflict between the "scientific" and Romantic or fictionalized traditions of national history.[65] Bankim's blatant attempts to politicize history ran counter to the strict scientific standards that scholars such as Bhandarkar had emphasized. Yet in many ways it was nineteenth-century writers such as Bankim, outside the historical profession, who had the greater impact on the popular historical consciousness of the twentieth century. Scholars have shown that the principles of academic history, not only in India but also in France, Britain, and elsewhere, evolved out of the creative tension between the scientific and the popular, with the former honing the fundamentals of the discipline as a knowledge form against the "fictionalized" accounts.[66] But if history was to be an agent of liberation, room had to be made for the emotional and imaginary in the depiction of the past. This was shown by the fact that many adherents of scientific history in early twentieth-century India were also authors of historical romances, although they were clear to keep these writings separate from their scholarly works.

The role of religion in nationalist historiography

A recurrent theme to emerge among the nationalist leaders of the twentieth century, by way of Bankim, was the role of the *Bhagavad Gita* as a source of inspiration.[67] Krishna's "way of the warrior" speech to Arjuna in the *Gita* found much appeal among some of the insurrectionist nationalist leaders in search of martial heroes. Thus the Maharashtrian nationalist Bal Gangadhar Tilak (1856–1920) agreed with Bankim that Krishna was a historical figure. Significantly, Tilak also glorified the historical, not the mythological, Maratha leader Shivaji (1627/30–1680), whose resistance against the Mughal emperor Aurangzeb he extolled as a battle for the survival of Hinduism, thus giving rise to the Shivaji cult that became commonplace among nationalists and communalists alike in the early twentieth century.[68] Tilak's concept of *swaraj* (self-rule), which was directed against the British, also rested on a version of India that was Hindu and Vedic, and his attempts to revive religious festivals such as the Lord Ganesha processions were motivated by a politicized concept of religion. Highly aware that collective identity was to some degree, if not entirely, a construction, Tilak ignored the many gods, traditions, and rules of social stratification that characterized Hinduism and defied homogenization. The task was to construct a narrative that bypassed evidence of such pluralism. British assertions that the political unity of India was based on their own achievement could be countered only by claims of national unity resting on a common culture. Such claims were not necessarily exclusivist. During the 1920s, as we will see later, several books focusing on the political and cultural formations of ancient India emphasized the geographic space encompassing shrines, pilgrimage sites, social institutions, and imperial formations that bound a people together but that was open enough to accommodate other cultures and traditions within it. But the emphasis on an ancient and therefore pre-Islamic past increasingly led to the identification of Indian unity with Hinduism. The unity of India was the unity of the Hindus. As Tilak claimed, this "unity has disappeared bringing on us great degradation, and it becomes the duty of leaders to revive that union."[69]

This duty was embraced by V. D. Savarkar (1883–1966). A terrorist, historian, and "national hero" to those of the Hindu Right, Savarkar's solution to India's unwieldy pluralism was to merge "Hinduness" (*Hindutva*) with geography, racial connection, and shared culture based on high Hindu, that is, Vedic tradition. "Hindutva is not a word but a history," he claimed, of which "Hinduism is only a derivative." An avid admirer of Garibaldi and Mazzini (whose biography he had translated into Marathi), Savarkar took the nationalist discourse one step further by formulating an ethnic identity based on the religious practices of a people bound within a particular geographical area. A Hindu is:

> he who looks upon the land that extends . . . from the Indus to the Seas, as the land of his forefathers, his Fatherland, who inherits the blood

of that race whose first discernable source could be traced to the Vedic *Saptasindhus* (seven rivers) and which on its onward march, assimilating much that was incorporated and ennobling much that was assimilated, has come to be known as the Hindu people, who has inherited and claims as his own the culture of that race.[70]

Hindutva therefore comes into existence both at a point of origin and through time, through history, and it is this common history that underlines the claim to nationhood, not just in the metaphorical sense but also in acts of resistance, as in the Indian uprising of 1857–1858, which the British called a "mutiny" and Savarkar *The Indian War of Independence*, the title of his historical monograph of 1909 and the first of such books to question the mutiny version of that event.

Savarkar's idea of *Hindutva* proposed a master narrative for the emergent nation-state, the basis for a comprehensive history of India. It was, of course, unabashedly sectarian and exclusivist. Its high-caste Hindu ideology averred a majoritarian version of the nation that marginalized the other religions and castes, and, indeed, Savarkar is the acknowledged ideological mentor of Hindu political fundamentalism. But as we have seen, such ideas had their nineteenth-century antecedents. What is striking in Savarkar is the ethnicizing of *Hindutva* in terms of a sacralized geography. India was the true home of the Hindus because it was the country of their salvation (*punyabhu*). Muslims and Christians, although a part of the Indian population, were of divided loyalties, because the lands holy to them lay elsewhere.

The nation as history and history as science

The insistence on unity and homogeneity impacted historical writing insofar as the nation as a comprehensive and discrete entity became the focus of historical research, although partisan accounts of regions, castes, and religious communities flourished as well. But the gaze went toward the distant past. As Sumit Sarkar states, nationalist historiography in the preindependence period "developed on sites some distance from what, on logical grounds, should have been its proper location: the rich and growing traditions of contemporary anticolonial movements . . . and the history of colonial India consequently remained very much a narrative of viceroys, Afghan or Burmese wars, and administrative and 'constitutional' reforms."[71] Partly this was due to the watchful eye of the colonial state, and it has been rightly argued that, prior to 1947, nationalist historical writing was not as advanced as the movement itself.[72] For many of the historians of the 1920s onward, such as R.K. Mookerji (1880–1964) and K.P. Jayaswal (1881–1937), ancient India was the focal point, and the point was the portrayal of a civilization that disabused negative colonial portrayals, especially that of Oriental Despotism. Jayaswal pointed to the highly evolved political systems of ancient times, of the *ganas* and *sanghas* that were the incontrovertible proof of republican polities. Mookerji went further and, opposing the British view that India lacked unity prior to the arrival of the British, argued that auguries of the nation-state could be found in the ancient kingdoms of Ashoka, Chandragupta, and Harsha, who now began to appear as proto–freedom fighters. It would not be an exaggeration to say that most of the academic writing of this time was a counterhistoriography to the colonialist one, which was becoming more strident in the face of nationalist agitation. Both Vincent Smith's *Oxford History of India* (1919) and the six volumes of the British-sponsored *Cambridge History of India* (1922–1932) were thoroughly colonialist in their assumptions. Anglophone historical writing also endeavored to mute the radical implications of the economic nationalists with their own economic histories. Most influential among these was W. H. Moreland's *The Agrarian System of Moslem India* (1924), which attempted to argue that the pre-British economy was small and its trade networks hampered by lack of infrastructure and transport. This view was challenged by Jadunath Sarkar (1870–1958) who, despite his critical views of the emperor Aurangzeb, argued that the Mughals broke the isolation of the provinces and contributed to the modernization of India.

Sarkar, one of the most prolific historians of his generation, was regarded by his contemporaries as the Indian Ranke and was a most ardent advocate of modern scientific historiography. In a 1915 speech, he informed his audience that the "best method in historical studies is the scientific method" and added, ". . . I shall seek truth, understand truth and accept truth. This should be the firm resolve of an historian."[73] Sarkar's interests lay in the seventeenth and eighteenth centuries, primarily in the Mughals that perforce also directed his attention toward Aurangzeb's adversary Shivaji, who was depicted by Sarkar as a heroic figure.[74] However, unlike some of his contemporaries, such as the Maratha historian G. S. Sardesai (1865–1959), Sarkar was vehemently against a partisan reading of the sources. Sarkar was very critical of Sardesai's use of the Marathi *bakhars*, or historical ballads, which, on the basis of the principles of source criticism, were unsupported by the evidence. Sarkar regarded both Sardesai's reading of Shivaji as well as the writings of K. P. Jayaswal too motivated. Jayaswal's writings, he wrote, are "ninety-nine percent nationalist brag and moonshine."[75]

At the behest of Rajendra Prasad, the first president of independent India, Sarkar was invited as chief editor of a planned two-volume history of India, which ceased publication after only one volume. However, in 1935, the Indian History Congress, the first all-India association of historians, was established and with it the Rankean model of history, with its emphasis on politics, precision, and public archives, became the unquestioned paradigm among professional historians.

The hold of this paradigm among Indian academic historians in the 1920s and 1930s has received much attention.[76] Kumkum Chatterjee has shown that by the late nineteenth century, colonial education had produced a generation of Indian scholars for whom "the practice of history was inexorably associated with rational-positivist history grounded in verifiable facts."[77] Such views no doubt countered the colonialist charge that Indians lacked historical sense, but they also indicated a commitment to a particular type of history, one based on rational analysis and "hard evidence," in particular archaeological, numismatic, and epigraphic evidence, which was seen as being more reliable than textual and especially preprint culture material. In fact, many of the hard evidence enthusiasts were archaeologists, and the spectacular discoveries of the Indus Valley cities of Harappa and Mohenjodaro in the 1920s appeared to give strength to their reputations and views. But the paradigm of a rational-positivist history did not go unchallenged as newer forms of romantic history emerged.

The romance of the local and the emergence of alternative narratives

In the late colonial period, there were two sets of competing frameworks of history. The first was the colonialist history and the indigenous response to it, which we have already addressed. The second, related to the nature of historical writing itself, was an internal controversy within indigenous writing based on the dichotomies of *samaj/rashtra* (social and cultural history versus state-centered history) and romantic versus scientific history. These dichotomies also underlined a divide between professional historians and amateurs.

Kumkum Chatterjee has shown how acrimonious and public this divide was in the Bengal region during the 1920s and 1930s.[78] We have seen that by the late nineteenth century, there was an interest in social historical topics among Bengali writers with a strong romantic and populist bent. In the twentieth century, particularly after the *Swadeshi* upsurge, there was a resurgence of interest in populist history, a "folk history" of the Bengali people, based not on official archives and administrative records but on local myths, tales, genealogies, arts, crafts, customs, and material culture. One prominent example of such writing was Dineshchandra Sen's *Brihat Banga* (1935), the result of two decades of research and wanderings through the Bengali countryside. Sen called his work a "true history," a history that celebrated and privileged the folk culture of the Bengali people and equally the repositories of their traditions over texts, archives, and elites. Yet the bulk of *samaj*-oriented social and cultural history had the Bengali Hindu middle class (*bhadralok*) as its focus, rather than the common people.[79] Additionally, it appears that the social history thrust developed outside of the world of the formal historical profession, among autodidacts and those with an antiquarian bent. In this outlook, real history was not only an ethnographic undertaking, it was also indigenous in inspiration, as opposed to the Persian and colonialist histories, which were both foreign and state-centered (*rashtra*-oriented) history and would only alienate Indians from their own culture.[80] This, then, was a nationalist historiography of a different kind, a rebuttal to colonialist historiography at another level, one that could also be found in other modernizing nation-states across Asia as well, as Chatterjee had shown. It was also an effort to discover an authentic culture, untouched by foreign influences, and suggests a localized and regionalized cultural nationalism that ran parallel to the "official" nationalism of the political organizations. Of course, much of the writing was uncritical since the culture that it portrayed was idealized and romanticized. Together with the historical novel, these works increased the popularity of the genre of history. Yet so strong was its antipathy to that other statist, rationalist-positivist paradigm that it could not conceive that *samaj* and *rashtra* might be linked, preferring to see the social and cultural as untouched and untainted. But despite their differences, both modalities shared certain common assumptions. First, the past that they focused on tended to be Hindu and upper caste, a serious omission since it involved a region with a huge Muslim and lower-caste population. Second, they shared the belief in an Indian and Bengali agency in the writing of history. No colonial narrative could capture the essence of the Indian past.

The populist writers made additional claims. First, history was not the exclusive turf of the so-called professional historians. The amateur enthusiast was equally qualified to write sound history. Second, just as history was to be the story of ordinary people, so was its audience. The methodological rigor of formal history writing had no appeal for readers because it lacked emotion and heart. "What these scholars valorized was rather an instinctive, nonformalized manner of recovering the past, unfettered by structured methodology or criteria and evaluation."[81] Since specialized training in the discipline was not a requirement, the late colonial era witnessed the burgeoning of a large number of local histories, as well as the founding of locally sponsored literary and historical societies, such as the Bangiya Sahitya Parishad, established in 1900. It should be noted that at this time government funding for pure research did not go beyond the establishment of institutions like the Asiatic Society and the Anthropological Survey, and furthermore, history was not a university subject at the postgraduate level until after World War I, and most graduate level departments were established only after the war. Academic journals were few, and the colonial government resisted opening up the records to Indian students.[82] Local cultural organizations such as the Bangiya Sahitya Parishad therefore played an important role in the public sphere. By contemporary standards, such efforts were meager, no doubt, nor can one make mammoth claims for the quality of the output. "Inadequate funding for full-time research, confinement within national or regional parameters in the absence of opportunities for wider contacts, the restrictive aspects of a nationalist paradigm shot through with unstated class and high-caste assumptions (quite often sliding into communalist attitudes), all exerted a price. The 'best' scholarship of those times, with rare exceptions, appears unacceptably limited, parochial and un-self-questioning today."[83]

It has been argued that regional histories flourished in the late colonial period because the Education Department approved of a history that fragmented India and thus confirmed the colonialist view that India prior to the advent of the British was nothing more than a "geographical expression."[84] But the enthusiasm for the local also reflected important political concerns. In Bengal, the Partition of 1905 and the political agitation that followed suggested that there was a need to establish the historical integrity of the region for the sake of its geographical integrity. In Western India, there emerged a long string of histories celebrating the Maratha kings and their struggles against both the Muslims and the English. In the South, another sort of traditionalism emerged, one that prioritized Dravidological research and Tamil culture. The region and the nation emerged in tandem in late colonial Indian historiography, invoking different icons and emotive references. Whereas Hindu nationalism looked to the Vedas and the Brahmanical discourse, the cultural identifications of regions such as Bengal were the local gods and cults (*Kali,* the*Vaishnav* sects, and so on). Of course, individuals and groups could and did identify with both representations of the community and had overlapping identities. This complex and sometimes tension-ridden relationship between the national and regional in the context of anti-imperial politics is a subject for further examination.

In South and Western India, there also developed another narrative that questioned the high-caste Hindu and North Indian presumptions of the bulk of nationalist historiography. This narrative claimed that Brahminical dominance and Aryan imperialism had suppressed and subverted the indigenous regional cultures and peoples. Thus the theme of caste conflict was inserted into the historiography of this period, and it found political expression as well with the formation of various lower-caste political associations. But these histories, of mediocre quality, were generally ignored by academic historians. The same was true of Islamic writing, which now more than ever was moving toward a "two-nation" concept of nationalist writing that was at the same time highly state-centric, since, as the poet Muhammad Iqbal (1877–1938) asserted, in Islam, "Church and State were organically bound with each other."[85] But this was not the only view among Muslim intellectuals. Sayyid Ab'l-ala-Maududi (1903–1979) regarded South Asian Muslims as a separate religious community but did not see them as a nation, speaking instead to the universalizing mission of Islam, which went beyond the narrow confines of the nation.[86]

The nation reimagined: The Nehruvian synthesis

By the 1930s, the claim that Indians lacked historical consciousness could no longer be made. At the 1939 meetings of the Indian Historical Congress, it was stated that "no subject is perhaps studied in the Indian universities of the present day with the same assiduity as the history of India." This estimation was probably correct and no less remarkable given the paucity of official backing. Of course, after independence, official sponsorship was much more forthcoming. The postcolonial Indian government was quick to recognize the role of history in the task of nation-building, in correcting the colonialist narratives, and in documenting the "freedom struggle" against the colonizers. In this enterprise, India's historians had the unstinting support of its first prime minister, Jawaharlal Nehru, an innovative thinker and a historian of no small repute. His *Glimpses of World History* (1934) had been one of the few works of his generation to go beyond the usual Eurocentric surveys to encompass all the major civilizations. In *The Discovery of India* (1946), written in jail and at a juncture when India's independence was imminent, Nehru grappled with concept of the Indian nation and what it meant to be an Indian.

"There is not, and never was an India." This declaration by John Strachey (1823–1907), an administrator of the British *Raj*, had been a constant refrain among colonial commentators, and it was based on a conception of India as a continent that was fractious, unwieldy, and diverse. Nehru's response was to propose a complex, fluid, and layered definition of India and Indian-ness that was the very fruit of history's journey. His India was an "ancient palimpsest on which layer upon layer of thought and reverie had been inscribed, and yet no succeeding layer had completely hidden or erased what had been written previously."[87] The result was a "fusion" culture that had a civilizational identity without quite being a "melting pot." India indeed consisted of many communities, but these communities were not exclusive entities and were constantly engaged with one another. The extension of this concept to the temporal dimension implied that there could not be any unfortunate and intervening period of Indian history that was at variance with an otherwise autochthonous past – a past whose exclusive (and imagined) boundaries the Hindu nationalists sought to delineate as the dominant characteristic of India.

The novelty and advantage of Nehru's definition of India were that it provided a medium – one of openness and multiculturalism – that envisaged a quilting of India's many communities into a political fabric in which all could have a sense of civic citizenship. The role of the constitution and the federal democracy was to ensure that this fabric retained its integrity without any tendency toward domination by any major ethnic group. An implication of this was the concept of regional plurality and the freedom of each community to grow without external impositions. Further, it was open to the exigencies and demands of modernity and its counterpart, the modern nation-state, the guarantor of the entity that was India. Unlike the Hindu nationalists and even Gandhi, Nehru did not shy away from India's encounter with the West. In the intermingling of India's many cultures through time and history, even colonialism and the West were to be included to the extent that they had deposited the imprint of modernity. Nehru eschewed both the antihistorical and antimodernist impulses of his mentor Gandhi. India's economic development was contingent on its acceptance of the modernist project.

Postindependence historiography: Old and new trajectories

History in the postindependence period became a national project endorsing both the sovereignty of the nation and the autonomy of the Indian point of view. Government-sponsored history ventured into two major areas. The first related to the nationalist movement, now referred to as the "freedom struggle." The second major project went in the biographical direction, starting with a collection of Gandhi's works and speeches, and later moving on to other national figures like Vallabhai Patel, B. R. Ambedkar, and others.[88] The third nationalist project, sponsored not by the government but by private institutions (with some financial support from the government) and in some ways the largest and most controversial of the projects, aimed at a multivolume comprehensive history of India from ancient times to the present, a task that was well overdue considering that the last such project had been James Mill's eight volumes on India. As nationalist historiographies, all three projects were in the nature of hagiographies.

The freedom struggle initiative took place soon after independence. In 1950, it was decided by the chair of the committee that initiated the project, the well-known historian and educational adviser Tara Chand, that the phrase "freedom struggle" instead of "independence movement" better captured Indians' agency on the road to liberation. It has been suggested that Tara Chand was no doubt aware that among some sections it was felt that Indians did not have to fight very hard for their freedom; otherwise, Gandhi's nonviolent tactics would not have worked.[89] Tara Chand was conscious of the historical character of nationalism and conceded that India's national consciousness was the result of the impact of the West, although he also emphasized that in the West itself nationalism was a recent phenomenon. His view of history was broader and more critical than many of the other nationalist historians. His study of the influence of Islam on Indian culture reflected his disapproval of the religious contours of Indian nationalism.

Eventually the freedom struggle project, instead of being a collaborative undertaking, fell to Tara Chand to complete single-handedly. The first of his four volumes of *History of the Freedom Movement* appeared in 1961. It was also decided at this time that state governments should collect material for the regional histories of the freedom struggle, and in due course a number of such studies appeared, often competing with one another to occupy center stage in the fight for freedom (thus the Uttar Pradesh histories tried to utilize the Mutiny of 1857–1858 as the core event in the awakening of national consciousness). Bipan Chandra has pointed out that much of this writing was Whiggish, in that it exhibited a tendency to portray the national movement as the product of a love of liberty and freedom that was old and deeply ingrained in the character of Indians (or their regional counterparts). Thus, while Tarachand saw nationalism as an import, Oriya historians traced the origins of the Oriyan national movement to a love of liberty that went back to Asoka's invasion of Kalinga in the third century BCE.[90]

There was still a comprehensive history of India to be written, however. In 1951, the first of 11 volumes of *The History and Culture of the Indian People* came into print. The publisher of the series was the Bhartiya Vidya Bhavan, an educational institution dedicated to the promotion of Indian and specifically Hindu culture and values. The founder of the institution was the Gujarati literary figure and scholar K. M. Munshi (1887–1971), whose novels celebrated the glory of India's Hindu ancestors and their eclipse under Muslim rule. Munshi had long been interested in a comprehensive history of India that would capture her (Hindu) "soul" and was able to secure the financial support of the wealthy industrialist G. D. Birla for this project. The well-known Bengali historian Romesh Chandra Majumdar (1888–1980) was appointed general editor of the *History and Culture* volumes and, between the two, oversaw "the most ambitious history of India by Indians ever attempted."[91]

This history turned the palimpsest model of Indian culture put forward by Nehru on its head. Where Nehru celebrated the country's multicultural past and its "unity in diversity," the Bhavan-sponsored volumes proclaimed an India that was primarily Hindu, prey to outside invasions but always resilient, culturally and spiritually vital despite extraneous influences.[92] Majumdar rejected the "composite culture" of Nehru, seeing it as the ideology of a government struggling to erase the memory of Partition while pandering to its minorities. Majumdar, of course, rejected the colonialist narratives as well but not the tripartite division of India's past or the characterization of the Muslim period as the "dark age" that was "accompanied by a marked decadence of culture and the disappearance of the creative spirit in art and literature."[93] Majumdar's communalist antipathies led him to argue, when dealing with the nationalist phase of Indian history, that the Mutiny of 1857–1858 in no way represented a fraternal uprising of Hindus and Muslim Indians against the British. Like Tara Chand but from a completely different political motivation, he argued that nationalism was a Western idea, and in one sense he was even grateful to the British because they had relieved India of the tyranny of Muslim rule.

The communalist interpretation of the Indian past ran counter to the official discourse. It was also opposed by other well-known academic historians. In 1969, Romila Thapar, Harbans Mukhia, and Bipan Chandra authored *Communalism and the Writing of Indian History*, in which they disputed some of the common assumptions of the communalist position, both within the guild and in Hindu political organizations like the Rashtriya Swayamsevak Sangh (RSS). Romila Thapar, regarded as one of the most prominent historians of the ancient period, confirmed in her scholarship views that were hotly denied by the communalists, including, among other things, that the Aryans had come from outside of India and ate beef and that Vedic culture was the product of an admixture of outside and indigenous elements. She and others pointed to the constructed character of the communal conflict, and the culprit here was the colonial state.

Indian Muslim historians such as Abul Hasan Ali Nadwi (1914–1999) also emphasized the "syncretic" nature of Hindu-Muslim relations and the positive contributions of the Muslim impact. The declaration of Pakistan as a Muslim state in 1956, however, meant that Pakistani writing would have to focus on the creation of a separate history for Muslims, which "resulted in the virtual abandonment of historical writing in the future Pakistan."[94]

Toward a social science history

The Indian secular historians were, of course, heirs to the Nehruvian tradition, which was also anticolonialist and somewhat to the left. By the 1960s, this tradition had also come to embody some of the best work in terms of scholarship. A "paradigm shift," to quote Romila Thapar, occurred with the publication, in 1956, of D. D. Kosambi's (1907–1966) *Introduction to the Study of Indian History*. Although a Marxist, Kosambi was by no means a dogmatic one. Certainly he did not accept Marx's theory of the Asiatic Mode of Production, but his focus on social formations, class conflict, and material life took the discourse to another level of inquiry, away from ruling dynasties, wars, good kings and bad. Kosambi's *Introduction* reinterpreted the "medieval"/Muslim period of Indian history in terms of an Indian form of feudalism that was also accompanied by important technological changes. His work generated further investigations into Indian feudalism by historians such as R. S. Sharma and Irfan Habib, as well as lively interest among medieval historians in other parts of the world in alternate forms of feudalism. Further, the emphasis on social formations led to the first interrogations of the tripartite periodization of Indian history.

At the same time, the freedom struggle, while continuing to draw attention, become less of an obsession as other issues and concerns pertaining to the 1960s and 1970s directed scholars toward other issues and concerns. The rise of the political Left, as well as the growing fractiousness of Indian politics in general, signaled, among other things, by the Congress Party's decline in influence, and, lastly, the failures of "development," redirected attention to the question raised by the economic nationalists at the turn of the century, namely the failure of colonialism to develop the Indian economy. Bipan Chandra, a professor at Jawaharlal Nehru University, established in 1969 and reputed for its left-centric student politics, drew attention to the relationship between the structures of international capitalism and underdevelopment in the postcolonial era, that is to say, neocolonialism. Such investigations were also provoked by the "neocolonialist" narratives of scholars such as the American economic historian Morris D. Morris, who argued on behalf of the benefits of colonial rule. Bipan Chandra, who was on the left but also recognized the idealistic dimensions of the Indian nationalist movement, also questioned the views of a new generation of Cambridge historians, for whom the Indian nationalists were a group of fractious and power-driven politicos, who often collaborated with the British but whose primary ambition was to step into their masters' shoes.[95] "Men and women make history," Chandra claimed, "not only because of material forces and interests but also through and because of ideas" and warned against the "error of disregarding ideas and ideologies . . . of taking the mind out of history," for it also had the negative aspect of leading the historian "to ignore the traditions and values of democracy, civil liberty, secularism, humanism and reason which were embedded in the national movement from its inception."[96] The most discerning of the Indian Marxist historians recognized that a cookie-cutter approach to Marx's categories was counterproductive, that while Marx's general understanding of the dynamics of history had value, the Western and European trajectory of development may not apply to the Indian situation.

During this time, there was also a reemphasis on the social and cultural, but it tended to be confined to the precolonial period and was heavily influenced by anthropological and sociological frameworks and in particular to the work of M. N. Srinivas (1916–1999), whose concept of "sanskritization" allowed for a formulation of social change and historical development within the parameters of a specific cultural practice. For the colonial period, it was still the nationalist paradigm that predominated, and one reason for this was, as Sumit Sarkar suggests, "the social, inevitably constituted in large part also by 'internal' tensions, presented more intractable material for a nationalist historiography committed to a saga of a basically united people."[97] A section of Marxist historians did, of course, focus on the class struggles of workers and peasants for the colonial period, but most tended toward a largely mechanical Leninist application. The region continued to receive attention in the form of a provincial historiography that had sanction within the federal structure of the Union and was to be differentiated from postindependence political separatism. A number of scholarly journals also emerged, such as the *Indian Economic and Social History Review* (1963), which was devoted mainly to the colonial period. Additionally, non-Marxist studies in the area of "economic history" appeared. Among the first and well-known of such works was Dharma Kumar's *Land and Caste in South India* (1965), which utilized anthropological and quantitative techniques to produce a picture of economic and demographic change under colonial rule. It was only in the 1970s, however, that newer concerns and perspectives were brought into the area of the social, in which issues of gender, caste, worker, and "peasant insurgency" independent of mainstream nationalism were brought into focus.

Notes

1 Bernard Lewis, *The Emergence of Modern Turkey* (London, 1968), 181–182. Also, Selçuk Akşin Somel, *The Modernization of Public Education in the Ottoman Empire, 1839–1908: Islamization, Autocracy and Discipline* (Leiden, 2001).

2 Cf. Carter Vaughn Findley, "An Ottoman Occidentalist in Europe: Ahmed Midhat Meets Madame Gulnar, 1889," *American Historical Review*, 103:1 (February 1998), 15–49.

3 Lewis, *Emergence of Modern Turkey*, 189–191, 333–343; Erik J. Zürcher, *Turkey: A Modern History* (London, 1993), 71–72.

4 Jack A. Crabbs, Jr., *The Writing of History in Nineteenth-century Egypt: A Study in National Transformation* (Cairo, 1984), 156–162; Thomas Mayer, *The Changing Past: Egyptian Historiography of the Urabi Revolt, 1882–1983* (Gainesville, 1988), 7–8.

5 Supraiya Faroqhi, *Approaching Ottoman History: An Introduction to the Sources* (Cambridge, 1999), 176; Geoffrey Barraclough, *Main Trends in History* (New York, 1979), 128.

6 Lewis, *Emergence of Modern Turkey*, 333, 343.

7 Bernard Lewis, "History Writing and National Revival in Turkey" in his *From Babel to Dragomans: Interpreting the Middle East* (London, 2004), 424–426; and Alastair Bonnett, "Makers of the West: National Identity and Occidentalism in the Work of Fukuzawa Yukichi and Ziya Gökalp," *Scottish Geographical Journal*, 118:3 (2000), 165–182.

8 Lewis, "History Writing and National Revival in Turkey," 425–426. Ercüment Kuran, "Ottoman Historiography of the Tanzimat Period" in Bernard Lewis and P. M. Holt, eds., *Historians of the Middle East* (Oxford, 1962), 428–429.

9 Speros Vryonis, Jr., *The Turkish State and History: Clio Meets the Grey Wolf* (Thessaloniki, 1991), 68–69.

10 Nancy Elizabeth Gallagher, ed., *Approaches to the History of the Middle East: Interviews with Leading Middle East Historians* (Reading, 1994), 154.

11 See Cemal Kafadar, *Between Two Worlds: The Construction of the Ottoman State* (Berkeley, 1996), 33.

12 Vryonis, *Turkish State and History*, 70–77.

13 Cf. Kafadar, *Between Two Worlds*, 35–44. Also, Leslie Peirce, "Changing Perceptions of the Ottoman Empire: The Early Centuries," *Mediterranean Historical Review*, 19:1 (June 2004), 6–28.

14 Bonnett, "Makers of the West."

15 Crabbs, *Writing of History in Nineteenth-century Egypt*, 186–188; Gamal el-Din el-Shayyal, "Historiography in Egypt in the Nineteenth Century" in Lewis and Holt, *Historians of the Middle East*, 414–416.

16 Crabbs, *Writing of History in Nineteenth-century Egypt*, 188–192; Donald M. Reid, *Cairo University and the Making of Modern Egypt* (Cambridge, 1990), 22–24.

17 Crabbs, *Writing of History in Nineteenth-century Egypt*, 153.

18 Ibid., 191; Reid, *Cairo University*, 35–37.

19 Reid, *Cairo University*, 83.

20 Anthony Gorman, *Historians, State and Politics in Twentieth Century Egypt: Contesting the Nation* (London, 2003), 21.

21 Youssef M. Choueiri, *Modern Arab Historiography: Historical Discourse and the Nation-State* (London, 2003), 77.

22 Cited in Gorman, *Historians, State and Politics in Twentieth Century Egypt*, 27.

23 Jack Crabbs, Jr. "Politics, History, and Culture in Nasser's Egypt," *International Journal of Middle East Studies*, 6:4 (October 1975), 389. This assessment, however, is disputed by Youseff Choueiri in his *Modern Arab Historiography*, in that Ibrahim Sabrī's work was marred by his political involvement with the Wafd, 77–78.

24 Lewis, "History Writing and National Revival in Turkey," 428.

25 Cf. Choueiri, *Modern Arab Historiography*, 71–72; Marion Farouk-Sluglett and Peter Sluglett, "The Historiography of Modern Iraq," *The American Historical*

Review, 96:5 (December 1991), 1408–1421; also Barraclough, *Main Trends in History*, 128–129.

26 Firuz Kazemzadeh, "Iranian Historiography" in Lewis and Holt, *Historians of the Middle East*, 430–432; Touraj Atabaki, "Agency and Subjectivity in Iranian National Historiography" in Touraj Atabaki, ed., *Iran in the 20th Century: Historiography and Political Power* (J. B. Taurus, 2009), 69–92. About the quest of Iranian thinkers and historians for modernity, see Farzin Vahdat, *God and Juggernaut: Iran's Intellectual Encounter with Modernity* (Syracuse, 2002), 25–128.

27 For a monograph on the subject, or the pharaonism of the 1920s, see Donald M. Reid, *Whose Pharaohs? Archaeology, Museums, and Egyptian National Identity from Napoleon to World War I* (Berkeley, 2002).

28 Mayer, *Changing Past*, 10–27.

29 Joan Judge, *Print and Politics: "Shibao" and the Culture of Reform in Late Qing China* (Stanford, 1996).

30 Douglas Reynolds, *China, 1898–1912: The Xinzheng Revolution and Japan* (Cambridge, MA, 1993).

31 See Joshua Fogel, ed., *The Role of Japan in Liang Qichao's Introduction of Modern Western Civilization to China* (Berkeley, 2004) and Paula Harrell, *Sowing the Seeds of Change: Chinese Students, Japanese Teachers, 1895–1905* (Stanford, 1992).

32 Liang Qichao, "Xin shixue (New Historiography)" in his *Liang Qichao shixue lunzhu sanzhong (Liang Qichao's Three Works in History)* (Hong Kong, 1980), 3–9. Cf. Q. Edward Wang, *Inventing China through History: The May Fourth Approach to Historiography* (Albany, 2001), 42–50.

33 Liang, *Xin shixue*, 10–15. Cf. Xiaobing Tang, *Global Space and the Nationalist Discourse of Modernity: The Historical Thinking of Liang Qichao* (Stanford, 1996).

34 See Q. Edward Wang, "China's Search for National History" in Q. Edward Wang and Georg G. Iggers, eds., *Turning Points in Historiography: A Cross-Cultural Perspective* (Rochester, 2002), 185–203. Cf. Yü Ying-shih, "Changing Conceptions of National History in Twentieth-century China" in Erik Lönnroth, Karl Molin, and Ragnar Björk, eds., *Conceptions of National History* (Berlin, 1995), 155–174; and Zheng Shiqu, *WanQing guocui pai: wenhua sixiang yanjiu (The National Essence School of the Late Qing: A Study of Intellectual History)* (Beijing, 1997), 161–237.

35 Hu Fengxiang and Zhang Wenjian, *Zhongguo jindai shixue sichao yu liupai (Trends and Schools in Modern Chinese Historiography)* (Shanghai, 1991), 256–271.

36 Hu Shih (Shi), *The Development of the Logical Method in Ancient China* (New York, rep., 1963) and his "Shiyan zhuyi (Experimentalism)"; "Du Wei xiansheng yu zhongguo (Mr. Dewey and China)," "Qingdai xuezhe de zhixue fangfa (Qing Scholars' Research Methods)" in idem, *Wenti yu zhuyi (Problems and Isms)* (Taipei, 1986). Cf. Wang, *Inventing China through History*, 53–66.

37 Anthony Grafton, *Defenders of the Texts: The Traditions of Scholarship in An Age of Science, 1450–1800* (Cambridge, MA, 1991); Hu Shih (Shi), *The Chinese Renaissance* (New York, rep. 1963, orig. 1934); and Jerome Grieder, *Hu Shih and the Chinese Renaissance: Liberalism in the Chinese Revolution, 1917–37* (Cambridge, MA, 1970).

38 Gu Jiegang (Ku Chieh-kang), *The Autobiography of a Chinese Historian*, tr. Arthur Hummel (Leyden, 1931) and Gu Jiegang, "Huangdi (Yellow Emperor)" in Gu Jiegang, ed., *Shilin zashi chubian (Essays in the Forest of History)* (Beijing, 1963, 1st ed.). Cf. Laurence Schneider, *Ku Chief-kang and China's New History: Nationalism and the Quest for Alternative Traditions* (Berkeley, 1971); and Tze-ki Hon, "Ethnic and Cultural Pluralism: Gu Jiegang's Vision of a New China in His Studies of Ancient History," *Modern China*, 22:3 (July 1996), 315–339.

39 Gu, *Autobiography of a Chinese Historian*, 65–66.

40 See Qian Wanyue, " 'Cenglei de zaocheng shuo' yu 'jiashang' yuanze' " ("The Theory of Gradual Expansion" and the "add-on principle"), in Gu Chao, ed., *Gu Jiegang xueji (Essays on Gu Jiegang's Scholarship)* (Beijing, 2002), 195–200.

41 Fan-sen Wang, *Fu Ssu-nien: A Life in Chinese History and Politics* (Cambridge, 2000), 114–125; Wang, *Inventing China through History*, 121–129.

42 Margaret Mehl, *History and the State in Nineteenth-century Japan* (New York, 1998), 140–147; Nagahara Keiji, *20 seiki Nihon no rekishigaku (20th Century Japanese Historiography)* (Tokyo, 2005), 54–56.

43 Hyung Il Pai, *Constructing "Korean" Origins: A Critical Review of Archaeology, Historiography, and Racial Myth in Korean State-formation Theories* (Cambridge, MA, 2000), 35–41.

44 Hugh Borton, "Modern Japanese Economic Historians" in W. G. Beasley and E. G. Pulleyblank, eds., *Historians of China and Japan* (Oxford, 1961), 288–306.

45 Naramoto Tatsuya, "Bunka shigaku (Cultural History)" in Association of Historical Research and Association of the Study of Japanese History, ed., *Nihon rekishi Kōza (Lectures on Japanese History)* (Tokyo, 1968), vol. 8, 221–245; Nagahara, *20 seiki Nihon no rekishigaku*, 81–87.

46 Ueda Masaaki, "Tsuda shigaku no honshitsu to kadai (The Nature and Themes of Tsuda's Historiography)" in *Nihon rekishi kōza*, 247–288; Masubuchi Tatsuo, *Nihon no kindai shigakushi ni okeru Chūkoku to Nihon: Tsuda Sōkichi to Naitō Konan (China and Japan in Modern Japanese Historiography: Tsuda Sōkichi and Naitō Konan)* (Tokyo, 2001), 16–17.

47 Yong-ha Shin, *Modern Korean History and Nationalism*, tr. N. M. Pankaj (Seoul, 2000), 223–272; Chow Tse-tsung, *The May Fourth Movement: Intellectual Revolution in Modern China* (Cambridge, MA, 1960); and Vera Schwarcz, *The Chinese Enlightenment: Intellectuals and the Legacy of the May Fourth Movement of 1919* (Berkeley, 1986).

48 Pai, *Constructing "Korean" Origins*, 35–56.

49 Ibid., 261–262.

50 Ibid., 63–64.

51 Martina Deuchler, *The Confucian Transformation of Korea: A Study of Society and Ideology* (Cambridge, MA, 1992), 107–108.

52 Pai, *Constructing "Korean" Origins*, passim.

53 Chizuko T. Allen, "Northeast Asia Centered around Korea: Ch'oe Namson's View of History," *Journal of Asian Studies*, 49:4 (November 1990), 787–806.

54 Ibid., 794, note 5; Shin, *Modern Korean History and Nationalism*, 214. Cf. Boudewijin Walraven, "The Parliament of Histories: New Religions, Collective Historiography, and the Nation," *Korean Studies*, 25:2 (2002), 157–178.

55 Allen, "Northeast Asia Centered around Korea," 789; Shin, *Modern Korean History and Nationalism*, 211.

56 Remco E. Breuker, "Contested Objectivities: Ikeuchi Hiroshi, Kim Sanggi, and the Tradition of Oriental History (*Tōyō shigaku*) in Japan and Korea," *East Asian History*, 29 (June 2005), 69–106.

57 Pai, *Constructing "Korean" Origins*, 65.

58 Arif Dirlik, *Revolution and History: Origins of Marxist Historiography in China, 1919–37* (Berkeley, 1978).

59 P. J. Honey, "Modern Vietnamese Historiography" in D. G. E. Hall, ed., *Historians of South East Asia* (Oxford, 1961), 94–104.

60 Tōyama Shigeki, "Yuibutsu shikan shigaku no seiritsu (The Establishment of Materialist Historiography)" in *Nihon rekishi kōza*, 289–323; Nagahara, *20 seiki Nihon no rekishigaku*, 88–101.

61 Takamure Itsue, *Bokeisei no kenkyū (A Study of Matriarchy)* (Tokyo, 1938); Eiji Oguma, *A Genealogy of "Japanese" Self-images*, tr. David Askew (Melbourne, 2002), 156–171.

62 About Nishida Kitarō's role in justifying Japan's militarism, there have been different views. A recent and succinct discussion on the subject is found in Christopher S. Goto-Jones, *Political Philosophy in Japan: Nishida, the Kyoto School, and Co-Prosperity* (London, 2005).

63 M. K. Gandhi, "My Jail Experiences-XI," in *Young India* (September 11, 1924), in Collected Works CD-ROM. Available online at http://www.gandhiserve.org/cwmg/VOL029.PDF (p. 134 of vol. 29).

64 Cited in Michael Gottlob, ed., *Historical Thinking in South Asia: A Handbook of Sources from Colonial Times to the Present* (New Delhi, 2003), 27.

65 See Stefan Berger, ed. *Writing the Nation: Towards Global Perspectives* (Houndmills, 2007), introduction and other chapters, as well as the sections on East and Southeast Asia (ch. 1 in this book) that discuss the similar tension in nationalist historiographies in other parts of the world.

66 Dipesh Chakrabarty, "The Birth of Academic Historical Writing in India" in Stuart Macintyre, Juan Maiguaschca, and Attila Pok, eds., *The Oxford History of Historical Writing. Vol 4: 1800–1945* (Oxford, 2011). See also Stephen Bann, *The Clothing of Clio: A Study of the Representation of History in Nineteenth Century Britain and France* (Cambridge, 1984).

67 As pointed out by Vinay Lal, the role of the *Gita* in nationalist thinking is yet to be explored in detail. See Vinay Lal, *The History of History: Politics and Scholarship in Modern India* (Oxford and New Delhi, 2003), 76 n.98.

68 After the creation of the new state of Maharashtra in 1960, Shivaji was celebrated as the father of the "Maratha nation-state" and the "architect of freedom" in several commemoratory volumes authored by historians. Critical or nonhagiographic accounts of Shivaji encountered virulent opposition by communal pro-Shivaji elements. In 1974, one Marathi historian at Marathwada University was dismissed from his position for disputing some Shivaji myths (see Lal, *The History of History*, 105). More recently, after the publication of James Laine's *Shivaji* (2003), Indian scholars in support of his book have been harassed and scholarly institutes in Maharashtra such as the Bhandarkar Institute with its large archival collection ransacked. The then Maharashtra government also called for the arrest of Laine, a professor of religious studies at Macalaster College, Minnesota.

69 Quoted in Michael Gottlob, "India's Unity in Diversity as a Question of Historical Perspective," in *Economic and Political Weekly*, March 3, 2007.

70 Cited in Gottlob, *Historical Thinking in South Asia*, 155.

71 Sumit Sarkar, *Writing Social History* (New Delhi: Oxford University Press, 1997), 32.

72 Bipan Chandra, "Nationalist Historians' Interpretations of the Indian Nationalist Movement" in Sabyasachi Bhattacharya and RomilaThapar, eds., *Situating Indian History: For Sarvapalli Gopal* (Delhi, 1986), 197.

73 Cited in Lal, *The History of History*, 98.

74 For his researches, Sumit Sarkar consulted material in eight languages: Persian, Marathi, Hindi, Sanskrit, English, French, Dutch, and Portuguese.

75 Cited in Chakrabarty, "The Birth of Academic Historical Writing," 531.

76 Lal, *The History of History*, 31–35; also, Kumkum Chatterjee, "The King of Controversy: History and Nation-making in Late Colonial India," *American Historical Review*, 110:4 (December 2005), 1454–1475.

77 Chatterjee, "The King of Controversy," 1458.

78 Chatterjee, "The King of Controversy," 1455.

79 Sarkar, *Writing Social History*, 25.

80 Chatterjee, "The King of Controversy," 1462.

81 Ibid., 1464.

82 Chakrabarty, "The Birth of Academic Historical Writing," 523.

83 Sarkar, *Writing Social History*, 34–35.
84 C. A. Bayly, "Modern Indian Historiography" in Michael Bentley, ed., *Companion to Historiography* (London, 1997), 682.
85 Cited in Gottlob, *Historical Thinking in South Asia*, 40.
86 Ibid., 56.
87 Jawaharlal Nehru, *The Discovery of India* (Oxford, 1988), 58.
88 Gandhi's *Collected Works* in 100 volumes was completed in 1994 and is now available on CD-ROM.
89 Lal, *The History of History*, 85.
90 Chandra, "Nationalist Historians' Interpretations," 197; Lal, *The History of History*, 86.
91 Lal, *The History of History*, 92.
92 According to Majumdar, other ancient civilizations and cultures had perished, but in India there was a continuity of history and civilization.
93 The Muslim period was, to quote him once more, "the darkness of the long night, so far as Hindu civilization is concerned, a darkness which envelops it even now." Quote in Lal, *The History of History*, 95.
94 Bayly, "Modern Indian Historiography," 683.
95 Anil Seal, *The Emergence of Indian Nationalism: Competition and Collaboration in the Later Nineteenth Century* (Cambridge, 1968).
96 Chandra, "Nationalist Historians' Interpretations," 206–207.
97 Sarkar, *Writing Social History*, 39.

6 New challenges in the postwar period
From social history to postmodernism and postcolonialism

The Cold War and the emergence of the new world order

We are dividing the period 1945 to 1989/91 into two sections with the period around 1968 as a turning point. The three dates have significance not only in the West but globally. The defeat of the Axis in 1945 marked the end of the attempts of Nazi Germany and Imperial Japan to establish their domination over Europe and Asia respectively. It ushered in a new high point of American as well as of Soviet power, the dependence of Western Europe and Japan on the United States, the direct control of much of Eastern Europe by the Soviet Union. In the years that followed, the United States experienced an unprecedented prosperity that, unlike during the interwar period, was not interrupted by economic crises. This prosperity was later shared by Western Europe and by Japan as these areas, with American aid, arose from the destruction of war. At the same time the prewar great powers, France, Great Britain, Germany, and Japan lost their influence on international politics. These years were marked by the dissolution of the old empires as India, Pakistan, and Sri Lanka attained independence from Great Britain in 1947, Indonesia in 1949 from the Netherlands after a brief military conflict, and the Congo in 1960 from Belgium. The French tenaciously sought to maintain their hold on Algeria and Indochina. By the mid-sixties most of the former colonies in Africa, South and East Asia, the Middle East, the Caribbean, and Oceania had gained self-determination. China was unified politically with the establishment of the communist People's Republic in 1949. International relations were overshadowed by the Cold War, which was a conflict not merely between two sets of alliances, as had existed before 1914, but between two social systems, each seeking to define itself ideologically. China emerged as a second major communist power. It is striking that, notwithstanding the enmity between the two systems, no armed conflicts occurred in Europe, in part undoubtedly prevented by the fear of nuclear war. Instead, proxy wars took place in the former colonies in Africa and Asia. The relative stability in Western Europe and North America, as well as in the Soviet Union and the countries dominated by the Soviet Union, was undermined by increasing challenges to the status quo in the Western as well as the Soviet spheres with the emergence of the Civil Rights Movement in the United States, the opposition to Western involvement in the Vietnam War, and the growing disenchantment of a younger generation throughout Europe, Japan, and North America with the culture of a highly industrialized, commercialized culture and in Eastern Europe with resistance to the rigid dictatorship imposed by the Soviet Union. This discomfort manifested itself in the mass student protests of 1968 throughout the West, with high points in Berkeley, Paris, West Berlin, Mexico City, and Tokyo, as well as the Prague Spring. This student activism was predated by the notable role played by the Red Guards, or radical college students, in China's so-called Great Proletarian Cultural Revolution that began in 1966, following Maoist ideology, which incidentally also had a widespread influence outside China. These uprisings were put down everywhere and yet left their impact on the general mood in the years that followed.

Varieties of social history (1945–1968/70) in the West

As for historical thought and historical writing, the first two decades after 1945 reflected a broadly shared sense of confidence, at least in the West, and identification with the culture of the industrial society, a renewed effort to transform historical studies into a rigorous science, a science that, in its reliance on empirical research and analytical methods, resembled more closely the methodologies of the sciences proper than that of the Rankean approach, which had been part of the professionalization of historical studies before. For many historians in the period after 1945, history was to become a social science, although at least four models, partly following national lines, understood the scientific character of history differently. We shall distinguish between an American, a French (*Annales*), and a West German conception of historical social science and Marxist approaches that crossed national lines and were sufficiently divergent so that they could not be easily defined. Despite the uncertainties dominant in continental philosophy and the theoretical relativism of some American historians in the prewar period, such as Carl Becker and Charles Beard, none of these orientations gave up the belief in the possibility of objective historical knowledge.[1] They were confident that there was a real historical past, although they recognized the subjective elements that went into the reconstruction of this past. Moreover, all of these orientations, with the partial exception of the *Annales*, viewed history as a progressive process of modernization leading to its fulfillment in the West.

This confidence in scientific method and in modernization came under increasing attack in the second half of the 1960s, as the disenchantment with the modern industrial civilization led to a questioning of the scientific ideal and of the idea of modernization as progress that were fundamental to this civilization. Although many professional historians continued to do research and to write in the traditional manner, and many others followed the established social science approaches into the 1970s and 1980s, the latter period marked a pronounced turn in historical studies away from the study of society to that of culture, requiring new and different methods in order to understand the values that motivated societies. A similar turn to culture also occurred in worldwide Marxist historiography in postwar years.[2] The Soviet decision in August 1968 to crush the "socialism with a human face" of the Prague Spring marked the acceleration of the decline of Soviet power on the economic and ideological planes. The Marxism that the Soviet Union represented had lost its credibility not only in the West but also within the Soviet empire and beyond, such as in Japan, to which we will turn in the next chapter. Only in the formerly colonial countries struggling against Western intrusion and to an extent in the regions of Latin America seeking radical reforms did elements of Marxism play a significant role.

The United States: From consensus to the new left

The period immediately after World War II was marked on the one hand by a great surge in confidence in the solidity of the institutions and values of America, which had come out of the war victorious and resulted in America's rise to world power, on the other hand, by a sense of emergency in the face of the Cold War and of what was interpreted as a massive threat to the "free world." The dominance of the Progressive historians, who had played a central role in American historiography since the early twentieth century, had ended. Their place was taken by what has been described as the "Consensus School."[3] The Progressive school, as exemplified by Charles Beard, had seen America as a divided nation in which vested interests held sway over a broad populace. There was the confidence that in the long run the power of the vested interests would be curbed and a better, more just society would emerge. The Progressive historians, despite their focus on economic factors, were nevertheless not Marxists insofar as they saw this process in terms of reforms rather than revolution and rejected the Marxist reliance on historical laws to bring about the transformation of society.

The Consensus historians – Louis Hartz (1919–1986), Richard Hofstadter (1916–1970), and Daniel Boorstin (1914–2004), among others – reflected the conservative political and social mood of the 1950s and the reaction against the reforms of the New Deal but also the need to defend America against what they viewed as the imminent threat of communism to American freedom. They stressed the uniqueness of American history, which differed fundamentally from European class society. Since America did not have a feudal past, it could develop from its beginnings as a society of equals participating in a democratic political order. Except for the Civil War, they claimed, America had been free of major conflicts, and the Civil War could have been prevented if ideologically motivated abolitionists had not forced the issue.

Consensus historians continued to write history in traditional ways. Side by side, there developed an increasingly important social science orientation that shared important tenets of Anglo-American analytical philosophy. Carl Hempel (1905–1997) applied the concepts of analytical philosophy to historical inquiry in what came to be known as the Covering Law theory.[4] According to it, there is only one form of scientific reasoning, which applies to history as well as to other areas of study. All events have causes. To merely narrate a chain of events is inadequate. Instead, the historian must seek to link individual events to their causes. But the question arises whether this is possible, whether there are not elements of human activity and volition that defy such reduction. Hempel finally was forced to admit this. But the conclusion that Karl Popper (1902–1994) drew was that because there was only one logic of rational inquiry, history could not be a science.

Historians who wanted to apply social scientific approaches did not go as far as Hempel or Popper but nevertheless sought to formulate models, preferably quantitative, that would define general tendencies of social behavior with generalizations that could be tested empirically. Agreeing with Popper that the truth of statements in history or the social sciences could never be established positively, they maintained that statements must be formulated in such a way that they could be tested empirically; they could be demonstrated to be false if that turned out to be the case.[5] The task of the social scientific historian was not to narrate events but to propose theoretical explanations that link the events to a larger causal nexus. Here quantification plays a key role. With the aid of the new technical tools, the computers, large amounts of materials could be coordinated mathematically. History was thus transformed into a science that resembles the natural sciences in its rigor. Robert Fogel (1926–2013) and Stanley Engerman in their study of American slavery, *Time on the Cross*, raised the question whether slavery was economically in decline by the time of the American Civil War, as had often been maintained. They challenged this proposition and argued that the time had come when historical questions were no longer open to conflicting interpretations but could now, with the help of computer techniques, be answered with a high degree of certainty. Using extensive quantitative data on nutrition, housing, and health, they compared the conditions of the life of slaves positively with those of industrial workers in the Northeastern United States at the time. It was widely argued that only quantitative history deserved to be considered scientific. Quantitative methods were applied to the study of elections, of family patterns, of social mobility and migration, and, of course, of economics. The term "cliometrics" was coined to designate these new tendencies. In 1959, Robert Fogel and Douglass North (1920–2015) in *Railroads and American Economic Growth* (1964) sought to test empirically a counterfactual question of how the industrialization of America would have proceeded if railroads had not been constructed and other forms of communication and transportation, such as river and canal traffic, would have taken their place.

Modernization theories during this period played an increasing role in historical sociology and economics. These theories depended less on computer techniques than on a conception of historical development that went back to the Enlightenment and is paradoxically indebted to Marx and Engels. Walt Rostow (1916–2003) in *Stages of Economic Growth* (1960) proceeded despite its subtitle "A Non-Communist Manifesto" from Marx's assumption that "the country which is industrially more developed only shows the less developed one the picture of its own future,"[6] replacing mid-nineteenth-century capitalist England with mid-twentieth-century capitalist America. Ultimately, the whole world would follow the example of America in a modernization process, leading to a free market economy and a liberal, parliamentary democracy. The Vienna-trained economic historian Alexander Gerschenkron (1904–1978), in *Economic Backwardness in Historical Perspective* (1962), warned that countries that were industrialized later under different political and social conditions could not be fitted into this pattern. Nevertheless, Rostow's vision, which fitted ideologically well into the Cold War, survived among certain theorists such as Francis Fukuyama in his famous essay "The End of History?" that was published in 1989, months before the Berlin Wall fell.[7] A great deal of historical sociology in the United States in the 1950s and 1960s operated with a conception of a master narrative that portrayed the irresistible "modernization" of scientific thought, economic growth, and secular outlook, which not only the positivists of the nineteenth century but also Max Weber had foreseen, although Weber was much more aware of the dangers inherent in progress and of the distinct character of other civilizations than the post-1945 American sociologists. For modernization theorists, history was a unilinear process, and the West, especially America after World War II as the most modern society, was the pinnacle of this process. Modernization thus became largely identical with Westernization worldwide.

Yet the optimism and complacency of the Consensus historians and a great number of the social science historians gave way to increasing tensions within American society and abroad. Until the, blacks had been largely ignored by white historians or were dealt with paternalistically as racially inferior, as in the work of William A. Dunning (1857–1922)[8] and Ulrich Phillips (1877–1934)[9] and their students such as the already mentioned John Randall, who sought to document the racial inferiority of blacks. Now a number of black historians, such as W. E. B. Du Bois and John Hope Franklin (1915–2009), turned to the history of slavery and racial oppression, as did white historians, such as Stanley Elkins (1925–2013) and Kenneth Stampp (1912–2009). Elkins, in the very controversial book *Slavery: A Problem in American Institutional and Intellectual Life* (1959), compared American slavery with Nazi concentration camps. John Kenneth Galbraith's (1908–2006) *The Affluent Society* (1958) was followed by Michael Harrington's (1928–1989) *The Other America: Poverty in the United States* (1962), which pointed at the many disadvantaged in America.

The Consensus historians, as well as the earlier Progressive historians, were now challenged by a new left in the face of domestic unrest, specifically the Civil Rights Movement and America's involvement in the morass of the Vietnam War. Gabriel Kolko (1932–2014), in *The Triumph of Conservatism*[10] (1963), undertook to demonstrate that the Progressive era did not mark a movement toward a more democratic society, as had generally been argued, but a process of more effective control of the economy by capitalist institutions, accompanied by reforms that actually led not to greater democracy but to government in the interest of vested economic interests. But the main thrust of the new left was in the area of foreign affairs in the shadow of the Vietnam War. Rejecting the image of the Cold War as a defense of the free institutions of the West against Soviet and Chinese aggression, historians such as William Appleton Williams (1921–1990), Walter La Feber, and Gabriel Kolko[11] sought to demonstrate the extent to which American foreign policy followed the aims of vested interests and that in its relation to the less developed countries, it was thoroughly imperialistic. At the same time, they did not support the Soviet Union but were fully aware of its repressive character. Nevertheless, they had great sympathy for the struggle for self-determination of countries formerly or still dominated by the West, such as Vietnam.

From the tense political atmosphere of the late 1960s in the United States and the student movement, there emerged an orientation in historical writing that defined itself as Radical.[12] Although relatively marginal, it contributed to the historical and social outlook of the seventies. It aimed at a "history from below" that would concentrate on those segments of the population that had been almost entirely ignored by Progressive and Consensus historians alike. Howard Zinn (1922–2010) tried to rectify this in his *A People's History of the United States from 1492 to the Present* (1980). Part of Radical history was also a greater concern with women with a broader feminist conception, about which we shall say more later in this chapter. The notion of the United States as "one nation indivisible under God with liberty and justice for all" gave way to a perception of a multicultural society with different segments often deprived of equal access to liberty and justice and calling for histories of their own. The challenge remained of writing a history that recognized the many sides of American society, in terms of class, ethnicity, and gender, without necessarily giving up a sense of national community but redefining the nation.

France: The Annales

We must avoid speaking of an *Annales* paradigm, which would suggest that there is a clear conception of how to ask questions guiding scholarly and scientific inquiry and presupposing a clear methodological way to proceed in dealing with these questions.[13] Instead, historians in this movement have gone in very diverse directions. Peter Burke credits it with having produced "a remarkable amount of the most innovative, the most memorable and the most significant historical writing of the twentieth century."[14] It has been suggested that its significance and its impact on historical studies not only in France but internationally were comparable only to that of the Ranke school in the nineteenth century. At its center was the perception of history as a social science or an all-embracing "human science," but a science that differed markedly from the social science approaches just discussed in the United States. As we saw in Chapter 4, what held the historians who followed these approaches together was originally the *Annales* journal founded by Marc Bloch and Lucien Febvre in 1929 and then, after World War II, the elaborate institutional framework built around the journal.

Prior to World War II, the *Annales* were marginal to the French historical profession even after Febvre and Bloch moved to Paris in 1933 and 1936, to the Collège de France and the Sorbonne respectively. The dominant historiography still largely followed conventional lines of narrative political history of events. With Bloch murdered by the Nazis in 1944, Febvre after the war assumed leadership of the *Annales* and succeeded in 1947 in organizing a special section of the Ecole Pratique des Hautes Etudes, the Sixth Section, of which he became president and which enabled him to organize research along the lines history should be written from his perspective. History for him was inseparable from the social sciences. The borderline between them was to be erased. Within the Sixth Section, which after 1972 was reorganized as Ecole des Hautes Etudes en Sciences Sociales, scholars in the social sciences and the humanities were recruited to make possible close cooperation among historians, not only as had already been earlier the case with economists, sociologists, and geographers but also with anthropologists, psychologists, psychoanalysts, and importantly now also art historians, literary critics, and specialists in the new semiotic discipline. History was to become a comprehensive social science, or, as it was also called, a "science of man"; this "New History" was to provide a central thread to the various other disciplines. The isolation not only of history but of the various disciplines in the social sciences and the humanities was to be overcome in the science of man. At the same time this science was not to have a systematic character; in other words, there was no aim at a unitary science; rather, it included various approaches that explored different aspects of human existence without losing contact with each other. In 1956 after the death of Febvre, his student Fernand Braudel (1902–1985) assumed the editorship of the *Annales* and the presidency of the Sixth Session. As Peter Burke suggested, the *Annales*, which had begun as the journal of a "heretical sect," took over the French historical establishment.[15] In 1968 a central edifice was opened, the Maison des Sciences de l'Homme (House of the Sciences of Man) on the Paris Left Bank in which the scholars in the various disciplines were housed and conditions for formal and informal exchanges were excellent.

For the decade and a half after Febvre's death, Braudel was the leading person in the *Annales* circle. His reputation had been well established with the publication in 1949 of his three-volume monumental *The Mediterranean and the Mediterranean World in the Age of Philippe II*.[16] Braudel had begun the study in the early 1930s as a dissertation. The focus originally was on the foreign policy of Philippe II of Spain (1527–1598), a still relatively traditional diplomatic history. Its completion was delayed by two interruptions, the first a two-year teaching spell at the University of São Paulo in Brazil where he befriended and was deeply influenced by his French colleague, the anthropologist Claude Lévi-Strauss (1908–2009); the second several years in a German internment camp, where he nevertheless had the leisure to rethink the study and write a major part of the draft. The completed study moved in a very different direction from the original conception. He turned emphatically away from narration to a concern with the fundamental structures that define history. He also turned away from the traditional Newtonian idea that saw time as unilinear and progressive and instead insisted that different historical settings require different understandings of time. The book was divided into three distinct sections reflecting three different conceptions of time. Braudel was not interested in the rapidly changing course of events, which marked traditional historiography, but in aspects resisting or slowing change, in what he called *longue durée* (long duration).

Like Bloch, he wanted to place history on a firm material basis, but what he understood as material differed radically from Marx. Although economics played a very important role in Braudel's history, it rested on a basis much more rooted in the material world than Marx's means and conditions of production. The first section of the book deals with the geographic setting of the Mediterranean Sea and the land surrounding it on the European, the North African, and the Near Eastern shores. But Braudel was no economic determinist; like Bloch, he rather relied heavily on the "human geography" of Paul Vidal de la Blache.[17] For him, the Mediterranean world consisted not only of the sea, mountains, and plains, but also of settlements, roads, and ports. Geography was thus not merely a natural but also a human and therefore a historical science. What interested Braudel was not the course of events but the structures within which human history takes place. In the first section on geography, these structures are largely immutable. When he turned to economy and society in the second section, he again was interested in long enduring structures but also recognized movement and sought to recognize a lawful character in these changes. Drawing from the economic theories of Clément Juglar (1819–1905) and Nikolai Kontradieff (1892–1931?),[18] he searched for recurring patterns in economic activity in the form of shorter and longer business cycles. Braudel operated with a conception of history and society that, because he considered it to be materialistic, he identified it with a scientific outlook. He had little to say in this section about civilizational aspects. Finally, in the third section Braudel returned to his original concerns with the diplomatic and military aspects of Philip II, yet almost apologetically referred to the account of the political events as superficial, not touching on the long enduring structures that underlie history. Nevertheless, Braudel contributed several important ideas to French historical discourse in the 1950s and 1960s: the commitment to a science of man that turned away from events and great individuals to social structures, from narration to analysis, from history as a self-defining discipline to a broad interdisciplinary approach, and he incidentally moved beyond the concentration on the nation-state to a broad cosmopolitan view that in his book on the Mediterranean deals with all the areas bordering on the Mediterranean.

The conception of the study of man as a science was reflected in the Sixth Section, whose members referred to their research institutes as laboratories. In the 1960s, the *Annales* dedicated a series of issues to human biology from a historical perspective. In 1951, the Sixth Section launched three important series, reflecting Braudel's outlook on (1) ports, routes, and traffic, (2) business and businesspeople, and (3) money, prices, and conjunctures. Pierre Chaunu (1923–2009) followed Braudel's study of the Mediterranean with a 12-volume work, *Sevilla and the Atlantic*,[19] measuring the tonnage of goods transported between Spanish ports and the Spanish colonies in the New World between 1504 and 1650.

Braudel next engaged in a three-volume study of what he described as a "history of material culture,"[20] centering on the rise of capitalism. Although as expected this work focused on the early Italian centers, followed by Antwerp, Amsterdam, and London, it is important to note that Braudel proceeded from a global perspective, introducing comparisons with developments in China, India, the Muslim world, and Latin America. The first volume dealt with the material aspects of everyday life – food, clothing, housing, health, tools, money, and towns – however, leaving out the mental outlooks that played such an important role in Bloch's and Febvre's writings. Only in his last uncompleted, posthumously published work, *The Identity of France*,[21] did Braudel turn specifically to France, but as the subtitle "space and history" suggests, not to France as an integrated nation but as constituted by regions, each with a character of its own.

Braudel's interest in economic history was reinforced by Ernest Labrousse (1895–1986), a member of the Sixth Section, who already in the 1930s undertook an extensive study of prices[22] that followed upon François Simiand's (1873–1935) earlier studies.[23] Labrousse, from a Marxist perspective, focused on the eighteenth century and sought to establish a relationship between the movement of prices and the outbreak and course of the French Revolution, as Georges Lefebvre had done earlier, but on a quantitative basis.

Important members of the *Annales* circle in the 1950s and 1960s turned to regional studies. Like Braudel, they avoided national history and also a confrontation with the modern period, although isolated studies like those of Charles Morazé (1913–2003) dealt with the triumph of the bourgeoisie[24] and Marc Ferro with World War I and the Russian Revolution.[25] Yet the methodologically innovative works in the tradition of Febvre and Bloch focused on regions in France before the French Revolution. This was undoubtedly due in part to methods suitable to relatively immobile societies but not to the rapid transformations in an industrial age. While the *Annales* in the 1930s had also dealt with contemporary problems, Italian fascism, Soviet communism, the New Deal, urbanization, and problems of the underdeveloped world, the issues of the journal after 1945 paid little attention to the world of the twentieth century. This may have reflected a certain discomfort with the modern world, shared broadly by segments of twentieth-century opinion. The *Annales* circle was committed to transforming history into a scientific discipline, and this ultimately involved a commitment not just to quantification but also to a social science that did not, like many of the American social scientists, involve an idea of progressive advancement into modernity. Although the *Annales* historians in no way romanticized the agrarian society of the past, as the German advocates of *Volksgeschichte* had done, but also saw the negative sides of this period, they chose it, along with the Middle Ages, as a prime area for research. Pierre Goubert's (1915–2012) study of the town of Beauvais and of the surrounding area[26] echoes Febvre's attempt in his dissertation on Franche-Comté to write a "total history" of a region. But it is different, much less total and more selective, operating with Braudel's concepts of "structure" and "conjuncture," less interested than Febvre in religion and politics than in long- and short-term fluctuations of prices, production, and population in the period from 1600 to 1730, as well as the effect of these fluctuations on different social classes. Goubert sought to demonstrate how in a traditional society population growth resulted in recurrent subsistence crises in more or less regular cycles of 30 years, leading to conscious attempts to limit growth through delayed marriages.

Independently of the *Annales* circle but integrated into *Annales* studies like that of Goubert was the development in this period of historical demography that differed from older statistical accounts of population in empirically studying population cycles in the broader context of economic and social structures and development. In France a National Institute for Demographic Studies was founded under the guidance of Louis Henry (1911–1991); in Great Britain a similar Cambridge Group for Population and Social Structure came into being under Edward Wrigley, Roger Schofield, and Peter Laslett (1931–2001). An important tool for the analysis of social structure was family reconstitution made possible through the use of parish records. In Japan a group around Akira Hayami in Kyoto and Tokyo undertook something similar using the records of Buddhist temples since 1600.[27] Lacking in Braudel's study of the rise of capitalism was any examination of the mental set of early capitalists. Robert Mandrou (1921–1984) did exactly this in a study of early modern capitalists but also more broadly of popular attitudes, including reading habits.[28] Beginning in the 1960s, a great deal of work

within the *Annales* circle turned to the "history of mentalities." These studies continued into the 1970s and proceeded on the assumption that historical studies must be quantitative to be "scientific." The basic theme in these
studies was dechristianization as reflected by attitudes toward death. To
understand the transformation of consciousness, they fed thousands of wills
into computers, thus creating a series. In this sense, scientific history would
be "serial history," as undertaken in the publications of Michel Vovelle and
Pierre Chaunu (1923–2009).[29] Relatively soon, the *Annales* received considerable attention abroad, in Italy, Spain, and Latin America, but particularly
in Mexico and Brazil, and, as we shall see later in this chapter, in Eastern
Europe, especially in Poland and Hungary, and even in the Soviet Union.

Germany: From Historismus to a critical historical social science

The same effort to transform history into a social science as in the United
States and France also dominated historical studies in West Germany after
1945. But the transition was more abrupt because German historians, committed to the tradition of historical thought that saw the highpoint of German history in Bismarck's creation of a Prusso-German nation-state, for a
long time opposed democratization and resisted all attempts at introducing
social science methods.[30] This changed after World War II. At first there was
no break with the historical profession before 1945. The liberal historians
who had been forced to emigrate after 1933 were for the most part not
invited to return; only the ultranationalist Hans Rothfels (1891–1976), who
had been close to the Nazis but had to leave Germany in 1939 because of
his Jewish ancestry, came back.[31] The old guard, chief among them Gerhard
Ritter (1889–1967), continued to dominate the profession. However, the
younger historians, among them Werner Conze (1910–1986) and Theodor
Schieder (1908–1984), who during the Nazi period had pursued a racially
oriented social history (*Volksgeschichte*), after 1945 gave historical studies a new direction. While the historical establishment had bitterly fought
attempts to introduce social science concepts into historiography, and Ritter even then emphatically rejected the *Annales*, which he considered to be
close to Marxism, as well as American social sciences,[32] they, as mentioned
in Chapter 4, were quite willing in the Nazi period to accept the proponents
of *Volksgeschichte* because they shared the criticism of democratic institutions. Now after 1945, they saw Nazism not as a peculiarly German but as
a generally Western phenomenon, with its roots in modern mass society.
Nazism came to power, they claimed, not because Germany before 1933
had been insufficiently democratic but because it had been too democratic.[33]
After 1945, the proponents of *Volksgeschichte* repudiated their adhesion to
racial theory, or quietly passed over it, and turned from their romantic view
of medieval agrarian communities to what they considered to be a realistic
comprehension of the modern industrial world.[34] They, foremost Werner
Conze and Theodor Schieder, now became mentors of a new generation

of historians, including Hans-Ulrich Wehler (1931–2014), Hans Mommsen (1930–2015), and Wolfgang Mommsen (1930–2004), who began their university training in the post-1945 period.[35] In 1957 Werner Conze founded the Work Circle for Modern Social History, which involved many of the younger historians, and which devoted itself to the study of modern German industrial society. An even younger generation, foremost Jürgen Kocka, trained by the democratically oriented Gerhard A. Ritter (1929–2015) – no relation to Gerhard Ritter – appeared on the scene. Conze and Schieder largely avoided a study of the German sources of Nazism, which they saw, like Gerhard Ritter and Rothfels, as a generally Western expression of modernization.

Yet the younger historians trained by Conze and Schieder, as well as the students of Gerhard A. Ritter, saw this differently.[36] The key problem they confronted was that of the rise of Nazism. They saw it not as a general European phenomenon but as one with deep roots in German history. They also viewed modern history in terms of modernization but saw modernization differently from Conze or Schieder. It meant also democratization. As Wehler maintained: "The progressive economic modernization of German society should have been accompanied by a modernization of social relations and politics. Industrialization with its permanent technological revolution should have brought with it a development in the direction of a society of legally free and politically responsible citizens capable of making their own decisions," which in the German case it clearly did not.[37] This suggested that economic modernization was accompanied, as it was in Great Britain, the British dominions, the United States, and much of Western Europe, by the achievement of parliamentary government. The question arose why Germany followed a separate path (*Sonderweg*) that diverged from the West. Answering this question required a specific social science approach, which involved a break with the old German traditional narrative, with its *Historismus*,[38] centered on politics, and a turn to an analytic social science. Unlike the older German historians, Wehler and the historians of his generation spent considerable time in the United States and in Great Britain and were very much aware of social science discussions in those countries and to a lesser extent also in France. At the same time, they also drew on German sources of social thought, on Marx, without being Marxists, on Max Weber, and on the historians and social scientists who were driven from Germany after 1933. Their conception of social science differed from that of the mainstream of social science in America by linking social studies much more closely to politics. They also broke with the postulate that social scientific research must be free of value judgments and called for a history and a sociology with a clear value orientation. In this connection they were deeply influenced by the so-called Critical Theory of the Frankfurt School of Max Horkheimer (1895–1973) and Theodor Adorno (1903–1969),[39] who had been forced into emigration by the Nazis but returned to Germany after the war. They maintained that a rational approach to the study of human affairs involved not only methodological procedures but also the question to what extent social institutions are reasonable in terms of human needs and dignity. Unlike the representatives of the American tradition of behavioral social sciences, Wehler wanted to approach society with clearly formulated questions related to social change. To him, there was thus a close relation between social science and social practice.

In the course of the late 1960s and the 1970s, an increasing number of younger West German historians accepted these premises and collaborated together with sociologists, economists, and political scientists, often referred to as the Bielefeld School because there Wehler and the younger Jürgen Kocka founded a loose interdisciplinary association of researchers. They focused on the historical and social developments to explain the catastrophic course of German history in the first part of the twentieth century. They located a basic explanation in the factors that led to the unification of Germany under Bismarck that prevented the democratization of Germany and left powerful premodern classes, the landed East Prussian landed aristocracy, and the military cooperating with the emergent great industrial sectors in a powerful position to curb the growing strength of the working classes. These questions had already been raised in the Weimar Republic by one of Meinecke's students, Eckart Kehr (1902–1933), who in his dissertation of 1930 argued that not considerations of national security and foreign policy motivated the German construction of the battle fleet, which ultimately led to the confrontation with Great Britain, but concerns of domestic policy, aiming at consolidating the position of the dominant elites.[40] Wehler in the 1960s published the writings of Kehr as a basis for the new critical historiography.[41] Similar questions related to the political consequences of the contradiction between Germany's modern economy and her premodern social structure were raised by other historians from the Meinecke circle, such as Hans Rosenberg (1904–1988), later at the University of California at Berkeley, who never returned to Germany permanently but held a number of important seminars there attended by many of the younger historians, by which he served as a bridge between critical American and German social science approaches.

An impetus to the new critical history was offered by Fritz Fischer (1908–1999), older and not a member of the Bielefeld school, in fact with a Nazi past, who nevertheless through his research in the 1950s came to the conclusion, in *Germany's War Aims in the First World War*,[42] that Germany was primarily responsible for the outbreak of war in 1914. His method of archival research was traditional and had little in common with social science methods, but his examination of the broader framework in which this decision to go to war was made supported the interpretation of German foreign and military policy of the critical school. Fischer concluded that the imperial government had yielded to a broad consensus of economic interest groups, from industry and agriculture to the labor unions, which favored the extension of German political and economic hegemony over much of

Europe, particularly Eastern Europe, thus foreshadowing policies actually carried out by Nazi Germany in World War II, and which were aimed at supplanting Great Britain and France as the major colonial power. Fischer's book was met by vigorous opposition by conservative historians, foremost Gerhard Ritter, but his theses, even if modified, were taken seriously by a broad segment of the younger historians.

By the mid-1970s, the critical school had a firm basis not only in Bielefeld but also at other universities and centers of research. In 1975 it launched a journal, *Geschichte und Gesellschaft (History and Society)* that raised methodological issues and examined aspects of modern history. In contrast to much of the work of the *Annales* and of the British *Past and Present*, its focus and that of the book series "Critical Studies" associated with it, was not on the medieval or modern world but on the processes of transformation in modern industrial societies.[43]

The 1970s and 1980s: The cultural turn and postmodernism

From social science history to the cultural turn

In 1966, Emmanuel Le Roy Ladurie, a student of Braudel, soon to be his successor as director of the *Ecole des Hautes Etudes en Sciences Sociales*, published a two-volume dissertation on the peasants of Languedoc,[44] the Southern region of France, from the time immediately preceding the Black Death in the early fourteenth century to what he considered the agricultural revolution of the eighteenth century, followed the next year by a smaller second dissertation on the history of climate since the year 1000.[45] Both reflected Braudel's concern that the prime task of historical composition is not to relate the actions of persons but to reconstruct the long enduring structures in which history transpires, along with the regular cycles, the ups and downs (*conjonctures*) within these structures. But in *The Peasants of Languedoc*, Le Roy Ladurie went beyond Braudel in an attempt to transform history into a rigorous empirical science following the model of the natural sciences. The core of this science rested not in grandiose explanations of reality but in the formulation of concrete theoretical questions regarding the subject matter under inquiry. Here Le Roy Ladurie proceeded from the Malthusian thesis regarding the close relationship of agricultural productivity, population, and the availability of food, which he held operated in the period under investigation when food production remained static until the agricultural innovations beginning in the eighteenth century. Employing statistical data on population, land prices, food prices, and wages, he traced the cycles of relative plenty followed by increases in population and consequent scarcity of food that operated independently of human intervention. While the first volume presented and analyzed the developments in the time period under study, the second volume was statistical, providing the basis for the first volume. In his separate history of climate, he utilized data from tree rings to link the production of food to hard, natural causes. Soon afterward, Le Roy Ladurie quite dogmatically asserted that no history that does not rely on quantifiable data can claim to be "scientific."[46]

Yet the Malthusian analysis in *The Peasants of Languedoc* focusing on anonymous, impersonal forces was accompanied by an examination of how the conditions created by these forces translated into states of social consciousness reflecting the subordination of the peasantry and resulting in social conflict. Most striking is a brief five-page account of the disorders during the carnival in the Provence town of Romans in 1580, which he later expanded into a book.[47] Here Le Roy Ladurie moves in a very different direction, telling a story with real actors, portraying the conflict between the Huguenot bourgeois merchant elite ruling the town and the poor Catholic urban population supported by the influx of the surrounding peasantry. But the conflict was fought out not over overt political and economic issues but symbolically with each side in the carnival; assuming the role of animals intent on destroying the other. Not economics but psychoanalysis offered a key to understanding the struggle that ended in the massacre of the masqueraded poor.

The view of history as a rigorous social science was still held by many historians primarily but not exclusively in the United States in the 1970s and well into the 1980s. The British historian Geoffrey Barraclough (1908–1984), in a survey of historiographical trends for UNESCO, commented in 1979 that "the search for quantity is beyond all doubt the most powerful of the new trends in history, the factor above all others which distinguishes historical attitudes in the 1970s from historical attitudes in the 1930s."[48] We already mentioned that Robert Fogel and Stanley Engerman in a quantitative study of slavery, *Time on the Cross* (1974),[49] on the profitability of the slave economy and the living conditions of the slaves, wanted to put an end to divergent historical interpretations and place history on an objective, scientific basis. The book was briefly hailed as a breakthrough but was soon subjected to massive criticism by quantifying historians because there were mistakes in its data but more seriously because a study of slavery, or of social conditions generally, has to take qualitative factors into consideration.[50] This did not prevent Fogel from being appointed to an endowed chair at Harvard University and in 1994, together with Douglass North, being awarded the Nobel Prize in Economics. In an exchange with the traditionalist British historian Geoffrey Elton (1921–1994), Fogel raised the question in what directions historical studies would and should go, either in the manner of the Rankean School with its reliance on the critical examination of documentary sources or as the strict social science that Fogel championed. Both posited a sharp dividing line between history and literature, between the scholar or scientist and the amateur. Historical studies for Fogel had to adopt the mode of the rigorous sciences; it required experts and a technical discourse accessible to the trained specialist but not to the general educated reading public.[51]

By the early 1970s, a good deal of historical writing, including that of Le Roy Ladurie, had moved away from the social science models of the 1960s to which Fogel still clung. In 1975, only nine years after *The Peasants of Languedoc*, Le Roy Ladurie published *Montaillou: An Occitan Village*.[52] This was a very different history, not one on a large scale, covering a region such as the Provence over several centuries but a very small isolated village of barely 200 souls, a history in which individuals and individual families were at the center. The sources are not hard quantitative data but the testimonies of villagers as recorded in Inquisition records. The occasion of the Inquisitional hearings was the attempt of the Catholic Church to suppress the Cathar heresy that had a strong foothold in the village. The opening chapters of the book deal in *Annales* manner with the geographic setting, the economy, and the social setting, the *domus*, the home of the extended family, to which the villagers were tied. But beyond this introduction, we encounter individuals, male and female, and through their testimonies learn about their experiences, their outlooks on life, their sexual attitudes and practices, their superstitions, and their concepts of death – in brief a history from below of everyday life. And this book was deliberately written for a broad public and in fact became a best seller with over 500,000 copies sold in France.

Two other books can be mentioned that reflect the new orientation in historical writing, Carlo Ginzburg's *The Cheese and the Worms: The Cosmos of a Sixteenth Century Miller* (1975)[53] and Natalie Davis's *The Return of Martin Guerre* (1984).[54] Like Le Roy Ladurie in *Montaillou*, both avoid the reconstruction of larger impersonal historical processes and instead focus on the life experiences of individuals from humble social origins in social settings not of their choice but who react actively to this setting in which they find themselves. In *The Cheese and the Worms*, the central person is a miller, Domenico Scandella, commonly called Menochio. Born in 1532 in a village in the region of Friuli under the shadow of Venetian domination, he creates, with a very active imagination, a picture of the world that conflicts with Catholic orthodoxy and results in two inquisitional trials and his death on the stake. Ginzburg's sources are the testimonies of the trials. He traces the outlines of two cultures, that of the educated elites of the time and that of the peasantry, and the interaction of the two through Menochio's readings. Menochio is unusually well-read, has read a great number of the philosophic and scientific classics, but, as part of the peasant world to which he belongs has reinterpreted them through the eyes of that world. A key concern of Ginzburg is the interplay of elite and popular culture. Yet the question occurs to what extent he reads his own romantic conceptions of a peasant culture into Menochio's testimony. He assumes the existence of an age-old Mediterranean peasant culture, from which Menochio inherited his earthy view of religion, an assumption for which Ginzburg has no basis in the sources, and explains Menochio's execution as having resulted less from his heretical beliefs than from the desire of the modernizing, capitalistic world of Venice to root out the archaic peasant culture that Menochio represented. Yet the book reads less as a cumbersome scholarly treatise than as a fascinating literary work, as which it was received.

The same is true of Natalie Davis's *The Return of Martin Guerre*. It reads as a novel and is intended as that, as well as as a contribution to the social history of the Southern French countryside at the time of the Reformation. At the center is a peasant woman, Bertrande de Rols, who is abandoned by her husband, Martin Guerre, who had treated her miserably. She remains chaste for years until a man claiming to be Martin Guerre appears in the village and is accepted by her and by the majority of the villagers as such. A loving relationship results. Davis suspects fully that Bertrande knew that the impostor was not her husband, but she and the supposed Martin Guerre "invented" their marriage and lived happily together until the real Martin Guerre returned. She interprets Bertrande's actions as a woman's strategy in a world dominated by men. At the same time, Davis reconstructs the relationships among the villagers so that this becomes a portrayal of rural history in that corner of France at that point in time. Again this book, like *The Cheese and the Worms* and *Montaillou*, was widely read in a host of languages and was turned into a film. Nevertheless, the question was soon raised whether this was a serious work of history or rather an entertaining but anachronistic story in which Davis projected the feminist attitudes of a late twentieth-century middle-class woman onto the behavior of a sixteenth-century peasant woman.[55] Davis did not invent the story out of the blue but based it on the recollections of the judge who presided at the trial leading to the conviction and execution of the impostor. In an exchange in the *American Historical Review*, her critic argues that she had gone far beyond the documentary evidence. Davis admitted that she had used her imagination in reconstructing the peasant world in which Bertrande de Rols lived. Nevertheless, she maintained that wherever she lacked the sources, she could draw upon similar villages for which there was evidence. She admits that imagination and "invention" had an important place in her reconstruction of the village and of the motivations of Bertrande de Rols but argues that "invention" is inevitable in recreating a real past with real people and that this invention is not the arbitrary creation of the historian but carefully follows the "voices" of the past as they speak through the sources.[56] In her defense, it could be noted that Ranke also frankly recognized the role of imagination guided by the sources in reconstructing the thought processes of his historical actors.

In this spirit, Lawrence Stone in 1979 in an article, "The Revival of Narrative" in *Past and Present*,[57] the leading British journal of social history, proclaimed, perhaps prematurely, the death of the social science paradigm. The belief, central to social science history, that "a coherent scientific explanation of change in the past" is possible, he claimed, was now widely rejected. In its stead, historians turned increasingly to the diverse aspects of human existence that had been previously neglected. The conviction took hold that "the culture of the group, and even the will of the individual, are potentially at least as important agents of change as the impersonal forces of material output and demographic growth."[58] This interest in concrete human individuals as agents of history ushered in a return to narrative history. But these new histories were quite different from the older narratives. While in the latter, the focus was on politics and political personalities, the new narratives dealt with common people, at times as we saw in *The Cheese and the Worms*, with persons who were far from the ordinary, such as Menochio.

There now was a shift in historical studies from the analysis of institutions to spheres of culture, often described as a "cultural turn"[59] that, however, went in different directions. Culture was now understood anthropologically in terms of the behavior of human subjects in a society. There had been many social histories of culture, Marxist as well as non-Marxist, going back to the nineteenth century, but what occurred was the replacement of these social histories of culture by cultural histories of society.[60] Often but not necessarily, this meant a retreat from political history. Thus the role of culture played an important role in the causal analysis of the French Revolution. As we already saw, the Marxist interpretation of the Revolution as a bourgeois revolution, which had dominated French historiography since Albert Mathiez's (1874–1932) and Georges Lefebvre's work in the 1920s, was challenged in the 1960s by Alfred Cobban (1901–1968)[61] but still on economic grounds. François Furet (1927–1997), who in his earlier years had been a member of the Communist Party, later occupied a key position in the repudiation of Marxist as well as non-Marxist economic interpretations of the French Revolution. In a bitter attack in 1971 in the *Annales*, he lashed out against the dogmatism of Albert Soboul (1914–1982), the most important exponent of a Marxist class analysis of the French Revolution, and stressed the role of an ideology that cut across class lines as a causal factor.[62] It is striking how Furet who, like Le Roy Ladurie, had been an ardent advocate of quantitative methods in the late 1960s, in the 1970s in a series of books turned away from quantification to the role of politics, ideas, and culture that did not lend themselves to quantitative analysis.[63] The primacy of economic and sociological categories was replaced in the works of Maurice Agulhon (1926–2014)[64] and Mona Ozouf[65] by studies of the symbolism of the revolutionary and the republican heritage. In this turn to the cultural analysis of the French Revolution, Lynn Hunt's *Politics, Culture, and Class in the French Revolution* (1984) is important. In its Introduction, she explains that she conceived this work originally as a social history of the French Revolution that, however, "increasingly turned into a cultural analysis in which the political structures . . . became but one part of the story."[66]

Postmodernism and the linguistic turn

While these reorientations in historical writing occurred in the 1970s and 1980s, a very lively discussion took place at the same time about the nature of history and the possibilities of historical knowledge. The new theoretical positions that emerged have, since the 1980s, been referred to as postmodernism, although the exponents of postmodernism are too diverse to speak of a group or of a movement. Nevertheless, there are a number of ideas pointing in the direction of radical historical and epistemological relativism that are shared by thinkers identified as postmodernists. The postmodernist discussions took place primarily within the circles of academic literary theorists, first in France in the 1960s and then particularly in the United States, and were taken up to a lesser extent by philosophers, historical anthropologists, and linguists. Historians discussed these ideas and, as we already saw, shared much of the criticism of the modern world and of its scholarly approaches. But in their practice as historians they could not accept the idea that history is nothing more than a form of fiction, although they realized that imagination entered every historical narration where the sources were inadequate, but that these elements of imagination were not fictional but, as Natalie Davis had pointed out, were guided by the documentary "voices of the past"[67] to reconstruct and understand the past better, even if admittedly imperfectly,

Postmodernism has to be understood in the context of the critical attitude toward the modern late industrial capitalist society. It was fueled by the protest movements of the 1960s, the Civil Rights Movement in the United States, the opposition to the Vietnam War, feminist activism, and finally gay liberation. The term "postmodern" was widely used only after Jacques-François Lyotard's (1924–1988) *The Postmodern Condition* (1984), in which he defined postmodernity as "incredulity towards metanarratives" such as the ideas of progressive development toward perfection, the idea that there is one "History," held by both defenders of liberal capitalism and of Marxist socialism.[68] As Keith Jenkins formulated it subsequently, "postmodernity is not an ideology or position we can subscribe to or not, postmodernity is precisely our condition: it is our historical fate to be living now." It is the response to the "general failure of modernity . . . of the attempt from the eighteenth century in Europe, to bring about through the application of reason, science, and technology, a level of social and political well-being. . . . In fact history now appears to be just one more foundationless, positioned expression in a world of foundationless, positioned expressions."[69] In short, postmodernism represents a profound disillusionment with the Enlightenment project and with the progress of science that is at the core of the modern worldview.

The term "postmodernism" largely replaced the term "poststructuralism" in the course of the 1980s, although the latter represented similar assumptions on the nature of history and historical knowledge. The term "postmodern" emphasizes more strongly than poststructuralism does that the modern world as we have known it has come to an end, that we live in a fundamentally different world today, although its critics could argue that this contemporary world is unthinkable without the modern world out of which it grew and from which it has never emancipated itself. Poststructuralism emerged in France in the 1960s as a reaction to structuralism but in fact continued basic assumptions of the latter. We already saw Fernand Braudel's structuralist approach to history. Braudel wished to overcome the narrative, event-, and person-oriented approach of conventional historiography and replace the idea of history as a unilinear progressive process. These concerns also play a central role in the structural cultural anthropology of Claude Lévi-Strauss, for whom, similarly as for Clifford Geertz (1926–2006), cultures have to be seen in terms of their symbolisms that require interpretation. Cultural anthropology had traditionally since the nineteenth century drawn a sharp distinction between supposedly primitive, nonliterate peoples without a history,[70] who constituted the subjects of their study, and civilized peoples, particularly in the modern West, with a progressive history. Lévi-Strauss revised this picture and showed that these allegedly primitive peoples in fact had conscious worldviews and sets of values and denied that modern scientific rationality possessed an advantage over the mythical thinking of supposedly primitive peoples in answering questions of the meaning of life.[71]

Structuralists, poststructuralists, and postmodernists saw in language a key to the constitution of societies and cultures. This led to the so-called linguistic turn. This turn took on several more and less radical forms. Traditionally, language had been seen as an instrument for referring to a real world. The poststructuralist and postmodern theorists saw in language an autonomous system not dependent on reality but in fact constructing reality. This idea of language as an autonomous system that possesses a syntactic structure goes back to the Swiss linguist Fernand de Saussure's (1857–1913) *Course in General Linguistics* (1916).[72] De Saussure did not go so far as to deny that the signs, that is, sounds that make up language, and the objects (signifiers) to which they refer have no reference to reality but held that language is not a means for communicating meaning, but on the contrary meaning is a function of language. In other words, men do not use language to convey their thoughts, but what men think is determined by language.

A good deal of historical writing in the 1970s and 1980s recognized the important role language played in shaping history, without, however, accepting the radical position that language had no reference to reality but created reality. They did, however, assign language an important place in the shaping of historical consciousness. Thus Quentin Skinner[73] at Cambridge and John Pocock[74] at Johns Hopkins gave intellectual history a new direction by moving away from the traditional history of ideas to an analysis of the discourse of political thought. Reinhard Koselleck (1923–2006), with German collaborators, published a multivolume encyclopedic work, *Geschichtliche Grundbegriffe (Basic Historical Concepts)*,[75] in which a selected number of concepts in the political and philosophical language in Germany between the middle of the eighteenth and the middle of the nineteenth centuries were examined to gain an understanding of the fundamental changes that took place in this period, which Koselleck considered crucial in the transformation from an older to a modern social and cultural order. We have already seen the role that Lynn Hunt, Maurice Agulhon, and Mona Ozouf assigned to language, along with signs and symbols for the analysis of the French Revolution and French republican traditions. William Sewell, in *Work and Revolution in France: The Language of Labor from the Old Regime to 1848* (1980),[76] deals with the decisive role of language in shaping the revolutionary consciousness of workers. Gareth Stedman Jones, like E. P. Thompson, deals with the formation of the English working class in *Languages of Class: Studies in English Working Class History 1832–1982* (1983).[77] He acknowledges Thompson's contribution to freeing class from its immediate link to an economic base but places much greater emphasis on the role of language in the constitution of class consciousness. Concentrating on Chartism, he argues that the rise and decline of the Chartist movement was less determined by economic deprivation than by political language. In a similar way, Thomas Childers examines the election campaigns in the Weimar Republic that led to the rise of the Nazis to power and stresses that basic terms did not designate realities soberly but were filled with emotional and political content such as blood, honor, nation, and folk (*Volk*).[78]

Yet while Sewell, Stedman Jones, and Childers emphasize the extent to which language not only describes but constitutes social reality, they all accept the existence of such reality and see in language a tool for examining it. But theorists proceeding more closely from postmodernist assumptions deny this. They view language as an autonomous syntactic system that is self-contained and does not reflect reality but creates it. Yet carrying this idea even further, Jacques Derrida (1930–2004) argued that there is no system or coherence to language. The historian, or for that matter any reader, is confronted by texts, not by objective reality. We have already noted how Clifford Geertz viewed cultures as texts that had to be read as such. In an often cited formulation, Derrida wrote "there is nothing outside the text."[79] But the text, he believes, can be read very differently by different readers. It has to be "deconstructed" to point at its inner contradictions. As Foucault in a similar way pointed out, the text is independent of its author.[80] Hence what the author intended is irrelevant.

What is the significance of this for historical writing? Roland Barthes (1915–1980) already stressed in the 1960s that from the linguistic character of history followed that there was no distinction between history and literature or between fact and fiction. He complained that "the realism of historical discourse is part of a cultural pattern . . . [that] points to an alienating fetishism of the 'real.'"[81] Hayden White, in *Metahistory: The Historical Imagination in Nineteenth-Century Europe* (1973), did not go as far as Barthes in denying that there are historical facts but stressed that any attempt to write history required poetic imagination. Still thinking in structuralist terms, which he later modified in the direction of Derridean postmodernism, he asserted that the way history is written is determined by a limited number of rhetorical patterns. History for him is thus basically a product of the poetical imagination.[82] "Historical narratives," he wrote in 1978, "are verbal fictions, the contents of which are as much *invented* as *found* [White's emphasis]."[83] Historiography must therefore be seen as a literary genre following literary criteria. But this leaves no criteria for historical truths. Decisions of what is to be accepted as truth, he argues, are determined by aesthetic and moral perspectives rather than by evidence. This leads White into a very difficult situation when challenged by Saul Friedländer[84] and Christopher Browning on how the Holocaust can be dealt with historically. White does not claim that there was no Holocaust; to do so would be "morally unacceptable as it is intellectually bewildering."[85] But he still maintains that there is no way in which the history of the Holocaust can be objectively reconstructed. It must follow the rhetorical patterns of all historical accounts, which means that once it goes beyond the factual basis to produce a narrative, it becomes interpretative and can no longer be proved or disproved. As long as interpretations do not distort the facts, there are no objective bases on which they can be compared. Christopher Browning, who in *Ordinary Men* reconstructs how a Hamburg police battalion carried out mass killings in Poland,[86] challenged White, emphasizing that the Holocaust is not primarily a construct of the historian. Rather, he notes, "There is a constant dialectical interaction between what historian brings to the research and how the research affects the historian."[87]

The position of theorists whom we have loosely termed postmodernists contains two insoluble contradictions, one related to the question of historical knowledge, the other to that of ethical judgments. It is easy to declare history merely a form of literature. Of course, written history has literary aspects, but it is more than mere imaginative literature. It always involves an attempt to reconstruct a past dealing with real human beings and real settings in a historical context, no matter how complex and indirect this operation is. There is no history without research. There have been exponents of a theoretical postmodernist position, but when they wrote history, as Joan Scott did of nineteenth-century French women, she sought out perspectives of women in France as historical agents, shaping their lives and participating in the political and social scene that had been previously neglected. She turned to sources according to established forms of research, even if she may have interpreted this research differently. But in the final analysis, historical narratives had to stand the test whether they indeed were truthful representations or figments of the imagination. Simon Schama, in *Dead Certainties: Unwarranted Speculations* (1991),[88] tells multiple stories about the death of a British general in the French and Indian War and about various suspicions of a murder involving a mid-nineteenth-century Harvard professor, none of which can be proved or disproved and thus raise an important question relating to the very possibility of historical knowledge. Jonathan Spence, in

The Question of Hu,[89] strayed from his serious studies of Chinese history in the Ming and Qing dynasties to tell the story of a Cantonese Catholic, Hu, who in the early eighteenth century finds himself transposed to Europe. Proceeding from documentary sources, he tried to reconstruct Hu's state of mind. But basically he does something similar to what Natalie Davis did in *The Return of Martin Guerre*. He employed his imagination not capriciously but filled in what seemed likely.

There is, moreover, a contradiction between the emphatic rejection of Enlightenment values and the actual values that the theorists we have dealt with in this section have adopted. The modern world, the product of Enlightenment, is seen in terms of domination, class, the subordination of women, the repression of marginal groups and individuals, including homosexuals, who do not conform. It is one of the positive contributions of postmodernist theories to have pointed at these aspects of repression and exploitation that also became the theme of a good deal of social and cultural history that did not share the postmodernist extreme epistemological relativism. But in their justified critique of the negative sides of modern civilization and of the ways in which knowledge – scientific, technical, societal, and humanistic – have been used as instruments of domination, Barthes, Foucault, White, Paul De Man (1919–1983),[90] Lyotard, Jean Baudrillard (1929–2007), and particularly Derrida, turned to philosophers of the extreme right such as Friedrich Nietzsche, who had nothing good to say about women, and Martin Heidegger, who in 1933 joined the Nazis. Both were outspokenly anti-democratic. Derrida, a man of the Left, nevertheless invoked Nietzsche and particularly Heidegger as important sources of his thought. From Heidegger he accepted the condemnation of the Western tradition of philosophy and rational thought since its Greek beginnings, not only the Enlightenment, as "logocentric," to be replaced by a mythical approach, which to Heidegger lay at the core of the spiritual revolution represented by Nazism. Scott turns to Derrida to lay the foundations for a feminist reading of history. She argues that sex is not a natural given but a social and cultural construct in a historical setting. She then points to the male-dominated character of language and much of the intellectual heritage of the West. But she carries this further, endorsing Derrida's conception of language, as she understands it, as a foundation for a feminist politics, failing to understand that Derrida posits a linguistic determinism that leaves little space for an active political program. She further sees the world in its complexity as fully a construct of language, criticizing Gareth Stedman Jones, who had stressed the central role of language in class consciousness, for "slipp(ing) back to the notion that language reflects a 'reality' external to it, rather than being constitutive of that reality."[91]

But if you follow Scott, how is it possible to write history, even feminist history? And as we have suggested, the history she writes assumes, as does feminist history generally, that there is a real world with real people, deeply influenced by language but not a pure construct of language.

Microhistory, the history of everyday life, and historical anthropology

The turn to culture also involved a focus on small-scale history, away from large-scale structures and developments as they had been pursued until then by social scientists, Marxists, and many *Annales* historians. In Italy, an important group of historians gathered around the journal *Quaderni Storici*, champions of a "microhistory" (*microstoria*), in contrast to the macrohistorical approaches that had previously dominated much social history. Almost all of the Italian microhistorians, including Carlo Ginzburg, Giovanni Levi, and Edoardo Grendi (1932–1999), distanced themselves from "the optimistic (Marxist) belief that the world would be rapidly and radically transformed along revolutionary lines."[92]

This repudiation of a Marxist philosophy of history also involved a broader rejection of the notion widely circulated in Western historical thought generally of a world history climaxing in the modern West, as the only center of true civilization. There remained a residual Marxist perspective that stressed the exploitative character of this modern capitalist civilization. A part of this civilization was also its particular conception of scientific logic that led some critics, as diverse as Martin Heidegger, Roland Barthes, Paul Feyerabend (1924–1994), and Ashis Nandy, to suggest that there is no distinction between truth and fiction. The Italian microhistorians did not go so far. Levi stressed that it was "important to refute relativism, irrationalism, and the reduction of the historian's work to purely rhetorical activity that interprets texts and not events themselves."[93] Ginzburg took a similar position. But while the social sciences tended to formulate generalizations as causal explanations, microhistory examined how these generalizations applied to the local scale. In his study of an early modern Italian village, Levi demonstrated that the transfer of landed property did not mechanically follow the classical laws of the market but was also affected by noneconomic factors, moral, religious, and highly personal ones, what Pierre Bourdieu (1930–2002) would call "symbolic capital."[94]

Much more than in the previous periods, there was an intense exchange carried on among historians in the various Western countries, including also Eastern Europe, participating in the new trends. The counterpart to *Microstoria* in Germany was *Alltagsgeschichte*, although there were also differences. The proponents of *Alltagsgeschichte* shared with *Microstoria* the critique of established social science approaches, in Germany that of historical social science, with its center at the University of Bielefeld and the journal *Geschichte und Gesellschaft. Alltagsgeschichte* did not possess the strong institutional basis of the Bielefeld School, but its most important proponents were attached to the Max Planck Institute for History in Göttingen. In the 1980s, there was a lively exchange between adherents of the two orientations. The proponents of *Alltagsgeschichte* criticized historical social science on very similar grounds as the proponents of *Microstoria* criticized social science history, that it was impersonal, overly abstract, and had too little interest in the life and experience of common people. But the historians of the Bielefeld School and the practitioners of *Alltagsgeschichte* shared a commitment to the emancipatory function of historical studies; for the Bielefeld historians and the social scientists in various disciplines associated with them, this generally meant the reform course of social democracy in an industrial society, while the adherents of *Alltagsgeschichte* tended to be further to the Left in the direction of greater local popular control and environmental reform. Hans Medick at the Max Planck Institute went further in his criticism of social science approaches than did Giovanni Levi in Italy and moved in the direction of historical anthropology, agreeing with Clifford Geertz in his insistence that the study of culture involves not causal explanation but interpretation of meaning. Citing agreement with Max Weber that "man is an animal suspended in webs of significance which he himself has spun," Geertz nevertheless totally misunderstood the methodological consequences that Weber had drawn for the study of culture. While Weber called for a strict rational approach by which inquiry was guided by clearly formulated theory-oriented questions, Geertz called for a "thick description," a direct anthropological confrontation with the cultural phenomena as an "other," letting the culture speak directly, as a "text," the significance of which needed to be "explicated," not explained.[95]

The History Workshop *movement*

The history of everyday life for the most part reflected a Marxist heritage, although as we already saw, it had freed itself of economic determinism and the political dogmatism of the Communist party. In 1976, the *History Workshop* was founded in Great Britain with the subtitle, *A Journal of Socialist Historians*. In fact, the journal reflected these changes. At first the journal saw itself indebted to E. P. Thompson's approach to labor history but soon went beyond it. What distinguished it from other British historical journals was not its socialist commitment, which was shared by many of the editors and contributors to *Past and Present*, but its resolve to bridge the gap between academics and the broader public and to encourage the latter to write history. Fairly soon they became aware that the Marxist conception of an industrial working class, still held by Thompson, no longer understood the changes that were taking place in the economic and political spheres. Hence they soon became concerned with the effect of the new economic realities on aspects of everyday life, including private life and sexuality. The exploitation of women not only as part of the labor force but also within a society still dominated by men moved them in a feminist direction. Not only was increasing space given to the experiences of women, but women also contributed many of the articles and occupied an important place on the editorial board. In 1982 the subtitle of the journal was changed to *A Journal of Socialist and Feminist Historians*. In 1995 the subtitle was dropped altogether, recognizing that the original Marxist analysis of an industrial society no longer corresponded to the changed realities of the modern world. In the opinion of the editors, the conditions under which radical historians could identify themselves as Marxists or even socialists no longer prevailed. The challenges of the contemporary world – environmental, ethnic, sexual – had become so complex that the terms "socialist" and "feminist" with the connotations they carried no longer sufficed. Nevertheless, the journal maintained its critical stance. It also sought, although with limited success, to involve working people, women and men, in digging up their local past. Almost all of the contributors, however, continued to be academics. But the *History Workshop* idea spread to the European continent with local workshops founded in Germany and Sweden and two journals in Germany.[96] All this involved a turn to historical anthropology, In Italy *Quaderni Storici* and in Russia the newly founded *Odysseus* moved in a similar direction.

Feminist and gender history

The late 1960s also saw an increased interest in the history of women.[97] Prior to the professionalization of the discipline in the West, there had been women's history and women historians, both in the West and elsewhere, at a time when women were regarded as keepers and recorders of tradition. But as historical writing became an academic discipline focused on the rise of the nation, women as subjects of history were relegated to the background. Women, of course, continued to write about women, both within and outside the profession. Two main trends developed, one centering around middle-class women in movements for political reform, such as suffrage, the legal status of women, widened educational opportunities, and abortion rights, the other dealing with the condition of working-class women as part of the workforce. But before the 1960s most histories paid little attention to the active role of women in history or their problems. Historical writing, even social history, centered around men.

It was only in the 1960s, as part of the general social unrest marked by the Civil Rights Movement in the United States, the opposition to the Vietnam War, and most significantly the second wave of feminism, that women's roles and concerns gained attention. This history from its beginnings, like much of the everyday history we just discussed, pursued a clear political mission, namely to end the "invisibility, powerlessness, and subordination" of women, creating a "her-story" in which women appeared as active subjects in history, not merely as its passive objects, and that exposed the hierarchy inherent in most traditional historical accounts.[98] Few of the feminist historians, with the exception of those in the Eastern bloc, were Marxists, yet they viewed all existing societies, past and present, as oppressive and saw their work as historians as contributing to combating this oppression. But the stories they told and the questions they asked were different. American and British historians tended to concentrate on suffrage. The Italians,

French, and Germans looked at the division of labor under capitalism. For Indian historians, the emphasis was on prominent nationalist women.

As in the new social history, her-story emphasized agency; women were to be seen as significant historical actors and brought into the light. The titles of books published, such as *Hidden from History* (Sheila Rowbotham) and *Becoming Visible* (Renate Bridenthal, Claudia Koonz, and Susan Stuard), exemplified this intention. Yet it soon became clear that in the political and public sphere, where women tended to be excluded, there were limits to this enterprise. It was in the private sphere and domestic arena where women's lives and experiences could be found, and here the new social history, which looked at nontraditional sources to uncover the lives of ordinary people, gave inspiration. But rather than seeing women as victims of patriarchy, circumscribed to the home, scholars now found women who wielded power within their homes and indirectly, through their men, without. The once ordinary private sphere became the locus of a different type of political behavior. However, as Julie Des Jardins has shown, the separate spheres paradigm "did not identify patriarchal forces with much precision, nor did they account for women experiencing them differently across class and context."[99] It accounted to a significant degree for the lives of upper-class women in the West, but what about poor, non-White, Third World, and lesbian women? Further, could Western categories of freedom and oppression be applied to other cultures and societies, where spheres of influence and sexual organization functioned differently?

Her-story did little to challenge traditional assumptions about the practice of history. It did challenge conventions of periodicity and progress (did women experience a renaissance during the Renaissance?) but remained fundamentally true to masculinist prescriptions of the profession. This resulted in the marginalization of women's history, even as Women's Studies departments were established in many universities during the course of the 1970s. Women's history came to be regarded as a neglected but important addendum to the curriculum, but an addendum nevertheless, "pulling them [women] from their contexts . . . isolated and peculiarized,"[100] a section within a textbook chapter with no discernible connection to anything else.

Neither did her-story convincingly explain varying and evolving patterns of oppression and hierarchy. One still had to account for changing relations between the sexes, theorized weakly by static explanations of patriarchy, whether of the Marxist or other variety. It came to be realized that essentialist notions of sex – biological sex – stood in the way. Whereas sex was a matter of biology and therefore immutable, gender was socially constructed, learned, and expressed variably in different cultures, expressed in contradictory and uneven relations of power, entrenched in the institutions of the culture, in its accepted ways of logical reasoning, and also in its language.[101]

Joan Wallach Scott's "Gender: A Useful Category of Historical Analysis," which appeared in 1986, marked an important theoretical break in women's history. Of course, women's history as her-story continued to be written, but now gender as constructed sex became more than a means to understand women's lives and experiences, as it came to include the symbolic system of registers, locations, and contested meanings between and among the sexes. Linguistic and deconstructive analyses of gendered meanings could be used to bring to light asymmetries of authority and power. Sexual tropes such as "manliness" and "effeminacy" revealed and reinforced hierarchies not only in the relations of the sexes but also in class relations and race relations, metropole and periphery. An important book to analyze the complex relationship between gender, race, and empire was Anne McClintock's *Imperial Leather* where she states that race, gender, and class ought to be seen as "articulated categories" that come into existence "in and through relation to each other" and that feminism is "as much about class, race, work, and money, as it is about sex," just as "gender is as much an issue about masculinity as it is of femininity."[102] Gender thus went beyond the original concerns of feminist historiography in the direction of a wider and more culturalist conception of the discipline.

Socially constructed notions of gender and gender-constructed notions of the social and cultural presented a circulatory logic that exposed the relativistic implications of the enterprise. If neither men, women, society, nor culture were fixed, neither could the histories that historians wrote be so. As Scott pointed out, history was "participant in the production of knowledge about sexual difference."[103] This has also turned history into what Julie Des Jardins has called a "daunting enterprise," "unlocking possibilities" while at the same time cautioning historians not to make too much of what they have uncovered. Yet gender has also shown how historical writing had been a masculinizing enterprise, how masculine notions of scientificity, objectivity, and logic, as applied to equally masculine topics such as wars, nations, and their leaders, had defined the discipline for so long. At the same time, it questioned conventional notions of masculinity. A big step forward in gender studies was so-called queer science, as historians focused on homosexuality, transsexuality, and other nonconformist forms of sexual orientation. Conventions of manhood were also studied to reveal forms of constraint and pressure. Through the lens of gender, therefore, a "men's history" emerged.

Postcolonialism[104]

The period after 1970 saw not only a greater interest in the history of the non-Western world, the beginnings of a globalization of history about which we shall write more in Chapter 8, but also a more critical assessment by historians in parts of the world that, like India, had previously been colonies or, like China, had been subjects of imperialist pressures. The critique of the West and of Western historiography had already, as we have seen, been increasingly voiced in Western and non-Western historical thought. In brief, the idea of a unilinear historical development, a world history that culminated in the civilization of the modern West, was widely rejected. The Western progressive idea of history was seen as part of an ideology that viewed the societies and cultures of the non-Western world as inferior and thus provided an ideological legitimization for colonialism and imperialism. Colonialism involved not merely political control over the colonized peoples but also cultural hegemony aimed at forced modernization along Western lines. By the 1970s, almost all of the previous colonies had attained independence but remained dependent economically on the former colonial powers and inherited a great deal of the administrative infrastructure imposed by the latter. There was no return to precolonial political structures – borders especially in Africa ignored older tribal lines and created artificial nation-states – and the educational systems followed Western models.

The term "postcolonialism" has been applied to designate the critique of Western historical institutions and patterns of thought in the postcolonial era, but postcolonial currents are too diverse to permit a clear definition. Nevertheless, they have several characteristics in common, first of all the attribution of colonialism to the economic penetration of capital in the world market. This idea admittedly derives from Marx. Yet few postcolonial thinkers are orthodox Marxists who see colonial subjugation primarily as a function of the capitalist world market. Almost all emphasize the cultural aspects of economic and political domination and also maintain that this domination has by no means ended. An important forerunner of postcolonialism was Frantz Fanon (1925–1961), born in Martinique, educated as a psychiatrist in Lyon, and, unlike the other writers whom we shall mention, an active revolutionary who participated in the Algerian insurgency against the French. His *The Wretched of the Earth* (1961)[105] was an open call for revolution that could be carried through only by violence. The book was taken very seriously by anticolonialist activists in Black Africa but also became an important document for black liberation movements in the United States as well as for the radical students' movement in Europe.

By the 1970s, Fanon's *The Wretched of the Earth* was a classic but belonged to history. Postcolonialism was now almost strictly the work of academics, although their writings exerted an influence, difficult to measure, on the reshaping of political attitudes and perspectives. It must be noted that many of the practitioners of postcolonial historiography came not from the former colonies but from the West. As a matter of fact, the majority of postcolonial historians and social theorists, particularly in India, have been trained in the West or in Western-style institutions. In many cases they have pursued a career at Western universities and have written in English or in fewer cases in French, rather than in their native languages, so that it may be argued, rightly or wrongly, that postcolonialism reflects Western as much as non-Western attitudes.

To do justice to the understanding of the past in the formerly colonial world or in countries like China subjected to external pressures requires an examination of the writings in non-Western languages, which we can do only for China and Japan. In the following pages, we shall limit ourselves to two important English-language expressions of postcolonial thought: Edward Said's *Orientalism* (1978)[106] and the Indian *Subaltern Studies* founded in 1982.

Postcolonial thought cannot be understood without its Marxist heritage, the stress on the capitalist world market originating in the West and the resulting Western control over the non-Western world, the "periphery," as the American sociologist and Africanist Immanuel Wallerstein defines it in his *The Modern World System*.[107] Wallerstein operated with an orthodox Marxist conception of the world market driven by the need of capital in the West to achieve maximum accumulation, requiring the economic exploitation and political domination of the non-Western world. Accumulation requires low wages. Wallerstein thus explains racism in the periphery and at home in terms of the need of capitalism to reduce labor costs and then argues that the subordination of women under capitalism had similar roots because the unpaid labor in the home made it possible to reduce the wages of the males. Wallerstein's work received considerable attention in Latin America where it fitted in well with *dependencia* theory seeking explanations for the stultified economic development of Latin America. Yet Wallerstein's heavy reliance on an economic interpretation of the subordination of the non-Western world was relatively isolated within the discussions of colonial and postcolonial dependency that gave greater attention to the interplay of economy and culture, never, however, ignoring the imperialist context of Western political, economic, and cultural domination.

Said's *Orientalism* exerted an immense influence on the postcolonial discussions of the 1980s. Forced as an adolescent to flee from his Palestinian home, educated in Cairo and Great Britain, Said spent his career as a professor of English literature at Columbia University in New York City.[108] He was a politically engaged intellectual, deeply involved in the fate of the Palestinians. In *Orientalism* he examined the political function of the scholarship on the Near East and more generally on Asia. He recognized the role of capitalist imperialism on the treatment of the non-Western world but assigned a much greater role to ideas, particularly to scholarship, than Marxists do. He proceeded from a conception derived from Nietzsche and Foucault that knowledge is never neutral but is an instrument of power. Turning to the academic studies of the Orient, he argued that the scholarship dealing with the Near East was designed not only to legitimate Western expansion and domination but in fundamental ways initiated such policies. He argued that British and French Orientalist scholarship, on which he focused, did not represent the Orient realistically as it existed but created – or better said, invented – an image that served its political purposes. A sharp distinction was drawn in this scholarship between a civilized, rational, and civil West and a backward, superstitious, cruel, and effeminate East. The Orient thus appeared as an "Other." And this scholarship deeply influenced Western ideas of history. Said pointed out that the ideas of Western, specifically academic scholarship were simplistic. But the question is often asked whether Said did not present an overly simplistic picture of Oriental studies; he did not deal with the rich tradition of Oriental studies in Germany and the United States, which had no immediate colonial interests in the Near East, the extent to which Orientalist studies, also in France and Great Britain, did not fall into this pattern and, as in the case of Max Müller (1823–1900) and other early Indic scholars, actually admired what they considered the depth of Indian civilization, although they too tended to view Indian mysticism as belonging to the childhood of humanity and thus like the Orientalists affirmed the normative character of the modern West.

The Subaltern Studies

It is striking that *Orientalism* was received with such enthusiasm in the West as well as in the East, as a "landmark event" in the shaping of postcolonial scholarship.[109] Undoubtedly, this had a good deal to do with the general intellectual climate in both West and East, but perhaps we should not say East but refer to Anglophone India, which in many ways participated in Western discussions. An extreme expression of this are the writings of Ashis Nandy at the University of New Delhi, also a frequent fellow at institutions in Great Britain and Germany, who, as we already mentioned, rejects the Enlightenment tradition of the West outright, holds it responsible for the mass violence and genocides of the twentieth century, and calls for a return to premodern ways of thinking, away from modern rationalist and secular outlooks. Part of the modern historical outlook is the dominance of the "modern nation state, secularism, the Baconian concept of scientific rationality, nineteenth century theories of progress, and, in recent decades, development. We must again respect cultures that have lived with open-ended concepts of the past or depended on myths, legends, and epics to define their cultural selves."[110]

The *Subaltern Studies*,[111] founded in 1982, did not go so far. Its purpose, as its editor Ranajit Guha, at the time at the University of Sussex, explained in the opening issue in 1982, was to break with the dominant Indian historiography, which he described as elitist, that saw the emergence of Indian nationalism and the achievement of Indian independence as the work of leading political figures and intellectuals whom Guha, using Marxist terminology, defined as bourgeois. Using the term "subaltern" derived from Antonio Gramsci's *Notes on Italian History*, the *Subaltern Studies* were to concentrate on the subordinated parts of the population, the peasants, lower castes, tribals, and other marginalized groups who had been generally ignored in the conventional elite historiography of the Indian nation. The very notion of the nation copied by Indian "bourgeois" history from British models was now questioned. India consisted of a very diverse population, each with its own traditions. At the center of subaltern history was the assertion that the subordinate classes had not been passively mindless subjects but were "agents" who possessed a political consciousness and actively made their history. Elite histories "fail to acknowledge, far less interpret, the contribution made by the people *on their own*, that is *independently of the elite*"[112] in the making of modern India. Guha presented a model of how these uprisings were to be studied in *Elementary Aspects of Peasant Insurgency in Colonial India*.[113] Further, since the subordinates left few written documents, Guha developed, in an essay titled "The Prose of Counterinsurgency," methods for teasing out subaltern consciousness from official records documenting insurgency, which were to be read "against the grain" as much for their assertions as for their "silences." This emphasis on the textual properties of archival documents in the context of knowledge-power brought subaltern historiography into a deep engagement with postmodern literary theory.

As stated, the movement represented by the *Subaltern Studies* was Leftist in inspiration. But it was also a part of the general disillusionment with orthodox Marxist theory and practice that arose in the West in the 1970s. As did E. P. Thompson, whose visit to India in 1976 had an enormous impact on Indian scholars, the *Studies* sought to rescue the so-called subaltern from the "condescension of posterity," including the condescension of the "official" Left historians with their exclusive concentration on economic conditions and Left organizational leadership. Written exclusively in English, the *Studies* involved not only Indian but also British and American historians and social scientists, including historical anthropologists, forming a loose but still cohesive group across the continents with a shared conception of history. The question can, of course, be raised whether this group did not also represent an elite, namely an academic elite, more closely linked by language and training with British rather than with Indian traditions This point was raised by Gayatri Chakravorty Spivak, a member of the group who noted the inherently paradoxical position of intellectuals "speaking for" the subalterns rather than allowing them to speak for themselves. The striking similarity between the Subaltern approach and the history-from-below movement of the British Marxists was also noted; there was hardly anything postcolonial about it.

Members of the group, however, argued that although *Subaltern Studies* "did not begin self-consciously as a postcolonial project," the nature of its "intervention" inevitably pointed to and developed into a critique of colonial and Western knowledge practices.[114] Implicated in the analysis of anticolonial movements of subaltern groups was a wider critique of state, nation, modernity, and the Eurocentric presumptions that underlay these concepts. Elitist representations of the past, even nationalist ones, were derived from colonial and Eurocentric discourses, privileging certain concepts and categories and denying other imaginings of state or nation or modern. At the root of the problem, *Subaltern Studies* argued, was the presumed universality of Europe's historical experience including and especially the institution of the modern nation-state, as also conceptions of historical evolution modeled on European trajectories. Following the critique of Eurocentric history was an interrogation of the modern discipline of history itself, not to the extent of Nandy, who rejected it altogether, but as a theoretical category laden with power.

These concerns were raised by Dipesh Chakrabarty in an article published in 1992,[115] to be included later in the influential monograph titled *Provincializing Europe*. While addressing the historiography of the non-Western world, Chakrabarty stated, "There is a peculiar way in which all these other histories tend to become variations on a master narrative that could be called 'the history of Europe.'"[116] The task was to "provincialize" Europe, to repudiate "Europe as History," the template for the understanding of other cultures. Chakrabarty noted that Ranajit Guha's original contribution had been a fundamental rethinking of the nature of colonial capitalism, that the European category of a universalist capitalist path, suggesting prescribed stages of social and economic development, did not apply to the colonial situation. "The global history of capitalism does not have to reproduce everywhere the same history of power." In colonial India, the bourgeoisie, unlike its European counterpart, was dominant without a hegemonic ideology, exerting power in a manner that recalled precolonial relations of domination and subordination. Yet these "precolonial" practices could in no way be regarded as retrograde, "backward," or inconsistent with capitalist modernity but – and here *Subaltern Studies* parted ways with English Marxism – were to be seen as a different type of modernity, one that moreover, survived into the postcolonial period.[117] Similarly, Subaltern analysis of nationalist historiography and subaltern resistance disclosed enormous divergences in aims and values. Subaltern insurgency revealed a consciousness at odds with that of the nationalist elites, whose notions of nation, state, and civil drew inspiration from the West with its supposed secularism, rationalism, and forms of civil society, a heritage of the Enlightenment. This led to an interrogation of nationalism and the "nation-state" project, which was opposed to its binary counter, the community or "fragment," located "outside the thematic of post-Enlightenment thought" and that resisted "the state-centered drive to homogenize and 'normalize' in the name of a unitary national culture and political community."[118] This development indicated a convergence between *Subaltern Studies* and postmodernist critiques. In 1988, Guha retired from the editorial team of the project, and in the same year an anthology of the *Studies* was published with a foreword by Edward Said, describing the work as "intellectually insurrectionary." But criticisms of the project also appeared. Sumit Sarkar, a one-time member who broke away from it when it turned to postmodernism, was critical of its one-sided culturalism. The concept of the subaltern had been adopted to avoid the pitfalls of economic reductionism in the context of the largely precapitalist conditions of colonial India, while at the same time retaining the concepts of domination and exploitation. "What is conveniently forgotten," Sarkar argued, "is that the problems do not disappear through a simple substitution of 'class' by 'subaltern' or 'community.' Reifying tendencies can be actually strengthened by the associated detachment from socio-economic contexts and determinants out of a mortal fear of economic reductionism." Sarkar added that even Gramsci's subalterns "are emphatically not unrelated to 'the sphere of economic production.' "[119]

Further, divorced from its socioeconomic contexts, domination increasingly came to be seen as a cultural force, the "virtually irresistible" power-knowledge of the modern bureaucratic nation-state, whose roots lay in the post-Enlightenment West. But, as critics point out, such an isolated and valorized concept of the fragment overlooks its own internal tensions and contradictions, its own structures of domination and subordination, as well as the wider social formation in which it lies embedded and that often includes the reach of the colonial state. Historians concerned with broader issues of political economy also point out that the perspective of the fragment does not acknowledge "that global capitalism and local communitarianism were locked not in an adversarial but a dialectical relationship."[120]

The postnationalist celebration of the fragment in *Subaltern Studies* clearly resonated with the postmodernist critique of progress and modernity, as the fragment had to be by necessity precolonial in its identity. As we saw earlier, this antimodernism was very much at the crux of Ashis Nandy's position. Less extremely, Gyanendra Pandey, another member of the group, asserted, "Part of the importance of the 'fragmentary' point of view lies in this, that it resists the drive for a shallow homogenization and struggles for other, potentially richer definitions of the 'nation' and the future political community."[121] The repudiation of the Enlightenment also gave rise in the writings of some Subaltern scholars to a critique of the project of history itself as a European form of knowledge. It was Guha, following Said and Foucault, who first raised the question of the relationship between history writing and imperialism,[122] and others such as Gyan Prakash (1952), Partha Chatterjee, Shahid Amin, David Arnold (1945), among others, have also explored the issue of "colonial discourse" in various realms. Yet none go so far as Nandy or Vinay Lal, who reject the legitimacy of the historical enterprise, nor do they desire to reverse the hierarchy, substituting India for Europe. As Chakrabarty argues, the master narrative of Europe cannot be wished away. But one could, acknowledging that " 'Indian' history itself is in a position of subalternity,"[123] through a deconstructive reading of history as a colonial discipline locate the cracks and fissures that redefine the narrative from a subaltern perspective.

Subaltern Studies thus shifted from its original goal of rescuing subaltern agency to a more fundamental critique of academic history, seen as a Eurocentric history. Yet this "rethinking does not entail," as Gyan Prakash states, "a rejection of the discipline and its procedures of research."[124] Perhaps this has something to do with the fact that for all its critique of colonial culture and institutions, the India of the Subaltern school still has integrated a great deal of the British heritage – the educational system, the legal patterns, parliamentary institutions, and civil liberties, to mention only a few. Thus much of the Enlightenment tradition had become a part of modern Indian political culture. Subaltern scholars, as serious historians, accept international standards of historical scholarship. Thus while Dipesh Chakrabarty sought to demonstrate the parochialism of a Western view of historical development in terms of stages toward modernity for which colonial cultures represented the premodern forms destined to give way, he at the same time acknowledged that Western forms of science and social scientific rationality had generally been adopted in the formerly colonized world, particularly in South Asia. He thus notes "that today the so-called European intellectual tradition is the only one alive in the social science departments of most, if not all, [Indian] universities." Thus few, if any, Indian social scientists would base their theories on older Indian thinkers. One result of European colonial rule in India has been "that the intellectual traditions once unbroken and alive in Sanskrit or Persian or Arabic are now truly dead."[125]

One final observation must be made with regard to the political implications of the late Subaltern position. The valorization of the fragment and the premodern has found an undesirable but not unexpected endorsement in the right-wing religious-chauvinistic forces as represented by the *Hindutva* movement whose political wing has come to power in several of the Indian states at various times. While the Subaltern Group has spoken out and campaigned against this movement, seeing it as a "modern" construct of late and postcolonial times, the religious right wing has found it all too easy to appropriate the subaltern critique of the secular liberal nation-state as a Western import alien to "authentic Indian tradition." It must be noted that Ashis Nandy himself sees secularism as a form of statism and thus inherently intolerant, although various scholars have pointed out that the meaning of secularism in the Indian context is entirely different, referring mainly to religious pluralism and tolerance. The mingling of myth with history as a form of Indian historiography also services the *Hindutva*'s rewriting of the Indian past in the service of the political project of an idealized Hindu society. "Subalternism," writes Aijaz Ahmad, "has had a curious career, starting with invocations of Gramsci and finally coming into its own as an accomplice of the anti-Communist right."[126]

Latin America: From dependencia *theory and beyond*

In the period since the late 1960s with which we are dealing, a great deal of historical writing in Latin America moved in directions parallel to those that we have described in preceding sections on the West and on India, and will discuss in Africa, from narrative histories centering on political elites, to macrohistorical structural and Marxist approaches, to small foci in which the submerged classes appear on the historical scene in their cultural settings. In many ways, Latin America has been part of the West since the Spanish and Portuguese conquests in the sixteenth century. However, in a recent essay, Mark Thurner argues that the history of Latin American historiography has been written from a modern Western perspective that ignores an Indo-Iberian approach to history that preceded Western conceptions and was not directly influenced by them.[127] Yet there were also marked differences. And Latin America never has been a unit, but has rather been divided by ethnicities, some in the Southern tip with close ties to Europe, others with large indigenous populations, and especially in Brazil and the Caribbean also descendants of African slaves. This expressed itself in historiographical diversity, a diversity that, however as we shall see, should not be overstressed. With the professionalization of historical studies, these studies increasingly followed the patterns of Western historiography, particularly the French *Annales*, Marxist, and North American social science approaches to history, even where they continued to focus on local and regional themes.

There have been very few attempts to write histories of Latin America as a whole.[128] Latin American historians have primarily dealt with their own nation or region and seldom went beyond national borders. It is striking that the recently published fifth volume of the *Oxford History of Historical Writing* (2011) on historical writing since 1945 has separate chapters on Argentina, Brazil, and Mexico, but none dealing with Latin America as a whole, although there are many common traits, and there is a good deal of transnational interaction.[129] Juan Maiguashca in volume 4 of the *Oxford History of Historical Writing* (2011) between 1800 and 1945 deals with currents of historiography common to Spanish South America.[130] Only very recently has a study appeared that deals with historiographical trends in Latin America across national lines in the contemporary period. Jurandir Malerba's critical survey concentrating on the period since the 1960s, first published in Portuguese in 2009 and in Spanish in 2010, constitutes such a study.[131] A discussion of major trends in Latin American historiography from the Conquista until now has very recently been published by the Chilean historian Felipe Soza.[132]

What the diverse parts of Latin America have in common is a colonial past, which for most ended almost two centuries ago with the independence of numerous states with few connections among them. And then there was the common Spanish language in all Latin American states with the exception of Portuguese-speaking Brazil and small English-, French-, and Dutch-speaking enclaves. Economic development differed in the various parts of Latin America. For the most part the Latin American states did not experience industrial modernization at the same time as Western and Central Europe and North America. Agrarian peasant societies continued to be widespread, although there were islands of industry linked to free market economies closely interwoven with the capitalist world market and dependent on it. In contrast to Europe in the early post-Renaissance period, when historiography in a humanist tradition tended to be secular and went back to classical models of narrative political history in the manner of Thucydides, much history writing in Latin America in the post-Columbian period was dominated by Jesuit scholars and to an extent also by clerics from other Catholic religious orders. It was a strong point of this historiography that, particularly in the early period after the Conquest but still into the seventeenth and eighteenth centuries, it paid major attention to pre-Columbian societies and cultures and the interaction of the indigenous populations and the new European settlers in colonial times[133] and thus also dealt much more intensively with aspects of life and culture than the traditional historiographies of the mother countries that concentrated on politics and political leaders.[134] But Enlightenment ideas that played an important role in the fashioning of historical writing and historical interest in Europe in the eighteenth century asserted a more limited influence on historical thought in Latin America.

Independence marked a change, although much of the pattern of social relationships between the elites and the broad masses of the population remained unchanged but was by no means uniform throughout Latin America. Notwithstanding regional diversity, there were certain similar developments. The role of the clerics was replaced by persons from public life. And they often wrote history with the intent to create a sense of national but not Latin American identity. As yet, historical writing was little affected by the professionalization that already had transformed historical studies elsewhere.

In contrast, history in the period from independence in the 1820s to the early twentieth century was written primarily by amateurs largely from the elite. This was largely history from above, focusing on the national state and its leaders. This historiography has often been described as liberal. In some ways, liberalism was a European import. Enlightenment ideas entered and with them the call for a secular outlook free of the earlier religious orientation under the colonial regimes. Much of this new historiography involved a critique of the autocratic Spanish and Portuguese rule, a call for constitutional government associated with the guarantee of civil law and the rights of property associated with classical liberalism.[135] Few historians had a hemispheric perspective. Such a perspective was also precluded by the growing utilization of archives that necessitated a concentration on national and, increasingly, regional history for which archival sources were available. Much of this historiography was positivistic in its narrow dependence on these sources. Very belatedly, only in the course of the first half of the twentieth century, did professionalization set in and archives became more available in the national capitals and the countryside. At the same time, the dominant liberalism of much of nineteenth-century historiography was challenged throughout Latin America by what has been labeled "revisionist" outlooks that rejected the modernizing and cosmopolitan tendencies of much of Latin American historiography and replaced it by a more traditional and authoritarian outlook.[136] The recent documentary film exalting Augusto

Pinochet's dictatorship, presented in June 2012, shows that revisionism is by no means dead. Yet both liberal and revisionist historiography were largely the work of nonprofessional historians who were not guided by strict methodological procedures but who were rather ideologically motivated.

The first important steps toward the professionalization of historical studies occurred in the early twentieth century beginning at the Universities of La Plata and Buenos Aires in Argentina. Universities had been founded in the Spanish colonies as early as the fifteenth century. But they were not yet universities in the modern sense in which teaching was closely related to research. In Brazil, universities were not established in the colonial period.[137] But a degree of institutionalization occurred already in Brazil as early as in the nineteenth century, with the foundation of the Instituto Histórico e Geográfico Brasileiro in 1838; a similar institution was the Universidad de Chile, founded in 1842. Although the strict recourse to scholarly method that marked professional historical studies came later, both supported and funded historical studies under a more or less institutionalized framework.[138] In Argentina in 1908, the University of La Plata commissioned two well-known amateur historians, Ricardo Rojas (1882–1957) and Ernesto Quesada (1858–1934), to prepare a report on the way in which European and North American universities taught history and historical research to advanced students. Rojas surveyed European and North American universities generally, while Quesada visited all major German universities.[139] The result was to base the study of Argentinian history for the first time on a critical reliance on primary sources, essentially following the Rankean model.[140] Subsequently, other Latin American universities, particularly in Mexico, Chile, Peru, Venezuela, and Cuba, followed suit.[141] A new and different impulse came from the University of São Paulo, considered the first modern Brazilian university, founded in the 1930s, that introduced anthropological and cultural approaches as they were pursued by the French *Annales* School.[142] The University of São Paulo thus participated in the transformation of historical studies that was occurring in Europe and North America, particularly in France. It is of significance that Claude Lévi-Strauss and Fernand Braudel were among the early visiting professors at São Paulo. The period that followed saw the introduction of theories of social change that replaced the earlier positivism.

Two sets of historical theories were increasingly adopted by historians and social scientists after 1945 to deal with the social and economic condition in Latin America, forms of modernization theory and of Marxism, reflecting two different political orientations. Both theories shared the conviction in the irresistible movement of modern society worldwide toward economic growth and social and political modernization but viewed this development from different perspectives. Modernization theories generally held that Latin America must follow the path set by Western European and North American societies. In the process, Latin America would become modernized, and modernization signified Westernization in the cities and ultimately in the countryside. Driven by the alliance of multinational, state, and local capital, this process would lead to widespread industrialization and to a marked decline in urban and rural poverty. Yet by the mid-1960s, it became apparent that this developmental strategy worked neither on the industrial plane nor in the diminution of the great disparity in incomes, which in fact tended to increase. Nor did the expectation that the infusion of international and local capital would result in significant industrial growth and decrease the age-old condition in which the unequal division of trade between the developed economies of Western and Central Europe and North America, and soon also Japan, and less developed Latin America, would be overcome. At this point, Marxist-oriented "dependence" theories confronted modernization theories, challenging its optimism regarding the positive effects of capitalism on Latin American development.[143]

Dependence (*dependencia*) theory in the 1960s had Western proponents, particularly André Gunder Frank (1929–2005), born in Germany from where he fled from the Nazis as a child. Educated in economics at the University of Chicago, he spent most of his career after 1962 in Latin America where he taught at the universities of Brasília, Mexico City, and Santiago de Chile.[144] Perhaps the most important Western dependence theorist was Immanuel Wallerstein, whose *The Modern World System* has already been mentioned but who had no direct connections to Latin America.[145] Yet the primary proponents were Latin American, foremost the Argentinians Raúl Prebisch (1901–1986), the Brazilians Fernando Henrique Cardoso, who incidentally was president of Brazil from 1995 to 2002, Theotonio Dos Santos, and Ruy Mauro Marini (1932–1997), and the Mexican Pablo González Casanova,[146] to name only three. The core of the argument was that the infusion of capital into Latin America on the whole did not result in economic development but on the contrary stifled it and heightened the dependence of Latin America on world capitalism.[147]

Yet *dependencia* was still a structural form of Marxism in which individuals remained invisible. The period beginning in the 1950s saw increasing social unrest in various parts of Latin America: the Guatemalan revolt of 1954, soon suppressed through U.S. intervention; the Cuban Revolution of 1959; the Sandinista movement in Nicaragua; the election of Salvador Allende (1908–1973) to the presidency of Chile in 1969, ended by the military coup of General Augusto Pinochet (1915–2006) in 1973 supported by the United States; the student demonstrations at the Mexico City Olympics in 1968; insurgencies in various countries, all of them inspired to some degree by Marxist ideals of social justice. The turn to a history-from-below, which we have previously followed in Western Europe and North America, as well as in India, also occurred in Latin American historiography, in part adopting models from abroad. In fact, historiography in Latin America very closely followed the transformation of historical studies in Western Europe and North America. Thus beginning in the 1950s but partly already earlier, there occurred a shift away from the traditional narrative history of events focusing on politics and political leaders to social and economic history. But the prime model was not North American social science–oriented history but the French *Annales* with its much broader conception of society as a totality encompassing economic but also social and cultural aspects, forming interdisciplinary sciences of man *(sciences de l'homme)*. The late 1960s, for which 1968 was a symbolic date, were marked by a profound change in historical outlook, in historical practice, and in the choice of topics that Latin American historians shared with historians in Western Europe and North America. A significant part of this reorientation was the turn away from historical sociology and economics, which had played a significant role in the early history of the *Annales*, to culture and historical anthropology.[148]

There took place in the late 1960s a radicalization of historical writing that went further in Latin America than it did in Europe or in North America but followed closely European and North America patterns. This radicalization had roots in European, particularly French and to an extent Marxist, thought but took on forms that were sometimes specifically Latin American. Despite variations reflecting regional differences and problems, these ideas were shared broadly by historians in Latin America generally.[149] The unrest of the late 1960s brought with it the rise of a feminist movement, the struggle against ethnic discrimination, postcolonialism, and a critique of the social and economic status quo, which influenced the way in which history was written. Inevitably, this led to the merger of *Annales* ideas and cultural anthropology with the economic critique of Marxism. But Marxism assumed a form corresponding more closely to specific Latin American conditions.[150]

We must distinguish between two different forms of Marxism, one that expressed itself in revolutionary practice, the other in theoretical formulations within an academic framework. The first is closely related to the Cuban Revolution and the legacy of Che Guevara. It was by no means restricted to Cuba but played a role in revolutionary struggles in Nicaragua and left governments in Venezuela, Ecuador, and Bolivia, and earlier in the reform movements under Jacobo Arbenz (1903–1971) in Guatemala and Allende in Chile. It moved away from the traditional Marxist conception of the class struggle in an essentially industrial society to the insurgency of predominantly peasant populations, as in Nicaragua and in the Zapatista autonomy movement in Mexico. On the other hand, in the more urbanized areas not only in Argentina, Chile, Brazil, but also in Mexico, Marxism increasingly was concentrated in academic institutions. Forced into exile during the periods of military dictatorship in Argentina (1966–1983), Brazil (1968–1985), and Chile (1973–1990), which interrupted movements of social reform and led to the temporary purge of reform-minded intellectuals from the universities, Marxist historians whose work until then had been geared directly or indirectly to political action, now, to cite Juan Maiguashca, "turned to interpreting the world rather than changing it. Thus Latin American Marxist 'academic' history was born, complete with footnotes, bibliographies, subject indexes and other scholarly accoutrements."[151] By the end of the 1980s, Marxist history had gained academic respectability and in some places had become a new establishment.

But Marxism in Latin America, both in its insurrectionary and its academic form, differed despite its European roots noticeably from European forms of Marxism. It was much more indebted to Antonio Gramsci (1891–1937) than to Karl Marx. From Gramsci, it took over the idea of cultural "hegemony" and the focus on the "subaltern classes" that went far beyond the orthodox Marxist notion of a revolutionary proletariat to include the masses of the poor.[152] At the same time, the work of Edward P. Thompson (1924–1993) received considerable attention. The workers were no longer seen as determined primarily by economic forces but as helping to shape the world in which they lived.[153] The focus now shifted from a macrohistorical approach that concentrated on impersonal structures to a microhistory. Increasingly, a "history from below," of *los de abajo*, not only of the industrial proletarians but also of peasants, as well as of women and marginal groups and individuals including vagrants and criminals, became the subjects of historical writing. For the first time, significant work was done on the history of slavery in Brazil and Cuba but also elsewhere, dealing with the slaves as historical agents, as Eugene Genovese (1930–2012) had done in the United States,[154] and focusing on the culture the slaves created in captivity. Of course, this was not a peculiarly Latin American movement but, as we have seen, reflected new outlooks and orientations characteristic of important segments of the historiography of the 1970s and 1980s generally. The urban elites as central subjects of historical treatment gave way to a concentration on the impoverished. As a result, we now know more about the "hard-drinking, rock throwing mob, and the urban artisan"[155] than we did in traditional forms of Marxist analysis.

And this takes us to the most recent period, the last decade of the twentieth century and the first decade and a half of the twenty-first century. In this period a tremendous extension of centers of higher learning took place, with important research universities established throughout Latin America, with two outstanding universities—the University of São Paulo and the Colegio de Mexico. Again we see a close relation between historiographies in Latin America and in the Western world generally, perhaps even closer than before.[156] As we have seen, this relationship existed since the professionalization of historical studies in Latin America in the 1930s but was intensified in the period of military dictatorship in Argentina, Brazil, and Chile, during which scholars in these countries took refuge in Western Europe and the United States. In reverse, Spanish, German, and Italian scholars had taken refuge in Latin America, particularly in Mexico, during the period of Fascist dictatorship in those countries in the 1930s and 1940s.[157] At this point came, the work of Tulio Halperin Doughi (1926–2014), perhaps the most important Argentinian social and political historian of the twentieth century, who in 1972 in exile became a faculty member at the University of

California, Berkeley, and returned to the University of Buenos Aires after Argentina's return to democracy.[158]

The years around 1990 marked the collapse of the Soviet Empire and with it that of Marxism-Leninism as a political and social doctrine, But this had little effect on the writing of history. Marxism-Leninism had been largely discredited already before 1990, also in Latin America, except to a degree in Cuba where it remained the official doctrine. The fundamental reorientation of historiography did not take place around 1990 but already, as we have seen, earlier in the late 1960s, part of the worldwide turn away not only from traditional political history but also from the North American model of empirical, quantitative social science history dealing with anonymous social structures and processes of historical change. It was accompanied by the student revolts of the late 1960s when history increasingly turned to the inclusion of those segments of the population, particularly women and ethnic minorities, who had previously been marginalized in historical studies. The composition of the student bodies and faculties changed and with it the introduction of new topics into historical studies, sex and gender, collective mentalities, and emotions. The three essays on Argentina, Brazil, and Mexico, as well as the section of Felipe Soza dealing broadly with Latin America, all agree about the extent to which historians in their respective countries followed the main currents of West European and North American thought, a turn that was intensified after 1990. "Recent years," Joel Horowitz writes on Argentina, "have seen the publication of works that reflect most of the major trends in Western historiography from the linguistic turn to gender studies, to private lives, to intellectual history, to postmodernism."[159] On this all three authors and Soza agree. They see a return to narrative history, as Gillermo Zermeño Padilla does in the chapter on Mexican historical writing, largely influenced by historians and theorists of history such as Lawrence Stone, Arthur C. Danto, Paul Ricoeur, Michel de Certeau, Hayden White, and Roger Chartier[160] The *Nueva historia Argentina*, a ten-volume work written by different historians, is cited as a prime example of this new cultural historiography.[161] The works of the Brazilian historian Laura de Mello de Souza is cited as a prime example of the application of cultural history to the history of mentalities.[162] As in France, the history of private life reasserts an important place, such as in the edited work of the Brazilian Fernando A. Novais, *Historia da vida privada no Brasil* (1997–1998). Political history reasserts itself after 1990 in the form of a "new political history," but a very different political history from the one that was largely repudiated earlier in Latin America, as it was in Western Europe and North America. This new political history turned away from a concentration on politics and elites to a consideration of the cultural context in which women and the lower classes, not only workers but also peasants, played an active role.[163]

1990 also witnessed the end of the Cold War and with it growing globalization, accompanied by an increased turn to comparative, transnational, and transcultural historical studies. This interest in global history was most marked in the United States and interestingly also in China,[164] to a lesser extent in Europe where national history still occupied an important but not exclusive place, but very little in Latin America. As Marshall Eakin notes, "[M]uch like the rest of Latin America, much of the historiography produced in Brazil concentrates on national history" and is "rarely comparative or cross-national."[165] And this despite the great influence that Fernand Braudel, whose work, except for his final book on the identity of France,[166] was transnational throughout, had on Brazilian and generally on Latin American historiography. An exception is the recently published *Comprender el Pasado. Una historia del escritura y pensamiento histórico*,[167] which attempts a history of historiography since its beginnings, but nevertheless, except for a chapter dealing with Chinese and Islamic historiography in its classical period, contains no mention of its later development, and except for the section by Felipe Soza on Latin America is still Western, not globally centered.

The period after 1990 saw a sharp decline in the role that Marxism played in Latin American historiography. This was not merely the result of the collapse of the Soviet Union and the sharp decline of the European Communist parties but of the general turn away from the economically focused history pursued by Marxism to the rise of cultural history, But Marxism too, as we have seen, had undergone a cultural turn in the last third of the twentieth century. The *Annales*, who had originally shared with Marxism a strong emphasis on social and economic structures, in an extreme form in Braudel's conception of the *longue durée*, were deeply affected by the new cultural approaches to history. Increasingly in the last 25 years, the classical theories of history and society, which had dominated Marxism, the *Annales*, and social science conceptions of modernization, were discredited.[168] In Latin America there was now a stress on a history of everyday life, essentially a history from below. And a great deal of historical writing concentrated on inequality and discrimination as they existed in past and present society. Workers, women, and the indigenous segments of the population became the focus of a growing body of historical writing, particularly in the last two and a half decades.[169] In Brazil and Cuba, important works dealt with the history of slavery, now from a culturalist perspective. And although most of this history no longer regarded itself as Marxist, it reflected a Marxist inspiration, but one that went beyond the materialist confines of traditional Marxism to a broader culturally oriented perspective encompassing a much wider segment of the population, including those whom traditional Marxism, with its narrow focus on a male industrial proletariat, had neglected.[170] In a way, Marx was replaced by Michel Foucault.

The emergence of modern historiography in Sub-Saharan Africa[171]

The development of historiography in Sub-Saharan Africa was different from that in every other area we have discussed. The period of colonialism was harsher than in India and connected with an even more pronounced racism. The creation of universities and the professionalization of historical studies began very late, only toward the end of the colonial period. Even more emphatically than in India, the colonial rulers insisted that Africa or at least Black Africa was a continent without a history, an opinion broadly shared by intellectuals and a broad segment of the population within Europe and North America. This racism was already well developed among certain Enlightenment thinkers. David Hume in the late eighteenth century considered "negroes to be naturally inferior to the white." He continued that "there never was a civilized nation of any other complexion than the white . . . No ingenious manufacturers among them, no arts, no science." Hegel, as we already saw, denied that India and China possessed historical development, but was even harsher on Africa. Africa, he wrote, is "no historical part of the World. . . . What we properly understand by Unhistorical, Undeveloped Spirit, still involved in the conditions of mere nature." As late as 1968, Hugh Trevor Roper, the Regius Professor of Modern History at Oxford, dismissed Africa "as the unrewarding gyrations of barbarous tribes in picturesque but irrelevant quarters of the globe."[172] He further wrote: "There is only the history of the Europeans in Africa. The rest is darkness and darkness is not a subject of history"[173] In fact, attention was paid to Africa in European and North American studies in the first half of the twentieth century with little or no concern for the African past but only as part of European expansion.

The task to which Black African scholars began increasingly to turn in the 1950s and 1960s was to demonstrate that Sub-Saharan Africa had a history that long preceded the colonial period.[174] Already in the late nineteenth and early twentieth centuries, Africans and Afro-Americans had begun to refute the Eurocentric stereotype of an unhistorical past. W. E. B. Du Bois (1868–1963) and Leo Hansberry (1894–1965) in the United States sought to discover an African identity through the ages, not with the aim of later African historians to research history with the purpose of nation-building but, for Du Bois, a historical sociologist and Marxist, with an outspoken anti-imperialist and anticolonial agenda and a militant advocacy of racial equality in the United States and Africa, to fashion a Pan-African identity transcending national and ethnic lines.[175] Oriented toward nationalism, a new African cultural elite in the late nineteenth and early twentieth centuries sought to join African roots with visions of progress that merged European ideas of democracy and economic growth with the rediscovery of African traditions. In British West Africa, Edward Wilmot Blyden (1832–1912),[176] already in the second half of the nineteenth century, attempted a similar synthesis. In the first half of the twentieth century, Léopold Senghor (1906–2001),[177] a French language poet and first president of independent Senegal (1950–1981), strove for what he called *négritude*, a recapture of what he considered the spirit of the African past and character, which he wanted to merge with the exigencies of modern civilization. This idea was drawn from Aimé Césaire (1913–2008), a Black poet from Martinique and hence part of the African diaspora. He is not the only example. George Padmore (1903–1959) exercised significant influence in the Pan-African movement. Another highly significant West Indian scholar was Walter Rodney, author of *How Europe Underdeveloped Africa*, who extends the Marxist-dependency school of writings.[178] To an outsider the definition of *négritude* may appear as an essentialist conception of Black Africa overlooking the ethnic, cultural, religious, and ethnic diversity of the Sub-Saharan continent. Nevertheless, the late years of the British, French, Belgian, and Portuguese colonies saw the growing commitment of an elite seeking independence to prove that Africa indeed had a history. The colonial period was seen as a relatively short episode in the long history of the African past.[179]

The professionalization of historical studies in Black Africa as a scholarly academic response to the colonial interpretation of African history came relatively late, only after the end of the Second World War, but then made rapid progress. The original impetus came from outside Africa, from Great Britain and North America, where non-African scholars had also freed themselves from the old imperial predilection to deal with Africa only in its relevance to European colonial domination and turned to an African history. It is important to note that in the endeavor to decolonize African historiography, an international community of scholars emerged including Western as well as Black African historians. Shortly after the end of World War II, the Institute of Oriental Studies in London was expanded to include African Studies in its name. In 1948 the University of London established three university colleges, in Nigeria, Ghana, and Uganda. Soon further universities were established in Nigeria, including one in Northern Nigeria with an Islamic focus. Other universities were established in the former British as well as in the formerly French colonies such as the University of Dakar (Cheikh Anta Diop University) and in the former Belgian Congo the University of Louvanium (University of Kinshasa). To begin with, the instructors in the former British colonies were largely British, but they were gradually although not totally replaced by Africans after the link between the African universities and London was terminated in 1962.[180] The professionalization of historical studies then made rapid strides. The most important early center was the University of Ibadan. From there Kenneth Onwuka Dike (1917–1983) and his slightly younger colleague Jacob Ajayi (1929–2014) both trained at the University of London, began in the 1950s to transform African studies into a rigorous academic discipline, consonant with international standards, and laid the foundations for what came to be known as the Ibadan School. Dike, in his London dissertation on *The Trade and Politics in the Niger Delta 1830–1885* (1956),[181] had extensively used oral as well as printed records and contributed to the acceptance of oral traditions as a legitimate source of historical inquiry, not merely as folklore. In 1952 Dike participated in the establishment of the Nigerian National Archive, the National Museum, and the Institute of African Studies in Ibadan. He helped launch the Ibadan History Series and the *Journal of the Historical Society of Nigeria.* Ajayi dealt with the making of elites in Nigeria in the nineteenth century, but the historians of the Ibadan School also explored precolonial history, using archival, oral, archeological, and linguistic as well as written Arabic sources. The Ibadan School had contributed to rejuvenating African studies, but professional associations and journals also came into existence elsewhere, such as the *Transactions of the Historical Society of Ghana.* The Nigerian Society launched a special periodical for teachers and students. International conferences brought together scholars of African studies from the various African countries, from Europe, and from North America.[182]

A measure of the increasing role of professional African scholars of African studies and the new direction in which African studies went was the eight-volume UNESCO *General History of Africa.*[183] The project was run under the academic control of an international scientific committee of experts; a majority of the editors of the eight volumes were Black Africans. The second volume dealing with the period before the seventh century was edited by an Egyptian, the following volume from the twelfth to the fifteenth centuries was co-edited jointly by a Moroccan and a Czechoslovak. All other volumes were edited by scholars from Sub-Saharan Africa: a first volume on Methodology and Prehistory by a scholar from Upper Volta, now Burkina Faso; two by Kenyans, including the last volume on Independent Africa; and one each by scholars from Guinea, Ghana, and Nigeria. It is also important to note that the majority of volumes deal with the precolonial period, thus establishing the continuity of Black African history.

A key question to which scholars turned was the establishment of a methodology for the early periods of Sub-Saharan African history with their paucity of written records. There were, of course, archeological and linguistic sources, and there are some archival ones. An important archive existed in Timbuktu in present-day Mali. Yet for Sub-Saharan Africa, the major problem with archival sources is their mainly external origin, that is, Arabic or European. Oral traditions constitute an important source for correcting the gaps in the external sources. As soon as Arabic and European writing became established in Sub-Saharan Africa, local scholars began to compile written records of oral traditions and write chronicles of current events. Comparative methods are required to test the coherence and contradictions among these sources. A much more complex methodology is required than for Western or Arabic historiographies, which can rely on more amply available written sources. But the oral sources should not be discounted. African studies require a broadly interdisciplinary approach, joining historical with archeological and linguistic methods, such as were employed in the regional studies inspired by the Ibadan school.[184]

But the Ibadan School soon was subjected to criticism, very much as the established historiographies in India and Latin America had been, for focusing on elites and neglecting the common people.[185] They had seen their mission as providing a basis for nation-building, which had led to proving the existence of African states in the precolonial past. There was a tendency to focus on heroic leaders such as kings and to distort the actual past in order to create myths of use in creating a national consciousness. The 1970s and 1980s saw greater attention given to social and economic history and an attempt to deal with broader segments of the population, not unlike what was done in this period elsewhere in the areas of the world we have discussed. Historiography in socialist Tanzania from the beginning tended to go in this direction. Some historians at the University of Dar es Salaam protested against the "bourgeois nationalist history"[186] of the 1960s. They wanted a history that gave greater emphasis to anticolonial resistance on the part of the broad segment of the population. One major project involved the Maji-Maji uprising in German East Africa in 1905–1907.[187] In Tanzania as in Nigeria, neo-Marxist approaches played an increasing role in the critique of the historiography of the 1960s. As in Latin America and in India, this critique expressed itself in dependence theories to explain the economic underdevelopment of Africa. An important impulse for the combination of dependency and Marxist theories was contained in the West Indian Walter Rodney's (1942–1980) *How Europe Underdeveloped Africa* (1972) that was adopted as the leading opinion by a new school of African historians and social scientists. Nevertheless, after socialist regimes in the 1980s and 1990s in such countries as Ethiopia, Tanzania, and Mozambique failed in their promise to transform their country along socialist lines, opinion moved away from traditional Marxist foci on the means of production and class to new theoretical paradigms such as those of Antonio Gramsci, Michel Foucault, Edward Said, and E. P. Thompson, an intellectual development similar to that which we saw in India and Latin America. In Africa, moreover, the focus increasingly shifted from analysis of class to that of ethnicity. At the same time the previous critique of colonialism and the colonial state increasingly gave way to a critique of the postcolonial state and its leadership.

The rise of an academic profession of historians in Francophone Africa was slower.[188] The most important center was the University of Dakar, then the only university in Francophone Senegal. There were several reasons for this delay. One was that Senghor's endorsement of *négritude* placed the focus on poetic and aesthetic approaches to the past rather than on rigorous historical studies. Another was that France maintained a great degree of control over university studies in its former colonies. Thus for a long time, there was not a single African who taught history on the university level in Francophone Africa. The high demands in France to qualify for university teaching – a second much more extensive dissertation was required of doctoral candidates in addition to a first dissertation so that candidates generally could not qualify until they were in their forties – meant that before 1979 no African historian was in a position to direct a dissertation. Notwithstanding this, by the 1970s an increasing number of historians, even without full French credentials, pursued serious historical studies. Francophone historians organized a continental association of African historians and in 1974 launched their own journal, *Afrika Zamani: Revue d'Histoire*

Africaine.[189] They followed the path of their Anglophone colleagues by first concentrating on politics and heroic leaders in the past, as part of nation-building, as the Ibadan School had done originally, and then turned to social, economic, and ethnological history. The slave trade and the role of Islam became important topics of study.

These are fragmentary examples from a vast continent. Nevertheless, certain generalizations can be attempted. The Eurocentric notion of Africa as a continent without a history has been laid to rest, incidentally by scholarship on Africa outside of Africa. In the 1960s, African historians tended to trace the rise of nationalism and of the nation-state on the model of the nationalism that had grown in Europe. By the 1970s, they focused more on the resistance against colonialism and the attempt in this resistance to recover the submerged authentic voice of Africa. Looking from the present in 2016 back to the 1970s and 1980s, there are two regrettable developments. On the positive side, the professionalization of African studies contributed to a sense of Black Africa identity. On the other hand, with its center in academe the historical profession lost close contacts with the broader population. The oil boom in the 1970s made possible an expansion of universities in Nigeria, less so in states without abundant oil resources. Then came the hungry years from the 1980s, economic decline, and a drastic reduction in resources, with the result that a great many – probably a majority of scholars – were forced to find employment outside academe, and quite a number actually emigrated, foremost to the United States, journals ceased publication, and libraries no longer could purchase even the most important books and periodicals. Thus what seemed so encouraging in the 1970s, the integration of African scholars into the international community, has now suffered serious setbacks.

Historical writings in South Africa[190]

The development of historical studies in South Africa in the period of decolonization is fundamentally different from that in the Black African countries we have discussed. The differences are obvious. While in Black Africa decolonialization was accompanied by the creation of an indigenous academic infrastructure, devoted to establishing the African past in the struggle against colonialism, in South Africa universities until the end of Apartheid in 1994 were strictly segregated. Many of the white universities dated back to the nineteenth century, with some predominantly Anglophone and others primarily Afrikan-speaking. This has changed to a degree with the end of Apartheid with black students attending formerly all-white universities. The few historically black universities such as the University of Fort Hare, founded in 1916, had been poorly funded and had produced few historians who could occupy an important position in the search for a historical past that would serve in the struggle for racial emancipation.[191] A Black historical consciousness found its expression elsewhere, less in academe, than, as

Michael Murray noted in 1988, in "the literary arena of drama, poetry, short stories, novels, and the like literature."[192] Unlike in Black Africa, the academic struggle against colonialism and racism was carried out largely by Anglophone whites. Nevertheless, there are close parallels in the path that historiography took after 1960 in the white-dominated South African academe and the universities in Black Africa. And in all of them, Marxist ideas, although not as an orthodox doctrine, inspired a great deal of historical thought and writing in the last third of the twentieth century.

South African historians, such as Wessel Visser of the historically Dutch-Afrikan University of Stellenbosch, have divided historical writing on the history of South Africa into several consecutive categories; a British imperialist, a white Anglophone settler or colonialist historiography contemporaneous with an Afrikaner nationalist history, in conflict with the South African British historians but sharing their colonialism and racism, followed in the wake of decolonization by what has been variously called a liberal school that as early as the 1930s recognized that Blacks too had a history going back into the precolonial past. It, however, maintained its faith in the development of a capitalist market economy that would free blacks from their poverty. The so-called liberal school was followed by a revisionist or radical school that would reject the assumptions of the liberal school from a Marxist perspective focused on the close relationship of capitalism and racism. Both the liberal and the revisionist or radical schools, composed almost entirely of white Anglophones, were deeply committed to the struggle against apartheid. Already before the end of apartheid, revisionist historiography turned away from a narrowly economic interpretation of class struggle to a broader cultural approach in which gender relations for the first time played an important role. Finally, while maintaining its critique of the inequalities and the racial discriminations inherent in the established status quo, historians abandoned much of the Marxist discourse of revisionist historiography without surrendering its political and social agendas.

Unlike in Black Africa, where the rediscovery of an African past was undertaken by black academicians, in South Africa it came from the liberal school and in an important way also from outside South Africa, particularly from England where many of the Anglophone historians had received an important part of their education. Although widely identified with the conviction that capitalism would ultimately overcome the economic impoverishment and backwardness of the black population, many historians associated with the liberal school, while clearly not Marxists, recognized the effect that industrialization and urbanization had on the white and the black working population, and in the 1960s and 1970s paved the way for the Marxist perspective of the 1980s and 1990s. An important summation of liberal thinking about South Africa was presented by the two-volume *Oxford History of South Africa*, published in 1969 and 1971.[193] As Wessel Visser, himself an Afrikaner, wrote, *The Oxford History* "dispelled for all time the myth that South African history began when the Portuguese seafarers rounded the Cape in 1487 – it demonstrated that Africans had indeed had a history before the coming of the white man."[194]

The *Oxford History* in many ways built on the ideas of William Miller Macmillan (1885–1974), a native of Scotland, largely educated in Great Britain, who spent his teaching life in South Africa, until in 1933 when he left the University of Witwatersrand in large part because of his outspoken opposition to segregation. Already in the 1910s, he began to address the problem of poverty among whites and blacks in South Africa. Macmillan examined how rural blacks were dispossessed of their land, were turned into farm laborers, or had to migrate to the industrializing cities, where they had to compete with poverty-stricken rural whites. For historiography, this meant an inclusive history that dealt with South Africa as a totality in which the fates of whites and blacks were interwoven.

Macmillan was no Marxist but an outspoken democratic socialist who very early joined the Fabian Society and the British Labour Party. Yet with his stress on the economic forces that created white and black poverty, he came close to the Marxism of the radical school. Neither Macmillan nor his pupil C. W. de Kiewiet (1902–1986), who in 1956 published *The Anatomy of South African Misery*,[195] were in any sense neoliberals. Yet the revisionists went further than they in their economic critique, encompassing a Marxist discourse absent from Macmillan's or de Kiewiet's studies of poverty. The 1950s and 1960s saw a growing black resistance against the South African government. This resistance increased steadily in the 1970s and 1980s and had support not only among blacks but also among whites, particularly English-speaking intellectuals. Among them were also members of the Communist Party of South Africa. Using Marxist concepts, they saw South Africa as "a class-ridden society created by international and South African capitalism . . . transforming a politically and economically independent pre-capitalist black population into wageworkers in a proletarianized urban community."[196] According to Martin J. Murray, an American Africanist, in an article in 1988, Marxism had replaced liberalism "as the dominant intellectual perspective in South Africa, . . . because liberalism has failed to acknowledge the connection between capitalism and apartheid."[197] The growth of Marxism closely followed the political turmoil of the 1970s, the 1972–1973 mass strike wave, and the 1976–1977 Soweto riots. It also in a limited way gave rise to a black nationalist historiography,[198] focusing on the white oppressors who deprived the black peoples of their land and transformed them into a landless proletariat. A large segment of the black student movement relinquished the idea of a multiracial South Africa. For them, South Africa was a black country for blacks alone.[199]

While the Marxist critique of capitalist exploitation and racism had concentrated on an analysis of class in economic terms, now greater emphasis was given to cultural factors accompanied by a move away from the focus on anonymous social structures to the lives of the victims of capitalist exploitation and racist suppression. As we have already seen in the chapter on

Western Marxism, basic aspects of a narrowly materialist interpretation of history and society were challenged in Antonio Gramsci's *Prison Notebooks*, written while he was incarcerated in Mussolini's prison, and the concept of a working class expanded to include much broader parts of the population, the so-called subaltern classes. It was this revision of Marxism that occupied an important role in Great Britain in the 1960s in the works of E. P. Thompson, George Rudé, Eric Hobsbawm, in the 1980s in the *Subaltern Studies* in India, and in the 1960s and 1970s in the works of Eugene Genovese[200] in the United States on the culture that the slaves made in resisting their servitude. These ideas deeply affected South African revisionist writings. In 1977 the *History Workshop* was founded in England, as its subtitle suggested, *A Journal of Socialist Historians*, in the spirit of the history workshop at Ruskin College, the labor college at Oxford University, devoted to the lives of working people, particularly those oppressed in a capitalist economy.[201] Five years later, *History Workshop* changed its subtitle to *A Journal of Socialist and Feminist Historians*. It thus moved away from the male orientation that dominated almost all historiography, Already in 1978, a *History Workshop* conference was convened at the University of Witwatersrand with the aim, as Belinda Bozzoli, the convener of the conference and herself one of the historians in the new direction,[202] declared, "to begin the process of recreating Witwatersrand from a grassroots perspective."[203] By the mid-1980s, a considerable number of works dealt with the impact of capitalism in close relation with the racist policies of the state on the everyday lives of a proletarianized population, white and black, in the new urban setting, giving considerable attention to its impact on women. Proceeding from the Marxist conception of class analysis, a number of English-speaking, and for the first time now also Afrikaner, and a small number of blacks began to study the submerged groups, such as white and black workers in the mines and in the rural population. Perhaps the most important author in this direction was Charles van Onselen who in 1982 in a history of the Witwatersrand dealt with the poor whites who came to the city, washermen and rickshaw peddlers, representing the most depressed segments of the population, and on the role of alcohol and prostitution in attracting white and black workers to the gold mines. Van Onselen was deeply influenced by E. P. Thompson's *The Making of the English Working Class* but moved in a very different direction, dealing with the classes most affected by the process of capitalist industrialization, the very people whom Marx would have discounted as the *Lumpenproletariat*, with whom Thompson did not deal.

The year 1994 marked the end of apartheid, but as one of the best observers of the South African historical scene, Christopher Saunders, observed, the transfer of power was not matched by any significant historiographical development.[204] In many ways, as we saw with the revisionists, a decolonization of historical writing took place already well before the end of apartheid. If some had expected that the end of apartheid would see a black nationalist history, similar to that which took place in the black African states with the coming of independence, that would stress the African contribution to the exclusion of others and that would see whites as merely intruders in an essentially African country, this did not happen. It has been suggested that the conditions under which apartheid was ended were very different from those under which the black African states obtained their independence. The end of apartheid involved a compromise between whites and blacks and the creation of a participatory democracy. Although previously all-white universities like Witwatersrand now admitted large numbers of black students, the majority of young blacks could not afford attending the universities. The government pledged to support proper education for all South Africans, irrespective of race and gender, but in fact black students, many of them very poor, continued to be educationally disadvantaged. Racial discriminatory patterns persist, as do tremendous social, economic, and educational inequalities that affect the white lower classes but even more the black ones.[205]

Notes

1 Peter Novick, *That Noble Dream: The "Objectivity Question" and the American Historical Profession* (Cambridge, 1988); John Higham, *History: Professional Scholarship in America* (Baltimore, 1983).

2 See *Marxist Historiographies: A Global Perspective*, ed. Q. Edward Wang and Georg G. Iggers (London, 2015), especially the Introduction.

3 On the Consensus School, see Ernst Breisach, *Historiography: Ancient, Medieval, & Modern* (Chicago, 1983), 388–391; Bernard Sternsher, *Consensus, Conflict, and American Historians* (Bloomington, 1975); Davis S. Brown, *Richard Hofstadter: An Intellectual Biography* (Chicago, 2006).

4 Carl Hempel, *Aspects of Scientific Explanation and Other Essays in the Philosophy of Science* (New York, 1965).

5 See Paul Arthur Schilpp, ed., *The Philosophy of Karl Popper*, 2 vols. (La Salle, 1974).

6 Karl Marx, *Capital*, vol. 1, "Introduction" in Robert C. Tucker, ed., *The Marx-Engels Reader* (New York, 1978, 2nd ed.), 296.

7 Francis Fukuyama, "The End of History?" *The National Interest*, 16 (Summer 1989), 3–18; *The End of History and the Last Man* (New York, 1992); also his "Reflections on the End of History, Five Years Later," *History and Theory*, 34:2 (1995), 27–43.

8 William A. Dunning, *Reconstruction: Political and Economic 1865–1877* (New York, 1907).

9 See Ulrich Phillips, *American Negro Slavery: A Survey of the Supply, Employment and Control of Negro Labor as Determined by the Plantation Regime* (New York, 1918).

10 Gabriel Kolko, *The Triumph of Conservatism: A Reinterpretation of American History 1900–1916* (New York, 1963).

11 See Breisach, *Historiography* on New Left historians, 391–393.

12 See Joseph M. Siracusa, "Radical History (United States)" in Daniel Woolf, ed., *A Global Encyclopedia of Historical Writing* (New York, 1998), 757–758, with bibliography.

13 Traian Stoianovich, *French Historical Method: The Annales Paradigm* (Ithaca, 1976).

14 Peter Burke, *The French Historical Revolution: The Annales School, 1929–89* (Cambridge, 1990), 1. See also André Burguière, *The Annales School: An Intellectual History* (Ithaca, 2009).

15 Burke, *The French Historical Revolution*, 31.

16 Second enlarged two-volume edition in 1966; English translation, 2 vols. (New York, 1972–1973).

17 Vidal de la Blache, *Principles of Human Geography* (New York, 1926).

18 The Russian economic theorist Kontradieff apparently died in a Soviet prison in 1930 or 1931.

19 Pierre Chaunu, *Séville et l'Atlantique*, 12 vols. (Paris, 1955–1960).

20 Fernand Braudel, *Civilisation materielle, économie, capitalisme*, 3 vols. (Paris, 1979–1987); English: *Civilization and Capitalism*, 3 vols. (New York, 1992).

21 Fernand Braudel, *L'identité de la France, espace et histoire* (Paris, 1986); English: *The Identity of France*, 2 vols. (New York, 1988–1990).

22 Ernest Labrousse, *Esquisse`des mouvements du prix et du revenus* (Paris, 1933).

23 François Simiand, "Méthode historique et sciences sociales," *Revue de synthèse historique*, 6 (1903), 1–22, English in *Review*, 9 (1985–1986), 163–213; also his *Recherchrs anciennes et nouvelles sur le movement général des prix du XVIe au XIXe siècle* (Paris, 1932).

24 Charles Morazé, *Les bourgeois conquérants* (Paris, 1957); English: *The Triumph of the Bourgeoisie* (New York, 1966).

25 Marc Ferro, *La revolution russe* (1967), English: *The Russian Revolution of February 1917* (Englewood Cliffs, 1972) and *La grande guerre 1914–1918* (Paris, 1969); English: *The Great War 1914–1918* (London, 1973).

26 Pierre Goubert, *Beauvais et le Beauvaisis* (Paris, 1960); there does not appear to be an English translation, but see his *Louis XIV and Twenty Million Frenchmen* (New York, 1970).

27 Hayami Akira, *Kinsei nōson no rekishi jinkōgakuteki kenkyū* (*A Historical Demographical Study of the Modern Countryside*) (Tokyo, 1973). In addition, Hayami helped the Ministry of Internal Affairs of Japanese government in compiling a multivolume study of Japanese population data; see *Kokusei chōsa izen Nihon jinkō tōkei shūsei* (*Data on Japanese Population Before the National Census*) (Tokyo, 1992).

28 Robert Mandrou on early capitalists, outlook and behavior, see his *Les Fuggers propriétaires fanciers en Souabes 1500–1618: Etudes de comportements socioéconommiques al la fin du XVIe siècle* (1968); on psychology of early modern France, see his *Introduction à la France moderne 1500–1640, essai de psychologie historique* (Paris, 1974); on popular culture, see his *De la culture populaire aux 17e et 18e siècles* (Paris, 1964); on witchcraft and the law, see his *Magistrats et sociers en France au 17e siècle* (Paris, 1968).

29 Michel Vovelle, *Piété baroque et déchristianisation* (Paris, 1973); Pierre Chaunu et al. eds., *La Mort à Paris* (Paris, 1978).

30 Georg G. Iggers, *The German Conception of History: The National Tradition of Historical Thought from Herder to the Present* (Middletown, 1983).

31 See Jan Eckel, *Hans Rothfels: Eine intellektuelle Biographie im 20. Jahrhundert* (Göttingen, 2005).

32 Gerhard Ritter, "Scientific History, Contemporary History, and Political Science," *History and Theory*, 1 (1962), 261–279.

33 Gerhard Ritter, *Carl Gördeler und der deutsche Widerstand* (Stuttgart, 1954); English: *Carl Goerdeler's Struggle against Tyranny* (Freeport, 1970); Hans Rothfels, *The German Opposition to Hitler* (Chicago, 1948): Jam Eckel, *Hans Rothfels/ Eine intellektuelle Biographie im 20. Jahrhundert* (Göttingen, 2005).

34 See Winfried Schulze, *Deutsche Geschichtswissenschaft nach 1945* (München, 1989); particularly ch. 16, "Von der 'politischen Volksgeschichte' zur 'neuen Sozialgeschichte,'" 281–301.

35 On the role of German historians such as Werner Conze and Theodor Schieder under Nazism and their postwar students, see Rüdiger Hohls and Konrad H. Jarausch, eds., *Versäumte Fragen: Deutsche Historiker im Schatten des Nationalsozialismus* (Stuttgart, 2000).

36 See Georg Iggers, ed., *The Social History of Politics: Critical Perspectives in West German Historical Writing since 1945* (Leamington Spa, 1985).

37 Hans-Ulrich Wehler, *Das deutsche Kaiserreich* (Göttingen, 1973), 17; a shortened English version: *The German Empire, 1871–1918* (Leamington Spa, 1983).

38 Frederick C. Beiser, *The German Historicist Tradition* (Oxford, 2011); Georg G. Iggers, *The German Conception of History: The National Tradition from Herder to the Present* (Middletown, 1968); Georg G. Iggers, "Historicism: The History and Meaning of the Term," *Journal of the History of Ideas*, 56 (1995), 129–152.

39 See Martin Jay, *The Dialectical Imagination: A History of the Frankfurt School and the Institute of Social Research 1923–1950* (Boston, 1973); John Abromeit, *Max Horkheimer and the Foundation of the Frankfurt School* (Cambridge, 2011).

40 Eckart Kehr, *Schlachtflottenbau und Parteipolitik, 1894–1901* (Berlin, 1930; rep. 1966).

41 Eckart Kehr, *Das Primat der Innenpolitik*, essays ed. Hans-Ulrich Wehler (Berlin, 1965).

42 Fritz Fischer, *Der Griff nach der Weltmacht* (Düsseldorf, 1961); English: *Germany's War Aims in the First World War* (New York, 1967).

43 See Foreword to first issue, 1975.

44 Emmanuel Le Roy Ladurie, *Les Paysans du Languedoc* (Paris, 1966); English: *The Peasants of Languedoc* (Urbana, 1976).

45 Emmanuel Le Roy Ladurie, *Histoire du climat* (Paris, 1967); English: *Times of Feast, Times of Famine* (New York, 1971).

46 Emmanuel Le Roy Ladurie, *The Territory of the Historian*, tr. Ben and Sian Reynolds (Chicago, 1979), 15.

47 Emmanuel Le Roy Ladurie, *Carnival in Romans*, tr. Mary Feeney (New York, 1980).

48 Geoffrey Barraclough, *Main Trends in History* (New York, 1979), 89.

49 (New York, 1974).

50 See Herbert Gutman, *Slavery and the Numbers Game: A Critique of Time on the Cross* (Urbana, 1975).

51 Robert Fogel and Geoffrey Elton, *Which Road to the Past? Two Views of History* (New York, 1983).

52 English: *Montaillou: Cathars and Catholics in a French Village 1294–1314* (New York, 1978).

53 English: (New York, 1975).

54 (Boston, 1983).

55 Robert Finlay, "The Refashioning of Martin Guerre," *American Historical Review*, 93:3 (June 1988), 553–571; Natalie Davis's rejoinder, "On the Lame," ibid., 572–603.

56 Natalie Zemon Davis, *The Return of Martin Guerre* (Cambridge, MA, 1983), 5.

57 Lawrence Stone, "The Revival of Narrative: Reflections on a New Old History," *Past and Present*, 85 (November 1979), 3–24.

58 Ibid., 9–19.

59 See Peter Burke, *What Is Cultural History?* (Cambridge, 2004).

60 Roger Chartier's remarks in this regard were referred to in Burke, ibid., 74.

61 Alfred Cobban, *The Social Interpretation of the French Revolution* (Cambridge, 1965); see also his, *Historians and the Causes of the French Revolution* (London, 1957).

62 François Furet, "Le Catéchisme révolutionnaire," *Annales Economies: Sociétés. Civilisations*, 26 (1971), 255–289.

63 François Furet, *Interpreting the French Revolution*, trans. Elborg Forster (Cambridge, 1981); see also with Mona Ozouf, ed., *The Transformation of Political Culture*, 3 vols. (Oxford, 1989).
64 Maurice Agulhon, *La République au village* (Paris, 1970); on political symbolism, see his *Marianne au combat* (Paris, 1979); English: *Marianne into Battle: Republican Imagery and Symbolism in France 1789–1880* (Cambridge, 1981).
65 Mona Ozouf, *La Fête révolutionnaire 1789–1799* (Paris, 1976); English: *Festivals and the French Revolution* (Cambridge, MA, 1988).
66 (Berkeley, 1984), xi.
67 Davis, *Return of Martin Guerre*, 5.
68 Jean François Lyotard, *The Postmodern Condition: A Report on Knowledge* (Minneapolis, 1984).
69 Keith Jenkins, ed., *The Postmodern History Reader* (London, 2000), "Introduction," 3, 4, 6.
70 Eric R. Wolf, *Europe and the People without History* (Berkeley, 2010).
71 Claude Lévi-Strauss, *Savage Mind* (Chicago, 1968).
72 English: (London, 1983).
73 See e.g. Quentin Skinner, *Foundations of Modern Political Thought*, 2 vols. (Cambridge, 1978).
74 See e.g. John Pocock, *The Macchiavellian Moment: Florentine Political Thought and the Atlantic Republican Tradition* (Princeton, 1975).
75 Otto Brunner, Werner Conze, and Reinhart Koselleck, eds., *Geschichtliche Grundbegriffe*, 8 vols. (Stuttgart, 1972–1997)); see also Melvin Richter, *The History of Political and Social Concepts: A Critical Introduction* (New York, 1995).
76 (Cambridge, 1980).
77 (Cambridge, 1983).
78 Thomas Childers, "The Social History of Politics in Germany: The Sociology of Political Discourse in the Weimar Republic," *American Historical Review*, 95:2 (1990), 331–358.
79 Jacques Derrida, *Of Grammatology* (Baltimore, 1976), 158.
80 Michel Foucault, "What Is an Author?" in José Harari, ed., *The Foucault Reader* (New York, 1984), 101–120.
81 Roland Barthes, "The Discourse of History," tr. Stephen Bann, in E. S. Shaffer, ed., *Comparative Criticism: A Yearbook*, vol. 3, (Cambridge, 1981), 3–20.
82 Hayden White, *Metahistory: The Historical Imagination in Nineteenth-century Europe* (Baltimore, 1973); see Introduction "The Poetics of History," 1–42.
83 Hayden White, "Historical Texts as Literary Artifact" in his *Tropics of Discourse: Essays in Cultural Criticism* (Baltimore, 1978), 82.
84 Saul Friedländer, ed., *Probing the Limits of Representation: Nazism and the "Final Solution"* (Cambridge, MA, 1992).
85 Cited in Christopher Browning, "German Memory, Judicial Interrogation, and Historical Reconstruction: Writing Perpetrator History from Postwar Testimony" in Friedländer, *Probing the Limits of Representation: Nazism and the "Final Solution,"* 32.
86 Christopher Browning, *Ordinary Men: Reserve Police Battalion 101 and the Final Solution in Poland* (New York, 1992).
87 Browning, "German Memory," 31.
88 (New York, 1991).
89 (New York, 1988).
90 De Man wrote for a collaborationist paper under the Nazis in occupied Belgium, including explicitly anti-Semitic articles.
91 Joan Wallach Scott, "On Language, Gender, and Working Class History" in her *Gender and the Politics of History* (New York, 1999), 53–67.

92 Giovanni Levi, "On Microhistory" in Peter Burke, ed., *New Perspectives on Historical Writing* (University Park, 1992), 93.
93 Ibid., 95.
94 Giovanni Levi, *Inheriting Power: The Story of an Exorcist*, tr. Lydia Cochrane (Chicago, 1985).
95 Clifford Geertz, "Thick Description. Toward an Interpretative Theory of Culture" in his *The Interpretation of Cultures: Selected Essays* (New York, 1973), 3–30.
96 *Geschichtswerkstatt* and *Werkstatt/Geschichte*.
97 See Bonnie Smith, *The Gender of History: Men, Women, and Historical Practice* (Cambridge, MA, 1998).
98 See Joan Wallach Scott, "Women's History" in Burke, *New Perspectives on Historical Writing*, 45.
99 Julie Des Jardins, "Women's and Gender History" in Axel Schneider and Daniel Woolf, eds., *Oxford History of Historical Writing* (Oxford, 2011), V. 5, 146.
100 Ibid., 145.
101 See Scott, "Introduction," *Gender and the Politics of History*, 1–11.
102 Anne McClintock, *Imperial Leather: Race, Gender and Sexuality in the Colonial Context* (Routledge, 1995), 5 and 7.
103 Scott, *Gender and the Politics of History*, 2.
104 See Robert Young, ed., *Postcolonialism: A Historical Introduction* (London, 2001); Prasenjit Duara, ed., *Decolonization: Perspectives from Now and Then* (London, 2004).
105 Frantz Fanon, *The Wretched of the Earth* (New York, 1961).
106 3 vols. (Minneapolis, 1974–1989).
107 See also Immanuel Wallerstein, *The Capitalist World Economy: Essays* (New York, 1979).
108 See Edward W. Said, *Out of Place: A Memoir* (New York, 1999).
109 See Prasenjit Duara, "Postcolonial History" in Lloyd Kramer and Sarah Maza, eds., *A Companion to Western Historical Thought* (Malden, 2002), 418.
110 Ashis Nandy, "History's Forgotten Doubles," *History and Theory*, Theme Issue 34, p. 44; see also Vinay Lal, *Dissenting Knowledges: Open Futures: The Multiple Selves and Strange Destinations of Ashis Nandy* (Delhi, 2000).
111 On the Subaltern Group, see also Vinay Lal, "Subalterns in the Academy: The Hegemony of History" in his *The History of History: Politics and Scholarship in Modern India* (New Delhi, 2003), 186–230; also Dipesh Chakrabarty, *Habitations of Modernity: Essays in the Wake of Subaltern Studies* (Chicago, 2002).
112 Ranajit Guha, ed., *Subaltern Studies I: Writings on South Asian History and Society* (Delhi, 1982), 3.
113 (Delhi, 1983).
114 Gyan Prakash, "Postcolonial Criticism and History: Subaltern Studies," Axel Schneider and Daniel Woolf, eds., *The Oxford History of Historical Writing* (Oxford, 2011), vol. 5.
115 Dipesh Chakrabarty, "Postcoloniality and the Artifice of History: Who Speaks for the Indian Pasts?" *Representation*, 37 (Winter 1992).
116 Ibid., 1.
117 Chakrabarty, "Subaltern Studies," 22.
118 Gyanendra Pandey, "In Defence of the Fragment: Writing about Hindu-Muslim Riots in India Today," *Representations* 37 (Winter 1992), 28–29.
119 Sarkar, *Writing Social History*, "The Decline of the Subaltern in *Subaltern Studies*," 88–89.
120 Sugata Bose and Ayesha Jalal, *Modern South Asia: History, Culture, Political Economy* (Delhi, 1997), 9.

121 Pandey, *Representations*, 28–29.
122 Ranajit Guha, *An Indian Historiography of India: A Nineteenth Century Agenda and Its Implications* (Calcutta, 1988).
123 Chakrabarty, "Postcoloniality and the Artifice of History," 1.
124 Prakash, "Postcolonial Criticism," 90.
125 Dipesh Chakrabarty, *Provincializing Europe. Postcolonial Thought and Historical Difference* (New Jersey: Princeton University Press, 2008), 5–6.
126 Cited in Latha Menon, "Saffron Infusion: Hindutva, History and Education," *History Today*, 54:8 (August 2004).
127 Mark Thurner, "An Old New World for the History of Historiography," *Storia della Storiografía*, 67:1 (2015), 29–50; also idem, *History's Peru: The Poetics of Colonial and Postcolonial Historiography* (Gainesville, 2012).
128 The UNESCO *Historia general de América Latina*, 9 vols. (Madrid, 1999–2008) and *The Cambridge History of Latin American History*, 11 vols. (Cambridge, 1984–2008) should be mentioned as comprehensive histories of Latin America, although neither deals directly with historiography, except for vol. 9 of UNESCO, Estevão de Rezende Martins, ed., and not in any comprehensive way. See also See George L. Vásquez, "Latin American Historiography (Excluding Mexico and Brazil) – Writing on the Precolonial and Postcolonial Periods from the Sixteenth Century to the Present Day" in D. R. Woolf, ed., *A Global Encyclopedia of Historical Writing* (New York, 1998), vol. 2, 534–542; Juan Maiguashca, "Latin American Historiography (Excluding Mexico and Brazil) – the National Period 1820–1990," ibid., 542–544. See the special issue of *Storia della Storiografía*, "New Themes in Latin American Historiography," 67:1 (2015). For a critical perspective on contemporary Latin American historiography, see Jurandir Malerba and Carolos Aguirre Rojas, eds., *Historiografia contemporânea em perspectiva crítica* (Bauru, 2007).
129 Joel Horowitz, "Argentine Historical Writing in an Era of Political and Economic Instability"; Marshall C. Eakin, "Brazilian Historical Writing," 440–453; Guillermo Zermeño Padilla, "Mexican Historical Writing" in Schneider and Woolf, *The Oxford History of Historical Writing*, vol. 5, 422–439, 440–453, 453–472.
130 Juan Maiguashca, "Historians in Spanish South America: Cross-References between Centre and Periphery" in Macintyre, Maiguashca, and Pók, eds., *Oxford History of Historical Writing*, vol. 4, 463–490.
131 Jurandir Malerba, *História na América, ensato crítica historiográfica* (Rio de Janeiro, 2009).
132 Jaime Aurell, Carolina Palmaceda, Peter Burke, and Felipe Soza, *Comprender el pasado: Una historia de la escritura y el pensamiento histórico* (Madrid, 2013), especially Soza, "La historiografia latinoamericana," ibid., 341–437.
133 See Jorge Cañizares Esguerra, *How to Write the History of the New World* (Stanford, 2002); Turner, "An Old New World for the History of Historiography"; and Alan Durston, "Indigenous Languages and the Historiography on Latin America," *Storia della Storiografía*, 67:1 (2015), 51–66.
134 See Vásquez, "Latin American Historiography."
135 Maiguashca, "Latin American Historiography," 542–543.
136 Cf. Horowitz, "Argentine Historical Writing," 422.
137 See Eakin, "Brazilian Historical Writing," 440.
138 Ciro Flamarion Cardoso, "Brazilian Historical Writing and the Building of a Nation" in Macintyre, Maiguashca, and Pók, *Oxford History of Historical Writing*, vol. 4, 447–462.
139 Soza, "La historiografia latinoamericana," 417–418.
140 On Ranke, see Padilla, "Mexican Historical Writing," 455–460.

141 Juan Maiguashca, "Historians in Spanish South America: Cross References between Centre and Periphery" in Macintyre, Maiguashca, and Pók, *Oxford History of Historical Writing*, vol. 4, 482–484.
142 See Eakin, "Brazilian Historical Writing," 440.
143 See Peter Evans, *Dependent Development: The Alliance of Multinational, State, and Local Capital* (Princeton, 1979).
144 "André Gunder Frank" in *Wikipedia*, last updated June 5, 2015.
145 Immanuel Wallerstein, *The Modern World System* (New York, 1974), other updated volumes 1980, 1989, 2004, 2011, with a further volume upcoming.
146 See note 129 for the three articles on Latin American historical writing, *Oxford History of Historical Writing*, vol. 5, 422–472.
147 See e.g. André Gunder Frank, *Capitalism and Underdevelopment in Latin America* (Monthly Review, 1967); Vincent Ferrero, "Dependency Theory: An Introduction" in Giorgio Secondi, ed., *The Development Economics Reader* (London, 2008), 58–64.
148 Soza, "La historiografía latinoamericana," 440.
149 Jurandir Malerba, *La historia en América Latina: Ensayo de crítica historiográfica* (Rosario, 2010).
150 Juan Maiguashca, "Latin American Marxist History; Rise, Fall, and Resurrection" in Q. Edward Wang and Georg G. Iggers, eds., *Marxist Historiographies: A Global Perspective* (London, 2015), 104–124. On Marxist historiography in Latin America, see Sergio Guerra Vilaboy, "O fondadores de la historiografía marxista na América Latina" in Malerba and Rojas, *Historiografia contemporânea em perspectiva crítica*, 315–350.
151 Maiguashca, "Latin American Marxist History," 107.
152 See Florencia E. Mallon, "The Promise and Dilemma of Subaltern Studies: Perspectives from Latin American History," *American Historical Review*, 99:4 (1994), 1491–1515.
153 Edward P. Thompson, *The Making of the English Working Class* (London, 1964).
154 Eugene Genovese, *Roll, Jordan, Roll: The World the Slaves Made* (New York, 1974).
155 See Knight, "Latin America," 740.
156 See footnote 129 for three chapters on Latin America in *Oxford History of Historical Writing*, and Soza in footnote 132.
157 Felipe Soza, "The Association of Chilean Historians in the United Kingdom 1980–1989," *Storia della Storiografia*, 67:1 (2015), 101–118.
158 Horowitz, "Argentine Historical Writing," 426, 427, 430, 434, 436.
159 Horowitz, "Argentine Historical Writing," 437.
160 Padilla, "Mexican Historical Writing," 469. See also Soza, 428.
161 Horowitz, "Argentine Historical Writing," 437.
162 Eakin, "Brazilian Historical Writing," 449.
163 Padilla, "Mexican Historical Writing," 461–464; Soza, 429.
164 For a comparison of the role that global perspectives on history and historiography occupy in the United States and China today and the lesser role they play in Germany, see Dominic Sachsenmaier, *Global Perspectives on Global History* (Cambridge, 2011).
165 Padilla, "Mexican Historical Writing," 459.
166 Braudel, *The Identity of France*, vol. 1 on *History and Environment*, vol. 2 on *People and Production*.
167 (Madrid, 2013).
168 Padilla, "Mexican Historical Writing," 470.
169 See Eakin, "Brazilian Historical Writing," 464; and Soza, "La historiografía latinoamericana," 428, See also Alan Knight, "Subalterns, Signifiers, and

Statistics: Perspectives on Mexican Historiography," *Latin American Research Review*, 37 (2002), 136–158.

170 Cf. Marcel van der Linden and Karl Heinz Roth, eds., *Beyond Marx: Theorizing the Global Labour Relations in the Twenty-first Century* (Leiden, 2013).

171 For a good historical and bibliographical overview of historical studies about and in Africa, see Joseph C. Miller's 1999 Presidential Address "History and Africa/Africa and History," *American Historical Review*, 104:1 (1999), 1–32; more important and current, Toyin Falola, "African Historical Writing" in Schneider and Woolf, eds., *Oxford History of Historical Writing*, vol. 5, 399–421. The present section rests very heavily on Toyin Falola's article. We thank him for having read and commented on the draft of our section.

172 Cited in Toyin Falola, "Nationalism and African Historiography" in Q. Edward Wang and Georg G. Iggers, eds., *Turning Points in History. A Cross Cultural Perspective* (Rochester, 2002), 211–212.

173 Cited in Ibid., 402; Broadcast Lecture by Hugh Trevor-Roper, reprinted in *The Listener* (28 November 1963), 123.

174 See the recent section on African historiography in Markus Völkel, *Geschichtsschreibung: Eine Einführung in globaler Perspektive* (Köln, 2006), 360–372; see also UNESCO, *General History of Africa* (London, 1978–2000).

175 David L. Lewis, *W.E.B. Du Bois: Biography of a Race, 1868–1919* (New York, 1993); also William Wright, "The Socialism of W.E.B. Du Bois," PhD dissertation, State University of New York at Buffalo, 1985.

176 Falola, "Nationalism and African Historiography," 213.

177 Ibid., 214–215.

178 Walter Rodney, *How Europe Underdeveloped Africa* (London, 1972).

179 See J. F. Ade Ajayi and E. J. Alagoa, "Sub-Saharan Africa" in Georg G. Iggers and Harold T. Parker, eds., *International Handbook of Historical Studies: Contemporary Research and Theory* (Westport, 1979), 411.

180 On the beginnings of academic history in Africa, see Ade Ajayi and Alagoa, "Sub-Saharan Africa," which was written by two of the most important historians of the Ibadan School. See also Andreas Eckert, "Historiker, 'nation building' und die Rehabilitierung der afrikanischen Vergangenheit. Aspekte der Geschichtsschreibung in Afrika nach 1945" in Wolfgang Küttler, Jörn Rüsen and Ernst Schulin, eds., *Geschichtsdiskurs*, vol. 5 (Frankfurt/Main, 1999), 162–190.

181 Kenneth Onwuka Dike, *The Trade and Politics in the Niger Delta 1830–1885: An Introduction to the Economic and Political History of Nigeria* (Oxford, 1956).

182 See Falola, "Nationalism and African Historiography," and Ajayi and Alagoa, "Sub-Saharan Africa."

183 UNESCO, *General History of Africa*; about the composition of the editorial staff, see Ajayi and Alagoa, "Sub-Saharan Africa," 417.

184 See Ajayi and Alagoa, "Sub-Saharan Africa."

185 See Andreas Eckert, "Nationalgeschichtsschreibung und koloniales Erbe. Historiographie in Afrika in vergleichender Perspektive" in Christoph Conrad and Sebastian Conrad, eds., *Die Nation schreiben. Geschichtswissenschaft im internationalen Vergleich* (Göttingen, 2002), 78–111.

186 Ibid., 96.

187 Ibid., 98.

188 Eckert, "Nationalgeschichtsschreibung."

189 Ajayi and Alagoa, "Sub-Saharan Africa," 413.

190 For the section on South African historiography, see Martin J. Murray, "The Triumph of Marxist Approaches to Social and Labour History," *Journal of Asian and African Studies*, 23:1 (1998), 79–101 and Wessel Visser, "Trends in

South African Historiography and the Present State of Historical Research," Paper presented at the Nordic Africa Institute, Uppsala, Sweden, September 23, 2004, and an extensive telephone conversation with Prof. Visser on January 13, 2015 on present trends. We are grateful to Professor Christopher Saunders for his careful reading and critical comments on this section. See also, Hans Erik Stolten, ed., *History Making and Present Day Politics: The Meaning of Collective Memory in South Africa* (Uppsala, 2007).

191 See "The Dilemma of the Black Universities in South Africa," *South African Journal of Higher Education*, 20:3 (2006), 442–460.

192 Murray, "Triumph of Marxist Approaches to Social and Labour History," 98.

193 The eight-volume *Cambridge History of Africa* (Cambridge, 1975) also deals extensively with the early history of Africa, as does the two-volume *Cambridge History of South Africa* (Cambridge, 2010–2011).

194 Visser, "Trends in South African Historiography and the Present State of Historical Research," 8.

195 (London, 1956).

196 Visser, "Trends in South African Historiography and the Present State of Historical Research," 8.

197 Murray, "Triumph of Marxist Approaches to Social and Labour History," 79.

198 Visser, "Trends in South African Historiography and the Present State of Historical Research," 14.

199 Ibid., 15.

200 Eugene Genovese, *Roll, Jordan, Roll. The World the Slaves Made* (New York: Vintage, 1974).

201 See most recently He Wuyi, "Raphael Samuel's Idea of a People's History," *Storia della Storiografia*, 66:2 (2014).

202 Belinda Bozzoli, *Labour, Townships, and Protest: Studies in the Social History of the Witwatersrand* (Johannesburg, 1979), more recently her *Theatres of Struggle and the End of Apartheid* (Athens, OH, 2004).

203 Murray, "Triumph of Marxist Approaches to Social and Labour History," 94.

204 Christopher Saunders, "Four Decades of South African Academic Historical Writing" in Stolten, *History Making and Present Day Politics: The Meaning of Collective Memory in South Africa*, 286. This book deals extensively with the reorientation of historical thought in postapartheid South Africa.

205 See R. Ilorah, "The Dilemma of the Historically Black Universities in South Africa," *South African Journal of Higher Education*, 20–3 (2006), 442–460.

7 The rise of Islamism and the ebb of Marxism

Historical writings in late twentieth-century Asia, the Middle East, and the West

The ebb and flow of Marxist historiography in East and Southeast Asia

Reinventing Japan: Postwar reform of historical education and writing

Japan's defeat in World War II inaugurated a new era in world history. It also opened a new chapter in Japanese historiography and in East and Southeast Asian historiography in general. During the period of U.S. occupation of Japan (1945–1952), General Douglas MacArthur, while helping retain the Japanese Emperor, did everything else to undermine the Japanese traditions, political and cultural alike, deemed by him as culpable for the country's aggressive and militarist behavior in the first half of the twentieth century. In 1947, under his direct supervision, the SCAP (Supreme Commander of Allied Powers) drafted a new constitution for Japan, promoting women's and workers' rights and expanded suffrage, on which a new Diet was elected. The constitution guaranteed freedom of expression and press, public assembly, political parties, and organizations. As union movement and socialist activities came back to life, Marxist historiography also boomed, enjoying the freedom it never had had before in the country. The main task the Marxist historians tackled at the time was to criticize and condemn prewar and wartime historiography and historical education, which also led them to scrutinize the course of Japanese modernization. And their endeavor was joined by the "modernist" historians, another important historical school developed in postwar Japan.

In wartime, the imperial historical school had dominated the field of historical study and imposed its historical views on the writing of history textbooks. The publication of *An Introduction to National History* (*Kokushi gaisetsu*), a secondary school text published in 1943 by the Ministry of Education, was a good example. It made a blatant attempt to inculcate Japanese students with the holiness of the national body in Japan, centering on the sacrosanctity of the Japanese imperial house. Some members of the cultural history school (Tsuda Sōkichi excepted) also developed the so-called overcoming the modern (*kindai no chōkoku*) thesis, aiming to prove that Japan's unique cultural tradition, in which the sacred imperial house occupied the centerpiece, could enable the country to transcend the Western model of modernity. After World War II, in order to reform Japan's historical education, it thus entailed that the sanctity of the Japanese imperial power be stripped away. In 1946, the newly organized Ministry of Education issued a "New History" textbook, entitled *The Course of [Our] Nation* (*Kuni no ayumi*) that, using archaeological findings, opens with a description of early cultures on the Japanese archipelago, leaving out the age of gods, or the divine origin of the imperial house.[1] This move was unprecedented and significant, for ever since the Meiji Restoration, the majority of Japanese history textbooks had traced the country's origin in mythology, either unable or unwilling to break away from the monarch-centered tradition of dynastic historiography. Incidentally, after the war, the Emperor also came forward to declare that he and his ancestors were not of divine descent.

Aside from reforming the historical education, postwar Japanese historians faced another daunting task: how to explain their country's recent past, or its belligerent behavior toward its neighbors from the late Meiji period to the outbreak of World War II in Asia in 1937. Marxist historians again took the lead in launching historical investigations. In 1946 Ishimoda Shō (1912–1986) published *The Formation of the Medieval World* (*Chūkoteki sekai no keisei*), a work for which he had done most of the research during the war, in spite of being blacklisted by the government. The first volume of a series of books the author later would complete, *The Formation of the Medieval World* traces the development of feudal landownership in medieval Japan. Ishimoda expressed sympathy for the peasants victimized by the formation of large ownerships. Yet pursuant to his Marxist belief in the ineluctable transition from slavery to feudalism, he considers the whole process a necessary phase in the telos of human progress. If this pessimist and determinist overtone reflected his gloomy mood in researching the topic under militarist rule, the book's criticism of feudalism also mirrored the milieu of postwar Japan, one rife with doubts and criticisms about the country's past.[2] In the same critical spirit of the postwar era, Tōyama Shigeki (1914–2011) and Inoue Kiyoshi (1913–2001) published studies of the Meiji Restoration. Tōyama's study reveals, among others, the imperial system's damaging impact on modern Japanese history, whereas Inoue's analyzes the Restoration against the backdrop of the non-Western peoples' struggle against Western colonialism in an international context. Building on the work of prewar Marxist historians, both studies opened up new ground in the study of Meiji history.[3]

On the "modernist" side, Ōtsuka Hisao (1907–1996), an expert on European economic history, examined the transition of Japanese economy from the feudal period to modern time. Inspired by Max Weber's "ideal-type" approach, he analyzed the characteristics of each period and demonstrated their fundamental difference. His interest in describing the phasic social development in history also bore the Marxist influence. From a different angle, Maruyama Masao (1914–1996), an intellectual historian, launched his study of Japan's intellectual and cultural change in the Tokugawa period. He set forth the thesis that Japanese intellectual tradition had provided the "spiritual structure" for prewar militarism and statism, for it had not been completely revamped to allow such modern ideas as individualism and liberalism to take deep root in Japanese society.[4]

Regarding Japan's modernization as an aberration, accountable for its militarism and imperialism over the early twentieth century, both the Marxists and the "modernists," willy-nilly, looked for the "normal" and "mature" growth of modernism in Euro-American history, for which they consulted the writings of Maurice H. Dobb (1900–1976) and Paul M. Sweezy (1910–2004). To the Marxists, Marx's theory of social development, such as the transition from slavery to feudalism and continually to capitalism, was essential to their analysis of Japanese history. Araki Moriaki (1927–1993), for example, established his career in examining Japan's slavery system and its transition to feudalism. In order to explain the driving force for such social development, Marxist historians also developed the thesis of the "people's struggle," drawing attention to peasant rebellions and other mass movements to depict and explain change and progress in history.[5]

The alliance between the Marxists and "modernists" in the postwar era suggested that the former, thanks to the unprecedented freedom they enjoyed, now could exchange and collaborate much more freely and openly with their empiricist-oriented colleagues, or the mainstream of Japan's historical profession. Indeed, despite the war, the modernists had expanded their careers, for their research interest was not deemed as inimical as the Marxists' by the militarist government. In the postwar period, both groups worked together to produce several important book series on Japanese history, most notably the *Iwanami Series on Japanese History* (*Iwanami Kōza: Nihon Rekishi*) by Iwanami Shoten, a prestigious academic publisher in Japan.

The liveliness of postwar Japanese historiography was also manifested in the revival and establishment of historical associations. Again, Marxist historians were the vanguard. In 1946, Ishimoda Shō, Tōyama Shigeki, and others reorganized the Association for Historical Study (*Rekishigaku kenkyū kai*), which had appeared in 1932 but was subsequently disbanded in 1944 under militarist rule. The newly organized Association also established a branch on historical education, with which its members worked on cleansing the influence of the imperialist historical school in history teaching and textbook writing. Other historical organizations also cropped up after World War II. The Association for the Study of Japanese History (*Nihonshi kenkyū kai*) was a notable example, for it was founded mainly by and for amateur historians. All these associations published their own journals. Meanwhile, such old journals as the *Historical Journal* (*Shigaku zasshi*) (founded 1889) were also refurbished to tailor to the new interest of historians of the younger generation. By 1950, in order to rejoin the International Congress of Historical Sciences (CISH), Japanese historians formed the Japanese Association for Historical Study (*Nihon rekishigaku kyōkai*), with a goal to coordinate all existent historical societies. In 1960 the Association, for the first time in postwar Japan, sent a delegation to attend the Tenth CISH in Stockholm. Since then, Japanese historians have regularly attended CISH's quinquennial conventions and played an active part in its organizations and activities.[6]

The dominance of Marxist historiography in the People's Republic of China

If the revival of the Marxist school and historical organizations marked the advance of Japanese historiography in the postwar period, the same trend could also be observed in postwar Chinese historiography. But there were key differences. After its "bitter" victory over Japan in World War II, China succeeded in recovering Taiwan and restored its sovereignty over foreign spheres of influences on the mainland. But despite U.S. assistance, the nationalist government led by Chiang Kai-shek (1888–1975) was unable to engineer a quick economic recovery, which led to social unrest and political protests. Having gained popularity during and after the war and received Soviet assistance, the Chinese communists successfully expanded their bases from Manchuria to other parts of the country. In the ensuing civil war between the nationalists and communists, the latter, under Mao Zedong's (1893–1976) leadership, was victorious; after expelling Chiang and his remaining army to Taiwan, Mao established the People's Republic of China (PRC) in 1949.

This change of power in China exerted a significant impact on the development of Chinese historiography. It caused, inter alias, the final dissolution of the embattled Historical Source School on the mainland. In the wake of Chiang's defeat, Hu Shi, Fu Sinian, and other academic leaders left for Taiwan, Hong Kong, and/or the West, out of their distrust of communism. However, many of their colleagues and cohorts, including Gu Jiegang and Chen Yinke (Yinque, 1890–1969), an acclaimed historian and Fu's right arm at the Institute of History and Philology, stayed behind, partially because of their disappointment at Chiang and partially because of their attachment to Chinese culture. After retreating to Taiwan, Fu Sinian headed the Taiwan University, established by the Japanese in 1928, and used it as a base to revive the Historical Source School. The other base was the Institute of History and Philology, which Fu brought to the island, following the nationalists' retreat. Though Fu died in 1950, his effort was not spent in vain. The school began to dominate the historical field in Taiwan; Hu Shi's presidency of the Academia Sinica, to which the Institute of History and Philology belonged, during 1958 and 1962 also reinforced its position and spread its influence.[7]

Yet on the mainland, it was the world of Marxist historians. Following their victory, the communist leaders founded the Chinese Academy of Sciences, headed by Guo Moruo (1892–1978), a Marxist historian of ancient China. It was aimed in part to compete with the Academia Sinica and in part to copy the Soviet model (*Akademiya nauk*). From the early 1950s to the early 1960s, Chinese historians regarded Marxist historiography in the Soviet Union as the exemplar and followed it closely. They invited Soviet historians to China as advisors and supervisors at the Academy, and many universities translated Russian historians' works, including such party doctrines as *Dialectical and Historical Materialism*, attributed to Joseph Stalin, and *A Brief Course on the History of the Soviet Communist Party (Bolshevik)*. There also appeared journals specializing in translating works of Russian historians. In a word, Russian works on Marxist historical theory and historiography were placed on the pedestal in juxtaposition with the works of Marx, Engels, Lenin, and Mao.

Chinese historians' enthusiasm for Soviet Marxist historiography mirrored the two countries' friendship in the period. Yet notwithstanding the zeal, Chinese Marxists were also eager to make their own distinct contribution, for they had approached Marxism from variegated sources, not exclusively from Russia. Guo Moruo, for instance, was probably more familiar with Japanese works on Marxism, such as that of Kawakami Hajime, for Guo had spent considerable time in Japan, first in the 1910s and again in the 1930s. Pursuant to the Marxist theory on social development, Guo focused his study on proving the existence of slavery in ancient China and portraying its subsequent transition to feudalism, an attempt reminding one of Araki Moriaki's research. But insofar as his use of sources was concerned, Guo was also influenced by the empirical ethos fostered by the Historical Source School. More specifically, his work carried on the pioneering research by Wang Guowei and others on ancient China, which compared conventional written sources with the inscriptions found on newly discovered Shang oracle bones. Indeed, from the 1930s on, while establishing himself as a leading Marxist historian, Guo also garnered a reputation as an expert on oracle bone study, a highly specialized field, for his ability to recognize and decipher these ancient inscriptions.[8]

Though a Marxist like Moriaki, Guo Moruo's theory on the transition from slavery to feudalism in ancient China differed from that of the Russian China experts in one area – *when* it actually took place. That is, though they both maintained that Marx's thesis on phasic social development in history was universally applicable, they could not agree on when the slavery-feudalism transition occurred in Chinese history; nor could, interestingly, the Chinese Marxist historians among themselves. While Guo Moruo proposed that the slavery-feudalism transition had occurred at the end of the Zhou dynasty (eleventh century–256 BCE), Fan Wenlan (1893–1969), a veteran Marxist who had joined the communist movement in Yan'an, argued that it had taken place several centuries earlier. Their difference precipitated a vigorous discussion in the Marxist historical community, for it was pertinent to the large question of whether or not Marxist historical theories were applicable to interpreting Chinese history. Additionally, Fan Wenlan hypothesized that the formation of the Chinese nation had occurred in 221 BCE, when the Qin dynasty unified China proper, even though the accepted notion was that, drawing on the European historical experience, nation-states did not appear until modern times. This notion had been endorsed and expounded by Stalin in his *Marxism and the National and Colonial Question*. By stressing that the Chinese nation had predated all the rest in the world, Fan was making a veiled attempt to question the universality of Western history and glorify the uniqueness and longevity of Chinese history.[9]

Thus, PRC historians were at once Marxists and nationalists; even though their country was moving resolutely in the socialist direction and becoming a committed member of the Soviet bloc in the Cold War divide, Marxist historians in China did not follow slavishly their Russian colleagues in developing new interpretations of Chinese and world history. Their works were animated by the similar nationalist stirrings that had motivated their non-Marxist counterparts and cohorts. However, after the founding of the PRC, non-Marxist historians faced a good deal of hardship. They were asked to go through a seemingly never ending "thought reform" process, in which they repeatedly had to make self-deprecatory criticisms. Many of them endeavored to embrace and adapt to the new ideology, often sincerely and seriously. But it remained hard for them to gain the party's trust. In the early 1950s, Gu Jiegang, for example, was recruited to the Chinese Academy of Sciences in Beijing and became a research fellow of history. But the "research" he was allowed and urged to conduct in the period consisted mainly of endless self-criticisms of his "illicit" friendship and collaboration with Hu Shi, his mentor but now a bête noire of Marxist historians, in propagating the Historical Source School.[10]

Chen Yinke, another noted non-Marxist historian, fared somewhat better. A polyglot who had spent many years in Euro-America pursuing modern education, he had garnered the reputation as an outstanding evidential scholar of the modern age, Aside from his Western education, Chen, a scion of an eminent literati family, had also received solid training in classical Chinese learning. After his return from the West in 1926, Chen taught Chinese Buddhism and Tang history. His erudition impressed not only his students but also his colleagues and peers. Drawing on multilingual sources, his exacting, philology-based research also won him high scholarly acclaim. In the early 1950s, the Chinese Academy of Science approached Chen and asked him to lead one of its history institutes. Chen declined the offer. The government retained its interest in him and even provided him with research assistants, for he by then had already lost his eyesight. During the 1950s and the early 1960s, Chen continued to produce well-researched studies. However, his non-Marxist stance, which he seemed able to maintain, had marginalized considerably his influence in the historical community.[11]

Indeed, though impressive for the mastery of multilingual sources, Chen Yinke's study no longer commanded the interest of historians in the PRC during the 1950s and the 1960s. In addition to the discussions on historical periodization and the origination of Chinese nation, Chinese historians were then engrossed with the study of peasant rebellions. Together with the studies of the vicissitudes of feudal landownership and the emergence of the so-called capitalist sprouts in late imperial China, these five subjects, or "five golden flowers" as they were known at the time, dominated the landscape of PRC Marxist historiography. To conduct these studies was to expound the applicability of Marxist theory to the study of Chinese history and finesse the incongruity between the Marxist framework and the knowledge of Chinese history preserved in the extant body of historical literature. In order to foreground the role of peasant rebellions in history, for example, Marxist historians sifted the dynastic historical sources for any useful records. By reconstructing the history from this peasant-centered perspective, they jettisoned the elitist approach of the Historical Source School and the monarch-centered tradition in dynastic historiography.[12] Like its Japanese counterpart, this "people's struggle" approach was aimed to extend the Marxian class struggle theory in historical writing.

China's honeymoon period with the Soviet Union did not last long. Khrushchev's de-Stalinization project startled Chinese communist leaders, and beginning in the early 1960s, the two countries' relationship soured. On a more personal level, Mao was frightened by what Khrushchev did to Stalin after his death. To prevent it from happening to him, he launched the Great Proletarian Cultural Revolution in 1966, using young students to search for and chase down Chinese "Khrushchevs" in his party. This political upheaval, which came to an end only after Mao's death, paralyzed historical study. In fact, it was catalyzed by a scathing literary campaign organized by Mao against the *Dismissal of Hai Rui* (*Hairui baguan*), a historical play written by Wu Han (1909–1969). Wu, an erstwhile follower of Hu Shi, was a noted expert on Ming history and, after joining the communist movement in the late 1940s, became deputy mayor of the Beijing municipal government. Wu's metamorphosis was once regarded as a model for other non-Marxist historians in the PRC. But his play apparently irked Mao. As a first sacrifice to Mao's campaign, Wu's death foreboded the plight his peers and the nation as a whole were to endure during this decade-long (1966–1976) caesura in Chinese history.[13]

Challenges to Marxist historiography and Eurocentrism

In Japan, the fallout of de-Stalinization injected a new turn to the development of Marxist historiography. The so-called reverse course, occasioned by the advent of the Cold War, also curtailed labor and communist movements and caused the resurgence of political conservatism. Against the changing political atmosphere, marked by the failure of the Socialist Party and other leftist organizations and radical students to prevent the ratification of the Treaty of Mutual Cooperation and Security between the U.S. and Japan in 1960, Japanese Communist Party and Marxist historians engaged in self-criticism, which led to a new look at their previous work on Japanese history. In a debate on the history of the Shōwa period (1926–1989), for example, Marxist historians were criticized by their non-Marxist opponents for their at times dogmatic application of the class struggle theory. The critics charged that Marxist historiography emphasized structural changes in history at the expense of real people's lives. That is, while Marxist historians intended to examine history from the perspective of the "struggle of the people," they often fell short of depicting concretely how the life of the real people changed in their historical narrative.

The debate on Shōwa history had broad implications for the advance of Marxist historiography in Japan's historical community. Goaded by their critics to examine the movement of history from a variety of angles, Marxist historians began to cast doubt on the social development theory, one of the cornerstones of Marxist historical theory. They took note of the fact that while the continuous transition from slavery to feudalism and to capitalism outlined the evolution of world history, the progress was not always unilinear and one-directional. At times, they argued, two or more modes of production (e.g., feudalism and capitalism) and class relations (e.g., peasants vs. landlords and workers vs. bourgeoisie) coexisted in one time period. In addition, the historical evolution in one particular region tended to acquire distinct characteristics, shaped by factors unique to itself and its surrounding areas.[14]

These discussions opened up new vistas of enriching the study of Marxist historiography. More importantly, they engendered, perhaps for the first time, criticisms of Eurocentrism, a major ideological influence underpinning the development of Marxist and "modernist" historiographies. As previously mentioned, the modernist historians had often received a Western education and, after their return to Japan, established their careers in teaching and researching European history. As Marxist historians championed Marxist theories of history, grounding in the European historical experience, the modernists also set forth their interpretive theories of Japanese history against the backdrop of European history. Ōtsuka Hisao's study was a typical example. Following Max Weber, he focused his research on proving Japan's "distorted modern" (*yuganda kindai*) as a foil to the "normal" modernization in Euro-America. Though his work shed light on the socio-economic factors leading to the rise of Japanese imperialism, it also reiterated the Eurocentric idiom about the "backwardness/stagnation" of Asian history.[15] Buoyed by the new critical spirit, Marxist historians, e.g., Eguchi Bokurō (1911–1989), questioned such a modernist thesis. In search for an alternative to the Eurocentric approach, efforts were now made to (re) situate Japanese history in the context of East Asia for (more?) intelligent comparison. Takeuchi Yoshimi (1910–1977), a China scholar, for example, went as far as to argue that the dismal failure of Japan's prewar attempts at modernization should open the eyes of Japanese historians to the progressiveness of modern Chinese history, exemplified by the inception of the PRC and its iconoclastic stance toward and action against tradition.[16]

But throughout the 1960s, many Japanese historians seemed still convinced that the Western model of modernization was the exemplar against which their country's history should be analyzed and compared. As Japan's economy entered a period of explosive growth, catapulting the country into the echelon of the industrialized world, Japanese historians became increasingly intrigued by the "modernization theory" advanced by Western scholars. Inspired by the works of such American Japan experts as John W. Hall (1916–1997), E. Herbert Norman (1909–1957), and Ronald P. Dore, they organized an International Symposium on Modern Japan in 1960, at which the participants reached an agreement on: (1) Beginning in the Meiji Restoration, Japan's modernization project was a successful one, and (2) this successful modernization paved the way for Japan's impressive postwar economic expansion.[17] In other words, instead of considering Japan's modernization during the Meiji, Taishō, and early Shōwa periods a failure, responsible for spawning militarism and imperialism, the historians now adopted a much more positive and uplifting teleology about the country's past.

Like the Marxist group, the modernist school led by Ōtsuka Hisao thus was under increasing scrutiny because of its emphasis on Japan's "abnormal modernity." Many of its critics were based in Kyoto and their challenge to Ōtsuka, who had established his sterling career in Tokyo, also reflected the rivalry between Tokyo University and Kyoto University, two academic powerhouses in modern Japan. Indeed, the once influential Kyoto School seemed to have resumed life beginning in the 1960s. And its membership was no longer dominated by the students of philosophy as in the prewar period. Insofar as its influence in historical study was concerned, the work of Iwanishi Kinji (1902–1992), an anthropologist trained in biology, and Umesao Tadao (1920–2010), a historian-cum-ethnographer, was most relevant, even though both of them were indebted to Nishida Kitarō's philosophical theories. In contrast to the deterministic streak embedded in the interpretation of both the Marxist and modernist schools, these scholars were more interested in drawing attention to human agency in the evolution of history and its interaction with the immediate ecological environment. Their theories opened the vistas of interpreting the course of Japanese civilization from different perspectives, such as seeing it as an ocean civilization instead of a land civilization and distinguishing it from its neighbors and challenging the universal application of Marxist and modernist theory that tended to flatten regional differences and historical specificities.[18]

The attempt to draw a positive picture of Japanese culture and history also characterized the work of Nakane Chie, a prominent women sociologist, who contrasted the characteristics of modern Japanese society and culture with those of Chinese and Indian societies, in hopes of explicating Japan's economic success.[19] When historian Ienaga Saburō (1913–2002) portrayed less positively Japan's modern history in his college and secondary school textbooks, he was censored by the Ministry of Education. Having failed to acquire the official approval, which is still the case in textbook writing, his book was subsequently prohibited from circulation. Ienaga later had to challenge, repeatedly, the Ministry's decision in court in order to get it reinstated. Not uncoincidentally, the same period saw the publication of Hayashi Fusao's (1903–1975) new study of World War II in Asia, in which he attempted to trivialize Japan's aggression.[20] In short, beginning in the 1960s, historical writing in Japan experienced a twofold development. On the one hand, Marxist historiography went through a positive transformation, fostering the studies of women's history, local history, folklore and popular culture, and minority groups. On the other hand, buoyed by Japan's economic boom and its growing importance in Cold War politics, Japanese historians of the younger generation and the society as a whole became increasingly less willing to look at the country's past with a critical eye.

Between Marxism and nationalism: Academic history in Vietnam

The leadership change in the socialist bloc also affected the development of Marxist historiography in other Asian countries, though its extent varied one from another. In postwar or postcolonial Vietnam, for instance, the Democratic Republic of Vietnam (DRV) in the north maintained a cordial relationship with and received aid from both the Soviet Union and China after Stalin's death. Yet in its historical practice, a discernible change occurred in the post-Stalin years. Like their Russian and Chinese counterparts, DRV historians embarked on Marxist historiography under the government aegis. As early as 1953, before they administered the coup de grâce to the French colonial regime, Ho Chi Minh (1890–1969) and other Vietnamese communist leaders had organized the Committee for Literary, Historical and Geographical Research, which, wittingly, also had an archaeological unit. The Committee's primary task was to compile a national history, as shown in its name change to Institute of History in 1959. The appearance of this "New History," however, took almost three decades. Like their Chinese counterparts, Vietnamese Marxist historians were vexed by the difference between the Marxist theoretical framework and their country's historical development. In order to conform the development to the "universal" course of historical evolution adumbrated by Marx, they raged heated discussions on periodization, aiming to identify the successive five-stage transition in Vietnam's past. In so doing, they consulted, in particular, Stalin's *Marxism and the National and Colonial Question* because, compared with Marx's approximation, Stalin was more adamant about the universal existence of these five stages (primitive communism, slavery, serfdom, capitalism, and socialism/communism) in world history. It was not until after Stalin's death and the advent of de-Stalinization that most Vietnamese Marxist historians came to agree that some modifications were necessary to Stalin's thesis and that Vietnamese history, for example, had not experienced slavery; it had moved directly from primitive communism to feudalism. During the late 1970s and the early 1980s when the national history finally appeared, it simply ditched the five-stage theory as its interpretive framework.[21]

However, the tradition of dynastic historiography and the legacy of French colonialism remained a serious challenge, for both stood as obstacles to the construction of a new, nationalist historical narrative. In such dynastic histories as Ngo Si lien's *Complete Version of the Historical Records of Great Viet*, one found a certain embryonic form of Vietnamese nationalism; Ngo, for instance, traced the birth of Vietnam in 2879 BCE in order to predate China's Xia dynasty (ca. 2207–1600 BCE). But overall, the dynastic historical corpus in Vietnam reeked of Chinese, Confucian influence. Yet at the same time, these historical sources, including certain Chinese dynastic histories, remained indispensable for the Vietnamese Marxist historians to weave together a continuous narrative of Vietnamese history from its antiquity to the present. Moreover, that China had traditionally exerted enormous influence in Vietnam became a contested issue because in the early part of the twentieth century, both the French Orientalist scholars and Western-influenced Vietnamese writers had labeled Vietnam a "poor" copy of China. Worse still, prior to the country's unification in 1976, South Vietnam had repeatedly reissued Tran Trong Kim's *Brief History of Vietnam*, a representative work of the colonial school. But to Marxist historians, Tran's work was an example of "feudal colonialism" for its traditional structure and Francophilic stance. Tran became a target of attacks also because he had collaborated with the French and Japanese colonizers in the 1930s and the 1940s.[22]

Thus, a palpable nationalist overtone is ingrained in Vietnamese Marxist historiography. In order to demonstrate that the Vietnamese had maintained a distinctly glorious record in fighting off the invaders, the historians decided to commence their country's feudal period with the Trung sisters' rebellion against the Chinese Han army in 40 CE They also ended this period with a landmark victory – their country's defeat of the Japanese in 1945. Though incredibly long as a period of feudalism, they argued, this history proved that Vietnam was a "shining example" of world revolutionary history, for Vietnam was the *only* country that established socialism by defeating a colonial power in a revolution. In fact, the historical longevity was also something they desired, for it demonstrated that, contrary to the claims of the Orientalists and prewar historians, Vietnam was not China's cultural colony and that the Vietnamese not only could but indeed had established independent states even earlier than did the Chinese. Thus, Ngo Si lien's tenuous assertion about Van Lang's founding of Vietnam in 2879 BCE remains quite appealing; it has motivated both historians and archaeologists in today's Vietnam to look for its evidence.[23]

The resurgence of national history

Nationalism has also characterized the advance of Korean historiography in the postwar period. After Japan's surrender in 1945, the Koreans gained independence, though their country has remained divided to this day, reflecting and extending the Cold War arrangement. Despite the ideological differences between the governments in North and South Korea, both countries' historians have faced the same colonial legacy and thus embarked on essentially the same project on reconstructing a new historical narrative, wherein the longevity of an independent Korean history and the indomitable spirit of the Korean people are lionized. The creation myth surrounding Tan'gun thus monopolizes the attention among historians and archaeologists, not only because it was advanced by such renowned Korean historians as Sin Ch'ae-ho for rebutting the Japanese belittlement of Korean history and culture but also because the Tan'gun religion (*Tan'gun-gyo*), or the worship of Tan'gun as a deity and savior for modern Koreans, was a major resistance movement during Japan's colonial rule and because in today's South Korea, the religion still has a great popularity. In North Korea, the lore of Tan'gun also has a great appeal because Paek Nam-un (1895–1970), a prominent Marxist historian, used the Tan'gun myth to dissect and describe ancient Korean society as a specimen of primitive communism from the Marxist perspective. After the establishment of North Korea, Paek held such prestigious positions as Minister of Education and president of the Korean Academy. During 1993–1994, when the top leadership was passed down from Kim Il-sung to his son Kim Jong-il, North Korean archaeologists conducted an excavation of the alleged Tan'gun's tomb near P'yongyang and claimed propitiously that they had found the remains of Tan'gun and his mother – the female bear. Moreover, using the method of electron-spin resonance (ESR), they also pushed Tan'gun's dates further back from the third millennium BCE to the fifth millennium BCE.[24]

South Korean historians and archaeologists have disputed these findings. However, they are equally fervent and animated about the belief in Tan'gun as the progenitor of the Korean people. In fact, despite the glaring discrepancy between the dates of Tan'gun according to the lore and the extant written historical records dated no earlier than the first century BCE, Korean historians and textbook writers have incorporated the Tan'gun tale in their narratives of Korean history. Korean students today are taught that Tan'gun founded the Korean state in 2333 BCE and that the Koreans are the chosen people (*paedal*) because Tan'gun's father descended from Heaven, much as Sin Ch'ae-ho and Ch'oe Nam-son argued back in the 1930s.[25] From the 1960s, as South Korea embarked on the path of modernization, this nationalist historiography also drew heavily on the modernization theory; the latter prompted its historians to seek elements in Korea's past for explaining its modern historical development. This attempt, however, occasioned contested results; some historians chose to expand the anticolonial and nationalist narrative, whereas others, inspired by postcolonial theory and pro-American political position, argued the need to experiment with postnationalist historiography, of which *minjung* (people), or the subaltern, should take a central place in constructing Korea's national past.[26]

Beginning in the 1970s, in a different form, nationalism also revived to exert a notable impact on the development of Japanese historiography. Thanks to Japan's impressive economic growth, Japanese historians by then seemed to have come out of the shadow of postwar pessimism about their country's history. The formation and vicissitude of the Japanese state in ancient and medieval times once again commanded interest among historians. In place of the harsh criticism characterizing the writings of Marxist historians, we find more in-depth and more balanced analysis tinged at times with a sympathetic and romanticized tone. The once notorious imperial system has also drawn new attention; increasingly, it is not viewed as one of Japan's "ills" but a way to understand Japan's distinct political structure and system.[27]

Nowhere is this new direction of Japanese historiography seen more clearly than in the changes of historical education and history textbook writing. In present-day Japan, the textbook market is open to publishers, whereas the Ministry of Education retains its role in screening and vetting the content of a textbook. Motivated by the slogan of "reexamining [our] history" or "thinking better of [our] history" (*rekishi no naoshi*), which is gaining currency in the historical circle and among the general public, some history textbooks, most notably the *History of the Nation* (*Kokumin no rekishi*) written by Nishio Kanji and published by a conservative publisher in 1999, have offered a revisionist view of Japan's modern history by playing down the country's responsibility for starting World War II in Asia and whitewashing the various atrocities committed by its army against the peoples in China, Korea, and elsewhere. Despite its "New History" pitch, Nishio's book has garnered only a negligible market share. However, it has sold well in regular bookstores, and its author's stance toward the war and modern Japanese history in general has also influenced other textbook writers.[28] More broadly, the emergence of this attempt to whitewash Japan's war crimes and reinterpret its role in World War II had a good deal to do with the "victim consciousness" propagated by Japanese politicians, as well as by some members of the Japanese academic community in the postwar years. That Hiroshima and Nagasaki were bombed and Japan as a whole was occupied by the United States was an important factor, which was used as a pretext to portray "Japanese nation as the real victim of the war." It enabled nationalist and revisionist historians to gain public influence in today's Japan.[29]

The Annales *school, postmodernism, and new changes in Japanese historiography*

The new direction in post-1970s Japanese historiography has manifested the influence of postmodernism and such new trends in Western historiography as the *Annales* School and social history. After over two decades of economic expansion, by which Japan was vaulted to the world of industrialized nations, the Japanese now saw the price they had paid for their country's modernization: pollution, urban congestion, high crime rate, moral decline, and desertion of the countryside. Influenced by the discussions of postmodernism (from the 1970s on, the word "postmodern" has become a catchphrase in Japan's academia and news media), historians have made a concerted effort to search for new ways in representing the past, characterized by the so-called total history approach.

Different markedly from the political and economic foci of the Marxists and the modernists, this total history interest bears clear imprints of the *Annales* School. Indeed, not only were the works of Lucien Febvre and Marc Bloch rendered into Japanese, but Fernand Braudel's monumental *Civilisation matérielle, économie et capitalisme: XVe-XVIIIe siècle* also appeared in Japanese between 1985–1999, inspiring Amino Yoshihiko (1928–2004), one of the most prolific historians in contemporary Japan, to produce, among others, his *Emperor and Non-peasants in Medieval Japan* (*Nihon chūsei no hi nōgyōmin to tennō*), a landmark study of medieval Japanese society. In contrast to the Marxist interest in the class conflict between the landlords and peasants, Amino centers his study on the nonagrarian population. Having offered a more vivid "image" (*katachi/zō*) of medieval Japanese society, he romanticizes the lives of the merchants, artisans, fishermen, blacksmiths, courtesans, and prostitutes, or the nonagrarian segments of the population. The emperor also acquires a benign image because it was he who warranted the legal statuses of these people. By romanticizing the past, Amino hopes to foster a more positive understanding of premodern Japan, one that alters its accepted image as a mere liability to progressive history and modernization in earlier scholarship.[30]

Braudel's masterpiece also inspired Kawakatsu Heita, a noted economic historian in the loosely knit Kyoto School in postwar times, to propound an oceanic outlook on Japanese history. Like his predecessors Iwanishi Kinji and Umesao Tadao, Kawakatsu draws particular attention to Japan's ecological surroundings and their impacts on its historical and economic development. Along with Hamashita Takeshi, another distinguished member of the Kyoto School, he proposes to examine the dynamism of intra-Asian trade within the Sinic world and Japan's economic exchange with the Chinese mainland in particular, before and after Western arrival.[31] This research has led them to problematize the modernization theory that saw the expansion of capitalism, or modern economy, as a one-way street, from the West to the non-West. Instead, like Andre Gunder Frank (1929–2005) and Immanuel Wallerstein, these Kyoto-based historians emphasize the role of Asia in evolving modern capitalism worldwide. Tsunoyama Sakae's (1921–2014) *Tea and World History*, appearing in 1980, is an inspiring and illuminating example in this regard.[32]

In addition to the *Annales* School, Japanese historians were exposed to the social history in Anglo-America and the social science history in West

Germany. If Ninomiya Hiroyuki (1932–2006), who had studied in France during the 1960s, is an exponent of the *Annales* School, Abe Kinya (1935–2006), a student returned from Germany, helped introduce German social science history into Japan; in his own writings, Abe advocated the study of *seken* (civil society/human world) as both a historical subject and perspective.[33] In addition, during the late 1970s, Jürgen Kocka and Reinhart Koselleck, leading exponents of social science history in West Germany, were invited to give lectures in Japan, as was Jacques Le Goff, a prominent member of the *Annales* School. Though the *Annales* School and the social science history pursued slightly different agendas, together they helped, as Ninomiya summarizes, redirect the interest of the Japanese historian in three areas: (1) from universality to local knowledge; (2) from abstract concepts to the daily world; and (3) relativizing the model of European modernization.[34]

Yet the outside influence was not the sole factor in reorienting the direction of historical study in contemporary Japan, for from the late 1960s, if not earlier, Japanese historians had already made serious attempts to broaden their field from political history to sociocultural history; the latter was known as people's history (*minshūshi*) in their terminology. Though influenced by Marxist historical theory, the advocates of this "New History" – Yasumaru Yoshio, Irokawa Daikichi, and Kano Masanao – are not Marxist historians, nor are they teaching at such academic powerhouses as Tokyo or Kyoto Universities. Uninterested in pursuing empirical study of a specific topic, these historians are more inclined to analyze the pros and cons of Japan's modernization in a comprehensive manner. Meanwhile, they are turned off by the Marxist approach because, to them, Japanese Marxist historians objectified and dehumanized history, reducing the dynamics of history into a few changing variables dictated by a destined telos. Indebted more to Yanagita Kunio's folklore study of the prewar years, these historians have attempted instead to reconstruct the everyday life and mentality of the common people.[35] Thus, "history of everyday life" (G. *Alltagsgeschichte*; J. *seikatsushi*) and "history of mentalities" (F. *Histoire de mentalité*; J. *seishinshi*) are as much imported from Germany and France as they are homegrown in Japan.[36]

Toward the end of the twentieth century, two interesting developments were mapping the landscape of Japanese historiography. One is the rapid expansion of women's history and the other the growing interest in the history and life of minority groups and social outcasts. As shown in Takamure Itsue's groundbreaking work in the 1930s and Inoue Kiyoshi's in the 1940s noted previously in the chapter, the field of women's history grew concomitantly with Marxist historiography. Entering the 1970s, the promoters of people's history and social history have also collaborated with the scholars in women's and gender history. Kano Masanao, for example, took an interest in Takamure Itsue and her study of the life of Japanese women.[37] The boom of the field, along with the study of history in general, has also benefited from

the fact that more and more Japanese women are pursuing advanced education and professional careers, a new social phenomenon in today's Japan.
Concomitantly, from the 1980s women's and also gender history received
more and more institutional support at various universities. While Marxism and nationalism remain influential, many women's historians in Japan
are also inspired by the postmodernist and poststructuralist theories advocated by such scholars as Judith Butler and Joan Wallach Scott. Meanwhile,
they have also voiced concerns and criticisms of the "gap" between Western
theory and Japanese reality. That is, few are intent on embracing Western
feminism wholesale in studying Japanese women, past and present.[38]

Discussions of ethnic and racial differences in public used to be taboo in
Japan, for ever since the Meiji Restoration, the country had always emphasized its cultural and national homogeneity, both at home and abroad. It
was not until the postwar years that scholars began to venture into the study
of the lives of Japan's "subaltern" groups, including the so-called untoucha-
bles (*eta*), nonhumans (*hinin*), and such ethnic minorities as the Koreans
and the Chinese. Since some of these groups live either in the cities or its
outskirts, the studies of their lives or ethnic history have grown in tandem
with the interest in urban history, another new booming subfield, as well as
the history of everyday life.[39]

China's search for alternatives to Marxist historiography

Since the late 1970s, Chinese history and historiography, too, have embarked
on a new course. The Cultural Revolution came to an end in 1976, after
Mao's death. In 1978 Deng Xiaoping (1904–1997), China's new leader,
launched economic reform in the country by opening, cautiously, its door
to the (Western) world. As Western countries began to receive Chinese students enthused to update their scientific knowledge, Western culture also
found its way into Chinese classrooms where it surprisingly encountered a
receptive audience. Having endured a decades-long period of chaos and several decades of self-imposed isolation, Chinese intellectuals, while brooding
painfully over their recent historical experience in the Cultural Revolution,
became quite curious about the newly rediscovered outside world.

At the Chinese Academy of Social Sciences (CASS), now independent
from the Chinese Academy of Sciences, Zhang Chunnian and Chen Qineng,
research fellows at the World History Research Institute, launched *World
History (Shijie lishi)* and *Newsletter of the Study of World History (Shijie
lishi dongtai)* in 1978–1979, aiming not only to promote the study of foreign history but also to introduce to Chinese history students new ideas and
trends of historical study in the Western world. Zhang Zhilian (1918–2008),
a professor of European history at Peking University, also arranged, in his
visits to Euro-America, such historians as Georges Duby, Jacques Le Goff,
François Furet, Charles and Louis Tilly, Immanuel Wallerstein, Georg Iggers,
Lynn Hunt, Arthur Schlesinger, Jr., Eric Hobsbawm, and E. P. Thompson to

lecture at his university and other institutions. Having interviewed Fernand Braudel in his twilight years in Paris, Zhang has become a major proponent of the *Annales* School in China. In addition, China rejoined the CISH in 1980; since then, its delegation has regularly attended the quinquennial CISH congregations.[40]

The so-called culture fever (*wenhua re*) discussion epitomized the ethos of 1980s China, characterized by its fervor for importing foreign cultures into China and for renewing China's own cultural tradition. Indeed, after Chinese universities reopened their doors to the Chinese youth who had lost their opportunity to study during the Cultural Revolution, the country now witnessed a robust cultural revival. In the field of history, the influx of new ideas contributed to the dissolution of the hegemony of Marxist historiography. Impressed by the "novel" approaches developed in Western historiography, Chinese historians of the younger generation engaged in heated discussions on historical methodology, in hopes of finding an alternative to the jaded Marxist approach.[41]

The modernization theory, though already chastised in other parts of the world, caught fire in the Chinese historical community, partly because it was "new" to the Chinese and partly because the country was pursuing a vigorous pace of modernization. Motivated by the desire to catch up with the advanced world and make up for the valuable time lost in the Cultural Revolution, Chinese historians and scholars looked to the theory for valuable lessons to guide their belated search for modernity.[42] This motivation was also shared by the public. In 1988, led by Jin Guantao, a former science student noted for his role in inaugurating the discussion on historical methodology, a group of young scholars put together a TV series on Chinese history, entitled *River Elegy* (*Heshang*), in which they taunted the Chinese cultural tradition and implored their compatriots to embrace industrialization and modernization *qua* the Western model. When the series was aired on China's central TV station, it captivated the audience and became an instant hit, though its iconoclasm vexed the government and displeased some members of the historical community.[43]

If the Western modernization is inspiring, so is its advocacy of democracy. In the heat of the prodemocracy movement in 1989, Chinese students erected a Statue of Liberty on Tiananmen Square, China's symbol for political power, demanding political freedom and transparency. When the movement was crushed with bloodshed, the culture fever discussion was also cooled. One of the casualties in its aftermath was the *History and Theory* (*Lishi yu lilun*), a journal launched by Chen Qineng and his colleagues at the World History Institute of the CASS in 1987. But in two years, under a new name *Historiography Quarterly* (*Shixue lilun yanjiu*), it came back to life and remains to this day a main venue for channeling new theories of history from the West and elsewhere into China.

All the same, the academic atmosphere has changed markedly since the 1990s. If the 1980s was characterized by the initial excitement among

Chinese academics for rediscovering the world, the 1990s saw the revival of empirical scholarship, manifest in the renewed interest in the Qing tradition of evidential learning and the legacy of the Historical Source School in the Republican period. Having regained their statures in today's Chinese academic world, Hu Shi, Gu Jiegang, Fu Sinian, as well as Liu Yizheng and Qian Mu, have become protagonists of numerous biographical studies. Chen Yinke seems to be especially well respected, not only because of his ability to straddle both classical Chinese learning and modern Western scholarship but also because he maintained, despite political pressure, his liberal belief in academic freedom and resisted the Marxist indoctrination, which was a rare example among his cohorts in the PRC. At Peking University, where Chen had taught along with Hu, Gu, and Fu, his disciples, Ji Xianlin (1911–2009), Zhou Yiliang (1913–2001), and Tian Yuqing (1924–2015), have garnered a celebrated status in post-Mao and post-Deng China for carrying on the tradition of empirical scholarship. At present, this scholarship is being continuously expanded on by the work of their students, such as Yan Buke, an expert on post-Han China, and Rong Xinjiang, a Tang Buddhist scholar; both are teaching at Peking University.[44]

Accompanying the revival of empirical scholarship, sociocultural history has become a major trend in contemporary Chinese historiography, well poised to take over the position occupied by the Marxist school in the earlier periods. And its advocates are widespread across the country and some of them, such as Chen Chunsheng and Liu Zhiwei at Zhongshan University in Guangzhou, have collaborated closely with China scholars from the West. In addition, these sociocultural historians have worked with overseas Chinese historians in Hong Kong, Taiwan, Japan, and Euro-America. The latter have contributed, for example, to such publications as the *New Historiography* (*Xin shixue*), edited by Yang Nianqun, a professor at People's University in Beijing, and the *New Social History* (*Xin shehuishi*) series, edited by Sun Jiang and Huang Donglan in Japan, in collaboration with Wang Di, a Chinese-American professor. As an attempt to shift the historical interest from class struggle to the life and culture of the common people, sociocultural history rose initially in the late 1980s amid the culture fever discussion. But its latest development, as shown in part by the aforementioned publications, has suggested that its practitioners have developed a strong interest in the new developments in Western historiography associated with postmodernism and postcolonialism. Advocating history's alliance with anthropology, psychology, and literature, these historians have made headway in promoting women/gender history, local history, cultural studies, semiotic analysis, and psychoanalysis.[45]

In sum, from the 1970s on, the once dominant influence of Marxist historiography has noticeably waned across East and Southeast Asia, whereas the nationalist influence remains consistent and forceful. Powered by the nationalist impulse, Asian historians have made persistent efforts to bolster national prestige and esteem through history and history textbook writing, which have caused at times disputes and controversies among the countries.[46] In addition, thanks to the galloping pace of globalization, historians of the region have engaged in more active dialogue with their counterparts across the world, much more than any previous period. However, as a distinct characteristic of the region's historiographical practice, the tradition of official history writing, or writing history collectively under government aegis, remains quite alive. The mammoth project launched recently in China on compiling a multivolume history of the Qing dynasty is a telling example, as is the aforementioned Vietnamese project on a standard narrative on its country's history. The same practice is also observed in Japan, though mostly at the local and county levels.[47] This juxtaposition between the "old" and the "new" has characterized the development of East and Southeast Asian historiography in modern times and will most likely continue to do so in the foreseeable future.

Islamism and Islamic historiography: The Cold War and beyond

Globalizing Muslim historiography

In our discussion of the development of modern Islamic historiography, we have so far managed to concentrate on Muslim historians living and working in the Middle East (though we have also mentioned Syrian Christian intellectuals' contributions and, from time to time, the European Orientalists' work as a foil to that of their Muslim interlocutors). But after World War II, particularly after the 1970s, it seems increasingly difficult to maintain this approach, for more and more historians of Middle Eastern origin have been working, either short or long term, in the Western academic world. Many Muslim historians at work today, like their Indian and, perhaps to a lesser degree, East Asian counterparts, have not only had exposure to Western education in their school years but have also often played a leadership role in promoting Middle Eastern studies in the West. This had rarely been seen in the careers of their teachers' generation.

This new change reflects, by all means, the advent of globalization across the world. But it is also specific to the Middle East in that the region had begun its cultural exchanges with the West ever since the late seventeenth century and that in recent decades, as higher education in the United States and some European countries experienced a noted growth of foreign student population, some of the students from the Middle East chose not only to receive Western education but also "to remain there and take up university teaching positions," for "the political, economic, and social problems of their home countries often made the choice to remain not merely appealing but almost compulsory."[48] In addition, given its geographical proximity, the Middle East had extensive exposures to Western cultural influences not only in the Maghreb, where the French colonial influence had been well present, but also in parts of the Mashriq and Anatolia. In an interview, Halil Inalcik, a prominent Turkish historian who taught for many years at the University of Ankara and also at Chicago and Harvard, recalls that when he was a student in Turkey, via such European-trained historians as Mehmet Fuat Köprülü and Bekir Sitki Baykal (1908–1987), he had already been exposed to European scholarship and to an extent comparable to that of his European colleagues he later met.[49] This Westernization of Turkish historiography and of the modern historical practice in the region as a whole has enabled historians of Middle Eastern origin to work and develop a career in the West. Cemal Kafadar, a collaborator of Inalcik's from a younger generation in Turkey, is now teaching at Harvard, as is M. Sükrü Hanioglu at Princeton, where he is currently the director of Near Eastern Studies. Suraiya Faroqhui, an expert on Ottoman history, is teaching at Ludwig Maximilian University in Munich and incidentally was born in Berlin. From the early twentieth century, people from the Middle East had begun to immigrate to Western countries; some of the leading historians of Middle Eastern studies were children of these immigrants. Albert Hourani (1915–1993), a long-term director of the Middle East Center at St. Antony's College in Oxford, for example, was born into a Lebanese immigrant family in Manchester, England. Charles Issawi (1916–2000), Hourani's classmate at Oxford and an eminent economic historian of the Middle East, was born and bred in Cairo and later emigrated to the United States and taught many years at Columbia, as was Afaf Lutfi al-Sayyid Marsot who, after receiving her education in Egypt and later at Stanford and Oxford, developed a successful teaching career at UCLA.[50] Hanna Batatu (1926–2000), a well-respected expert on modern Iraqi history, was born in Jerusalem; having emigrated to the United States in his early twenties, he established an outstanding career respectively at American University of Beirut and Georgetown.

Having played a major part in promoting the study of Middle Eastern history, these diasporatic scholars are not necessarily Muslims (Hourani and Issawi are Christians, as many Syrians are), nor have they taken an interest in the field simply because of their family background or cultural origin. Hourani and Issawi, for example, had been little interested in Islamic culture in their college days at Oxford. It was in the aftermath of World War II, especially amid the mounting concern over the situation in Palestine, that they, like their many cohorts, began taking a serious scholarly interest in the region. Globalization played an important role in transforming the writing of history also because the transformation occurred unevenly in the Muslim world. In the case of Saudi Arabia, for instance, many foreign (also Muslim) scholars made the earliest attempts at a Saudi national historiography in the postwar years.[51]

The interplay of history and historiography

Indeed, it is generally agreed that Middle Eastern studies, as well as the study of history in the region, entered a period of explosive growth after World War II that had much to do with the ever changing political landscape in the Middle East. First of all, following the examples of Turkey and Egypt, the trend of national independence continued with an ever greater momentum and at times assumed a violent, revolutionary form. During and after World War II, Saudi Arabia, North Yemen, Syria, Jordan, Lebanon, Iran, Iraq, Libya, and Morocco all became independent, as did Israel, whose independence in 1948, however, stirred up a high degree of animosity in the Muslim world. The Arab-Israeli War ensued, which ended in Israel's victory, though the conflict, mainly between the Israelis and the Palestinians, has continued to this day. Due to the unpredictable political conditions, not only did students of Middle Eastern origin choose to remain in the West when possible, but some mature scholars also sought to advance their careers in Western universities. The fact that in post–World War II years, English has become the paramount language, replacing French and German, used in publications on the Middle East is a reflection of American hegemonic power. But this also is the result of many Middle Eastern scholars, working in the West, having increasingly published their works in English.[52]

Second, in the eyes of most Muslims, Israel represents an agent of British and U.S. power; its existence reminds them of the persistent colonialist and imperialist legacy in the region. That is, though most countries in the Middle East have gained independence from Western powers in postwar years, the anti-Western sentiment remained palpable and pulsating, driving the tides of pan-Arabism and Arab nationalism.[53] In a secularized way, pan-Arabism resembled pan-Islamism advocated by Namık Kemāl and Sayyid Jamal al-Din al-Afghani (1838–1897) and propagated by the Young Ottomans at the turn of the twentieth century.[54] The formation of the Arab League in 1945 was but one indication of this movement's political strength. From the 1950s, first Egypt and then Iraq assumed its leadership, and pan-Arabism exercised a major impact on the writing of history.[55] In Egyptian historiography, for instance, pharaonism, which had prevailed in the 1920s with the intent of glorifying pharaonic Egypt for creating and bolstering national identity and respect among modern-day Egyptians, gave way to a renewed interest in the Islamic influence in the country's history and culture.[56] A similar change has also occurred in other countries in the region, in that Islam is now accorded much more attention and is also evaluated much more positively than before in historical writings. Even in Turkey, where attempts to turn the country into a European nation have been continually made after the death of Kemal Atatürk, interest in Islamic history, or the Islamic period of Turkish history, has been steadily on the rise, reinforced from time to time by the frustration of the country's hitherto unsuccessful bid for the EU membership.[57] Yet the best example of the movement's potency in promoting pan-Arabic solidarity was shown in the OAPEC's (Organization of Arab Petroleum Exporting Countries) oil embargo against the West, Israel, and Japan in 1973. This embargo suggests that despite their differences and disputes – some went back for centuries – the Muslim world has no longer been so fragmented as in the early part of twentieth century. Instead, it has become fully able to take concerted actions against the West's hegemony and dominance. And from the 1970s on, this challenge to the West, with respect to its intellectual resource, has drawn increasingly from the region's historical heritage and religious belief in Islam. That is, Islam has resurged in the region; its strength was seen not only in the 1979 Revolution in Iran, which ousted the pro-American, reform-minded monarch[58] but also in the founding and frequent meetings of such international organizations as the Organization of the Islamic Conference and the World Muslim Congress, as well as the existing Arab League, the OAPEC and OPEC (Organization of the Petroleum Exporting Countries), among Muslim countries. Since the 1990s, the activeness of these organizations, which have found few counterparts in other parts of the world, has reached an unprecedented high level.[59]

Third, during the 1950s and the 1960s, Cold War politics, the influence of the Soviet Union and of Marxism and socialism in general, shaped the history and politics in the modern Muslim world. In its confrontation with the Western world, the Soviet Union considered the Middle East, to which it had had a historical tie, an important front. To many political and intellectual leaders in the Middle East, the anti-Western stance of the Soviet Union and the prospect of socialism as an alternative to capitalism were both inspiring and encouraging. Having had the experiences in dealing with Western colonialism and imperialism, these leaders appeared quite motivated to seek an alternative route to modernity than the Western model. Buoyed by the radicalism and populism prevalent at the time, Egypt, for example, experienced a regime change in the Free Officers' Revolution (1952–1956), which was followed by Gamal Abdel Nasser's (1918–1970) experiment with socialism, or Nasserism. In its wake, Iraq witnessed the Revolution of 1958, led by Abdul Karim Qassim (1914–1963), which toppled the monarchy and founded a republic. Though Qassim was no Communist, he received support from communist organizations in his country and from the Soviet Union and attempted several socialist policies by confiscating the rich and helping the poor. In the cultural arena, Marxist ideas gained considerable ground. Under its sway, many Muslim Marxist historians vilified the work and interpretations of European Orientalists about their culture and history and attempted new ones. Their work, though at times doctrinaire and simplistic, gave rise to the interest in socioeconomic history, which, from the late twentieth century to the present, has superseded political, diplomatic, and intellectual history as the main trend of historical study in the region. This new trend has also helped broaden the field of history and strengthened its tie with the public and society; many of the histories reflecting the trend have been written by nonacademic historians who did not belong to the establishment in the profession.[60]

Fourth, the post-World War II developments in Western historiography, especially the growing influence of the *Annales* School in France, influenced the rise of the socioeconomic history trend and, in more recent decades, the interest in cultural and gender history, in modern Islamic historiography.[61] Coupling with the Marxist influence, the *Annales* School helped reorient the direction of the study of Middle Eastern history by drawing a lot of attention to socioeconomic structure as a key factor for generating fundamental changes in history. It prompted Middle Eastern historians to reconsider the Orientalist approach and attempt the integration of social science theories and methods and careful source criticism in historical research. An international conference, called Orientalism and History, held at Cambridge in 1954, suggested this new endeavor. Claude Cahen (1909–1991), a Marxist historian and a participant in the meeting, advocated studies of "fiscal institutions, land taxes, the social categories of landowners, the economic and technical forms of culture, the history of cities, and the professions and patterns of work and commerce."[62] These subjects clearly extended the main interest of the *Annales* School and were to adumbrate the future trend of research interest among the scholars of the Middle East. Albert Hourani's long-spanning career seems to be quite illustrative in this regard. During the postwar years, he entered the field of Middle Eastern studies with an interest in political history, only to change to intellectual history in the late 1950s, which resulted in the publication of his well-known *Arabic Thought in the Liberal Age, 1789–1939* (1962). By the mid-1960s, he embarked on social history, because, in his recollection, "students who were going to Oxford wanted to do other kinds of subjects, to read other kinds of books. I began to think there are other sorts of history."[63] This interest shift in Hourani is also shown in the work of Halil Inalcik. Having had a solid early training in Orientalist scholarship, Inalcik later developed, thanks to the influence of Marxian theory of history, an influential theory that draws considerable attention to the role of the *çift-hane* (big farms) in shaping the agrarian social structure of the Ottoman Empire.[64] From the 1970s, therefore, "a whole system of new theories, models and approaches" has emerged in the historical study of the Middle East, which is marked most notably by the rise of women's and gender history, history from below or the history of everyday life, new cultural history, and colonialism and postcolonialism studies.[65] In the case of women's history, a burgeoning subject in Middle Eastern studies, for example, scholars have directed attention to the multifaceted role women played in region's history, including owning property and exercising social power and how by involving women's roles, one can reconsider historical periodization and reopen the discussion on some important yet often taken-for-granted themes and methods, such as the once dominant nationalist approach to historiography.[66]

Edward Said and the critique of Orientalism

In the field of Middle Eastern studies, critical reconsideration and evaluation of Orientalist scholarship thus predated the publication of Edward Said's (1935–2003) seminal book *Orientalism* of 1979,[67] though this by no means diminishes the book's decisive and lasting influence in reshaping the direction of Middle Eastern studies and beyond. The revolt against positivist scholarship prevailing in the modern West until the 1960s, in which Orientalism was an integral part, had already found its exponents in the radical student movements of the 1960s; the self-critical attitude held by the Western youth toward capitalism opened the eyes of many Middle Eastern intellectuals to the hypocrisy and hegemony of the Western model of modernization and scholarship. The devastating defeat of the Arabs in the Arab-Israeli conflict in 1967, which might well be viewed as a failed attempt to challenge Western dominance, also "exemplified in concrete terms," as Hisham Sharabi (1927–2005) put it, "the consequences of subordination and underdevelopment and cleared the way for a new critical self-awareness." This self-awareness gave rise to the shift of interest from the elite to the social and the ordinary and, more importantly, toward a critical attitude toward certain Western concepts and approaches, particularly the "values and insights implicit in an exclusively Western view or perspective on the (non-Western) world."[68]

Born in Jerusalem and brought up mainly in Egypt, Edward Said established a sterling career in the United States, another testimony to the success of the postwar diasporic generation of Middle Eastern scholars. Though he was not a historian, Said posited an important hypothesis about the work of the Orientalists as an attempt to forge an East–West dichotomy. Its bold argument has since opened up the historical discussion of the rise of academic scholarship in the West and its complicitous, though perhaps unwitting role in assisting the spread of Western imperialism to the non-Western world. In formulating his thesis, as many Middle Eastern scholars have duly pointed out, Said perhaps did not do full justice to Orientalist scholarship, but his finding nonetheless has exerted an immense influence in the study of Middle Eastern history and historiography and that of other non-Western regions.[69] Influenced by postcolonialism, which Said considered an important theoretical ally in reconceptualizing the changes in the contemporary world, Middle Eastern scholars and historians today, for example, are concerned not only about how the West presents the East but also vice versa, or the formation of Occidentalism, and have examined critically the presentation as a form of cultural re-presentation by analyzing its complex and paradoxical outcome in the respective contexts.[70]

In other words, before Said and Michel Foucault, whose thesis on the intrinsic relation between knowledge and power had inspired Said, many had been aware of the political influence in the process of cultural production. The acuteness of Said's argument and his deft adoption of Foucault's work thus are as much a result of Said's own analytical acumen as a reflection of the drastic changes the field of Middle Eastern studies has experienced since the 1950s. In 1963, for example, the Egyptian historian Anouar Abdel-Malek (1924–2012) had sounded the call for a critical overhaul of Orientalist scholarship in his "The End of Orientalism" article.[71] This is, however, not to say that the period prior to the 1950s had been uneventful; indeed, as we have discussed in Chapter 5 the study of Middle Eastern history, which was indispensable to the field's growth, was fraught with important changes that led to, inter alias, the formation of the historical profession in the Middle East. From the 1950s onward, the historical profession and historians in the Middle East have faced greater challenges in weathering through ideological influences and political interventions that in the meantime also characterized its own transformation.

The appeal of Marxism and socialism

It seems logical to start with Egypt, for the country in many regards has been a vanguard of many radical changes in the region; in a most recent survey of Middle Eastern historiography, Egypt is also "a focus of special attention."[72] As already mentioned, Turkey in this period has intensified its effort to become a member of the European Union, exemplified in the country's repeated bid for EU membership. Consequently, despite its dominant Muslim population, its government deliberately tried to set the country apart from its Arab Muslim neighbors both politically and religiously. By comparison, Egyptian political leaders, ranging from Muhammad Naguib (1901–1984), who was installed by the Free Officers as the first president of the republic in 1953, and Gamal Abdel Nasser to Anwar Sadat (1918–1981) and Hosni Mubarak, all perceived and projected themselves as the leader of the Arab world, even though their country, because of its pharaonic heritage and the existence of the Copts, had not been considered a bona fide Arab nation by some of its Arab neighbors. Nasser, for example, played an instrumental role in founding and propagating pan-Arabism through his leadership of the Arab League. The Egyptian leaders' domestic policy followed their outward ambitions, which in turn exerted a tremendous impact on directing the interest and study of Egyptian history among the historians. Since the founding of the republic, Egyptian historiography has encountered several notable turns. And the first one occurred almost as soon as the new government came into existence. As shown in Chapter 5, the construction of historical study as an academic discipline in Egypt was predicated on two influences: nationalism and Orientalism. Trained in the West by scholars mostly in Oriental studies, the first generation of professional historians adopted the nationalist teleology and applied it to interpreting the evolution of Egyptian history. Shafiq Ghurbāl, their undisputed leader, for example, built his career on studying Muhammad ʿAlī and his reform era, which he regarded as constituting a crucial step in Egypt's modernization pursuant to the Western model.[73] But after the Free Officers overthrew the monarchy, the government seemed to have pursued a different interest in interpreting modern Egyptian history, in that the khedives were now regarded as the villains and that the revolts against them, such as the ʿUrābī Revolution, were awarded accolades. The Revolution of 1919, led by the Wafd, did not fare anything better either, for it was not regarded as reflecting the will of the common people. To the Free Officers, the 'Urābī mutiny, though it failed, heralded their own action, with which they wanted to identify. After Nasser came to power, not only had this new interpretation gained more ground but the government also sponsored the project on restoring Islam as part of the country's cultural identity. Spelled out in the Charter of National Action, a document drafted by a committee put together by the government, this historiographical project was consistent with Nasser's introduction of many new policies, both at home and abroad, with the aim to search for an alternative model to the Western one in orchestrating the political and economic development in Egypt as well as in the Arab world as a whole.

Nasser's "turn to the Left" policy was not to the intellectual liking of Shafiq Ghurbāl and his peers or to mainstream academic historians, for it directly challenged their previous assessment of the historical development in modern Egypt. However, these historians also showed a willingness to adapt to the changed political climate. After the Arab League set up the Institute of Higher Arabic Studies, Ghurbāl, after retiring from Cairo University, became its second director, succeeding Sati' al-Husri (1880–1968), an outspoken exponent of Arab nationalism. In his later years, Ghurbāl also manifested a perceptible interest in Arabism. When Egypt and Syria were merged temporarily in 1958, Ghurbāl published a slim book, based on his lectures, outlining the history and characteristics of Arab nationalism and refuting the accepted claim that it was a mere imitation of European nationalism.[74] In response to the government initiatives for revisiting the country's past, he also edited, at the end of his life, the first volume of *The History of Egyptian Civilization*.

Despite these conciliatory moves, Ghurbāl and his generation were no longer deemed fit for taking the task directed by the government. 'Abd al-Rahmān al-Rāfi'i, the popular nonacademic historian of the same generation, fared a little better in that he continued publishing and in 1964, was also nominated for the Nobel Prize.[75] In any event, the influence of their generation was diminishing. Ahmad 'Izzat 'Abd al-Karim (1908–1980), Shafiq Ghurbāl's most celebrated student who earned the first PhD in history educated within the country, switched the focus of his study from political, institutional history to social and economic history, calling attention to the contribution of the masses. After this metamorphosis, 'Abd al-Karim succeeded in making himself a new leader of the Egyptian historical community from the 1960s.[76]

But 'Abd al-Karim was no short of competitors. Though he served on the committee that drafted the Charter of National Action, it was Muhammad Anīs (1921–1986), Shafiq Ghurbāl's junior colleague at Cairo University, who was eventually put in charge by the Nasser government for the project on rewriting Egyptian history. Having earned his PhD from the University of Birmingham, Anīs sometimes presented himself as a Shafiq Ghurbāl's student, though he obviously disagreed with Ghurbāl's general interpretation of modern Egyptian history. From a socialist-populist perspective, Anīs set out to establish his own school, the socialist school, and cast the evolution of Egyptian history in a completely new light. And he deemed it all necessary, for "this socialist view is the offspring of the current phase upon which our society boldly embarks."[77] Anīs posited that modern Egyptian history witnessed the class struggle of two forces, one representing the rich and the other the educated class aided by a military wing. The ʿUrābī Revolution of 1881 marked a turning point in Egyptian history, in that the two forces collided, signaling the country's transition from feudalism to socialism. Though the rich had initially gained an upper hand over its opponent because of foreign aid, it was eventually defeated in 1952 by the Free Officers. Egypt from then on had been ushered into a new historical era.[78]

This new interpretation of Egyptian history was music to the government's ears, for which Anīs was rewarded handsomely; in 1964, he was promoted to Chair Professor of Modern History at Cairo University. When he was commissioned to write a history of the Egyptian resistance to the French invasion in 1798, he was awarded a lucrative contract. Acting on his belief that history should be "in the service of socialist development," Anīs not only joined the Arab Socialist Union, then the only legal party in Egypt, but also served as Secretariat of the party's section on Propaganda and Socialist Thought. Thanks to his political clout, Anīs also set up the National Historical Documents Center and served as its first director. This move was both for promoting historical study as well as for controlling its production. After the center was opened, Muhammad Anīs, Ahmad ʿIzzat ʿAbd al-Karim, and others sent their students to work with the documents in writing their theses. Their work raised the level of and set new standards for Egyptian historical writing. However, the Center was not completely open to the public, nor was it fully accessible to foreign scholars.[79] As a professionally trained historian, Anīs was quite aware of the importance of source collection and criticism. Though his works were at times known to be aggressive and polemical, he wrote them on carefully assembled sources. But, again, he believed that the careful use of sources was for expounding the accepted theory or doctrine.[80]

The influence of Muhammad Anīs and his socialist school was extensive and at times suppressive. In 1963, when the school administered the government project for "the Revision of Modern Historical Writing," many of his colleagues felt that they had no choice but to participate. To echo Anīs's socialist interpretation of Egyptian history, Ahmad ʿIzzat ʿAbd al-Karim, for example, presented his analysis of the socialist nature of Ottoman feudalism in Egypt, a rather absurd assertion.[81] But the influence of the socialist school seemed not long lasting. Though Anīs more or less maintained his high public profile in the post-Nasser days, he was often absent from his post at Cairo University by taking on assignments outside the country.[82] After Nasser's death in 1970, Anwar Sadat, the new president, quickly launched a campaign to discredit Nasserism. Insofar as its influence on historical study was concerned, this de-Nasserization was conducive to new interpretations and different schools of thoughts for Sadat lifted the government control of press and allowed more academic freedom. Buoyed by this new political climate, Egyptian historiography embarked on a new course of development, characterized by, among other things, the endeavor to discover democratic elements in its past.[83] If democratization indeed occurred under Sadat, it was accompanied by the notable growth and diversification of higher education; many new universities had cropped up during the 1970s. And a good number of women, for the first time, entered universities, from them emerging the first generation of women historians (e.g., Afaf Lutfi al-Sayyid Marsot in the Middle East).[84]

But Sadat also purged Nasserists and socialists, though not as harshly as Nasser had done to his political enemies. The Marxist school of historiography, or the Marxian approach to historical interpretation, retained its attraction, and from the 1980s, when freedom of political expression was increased, it further expanded its territory of influence, attesting to the overall popularity of Marxism in the contemporary Muslim world. Rif'at al-Sa'id, a leading Marxist historian, for example, is among the most published historians in today's Egypt. Beginning in 1998, a multivolume history on the working class and the subaltern has been continuously published, with its fifth volume appearing in 2001.[85] Abdallah Laroui, an eminent Moroccan historian and a sharp critic of Orientalism, is famous for his Marxian approach to constructing a new narrative for his country's history.[86] The development of modern Iraqi historiography also offered testimony to the Marxist influence in the Middle East. Throughout the twentieth century, academic freedom has rarely existed in the country. Most accounts of Iraqi history have appeared either in the West or in other parts of the Middle East, such as in Cyprus and Damascus, and they are characteristically Marxist. In his definitive study of modern Iraqi history, Hanna Batatu chronicles in detail the rise of the Iraqi Communist Party and its widespread influence in the 1950s.[87] Last but not least, Marxism also played a notable role in motivating the Arab uprising of the 2010s. While many states in the Middle East embarked on the path of capitalist development, the resulting social problems (e.g., the widening gap between the rich and poor, environmental deterioration, and high crime rate) undermined the people's confidence in continuing along the path and turned them to the Marxist class struggle theory. Meanwhile, Marxist historians in the region are also inspired by the work of cultural Marxists in the West, which help them to note the interaction between economic base and superstructure or the increasing appeal of Islam and its sociopolitical impact on the populace.[88]

The Islamic revival: Islamism and nationalism

Another factor influencing the change in contemporary Islamic historiography is the resurgence of Islam. This renewed interest in Islam has been embedded in the endeavor pursued by many Muslim nations in post-World War II years to seek an identity distinct to their own cultural past that was also consistent with the general anti-Western sentiment prevalent in the region. In contrast to the nationalist historians of the previous generation, historians today seem increasingly interested in focusing their study on their countries' Islamic past, rather than the pre-Islamic period that their predecessors had worked on diligently and, perhaps also imaginatively, in the late nineteenth century and the beginning of the twentieth century. Except perhaps for those working in the tourist industry, pharaonic Egypt has subsequently lost its appeal to modern Egyptians. Indeed, pharaonism, once a fascinating subject among Egyptian historians, has now become almost irrelevant to the Egyptian imaginary of their national past.[89] In light of the prolongation of the Cold War and the growing tension in the Middle East, highlighted by the incessant Arab-Israeli conflicts over the decades, more and more Muslim historians have turned their back on the Western model of modernization that had inspired their predecessors. Though distinctly secular, Nasser's advocacy of pan-Arabism expressed this new interest at the political level, whereas at the cultural level, despite Nasser's death, the sentiment of seeking Arab solidarity continued to grow and gave rise to the reevaluation and rejuvenation of Islam. Already during Nasser's years, Tariq al-Bishri, a leading figure of the Islamic school in contemporary Egyptian historiography, had developed doubts on the modernist, Western-oriented interpretation of Egyptian history, accepted by the earlier generations. From the 1970s, he came out to reject the accepted notion that Islam was an obstacle and antecedent to modernization. Instead, al-Bishri now considered Islam a cornerstone for the Egyptian national identity. In more recent years, this new interpretation of the Islamic heritage has gained tremendous currency. Outside the academic circle, it has been promoted by the effective work of such grassroots organizations as the Muslim Brotherhood. "Its [al-Bishri's] use of a familiar religious idiom," as one observer puts, "and invocation of cultural authenticity has guaranteed it a wide appeal among the Egyptian public."[90] Among the academics, the onset of postmodern critique of the master narrative in historical interpretation from the 1970s also provided incentives for Muslim scholars to rethink the Islamic tradition and its relation with modernity.[91]

Indeed, this Islamic revival, which became visible and vibrant since the 1980s, is seen not merely in Egypt but elsewhere in the Middle East.[92] Take the example of Lebanon; tensions among its myriad ethnic and religious groups have, over the many decades, hindered its historians in developing a coherent and convincing narrative of the country's history. The knotty issue seems to be that each ethic group, particularly the Christian Maronites and Muslim Arabs, differed markedly in their takes on Lebanese history. Buoyed by Arabism, for example, Muslim historians emphasized the Islamic influence and characteristics, whereas the Maronites were determined to foreground their ancestors' accomplishments during the fifteenth and eighteenth centuries; they also searched their community's remote past in the Phoenicians. The Maronites' intention and interest received criticism from Kamal S. Salibi (1929–2011), a Christian Lebanese historian trained first at American University of Beirut and later, in the 1950s, at the University of London, where he worked with Bernard Lewis, then an upcoming authority on Middle Eastern affairs.[93] Armed with his Western education, Salibi set out to write a national history in an objective manner for his country. Entitling one of his books *A House of Many Mansions*, he intended to accord due acknowledgment to each ethnic group's contribution to the evolution of Lebanese history, though his bias for the Maronites and his hope for Lebanon to retain its Christian characteristics remain discernible.[94] But since the 1980s, provided the notable change in the political landscape, marked by the steady filtering of Syrian and Palestinian influences, Salibi has altered his view and recognized the increasing importance of Arabism. "Only in an Arab world where the bond of Arabism remains significant," he states, "can a country like Lebanon retain its special importance."[95]

Thus, though Nasser died in 1970 and Egypt afterward moved (insofar as its top leadership is concerned) in a new direction of democratization more or less on the Western model, pan-Arabism has not died down. Instead, it, as well as Arabism, has expanded its influence across the Middle East. Moreover, it has found a new leadership in Ba'athism in Syria and Iraq. The Ba'ath party, a pan-Arab party founded in the 1940s, came to power in both countries in 1963. In Iraq, after the party regained its power in 1968, the government fell in the hands of Saddam Hussein (1937–2006), who formally assumed presidency in 1979. In order to pursue a leadership role in the Arab world, Hussein projected himself as an ardent believer in Arabism and Arab unity. Having persecuted the Kurds in his country, he also suppressed the Shi'ites and, in his invasion of Kuwait, laid claim to the latter's territory. Pan-Arabism, therefore, was a means that Saddam Hussein and the Ba'ath party employed to consolidate their power base and exercise political influence both at home and abroad. Aided by oil wealth, the Iraqi government offered financial support to the historical community, in order to suborn the historians to produce panegyrical accounts of the rise and contribution of the Ba'ath party and reveal the evils of the previous Hāshimite dynasty for its collaboration with the British. This practice was also extended to recreating Iraq's past in order to foreground the country's Arab characteristics and cultural identity. In particular, having invoked the writings of Abu 'Uthman 'Umar ibn Bahr al-Jahidh (776–869), a historical thinker from the heyday of the 'Abbasid Empire, the government-sponsored historians glorified the history of the Empire, which happened to have centered on Baghdad, as a most legitimate and unalloyed reign of the Muslim world, hoping to boost Arab and Iraqi identity. That is, by linking Iraq's history directly to the 'Abbasid, it bolstered Iraq's stature as a legitimate leader of the Arab world in modern times.[96]

By ruling the country with an iron hand, Saddam Hussein inculcated the Iraqis with the doctrines of Arabism as a form of nationalism through school education and news media. Samir al-Khalil's *Republic of Fear: Saddam's Iraq* (1989, 1990) has offered a portrayal of this practice. Indeed, Hussein not only gave directives to the project on rewriting Iraqi history for extending support to his rule, he was also personally involved in it. In 1979, a book entitled *On the Writing of History* (Hawla kitabat al-Tarikh) was published by the Ministry of Culture and Arts, which consists of four essays written by Hussein himself and the rest by scholars who expound his view. According to Saddam Hussein, history is written for a purpose, which is to serve the national development and social progress. Certain individuals are to be glorified but only to the extent that their feats would advance the interest of the society as a whole. At the present time, Hussein maintained, this interest was to strengthen Iraq's Arab heritage through pan-Arab nationalism but without invoking separatism and sectarianism. In other words, though the minorities – the Kurds and the Christians – were entitled to their cultural and religious traditions, they should recognize that Iraq as a country belonged unmistakably to the Arab world.[97] If Arabism is a way for Saddam Hussein to overcome the sectarianism and localism that had previously plagued the country, it has, however, not proven successful, for the effort to revive Islam, its main agendas, seems to have reinforced loyalties to a particular Shi'i, Sunni, and Kurdish tribe, a group, or even the family, rather than to the Iraqi state, though given their suppressed situation, the Kurds have received the least study.[98] Iraq's ethnic and religious heterogeneity, since the U.S. invasion of 2003, has continued to pose serious challenges to the U.S. endeavor to stabilize the country and establish democracy.

History and politics: The challenges of nationalist historiography

If the characteristics of contemporary Iraqi historiography reflect and extend the impacts of political and economic changes, this is not an isolated case. Rather, similar changes also occurred in the Arab Gulf, Libya, Algeria, and Iran. Like Iraq, these countries obtained independence either in a revolution or through the revival of a tribal royalty and, during the 1960s and in the 1970s, they all benefited from the booming oil industry in the Middle East. In their effort at state formation and nation-building, history writing has played an instrumental role that has coincided with its own transition from a traditional form of learning to an academic discipline. Two models seem to have emerged in the process. One takes place mainly in such countries as Libya and Algeria. Following the examples of Egypt and Iraq and the earlier ones in Syria, military officers waged coup d'états against the reigning regimes, which typically were puppet governments set up by the West. This type of revolution occurred in Sudan in 1958, Yemen in 1962, Algeria in 1965, and finally Libya in 1969. After obtaining power, whose base was enhanced financially by the oil fortune, the leaders all resorted to nationalism and initiated and sponsored historiographical projects to condemn the previous regimes for collaborating with the West. In so doing, the historians underlined the rupture in historical memory and recreated and invented a national past in which resistance movement to Western intrusion figured centrally. The other model, which occurs principally in such countries as Kuwait and Saudi Arabia that have not experienced a revolution, deemphasizes and eschews such a revolutionary rupture in national history. By stressing the compatibility of traditional tribal culture and modern culture, it traces the national past mainly in the continuation of the royal house. Interestingly, this kind of historiographical project, which often delves into a nonliterary and oral folklore tradition, is often motivated by the intention to prevent exactly the same revolutionary revolts that took place in the neighboring countries for their potential threat to its own regime.[99]

All the same, historical studies in these oil-producing countries began to become professionalized from the late 1960s on, and the process bore the nationalist characteristics as we saw elsewhere in the Middle East. Under the aegis of the government, national universities were established, and from their graduates emerged the first generation of academic historians who subsequently also received advanced training either in Egypt, Lebanon, or Euro-America. Take Libya as an example. The first nationalist attempt at history writing occurred in prerevolutionary days. In 1968, the Faculty of Arts of the University of Libya organized its first academic conference, from which a volume titled *Libya in History* resulted; most of its essays dealt with the country's remote past. After 1969, when Mu'ammar al-Qadhdhafi (1942–2011) overthrew the monarchy, more attention was accorded to modern Libyan history, especially the period of Italian occupation, in order to lionize the Libyan resistance to colonial rule. For that purpose, the government established the Center for the Study of the *Jihad* of the Libyans against the Italian Occupation in 1978, whose main task was to offer new interpretations of Libyan history from a nationalist, revolutionary perspective. It sponsored oral history and other source collection projects; the former consisted mainly of interviews with the participants in the resistance movement. Between 1978 and 1982, the Center registered over 4,000 hours of such interviews. All this was aimed to help define the history of Libya as "that of a cohesive, nationalist, anti-imperialist society, loyal to its Arab and Muslim culture, opposed to Western political and cultural domination, and actively participating in world history." Since historical study in Libya did not become an academic discipline until the late 1960s and most of its historians were trained outside the country, the development of contemporary Libyan historiography has registered the influence of such trends as social and cultural history in Western historiography. However, al-Qadhdhafi's autocratic rule of the country, which became increasingly apparent from the 1980s, also meant that academic freedom was quite limited, if it existed at all, in its historical community. Thus the majority of historical works appearing in recent years, despite their professional appearance, are either subservient to or apologetic for the government's political needs and ideals.[100]

Extreme as it may appear, Libya's case as an example of political intervention in historical study seems not to be a far cry from the general development of Middle Eastern historiography in contemporary times. In Turkey, where academic historiography took root earlier than it did in many of its neighbors, the government also exercises pressure on the historians with respect to their writing of Turkish history. And the source of such pressure can often be traced in its top leadership, beginning in the reign of Mustafa Kemal, the country's founder. As mentioned earlier, throughout the twentieth century, Turkey has continued the effort initiated by Kemal to turn it into a European nation. To this end, it launched more political reforms, though not without bumps and setbacks, aiming to establish a representative government and improve political transparency. Having joined NATO in 1963, it also adjusted its foreign policy by allying with the West, for which the country was "awarded" the associate membership status by the EU in the same year. However, since then, its application for becoming a formal EU member has been a frustrating experience.

Ever since Mustafa Kemal, the Turkish government has never ceased to make history readily available to expand its political pursuit. In 1988, Turgut Özal (1927–1993), then Turkey's prime minister and later its president (1989–1893), published a book on Turkish history. Entitled *La Turquie en Europe*, it expands on the Turkish Historical Thesis introduced by Mustafa Kemal in regard to early Turkish history and civilization. It outlines the evolution of Turkish history from the Neolithic era to the present, covering five major periods: (1) from the Neolithic through the Hellenistic age, (2) Roman times, (3) the Byzantine Empire, (4) the Seljuk and the Ottoman, (5) modern Turkey. By linking the modern Turkish people with the Hittites and by extolling the Hittites as the major power player in Central Asia, or Anatolia, the geographical origin of human civilization, Özal, whose work undoubtedly had received assistance from professional historians, emphasizes the intrinsic and historical connection between Anatolia and Europe. Through the Ionians, he connects Greek civilization with Anatolia, or Central Asia, and proceeds to deny the Greek origin of Western civilization and supplant it with the Turkish, or the Central Asian. He also extends his argument to a later period, contending that in the Roman period, the spread of Christianity had its first success in Anatolia. All in all, Özal wants the book to drive home the point that Turkey not only had a historical tie with the development of European history, but it also, as the book's title suggests, was de facto *the* origin of European civilization.[101]

At once a sermon to the European community about Turkish history and culture and a plea for its consideration for Turkey's EU membership, Turgut Özal's *La Turquie en Europe* has something worth noting: its discussion of Islam's role in Turkish history. In contrast to Mustafa Kemal's secularism, Özal does not want to belittle Islam. On the contrary, he praises its high cultural and scientific achievement, to which, he insists, the Turks contributed, and states that this achievement bred and benefited the intellectual growth of European culture.[102] Indeed, though Turkey today remains interested in the EU membership, it has witnessed the same level of Islamic revival as that in other Muslim countries. Though loyal to the Turkish Historical Thesis, as shown in the book's main argument, Özal in his presidency also openly identified himself with Muslim symbols and policies. Despite its secular claim, the government established an Office of Religious Affairs beginning in the 1980s and provided funding for Islamic schools, which had risen sharply in recent decades. In contrast to Kemal's decision to ban the fez and veil, now Turkish girls are permitted to wear head scarfs. After Özal's death in 1993, this movement of (re)Islamization has picked up even more steam, exerting influence in reorienting the country's foreign policy of recent years. Since the 1990s, Turkey has considered itself more a "bridge" between East and West, or Asia and Europe, than an "authentic" European nation as it used to claim.[103] All this has impacted the direction of Turkish historiography. Ottoman history, for example, has garnered more attention and is treated more positively than before. The Research Center for Islamic History, based in Istanbul, is currently publishing a multivolume work on Ottoman history.[104] Having affirmed their Muslim identity, more and more historians, both in Turkey and abroad, have also questioned the image presented by the Orientalists about the "decline" of the Ottoman Empire beginning in the eighteenth century, which has gained currency also in Western scholarship on Turkish history.[105] More significantly, this revival of interest in Islamic culture led historians, from the 1970s, to discover the value of Muslim court archives in various provinces. Mingling with the influence of the *Annales* School in advancing social and local history, the discovery and use of this whole wealth of archival sources have been instrumental in making the "social-history revolution" in contemporary Ottoman historiography that transcends and transforms the national history paradigm.[106]

In conclusion, the most recent and important change in contemporary Islamic historiography is related to the Islamic resurgence, though its origin can be traced back in the post–World War II years. During the late 1980s and the 1990s, this resurgence has gained considerable strength. As a result, "[I]n 1995 every country with a predominantly Muslim population . . . was more Islamic and Islamist culturally, socially, and politically than it was fifteen years earlier."[107] The rise of Islam has been both a cause and effect of the historiographical changes shown in this chapter. Many of these changes are closely associated with the postmodern and postcolonial critiques of the Western cultural hegemony (in which modern historiography is an essential part) that we have observed from the 1970s. Granted, these changes have not yet produced a school like the Subaltern School in modern Indian historiography that has had a worldwide influence. Nor has the Islamic revival, with its inherent ecumenism in Muslim solidarity or Arab unity as shown in pan-Arabism, eroded the dominance of national history writing that characterized the major changes in Islamic historiography throughout the twentieth century. In fact, puts one observer, "[D]espite their claim to be supranational, most Islamist movements have been shaped by national particularities."[108] Meanwhile, we must note that while dominant, national history in the Middle East has not been written uniformly in the narrative form, as seen in many other parts of the world. Rather, local and dynastic histories from the past, as shown in the case of Saudi Arabia, remain a viable form for Middle Eastern historians, helping pluralize one's identity in the region. Equally important is that new fields like women's history, new cultural history, history of everyday life, and so forth are also being continuously explored, which are generating more and more appeal to the reading public.[109] In sum, the historiographical changes in the Middle East have undoubtedly contributed to the transformation of our historical mind in today's world. After all, Michel Foucault and Jacques Derrida, two principal inspirations of postmodernism, had spent part of their lives in Tunisia and Algeria respectively.[110] Edward Said, a key campaigner of postcolonialism, also was from the region. Given the intensity of their fight against the colonial and imperialist legacy, Muslim historians tend to subject their work to ideological influence and political pressure, perhaps more so than did their counterparts in other parts of the world. In light of the fact that many governments in the region remain autocratic, this situation will probably continue and pose more serious challenges to these historians in the foreseeable future.

Between orthodoxy and new directions: Marxist historiography in the West

The period between 1945 and 1968 was marked both by the consolidation of Soviet power, as it extended its control over Eastern Europe, and by an increasing crisis within the Soviet system and particularly in the orthodox Marxist worldview. The death of Joseph Stalin in 1953 and Nikita Khrushchev's speech at the 20th Congress of the Communist Party of the USSR in 1956 introduced a painful but imperfect process of de-Stalinization. At the same time, a series of revolts in East Germany in 1953, in Poland in 1956, and most violently in Hungary that same year, and finally in Czechoslovakia in 1968, marked not only discontent but also called into question orthodox Marxist ideology.

In the Soviet Union as well as in the countries under her control, the writing of contemporary political history and to a large extent also that of the earlier modern period leading to the present was under tight control by the party and the state.[111] The official doctrine of historical and dialectical Marxism was maintained, but there was movement. Historians had greater freedom in the Soviet Union from schematic views of history when they dealt with earlier periods of history.[112] Historians of these periods were still expected to confirm to Marxist dogma, but some writers broke through these confines and made significant contributions to cultural history that received wide attention internationally. One of these was the philosopher and literary historian Mikhail Bakhtin (1895–1975), who in *Rabelais and His World* (1941) explored popular culture in the French Renaissance, focusing on carnivalesque and grotesque aspects. It is interesting that this and his important works on semiotics contained no Marxist elements. Nevertheless he was able to write, although for a period in the early 1930s he was sentenced to "internal exile" in Kazakhstan. A further striking example that non-Marxist history could be written in the Soviet Union was the work of Aaron I. Gurevich (1924–2006), who in 1967 published a book on medieval Norway in which he stressed the primary role of cultural factors in explaining feudalism. He was disciplined but nevertheless in 1972 was able to publish his *Categories of Medieval Culture*[113] that in its focus on structures and mentalities came close to the *Annales*, which in fact in the same year published one of his seminal articles.[114] His subsequent studies of the popular basis of medieval culture followed.[115]

Although this movement away from Marxist orthodoxy still played a limited role in Soviet historiography, it soon occupied a significant role in Poland and Hungary. The close ties that had existed between Polish social and economic historians and the *Annales* before the war were reestablished after the thaw of 1956, and in an atmosphere of increasing openness contacts became very close. The Sixth Section sponsored studies by Polish students and scholars. Several historians published extensively in the *Annales*, most noteworthy Witold Kula (1916–1988), Jerzy Topolski (1928–1998), and Andrzej Wyczański (1924–2008). Kula's *Economic Theory of the Feudal System* was translated almost immediately into French with an introduction by Braudel,[116] and the basic *Annales* writings were translated into Polish. And Kula like Braudel possessed a universal outlook. In *Measures and Men*[117] Kula explored the symbolic significance of weights and measures throughout Western history. Topolski in his English-language journal, *Poznan Studies in the Social Sciences and the Humanities*, sought to initiate a dialogue between Marxists and non-Marxists on questions of theory and methodology. In Hungary, social and economic historians including Istvan Berend (1930) and György Ránki (1930–1988) established close contacts with Western social scientists, particularly in the United States.

Even in East Germany, where scholarship was still very tightly controlled, things began to move, even if slightly later. In 1980 Jürgen Kuczynski (1904–1997), a leading East German economic historian and a committed Marxist, began to write a series of six volumes on the everyday life of the German people.[118] Influenced by the interest in "Every Day History" (*Alltagsgeschichte*) in West Germany and the *Annales*, he complained in the introduction to that book that Marxists have written history too often from the top without sufficient concern for the life experiences of the common people, for "what they ate, their clothing, their dwellings, what went on in their minds every day, how they worked, when they rested and slept, what it was like when they were sick, into what circles they married, how they moved from place to place."[119]

While in the East there was a gradual opening away from orthodox Marxism, in Western Europe, particularly in France, but interestingly enough also in Great Britain, there was a paradoxical development: on the one hand the realization that Communism as a political system had failed and that Marxism as a philosophy had lost its credibility, on the other hand the belief that Marxism raised important questions for the pursuit of social history. Marxism was thus seen no longer in terms of its philosophy of history but, as Dennis Dworkin observed, "as a guide to historical study rather than as a substitute for it. This Marxist tradition," he continued, "has had a major impact on the writing of history in the twentieth century and has become part of the mainstream of historical thought in the West."[120]

In France, the Marxist explanation of the French Revolution as a "bourgeois" revolution had become the orthodox doctrine since Georges Lefevre's studies in the 1920s and remained so until it was challenged in the 1960s by historians who questioned that the bourgeoisie was a capitalist class and suggested that the bourgeoisie and landed aristocracy were much more closely intertwined than the Marxist thesis assumed.[121] The class composition of the elite that carried out the revolution was in fact much more complex, and Marx's analysis of the class character of the French Revolution in essence anachronistic. A new note was introduced by historians of British origin such as George Rudé (1910–1993)[122] and Richard Cobb (1917–1996),[123] who moved away from the focus on anonymous mass movements to a careful analysis from police records of the individuals involved in events like the storming of the Bastille.

Yet the most innovative reconstitution came from a group of young historians in Great Britain in the Communist Party's Historians Group in the years immediately after World War II, including among others Maurice Dobb (1900–1976), Christopher Hill (1912–2003), George Rudé, Edward P. Thompson (1924–1993), Dorothy Thompson (1923–2011), and Eric Hobsbawm (1917–2012). In 1952 they founded, together with non-Marxist historians such as Lawrence Stone (1919–1999), *Past and Present*, to this day the leading British journal of social history. It is striking that like in the *Annales* the main focus was on the early or premodern period, in this case the transition from feudalism to capitalism.[124] One of the great values of the journal was that it offered a place where Marxists and non-Marxists could enter into dialogue. Turning to the modern world, Hobsbawm wrote a comprehensive multivolume history from what he described as the dual French and Industrial Revolutions to the collapse of the Soviet Union.[125]

The revelations of Stalin's crimes and the suppression of the Hungarian uprising in 1956 resulted in almost all of the British members of the Communist Party's History Group except Eric Hobsbawm leaving the party and in the dissolution of the History Group. Nevertheless, they all continued to adhere to a Marxist interpretation of history. Marxism, however, took on new forms. The most important turning point to a new Marxist approach to the study of history was undoubtedly Edward P. Thompson, *The Making of the English Working Class* (1963). Thompson's study was in the tradition of Marxist historiography in proceeding with a concept of class conflict and seeing the formation of class affected by the changing means of production, in this case the Industrial Revolution. At the same time, Thompson, like other Marxists now, stressed that the writings of Marx needed to be reinterpreted in a changing world. Most important, however, was that he viewed class in cultural terms. The English working class was not primarily a product of the Industrial Revolution but entered the Industrial Revolution with traditions rooted in culture and thus as active agents shaped the industrial world into which they entered; hence the choice of the term "making" in the title. Moreover, for him, the working class was not an abstract, as it was in Marx's and Engels' *The Communist Manifesto*, but consisted of Englishmen, who had to be understood in terms of English history, in what Thompson called the "Peculiarities of the English."[126]

This stress on culture and human agency deeply affected new left social history not only in Great Britain but also in the United States, as in Herbert Gutman's (1928–1985) *Work, Culture and Society in Industrializing America* (1977), an attempt to break through much of traditional labor history that stressed trade unionism and neglected the working people and their variegated subcultures. In the United States, two important studies of slavery followed in the orientation of a cultural Marxism, Herbert Gutman, *American Blacks in Slavery and in Freedom* (1977) and Eugene Genovese (1930–2012), *Roll, Jordan, Roll: The World the Slaves Made* (1972), the latter strongly influenced by Gramsci's notion of hegemony.

Very soon, the limits of Thompson's form of cultural Marxism were recognized. He had still worked with a notion of class that did not take sufficiently into account ethnic diversity and the very complex composition of the working classes, reflecting very different social strata. Thompson was also criticized for neglecting the role of women, so that his working class was primarily male.[127] However, the core of Thompson's Marxism remained intact, namely the centrality of social conflict, the critique of the capitalist society, and the commitment of historical studies to the struggle for a more just world. These ideas were going to inform new left social history in Great Britain and the United States, as well as in India, Latin America, and Sub-Saharan Africa, by historians who gradually ceased to identify themselves as Marxists.

The collapse of the Soviet Union and of the communist regimes in its Eastern European subject states carried with it the definite demise of Marxism-Leninism as a historical doctrine. It became increasingly evident that the Marxist model of historical development had become increasingly irrelevant in the contemporary world. But, as we have seen, Marxism-Leninism had long before lost its intellectual credibility, and Marxist theory in Western Europe had moved away from Marxist orthodoxy to stressing the role of culture and recognizing that the development of a postindustrial capitalism had created social realities that no longer corresponded to Marx's conception of industrial economies with its clearly delineated bourgeois and proletarian classes. Marxism, moreover, had lost its foundation in a revolutionary proletariat that no longer existed in the form Marx had conceived it. He had expected to see the successful proletarian revolution in his lifetime. Instead, he had to experience a series of defeats with the unsuccessful Chartist movement, as well as the defeat of the 1848 revolutions and of the Paris Commune. As Richard Ashcraft wrote in 1978 in a review of Perry Anderson's *Considerations of Western Marxism*, "one unbroken link in the tradition of Marxism is certainly the defeat of the revolutionary working class within capitalist countries."[128] In the economically less evenly developed societies with large preindustrial agrarian populations, the classical Marxist analysis of classes fitted even less. After 1990 Marxism as a revolutionary movement was restricted to unevenly developed areas of Latin America and India and to some extent Sub-Saharan Africa. Elsewhere, but also in Latin America and India, the advocates of Marxist social theories were largely intellectuals generally found at the universities; Marxism became one philosophical orientation among others. But while Marxist ideas continued to occupy a role in the historiography of non-Western countries, it did so more in its Gramscian than in its orthodox form. In the West, historians who had long identified themselves as Marxists such as Perry Anderson, the editor of the *New Left Review*, and Eric Hobsbawm in his most recent collection of essays, *How to Change the World: Reflections on Marx and Marxism* (2011), concluded that Marxism in the form in which they had once understood it had failed to understand the economic and political realities of the twentieth and even more so of the incipient twenty-first century. Capitalism now appeared firmly entrenched; the revolutionary transversal that Marx and Engels had expected in their lifetimes now seemed totally out of the question. Yet as Hobsbawm stressed and Anderson would agree, the capitalist market economy has no answer to the major problem confronting the twenty-first century, "high-tech economic growth in the pursuit of unsustainable profit" at the cost of an increasing gulf between the wealthy and the large sections of the population and the increasing destruction of the globe's natural resources. Marxism in its orthodox form is no longer tenable as an answer to capitalism. Much of what Marx wrote, Hobsbawm notes, "is out of date and some of it is not or no longer acceptable." But it continues to offer an important contribution to the critical analysis of the problematic character of present-day capitalism. Thus Hobsbawm concludes his book: "Once again the time has come to take Marx seriously."[129]

Notes

1 Nagahara Keiji, *20 seiki Nihon no rekishigaku (20th Century Japanese Historiography)* (Tokyo, 2005), 124–145; and Yoshiko Nozaki, *War Memory, Nationalism and History in Japan: Ienaga Saburo and the History Textbook Controversy, 1945–2005* (London, 2005).

2 Ishimoda Shō, *Chūseiteki sekai no keisei (Formation of the Medieval World)* (Tokyo, 1957). Cf. Thomas Keirstead, "Inventing Medieval Japan: The History and Politics of National Identity," *Medieval History Journal*, 1:1 (1998), 47–71.

3 Tōyama Shigeki, *Meiji ishin (Meiji Restoration)* (Tokyo, 1951) and Inoue Kiyoshi, *Nihon gendaishi (Modern History of Japan)* (Tokyo, 1951).

4 Ōtsuka Hisao, *Kindaika no rekishiteki kiten (The Starting Point of the History of Modernization)* (Tokyo, 1948) and *Max Weber on the Spirit of Capitalism*, tr. Kondō Masaomi (Tokyo, 1976); Maruyama Masao, *Studies in the Intellectual History of Tokugawa Japan*, tr. Mikiso Hane (Tokyo, 1974).

5 Araki Moriaki, *Nihon hōken shakai seiritsu shiron (Historical Discussions on the Formation of Japanese Feudal Society)* (Tokyo, 1984); also Nagahara, *20 seiki Nihon no rekishigaku*, 145–166, 178–180.

6 See Kokusai rekishi kaigi Nihon kokunai iinkai (CISH/The Japanese National Committee), ed., *Nihon ni okeru rekishigaku no hattatsu to genjō (The Development and Status of Historical Study in Japan)* (Tokyo, 1959); and Nagahara, *20 seiki Nihon no rekishigaku*, 193–195, 292. Kabayama Kōichi has written *Rekishika tachi no Yūtopiya he: kokusai rekishigaku kaigi no hyakunenn (Toward Historians' Utopia: Centennial Anniversary of the International Congress of Historical Sciences)* (Tokyo: Tosui Shobō, 2007), which examined the history of Japanese historians' relationship with the International Congress of Historical Sciences.

7 Q. Edward Wang, *Inventing China through History: The May Fourth Approach to Historiography* (Albany, 2001), 199–202; and Wang Qingjia, *Taiwan shixue 50 nian, 1950–2000 (Historical Writings in Taiwan over the Past 50 Years, 1950–2000)* (Taipei, 2002), 3–42.

8 See Guo Moruo, *Zhongguo gudai shehui yanjiu (A Study of Ancient Chinese Society)* (Beijing, 1989) and *Shang Zhou guwenzi leizuan (Ancient Inscriptions of the Shang and Zhou Periods)* (Beijing, 1991).

9 See Fan Wenlan, *Zhongguo tongshi jianbian (An Abbreviated General History of China)* (Beijing, 1956) and Q. Edward Wang, "Between Marxism and Nationalism: Chinese Historiography and the Soviet Influence, 1949–1963," *Journal of Contemporary China*, 9:23 (2000), 95–111. Cf. Albert Feuerwerker, ed., *History in Communist China* (Cambridge, MA, 1968) and Dorothea Martin, *The Making of a Sino-Marxist World View: Perceptions and Interpretations of World History in the People's Republic of China* (Armonk, 1990).

10 Ursula Richter, "Gu Jiegang: His Last Thirty Years," *China Quarterly*, 90 (June 1982), 286–295; Gu Chao, *Lijie zhongjiao zhibuhui: wode fuqin Gu Jiegang (Against All the Odds: My Father Gu Jiegang)* (Shanghai, 1997) and Wang Xuedian and Sun Yanjie, *Gu Jiegang he tade dizimen (Gu Jiegang and His Disciples)* (Ji'nan, 2000).

11 Lu Jiandong, *Chen Yinke de zuihou ershi nian (Chen Yinke's Last Twenty Years)* (Hong Kong, 1996).

12 Wang, "Between Marxism and Nationalism." Cf. Feuerwerker, *History in Communist China*.

13 Tom Fisher, "'The Play's the Thing': Wu Han and Hai Rui Revisited" in Jonathan Unger, ed., *Using the Past to Serve the Present* (Armonk, 1993), 9–45.

14 Nagahara, *20 seiki Nihon no rekishigaku*, 169–170.

15 Sebastian Conrad, "What Time Is Japan? Problems of Comparative (Intercultural) Historiography," *History and Theory*, 38:1 (1999), 67–83.

16 Nagahara, *20 seiki Nihon no rekishigaku*, 173–185. Takeuchi Yoshimi, *What Is Modernity? Writings of Takeuchi Yoshimi*, tr. Richard Calichman (New York, 2004).

17 Nagahara, *20 seiki Nihon no rekishigaku*, 199–202.

18 Kawakatsu Heita, *Bunmei no kaiyō shikan (An Oceanic Perspective on Civilization)* (Tokyo, 1997).

19 See, for example, Nakane Chie, *Japanese Society* (Berkeley, 1970).
20 Nozaki, *War Memory, Nationalism and History in Japan*; and Hayashi Fusao, *Dai Tōa sensō kōteiron* (*On Affirming the Great War in East Asia*) (Tokyo, 1970).
21 Patricia M. Pelley, *Postcolonial Vietnam: New Histories of the National Past* (Durham, 2002), passim.
22 Ibid., 32–34, 36–40.
23 Ibid., 62–63. Cf. Nguyên Thê Anh, "Historical Research in Vietnam: A Tentative Survey," *Journal of Southeast Asian Studies*, 26:1 (March 1995), 121–132.
24 Hyung Il Pai, *Constructing "Korean" Origins: A Critical Review of Archaeology, Historiography, and Racial Myth in Korean State-formation Theories* (Cambridge, MA, 2000), 268–270.
25 Ibid., 57–58.
26 Cf. Henry Em, "Historians and Historical Writing in Modern Korea," *Oxford History of Historical Writing*, vol. 5, 659–677.
27 Nagahara, *20 seiki Nihon no rekishigaku*, 247–257.
28 Ibid., 264–285; Nishio Kanji, *Kokumin no rekishi* (*History of the Nation*) (Tokyo, 1999); and Nozaki, *War Memory, Nationalism and History in Japan*.
29 Sebastian Conrad, "Japanese Historical Writing," *Oxford History of Historical Writing*, vol. 5, 638–658; quote on 649.
30 Amino Yoshihiko, *Nihon chūsei no hi nōgyōmin to tennō* (Tokyo, 1984).
31 Kawakatsu Heita, *Bunmei no kaiyō shikan* and *Bunkaryoku: Nihon no sokojikara* (*Cultural Power: Japan's Potentials*) (Tokyo, 2006). Also Hamashita Takeshi and Kawakatsu Heita, eds. *Ajia kōekiken to Nihon kōgyōka, 1500–1900* (*Asian Trade Sphere and Japan's Industrialization*) (Tokyo, 2001). Some of their works are available in English: A. J. H. Latham and Heita Kawakatsu, eds., *Japanese Industrialization and the Asian Economy* (London, 1994) and idem, eds., *Intra-Asian Trade and the World Market* (London, 2006).
32 Tsunoyama Sakae, *Cha no sekaishi: ryokucha no bunka to kōcha no shakai* (*Tea and World History: Green Tea's Culture and Black Tea's Society*) (Tokyo, 1980). For Tsunoyama's career as a critic of the modernist school and the rise of the Kyoto School in general, see his *Seikatsushi no hakken: firudo waku de miru sekai* (*The Discovery of Everyday History: The World Seen from the Fieldwork*) (Tokyo, 2001).
33 See, for example, Abe Kinya, *Sekengaku no shōtai* (*An Invitation to the Study of "civil society"*) (Tokyo, 2002) and *Nihonjin no rekishi ishiki: seken to iu shikaku kara* (*The Historical Consciousness of the Japanese: From the Perspective of "civil society"*) (Tokyo, 2004).
34 Nagahara, *20 seiki Nihon no rekishigaku*, 219–220.
35 Carol Gluck, "The People in History: Recent Trends in Japanese Historiography," *Journal of Asian Studies*, 38:1 (November 1978), 25–50; Nagahara Keiji, "Reflections on Recent Trends in Japanese Historiography," tr. Kozo Tamamura, *Journal of Japanese Studies*, 10:1 (Winter 1984), 167–183; and Minshūshi Kenkyūkai, ed. *Minshūshi o kangaeru (Reflections on People's History)* (Tokyo: Azekura Shobō, 1988).
36 Hirota Masaki, "Pandora no hako: minshū shisōshi kenkyū no kadai (Pandora's Box: Issues in the Study of the History of Public Mentality)," Sakai Naoki, ed., *Nashonaru Hisutori o manabi suteru (Unlearning National History)* (Tokyo, 2006), 3–92.
37 Kano Masanao and Horiba Kiyoko, *Takamure Itsue* (Tokyo, 1977).
38 Cf. Hiroko Tomida, "The Evolution of Japanese Women's Historiography," *Japan Forum*, 8:2 (1996), 189–203 and Curtis Anderson Gayle, *Women's History and Local Community in Postwar Japan* (London, 2010).
39 Nagahara, *20 seiki Nihon no rekishigaku*, 232–235, 243–246.

40 Q. Edward Wang, "Encountering the World: China and Its Other(s) in Historical Narratives, 1949–89," *Journal of World History*, 14:3 (September 2003), 327–358.

41 Ibid.; also Jing Wang, *High Culture Fever: Politics, Aesthetics, and Ideology in Deng's China* (Berkeley, 1996).

42 Luo Rongqu's series of studies of the modernization theory are emblematic. See his *Zhongguo xiandaihua licheng de tansuo* (*An Exploration of the Chinese Search for Modernization*) (Beijing, 1992); *Xiandaihua xinlun* (*New Discussions on Modernization*) (Beijing, 1993); and *Xiandaihua xinlun xupian* (*New Discussions on Modernization: A Sequel*) (Beijing, 1997).

43 Wang, "Encountering the World," and Xiaomei Chen, *Occidentalism: A Theory of Counter-discourse in Post-Mao China* (New York, 1995).

44 Cf. Qu Lindong, "Historical Studies in China: the Legacy of the Twentieth Century and Prospects for the Twenty-first Century," *Chinese Studies in History*, 38:3–4 (Spring and Summer 2005), 88–113; Wang Xuedian, "Jin wushinian de Zhongguo lishixue (Chinese Historiography of the Past 50 Years)," *Lishi yanjiu (Historical Research)*, 1 (2004), 165–190; and Hou Yunhao, "20 shiji Zhongguo de sici shizheng shixue sichao (Four Schools of Positive/empirical Historiography in 20th Century China)," *Shixue yuekan (History Monthly)*, 7 (2004), 70–80.

45 Yang Nianqun, Huang Xingtao, and Mao Dan, eds., *Xin shixue: duo xueke duihua de tujing (New Historiography: The Prospect of Interdisciplinary Dialogue)* (Beijing, 2003); Sun Jiang, ed. *Xin shehuishi: shijian, jiyi, xushu (New Social History: Events, Memories and Narration)* (Hangzhou, 2004); Huang Donglan, ed. *Xin shehuishi: shenti, xinxing, quanli (New Social History: Body, Mentality and Power)* (Hangzhou, 2005), and Wang Di, ed. *Xin shehuishi: shijian, kongjian, shuxie (New Social History: Time, Space and Historical Writing)* (Hangzhou, 2006). Cf. Q. Edward Wang, "Historical Writings in Twentieth-century China: Methodological Innovation and Ideological Influence" in Rolf Torstendahl, ed., *An Assessment of Twentieth-century Historiography* (Stockholm, 2000), 43–69, especially 62–66, and Huaiyin Li, *Reinventing Modern China: Imagination and Authenticity in Chinese Historical Writing* (Honolulu, 2013).

46 Edward Vickers and Alisa Jones, eds., *History Education and National Identity in East Asia* (New York, 2005) and Laura Hein and Mark Selden, eds., *Censoring History: Citizenship and Memory in Japan, Germany, and the United States* (Armonk, 2000).

47 See "*Qingshi* (Qing History): Why a New Dynastic History," special issue in *Chinese Studies in History*, 43:2 (2009/10), and Masayuki Sato, "The Two Historiographical Cultures in Twentieth-century Japan" in Torstendahl, *Assessment of Twentieth-century Historiography*, 33–42.

48 R. Stephen Humphreys, "The Historiography of the Modern Middle East: Transforming a Field of Study" in Israel Gershoni, Amy Singer, and Y. Hakan Erdem, eds., *Middle East Historiographies: Narrating the Twentieth Century* (Seattle, 2006), 27.

49 Nancy Elizabeth Gallagher, ed., *Approaches to the History of the Middle East: Interviews with Leading Middle East Historians* (Reading, 1994), 155.

50 Ibid., 19–66, 91–108. For more examples of the postwar generation of Middle Eastern scholars, see Thomas Naff, ed., *Paths to the Middle East: Ten Scholars Look Back* (Albany, 1993).

51 Jörg Matthias Determann, *Historiography in Saudi Arabia: Globalization and the State in the Middle East* (London, 2014), 39–50. Also Youssef M. Choueiri, "Arab Historical Writing," *Oxford History of Historical Writing*, 5, 496–514.

52 Humphreys, "The Historiography of the Modern Middle East," 19–27.

53 Cf. Rashid Khalidi, "Arab Nationalism: Historical Problems in the Literature," *American Historical Review*, 95:5 (December 1991), 1363–1373.

54 Youssef M. Choueiri, *Arab Nationalism – A History: Nation and State in the Arab World* (Oxford, 2000), 101–102.

55 Cf. Yvonne Yazbeck Haddad, *Contemporary Islam and the Challenge of History* (Albany, 1982); Assem Dessouki, "Social and Political Dimensions of the Historiography of the Arab Gulf" in Eric Davis and Nicolas Gavrielides, eds., *Statecraft in the Middle East: Oil, Historical Memory, and Popular Culture* (Miami, 1991), 92–115.

56 Anthony Gorman, *Historians, State and Politics in Twentieth-century Egypt: Contesting the Nation* (London, 2003), 62; Shimon Shamir, "Self-view in Modern Egyptian Historiography" in Shimon Shamir, ed., *Self-views in Historical Perspective in Egypt and Israel* (Tel Aviv, 1981), 37–50.

57 Bernard Lewis, "History Writing and National Revival in Turkey" in his *From Babel to Dragomans: Interpreting the Middle East* (London, 2004), 428; Meltem Ahiska, "Occidentalism: The Historical Fantasy of the Modern," *The South Atlantic Quarterly*, 102:2/3 (2003), 351–379; and Geoffrey Barraclough, *Main Trends in History* (New York, 1979), 129.

58 Farzin Vahdat, *God and Juggernaut: Iran's Intellectual Encounter with Modernity* (Syracuse, 2002), 129–211. It offers a discussion of the intellectual foundation of the revolution.

59 Cf. Samuel Huntington, *The Clash of Civilizations and the Remaking of World Order* (New York, 1996).

60 Gorman, *Historians, State and Politics in Twentieth Century Egypt*, 79–111.

61 Gershoni, Singer, and Erdem, *Middle East Historiographies*, 3–18.

62 See Nancy Elizabeth Gallagher's introduction to her edited volume, *Approaches to the History of the Middle East*, 1–8.

63 Gallagher, *Approaches to the History of the Middle East*, 36; Albert Hourani, "How Should We Write the History of the Middle East?" *International Journal of Middle East Studies*, 23:2 (May 1991), 125–136.

64 Gallagher, *Approaches to the History of the Middle East*, 163; Halil Inalcik, "Village, Peasant, and Empire" in Halil Inalcik, ed., *The Middle East and the Balkans under the Ottoman Empire* (Bloomington, 1992), 137–160; also Supraiya Faroqhi, *Approaching Ottoman History: An Introduction to the Sources* (Cambridge, 1999), 187.

65 Israel Gershoni, Hakan Erdem, and Ursula Woköck, eds., *Histories of the Modern Middle East: New Directions* (Boulder, 2002), 2–3, and Gershoni, Singer, and Erdem, *Middle East Historiographies*, passim.

66 See Judith E. Tucker, "Problems in the Historiography of Women in the Middle East: The Case of Nineteenth-century Egypt," *International Journal of Middle Eastern Studies*, 15:3 (August, 1983), 321–336; Julia Clancy-Smith, "Twentieth-Century Historians and Historiography of the Middle East: Women, Gender, and Empire," Gershoni, Singer, and Erdem, *Middle East Historiographies*, 70–100.

67 Cf. Youssef M. Choueiri, *Modern Arab Historiography: Historical Discourse and the Nation-state* (London, 2003), 191.

68 Hisham Sharabi, ed., *Theory, Politics, and the Arab World: Critical Responses* (London, 1990), 21.

69 Gallagher, *Approaches to the History of the Middle East*, passim. For an extensive discussion on Said's work, its impact, and the critical responses and reviews of it by experts of the Middle East, see Zachary Lockman, *Contending Visions of the Middle East: The History and Politics of Orientalism* (Cambridge/New York, 2004). Also, Bryan S. Turner, *Orientalism, Postmodernism and Globalism* (London, 1994).

70 See, for example, Mohamad Tavakoli-Targhi, *Refashioning Iran: Orientalism, Occidentalism and Historiography* (Houndmills, 2001); K. E. Fleming, "Orientalism, the Balkans, and Balkan Historiography," *American Historical Review*, 105:4 (October 2000), 1218–1233; Carter Vaughn Findley, "An Ottoman

Occidentalist in Europe: Ahmed Midhat Meets Madame Gulnar, 1889," *American Historical Review*, 103:1 (February 1998), 15–49; Ahiska, "Occidentalism"; and in areas outside the Middle East, Stefan Tanaka, *Japan's Orient: Rendering Pasts into History* (Berkeley, 1993); Chen, *Occidentalism*; and Arif Dirlik, "Chinese History and the Question of Orientalism," *History and Theory*, 35:4 (December 1996), 96–118.

71 Clancy-Smith, "Twentieth-Century Historians and Historiography of the Middle East," 76.

72 Gershoni, Singer and Erdem, *Middle East Historiographies*, 7.

73 A detailed discussion of Shafiq Ghurbāl's view of Muhammad 'Alī is in Choueiri, *Modern Arab Historiography*, 77–114.

74 Choueiri, *Arab Nationalism*, 41–48.

75 Jack Crabbs, Jr., "Politics, History, and Culture in Nasser's Egypt," *International Journal of Middle East Studies*, 6:4 (October 1975), 403–404.

76 Gorman, *Historians, State and Politics in Twentieth Century Egypt*, 30–32.

77 Ibid., 32–34.

78 Thomas Mayer, *The Changing Past: Egyptian Historiography of the Urabi Revolt, 1882–1983* (Gainesville, 1988), 45–46.

79 Ibid., 73. Albert Hourani of Oxford, for example, recalled that he was denied access to the material. Gallagher, *Approaches to the History of the Middle East*, 29.

80 Gorman, *Historians, State and Politics in Twentieth Century Egypt*, 57–58, 74–78; Crabbs, "Politics, History, and Culture in Nasser's Egypt," 393–395; Mayer, *Changing Past*, 43–47.

81 Crabbs, "Politics, History, and Culture in Nasser's Egypt," 396–399.

82 Gorman, *Historians, State and Politics in Twentieth Century Egypt*, 33.

83 Mayer, *Changing the Past*, 59.

84 Gorman, *Historians, State and Politics in Twentieth Century Egypt*, 34–41.

85 Ibid., 94–96.

86 Choueiri, *Modern Arab Historiography*, 174–196.

87 Marion Farouk-Sluglett and Peter Sluglett, "The Historiography of Modern Iraq," *The American Historical Review*, 96:5 (December 1991), 1409–1410.

88 See Ervand Abrahamian, "Marxism and Middle Eastern History" in Edward Wang and Georg Iggers, eds., *Marxist Historiographies: A Global Perspective* (London, 2015), 219–228.

89 Israel Gershoni, "New Pasts for New National Images: The Perception of History in Modern Egyptian Thought," in Shimon Shamir, *Self-views in Historical Perspective in Egypt and Israel*, 51–58.

90 Gorman, *Historians, State and Politics in Twentieth Century Egypt*, 102–104.

91 See Inge Boer, Annelies Moors, and Toine van Teeffelen, eds., *Changing Stories: Postmodernism and the Arab-Islamic World* (Amsterdam, 1995). Also, Turner, *Orientalism, Postmodernism and Globalism*.

92 Cf. Haddad, *Contemporary Islam*. It offers both excerpts and an analysis of Muslim thinkers and historians across the region with regard to their positions and discussions on the relevance of Islam in modern times.

93 K. S. Salibi, "The Traditional Historiography of the Maronites" in Lewis and Holt, *Historians of the Middle East*, 225. This article is a part of the doctoral thesis Salibi completed at the University of London in 1953.

94 Cf. Kamal Salibi, *A House of Many Mansions: The History of Lebanon Reconsidered* (Berkeley, 1988).

95 Choueiri, *Modern Arab Historiography*, 125–167; citation on 166.

96 Dessouki, "Social and Political Dimensions of the Historiography of the Arab Gulf"; Eric Davis and Nicolas Gavrielides, "Statecraft, Historical Memory, and Popular Culture in Iraq and Kuwait" in Davis and Gavrielides, *Statecraft in the Middle East*, 94–95, 116–148.

97   Ibid., 138–140.

98   Cf. Farouk-Sluglett and Sluglett, "Historiography of Modern Iraq."

99   Dessouki, "Social and Political Dimensions of the Historiography of the Arab Gulf"; Davis and Gavrielides, "Statecraft, Historical Memory, and Popular Culture in Iraq and Kuwait," Davis and Gavrielides, *Statecraft in the Middle East*, 92–99, 140–145.

100 Cf. Lisa Anderson, "Legitimacy, Identity, and the Writing of History in Libya," ibid., 71–91, citation on 87.

101 Speros Vryonis, Jr., *The Turkish State and History: Clio Meets the Grey Wolf* (Thessaloniki, 1991), 11–66.

102 Ibid., 45.

103 Huntington, *The Clash of Civilizations and the Remaking of the World Order*, 144–149.

104 Faroqhi, *Approaching Ottoman History*, 197. Also, Riffat Ali Abou-el-Haj, "The Social Uses of the Past: Recent Arab Historiography of Ottoman Rule," *International Journal of Middle East Studies*, 14:2 (May 1982), 185–201; Barraclough, *Main Trends in History*, 129–130.

105 See Rifa'at 'Ali Abou-El-Haj's *Formation of the Modern State: The Ottoman Empire, Sixteenth to Eighteenth Centuries* (Albany, 1991). Also, Jane Hathaway, "Rewriting Eighteenth-Century Ottoman History," *Mediterranean Historical Review*, 19:1 (June 2004), 29–53.

106 Hathaway, "Rewriting Eighteenth-Century Ottoman History." Also, Enid Hill, ed., *New Frontiers in the Social History of the Middle East* (Cairo, 2001).

107 Huntington, *Clash of Civilizations*, 111.

108 Olivier Roy, *Globalized Islam: The Search for a New Ummah* (New York, 2004), 62.

109 Determann, *Historiography in Saudi Arabia* and Clancy-Smith, "Twentieth-Century Historians and Historiography of the Middle East," 86–87.

110 See Robert C. Young, ed., *Postcolonialism: An Historical Introduction* (Malden, 2001), 395–426.

111 Denis Kozlov, "Athens and Apocalypse: Writing History in Soviet Russia" in Schneider and Woolf, *Oxford History of Historical Writing*, vol. 5 (Oxford, 2011), 374–398.

112 Yuri Bessmertny, "August 1991 as Seen by a Moscow Historian, or the Fate of Medieval Studies in the Soviet Era," *American Historical Review*, 97:2 (June 1992), 803–816.

113 English: (London, 1985).

114 "Représentations et attitudes à l'égard de la propriété pendant le Haut Moyen Age," *Annales. E.S.C.*, 27 (1972), 523–548, and later his study on the birth of the individual in Medieval Europe; already earlier he had published "Wealth and Gift Bestowal among the Ancient Scandinavians," *Scandinavica*, 7:2 (1968), 126–138.

115 English: *Medieval Popular Culture: Problems of Belief and Perception* (New York, 1988); *Historical Anthropology of the Middle Ages* (Chicago, 1992); *The Origins of European Individualism* (Oxford, 1995).

116 *Théorie économique du système fédodal, pour un modèle polonaise, 16e–18e siècle;* preface by Fernand Braudel (Paris, 1970); English: Witold Kula, *Economic Theory of the Feudal System* (London, 1976).

117 Witold Kula, *Miary y Ludzie* (Warsaw, 1970).

118 Jürgen Kuczynski, *Geschichte des Alltags des Deutschen Volkes (1600–1945),* 6 vols. (East Berlin, 1980–1982). On new cultural history in East Germany in the 1980s, see Georg G. Iggers, *Marxist Historiography in Transformation* (Providence, 1991).

119 Ibid., 38.

120 Dennis Dworkin, "Marxism and Historiography" in D. R. Woolf, ed., *A Global Encyclopedia of Historical Writing* (New York, 1998), 599; cf. Dennis Dworkin, *Cultural Marxism in Postwar Britain* (London, 1997).

121 See Alfred Cobban, *The Social Interpretation of the French Revolution* (New York, 1964).

122 George Rudé, *Paris and London in the Eighteenth Century: Studies in Popular Protest* (London, 1970); *The Crowd in the French Revolution* (Oxford, 1959); with Eric Hobsbawm, *Captain Swing* (London, 1993).

123 Richard Cobb, *The Police and the People: French Popular Protest 1789–1820* (Oxford, 1970).

124 See Maurice Dobb, *Studies in the Development of Capitalism* (London, 1946).

125 Eric Hobsbawm, *The Age of Revolution, 1789–1848* (Cleveland, 1962); *The Age of Capital* (London, 1975); *The Age of Empire, 1875–1914* (New York, 1987); *The Age of Extremes: A History of the World 1914–1991* (New York, 1994).

126 E. P. Thompson, "Peculiarities of the English" in his *The Poverty of Theory and Other Essays* (London, 1978).

127 Joan Wallach Scott, "Women in *The Making of the English Working Class*" in her *Gender and the Politics of History* (New York, 1988), 68–90.

128 Richard Ashcraft, review of Perry Anderson, *Considerations of Western Marxism* in *Political Theory*, 6:1 (February 1978), 136.

129 Eric Hobsbawm, *How to Change the World: Reflections on Marx and Marxism* (New Haven, 2011), 12; 418–419. For a survey of the Marxist legacy in modern and contemporary historiography from a comparative perspective, see *Marxist Historiographies: A Global Perspective*.

8 Historiography in the early twenty-first century
A critical retrospect

The globalization of the world

Just as the political currents of the 1960s deeply influenced historical thought and writing worldwide, so the changed political constellation of the 1990s after the dissolution of the Soviet empire between 1989 and 1991 and the end of the Cold War presented historians with new challenges. The universal peace that the American political scientist Francis Fukuyama proclaimed in his essay, "The End of History?"[1] in which he predicted a worldwide, even if gradual, acceptance of American-style free enterprise and democratic institutions after the collapse of Soviet communism, did not materialize in the way he had foreseen. In fact, the years since 1989 have been marked on the international level by new forms of belligerent confrontation, not between states as in the Cold War, but with enemies, particularly in the Middle East, Afghanistan, the Balkans, and Africa, without clearly definable borders and involving various forms of terrorism. Samuel Huntington (1927–2008), in *The Clash of Civilizations*,[2] had written of an irreconcilable conflict between Islamic and Western – and incidentally also East Asian culture – but operated with very simplistic notions of a timeless Islam as a unified culture, overlooking the divisions in the Islamic world, its history, the effects of modernization, the role of economic factors, and finally the interrelation between Islamic societies and the modern West.

On one level, Fukuyama's prediction seemed to be at least partly correct: the extension of Western-style capitalism to large areas of the world as part of a process of globalization that had begun before 1989 and that forms the core of what has been described as the process of globalization. But with few exceptions, such as Taiwan and South Korea, globalization has not led to democratization. This process involved not only the worldwide transformation of the economy, intensified by the new information technology, but was accompanied by the increasing homogenization in everyday life, consumer behavior, patterns of urbanization, metropolitan architecture, popular culture in film and music, and the relation of the sexes and of the generations. Nevertheless, globalization took on different heterogeneous forms on the social and cultural levels, reflecting local circumstances and heritage. And these generated resistance against the effects of globalization on traditional ways of life that often involved violence. It is worth noting that in recent years, Fukuyama himself has also modified his earlier sanguine prediction of the worldwide historical development.[3]

The debate on globalization is in many ways reminiscent of the previous arguments concerning dependency and modernization. It is indisputable that the global culture of today originated with the structures of political and financial power situated for the most part in the West, but also in Japan, and that, despite their global dissemination, the forces of globalization, in terms of institutional organizations and power, are still centered in the developed world, which today includes China. A related question is whether the history of globalization, like that formerly of modernization, can be regarded as a new "master narrative." Like earlier in the debate on modernization, which we have followed in Chapter 6, analysts of globalization were divided between those who saw it positively and those who stressed its destructive sides. The former point to the benefits of greater access to technology, information, services, and markets, the positive outcomes of increasing productivity, the rise in global per capita incomes, and the like; the latter emphasize the increasing social and economic gulf within the Western societies, the dismantling of the welfare state, and particularly the failure to diminish poverty in large sections of Africa, Asia, and Latin America. Globalization has received tremendous attention in the popular media, although the scholarly literature on the subject is also large.[4] For many social scientists, it has become the most significant interpretative key for our time. All this calls for a historiography that can deal with the conditions in which we live today, which in many ways are different from those in the pre-1989 period.

More than in the period before 1990 but beginning already then, an international scholarly community came into existence, as non-Western scholars, foremost among them Indian, Middle Eastern, Latin American but also increasingly historians from Sub-Saharan Africa, occupy important academic positions at North American, British, and Australian universities. It is an important fact that the language of international communication is increasingly English. Scholars in the non-Western world have now increased input into these discussions, and, as we have already seen, the Indian *Subaltern Studies* offered direct impulses to Western and Latin American thought. In Middle Eastern studies, English has also become the paramount language among both Western scholars and scholars of Middle Eastern origins, eclipsing the once viable choices of French and German.[5] In return, Western, particularly North American and British, scholars cooperate closely, as to an extent they already did before 1990, with scholars in Latin America, Africa, and East Asia, so that studies in many fields have been increasingly internationalized. An active exchange across continental lines takes place at the International Congress of Historical Sciences that meets every five years (its 2015 meeting was held in Jinan, China, which was the first time for such gathering to take place outside Euro-America), as well as at other conferences. There are also regional collaborations among historians. In recent years, while the writing and revision of history text-books in Japan often precipitated protests and criticisms in its neighbors such as China and South Korea, efforts have also been made by the historians in these countries to work together in seeking a consensus and solving the controversies regarding the region's modern history. At times their effort also received government support, such as the bilateral and multiyear Joint History Research Project conducted between historians of China and Japan, as well as that between South Korea and Japan during 2000 and 2010. These collaborations have produced a level of consensus among the historians regarding their countries' entangled history. Yet it remains to be seen whether and to what level these scholarly agreements would also influence policy making and improve relationships among the nations in the region.[6]

There are still very definite limits to international exchanges. That English has become almost a sole international language is one of them, in spite of its apparent benefit. As a result, English language literature is widely read in the original or in translation across the world. Many of the important works in history or related social science and humanistic disciplines are translated from English into non-Western languages, as are important French and German books and articles. But very few Chinese, Japanese, Korean, Farsi, Turkish, or Arabic writings have been translated into English,[7] with the result that international communication is still dominated by Anglo-America, with little awareness of the theoretical discussions outside the West, with the exception of Anglophone scholarship in India. Yet much more than in social science disciplines, history continues to be written in national languages for national audiences. In recent years, the international communication among historians across the world has been facilitated considerably by the advance of computer technology, digitalization, and wide use of the Internet.

The reorientation of historical studies

Now to the main developments in historiography that address the changed conditions: In the period after 1990, after the end of the Cold War, we can identify several major trends or foci in historical writings across the world: (1) the divergent development between theory and practice, (2) new interest in oral history and the history of memory, (3) expansions of feminist and gender history around the world, (4) redefining the alliance between history and the social/natural sciences, (5) the transformation of the concept of the nation and the significance of global history, (6) the growing importance of environmental history, and (7) the examination of the role of emotions in history. However, while these are main trends of change in the ways history is written today, there is no dominating paradigm like the Rankean one in the nineteenth century but rather a considerable diversity and overlapping.

Thus the history of women and gender is unthinkable if emotions are not considered; nor can global history neglect the roles of environment and biology.

The divergence of theory and practice

The postmodernist challenge of modern historiography in the 1990s marked the rise of an epistemological relativism in historical circles around the world. In its extreme form, such relativism denies that there is a social reality and argues instead that all supposedly scientific explanations of social life were simply "exercises in collective fictionalization or mythmaking."[8] As we covered extensively in Chapter 6, critiques of modern Western historiography, which were inspired not only by postmodernism but also by postcolonialism and feminism, have encouraged historians to seek alternatives to the Rankean model of politico-diplomatic history centering on nation-states and to experiment with new approaches to history writing. Yet among working historians, few seem to have fully embraced the position of postmodernism, and, since the dawn of the twenty-first century, their interest in the postmodern critique of historiography has also apparently declined. Meanwhile, many have continued to explore new ways to study and write history for the rapidly changing and expanding world. The transformation that culturalism has undergone since its beginnings in the 1970s until today is an example, which helps demonstrate the successive assessments of the state of historiography. The cultural turn exerted a great influence on much historical writing in the half century from the late 1960s to the present, with historians expanding the scope of history, placing politics and society into a cultural context, recognizing the role of discourse and language in history without succumbing to the linguistic turn's denial of past reality and its reduction of history to pure literature, In 1989, Lynn Hunt edited *The New Cultural History*, which was followed by *Beyond the Cultural Turn* co-edited by her and Victoria Bonnell in 1999 and more recently her own *Writing History in a Global Era* in 2014. While the cultural and the linguistic turn occupied a dominant role in historical thought in the first of these three collections, she opens her work of 2014, 25 years later, with the observation that they have lost their vitality in a global era, as had the approaches of the *Annales*, Marxism, and American social science, which had been repudiated by the cultural and linguistic turns, thus "creating uncertainty how history will be written in the future."[9]

At this point it may be useful for us to distinguish between the role that the cultural and linguistic turns occupied in historical theory from that in historical writing. The theorists whose works philosophized about how history is written, such as Hayden White and Frank Ankersmit, as well as Roland Barthes and Jacques Derrida, did not write history, while the bulk of historians operated with theoretical assumptions without spelling them out. Over the past few decades, White and Ankersmit, two living theorists, have remained productive. In 1999, White published *Figural Realism*, which was followed by *The Practical Past* in 2014; both are collections of White's essays in recent years. In the former, he continues to compare history with literature and argues that figurative language used most in the latter can also refer to reality quite as faithfully as do other modes of discourse. Borrowing the idea from Michael Oakeshott (1901–1990), White in his latest book discusses the differences between the "practical past" and the "historical past." While most historians are eager to reconstruct the "historical past," he opines, they often fall short in demonstrating its function to society, for their method of delivery of historical knowledge is quaint and dull. He instead advocates the exploration of new methods in narrating and representing the past, or the "practical past," in order to revive history's relevance to the present. In a similar vein, Ankersmit of late has explored new ways to examine history's relation with reality. Instead of dwelling on the idea of how narrative history tends to misrepresent historical reality, he proposes in his *Sublime Historical Experience* (2005) that one should turn attention to "experience," or how the past is experienced by the people, instead of being narrated to them by the historian. As such, Ankersmit hopes to exercise an "intellectual empiricism," which operates on methodological as well as on aesthetic levels. Insofar as historical experience is concerned, one is related to the past through such binary categories as "loss" and "love," "discovery" and "recovery," and "pain" and pleasure." To him these types of experience accurately describe the stages by which one approaches the past from the present and renews and revives the tie between the two. More important, Ankersmit argues that such experience is precognitive as it precedes historical knowledge. As such, he sees the need for the historian to describe and analyze historical change not only on the rational but also on the emotional levels.[10]

Ankersmit's emphasis on "experience" (which is also discussed by others like Joan Scott, William Sewell, Jr., and Gareth Stedman Jones) is somewhat reflected in the study of emotions by historians of recent years, which we will cover below. After his retirement from University of California/Santa Cruz, Hayden White was invited to teach at Stanford University as a chair professor in the Department of Comparative Literature. This appointment suggests that while widely noted by historians for his *Metahistory*, White's influence remains outside the historical profession. Yet in the field of historical theory and philosophy of history, White and Ankersmit are commonly regarded as leading scholars as of today. While compiling for Routledge the *Fifty Key Thinkers of History* (2000), Marnie Hughes-Warrington, an Australian historian, acknowledges that "White's writings are historiographically provocative," even though "literary theorists seem to have shown more interest in White's works."[11] Both White and Ankersmit have become subjects of several studies by young as well as senior historians. In his *Hayden White: The Historical Imagination* (2011), Herman Paul, a Dutch historical theorist, offers an overview of White's career and influence, whereas Peter Icke in his *Frank Ankersmit's Lost Historical Cause* (2012) scathingly criticizes Ankersmit's turn to experience. To Icke, who studied with Keith Jenkins, an avowed postmodernist, Ankersmit's recent study marked a "retreat" from his earlier advocacy of postmodernism. Ernst Breisach, author of the widely adopted *Historiography: Ancient, Medieval and Modern* (1983), also offers his evaluation in his *On the Future of History: The Postmodernist Challenge and Its Aftermath* (2003). Breisach states that "postmodernism has proved to be neither a fad nor a product of an overheated intellectual fashion industry" and that "the extremity of postmodernist views made them falter but in the process they became useful by what they have pointed out."[12] Peter Burke, an acclaimed cultural historian, too, sees the impact of White's *Metahistory* 40 years after its appearance. "White's critiques of positivist historians and their illusions of objectivity, science and realism," observes Burke, "however shocking they may have seemed to the more conservative members of the profession 40 years ago, is now, I think, widely accepted."[13]

From the 1990s, Keith Jenkins and Alun Munslow, two English historians, have been rather prolific in promoting the postmodern critique of modern historiography. Not only have they edited such anthologies as *The Postmodern History Reader* (1997) and *The Nature of History Reader* (2004), but they have also authored several textbooks on related topics targeted at college students. Jenkins' *Rethinking History* (1991), for example, has run through a few printings, been translated into several languages, and been adopted by some schools in the West and beyond.[14] *Rethinking History*, the same-named journal launched by Munslow and Robert A. Rosenstone, an American historian, in 1997, has frequently featured novel approaches to historiography. Rosenstone is an exponent for the need to represent history through visual media, and, since 1989, he has worked with the *American Historical Review* to organize its regular forum on reviewing historical films.

Without question, most historians today remain committed to the pursuit of factual history and believe that there is an essential distinction between history and literature. Yet they are also increasingly receptive to the idea that besides the writing of narrative history, the past can be accessed, reconstructed, and re-presented by other forms of communication. This change is especially salient in the area of teaching, where historical knowledge is no longer being delivered in the form of lecture or through *Lesung* to which Ranke (despite his promotion of the *Seminar*) and his disciples were accustomed in their times. Instead, using PowerPoint slides and other multimedia tools has almost become a must for history teachers in classrooms at all school levels. Moreover, it has also become more and more common for scholars to do the same (oftentimes even demanded by the organizers) while they present their research papers at academic conferences. Thus, while presenting their research, more and more historians are, in their historical representations, turning to alternative methods to the narrative, which is increasingly seen by them as sedimented and even antiquated; the purpose for doing so is to demonstrate the knowledge of the past through more vivid visual images and with audio effects. Little wonder, therefore, that the *American Historical Review* has run film reviews for the past few decades. In 2012, the journal also published a forum on the "linguistic turn in historiography." To varying degrees, its participants acknowledge the impact of the postmodernist critique on heightening the epistemological awareness of the historian in researching and writing history and discuss how it was germane and conducive to engendering other "turns" (cultural, imperial, environmental, etc.) in historiography.[15]

All the same, insofar as their actual work is concerned, it seems historical theorists and historians by and large remain living in two separate worlds. A similar case can also be observed in other corners of the world. For example, a recent review of the influence of postmodernism, feminism, and postcolonialism in contemporary Japanese culture has centered on the literary works by novelists rather than those by historians.[16] But on rare occasions direct exchanges also took place. Chapter 6 mentioned the dialogues between Hayden White and Saul Friedländer on the study of the Holocaust in 1990 and 2013, which are worth mentioning again here.[17] The exchange centered on the question as to how one wrote the history of the Holocaust. Friedländer, who is quite aware of the various new methods in representing history, experimented with them in his two-volume *Nazi Germany and the Jews* (1997–2006), which White recognized as a major work of history with which he could identify. White at no point denied that the Holocaust occurred; in the exchanges, he reconciles his insistence that all "historical narratives (are) verbal fictions"[18] with his recognition that the Holocaust actually occurred. He now distinguishes between the traditional historians who were "interested in the past as an object of scientific study" and postmodern historians committed to what he calls a "practical past," a value-oriented history.[19] He fully accepts Friedländer's history of the Holocaust but chooses to compare it to a literary work, a great "modernist novel" akin to the novels of Joyce, Proust, and Kafka.[20] In a sense, there was nothing new in Hayden White's stress on the literary qualities of all historical narratives. Leopold von Ranke, considered the father of "scientific" history, had already in 1830 noted that history was both a science and an art, a science in establishing the evidential basis for historical narratives, an art in the composition of these narratives.[21] What White tries to foreground is how Friedländer breaks with the traditional form of the historical narrative that narrates a story following a timeline from a beginning to an end. White points out how Friedländer's history, similar to the modernist novel, fragments time and eliminates a plot. Instead of telling a continuous story, he lets the victims of the Holocaust speak. In a sense, Friedländer does this, but it is through the voices of the victims that he captures the reality of the Holocaust. As Friedländer stresses, "[N]o historian of the Holocaust would be ready to give up the 'scientific' rendering of events." "The historian's primary role," he continues, "is to carry out the quest for factual precision."[22] And this has also been the primary task of Friedländer's volumes on the Holocaust, although under the impact of the cultural turn he has a much broader view of how to write history but one that nevertheless does not give up the commitment to the pursuit of factuality in history. In sum, White continues to have a great impact on literary theory, particularly in Departments of Comparative Literature in the United States. To his supporters, such as Frank Ankersmit, Keith Jenkins, Alun Munslow, and Dominick LaCapra, he is likely to be hailed a "patron saint." Ankersmit, in his introduction to the recent *Philosophy of History after Hayden White*, states that "contemporary philosophy of history is largely what [Hayden] White has made it."[23] But in the surveys of the history field by the historians whose areas of research fall outside intellectual history, White and his associates have received less attention. Examples are *The Landscape of History: How Historians Map the Past* (2004) by John Lewis Gaddis who teaches diplomatic history at Yale, *From Herodotus to H-Net: A Story of Historiography* (2015) by Jeremy D. Popkin, a political historian at the University of Kentucky, and *The New Ways of History: Developments in Historiography* (2010), whose chief editor Gelina Harlaftis is a maritime historian in Greece.[24] These works help illustrate the divide between the work of a historical theorist and a working historian or between the fields of historical theory and historical writing. Compared with the decade of the 1990s, this divide is indeed widening instead of closing in more recent decades.

New interest in oral history and the history of memory

What distinguishes Saul Friedländer's study of the Holocaust is his attempt to experiment with new ways to enable readers to hear a variety of voices from the past. Similar attempts have also been made by many other historians, especially in studies of microhistory, everyday history, and women's history. These studies tend to begin with a focus on premodern and preindustrial periods but increasingly also deal with the more recent time, such as of Nazi Germany and Soviet Russia of the Stalin period, after it became possible in 1988 in the last stages of Perestroika.[25] Oral history interviews with survivors and those on the social bottom and margins played a significant role. Oral history was not new. Already in the 1930s, interviews had been carried out in the United States with surviving former slaves. In Germany, Lutz Niethammer and his team questioned inhabitants of the industrial Ruhr region in West Germany on how they experienced and remembered the Nazi years[26] and then in the last years before the collapse of the East German regime were permitted to interrogate survivors there. A rather impressive endeavor outside the Western academia perhaps is the Oral History Project, conducted at the Institute of Modern History in Academia Sinica, Taiwan, which began in the 1960s and has continued to this day, with nearly a hundred titles published, covering a good number of interviews of political, military, cultural, and intellectual figures in modern Chinese and Asian history, including survivors of political persecution.[27]

One question that naturally arose is to what extent these recollections could be trusted to convey a truthful image of a historical period. The turn to oral history is closely connected with the turn to history as memory. One question that, of course, immediately comes up, is that while the foundation of serious historical research is the intent of constructing a truthful picture of the past that can be tested with recourse to the evidence, even if it is inevitably incomplete, oral historians and the makers of historical memory are free of this obligation.[28] The turn to memory had origins in the work in the 1920s of Maurice Halbwachs (1877–1945), the student of Durkheim, on "collective memory" that inspired Lucien Febvre's and particularly Marc Bloch's concern with collective mentalities that became central to the conception of history of the French *Annales*. But it was only in the 1970s and 1980s that the history of memory achieved importance. It fitted in well with the turn to culture in historical writing and the role it assigned to interpretation. Coming from the *Annales* circle, a large number of the most distinguished French historians contributed to the seven-volume collection *Lieux de Mémoire* (*Sites of Memory*),[29] launched by Pierre Nora and published between 1984 and 1992, soon followed by an English translation and a collection of German memory sites.[30] The point for Nora was that the history of the French nation cannot adequately be represented by a narrative based on documentary evidence but involves the images that the French have of their past. Thus sacred sites, festivals, myths, songs, literature, and art all play a role in fashioning national consciousness. It is no longer the past as it occurred that matters but the past as it is remembered, which can mostly not be checked against what happened. In 1989 Saul Friedländer, a survivor of the Holocaust, launched *History and Memory* at Tel Aviv University, which became the most important journal for the studies of historical memory in which the Holocaust occupied an increasingly important place. Over the recent years, the journal has also featured articles on memory studies not only of Euro-America but also of other parts of the world. For instance, several studies that deal with traumatic experiences in late imperial and modern China, such as the Nanjing Massacre of 1937, one of the most horrific atrocities the Japanese army had committed in World War II against the Chinese, have appeared in *History and Memory*, as well as studies of transatlantic slavery in American and African history.[31] In a word, while the turn to memory among historians has resulted from a combination of elements, the experience of World War II and especially the events of the Holocaust and other major war crimes have been the major impetus for engendering the shift.

But a history of memory involves not only what is remembered but also what is forgotten or repressed, and that has received inadequate attention, as Paul Ricoeur (1913–2005) pointed out.[32] In this connection, the recent book by Christina Morina, *Legacies of Stalingrad: Remembering the Eastern Front in Germany since 1945* (2011) marks an important contribution, preceded by her mentor Jeffrey Herf's *Divided Memory: The Nazi Past in the Two Germanys* (1997).

Morina examines the selective memories of the Russian front in a divided Germany during the Cold War, which she considers together with the Holocaust the greatest crime, most destructive of human lives, and inseparably connected to the Holocaust committed by the Nazis. While in Soviet-controlled East Germany historians did deal with the crimes perpetrated by the German *Wehrmacht* but virtually ignored the genocide of the Jews, a West Germany generation of veterans stressed the suffering experienced by the Germans and similarly marginalized what was done to the Jews.[33] Both in the East and in the West, the common German soldier who was forced to fight was exonerated of crimes. In the West where greater freedom made criticisms possible, the few historians and literary writers who examined the crimes were treated as outsiders. Only slowly did historians and intellectuals and the media in the West and much later and less completely in the East turn to the Holocaust.[34] But selective memory was not restricted to Germany.[35] The Japanese were much slower than the Germans, who finally did confront the crimes perpetrated in World War II. Turkey until now vehemently denies the genocide it perpetrated on the Armenians in World War I. The French for a long time were silent about their cooperation with the Nazis in the deportation of the Jews, just to mention a few significant cases. Only now are historians and cultural scholars, primarily but not only in the United States and Brazil, confronting the slave trade and the slave past and the internment of Japanese Americans in World War II and only now are Australians turning to the treatment of the aborigines. Until recently and mostly published only overseas, Chinese scholars have begun publishing on the millions who died in the Great Famine following the Great Leap Forward under Mao Zedong (1893–1976). Yang Jisheng's *Tombstone: Reports on the Great Famine in 1960s China* first appeared in Hong Kong in 2008, which offers a graphic description of the famine in the wake of the Great Leap Forward at that time in China. While unavailable in mainland China, the book was subsequently rendered into English in 2012. In the meantime, several English titles on the same topic have also appeared, authored by Western scholars or Chinese scholars working overseas.[36] Although memory studies of Mao's China remain by and large off-limits, slowly and cautiously scholars have embarked on memory studies of several other periods in modern and contemporary Chinese history. Interest in memory studies has also appeared in Japan.[37] Overall, memory studies using oral historical sources have boomed in many historical circles. In addition to *History and Memory*, SAGE has published the scholarly journal *Memory Studies* since 2008, and Palgrave Macmillan has launched the book series "Memory Studies" in 2010 with five to ten titles a year. The recent trend in memory studies has shifted the focus from remembering and representing the past – which were the initial and primary incentives for conducting oral history projects – to examining how memory is preserved, received, and/or rejected. As such, advances in memory studies have helped raise concerns about history's relation with politics and morality, among other areas.

Expansions of feminist and gender history around the world

As we saw in Chapter 6, from the mid- to the late 1980s, histories of women had advanced from the prevalent notion of separate spheres to an analysis of gender as a "useful category of historical analysis."[38] Through the concept of gender, feminist historians sought to stress the culturally and socially "constructed" nature of sexual identity. Thus, although it had developed out of the feminist agenda, gender history went in a different direction, investigating asymmetries and relations of power through the gendering of institutions and social practices and the institutionalization of gender. Gender was constitutive, not merely reflective, of social change. The referents of gender thus went further than men and women, to look at the economy, the society, and the political realm. As we have noted, this understanding of gender also made possible men and masculinity objects of historical research. Whereas men had earlier been conceptualized as ungendered, being the main actors of what was considered to be historically significant – war, politics, and statesmanship – it was now shown that constructions of masculinity were critical for an understanding of these subjects as well as the wider set of social relations. There had, of course, been studies of men and masculinities earlier, but these had emerged from what came to be referred to as the "materialist" perspective, which regarded identities in terms of stable social and institutional bases. Poststructuralist conceptions of masculinity now attempted to configure the instabilities and contradictions of identity formation, and hence change.[39] Postcolonial analyses of the gendered nature of colonial discourse also yielded a rich vein of investigations into masculinity.[40]

Yet this interest in gender and men also generated unease among feminist scholars, who wondered whether the new developments would once again make women invisible, by creating a male-centered history that overlooked the gendered organization of power.[41] Other gender scholars argued differently. By denaturalizing the history of men and masculinities and by exposing the dynamics and asymmetries of power as expressed through these categories, the feminist agenda would be kept alive. Of more serious concern was the question of how to make sense of the gendered pasts of non-Western, preliterate, or subaltern groups whose experiences would have to be filtered through the lens of Western interpretative frameworks. Non-Western (notably Indian) historians and scholars have recurrently raised this issue, as the extensive debates on *sati* (immolation of a widow on her husband's funeral pyre) have shown.[42] Could Western discourse and categories of organizing experience at all capture the experiences of colonial subjects, including its men and women?[43]

As we saw earlier, postcolonial perspectives had been brought to bear on the analytics of gender. It had been shown how concepts of "masculine" and "feminine" were central to the colonial project, critical to the evolution of colonial dominance, and a justification for its much touted "civilizing mission."[44] Mrinalini Sinha has shown how the stereotyping of the "manly Englishman" and the "effeminate Bengali" enabled colonial resistance to Indian judges presiding over white defendants and Indian doctors' examination of English women.[45] But postcolonial feminists also recognized that colonial dominance was not the only source of oppression. They voiced concern that while postcolonialism showed interest in the subaltern male, it gave little attention to the distinct and separate oppression of women. Yet there was an inherent contradiction in this criticism. On the one hand – and this was seen very clearly among Indian feminist historians – there was unease with the postcolonial nostalgia for premodern community and its accompanying patriarchy. As one Indian feminist historian stated, "[T]he postcolonial stance of subaltern history leads to defense of tradition even when these practices are clearly harmful and violate the canons of justice. According to these scholars, who is to say that *sati* is bad? It is the prejudiced Western eye that says it is."[46] Here the postcolonial feminists emphasized the "double colonization" of colonial oppression and patriarchy and the marginalization and mischaracterization of women in nationalist discourse. They argued that the appropriation of traditional stereotypes of women in the formulation of Gandhi's passive resistance did little to help the cause of Indian women.[47] At the same time, they questioned the imposition of Western feminist models on colonized and Third World women and the homogenizing tendencies of Western feminism. Second-wave Western feminist theory had assumed that the concerns of white, middle-class women were the concerns of women everywhere, but from the very beginning, black American and British feminists and very soon Third World feminist theorists asked whether implicit in white concern was another type of paternalism and racism. This concern with persistent and hegemonic Western cultural and political influence, however, was expressed as a necessary corrective, not as a wholesale rejection. Asian feminist scholars generally acknowledged the inspiration they received from the West in advancing women's rights and interest in their own countries, but they also engaged critically with the paradigmatic influence of Western feminism by drawing attention to the key differences in women's experiences in Asia vis-à-vis those of the West.[48] Scholars of the Middle East argued for a more sensitive and sophisticated study of the historical experiences of Middle Eastern women, preferring to examine the veil in terms of the complicated perspective of Arab feminists. Of course, black feminists had long been critical of white feminists' neglect of the dimension of race. As Hazel Carby in her influential essay "White Woman Listen!" had put it, white feminists "write their herstory and call it the story of women but ignore our lives and deny their relation to us." Postcolonial feminist history and feminist historians of nonwhite races thus gave history a renewed political agenda, but one that was more cognizant of the fact that "female subordination occurred in different places and different ways" and that subordination was never uniform or constant.[49]

This careful attention to the inflections and connections of gender, race, empire, and sexuality produced intriguing analyses of the relations between Western women and indigenous women, as well as the consequences of interventions by the former. It drew attention to the Western women who, in campaigning for the rights of the "oppressed" female natives, grew aware of the oppression of their own condition "at home."[50] It showed how having Western women "on their side" often led to the repositioning of views on issues such as the veil and *sati* by indigenous women, who transformed these practices into symbols of anticolonial resistance.[51] White women's complicity with colonialism has also been a subject of much study, with enduring, tension-ridden, and problematic consequences for the feminist agenda.

Not surprisingly, older proponents of women's history wondered about the future of their discipline in an environment that questioned a unitary and shared feminist consciousness. Gender theory had also led to the same result, in that "more often women's plight is no longer the ends but the means for understanding nationhood, imperialism, and abstractions constituted through gendered discourse."[52] This has led to rifts in university departments, with many centers of Women's Studies turning into Gender Studies.

To obtain a comparative transnational view of feminist and gender historiography, we have looked at publications in a number of countries in recent years, as well as the programs of meetings of national historical associations. We looked at the journals more closely in the preceding section on the relation of history and the social sciences. In particular, we compared the annual meetings of the American Historical Associations in the years between 2006 and 2015 with those of the biannual German *Historikertage* (Historians' Conventions) in these years. We have chosen Germany because there historians had been much more reticent to break with older historical approaches. In that respect, Germany constitutes one end of a historiographical spectrum; American historiography with its openness to new approaches in history represents the other end. An example of this reticence is the publication of the massive volumes of *Geschichtliche Grundbegriffe* (*Basic Historical Concepts*) (1972–1996), co-edited by the renowned German historical theorist Reinhart Koselleck (1923–2006), which analyzes the transformation of German society between 1750 and 1850 in terms of underlying social and historical concepts but does not contain a single article dealing with conceptions of sex and gender in that period. Nevertheless, by now many German historians have turned to social and cultural history but in different directions than many of their American colleagues. Each of the biannual conferences had a theme; the conference of 2008 was devoted to social inequality, the 2010 conference to transcending borders, the 2012 conference to environmental resources, the 2014 conference to history by winners and losers. The 2008 program, as we just noted, was devoted specifically to social inequality in a global setting, with considerable attention paid to the challenges presented by migration in the industrially developed countries. There was a great concern about the social, cultural, and political interaction within Europe and less concern in the colonial world, although it too received attention. Women and women's concerns were by no means neglected, but they were more integrated into a social, cultural, and political context than they were in a great deal of American feminist history.

As we look at the annual programs of the American Historical Association and to a lesser extent also at the articles of the *American Historical Review*, we find a picture different from that in the European journals, namely an almost obsessive concentration on sexuality and gender at the expense of broader social and political aspects. The number of articles on aspects of sexuality and gender sponsored by the Committee on Lesbian, Gay, Bisexual and Transgender History but also by the American Catholic Historical Association and the American Society of Church History, the latter two introducing aspects of sexuality in dealing with missionary activity in non-Western societies, is amazing. Of course, feminist historiography has made important contributions to opening historical study to areas that were previously badly neglected. While it has expressed its concern with placing the history of women in a broader social context, in fact the narrow focus practiced in many of the programs at the meetings of the American Historical Association and some of the articles in the *American Historical Review*, has set limits to meaningful historical inquiry. In the meantime, we have seen the programs of the American Historical Association move to greater openness and diversity without fully giving up its strong focus on sexuality and gender. Moreover, if we consider the books reviewed in the *American Historical Review*, we receive a very balanced picture of the serious scholarship carried out by American historians, even where they deal with aspects of sexuality and gender. And this is also true of the important international journal, *Gender and History*, which in its editorial to the first issue in 1990 stated: "We seek particularly to encourage research not only on gender and women, but also on how other divisions – of race class, religion, ethnicity, and sexual orientation – have redoubted [*sic*] on both ideas of gender and the experiences of women."

One interesting development in recent years has been the attention paid by women and gender studies to "world" or "global" history. Gender scholars have found in this decentered and relatively new field an opportunity to rethink the founding categories of history in "engendered" terms. Indeed, it was felt that gender was particularly well suited to this project, insofar as it had already embraced postmodern and postcolonial perspectives, particularly in the Anglophone academic world, which included diasporic scholars such as those belonging to the transnational subaltern studies community. These scholars have played an important role in opening national resistance to gender, which previously had been regarded as a Western import.[53]

A path-breaking work in this engagement is Peter Stearns' *Gender in World History* (2000), which attempted to reveal not only how gender relations in diverse societies changed after international contact but also the pivotal role of gender in each of the analyzed societies in the context of changing relations of power.[54] Scholars in this area have also pushed the body into the foreground of analysis, focusing on the construction of gendered identities through bodily practices and consumption as a key element in the construction of imperial modernity, while recognizing how these practices emerged in a "multicentered" and hybridized manner.[55] Gendered bodies of colonizers/colonized thus become redolent with meanings, as sites of tension, collusion, domination, and resistance. Nevertheless, as an area of scholarly engagement gendered world history is still in its experimental stages, at the present moment more of an agenda rather than a ubiquitous trend, one that aims to introduce gender differences in the "leading categories" of world history in order "to avoid becoming passive latecomers in a new master narrative."[56]

Redefining the alliance between history and the social/natural sciences

To establish what is meant by social science approaches to history, we have examined the development of major social science–oriented journals in the period after 1990 as an indication of changing historiographical trends. What we observe is a return neither to the analytical social sciences dealing heavily with economics, social structures, and demography, although the concern with these areas was by no means given up, nor to the radical forms of the cultural and linguistic turn with its relativistic epistemological implications. Of course, we cannot generalize how the majority of historians have conceived history in the last twenty-some years; there is too much diversity. Nevertheless, the journals we have examined give us an idea in what direction historical thought and writing have gone in recent years. Indicative of the reorientation that has taken place is the French *Annales*, which in 1994 changed its subtitle from *Economies. Sociétés. Civilisations* to *Histoire. Sciences Sociales*. The reason given for the change was that it was too narrow and that historians must work closely not only with sociologists and economists but also with scholars in other disciplines and the humanities. Actually, the *Annales* had done this all along but now reiterated this stand. Already in an editorial in 1988 and a subsequent one in 1989, the *Annales* had spoken of a crisis of the traditional social sciences and noted that Marxism, structuralism, and quantification had lost their ability to give the study of historical studies a convincing foundation; indeed, all ideologies had lost their credibility. This did not mean a repudiation of social science, or rather of the social sciences in the plural, but on the contrary a broadening, an inclusion of aspects of culture that had not received sufficient attention. And this called for new approaches and methods, not merely those of economics, sociology, geography, and anthropology, which had been mainstays of *Annales* historiography, but also those of literary criticism, sociolinguistics, and political philosophy.[57]

For many years after 1945, the *Annales* had largely avoided dealing with contemporary themes, with which it had still dealt in the 1930s. It had felt it easier to deal with social structures in relatively stationary premodern societies than in those undergoing rapid change. Now its perspective became global, in two senses: (1) in terms of space and time, an interest in societies and cultures and their interaction all over the world, and (2) in terms of Western and non-Western, the interaction of the two, as well as an occupation with all epochs of history from earliest antiquity until now. Not only society and economy were treated but also religion, the arts, and the humanities. Although the *Annales* did not ignore sex and gender and devoted a special issue to gender,[58] these topics did not occupy as central a role as they did in American and also to an extent British journals. The *Annales* were also free of the ideological orientation that had earlier marked *Past and Present* in Great Britain and to an even greater extent the *History Workshop*. *Past and Present* in its beginning had been an organ in which Marxist and non-Marxist historians discussed questions posed by Marxists regarding the emergence of a capitalist society, with the focus on England. Now the scope of the journal was much broader; similar to the *Annales*, its articles dealt with topics covering the range from earliest to contemporary times and dealing with the interaction of the Western and non-Western worlds. The German *Geschichte und Gesellschaft*, founded in 1975, had conceived itself as a journal dedicated to what it termed "historical social science" (*historische Sozialwissenschaft*) and strongly influenced by the analytical sociology of Max Weber and had understandably placed a great emphasis on examining Germany's disastrous past. It now broadened its topics to include great parts of the world past and present without losing sight of the problems of modern Germany and Europe. The Holocaust was not forgotten. Among the topics dealt with is also the role of sentiments. The major American journals dealing with social history, the *Journal of Interdisciplinary, Comparative Studies of History and Social History*, *Social Science History*, and *Social History* have gone in similar directions. An examination of two major journals dealing with Latin American history, the *Hispanic American Historical Review* and the *Latin American Research Review*, and two dealing with African history, the *Journal of African History* and *The Journal of Modern African Studies*, point in similar directions, but with greater concern with questions of race and ethnicity and the history of slavery, which also occupies an important role in the Western journals we have mentioned. Even the relatively traditional German *Historische Zeitschrift* recently had an article on lynch justice in the United States.[59] To sum it up, the social sciences continue to play an important role, yet there seems to be a much greater openness and diversity today than was the case of much analytical social sciences after 1945 or of the culturalism of the 1970 and 1980s.

It is striking how political history has been neglected, particularly in recent American historiography. Thus neither volume 4 of the *Oxford History of Historical Writing* (2011) dedicated to historical writing between

1800 and 1945 nor volume 5 (2011) dealing with the period since 1945, the most up-to-date and comprehensive histories of historiography, contain a chapter on political history and largely ignore the topic. Likewise, the seven-volume *Cambridge World History*, published in 2015, with Merry Wiesner-Hanks serving as editor-in-chief, also significantly downplays the role of politics in general and that of nation-states in particular, while charting historical development around the globe. Its volume 6, coedited by Jerry Bentley (1949-2012), Sanjay Subrahmanyan, and Merry Wiesner-Hanks, covers world history between 1400 and 1800, under the heading of "The Construction of a Global World." In two parts – "Foundations" and "Patterns of Change" – it foregrounds such themes as migration trade and exchange, religious change in "macro-regions" at the expense of the rise of nation-states in Europe. Of course, political history is included in the volume. But instead of discussing nation-building in the West, it directs readers' attention to "large-scale political formations," or empires, in Iberia, Russia, China, and the Middle East during the period. Some explanations of this approach are found in Jack A. Goldstone's chapter, entitled "Political Trajectories Compared," in the volume. "The universal expectation in the twenty-first century is that everyone is a citizen of some country . . . Yet, the rise of such modern states," writes Goldstone, "is a relatively recent development. By 1800, the process of creating such states was still new and incomplete." Great Britain and France were two lonely examples with "pre-modern" elements in their governments, whereas Prussia did not become Germany until 1871 and Japan, China, Russia, Turkey, and India did not form their nation-states until the twentieth century.[60] Moreover, political history remains thinly covered in the subsequent volume of the *Cambridge World History*, which spans the period from 1800 to the present. Of its seven parts, only one is devoted to "Politics," under which one chapter is "On Nationalism," discussing the spread of the ideology across the world rather than the success of the nation-building model of Euro-America. The other six chapters discuss such topics as imperialism, non-Western responses to European expansion, decolonization, genocide, Communism, and fascism, all designed to transcend the nation-state focus and Eurocentrism. Indeed, under the editorship of J. R. McNeill and Kenneth Pomeranz, volume 7 of the *Cambridge World History* allots sufficient space describing material and economic conditions of social/cultural developments and globalization in recent centuries.

Of course, political history is by no means dead and continues to be an important concern. We have discussed the revival of political history in Latin America in Chapter 6, a political history focused not on the elites but on the broad masses of the population, How can one ignore the calamities of the twentieth century, two world wars, Nazism, Stalinism, and Maoism, and the genocides, all of which require a political context in order to be understood? Reliance on archival sources, although essential to establish the facts, does not suffice. Nor can military and diplomatic history be ignored. But much of the historiography of politics reflected the transformation of historical thought generally. Increasingly, the older history from above, which depended closely, even exclusively, on archival sources, gave way not to the abrogation of political history but to the cross-fertilization of political, social, and cultural history and the extension of its scope to include broad segments of the population. Not only has political history seemed to have reignited the interest among historians in Latin America, Africa, and Asia, but new schools of historical research, such as the boom of memory already mentioned, have also turned historians around the world to the power of political condition and constraint. For memory studies tend to focus on how certain remembrance occurs whereas others become suppressed and rejected, political influence and manipulation from the state have received ample attention among scholars. So much so that some have criticized that memory is being transformed into a "'natural' corollary of political development and interests" or that "memory thus becomes a prisoner of political reductionism and functionalism."[61] Meanwhile, Jan and Aleida Assman's recent postulation on the construction of "cultural memory," which expands on as well as modifies Maurice Halbwachs' well-known theory of "collective memory," has also turned historians' attention to the benefit of anthropology, sociology, and communication theories for memory studies.

Indeed, the issue seems not that historians of today are no longer interested in allying with social sciences; rather, they are seeking new ways to redefine the entrenched alliance between them and making new efforts to update historical methodology, which also includes borrowing methods from the natural science in recent decades. This redefinition involves, as it were, attempts to delink the traditional association between social science theory and the nation-state focus in historical writing. At least in the modern West, observes Kevin Passmore, endeavors to borrow and apply social science methods in historical research, which began in the early twentieth century, were initially for the purpose of adumbrating the progress of nation. To this end, historians were drawn to the works of Gustave Le Bon (1841–1931), Max Weber, Émile Durkheim, as well as Karl Marx, in hopes of better explaining the causes and characteristics of human evolution on both the national and the international levels. This tradition became amplified as well as modified in post-World War II years, but from the late 1970s, or as the cultural and linguistic turn in historiography were emerging, historians began exploring new areas of research, which impelled them to transcend the national focus and reexamine history's alliance with such "old" social sciences as sociology, economics, and political science, just as the latter were experiencing the "historical turn" in their disciplines.[62] Indeed, some historical theorists have argued rather convincingly that historians, too, have a good deal to offer to social scientists by introducing and expounding the dimension of temporality. If there has been a "historicization" of those social science disciplines, then this process has also proven to be valuable for resuming and reassuring history's alliance with them.[63] In fact, according to Gabrielle Spiegel, new directions in historical writing are occurring after the linguistic turn, as more and more historians are taking interest in the roles of self, structure, agency, and experience in historical movement, for which they once again become eager to absorb and appropriate methodological elements from neighboring disciplines. The onset of globalization, reckons Lynn Hunt, has not lessened but increased the importance of the relationship between self and society in historical examination, for such analysis historians are (and are getting better at) seeking inspirations from new advances in biology and psychology.[64] The growing interest in environmental history and the history of emotions, two genres in historical writing that have experienced exponential growth as of late, which we will discuss later in the chapter, have also turned historians to useful and relevant developments in both the social and the natural sciences.

The transformation of the concept of the nation and the significance of global history

Despite the continuing focus on the nation in much historical writing, the conception of the nation underwent changes in the face of the increasing number of ethnic minorities in post-1990 Western and Central Europe and in the English-speaking countries. Many historians no longer viewed nations as homogeneous but as heterogeneous, multicultural societies. Moreover, the view of Europe as a homogeneous unit overlooked the many regional, linguistic, and cultural differences that mark Europe. The same, of course, also applies to Latin America, Africa, and major Asian regions. There was an increasing tendency to approach history from a multicultural perspective. An example of this are the major textbooks of American and world history used in American high schools, which emphasize the ethnic cultures that compose the United States and give attention to the role of minorities and women and that thus in this respect differ markedly from earlier textbooks.[65] In India, the *Subaltern Studies* turned away from the conception of the nation-state as the unit with which historians were to deal. The very diversities within India, the complex division among class, caste, and other lines had to be taken into consideration. From the perspective of the *Subaltern Studies*, much of anticolonial historiography had merely replaced British elites with Indian elites ignoring the large subaltern sections of the population as active agents in the anticolonial struggle. We saw similar redefinitions of the nation-state in Tanzanian Marxist historiography that, like the Subaltern Group, stressed the diversities that made up Tanzania and stressed the active role of the subordinate classes in the struggle for national independence.[66] This did not mean a decline in nation-oriented histories. But increasingly historians have written transnational histories that avoided the nation as the unit of study and instead investigated relationships, transfers, and interactions independent of national lines in what French historians have recently called *histoire croisée* (entangled histories).[67]

A salient example of this historiography in a global age is the nine volume series, *Writing the Nation*, funded by the European Science Foundation, which offers the most important analysis of the role of national narratives in nineteenth and twentieth century historiography. While the series reconstructs the nation oriented historiography of all of the many European states, it does this from a comparative, transnational perspective, examining the role which ethnicity, class, religion, and gender occupied in each of these national histories.[68]

One marked change since the end of the Cold War has been the increased attention given to world history and to global history away from traditional nation- and Western-oriented history.[69] The first half of the twentieth century saw two important attempts to write world histories, foremost those of Oswald Spengler[70] and Arnold Toynbee,[71] which centered around a comparison of civilizations, among which the West was only one. These works were discounted by professional historians because they were based on broad generalizations rather than on solid scholarship. Yet they offered an important impulse to historical thinking by presenting other civilizations as equally worthy of consideration as the West. It was only late in the second half of the twentieth century and particularly since the end of the Cold War[72] that world history assumed a professional character. A very significant early contribution to the scholarly study of cross-cultural interaction and diffusion was William H. McNeill's *The Rise of the West: A History of the Human Community* (1963), which notwithstanding its title was comparative and helped set a pattern for later writing of world history. McNeill sought to show that contacts between peoples of different societies and cultural traditions involving the interchange of ideas and skills were a key factor in world history.[73] He was attracted by Toynbee's broad approach to world history and actually worked with Toynbee but avoided the latter's attempt to establish regularities in world history, which for him rested on speculation. Although in its scope and its intercultural approach McNeill's book was a pioneer work, it was soon criticized, also by McNeill himself, for not being comprehensive enough, for example for excluding Africa from the larger pattern of world history and focusing on elites. In a subsequent work, *Plagues and Peoples* (1976), he dealt with the effects of infections and contagious diseases across societal and cultural lines and the disruptions brought about by these diseases of established political, trade, and social orders as important guides to historical study. Here for almost the first time a theme was addressed, involving biological and environmental factors, that had been largely neglected by historians but now would become important areas of study.

The year 1982 saw the founding of the World History Association and its *Journal of World History* founded with international contributors in 1990 with Jerry Bentley as editor. The journal became the most important organ of the new world history that also contained reviews of the relevant books. Its purpose, as stated on the first page of every volume, was to analyze history "from a global point of view," treating as its key themes "large-scale population movements and economic fluctuations; cross-cultural transfer of technologies, the spread of infectious diseases; long distance trade; and the spread of religious faiths, ideas, and ideals."[74] Particularly after 1990, the term "global history" became increasingly popular. In 2006, a *Journal of Global History* was founded in the same year as the *Globality Studies Journal*. Already in 1991, a bilingual journal, *Comparativ Zeitschrift für Globalgeschichte und vergleichende Gesellschaftsforschung*, was founded in Germany. As yet there is no consensus on what global history actually means and on at what point one can start speaking of a global history.[75] The term "global history" overlapped with "world history" and was often identical with it but tended to deal more frequently with the period after the explorations of the fifteenth century and often referred to the process of globalization since the last third of the twentieth century.[76] World history can include studies of premodern societies and cultures, themes that interest both journals; they could thus deal with exchanges of commodities, foods, and diseases in the Pacific realm long before the arrival of the Europeans. In historiographical practice, it meant that historians increasingly crossed national borders and dealt with cultures and societies outside the Western world. But also climate and environment played an important role, particularly for comparative studies of early periods of history. These are themes also suitable for the *Journal of Global History*. The editorial to the first issue of the journal and the historiographical essay that follows seek to establish its special role. It wants to overcome the fragmentation of regional and narrowly specialized studies that have marked historiography. In the past two centuries, it notes that "all historiographical traditions converged either to celebrate or react to the rise of the West." It now wants to pursue a truly global history based on "serious scholarship."[77]

This interest in transcending the nation-states pattern in historiography also spread to other parts of the world, although acquiring a slightly different meaning and following a different trajectory. In East Asia, efforts are made by historians to find alternatives to the dominating national history paradigm, as well as that of Marxism, and thus break free from the stifling ideological constraints on the work of the historian. In Japan, for example, the turn to sociocultural history, which since the 1980s has given rise to the effort to portray the everyday life of the common people and especially of the subaltern class, has coincided with the rise of urban history, one of the liveliest subfields of historical study during recent decades. Since the mid-1990s, this interest in sociocultural history has joined force to introduce "cultural studies" and postcolonial studies from the West to Japan. These advances have helped some Japanese historians to critically examine the legacy of Japanese colonialism in East Asia in the first half of the twentieth century and how these reflected the government control of textbook writing and publications.[78]

If the development of cultural history and cultural studies in Japan has benefited from cross-cultural dialogues in the international historical community, the same can be said about recent historiographical changes in China. The publication of the book series "New Social History" ("*Xin shehuishi*") beginning in 2004, for example, was a result of close collaborations among Chinese scholars working overseas and at home, as mentioned in the previous chapter. Across the Taiwan Straits, studies of Chinese history in recent decades have also shown a similarly robust interest in sociocultural history, thanks to the more frequent exchanges between Taiwanese historians and their Western counterparts. Compared with the historians in the People's Republic, historians in Taiwan indeed are more receptive of influences of Western historiography; inspired by the *Annales* School, a turn to sociocultural history had actually occurred in its historical circle in as early as the 1980s.[79] On the mainland, the culture fever movement of the 1980s gave rise to the study of social history, with an augmented interest in the change of social and cultural life, as an alternative to the Chinese Marxist historiography of the earlier period. Indeed, the trends of both social and cultural history have enabled Chinese historians, particularly those of the younger generation, to circumvent the Marxist orthodoxy in historical study upheld and imposed by the government, for from the 1990s Chinese leadership has increasingly turned to nationalism as an official ideology in maintaining their rule of the country. Thus, in mainland China today, pursuing the interest in social, cultural, and economic history, instead of national history – that is, the role of revolutions in effecting changes in the modern period – becomes an effective way for the historian to sidestep the political imprint on historical writing.[80]

Another example of late is the aforementioned *The Cambridge World History*. In contrast to Lord Acton's *Cambridge Modern History* and its sequel – *New Cambridge World History* of the 1950s and the 1970s – this book downplays the historical significance of the rise of modern Europe in world history. It takes "regional, topical and comparative" approaches and assembles a group of authors not only of a variety of disciplines but also from many countries across the world.[81] While following a broad chronological framework, beginning in the Paleolithic times, it charts the rise of cities, empires, and states and discusses the complex interactions between human activity and the environment through the past millennia.

This turn to comparative transcultural global history increasingly marked history worldwide. Among the broadly comparative works based on solid scholarship, the most comprehensive history yet written is Jürgen Osterhammel's *The Transformation of the World: A Global History of the Nineteenth Century*, which first appeared in German and subsequently in English.[82] K. N. Chaudhuri's *Asia before Europe: Economy and Civilization of the Indian Ocean from the Rise of Islam to 1750* (1990) and André Gunder Frank's *ReOrient: Global Economy in the Asian Age* (1998) both argue forcefully that before the capitalist West, India and China had played the crucial part in driving the world economy. Kenneth Pomeranz's well-acclaimed *The Great Divergence: China, Europe and the Making of the Modern World Economy* (2000) extends Chaudhuri and Frank's thesis and contends further that economic development in both the West and the East, or China, had followed a similar pattern until around 1750 and that the West leaped ahead of the East not because of its distinct cultural tradition, political development, or anything else but because of its discovery and colonization of the New World, which enabled Europeans to diverge from their Asian counterparts and grow along the new resource-intensive and labor-saving paths of industrialization.

Two countries with very different historiographical traditions, the United States and China,[83] stood out as centers for the pursuit of world or global history, directed not only to research but also to instruction. In the United States, undergraduate courses in Western Civilization, which had been widely introduced shortly after World War I, now gave way to courses in world or global history. In China, institutes of world history were established as early as the 1950s, along with, in more recent years, centers of global history studies at some universities. In 2011, the World History Association held its annual convention at Capital Normal University in Beijing, which has a vibrant global history research center. Several hundreds of scholars attended the convention from overseas, along with an equal number of Chinese participants. As we pointed out in the Introduction for the first time after 2006 a number of histories of historiography appeared that encompass historical writing throughout the globe from its beginnings. Going beyond this, a small circle of historians around the world pursued what they called "Big History" (David Christian, Fred Spier, and Cynthia S. Brown). While historians traditionally had considered the past prior to writing as prehistoric, they now wanted to go back to the very beginnings of the universe, the Big Bang, and trace it through the creation of the solar system, the first appearance of human life, and its evolution to the modern period. Such an approach, as shown in Christian's *Maps of Time: An Introduction to Big History* (2004) and Brown's *Big History: From the Big Bang to the Present* (2012), has to break with the established methods of historical inquiry that focuses on humanity. It wishes to link history more closely to the natural sciences and give it a material basis (Fred Spier, the Dutch author of *Big History and the Future of Humanity* [2010], began as a scientist before turning to history). To an extent, William H. McNeill had already attempted this examination of how the environment played its part on human activities in *Plagues and Peoples*. McNeill also endorsed David Christian's *Maps of Time*; in 2003, he coauthored, with his son John R. McNeill, *The Human Web: A Bird's-eye View of World History*, which gives a broad overview of world history from prehistoric times to the present, ending with some interesting discussions of the foreseeable future.

The growing importance of environmental history

In this connection, perhaps we need to turn to the rise of environmental history, which is at once a subfield of history and a path that links history with natural and social sciences. For most practitioners of the genre, the "environmental or ecological turn" in historiography occurred in the 1970s, marked not only by the aforementioned William McNeill's *Plagues and Peoples* but also by Alfred Crosby's *The Columbian Exchange: The Biological and Cultural Consequences of 1492* (1972) and Donald Worster's *Nature's Economy: A History of Ecological Ideas* (1977). In 1986, Crosby also expanded his thesis and attempted a larger scale of research in writing the *Ecological Imperialism: The Biological Expansion of Europe, 900–1900*. All three authors were then teaching in the United States and in 1976 came the American Society for Environmental History. Indeed, environmental history, at least in its formative years, seemed to have received more attention in American academia; "environmental history" was also coined by the American historian Roderick Nash for the English-speaking world. Some have traced this American tradition to the last years of the nineteenth century, when Frederick Jackson Turner put forth his "frontier thesis" in summarizing the characteristics of American history and culture. To be sure, Lucian Febvre, cofounder of the *Annales* School, also directed, in his *Geographical Introduction to History*, ample attention to the part that the natural environment played in human history. Febvre's idea later became amplified in Fernand Braudel's *Mediterranean* and even further in Emmanuel Le Roy Ladurie's series of works on climate history. But strangely, from 1980s the *Annales* journal published few articles on environmental history.[84]

The study of environmental history reached a height in the United States from the 1990s. By the time John R. McNeill wrote his survey of the field in 2003, there had appeared a half dozen research centers of environmental history in American universities. The American Society for Environmental History also swelled to over a thousand members. Meanwhile, the field became increasingly internationalized with historians of Europe, Asia, Latin America, Africa, and the Middle East coming on board. Not only have research centers been established in universities across continents, but professional associations (e.g., European Society for Environmental Historians founded in 1999) of environmental history have also attracted more members. In South Asia and Africa, this trend has been especially robust. For instance, scholars writing from an Indian perspective focused on the politics of environmental ideas, manifested in the colonial context allegedly as a movement to protect native wildlife over native people and, during the postcolonial period, in a growing polarization between the environmentalism of the affluent and the environmentalism of the poor.[85]

In addition to this political approach to environmental history, cultural/intellectual and material approaches have been attempted to analyze the relationship of history and its environment. The former looks at how humans perceive their physical surroundings both by nature and human construction in art and literature, whereas the latter, already shown in the works of Crosby, William McNeill, and more recently in Jared Diamond's popular *Guns, Germs and Steel: The Fates of Human Societies* (1999), describes how human history is conditioned and constrained by biological and natural conditions. Keith Thomas, the Cambridge anthropologist-cum-historian, wrote *Man and the Natural World: Changing Attitude in England, 1500–1800* (1983), which is regarded (less so by the author himself) as an early endeavor in experimenting with the cultural variety of environmental history study. Like Thomas, Simon Schama may not consider himself an environmental historian per se. Yet his *Landscape and Memory* (1996) is an elegant history of how nature was appreciated and presented in European painting, sculpture, and architecture. In contrast to many environmental historians who tend to hold a "declensionist" view of humans' relation with nature, Schama in his book hopes to convey the message that while much has been lost, a good deal has also been well remembered. And his writing is to reveal "the richness, antiquity, and complexity of our landscape tradition."[86]

As in Europe, landscape has also played its part in the cultural tradition in China and East Asia in general. In his comprehensive survey, *The Retreat of the Elephants: An Environmental History of China* (2004), Mark Elvin pays close attention to landscape painting and poetry in describing the Chinese perception of nature. Meanwhile, his book offers detailed descriptions of the change and decline of China's natural environment in the face of continuous farming and cultivation over the millennia. To examine the interactions between human action and the environment is a common approach seen in the material variety of environmental history. Edmund Russell's *Evolutionary History: Uniting History and Biology to Understand Life on Earth* (2011) represents a global undertaking, whereas John Iliffe's *Africans: The History of a Continent* (1998) centers on one continent; Iliffe also discusses not only how the Africans changed the environment but also how they met the natural challenges (aridity, disease, drought, etc.) on the continent with degrees of success and failure. Indeed, the relatively harsher living conditions in Africa, which was worsened by European colonialism, has inclined its historians to portray African history via an environmental view. A critical examination of the European colonial legacy also figures centrally in the environmental studies in Latin America.[87]

Without question, the development of environmental history in recent decades has coincided with the general trend of worldwide historiography. The study of the environment, for instance, behooves the historians to transcend the nation-state focus in Rankean historiography. "For many sorts of history, including most environmental history," puts John R. McNeill, a noted figure in the emerging field, "the nation-state is the wrong scale to operate." For "ecological processes unfold with no regard to borders."[88] Like McNeill, many environmental historians tend to adopt a global approach to history writing. J. Donald Hughes' *An Environmental History of the World: Humankind's Changing Role in the Community of Life* (2009), *The Environment and World History* (2009), edited by Edmund Burke III and Kenneth Pomeranz, and Anthony Penna's *The Human Footprint: A Global Environmental History* (2010) are examples. Likewise, scholars interested in global history, such as many of the contributors to *The Cambridge World History* previously mentioned, have also increasingly looked at historical development from environmental perspectives. In 2007, several environmental historians explored the idea of "Anthropocene" to describe the detrimental impact of modernization on the globe. They believe that from 1800 with the onset of industrialization, human activity had become a "global geophysical force" that fundamentally changed the earth system – the unprecedented high level of atmospheric carbon dioxide concentration serves as an alarming indication.[89] While the Anthropocene is identical with the modern age, it marks the environmental approach to historical periodization, comparable to the endeavor made by the global historians in transcending the nation-state focus in historiography. Moreover, the study of environmental history has helped historians to forge a new alliance between history and the social as well as natural sciences; the latter now include not only biology, archaeology, and ecology but also forestry, climatology, and palynology.

The examination of the role of emotions in history

Another example of how history joins with natural science is the study of emotions. At the 22nd International Congress of Historical Sciences held in Jinan, China, in 2015, "Historicizing Emotions" was one of the four major themes. Indeed, since the 1980s, a growing number of historians have turned their attention to the role of human emotions in history. Peter Stearns, a social historian and founder of the *Journal of Social History* in the United States coined (together with his wife Carol Stearns) the term "emotionology," in their *American Historical Review* article in 1985, arguing that the historical study of emotions can extend and expand on the study of social history and psychohistory, shifting attention from the "conventional sociological models of stratification and mobility" to the emotional aspect of "past mentalities." By "emotionology," they mean the social standard on collective emotions in a given period.[90] In addition to social history, the interest in emotions was shown early in Lucien Febvre's work on sensibility. As such, the *Annales* historians' works on the history of *mentalités* could be viewed as a precursor.[91] Other sources of inspiration were Nobert Elias's (1897–1990) *The Civilising Process*, which describes how humans learned to control their emotions on various occasions. In his *The Waning of the Middle Ages* (1919), Johan Huizinga (1872–1945) provides vivid descriptions of medieval life, in which emotional expressions (weeping and anger) by people would be viewed as rather direct and unrestrained by modern standard.

Yet the recent trend of emotional studies in history also has clearly departed from those early examples. In contrast to Elias and Huizinga's emphasis on the demarcation between medieval and modern life, historians of emotion of late tend to downplay the significance of modernity. Since emotion exists in all cultures, they don't see the need to identify one particular mode of expression as "civilized" in contrast to the "crude" or "uncivilized" other(s), nor do they want to stress a linear progress in structuring emotions in human history. For instance, in medieval Europe, family relations were conventionally portrayed as based on "purposive rationality," or lacking emotional connections and expressions. But the works of

Hans Medick, David Sabean, Louis Tilly, and Jack Goody challenged this view.[92] With respect to marital love, it has long been taken as a modern phenomenon that also distinguishes Western culture from others. In China and Japan, for example, marriages based on love, or "love marriages," did not become widely practiced until the postwar years of the 1950s and 1960s. But expressions of emotions – "affection" (*qing*) and "desire" (*yu*) – were far from absent in Chinese familial and other relationships in premodern periods but were actually abundant in literature and other types of writings, especially in the Ming (1368–1644) and Qing (1644–1911) dynasties.[93] And, if love-based marriage appeared first in the West, it also went through various forms of development; that is, emotions have their own history. In seventeenth-century New England, scholars find, couples were quite restrained in showing their affection toward each other lest their love for God be lessened. By contrast, from the twentieth century, love has become a celebrated ideal for marriage in the United States, even to the degree of "killing" the marriage; some couples quickly dissolve their union as soon as they believe their love no longer exists.[94]

On September 10, 2001, William Reddy published his *Navigation of Feeling: A Framework for the History of Emotions*, and then the very next day, the 9/11 attack shocked the world. While a clear coincidence, it serves, in the words of Jan Plamper, "both the instant and the catalysis contributed to the present global boom in the study of the history of emotions."[95] Indeed, in the immediate wake of the 9/11 attack, emotions ran quite high among the American populace that invariably also influenced the policy-making process by the government. Reddy is an American historian who teaches at Duke University and has produced pioneering works in emotions history. In his *Navigation of Feeling* and several other studies, Reddy describes various types of "emotional regimes" that set up normative ways to regulate the expression of human emotion. One example was in prerevolution France where the royal court exhibited and exercised its power through ritual ceremony, whereas in today's world a stewardess, for instance, is usually required to wear a smile for serving the passengers. Reddy believes that outside the "emotional regime," there is also "emotion refuge" where people enjoy their "emotional liberty" with (relatively) unrestrained utterance and gesture. Different from Reddy's bifurcated approach, Barbara Rosenwein, another American historian, instead proposed, in her *Emotional Communities in the Early Middle Ages* (2007) and most recently *Generations of Feeling: A History of Emotion* (2015), the "emotional communities" concept, arguing that emotional expressions varied depending on circumstances (with the family, at church or school, dining out, etc.).

Yet unlike the study of environmental history, emotions history from its outset has had an international appeal. In fact, while William Reddy, Barbara Rosenwein, and Peter Stearns are without questions its major advocates, the study of emotions history in the United States remains more of an individual choice. By contrast, research centers of the history of emotions have appeared in many European countries and Australia, where the study is conducted collectively. The Center for the History of Emotions, Max Planck-Institute for Human Development, Berlin, is but one example, which is directed by Ute Frevert, author of several studies on honor, manliness, and gender. Incidentally, Frevert organized the "Historicizing Emotions" panels at the International Congress of Historical Sciences in Jinan in 2015. The ARC Centre of Excellence for the History of Emotions, a nationwide research organization across several university campuses in Australia, is another example, as well as the Amsterdam Centre for Cross-disciplinary Emotion and Sensory Studies and Les Émotions au Moyen Age (EMMA) in Canada.

There is also an important similarity between the studies of environmental and emotions history, which is their interdisciplinary approach and strong interest in seeking the alliance between history and natural science. In his *History of Emotions: An Introduction* (2015), which first appeared in German as *Geschichite und Gefühl*, Jan Plamper, who was born in Germany, received his education in the United States, and now teaches in London, describes in detail how the study of human emotions has been a heavily researched field in neuroscience and how the study has influenced the work of the historian. Meanwhile, he also alerts readers about the key difference between historical and scientific studies of emotion. While neuroscientists search for universal patterns of emotional behavior associated with, say, brain cell activity, historians are inclined to seek the historicity of emotion. That is, the latter believe that although emotion exists throughout human history, it has also experienced marked changes in different periods.[96] In other words, quoting Michel Foucault, "We believe that feelings are immutable, but every sentiment, particularly the noblest and the most disinterested, has a history."[97]

Indeed, in addition to its indebtedness to social history, the rising interest in the history of emotions has extended the trends of New Cultural History and feminist and gender history over the recent decades. And all these new schools, to varying degrees, have registered the influence of postmodernism in historical writing. In 2012, *American Historical Review* ran a forum on The Historical Study of Emotions. Most of its participants acknowledge that the linguistic turn in historiography of the 1990s played a role in turning their attention to emotions history. Interestingly, two years earlier, *History and Theory* had run a similar interview, of which the interviewees believe that an "emotional turn" has possibly occurred in the field of history.[98] Peter Stearns is one of them who pronounces with his co-editor in a volume that the study of emotions has constituted "a new direction in history," in that it has gone beyond, for the first time, examining only the rational and external behaviors of individuals. Here Stearns echoes Barbara Rosenwein's 2002 observation that "[a]s an academic discipline, history began as the servant of political developments. Despite a generation's worth of social and cultural history, the discipline has never quite lost its attraction to hard, rational things. Emotions have seemed tangential (if not fundamentally opposed) to the historical enterprise."[99]

While expanding the scope of historical research, it seems the study of emotions has also put a new demand on historians to update how historical knowledge is delivered. Narrative, the celebrated form of historical writing in modern times, seems unable to convey effectively the emotions of historical actors. Julia Livingston, a historian of Africa where much information of the past is orally preserved and conveyed, admits how frustrated she becomes "by how distorted my own interviews seemed when they were stripped of their performative and emotional qualities and reduced to texts." Presenting his paper at the International Congress of Historical Sciences in Jinan, Alan Maddox of the University of Sidney played two songs for the audience, in order for them to feel the changing tone, or the "passion," of church music in the eighteenth century.[100] Indeed, as knowledge of the past and its study have been increasingly digitized (which incidentally was another major theme discussed in Jinan, China), it is probable that in the foreseeable future, historians are also going to diversify, update, and change their ways of delivering and presenting their research to readers and audiences. Instead of merely turning their research into narrative history, they may also adopt new means of communication that are currently being developed by the "digital humanities" project. This is a challenge not only for the historians of emotions but, to some extent, for all historians in the world.

Conclusion

In retrospect, the period after 1990 was marked by continuities in historical thought and writing but also witnessed significant reorientations. We have pointed at the sharp turn in historical thinking in the 1970s away from the analytical social sciences with their confidence in modern Western civilization as the high point of the process of historical development, which would serve as a model to the rest of the world, and the new cultural histories, which replaced methods for the explanation of social structures and processes with approaches that sought to interpret the meanings of underlying cultures. This, as we saw, involved an increasing skepticism regarding the possibilities of objective cognition in historical and social studies and deleted the strict border that the traditional social sciences had maintained between fact and fiction, historical studies and imaginative literature. In its most radical postmodern form, it denied the very possibility of historical knowledge that it demoted to pure ideology and myth. Yet the social context in which history was composed changed profoundly after the end of the Cold War, as economic globalization proceeded with the technological, political, social, and cultural transformations that accompanied it. Neither the traditional social sciences that dominated a great deal of historical and social studies in the 1950s and 1960s nor the culturalism and the linguistic turn that replaced them in the 1970s and 1980s appeared in a position to understand the profound changes that occurred since around 1990. Both were very one-sided in their approaches, the traditional social sciences in their neglect of local diversities and cultural patterns, culturalism in refusing to take into consideration the institutional context of culture.

In a sense, it seems that the process of globalization confirmed fundamental assumptions of classical modernization theories that saw the increased homogenization of economy, society, and culture on a worldwide scale. Yet the actual course of events in the period after 1990 went counter to the expectations of modernization theories. The latter had assumed that modernization on the economic level would be accompanied by the strengthening of civil society, a secular outlook, and political democracy. This assumed that Western development would also serve as a model outside the West. Yet the 1920s and 1930s, in which various forms of authoritarianism dominated much of continental Europe, including National Socialism in Germany and Stalinism in the Soviet Union, showed that this model did not even hold for the West. The period since the end of the Cold War has seen that this model of a civil society and democracy actually established itself in various parts of the world, with the European Union as perhaps a prime example; nevertheless, vicious civil wars and ethnic fighting persisted, in the Balkans in the 1990s, throughout large parts of Africa during this period, and in Syria after 2011. Rwanda and Darfur have demonstrated that genocides do not belong only to the past. Moreover, the earlier trend toward secularism has been reversed by strengthened religious fundamentalisms not only in the Islamic world but also in India, as an undercurrent even in China and in Western countries such as the United States, Poland, and Israel.

In other words, the complexity of the world under the impact of globalization and intercultural conflict required methods that were not met by postmodernist conceptions of history as primarily a form of imaginative literature nor, perhaps for a different reason, by the analytical social sciences as they were practiced before 1990. The globalization of recent decades requires approaches that take into account the major trends of change in the world in which all of us live and have lived. And in so doing, analytical approaches of the social sciences are indispensable, without which any meaningful study of globalization is impossible but which need to go beyond the concentration on structures and processes of the traditional American social sciences, the Braudelian *Annales*, or the various forms of Marxism and take into account the complexity and conflicts within the globalizations that play such a key role in shaping our world today. At present, it is still a bit too early to tell whether the various attempts to write global history would lead to a definitive transformation of the field of history. But the major trends of historical thought and writing that we have summarized here have already pointed to the need to call for new approaches to the writing of history, ones that not only challenge the often too readily accepted notion that the Western model remains the center of historical studies and radiates its influence all over the world but that also transcend the West/non-West dichotomy underpinning many well-intended comparative studies of history and historiography. It will present the changes in historical writing in a multipolar, global perspective, recognizing that the dynamics for its development have been generated by various sources and emerged from various corners of the world. Our book is an attempt to respond to such a call.

Notes

1 Francis Fukuyama, "The End of History?" *National Interest*, 16 (Summer 1989), 3–18; *The End of History and the Last Man* (New York, 1996); also his "Reflections on the End of History, Five Years Later," *History and Theory*, 34:2 (1995), 27–43.

2 Samuel P. Huntington, *The Clash of Civilizations and the Remaking of the World Order* (New York, 1996).

3 See Francis Fukuyama, *The Origins of Political Order: From Prehuman Times to the French Revolution* (New York: Farrar, Straus and Giroux, 2011) and, most recently, *Political Order and Political Decay: From the Industrial Revolution to the Globalization of Democracy* (New York: Farrar, Straus and Giroux, 2014).

4 Some of the popular works on the subject have become best sellers, including Thomas Friedman's *The Lexus and the Olive Tree* (New York, 2000, rev. ed.) and *The World is Flat* (New York, 2004); Benjamin Barber's *Jihad vs. McWorld* (New York, 1995); and Amy Chua's *World on Fire: How Exporting Free Market and Democracy Breeds Ethnic Hatred and Global Instability* (New York, 2003). With a few notable and recent exceptions, most of the theoretical literature on globalization has come from nonhistorians. This is partly due to the very contemporary nature of the subject and partly also because the common historical reference points of place and location are transcended by globalization.

5 R. Stephen Humphreys, "The Historiography of the Modern Middle East: Transforming a Field of Study" in Israel Gershoni, Amy Singer, and Y. Hakan Erdem, eds., *Middle East Historiographies: Narrating the Twentieth Century* (Seattle, 2006), 20.

6 In 2003, a new high school history textbook was compiled jointly by historians and published simultaneously in Japan, China, and South Korea. Since the adoption of history textbooks required "official" approval, this text remains a "supplementary reading." But its publication represents nonetheless an important step toward reaching an agreed-on account of the region's history. About the Joint History Research Project, see Q. Edward Wang, "Remembering the Past; Reconciling for the Future: A Critical Analysis of the China-Japan Joint History Research Project (2006–2010)," *The Chinese Historical Review*, 17:2 (Fall 2010), 219–237.

7 Dominic Sachsenmaier, *Global Perspectives on Global History* (Cambridge, 2011), 42.

8 See Victoria E. Bonnell and Lynn Hunt, eds., *Beyond the Cultural Turn: New Directions in the Study of Society and Culture* (Berkeley, 1999), Introduction, 3.

9 Lynn Hunt, *Writing History in the Global Era* (New York, 2014), 3.

10 Frank Ankersmit, *Sublime Historical Experience* (Stanford, 2005) and also his *Meaning, Truth, and Reference in Historical Representation* (Ithaca, 2012).

11 Marnie Hughes-Warrington, *Fifty Key Thinkers of History* (London, 2000), 355. It must be noted that most of the "key thinkers" on the list were from the Western tradition, with the exceptions of Sima Qian and Ibn Khaldun.

12 Ernst Breisach, *On the Future of History: The Postmodernist Challenge and Its Aftermath* (Chicago, 2003), 193, 205.
13 Peter Burke, "*Metahistory*: Before and After," *Rethinking History*, 17:4 (2013), 437–447, quote on 444.
14 Jenkins' *Rethinking History*, for instance, was quickly translated into Chinese after its appearance and adopted to teach courses on historical theory and mythology on college campuses in Taiwan from the 1990s.
15 See the essays by Judith Surkis, Gary Wilder, Durba Ghosh, James Cook, and Julia A. Thomas in *American Historical Review*, 117:3 (2012).
16 Fuminobu Murakami, *Postmodern, Feminist and Postcolonial Currents in Contemporary Japanese Culture* (London, 2004).
17 Hayden White, "Historical Emplotment and the Problem of Truth" in Saul Friedländer, ed., *Probing the Limits of Representation: Nazism and the "Final Solution"* (Cambridge, MA, 1992), 37–53. About Friedländer's study and its relations with other studies and postmodern theory, a useful discussion is in Michael Dintenfass, "Truth's Other: Ethics, the History of the Holocaust, and Historiographical Theory after the Linguistic Turn," *History and Theory*, 39:1 (2000), 1–20.
18 Hayden White, *Tropics of Discourse: Essays in Cultural Criticism* (Baltimore, 1985) 82. See also White: "No other discipline is more informed by the illusion that 'facts' are found in research rather than constructed by modes of representation and techniques of discoursivization than is history" in Bonnell and Hunt, eds., *Beyond the Cultural Turn*, 322.
19 White, "Historical Discourse and Literary Theory: On Saul Friedländer's *The Years of Extermination*" in Norbert Frei and Wulf Kansteiner, eds., *Den Holocaust erzählen: Historiographie zwischen wissenschaftlicher Empirie und narrativer Kreativität* (Göttingen, 2013), 51–78.
20 Ibid., 54.
21 Leopold von Ranke, "On the Character of Historical Science" in Georg G. Iggers, ed., *Leopold von Ranke, The Theory and Practice of History* (London: Routledge, 2011), 8.
22 Saul Friedländer, "Reply to Hayden White," ibid, 75–78.
23 Robert Doran, ed., *Philosophy of History after Hayden White* (London, 2013), 3.
24 There is a very brief mention of Hayden White in Norman J. Wilson, *History in Crisis? Recent Directions in Historiography* (Boston, 2014, 3rd ed.), 22, 117–118, 121. A similar case can be observed in Eileen Ka-may Cheng's *Historiography: An Introductory Guide* (London, 2012).
25 In 1988, in the last phases of the Soviet Union the human rights organization Memorial was founded by Andrei Sacharov, which began to conduct interviews with victims of Stalinism.
26 Lutz Niethammer, "*Die Jahre weiss man nicht, wo man die heute hinsetzen soll,*" *Faschismuserfahrungen im Ruhrgebiet. Lebensgeschichte und Sozialkultur im Ruhrgebiet 1930 bis 1960* (Berlin, 1983).
27 See http://mhorh.mh.sinica.edu.tw/index.php for the Oral History Project in Taiwan.
28 See Alan Confino, "History and Memory" in *The Oxford History of Historical Writing* (Oxford, 2011), v. 5, 36–53.
29 (Paris, 1986–1993).
30 Etienne François and Hagen Schulze, eds., *Deutsche Erinnerungsorte* (München, 2001).
31 See Lynn Struve, "Chinese Memory Makes a Martyr," *History and Memory*, 25:2 (2013), 5–31; Yinan He, "Remembering and Forgetting the War," ibid., 19:2 (2007), 43–74; Klaus Mühlhahn, "Remembering a Bitter Past," ibid., 16:2 (2004), 108–139; and Katharina Schramm, "The Slaves of Pikworo: Local Histories, Transatlantic Perspectives," ibid., 23:1 (2011), 96–130.

32 See Paul Ricoueur's introductory essay "Memory-Forgetting-History" in Jörn Rüsen, ed., *Meaning and Representation in History* (New York, 2006).

33 On conflicting memories on a European scale, see Arndt Bauerkämper, ed., *Das umstrittene Gedächtnis: Die Erinnerung an Nationalsozialismus, Faschismus und Krieg in Europa seit 1945* (Paderborn, 2012).

34 Dirk Moses, Binghampton, Kurt Pätzold, *Verfolgung, Vertreibung, Vernichtung: Dokumente des faschistischen Antisemitismus 1933–1942* (Berlin, 1984).

35 For a broadly comparative study of memory of recent history encompassing Europe, see Bauerkämper, *Das umstrittene Gedächtnis*; Geoffrey Cubitt, *History and Memory* (Manchester, 2007); and Marek Tamm, "Beyond History and Memory: New Perspectives in Memory Studies," *History Compass*, 11:6 (2013): 458–473.

36 Yang Jisheng, *Mubei: Zhongguo liushi niandai dajihuang jishi* (Hong Kong, 2009) and its English edition (New York, 2012). Also, Frank Dikötter, *Mao's Great Famine: The History of China's Most Devastating Catastrophe, 1958–1962* (New York, 2010); Zhou Xun, ed., *The Great Famine in China, 1958–1962: A Documentary History* (New Haven, 2012); and idem, *Forgotten Voices of Mao's Great Famine, 1958–1962* (New Haven, 2013).

37 It is worth mentioning that Nanjing University in mainland China has established a research center of memory studies in recent years. Some of its studies are featured in the special issue of *Chinese Studies in History*, 47:1 (2013). Japanese scholars have also turned to memory studies, as in the publication of *Rekishi to shite, kioku to shite: shakai undô shi, 1970–1985* (*As History, as Memory: Social Movements, 1970–1985*), ed. Kiyasu Akira, Kitahachi Atsushi, Okamoto Michihiro, and Tanikawa Minoru (Tokyo, 2013).

38 Joan Wallach Scott, *Gender and the Politics of History* (New York, 1999).

39 The number of works on men and masculinity is too numerous to name. An important article in the early literature is John Tosh's "What Should Historians Do with Masculinity? Reflections in Nineteenth-century Britain," *History Workshop Journal*, 38 (1994), 179–202.

40 Mrinalini Sinha, "Giving Masculinity a History: Some Contributions from the Historiography of Colonial India," *Gender and History* 11 (1999), 445–460.

41 Des Jardins, "Women and Gender History," 153.

42 See Lata Mani, *Contentious Traditions: The Debate on Sati in Colonial India* (Berkeley, 1998) and Joerg Fisch, "Sati and the Task of the Historian," *Journal of World History*, 18 (2007), 361–368.

43 Gayatri Chakravorty Spivak, "Can the Subaltern Speak?" in Cary Nelson and Lawrence Grossberg, eds., *Marxisms and the Interpretation of Culture* (Chicago, 1988), 271–317.

44 An excellent work on the relationship between colonialism and gender is Anne McClintock's *Imperial Leather: Race, Gender and Sexuality in the Colonial Context* (New York, 1995).

45 Mrinalini Sinha, *Colonial Masculinity: The "Manly Englishman" and the "Effeminate" Bengali in the Late Nineteenth Century* (Manchester, 1995).

46 Maithreyi Krishnaraj, "History through the Gender Lens" in Kirit S. Shah and Meherjyoti Sangle, eds., *Historiography Past and Present* (Delhi, 2005), 130.

47 Ketu Katrak, "Indian Nationalism, Gandhian 'Satyagraha,' and the Engendering of National Narratives" in A. Parker, M. Russo, D. Sommer, and P. Yeager, eds., *Nationalisms and Sexualities* (New York: 1992).

48 Dorothy Ko, "Women's History: Asia" in Kelly Boyd, ed., *Encyclopedia of Historians and Historical Writing* (London, 1999), vol. 2, 1314.

49 Maithreyi Krishnaraj, "Permeable Boundaries. Ideals, Images and Real Lives" in Alice Thorner and Maithreyi Krishnaraj, eds., *Women in Literature and History* (Hyderabad, 2000), 5.

50 Reina Lewis and Sara Mills, eds., *Feminist Postcolonial Theory: A Reader* (New York, 2003), 8.

51 Ibid., 8.

52 Desjardins, "Women and Gender History," 155.

53 Giulia Calvi, "Global Trends: Gender Studies in Europe and the US," *European History Quarterly*, 40 (4), 643.

54 Also important is the three-volume *Women's History in Global Perspective*, edited by Bonnie G. Smith, which appeared in 2005 as a comprehensive collection of articles on gender theory and empirical work from a global perspective.

55 Christopher Bayly, *The Birth of the Modern World, 1780–1914: Global Connections and Comparisons* (Oxford, 2004).

56 Calvi, "Global Trends," 641.

57 "Histoire et sciences sociales, un tournant critique?" *Annales ESC*, 43:2 (March–April 1988), 291–293; also, "Histoire et sciences sociales socials: Tentons l'expérience," ibid., 44:6 (November–December 1989), 1317–1323.

58 *Annales*, "Régime de genre" 3 (2012).

59 Manfred Berg, "Das Ende der Lynchjustiz im amerikanischen Süden," *Historische Zeitschrift*, 283:3 (2006), 583–616.

60 See *The Cambridge World History* (Cambridge, 2015), vol. 6, quote in Part 1, 447.

61 See Alon Confino, "Collective Memory and Cultural History: Problems of Method," *American Historical Review*, 102:5 (1997), 1386–1403; quotes on 1392–1393; also, idem, "History and Memory," *The Oxford History of Historical Writing*, 5, 36–51.

62 Kevin Passmore, "History and Social Science in the West," *The Oxford History of Historical Writing*, 5, 199–219.

63 See, for example, William H. Sewell, Jr., *Logics of History: Social Theory and Social Transformation* (Chicago, 2005); Herbert S. Klein, "The Old Social History and the New Social Sciences," *Journal of Social History*, 39:3 (2006), 936–944; and Philip T. Hoffman, "Opening Our Eyes: History and the Social Sciences," *Journal of the Historical Society*, 6:1 (2006), 93–117.

64 See Gabrielle M. Spiegel, ed., *Practicing History: New Directions in Historical Writing after the Linguistic Turn* (New York, 2005) and Hunt, *Writing History in the Global Era*.

65 See textbooks widely used today that stress the role of ethnic minorities and women, such as Andrew Clayton, Elisabeth Israels Perry, and Allan M. Winkler, *America Pathways to the Present* (Needham, 2003) and McDougal Littell, *The Americans* (New York, 2007) and contrast them with earlier white male–oriented textbooks such as John Spencer Bassett, *A Short History of the United States* (New York, 1929) and Allan Nevins and Henry Steel Commager, *America: The Story of a Free People* (Boston, 1942).

66 See Georg G. Iggers, "The Role of Marxism in Sub-Saharan and South African Historiography" in Q. Edward Wang and Georg G. Iggers, eds., *Marxist Historiographies: A Global Perspective* (London, 2015), 220–248.

67 Michael Werner and Bénédicte Zimmermann, "Beyond Comparison *Histoire Croisée* and the Challenge of Reflexivity," *History and Theory*, 45 (2006), 30–50.

68 Stefan Berger et al., eds., *Writing the Nation*, 9 vols. (New York, London, 2007–2015).

69 See the discussion of forms of world history and their development in recent historical thought and studies in Patrick Manning, *Navigating World History. Historians Create a Global Past* (New York, 2003); also, the brief but very concise article by Jerry H. Bentley, "World History" in Daniel Woolf, ed., *A Global Encyclopedia of Historical Writing* (New York, 1998), 968–970 and his "The New World History" in Lloyd Kramer and Sarah Maza, eds., *A Companion*

to *Western Historical Thought* (Malden, 2002), 393–416; and Sachsenmaier, "Global History and Critiques of Western Perspectives."

70 Oswald Spengler, *The Decline of the West* (New York, 1926).

71 Arnold Toynbee, *A Study of History*, 12 vols. (Oxford, 1934–1961).

72 See Jerry H. Bentley, *Shapes of World History in Twentieth-Century Scholarship* (Washington, DC, 1996).

73 On McNeill and Toynbee, see Bentley, ibid., 15.

74 See also Patrick Manning, *Navigating World History: Historians Create a Global Past (2003)* (New York, 2003).

75 Anthony G. Hopkins, "The History of Globalization – and the Globalization of History?" in Anthony G. Hopkins, ed., *Globalization in World History* (London, 2002), 11–46. See also Bruce Mazlish, *The New Global History* (London, 2006).

76 See Sachsenmaier, "Global History and Critiques of Western Perspectives."

77 Patrick O'Brien, "Historiographical Traditions and Modern Imperatives for the Restoration of Global History," *Journal of Global History*, 1:1 (2006), 3–39.

78 Cf. Narita Ryūichi, *Rekishi no sutairu* (*The Style of Historiography*) (Tokyo, 2001), 217–230, 275–288, 347–364; also Hirota Masaki, "Pandora no hako: minshū shisōshi kenkyū no kadai (Pandora's Box: Issues in the Study of the History of Public Mentality)" in Sakai Naoki, ed., *Nashonaru hisutori o manabi suteru* (*Unlearning National History*) (Tokyo, 2006), 3–92.

79 See Wang Qingjia, *Taiwan shixue 50 nian: chuancheng, fangfa, quxiang, 1950–2000* (*Writing History in Taiwan: Tradition and Transformation, 1950–2000*) (Taipei, 2002); and idem, "Jiegou yu chonggou: jin ershi nianlai Taiwan lishi yishi bianhua de zhuyao qushi" (Deconstruction and Reconstruction: Main Trends of Change in Historical Consciousness in Taiwan Over the Past Two Decades), *Hanxue yanjiu tongxun* (*Newsletter for Research in Chinese Studies*), 25:4 (November 2006), 13–32.

80 Cf. Huaiyin Li, *Reinventing Modern China: Imagination and Authenticity in Chinese Historical Writing* (Honolulu, 2013).

81 Merry Wiesner-Hanks' preface to *The Cambridge World History*, vol. 1, xv–xx.

82 See Jürgen Osterhammel, *Die Verwandlung der Welt: eine Geschichte des 19. Jahrhunderts* (Munich, 2009); its English version was translated by Patrick Camiller and published by Princeton University Press in 2014.

83 See Sachsenmaier, *Global Perspectives on Global History* which specifically deals with the advances of global history in the United States and Chjna.

84 J. R. McNeill, "Observations on the Nature and Culture of Environmental History," *History and Theory*, 42 (2003), 5–43. Also Richard White, "American Environmental History: The Development of a New Historical Field," *Pacific Historical Review*, 54:3 (1985), 297–335, and its sequel "Afterword Environmental History: Watching a Field Mature," *Pacific Historical Review*, 70:1 (2001), 103–111; and Alfred Crosby, "The Past and Present of Environmental History," *American Historical Review*, 100:4 (1995), 1177–1189.

85 Ramachandra Guha, *Environmentalism: A Global History* (London, 2000).

86 Simon Schama, *Landscape and Memory* (New York, 1996), 14.

87 See Mark Carey, "Latin American Environmental History: Current Trends, Interdisciplinary Insights and Future Directions," *Environmental History*, 14 (2009), 221–252.

88 McNeill, "The Nature and Culture of Environmental History," 35.

89 Will Steffen, Paul J. Crutzen, and John R. McNeill, "The Anthropocene: Are Humans Now Overwhelming the Great Forces of Nature?" *Ambio*, 36:8 (2007), 614–621.

90 Peter and Carol Stearns, "Emotionology: Clarifying the History of Emotions and Emotional Standards," *American Historical Review*, 90:4 (1985), 813–836.

91 Lucien Febvre, "La Sensibilité et l'histoire: Comment reconstituer la vie affective d'autrefois?," *Annales d'histoire sociale*, 3/1–2 (1941), 5–20. Lucien Febvre, "Sensibility and History: How to Reconstitute the Emotional Life of the Past" in ed. Peter Burke, tr. K. Folca, *A New Kind of History: From the Writings of Febvre* (New York, 1973), 12–26.

92 Jan Plamper, *The History of Emotions: An Introduction*, tr. Keith Tribe (Oxford, 2015), 55.

93 From the late 1980s, scholars in Academia Sinica in Taiwan have conducted a series of studies of affection and desire in Chinese culture and thought. See Hsiung Ping-chen, ed., *Lijiao yu qingyu: qian jindai Zhongguo wenhua zhong de hou/xiandai xing (Rites and Emotions: Postmodernity in Premodern Chinese Culture)* (Taipei, 1999). A brief survey of emotions in Chinese culture and history is provided by Norman Kutcher, "The Skein of Chinese Emotions History" in Susan Matt and Peter Stearns eds., *Doing Emotions History* (Urbana, 2014), 57–73.

94 See Susan Matt and Peter Stearns' Introduction to *Doing Emotions History*, 2. Also, Barbara Rosenwein, "Modernity: A Problematic Category in the History of Emotions," *History and Theory*, 53 (2014), 69–78.

95 Plamper, *History of Emotions*, 60.

96 Plamper, *History of Emotions*, chs. 2, 3, and 4.

97 Michel Foucault, "Nietzsche, Genealogy, History," *Language, Counter-Memory, Practice: Selected Essays and Interviews*, tr. Donald F. Bouchard and Sherry Simon (Ithaca, 1977), 153.

98 Julia Livingston, "AHR Conversation: The Historical Study of Emotions," *American Historical Review*, 117:5 (2012), 1487–1531 and "The History of Emotions: An Interview with William Reddy, Barbara Rosenwein, and Peter Stearns," *History and Theory*, 49:2 (2010), 237–265.

99 See Matt and Stearns, *Doing Emotions History*, 2–3 and Barbara Rosenwein, "Worrying about Emotions in History," *American Historical Review*, 107:3 (2002), 821–845, quote on 821.

100 See Julia Livingston's remarks in "AHR Conversation," 1489–1490. Alan Maddox's paper is entitled "Emotional Expression and the Passion at the Basilica of St Anthony of Padua in the Early Eighteenth Century," presented in the Historical Congress of Historical Sciences in Jinan on August 24, 2015.

Glossary

administrative historians   colonial officials in the service of the British East India Company and, later, the Crown who also wrote histories of India, with the aim to justify the imperial system.

Alltagsgeschichte   the history of everyday life, referring to a movement in Germany in the 1980s that turned against the macrohistorical explanations of social science history and focused on the history of common people on a local level.

Asiatic mode of production   term used by Karl Marx to characterize the social systems of India and China. In these systems, the state owned all the land because agricultural productivity could be maintained only by large-scale state-run public works, particularly irrigation. The absence of the private ownership of land inhibited social change and made these societies static.

Aufklärung   the German word for "Enlightenment" in the eighteenth century, committed to replacing traditional attitudes with critical thinking but still more religiously and less politically oriented than Enlightenment thinkers in France or Great Britain.

Bansei ikkei   a claim made by Japanese scholars about the continuous line of royal succession as a unique cultural phenomenon in Japanese history.

Bürgertum   the German middle class, defined more by education and culture than by social and economic status, as was the French *bourgeoisie*.

civilizational history (*bunmeishi*)   a form of nationalist history prevalent in Meiji Japan aimed to emulate the work of Henry Buckle and François Guizot and provide a narrative account for national evolution in history.

Confucian historiography   a tradition of historical writing abiding Confucian moral values and political ideals and emphasizing the role of history in espousing and explicating social hierarchy and political order.

Consensus historians   a group of historians in the United States in the 1950s and the 1960s, including Louis Hartz, Richard Hofstadter, and David Boorstin, who rejected the critical approach to American history of the Progressive historians and saw the United States as a distinct society, unlike Europe, free of social divisions and conflicts.

cultural turn the turn in studies of society and of history away from causal explanation to the interpretation of meanings that played an important role in historical theory in the 1970s and 1980s. In a moderate form, it stressed that society and history cannot be understood without taking cultural forces into account but that these cannot be separated from their social context. In a more radical form, it incorporates the linguistic turn (see *linguistic turn*), holding that language does not reflect social reality but shapes it and that there are multiple interpretations of all cultural manifestations that cannot be validated or disproved.

culture fever (*wenhua re*) an intellectual and cultural movement in 1980s China, associated with the country's Open Door economic policy. It aimed to introduce cultural and philosophical developments in the West to China as well as to revive the Chinese cultural tradition castigated and jettisoned during the Cultural Revolution (1966–1976).

dependencia a theory, indebted to Marxism, that holds in reference to economically less developed regions of the world that free market economies and investments by finance capital in these regions would not result in economic progress and the reduction of poverty but would stifle this development.

dynastic historiography a prevalent form of historical writing in East Asia and certain parts in the Middle East (e.g., Persia) that chronicled the rise and fall of a dynastic rule.

economic nationalism an economic critique of British rule in India developed in the late nineteenth century. It claimed that, far from benefiting India, British rule led to a "drain of wealth" and the "de-industrialization" of the country.

Egyptianization an effort to staff institutions of higher learning in modern Egypt with Egyptian scholars and critique the interpretation of Egyptian history by European Orientalists.

Eurocentrism a belief popular in Europe as well as in many regions outside Europe that since modern times, European civilization has been the vanguard and exemplar of historical development in and for the world.

evidential learning an intellectual movement beginning in eighteenth-century China and spreading to Korea, Japan, and Vietnam through the nineteenth century. It advocated a historicist approach to the study of Confucian classics, using the methods of philology, epigraphy, phonology, and etymology to reconstruct the context wherein the classics were created for obtaining an understanding of their true meaning.

flunkeyism (*sadae juŭi*) a theoretical characterization of the (excessive?) homage paid by the Koreans to the cultural and political influence from China, especially during the Chosŏn period.

Fürstenspiegel **(mirror for princes)** a genre of historical/literary writing in Persia.

Gymnasium a university preparatory secondary school in the German-speaking countries, generally with a focus on the humanities.

hadīth   traditions relating to the deeds and words of the Prophet Muhammad.

Hindutva   term coined by V. D. Savarkar to emphasize the ancient Vedic roots of Indian culture. *Hindutva*, or "Hinduness," emerged during the Indian nationalist movement and survived into the postindependence period as the Hindu right wing in Indian politics. It opposes the secular credentials of independent India and seeks to establish a Hindu-dominated state.

historism/historicism   a doctrine that developed in Germany in the nineteenth century that holds that history is the key to all knowledge.

History Bureau   a government office devoted to the compilation of dynastic histories in East Asia from approximately the sixth to the late nineteenth centuries.

Islamism   a set of political ideologies arisen in the late 1970s, championing that Islam is both a religion and a political system, that Islam remains an indispensable guidance to contemporary Muslim society, and that reception of Western cultural influence is un-Islamic.

isnād   "chain of transmitters/authorities" in early Islamic literature.

khabar   a form of historical literature among the early Muslims.

linguistic turn   the idea that language does not reflect reality but creates reality and endows it with meaning. In its moderate form, it suggested that social reality and history cannot be understood without recognizing the role that language plays in shaping this reality. In a more radical form, it denies that there is any social reality whatsoever.

logical positivism   an approach to philosophy formulated in Vienna in the 1920s by philosophers such as Moritz Schlick, Karl Popper, and Rudolf Carnap, according to whom philosophy must be based on strict science and who hold that all metaphysics is meaningless.

maghāzī   prophetic biography with a focus on Muhammad's military campaigns.

Methodenstreit   a controversy about historical method initiated by the German historian Karl Lamprecht who, in his *German History* in 1891, rejected the concentration of German historians on politics and gave a central place to society and culture. Lamprecht's initiative was rejected by much of the German historical profession but similar calls for a history that would take into consideration social, cultural, and economic factors were also raised in other countries at the turn of the twentieth century

microstoria (microhistory)   a movement in social history in Italy in the late 1970s and the early 1980s around the journal *Quaderni Storici*, which reacted against the then dominant social science history that analyzed large social groups through statistical methods. Instead, it focused on the concrete lives of common people in small-scale local settings.

Neo-Confucianism   a loose term referring to various schools of Confucian learning prevalent in Song and Ming China, as well as in Chosŏn Korea and Tokugawa Japan, that aimed to revive Confucianism in light of the advance of Buddhism whereas at the same time appropriating Buddhist ideas and practices.

New History the call of historians in the United States in the late nineteenth and the early twentieth centuries for a "New History" that would give greater attention to society, economy, and culture than the traditional history that placed politics and elites at the center.

new left an orientation among American historians in the 1960s and 1970s, including William Appleman Williams, Gabriel Kolko, Staughton Lynd, and others, critical of American capitalism and of American foreign policy in the Cold War.

Nissen dōsoron a theory advanced by Japanese historians in the early twentieth century about the same racial origin of the peoples in Japan and Korea.

Oriental Despotism term used by Marx to describe a specific form of class domination characteristic of the Asiatic mode of production where the need for large-scale waterworks led to despotic bureaucracies.

Orientalism a form of learning developed by modern European scholars specializing in cultures and histories of the "Orient," or the regions east of Europe (e.g., the Middle East and Far East). Also the title of Edward Said's seminal work in postcolonial theory that regards Orientalism as the ideological counterpart of imperialism and as a body of knowledge that appears objective when in fact it is politically motivated.

Ottomanism a form of nationalism prevalent in the Ottoman Empire at the turn of the nineteenth and twentieth centuries. Inspired by the ideals of the Enlightenment, it stressed equal citizenship among all the Ottomans.

people's history (*minshūshi*) a school of historical writing in modern Japan that originated in the Meiji period as an extension and ally of civilizational history and that boomed again in the postwar period due to Marxist influence.

pharaonism a historical interest in pharaonic, pre-Islamic Egypt as the foundation of modern Egypt, prevalent among Egyptian nationalist historians in the early twentieth century.

Philosophes a group of French eighteenth-century intellectuals, including Montesquieu, Voltaire, Rousseau, Diderot, and d'Alembert among others, who were authors of the *Encyclopédie* and saw in organized religions one of the main sources of superstition and intolerance and wished through philosophy and science to transform the world.

postcolonialism/postcolonial theory deals with the relationship between modern imperialism and culture. Postcolonial theory examines "Orientalist" scholarship and the power of "colonialist discourse" to set the terms of cultural representation. It contests and lays bare Eurocentric assumptions in scholarship.

postmodernism originally referred to architecture but here to literature, philosophy, and historical writing. The term began to replace poststructuralism in the 1970s. Both involved a rejection of earlier modernist concepts that involved the belief in the possibility of explaining reality through scientific analysis. Postmodernism in reference to historiography assumed that objective knowledge of past reality is not possible but is always a construct, that every historical text is subject to multiple interpretations, and that history is basically a form of imaginative literature not subject to standards of validation.

Progressive historians   historians in the United States in the first third of the twentieth century, most notable among them Charles Beard, James Harvey Robinson, Frederick Jackson Turner, Vernon Parrington, and Carl Becker, who wrote history in the service of social reforms aiming at greater democracy and benefiting the working masses and critical of traditional conservative American history.

Prussian School   German historians in the nineteenth century who pursued historical studies with the purpose of uniting Germany under Prussian leadership.

Puranas   literally, "tales of ancient times." A genre of Indian writings dating back to the fourth century till the early first millennium of the common era. Its themes are history, religion, mythology, tradition, and genealogy.

Rangaku   "Dutch learning," a form of learning in Tokugawa Japan that served as a window for the Japanese to gain knowledge of European culture via the works of Dutch scholars.

Rankean School   professional historians in the nineteenth and early twentieth centuries who took Leopold von Ranke's conception and practice of historical science as a model.

saj'   a rhymed prose used in Muslim historical writing.

samaj/rashtra   literally, "society" vs. "state." Historiographically, social history with an emphasis on local customs and folklore and state-centered history that emerged in India during the late nineteenth century as two opposing paradigms of historical writing.

sanskritization   term coined by the Indian sociologist M. N. Srinivas to denote the process by which lower castes or noncaste groups gained upward mobility by adopting the rituals and practices of the upper castes.

scientism   a positivist belief in the universal efficacy of scientific method in the studies of the humanities as well as of natural sciences.

sīra   Prophetic biography in early Muslim historiography.

social Darwinism   a doctrine that emerged with the British philosopher Herbert Spencer in the second half of the twentieth century that sought to apply Charles Darwin's theory of the survival of the fittest to the realm of politics and society. Spencer argued for a laissez-faire economy without any social programs. In Germany, social Darwinism was viewed in terms of racial conflicts and as a legitimation of imperialism and colonialism, as well as in other countries.

Social Democracy a German democratic socialist party, formed in 1875 that until 1958 considered itself a working-class party and after that sought to engage voters generally committed to social reforms and democracy.

Sonderweg an attempt by West German historians in the 1960s and 1970s, most important Hans-Ulrich Wehler, to establish that in Germany since Bismarck economic modernization was not accompanied by democratization as it was in other Western and Northern European nations and the United States. According to this theory, the failure on the part of Germany to follow the Western pattern contributed to the rise of the Nazis to power.

syncretism in the Indian context, the merging of different religious practices, including the worship of common saints. Syncretism belies the communal, or sectarian, version of Indian history that sees its different religious communities, particularly Hindus and Muslims, as antagonistic.

tabaqāt prosopography, a form of writing in Muslim historiography.

ta'rīkh chronography, a form of writing in Muslim historiography.

textbook historians college professors of the late nineteenth century who disputed the negative portrayals of the British historical narratives in the textbooks they authored for the Indian schools.

Tōyōshi (history of the East) a term coined by Japanese historians at the end of the nineteenth century to refer to a study of the history of Asia (Orient) in contrast to that of the West.

Turkish Historical Thesis an interpretation of Turkish/Ottoman history prevalent in the early twentieth century that stressed the historical and cultural connection between Turkey and Europe.

Turkism a form of Turkish nationalism emphasizing the rise of the Turks and the Ottoman Empire, hoping to make a secular departure from Islam.

Venia legendi the right to teach at a German university that generally required the successful defense of a second major dissertation in addition to the original doctoral dissertation.

veritable records historical records entered by court historians in East and Southeast Asia pertinent to the reign of the ruling monarch as primary sources for the compilation of dynastic historiography.

Volksgeschichte represented by a younger generation of historians in Germany in the Weimar Republic and under the Nazis for whom racial conflict and the drive of Germany for domination of the ethnic non-Germans constituted the center of their historiography.

Suggested readings

We have decided not to append an extensive bibliography to this book since the bibliographical information is contained by topics in the endnotes after each chapter. Instead, we are making suggestions for further reading. Wherever English translations of books originally not written in English exist, we have chosen the English title in the footnotes as well as in this section of suggested readings. The list of readings that follows is also comprised mainly of works written in European languages, particularly in English. It is not intended to be exhaustive but is consciously selective and serves as an introduction to the subject matter.

Theories of historiography

As far as questions of the theory and methodology are concerned, the most important source is the journal *History and Theory: Studies in the Philosophy of History*, founded in 1961. A recent examination of theoretical discussions is presented in Aviezer Tucker, *Our Knowledge of the West: A Philosophy of Historiography* (Cambridge, 2004). As for discussions of postmodernism and their bearing on the theory of knowledge, see Ernst Breisach, *On the Future of History: The Postmodernist Challenge and Its Aftermath* (Chicago, 2003), a comprehensive and balanced examination of postmodernism in the setting of Western intellectual history since the Enlightenment. A good survey from a point of view strongly endorsing postmodernism is found in Keith Jenkins, ed., *The Postmodern History Reader* (London, 1997); a very critical position is found in Richard Evans, *In Defence of History* (London, 1997); see also Nancy Partner and Sarah Foot, eds., *The Sage Handbook of Historical Theory* (London, 2013), Robert Doran, ed., *Philosophy of History after Hayden White* (London, 2013), and Aviezer Tucker, ed., *A Companion to the Philosophy of History and Historiography* (Malden, 2009).

Individual works

Ankersmit, Frank A., *History and Tropology: The Rise and Fall of Metaphor* (Berkeley, 1994).
Ankersmit, Frank A., *Meaning, Truth, and Reference in Historical Representation* (Ithaca, 2012).

Ankersmit, Frank A., and Hans Kellner, eds., *A New Philosophy of History* (Chicago, 1995).

Appleby, Joyce, Lynn Hunt and Margaret Jacob, *Telling the Truth about History* (New York and London, 1994).

Assmann, Jan, *Religion and Cultural Memory: Ten Studies* (Stanford, 2006).

Berger, Stefan, Heiko Feldner, and Kevin Passmore, *Writing History: Theory & Practice* (London, 2003).

Bloch, Marc, *The Historian's Craft* (New York, 1957).

Burke, Peter, *History and Social Theory* (Oxford, 1992).

Burke, Peter, *What Is Cultural History?* (Cambridge, 2004).

Carr, E. H., *What Is History?* (Middlesex, 1964).

Certeau, Michel de, *The Writing of History* (New York, 1988).

Chakrabarty, Dipesh, *Provincializing Europe: Postcolonial Thought and Historical Difference* (Princeton, 2000).

Chartier, Roger, *Cultural History: Between Practices and Representations* (Cambridge, 1988).

Collingwood, R. G., *The Idea of History* (Oxford, 1946).

Dilthey, Wilhelm, *Introduction to the Human Sciences* (Detroit, 1988).

Dirlik, Arif, Vinay Bahl, and Peter Gran, eds., *History after the Three Worlds: Post-Eurocentric Historiographies* (Lanham, 2000).

Droysen, Johann Gustav, *Outline of the Principles of History* (Boston, 1893).

Elton, Geoffrey, *The Practice of History* (London, 1967).

Evans, Richard J., *In Defence of History* (London, 2001).

Febvre, Lucien, *A New Kind of History and Other Essays* (New York, 1975).

Foucault, Michel, *The Order of Things: An Archaeology of the Human Sciences* (New York, 1970).

Fulbrook, Mary, *Historical Theory: Ways of Imagining the Past* (London, 2003).

Goldy, Jo, and David Armitage, *The History Manifesto* (Cambridge, 2014).

Goody, Jack, *The Theft of History* (New York, 2006).

Hegel, Georg Wilhelm Friedrich, *Lectures on the Philosophy of World History* (Cambridge, 1975).

Himmelfarb, Gertrude, *The New History and the Old: Critical Essays and Appraisals* (Cambridge, MA, 2004).

Hobsbawm, Eric, *On History* (London, 1997).

Hughes, H. Stuart, *History as Art and as Science: Twin Vistas on the Past* (New York, 1964).

Koselleck, Reinhart, *Futures Past: On the Semantics of Historical Time*, trans. Keith Tribe (Cambridge, MA, 1985).

Küttler, Wolfgang, Jörn Rüsen, and Ernst Schulin, eds., *Geschichtsdiskurs*, 5 vols. (Frankfurt am Main, 1993–1999).

LaCapra, Dominick, *History and Criticism* (Ithaca, 1985).

LaCapra, Dominick, and Steven L. Kaplan, eds., *Modern European Intellectual History: Reappraisals and New Perspectives* (Ithaca, 1991).

Lorenz, Chris, *Konstruktion der Vergangenheit: Eine Einführung in die Geschichtstheorie* (Cologne/Weimar/Vienna, 1997).

McNeill, William H., *Mythistory and Other Essays* (Chicago, 1986).

Megill, Allan, *Historical Knowledge, Historical Error: A Contemporary Guide to Practice*, with contributions by Steven Shepard and Phillipp Honenberger (Chicago, 2007).

Nietzsche, Friedrich, *On the Advantages and Disadvantages of History for Life* (Indianapolis, 1980).

Popkin, Jeremy D., *From Herodotus to H-Net, The Story of Historiography* (New York, 2015).

Rüsen, Jörn, ed., *Meaning and Representation in History* (New York, 2006).

Skinner, Quentin, *Visions of Politics, vol. 1: Regarding Method* (Cambridge, 2002).

Stanford, Michael, *An Introduction to the Philosophy of History* (Oxford, 1998).

Torstendhal, Ralf, and Iremline Veit-Brause, *History-Making: The Intellectual and Social Formation of a Discipline* (Stockholm, 1996).

Troup, Kathleen, and Anna Green, eds., *The House of History: A Critical Reader in Twentieth Century History and Theory* (New York, 1999).

Wang, Q. Edward, and Franz L. Fillafer, eds., *The Many Faces of Clio: Cross-Cultural Approaches to History, Essays in Honor of Georg G. Iggers* (New York, 2007).

White, Hayden, *Metahistory: The Historical Imagination in Nineteenth-Century Europe* (Baltimore, 1973).

White, Hayden, *Tropics of Discourse: Essays in Cultural Criticism* (Baltimore, 1977).

White, Hayden, *The Content of the Form: Narrative Discourse and Historical Representation* (Baltimore, 1987).

White, Hayden, *The Practical Past* (Evanston, 2014).

Young, Robert, *White Mythologies: Writing History and the West* (London, 1990).

THE CULTURAL AND LINGUISTIC TURNS

Bonnell, Victoria, and Lynn Hunt, eds., *Beyond the Cultural Turn: New Directions in the Study of Society and Culture* (Berkeley, 1999).

Brown, Callum G., *Postmodernism for Historians* (Harlow, 2005).

Burke, Peter, ed., *New Perspectives on Historical Writing* (University Park, 2001).

Burke, Peter, *What Is Cultural History?* (Cambridge, 2004).

Eley, Geoff, *A Crooked Line: From Cultural History to the History of Society* (Ann Arbor, 2005).

Hunt, Lynn A., ed., *The New Cultural History* (Berkeley, 1989).

Iggers, Georg G., *Historiography in the Twentieth Century: From Scientific Objectivity to the Postmodern Challenge* (Hanover, 2005, enlarged edition).

Jenkins, Keith, *Re-thinking History* (London, 1991).

Spiegel, Gabrielle, ed., *Practicing History: New Directions in Historical Writing after the Linguistic Turn* (New York, 2005).

Feminist and gender historiography

Canning, Kathleen, *Gender History in Practice: Historical Perspectives on Bodies, Class and Citizenship* (Ithaca, 2006).

Des Jardins, Julie, *Women and Historical Practice in America: Gender, Race, and the Politics of Memory, 1800–1945* (Chapel Hill, 2003).

Downs, Laura Lee, *Writing Gender History* (London, 2004).

Lerner, Gerda, *The Majority Finds Its Past: Placing Women in History* (New York, 1979).

Scott, Joan, *Gender and the Politics of History* (New York, 1988).

Smith, Bonnie, *The Gender of History: Men, Women, and Historical Practice* (Cambridge, MA, 1998).

Global histories of historiography

Syntheses

Crossley, Pamela Kyle, *What Is Global History?* (Cambridge, 2005).
Iggers, Georg G., Q. Edward Wang and Supriya Mukherjee, *A Global History of Modern Historiography* (London, 2016).

IMPORTANT REFERENCE WORKS

Kelly, Boyd, ed., *Encyclopedia of Historians and Historical Writing* (London, 1999).
Woolf, Daniel, ed., *A Global Encyclopedia of Historical Writing*, 2 vols. (New York, 1998).
Woolf, Daniel, *A Global History of History* (Cambridge, 2011).
Woolf, Daniel, ed., *The Oxford History of Historical Writing*, 5 vols. (Oxford, 2010–2012).

Others

Carbonell, Charles Olivier, *L'Historiographie* in *Qui Sais-Je* series (Paris, 1981), a very brief but comprehensive global history of historiography.
Christian, David, *Maps of Time: An Introduction to Big History* (Berkeley, 2004).
Jordan, Stefan, ed., *Lexikon Geschichtswissenschaft* (Stuttgart, 2002).
Offenstadt, Nicolas, *L'Historiographie* in *Qui Sais-Je* series (Paris, 2011).
Raphael, Lutz, *Geschichtswissenschaft im Zeitalter der Extreme: Theorien, Methoden, Tendenzen von 1900 bis zur Gegenwart* (München, 2003), deals briefly with historical studies outside the West in the twentieth century.
Russell, Edmund, *Evolutionary History: Writing History and Biology in Understanding Life on Earth* (New York, 2011).
Spier, Fred, *Big History and the Future of Humanity* (Chichester, 2010).
Völkel, Markus, *Geschichtsschreibung: Eine Einführung in globaler Perspektive* (Köln, 2006).
Wang, Q. Edward, and Georg G. Iggers, eds., *Turning Points in Historiography: A Cross Cultural Perspective* (Rochester, 2002).

Approaches to world and global history

Bentley, Jerry H., ed., *The Oxford History of World History* (Oxford, 2011).
Harneit-Sievers, Axel, ed., *A Place in the World: New Local Historiographies from Africa and South-Asia* (Leiden, 2002), raises important methodological questions.
Hopkins, Anthony G., ed., *Globalization in World History* (London, 2002).
Hunt, Lynn, *Writing History in the Global Era* (New York, 2014).
Mazlish, Bruce, *The New Global History* (New York, 2006).
McNeill, William H. *The Rise of the West: A History of the Human Community* (London, 1963), a pioneering work.
Olstein, Diego, *Thinking History Globally* (New York, 2015).
Osterhammel, Jürgen, *The Transformation of the World: A Global History of the Nineteenth Century* (Princeton, 2014).

Pomper, Philip, Richard H. Elphick, and Richard T. Vann, eds., *World Historians and Their Critics* (Middletown, 1995) and the same three editors, *World History: Ideologies, Structures, and Identities* (Malden, 1998).

Sachsenmaier, Dominic, *Perspectives on Global History* (Cambridge, 2011).

Spiers, Fred, *The Structure of Big History: From the Big Bang until Today* (Berkeley, 2010).

Torstendahl, Rolf, ed., *An Assessment of Twentieth-Century Historiography* (Stockholm, 2000).

Anthologies

Bentley, Michael, ed., *Companion to Historiography* (London, 1997).

Budd, Adam, ed., *The Modern Historiography Reader: Western Sources* (London, 2009).

Duara, Prasenjit, Viren Murthy, and Andrew Sartori, eds., *A Companion to Global Historical Thought* (Malden, 2014).

Erdmann, Karl Dietrich, *Toward a Global Community of Historians: The International Historical Congress and the International Committee of Historical Sciences*, ed. Jürgen Kocka and Wolfgang Mommsen (New York, 2005).

Green, Anna, and Kathleen Troup, eds., *The Houses of History* (New York, 1999).

Harlaftis, Gelina, *The New Ways of History: Developments in Historiography* (London, 2010).

Hoefferle, Carline, ed., *The Essential Historiography Reader* (Boston, 2011).

Iggers, Georg, and Harold T. Parker, eds., *International Handbook of Historical Studies: Contemporary Research and Theories* (Westport, 1979).

Küttler, Wolfgang, Jörn Rüsen, and Ernst Schulin, eds. *Geschichtsdiskurs*, 5 vols. (Frankfurt am Main, 1992–1999).

Rüsen, Jörn, Michael Gottlob, and Achim Mittag, eds. *Die Vielfalt der Kulturen* (Frankfurt am Main, 1998).

Rüsen, Jörn, ed., *Western Historical Thinking* (New York, 2002).

Stuchtey, Benedikt, and Eckhardt Fuchs, eds., *Writing World History, 1800–2000* (Oxford, 2003).

Wang, Q. Edward, and Georg Iggers, eds., *Marxist Historiographies: A Global Perspective* (London, 2015).

Histories of Western historiography

A number of general histories of historiography in English take historical writing back to antiquity. The most important ones are James Westfall Thompson, *A History of Historical Writing*, 2 vols. (New York, 1942); Harry Elmer Barnes, *History of Historical Writing* (New York, 1962); Ernst Breisach, *Historiography: Ancient, Medieval, Modern* (Chicago, 1983); and Donald R. Kelley, *Faces of History: Historical Inquiry from Herodotus to Herder* (New Haven, 1998), *Fortunes of History: Historical Inquiry from Herder to Huizinga* (New Haven, 2003), and *Frontiers of History: Historical Inquiry in the Twentieth Century* (New Haven, 2006). For a useful collection of texts, see Fritz Stern, *The Varieties of History: From Voltaire to the Present* (Cleveland, 1956).

Historians and historiography of Euro-America

Transnational histories of modern Western historiography

Two works that are still classics after over a century are George Peabody Gooch, *History and Historians in the Nineteenth Century* (London, 1913), which deals with historians in all of Europe and the United States, and Eduard Fueter, *Geschichte der Neuren Historiographie* (Leipzig, 1911), which covers European historiography since the Reformation.

Others

Berg, Manfred, *Grundriss der Geschichte* (München, 2013).

Butterfield, Herbert, *Man on His Past: The Study of the History of Historical Scholarship* (Cambridge, 1955).

Butterfield, Herbert, *The Origins of History* (New York, 1981).

Clark, William, *Academic Charisma and the Origins of the Research Universities* (Chicago, 2006).

Gazi, Effi, *Scientific National History: The Greek Case in Comparative Perspective (1850–1920)* (Frankfurt am Main, 2000).

Hobsbawm, Eric, *How to Change the World: Reflections on Marx and Marxism* (New Haven, 2011).

Iggers, Georg, *Historiography in the Twentieth Century: From Scientific Objectivity to the Postmodern Challenge* (Hanover, 2005, enlarged edition).

Iggers, Georg, *New Directions in European Historiography* (Middletown, 1975).

Lingelbach, Gabriele, *Klio macht Karriere: Die Institutionalisierung der Geschichtswissenschaft in Frankreich und in den USA in der zweiten Hälfte des 19. Jahrhunderts* (Göttingen, 2003).

Momigliano, Arnaldo, *The Classical Foundations of Modern Historiography* (Berkeley, 1990).

Momigliano, Arnaldo, *Studies in Historiography* (London, 1966).

Raphael, Lutz, *Geschichtswissenschaft im Zeitalter der Extreme: Theorien, Methoden, Tendenzen von 1990 bis zur Gegenwart* (Munich, 2003).

Skinner, Quentin, *The Foundations of Modern Political Thought*, 2 vols. (Cambridge, 1978).

Stuchtey, Benedikt, and Peter Wende, eds., *British and German Historiography 1750–1950* (Oxford, 2000).

National histories of historiography

France

Burguière, André, *The Annales School: An Intellectual History* (Ithaca, 2009).

Burke, Peter, *The French Historical Revolution: The Annales School 1929–1989* (Cambridge, 1990).

Den Boer, Pim, *History as a Profession: The Study of History in France 1818–1914* (Princeton, 1998).

Keylor, William R., *Academe and Community: The Foundation of the French Historical Profession* (Cambridge, MA, 1975).

Keylor, William R., *Jacques Bainville and the Renaissance of Royalist History in the Twentieth Century* (Baton Rouge, 1979).

Revel, Jacques and Lynn Hunt, eds., *Histories: French Constructions of the Past* (New York, 1995).

Stoianovich, Traian, *French Historical Method: The* Annales *Paradigm* (Ithaca, 1976).

Germany

Beiser, Frederick C., *The German Historicist Tradition* (Oxford, 2011).

Chickering, Roger, *Karl Lamprecht: A German Academic Life 1856–1915* (Atlantic Highlands, 1993).

Dorpalen, Andreas, *German History in a Marxist Perspective* (Detroit, 1985).

Haar, Ingo and Michael Fahlbusch, eds., *German Scholars and Ethnic Cleansing 1920–1945* (New York, 2005).

Iggers, Georg, *The German Conception of History: The National Tradition of Historical Thought from Herder to the Present* (Middletown, 1983), a critical oversight over the historical thought of the German historical profession.

Iggers, Georg, *Marxist Historiography in Transformation: New Orientations in Recent East German History* (New York, 1991).

Kessler, Mario, ed., *Deutsche Historiker im Exil (1933–1945)* (Berlin, 2005).

Kocka, Jürgen, *Sozialgeschichte in Deutschland seit 1945* (Bonn, 2002).

Lehmann, Hartmut, and James van Horn Melton, eds., *Paths of Continuity: Central European Historiography from the 1930s to the 1950s* (Cambridge, 1994).

Lehmann, Hartmut, and James J. Sheehan, *An Interrupted Path: German-Speaking Refugee Historians in the United States after 1933* (Oxford, 1991).

McClelland, Charles E., *State, Society and University in Germany 1700–1914* (Cambridge, 1980).

Meinecke, Friedrich, *Historism: The Rise of a New Historical Outlook.* trans. J. E. Anderson (New York, 1972).

Moses, John, *Politics of Illusion: The Fischer Controversy in German Historiography* (London, 1975).

Ranke, Leopold von, *The Theory and Practice of History*, ed. Georg G. Iggers (London, 2011).

Reill, Peter Hanns, *The German Enlightenment and the Rise of Historicism* (Berkeley, 1975).

Ringer, Fritz, *The Decline of the German Mandarins: The German Academic Community 1890–1933* (Cambridge, MA, 1969).

Ritter, Gerhard A., ed., *German Refugee Historians and Friedrich Meinecke: Letters and Documents 1910 to 1977* (Leiden, 1910).

Sabrow, Martin, *Das Diktat des Konsenses: Geschichtswissenschaft in der DDR 1949–1969* (Munich, 2001).

Schulze, Winfried, *Deutsche Geschtswissenschaft nach 1945* (Munich, 1993).

Schulze, Winfried, and Otto Gerhard Oexle, eds., *Deutsche Historiker im Nationalsozialismus* (Frankfurt am Main, 1999).

Wehler, Hans-Ulrich, ed., *Deutsche Historiker*, 9 vols. (Göttingen, 1971–1972).

Great Britain

Bentley, Michael, *Modernizing England's Past: English Historiography in the Age of Modernism* (Cambridge, 2005).

Butterfield, Herbert, *The Whig Interpretation of History* (London, 1931).

Clive, John, *Macaulay: The Shaping of the Historian* (New York, 1974).

Evans, Richard, *Cosmopolitan Islanders: British Historians and the European Continent* (Cambridge, 2009).

Kaye, Harvey J., *The British Marxist Historians* (Cambridge, 1984).

Kaye, Harvey J., and Keith McClelland, eds., *E. P. Thompson: Critical Perspectives* (Oxford, 1990).

Kenyon, John, *The History Men: The History Men in England Since the Renaissance*, 2nd ed. (London, 1993).

United States

For a critical history of the American historical profession and its theoretical and political assumptions, see Peter Novick, *That Noble Dream: The "Objectivity" Question and the American Historical Profession* (Cambridge, 1988).

OTHERS

Breisach, Ernst, *American Progressive History: An Experiment in Modernization* (Chicago, 1993).

Higham, John, *History: Professional Scholarship in America* (Baltimore, 1983).

Hofstadter, Richard, *The Progressive Historians: Turner, Beard, Parrington* (New York, 1968).

Kammen, Michael, ed., *The Past Before Us: Contemporary Historical Writing in the United States* (Ithaca, 1980).

Lewis, David Levering, *W.E.B. Du Bois: Biography of a Race, 1868–1919* (New York, 1993).

Meier, August, and Elliot Rudwick, *Black History and the Historical Profession 1915–1980* (Urbana, 1986).

Skotheim, Robert, *American Intellectual Histories and Historians* (Princeton, 1966).

Sternsher, Bernard, *Consensus, Conflict, and American Historians* (Bloomington, 1975).

Tyrell, Ian, *The Absent Marx: Class Analysis and Liberal History in Twentieth-Century America* (New York, 1986).

Eastern Europe and Russia

Boia, Lucian, *History and Myth in Romanian Consciousness*, trans. J.C. Brown (Budapest, 1997).

Mazour, Anatole G., *The Writing of History in the Soviet Union* (Stanford, 1971).

Mazour, Anatole G., *Modern Russian Historiography* (Westport, 1975).

Riis, Carsten, *Religion, Politics, and Historiography in Bulgaria* (Boulder, 2002).

Wieczynski, Joseph L., and George N. Rhyne, eds., *Modern Encyclopedia of Russian and Soviet History*, 55 vols. (Gulf Breeze, 1976–1993).

Jewish history

Brenner, Michael, *Propheten des Vergangenen: Jüdische Geschichtsschreibung im 19. und 20. Jahrhundert* (Munich, 2006).

Funkenstein, Amos, *Perceptions of Jewish History* (Berkeley, 1993).

Yerushalemi, Yosef Haim, *Zakhor: Jewish History and Jewish Memory* (Seattle, 1982).

Historians and historiography of non-Western regions

Transnational and transcultural historiographies

Breckenridge, Carol A. and Peter Van der Veer, eds., *Orientalism and the Postcolonial Predicament: Perspectives on South Asia* (Philadelphia, 1993).
Said, Edward, *Orientalism* (New York, 1978).

Islamic world

The tradition of historical writing in the Muslim world is surveyed by Franz Rosenthal, *A History of Muslim Historiography* (Leiden, 1968); A. A. Duri, *The Rise of Historical Writing among the Arabs*, ed. and tr. Lawrence I. Conrad (Princeton, 1983); and, more recently, by Chase Robinson, *Islamic Historiography* (Cambridge, 2003). Bernard Lewis and P. M. Holt, eds., *Historians of the Middle East* (Oxford, 1962) has chapters dealing with its modern transformation but outdated. More recent and comprehensive studies are by Youssef M. Choueiri, *Arab History and the Nation-State: A Study in Modern Arab Historiography 1820–1980* (London and New York, 1989) and by Israel Gershoni, Amy Singer, and Y. Hakan Erdem, eds., *Middle East Historiographies: Narrating the Twentieth Century* (Seattle, 2006).

OTHERS

Atabaki, Touraj, *Iran in the 20th Century: Historiography and Political Power* (London, 2009).
Crabbs, Jack, Jr., *The Writing of History in Nineteenth-century Egypt* (Cairo, 1984).
Determann, Jörg Matthias, *Historiography in Saudi Arabia* (London, 2014).
Gallagher, Nancy Elizabeth, ed., *Approaches to the History of the Middle East: Interviews with Leading Middle East Historians* (Reading, 1994).
Gorman, Anthony, *Historians, State and Politics in Twentieth Century Egypt: Contesting the Nation* (London, 2003).
Humphreys, R. Stephen, "The Historiography of the Modern Middle East: Transforming a Field of Study," in *Middle East Historiographies: Narrating the Twentieth Century*, eds. Israel Gershoni, Amy Singer, and Y. Hakan Erdem (Seattle, 2006), 19–36.
Lewis, Bernard, *History: Remembered, Recovered, Invented* (Princeton, 1975).
Lewis, Bernard, "History Writing and National Revival in Turkey," *From Babel to Dragomans: Interpreting the Middle East* (Oxford, 2004), 420–429.
Tavakoli-Targhi, Mohamad, *Refashioning Iran: Orientalism, Occidentalism, and Historiography* (New York, 2001).

East and Southeast Asia

There is no comprehensive survey of the historiographical traditions and their modern transformation in East and Southeast Asia. W. G. Beasley and E. G. Pulleyblank, eds., *Historians of China and Japan* (Oxford, 1961) has chapters dealing with the period covered in this book but is limited to historians in China and Japan and outdated. More important works have been published since then, especially on modern Chinese and Japanese historiography.

China

Dirlik, Arif, *Revolution and History: Origins of Marxist Historiography in China, 1919–1937* (Berkeley, 1978).

Duara, Prasenjit, *Rescuing History from the Nation: Questioning Narratives of Modern China* (Chicago, 1995).

Elman, Benjamin A., *From Philosophy to Philology: Intellectual and Social Aspects of Change in Late Imperial China* (Los Angeles, 2000).

Jenner, W. J. F. *The Tyranny of History: The Roots of China's Crisis* (London, 1992).

Li, Huaiyin, *Reinventing Modern China: Imagination and Authenticity in Chinese Historical Writing* (Honolulu, 2013).

Ng, On-cho, and Q. Edward Wang, *Mirroring the Past: The Writing and Use of History in Imperial China* (Honolulu, 2005).

Wang, Q. Edward, *Inventing China through History: The May Fourth Approach to Historiography* (Albany, 2001).

Japan

Brownlee, John S., *Japanese Historians and the National Myths, 1600–1945: The Age of the Gods and Emperor Jinmu* (Vancouver and Tokyo, 1997).

Mehl, Margaret, *History and the State in Nineteenth-Century Japan* (Basingstoke, 1998).

Numata, Jirō, "Shigeno Yasutsugu and the Modern Tokyo Tradition of *Historical Writing*," *Historians of China and Japan*, ed. W. G. Beasley and E. G. Pulleyblank (London, 1961), 264–287.

Tanaka, Stefan, *Japan's Orient: Rendering Pasts into History* (Berkeley, 1993).

Tanaka, Stefan, *New Times in Modern Japan* (Princeton, 2004).

Korea and Vietnam

Em, Henry, *The Great Enterprise: Sovereignty and Historiography in Modern Korea* (Durham, 2013).

Pai, Hyung Il, *Constructing "Korean" Origins: A Critical Review of Archaeology, Historiography, and Racial Myth in Korean State-Formation Theories* (Cambridge, MA, 2000).

Pelley, Patricia M., *Postcolonial Vietnam: New Histories of the National Past* (Durham, 2002).

South Asia

A comprehensive historiography on South Asia is Michael Gottlob, ed., *Historical Thinking in South Asia: A Handbook of Sources from Colonial*

Times to the Present (Oxford, 2003). A challenging postmodernist perspective is provided by Vinay Lal, *The History of History: Politics and Scholarship in Modern India* (Oxford and New Delhi, 2003).

OTHERS

Bhattacharya, Sabyasachi, *Approaches to History: Essays in Indian Historiography* (Delhi, 2011).

Chakrabarty, Dipesh, "The Birth of Academic Historical Writing in India," *The Oxford History of Historical Writing: Volume 4: 1800–1945*, ed. Stuart Macintyre, Juan Maiquaschca, and Attila Pok (Oxford, 2011).

Chatterjee, Kumkum, *The Cultures of History in Early Modern India* (New Delhi, 2009).

Guha, Ranajit, *An Indian Historiography of India: A Nineteenth Century Agenda and Its Implications* (Calcutta, 1988).

Guha, Ranajit, ed., *A Subaltern Studies Reader* (Minneapolis, 1988).

Guha, Ranajit, *Dominance without Hegemony: History and Power in Colonial India* (Cambridge, MA, 1998).

Inden, Ronald, *Imagining India* (Oxford, 1990).

Mantena, Rama Sundari, *The Origins of Modern Indian Historiography in India. Antiquarianism and Philology, 1780–1880* (New York, 2012).

Mukhopadhya, Subodh Kumar, *Evolution of Historiography in Modern India: 1900–1960* (Calcutta and New Delhi, 1981).

Phillips, C. H., ed., *Historians of India, Pakistan, and Ceylon* (London, 1961).

Rao, V. N., David Schulman, and Sanjay Subrahmanyam, *Textures of Time: Writing History in South India, 1600–1800* (New York, 2003).

Sarkar, Sumit, *Writing Social History* (New Delhi, 1998).

Warder, A. K. *An Introduction to Indian Historiography* (Bombay, 1972).

Latin America

Until now, there has not been a comprehensive history of Latin-American historiography in any language. Felipe Soza-Larrain, *La Historiografía Latinoamericana* is in the process of publication, but one can consult Felipe Soza, "La historiografía latinoamericana," *Comprender el pasado: Una historia de la escritura y el pensamiento histórico*, ed. Jaume Aurell, Catalina Balmaceda, Peter Burke, and Felipe Soza (Madrid, 2013), 341–350. For the period primarily since the 1960s, see Jurandir Malerba, *La historia en América Latina: Ensayo de crítica historiográfica* (Rosario, 2010). For a good history of Latin America, see also José de Moya, *The Oxford Handbook of Latin American History* (Oxford, 2011).

Africa

See the eight-volume UNESCO *General History of Africa* (London, 1978–2000), which includes discussions of historical writing in Sub-Saharan Africa. A brief but excellent bibliographical essay is contained in Markus Völkel,

Geschichtsschreibung: Eine Einführung in globaler Perspektive (Köln, 2006), 360–372, which counters prevalent conceptions that there were no indigenous traditions of historial writing in Sub-Saharan Africa other than traces in the Coptic civilization of Ethiopia. See also Toyin Falola, ed., *African Historiography: Essays in Honour of Jacob Ade Ajayi* (Essex, 1993), Adiele Afigbo, *The Poverty of African Historiography* (Lagos, 1997), and Andreas Eckert, "Historiography on a Continent without History. Anglophone West Africa, 1880–1940," *Across Cultural Borders: Historiography in Global Perspective*, ed. Eckhardt Fuchs and Benedikt Stuchtey (Lanham/ Boulder, 2002), 99–118.

Index